The Life and Letters of Benjamin Morgan Palmer

B. M. Palmer

The Life and Letters of Benjamin Morgan Palmer

THOMAS CAREY JOHNSON

The Banner of Truth Trust

THE BANNER OF TRUTH TRUST
3 *Murrayfield Road, Edinburgh* EH12 6EL
P.O. Box 621, *Carlisle*, *Pennsylvania* 17013, USA

*

First published 1906
This Banner of Truth Trust edition
first published 1987

ISBN 0 85151 522 3

*

Reprinted in Great Britain by offset lithography
at the University Printing House, Oxford

TO

HIS ONLY LIVING DAUGHTER AND HIS TWO GRANDDAUGHTERS,
"SWEET SOLACES OF HIS LATTER DAYS;"

TO

ALL WHO, HAVING HAD HIM AS PASTOR, LOVED AND ADMIRED
HIM IN THAT RELATION;

TO

ALL WHO REVERENCE IN THE CHRISTIAN, THE UNION OF THE
MOST CLEAR-CUT CONVICTIONS AS TO THE TEACHING OF
THE CHRISTIAN SCRIPTURES TOUCHING THE FAITH,
THE POLITY AND THE WORSHIP PROPER TO
THE PEOPLE OF GOD, WITH FERVID
LOVE FOR ALL MEN, EVEN OF
DIFFERING FAITH;

AND TO

ALL WHO TAKE A JUST PRIDE IN THAT WHICH WAS HIGHEST
AND BEST IN THE OLD SOUTH, HER BEAUTIFUL HOME-
LIFE THE SIMPLE BUT ELEGANT CULTURE AND
MANNERS OF HER LEADING CITIZENS, THEIR
INCORRUPTIBLE CIVIL INTEGRITY, AND
BURNING PATRIOTISM,

THIS VOLUME

IS MOST RESPECTFULLY DEDICATED.

PREFACE.

In the summer of 1903, the Rev. John W. Caldwell, Jr., paid me a call, during which he said that there was a plan on foot to prepare a memorial volume of his grandfather, the late Rev. Dr. B. M. Palmer, of New Orleans; that according to this plan the volume would contain the best of the biographical papers concerning him published soon after Dr. Palmer's death, a few of his best sermons and speeches, and a historical sketch of his services to the Church. He said, also, that in a family conference, they had concurred in thinking that I was the man to prepare the account of the ecclesiastical services.

I was naturally pleased at being thought worthy to perform this service in behalf of the memory of such a distinguished and noble man, but I felt that other men were probably much fitter for the task; and that it would be difficult to bring out his ecclesiastical services fully without dealing with his life and character as a man and a Christian, apart from which he could have given no such service to the Church. I also felt that such a volume as had been contemplated was an insufficient memorial of one so worthy; that a proper regard for his character, and work, and for the interests of Christianity, all dictated that an adequate biography should be prepared. I frankly stated all these views. I also said that, in my judgment, they should find a man to do the work who had been bred in the South Carolina belt of civilization. I ventured even to name a man who would do the work well. Mr. Caldwell agreed that a biography was really demanded to meet the proprieties of the case; but spoke of practical difficulties in the way of securing such an elaborate work. He said that I was believed to have the kinship of ecclesiastical view desired in a biographer. After considerable conversation, I declared that I could not even consider the matter further for six months; but that at the end of that time I would, if he pleased, see whether I could not assist him in having the biography prepared.

Accordingly, in January, or February, 1904, I wrote to a common friend in New Orleans, a gentleman who had known Dr. Palmer well, and admired him greatly; and told him of the conversation between Mr. Caldwell and myself; gave him my notion of the kind of work which should be prepared; repeated to him my view that a man from Dr. Palmer's own section of the country and one who had known him personally, should be discovered to reproduce his life. I said, however, that if those who wished to see his life reproduced could agree on no one else to do it, I would, because of my desire to secure the perpetuation of the Doctor's influence, undertake the biography, provided his friends in New Orleans would assume a certain specified financial risk.

Meanwhile, from other sources demands came that I should undertake this work. The following letter, written only a short while before its lamented author's death, will serve as an instance:

"*Rev. Thos. C. Johnson, D.D., Union Seminary, Richmond, Va.*

"MY DEAR DOCTOR: Dr. Palmer's life ought to be written, and, in my judgment, you are the man to write it. Let me say in advance, that this letter is penned on my own initiative and without consulting any member of the family.

"There has been much talk of a monument to Dr. Palmer. In my opinion the best is a Biography. Mrs. Caldwell observed to me when urging the matter some time since, that her father did not think much of biographies, as they were commonly unread; and that his long life as a simple, hard-working pastor had been too uneventful to furnish interesting material. The last was a huge mistake.

"Some of the items as they occur to me, I sketch:—product of a low-country civilization, a distinct variety; Levitical tribe, ministerial succession from Colonial times; Northern and Southern strains of blood in immediate ancestry; college escapade and estrangement from father and recoil from religion; spiritual conflict at conversion; life as a young pastor, choice of extempore preaching; long pastorate at a strategic point; life as professor, author; contributions to S. W. P., notably 'Christian Paradoxes,' 'Leaves from a Pastor's Portfolio;' review articles on every burning question, papers against Organic Union; agency in epochs, national and ecclesiastical; sermon at opening of the war; first General Assembly; anti-lottery speech; tragic end; obsequies, tributes, etc.

"Although in sympathy with Dr. Dabney on State and Church questions, he was, unlike him, an original secessionist, and, though strong in convictions and virile in expression, he was not so extreme in either; and his life furnishes material for the sketching of a portrait in which the skilful limner of Dabney need not repeat himself.

"Fraternally yours,

"R. Q. MALLARD."

Believing that the conditions stated in my letter to New Orleans would prove the occasion of the choice of some other man as Dr. Palmer's biographer, I was surprised by the early reception of letters saying that the conditions had all been complied with and that I was expected to do the work.

Having now no choice in the matter, I began at the earliest practical moment the study of the civilization of the far South and the collection of material bearing on Dr. Palmer's life. Much valuable matter was at once gathered through correspondence and by advertising for it. In June and July, 1904, I visited New Orleans, La., Charleston, McPhersonville, Walterboro, and Columbia, S. C., to gather material and converse with those who had known Dr. Palmer best. At every point, my mission secured me the greatest consideration and enthusiastic aid. In that most courteous of cities, New Orleans, there appeared so general a desire to help on the part of all who were informed of my business that space cannot be taken here to recount their names. Special mention must be made, however, of the proprietors of the great daily papers of the city, who kindly put their files at my command; of the guardians of the City Archives, who therein gave me access to mines of great value; of Rabbi Leucht, who granted some specially informing interviews; and, particularly, of Prof. John W. Caldwell and his family, who not only turned me loose in Dr. Palmer's study, opening his desks and revealing sometimes unconsciously, much as to his character, in the intimacies of social intercourse, but gave themselves to recalling, clarifying and verifying facts in connection with his life, affording me every possible assistance.

At Charleston, S. C., Mr. Alfred Lanneau and his sisters, Miss Mary Caldwell and Mr. Asher D. Cohen contributed valuable materials. At McPhersonville, the family of the Hon. Sanders Glover, and their cousin, Mrs. Kerr; at Walterboro, the Hon. C. G. Henderson and others; at Columbia, Miss Helen McMaster, Mrs. Clarkson, the Hon. Daniel Joseph Pope, Professor of Law in the University of South Carolina, who in his youth was a roommate of Dr. Palmer at the University of Georgia; and others.

Many ladies and gentlemen have loaned us valuable packages of letters; but, as their names for the most part occur in the body of the work, it has been deemed unnecessary to repeat them here.

Express mention must be made of aid rendered by Prof. Charles Woodward Hutson, of Texas.

The materials gathered, I went earnestly to work in the endeavor to master them and to reproduce the life of my noble subject in his environment. It was not an easy task. I am conscious of many imperfections in its execution; but I can claim the merit of having at least tried to present Dr. Palmer and his history in proportions corresponding to the objective facts.

Our friend, the Rev. D. K. Walthell, Ph.D., has prepared the index to the work. T. C. J.

Union Theological Seminary of Virginia.

CONTENTS.

LIFE AND LETTERS

OF

Benjamin Morgan Palmer

CHAPTER I.

THE ANCESTORS.
(1621-1818.)

WILLIAM PALMER I.—WILLIAM PALMER II.—WILLIAM PALMER III. AND THOMAS PALMER I.—REV. THOMAS PALMER.—REV. SAMUEL PALMER.—JOB PALMER.—REV. EDWARD PALMER.—SARAH BUNCE PALMER.

IT is vain to pour contempt upon the pride which traces one's history back to a noble heritage." Virtue receives a grace when it descends from sire to son:

> "And is successively, from blood to blood,
> The right of birth."

The history of Benjamin Morgan Palmer "was rooted in a strong, pure and gentle" lineage. The virtues which shone so luminously in him, had appeared before in his ancestral lines. The truthfulness of these assertions may be tested by a glance at the following sketches of his ancestors:

WILLIAM PALMER I., (——-1638).

In the year of our Lord 1621, when the Plymouth Colony was less than one year old, there came into the new settlement a second ship, laden with immigrants from the mother country of England. Amongst these was one William Palmer, whom, for convenience, we have called William Palmer I. We know little of him with certainty. Back in England, his home had been in Nottinghamshire. It would be interesting to know that he was related to Herbert Palmer, of the county of Kent, who was to sit as a member of the Westminster Assembly and to be known as the best catechist in all England. For in Herbert Palmer appeared certain prominent characteristics that have appeared, also, in some of the greater offspring of William Palmer I., notably the faculty of uniting breadth of affection with the tenacious maintenance of personal convictions. No such relationship is known, however.

Tradition says that this William Palmer I., who came over on the ship *Fortune,* bore the title of lieutenant. Though history tells us little of his life in the colony, it is no difficult task to imagine how he was occupied for the first years after his coming. "Fishing, hunting, and the collection of fuel and timber were the chief businesses of the colonists. These pursuits, which gave place to one another in turn, were interrupted by occasional traffic with the Indians." In his first midwinter the colonists "built a fort with good timber, both strong and comely, which was of good defence, made with a flat roof and battlements, on which their ordnance were mounted. It served them also for a meetinghouse, and was fitted accordingly for that use. It was a great work for them in their weakness and time of want. But the danger of the time required it, and also the hearing of the great massacre in Virginia made all hands willing to dispatch the same."[1] The settlers barricaded their dwellings. They enclosed the whole settlement, with the fort and space for a garden for each family, with a paling. They completed a military organization. They kept a watch and ward against the Indians. They struggled with weakness and famine. They prayed and worshipped, some of them in sincerity and truth, others in hypocrisy; for not all of the passengers on the *Mayflower,* and not all on the *Fortune,* were honest and worthy. The community was a mixed one.

That William Palmer I. belonged to the body of good men in the colony, and that he had in him worthy stock, there can be no doubt. Can an evil tree bring forth good fruit? His descendants in every generation have been men of worth, some of them men of mark. His line has given to the church more than thirteen ministers, viz.: Thomas Palmer, Samuel Palmer, Dr. B. M. Palmer, Sr. (uncle to Dr. B. M. Palmer of New Orleans), Edward Palmer, Benjamin Morgan Palmer, Edward P. Palmer, Edward Palmer Hutson, I. S. K. Axson, P. E. Axson, B. E. Lanneau, Wallace T. Palmer, Edward

[1] Bradford, *History of Plymouth Plantation,* p. 126, quoted in Palfrey's *History of New England,* I., p. 196-197.

Palmer Pillans, and John W. Caldwell, and others. His line includes Mrs. S. P. B. D. Shindler, the poetess, who wrote, "I'm a Pilgrim, and I'm a Stranger," "Passing under the Rod," and several prose works, some of which had large sale.

He had married some years before leaving England. His wife Frances followed him to the New World in August, 1623. At that time, the ship *Ann* and the little *James* arrived, having aboard "some who were the wives and children of such as were already here." Amongst these were Frances Palmer and her son William Palmer II., having come over in the *Ann*.

William Palmer I. and his wife Frances removed in the year 1632, taking their family with them, to Duxbury, a town situated on the other side of the harbor, at a distance of nine miles from Plymouth. A sense of security had spread, and property had increased, especially cattle. The settlers at Plymouth, who for the first years had lived compactly, had begun about this time to "disperse for the convenience of more pasturage and other accommodations." Later, the Palmers removed further up the coast toward Boston, to a place called Scituate. There the will of William I. was probated March 5, 1638.

WILLIAM PALMER II.

William Palmer II. was born, as we have seen, in England. He was married at Scituate, March 27, 1633, to Elizabeth Hodgkins. He removed to Yarmouth. He was one of the purchasers of Dartmouth. Tradition says that he removed to Newton, Long Island, in 1656, had born of him a son, in 1665, who was to become the Rev. Thomas Palmer; and that he died about the time of this son's birth; but there appears to be some solid evidence that he died as early as 1637.

WILLIAM PALMER III. AND THOMAS PALMER I.

William Palmer III. was born January 27, 1634, and his brother, Thomas Palmer I., in 1635 or '6. This William Palmer became heir of "Plymouth Estate," and settled at Dartmouth in 1660. He died in 1679. His wife bore the name "Susanna." His children were William IV., born 1663, John, born on the 18th of May, 1665, and "other children" not named. It has been conjectured, and with considerable probability, that one of these "other children" was Thomas Palmer, whose acquaintance we shall make as the Rev. Thomas Palmer; and that he was a twin brother of John, since the Rev. Thomas' birth year is certainly known, from his tombstone, to have been 1665. On the other hand it has been conjectured that, as William Palmer II. had a son born to him in 1635 or '6, who bore the name of Thomas Palmer, and as he is known to have inherited his father's lands at Scituate, he became the father of the Thomas Palmer born in 1665.

There are thus three views taken as to the connection between William Palmer II. and Rev. Thomas Palmer; and, notwithstanding the fact that several published "records" make Rev. Thomas Palmer to have been the son of William Palmer II., it is not deemed safe to assert that such was the connection. Mr. Alfred W. Lanneau, of Charleston, S. C., has given to this question much intelligent study and concludes, "that the Rev. Thomas Palmer was the son of William III. and not of William II.; and that he was a brother of John and of William IV." He writes, "My record of his life shows that he had a brother William when he moved to Middleboro."

THOMAS PALMER II. (1665-1743).

According to the testimony of his tombstone, this man was born in 1665. If not the son of William Palmer II., and of his wife, Elizabeth Hodgkins, he was the grandson, and probably through William Palmer III., as his father. He became a minister and settled at Middleboro, Mass., about 1696. He seems to have been a rash and headstrong man, and given to occasional intemperance. The discovery of these weaknesses provoked opposition to his settlement. He was ordained only after several years of preaching, probably May 2, 1702, his ordination being accomplished apparently through taking the opposition by surprise. The opposition continued. Council after council was held. Finally, in accord with the advice of the council of twelve churches, and also of that of "the anniversary convention of ministers in Boston, he was, by the church in Middleboro, June 30, 1708, deposed from the ministry, and excluded from their communion at the sacramental table." A section of the church stood by him, and he preached to his party in a private house for some time after his deposition. He lived out his days in the place; and, as he had considerable knowledge of medicine and skill in the healing art, he was employed for many years as a practicing physician among the people. Near the close of his life he was restored to the communion of the church. He died July 17, 1743.

His excellent wife, Elizabeth Sturvenant, had borne him eight children, the sixth of whom was to reflect much honor on his parents.

SAMUEL PALMER (1707-1775).

Among the children of Rev. Thomas and Elizabeth Sturvenant Palmer, was Samuel Palmer, their sixth child. He was born August 8, 1707, at Middleboro, Mass. He was sent to Harvard College for an education.

The Massachusetts colony had understood what was necessary in order to have the foundations of a permanent commonwealth. The people of that colony had hardly provided for the primal wants of life—food, clothing, houses, churches—before they began, through their legislative body, to tax themselves for the rearing of a college and its maintenance,—"the first body," says Mr. Edward Everett, "in which the people, by their representatives, ever gave their own money to found a place of education." They were the objects of suspicion on the part of the unfriendly home government. They were surrounded by hostile nations. But beyond their impending troubles, they looked to the needs of the future, and taxed themselves heavily to provide for those needs. "The generous project engaged the sympathy of John Harvard, a graduate of Emmanuel College, Cambridge, who, dying childless within a year after his arrival in Charlestown, bequeathed (1638) his library and the one half of his estate, it being in all about seven hundred pounds, for the erecting of the college." [2] For this beneficent act, the Court gratefully ordered the college to be called by the name of Harvard.

From this college Samuel Palmer was graduated in 1727. He prepared himself for the ministry, and perhaps, also, for the practice of medicine; and was settled at Falmouth, Mass., in 1730.

At a town meeting held June 30, 1730, it was agreed and voted that Mr. Samuel Palmer shall be the town's minister. "At the same meeting," says the ancient record, "the town made choice of nine men to consider of a suitable sum of

---

[2] Palfrey, *History of New England,* Vol. I., p. 549.

money for his encouragement, which gentlemen have agreed to give Mr. Palmer £200, settlement, to be paid in four years at £50 per year, in bills of credit, with £90 salary for the four years, and afterwards £100 per year so long as he shall remain the town's minister; and if the money should still grow worse, we will raise in proportion, and if it should grow better then to raise in proportion."

The town and the church made subsequent overtures to which he responded, September 1, 1731, as follows:

"To the church and other Christian inhabitants of the town of Falmouth, Brethren:—Since you have been pleased after my continuance for some time with you, to elect and make application to me to be your pastor and minister, presenting me with the act of the church, bearing date February 4, 1731, wherein is signified their choice of me, and desire of my continuance here to take the pastoral care of them, etc., and *also the concurring act and vote of the town* bearing date of March 2, 1730, wherein is expressed that the inhabitants of the town have legally chosen me to be their minister, etc., I do gratefully acknowledge the respect for, and affection toward me, which ye have so unanimously expressed and showed. And I have after humble and earnest supplication to the all-wise God to direct and guide me in the consideration of so weighty and important an affair and to influence my determination thereon—set myself seriously to consider of your invitation to me with the observable circumstances attending the same, asking advice thereon; and since there was such a unanimity as ye have signified to have been in your proceedings and a continuous affection toward me hath since been expressed, I cannot but conceive the voice of God to be therein,—that he united your heart and voice thus to apply yourselves to me, and, therefore, notwithstanding the discouragements otherwise arising I dare not gainsay, but must be willing to comply with your desire to take upon me this solemn charge and great work among you, as hearkening to, and obeying the voice of the great shepherd of the sheep, depending on him for assistance and strength to perform the same. And whereas the Lord hath ordained that they who preach the Gospel shall live of the Gospel, as they who waited at the altar were partakers with the altar, I do and shall expect that ye exercise toward me that charity, justice and liberality, which the Gospel of our Lord requires; to afford me a comfortable and honorable support and maintenance as God shall give you ability, and of what you are pleased of your bounty to bestow upon me to promote my settling comfortably among you, I shall thankfully accept. And now you abiding still by your choice of me to take charge of, and watch over you according to the rules of the Gospel, I shall account myself bound and devoted to labor for the good of your souls, desiring and expecting that your prayers be joined with mine, that I may not be given to you in anger but in love; as a blessing of our gracious and ascended Savior, and by him be made faithful and successful in this great work whereto I am called.[3] SAMUEL PALMER."

He was a methodical and regular worker, as is shown by the clear record of the history of the church of Falmouth which he kept from the day of his ordination. He was more,—a faithful pastor, a laborious minister, a man of prayer, whose praise was in all the churches. "His ministry was long continued and eminently successful."

As a minister must often do, in primitive communities, Mr. Samuel Palmer engaged in secondary forms of activity. He cared not only for the souls but for the bodies of men. He was for many years a practitioner of medicine. His library is said to have contained "some of the best medical works of his day," and he is said, like his father, to have had a "respectable knowledge of the healing art." It is not certain that he had received a diploma as a medical student. There is a probability that, doctors being scarce, he supplied himself with medical knowledge and practiced for the benefit of his parishioners very much as missionaries do at the present day. His useful life seems to have been sacrificed to his labors in this direction. In making a visit to a patient in a remote part of town, he exposed himself to severe weather, brought on a cold which was attended by fever and resulted in his death.

Mr. Palmer also indulged in farming. He owned a slave. This slave, who bore the name of Titus, was as well-known in his sphere as his master was in his. Between this Titus, or "Tite," as he was familiarly called, and his master there was a strong attachment; and the master treated the slave much as a companion, just as masters so often treated their more intelligent and characterful slaves farther south, down to year 1865. Many anecdotes of the relations between Titus and his master were long told in Falmouth. They carried on their farming operations together, Titus being foreman in these operations and the minister a rather indifferent aid. The parson was exceedingly fond of his pipe. Tite insisted that the

---

[3] For these extracts touching Rev. Samuel Palmer's settlement at Falmouth, see Jenkins' *Early History of the Town of Falmouth,* pp. 68, 72, 73.

pipe made the master absent-minded and consequently inefficient. They seem to have had their own way of doing things. For example, in plowing Titus was always at the helm, and gave the word of command to the minister who held the lines and drove the "team." The minister, whether under the influence of his pipe, as Titus supposed, or under some other spell, would suffer his horses to deviate from a straight line, and leave a most irregular furrow. Titus would lose patience and shrilly exclaim, "Why, Marster, it seems you might do a little better." As Titus' reproofs were very frequent, the neighbors enjoyed much laughing gossip about his "swearing at the minister."

The Rev. Samuel Palmer had married Miss Mercy Parker, June 1, 1736. By her he had three sons, the oldest, Thomas, the second, Joseph, and the third, Job, who removed to Charleston, S. C., and of whom we shall see more. Mr. Samuel Palmer's first wife dying, he married Miss Sarah Allen, in 1751. By the two marriages he had eleven children.

Nothing seems to have occurred to destroy the peace and harmony of the church during Mr. Palmer's ministry, which was closed by his death. He had been the faithful preacher and pastor for forty-five years in Falmouth.

The death of this excellent man was a heavy affliction to his church and town. He died April 13, 1775. Two days later he was buried, after which a day of fasting and prayer was appointed on account of the affliction by which the people had been bereft of their pastor. The town in further appreciation of Mr. Palmer's services allowed to his widow and family the use of certain public lands.[4] The following epitaph may be read on his tombstone in the old cemetery at Falmouth, Mass.: "Here lies interred the Body of the Rev. Samuel Palmer, who fell asleep April ye 13th, 1775, in the 68th year of his age and 45th of his ministry. His virtues would a monument supply, But underneath these clods his ashes lie."

JOB PALMER (1747-1845).

Mr. Job Palmer was for years the patriarch of the city of Charleston, S. C. He was a "man that was perfect

[4] We are indebted for this account of Mr. Samuel Palmer, also, to C. W. Jenkins' *History of Falmouth,* in the form of three lectures delivered in 1843.

and upright, one that feared God and eschewed evil." When ninety-three years of age he prepared a paper for his descendants, to which he made subsequent additions. In this document he gives the following clear account of his life:

"I was born in Falmouth in the County of Barnstable in Massachusetts, August 26 (15th new style), 1747. My father, Samuel Palmer, was pastor of the Congregational Church in that place. According to my views of religion now, I believe that real, vital religion was very low in Falmouth at the time when I left it, particularly among young people. [The winters were given up "to frolic, dancing and card playing."] Falmouth was my stated home until the twenty-third year of my age. In March, 1770, I left home and went to the city of New York. I continued there a short time, then went up North River to New Windsor, then back in the country about twelve miles to a place called Wallkill. I remained in that place and in its vicinity, through the summer and winter, and formed acquaintance with some pious people, particularly with a Mr. Blair, a pious Presbyterian minister whose preaching I generally attended. There I believe I received the first real religious impressions, or convictions of sin, that I ever experienced, excepting under one sermon I heard from Dr. Rodgers before I left New York. Those impressions were repeated from time to time under the preaching of Mr. Blair, and some other ministers. And I have reasons to believe that that preaching and some other religious exercises have been the means by which the blessed Spirit of God, at first, aroused my conscience to a sense of my danger, and, I would humbly hope, has led me to embrace the Redeemer, as my only hope of salvation, through his atonement and righteousness, and his intercession for the pardon of my many sins and follies.

"As I had no encouragement in my business to remain there, I returned to New York in the spring. Mr. Blair gave me a letter to Dr. Rodgers and his colleague, Mr. Trent. There my religious impressions were recommenced under preaching, and repeated frequently, and deepened.

"On the first of December, 1771, I was admitted to communion in the Presbyterian Church. By the advice of some friends, I concluded to go to Charleston, S. C., with Rev. Mr. Tennent, who had accepted a call to the Congregational Church there. [This was William Tennent, son of William Tennent, Jr., of Freehold, N. J. He soon wielded a commanding influence in Charleston in the pulpit and out of it. He was an active and flaming patriot. He "ably and effectively supported the Dissenting Petition, by a speech delivered in the House of Assembly, Charleston, January 11, 1777."] Dr. Rodgers and Mr. Trent gave me five letters to five persons, members of that church (the Circular Church to which Mr. Tennent had been called). These letters introduced me to the acquaintance of those persons, and I doubt not to the friendship of some of them. I was admitted to the first communion of that church after my arrival there. I arrived in Charleston in March, 1772. I pretty soon became acquainted with a number of the members of the church. In July, 1773, I was appointed clerk and sexton of the church and continued in the office until January, 1813 (thirty-nine years), when I resigned, and my son, Edward, was elected to supply my place.

"On the 23rd of October, 1774, I united in marriage with Miss Sarah Morgan, of Bermuda, your dear mother—grandmother, to some of you. She was ever dear to me, although an infirm and weakly woman, much troubled with the asthmatic complaint which, I suppose, was finally the cause of her death on February 21, 1797." [Of this marriage, he says elsewhere: "We lived in harmony, and, I believe, there were seldom any unkind words passed between us. We agreed in disposition. In respect to appearances in the world, neither of us was ambitious to make an appearance beyond what our circumstances would warrant. I mention these minute circumstances because I have no doubt that had we possessed the ambition of many others, perhaps in no better circumstances than ourselves, with my expensive family, I might years ago have been peeping through the grate of a jail, or confined within its bounds.

"You know," continues Mr. Palmer, "that the Revolutionary War commenced in the spring of 1775. From that time very little business was done in my line. I had some work on the fortifications, but from that time until Charleston was taken we had to rub pretty hard. After the fall of Charleston we carried on some work for several months. Then the British commander forbade all who would not take protection and acknowledge themselves British subjects, to do any mechanical business; and what we did was in a private way. In the spring of 1781, I, with a number of others, was put on board of a prison ship[5] in the harbor of Charleston, where we remained until a general exchange of prisoners took place. We were not allowed residence within the limits of British power. I then went with Mr. Thomas Legare and a number of others to Virginia, leaving our families in Charleston, intending to return by land and get them out. We returned to Camden and there heard that the British commander had obliged them to leave Charleston. Your mother, in her weak state, had to worry about to procure passage to Philadelphia. A number of ladies hired a small vessel to carry them thither. They

[5] Job Palmer's name occurs in the list of names on board the prison ship *Torbay*. The reader may see this list in McCrady's *South Carolina in the Revolution*, pp. 358, 359, footnote.

arrived at Philadelphia on the 11th of September, 1781. Fourteen days thereafter a child was born to us. On learning the destination of our families Mr. Legare and I set out for Philadelphia.

"When I returned from Philadelphia with my family, in the spring of 1783, after the British had left Charleston, I was applied to by a lady to open a singing school in her house, to instruct her daughters and some other young ladies in vocal music. I did so, and continued my school two afternoons in a week for a year or more. In the winter I opened an evening school for both sexes, two evenings in a week, and continued these schools in the winters, until the spring of 1788, when I, with my wife and one child, paid a visit to my friends in Falmouth, after an absence of eighteen years. Returning home in the fall, I taught a school for some winters afterward. The profits arising from these schools aided me considerably in the support of my family."]

"On March 27, 1798, I was united in marriage with Mrs. Esther Miller, aunt to some of you, to others great-aunt." [This lady was a sister to his first wife.] "She was an affectionate, tender wife to me, particularly in sickness, or any bodily distress. She departed this life June 16, 1832, a short time after the death of our daughter, Hetty Maria, by our marriage.

"On the fourth of November, 1814, I was elected one of the deacons of our church and continued active in that office until and including the celebration of the Lord's Supper in May, 1840, being then eight months in the ninety-third year of my age and the twenty-sixth year of my office as deacon. From that time I concluded to discontinue service at the Lord's table, unless there should be a deficiency of deacons at any time. Not that I was weary in serving my brothers and sisters in that ordinance; but I thought it proper for me to retire and let the younger deacons serve, of whom there was a sufficient number. . . .

"My dear descendants, I think you will believe that I have cause to feel a strong attachment to the church where I have performed the duty of clerk and sexton thirty-nine years, excepting the time the British army held possession of Charleston, in which I have been a deacon for twenty-six years, and in which I have enjoyed the privileges of a member in full communion for sixty-eight years.

"If I have discharged my duty faithfully in the situation I have occupied, I desire with gratitude to ascribe all the praise to God, who has disposed and enabled me thus to perform them.

"Job Palmer, aged ninety-three years and six months, March, 1841."

Mr. Job Palmer was deeply interested in the subjects of the deity of our Lord and the vicarious atonement. These doctrines were being condemned by many teachers, especially amongst the New England Congregationalists and their disciples wherever found. Mr. Palmer was particularly concerned that his own children should never accept the Unitarian views. The vigorous old man set himself to gather the evidences from the Scriptures bearing on this question. He arranged long lists of Scripture passages under the three heads: *First,* those texts that bear positive testimony to the supreme deity of Christ; *second,* those that yield "collateral evidence thereof;" and, *third,* those which speak of his coming into the world by the Father's appointment and with his own free consent, fulfilling the law of God and so magnifying it and making it honorable, dying to make atonement for all those who embrace him with true vital piety. He states that he has held this doctrine for sixty-three years, and sees no reason for the change, but that all his reading and reflection tend to fix him the more firmly in his faith in Christ's divinity.

The preface of this remarkable paper is in the following words:

"To my dear descendants who may see this paper after my death, I leave it and what it contains, as a memorial of my tender regard for them, and my earnest desire and prayer for their eternal welfare; and strongly recommend to them, and more especially to those of them, if any such there should be, who have doubts in their minds of the Supreme Divinity of the Lord Jesus Christ and of his suffering to make an atonement for sin, that they read the following passages of Scripture carefully, and prayerfully, that their minds may be led to a knowledge of the truth as it is in Jesus Christ, and that their hearts may be disposed to embrace it.

"As it hath pleased Almighty God to prolong my life to the advanced age of eighty-eight and to preserve to me my health and strength of body and other faculties of body and mind in so great a degree; and to give me the privilege, time, and disposition to read and search the Scriptures to discover the truth contained in them, it has been my desire and endeavor, while reading them, to select such passages from them as appeared to me sufficient evidence to establish the truth of certain doctrines, the belief of which appears to me, if not absolutely essential, yet very necessary for the salvation and comfort of those who are seeking salvation as they ought to do."

The paper was apparently written first when he was eighty-six years of age; but was re-written, enlarged and strengthened when he was eighty-eight. When it is remembered that he wrought it without the aid of modern Bible study helps, it appears no mean piece of work. Without collegiate education, Mr. Palmer evidently made himself a man of no small cultivation.

His occupation was that of a contractor and builder. In this business, he succeeded in supporting in comfort his large family. He was the father of sixteen children. He was a splendid type of simple-minded integrity and Christian character in the home and in the business world. Well may his posterity honor him. In the full possession of his faculties, almost to the last, he died at the age of ninety-seven.

Two of his sons entered the ministry. One of them was the Rev. Benjamin Morgan Palmer, Sr. He was for many years pastor of the Circular (Independent) Church of Charleston. He was a man of learned and deep piety; dogmatic and conservative; aggressive and masterful; somewhat of a pope in Charleston. But he was greatly beloved by his people. He was not without a glowing imagination and oratorical talent. His sermons, always written, were logical, concise and of a practical rather than a theoretical method. To the other ministerial son we must give more attention.

REV. EDWARD PALMER (1788-1882).

To Mr. Job Palmer was born in the city of Charleston, S. C., December 25, 1788, a son who received the name of Edward. He was the eighth of sixteen children. He received an excellent English education, which was not entirely arrested when, at the age of fifteen, he was taken into his father's business.

Upon reaching the age of twenty-three he preferred to engage in teaching, which calling he pursued for nine years with profit and success. On the first of January, 1812, he was united in marriage with Miss Sarah Bunce.

Though reared under the most favorable religious influences he did not make an early profession of faith in Christ. As far back as his memory could reach he was the "subject of frequent and deep convictions of sin and guilt." On three occasions—in the fifteenth, twentieth, and twenty-second years of his life—"the great controversy was well-nigh closed in the final surrender of his heart to God." He continued vacillating, nevertheless, "between hope and fear through succeeding years," until 1819; when, in his thirty-first year, he gave his testimony to wonder-working grace. This step involved another, that of "setting before others the great and glorious salvation." The manner of his call to the ministry may be related in his own words:

"I was at the time stated a member of several societies—one, a Musical Association; another a Young Men's Missionary Society—at which I had been called to deliver public addresses. On one of these occasions, Mr. Jonas King, afterwards a distinguished missionary to Greece, was present. At the close he accompanied me home, and in the course of conversation, asked me if I had ever thought of the ministry myself. I promptly replied: 'Look, my dear sir, at a fond wife and four lovely children, whom I am bound by every tender and holy tie to support, and then say whether that question can be asked.' To which he rejoined: 'If the Lord shall call, he will prepare the way.' Rev. Dr. Porter, of Andover Seminary, being also in the city, sent for me; and, after a long and interesting interview, not only encouraged the step, but imposed upon me the prayerful consideration of the matter; all of which culminated in my departure to the North in 1820."

"The magnitude of this decision" begins to dawn on one when he recalls the fact that, though Mr. Palmer was thirty-two years old, he was ignorant of the Latin grammar; that his preparation for the ministry involved a four years' course of preparation, and a long separation from his family. See him then at this mature age amongst the boys at Phillips Academy, Andover, Mass., for eighteen months. In September, 1821, he matriculated in the Seminary at Andover. So successful was he as a student during his years of preparation, that the faculty at Andover, without his knowledge of their intention, procured for him from Yale College the degree of Master of Arts.

He was licensed in July, 1824, by a Congregational Association, and in October of the same year, was ordained as an evangelist. In the fall of 1824, he was installed pastor of the church at Dorchester, about eighteen miles from Charleston, by the Congregational Association which then existed on the sea-board of South Carolina; but which with a portion of Harmony Presbytery, was formed in 1827 into the Charleston Union Presbytery. After two years and a half in this pastorate, he removed to a wider sphere of labor at Walterboro, S. C. In the fall of 1831, he accepted a call to the Presbyterian

Church at Stony Creek, in the District of Beaufort. There he remained until the year 1844, giving, however, toward the latter part of the period, a portion of his time to Walterboro. Returning to Walterboro in 1844, he served that field till 1855, then returned to Stony Creek which he served till 1861. Going back again to Walterboro in 1861, he continued to serve that people till 1874, his eighty-sixth year. In this year led by a sore domestic bereavement he resigned his pastoral office and was, thenceforth, cared for by his children. He retained his vigor, physical and mental, well beyond his ninetieth year.

Rarely has there been a man so much beloved within the circle of his acquaintances. He was loved by every class of society and by the representatives of every type of religious belief. He was an excellent preacher, a man of vast energy, singularly pure in his dispositions, and ever ready to go, like the Master, to the lowliest of the people with the everlasting Gospel. He was assiduous in his efforts in behalf of the African race. He was marked for the catholicity of his feelings in religion.

In his first wife, Sarah Bunce, he had united himself with a lady of extraordinary capacities and character.

SARAH BUNCE.

Sarah Bunce was the daughter of Captain Jared Bunce, who was born near Hartford, Conn., May 12, 1759. He used to say he could trace his ancestry back to an Alderman Bunce, who lived in London in the time of Cromwell. His mother was a Griswold and was connected with the Stanleys whose remote ancestor was Edward Stanley, Earl of Derby. Jared Bunce was a merchant in early life; but failed in business and went to sea. He commanded the packet *Georgia,* sailing between Philadelphia and Charleston, in both of which places he was well known and greatly beloved as an intelligent and remarkably cheerful Christian. Extant letters prove that he was a man of great independence and vigor of thought and expression. February 11, 1779, he married Lydia Pettiplace (now called Pettis in New England), a woman revered by her acquaintances alike for her piety and her intellectual worth.

The children of this couple seem to have been persons of the most lively and forceful intellectual and moral natures. Of their posterity have been Admiral F. M. Bunce, and his brothers, Edward and Jonathan. Three of Captain Jared Bunce's daughters married ministers: Mary Stanley Bunce married the Rev. Dr. Benjamin Morgan Palmer, Sr.; Sarah married the Rev. Edward Palmer, and Harriet the Rev. Allen Wright, a missionary to the Choctaws. These were all extraordinary women. Says Prof. Charles Woodward Hutson, a nephew: "Mrs. Wright I met twice, once as a boy; and again as a young man in my last year at college. She was the tallest woman I ever saw, and of most commanding presence. When I first knew her, she delighted me with wondrous tales of Indian life and vividly narrated folk-lore, and with the singing of hymns in Choctaw. On the later occasion I was almost constantly with her for the greater part of the summer, at Marietta, Ga., in the house of her nephew, the Rev. Edward Porter Palmer; and I have seldom met any one whose talk was more charming, whose literary taste was so pure and withal so enthusiastic. I have often wished that I had taken notes at the time of our conversation."

Mrs. Sarah Bunce Palmer was born in her father's home, in Weathersfield, Conn. She was a woman of remarkably strong and vigorous mind. By degrees she gave herself, as we shall see, a very thorough education and large culture. She was a great reader and "a deep thinker," a woman of rare native refinement. She possessed moral nerve, as appears from the following, amongst other things related of her: When she was about fifteen years of age, her father had his home in Philadelphia. Her mother had died, and the father had married a second time. The stepmother was amiable but incapable of governing the younger children, as Sarah and her older sister thought they ought to be governed. The father being absent at sea, these sisters thought the two younger ones should be sent to Weathersfield, Conn., for schooling and training. The fifteen-year-old Sarah dressed herself so as to look as old as possible, donned a "poke-bonnet," amongst other articles indicative of the state of aged womanhood, and successfully carried her two younger sisters from Philadelphia to Weathersfield, accomplishing her journey in safety. She became noted for her exalted character and for her devotion to her duties as a pastor's wife. Along with her uncommon intellectual intensity and her strength of will, she had a sunny disposition and a love for the beautiful, which made her a general favorite, especially with the young.

In physical appearance, she was a woman of medium height, slender, with a lofty and well-moulded brow, a penetrating, steel-blue eye, finely chiseled nose, firm mouth, flexible lips, strong but not stubborn chin.

In the next chapter but one we shall see that Benjamin Morgan Palmer, her son, inherited much from the civilization into which he was born and amidst which he grew up, much from the Palmers, from his great-grandfather Samuel down, something from the Morgans, but most of all from his mother.

CHAPTER II.

FEATURES OF THE CIVILIZATION AMIDST WHICH HE DEVELOPED.

(1818-1860.)

"I AM A SOUTH CAROLINIAN, YOU KNOW."—THE DISTINGUISHING FEATURES OF SOUTH CAROLINA CIVIL LIFE AND GOVERNMENT.—THEIR BELT OF INFLUENCE.—THEIR SOURCE THE LOW COUNTRY.—THIS THE REGION IN WHICH YOUNG PALMER GREW UP.—THIS REGION DESCRIBED GEOGRAPHICALLY AND HISTORICALLY.—THE PEOPLE OF THIS REGION.—THEIR LIFE ON THE PLANTATIONS AND IN THE SUMMER SETTLEMENTS.—THEIR EDUCATION, LIBRARIES, AND GENERAL CULTURE.—THEIR SPORTS AND RECREATIONS.—THEIR POLITICS.—THE MORAL AND RELIGIOUS TONE OF THE COMMUNITY.

I AM a South Carolinian, you know." Benjamin Morgan Palmer, in his mature years, was wont to make this statement from time to time, in explanation of views which he held and courses of action which he pursued. He thus evinced his consciousness of having adopted, and made his own, not a little from the distinguishing features of South Carolina civilization. And it is not unsafe to say that, in his political views, in his social ideals, in his manners, in a certain quality of heroic daring, and in the persistent maintenance of his views against all comers, he soon became, and ever remained, a noble exponent of much that was the best and highest in South Carolina civilization. Nor is there anything strange in this. His whole life, two or three years excepted, was spent within the sphere in which South Carolina ideals were dominant. The South Carolina type of civilization was a noble and impressive one; particularly impressive to one of ardent and imaginative temper, and the strong sense of justice, and absolute fearlessness in its defence, by which he was characterized. That type of civilization had produced the finest fruits, he knew: men of the first water, men of thought and action, of knightly spirit, and of bearing heroic to the point of sublimity.

However much alike the types of civilization in the several States of these United States may seem to the superficial foreign observer, the close student amongst the home born knows that every State has had its own individual type of civilization, a type "as distinct and persistent as that of the leading Greek cities." He knows, too, that amongst these States, three have possessed civilizations of marked and dominating individualities, viz.: Massachusetts, Virginia and South Carolina; and that, amongst these three, the South Carolina type stands out with especial distinctness, "with dauntless and defiant spirit, fiery temper, and venturesome chivalry."

The distinctive South Carolina features of civil life and government were a sentiment of independence in regard to the other states, "the centripetal character" of her government, the struggle between the aristocratic and democratic tendencies in the body itself, and the inviolability of the family relation.[1]

Her sentiment of independence in regard to the other states had been bred of her history. The colony of South Carolina was from her planting, in 1670, to 1733, when Oglethorpe established his colony of Georgia, the lonely and remote outpost between the other English colonies, and, on the one hand, the Spaniards at St. Augustine, and on the other, the French toward the Mississippi. Planted to assert the dominion of Great Britain against that of Spain in disputed territory, the immigrants had not yet settled on the Ashley when the Spaniards appeared and gave notice that the colony must fight for its existence. "France, also, advancing her claims to the territory eastward of the Mississippi and northward of Mobile, was disputing the westward limits of Carolina. The Indian tribes, with whom the Spaniards and French alike coalesced with greater facility than did the English colonists, presented the ready means of continual though unavowed hostility, and circumscribed the advance of the colony not only by open warfare, but by the dread of the hireling savage." [2] For safety against Spanish, French and Indians, coming singly or in combination, the colony of South Carolina had to depend on itself, for the most part. In the Great Indian War of 1715, North Carolina and Virginia gave indeed, little and feeble assistance. South Carolina down to the Revolutionary War, continued to fight her battles with relatively little outside help. The first

---

[1] These characteristics are ably illustrated by McCrady in his great work on South Carolina colonial history.

[2] McCrady, *History of South Carolina under the Proprietary Government*, pp. 683, 684.

British soldiers seen in the province of South Carolina, with the exception of Oglethorpe's regiment which had been raised by him for special service in Georgia, were those under Colonel Archibald Montgomery, sent in 1760 to aid in the war against the Cherokees. She had swept her coasts of pirates also, largely by the strategy and tactics, the daring and valor of her own men. During the Revolutionary struggle, her chief, and at times, only succorers were her own people, who developed an ability to endure and a skill and persistence in partisan warfare which has rarely been equalled in the annals of any people, and which unnerved and wore away the armies of her invaders. During this period she often feared that she had been utterly abandoned by the States to the north. Not without considerable assistance indeed, but largely by her own exertions, she achieved her own sovereign independence; and in the process of doing so had given vast encouragement and help to her sister States in their struggles. So circumstanced throughout most of her history as to be under the stern necessity of taking care of herself, she had responded to the necessity and had in doing so wrought into the very fiber of her being the sentiment of independence with reference to all other political bodies.

In like manner this sentiment had been impressed by the conflict with the Proprietary Government which had ended in successful revolutions on the part of the colonists and their overthrow of that government; and by the unceasing conflict thereafter with the royal government in behalf "of those natural rights that we all feel and know as men and as descendants of Englishmen." Not unnaturally, the provocations being great, about the time young Palmer wakes into vigorous mental life, we shall find Nullification running high in South Carolina. Not unnaturally, the provocations being great, about the time he reaches his early prime, we shall find Secession an accomplished fact; and that he himself is an outspoken and determined secessionist. Both facts are the outcome of the history of earlier South Carolina.

The centripetal character of the government is another distinguishing mark of South Carolina civilization. It also was induced by the treatment of the colony by the mother country, and by her isolation and exposure to invasion from all sides. In Virginia the colonial growth was by rural communities. There was no city, or town, life. In New England the colonists separated early into different towns, but in South Carolina the ever-impending danger of invasion by Spaniards, Indians, and French, "restricted the colonists for many years to distances within reach of Charlestown."

"When this danger was overcome by the increase of the population, and the founding and building up of the colony of Georgia, the unhealthfulness of the country along the river, increased, if not caused by the disturbance of the soil and the stagnant water of rice planting in the inland swamps, compelled the planters to reside in the summer in the town or in some high resinous pine land settlement apart, as they thought, from malaria. Thus, until the immigration of the Scotch-Irish and Virginians into the upper country by way of the mountains, from 1750 to 1760, the development of the colony was from one point, the circle enlarging as the population increased, but always with reference to the one central point,—the town—Charles Town.

"The development of Carolina thus presented the anomaly that, though it was a planters' colony, it was developed by way of city, or town, life. Boston was the largest town in Massachusetts, but there was organization and administration outside of it. For many years Charles Town practically embodied all of Carolina. Beaufort, the next town to be settled, was not attempted for more than forty years after the planting of the colony and Georgetown not until some years later. Until 1716 elections were generally held in the town for all the province, and representation outside of it—that by parishes—was not practically established until the overthrow of the proprietary government in 1719. No court of general jurisdiction was held outside of it until 1773, over a hundred years after the establishment of the colony. There was only one government for the province, the town and the church. The same General Assembly passed laws for the province, laid out streets, regulated the police for the town, and governed the church. Even after the colony had grown, and the upper country had been peopled from another source, every magistrate in the province was appointed in Charles Town until the Revolution of 1776, and after that, upon the adoption of the Constitution of 1790 and the change of the seat of government to Columbia, at that place. There was thus from the inception of the colony in 1665 to the overthrow of the State in 1865, for two hundred years only one government in South Carolina. There was no such thing as a county or township government of any kind."[3]

In the facts, that the controlling element of the original South Carolina settlers was from Barbadoes, and that under

---

[3] McCrady, *History of South Carolina under the Proprietary Government,* p. 7.

Yeamans, it brought with it a colonial system which had at its basis the institution of African slavery, and that upon this social order an attempt was made to engraft "a legally recognized aristocracy of Landgraves and Caciques, proposed by Locke and adopted by the Proprietors under the influence of Shaftsbury," we have the occasions of the emergence of another marked trait of South Carolina civilization,— "a strongly aristocratic tone with a party for sustaining prerogative," and on the other hand from the very outset "a party of the people who based their rights upon the dogma of a strict construction of chartered or constitutional provisions." We shall find that Palmer, like the dominant party of his state, was a strict constructionist.

Again, the hostility of the Spaniards, the French and the Indians, "necessitated, from the beginning, a military organization of the people." This was made the more necessary by the increasing number of negro slaves,—savages,—a source of weakness in time of danger, for a long period, till the institution became thoroughly settled, a constant source "of care and anxiety." The colonists were long afraid of a negro rising on occasion of a war with the Spanish, French, or Indians. Under these spurs a military police organization of the whole people was effected, and "continued from 1704 until the emancipation of the negroes as the result of the war of secession."

"Under this system the province, and afterwards the state, was divided into military districts, the chief of each of which was a colonel, and these again into other districts, or beats, under captains. The captain was the police officer of his district, or beat, and was charged with the patrol and police of his beat and the enforcement of the regulations in regard to slaves. The regimental and company military precincts were thus coincident with the police districts and the two formed one system. . . . This system gave a military organization to the people which was much more effective and exacting than ordinary militia enrollment and muster. So imbued was the system of government brought from Barbadoes with a military spirit that the high sheriff of the province retained the military title of 'provost-marshal' for a hundred years—indeed, until the American Revolution. To this source may be traced the prevalence of military titles in the South, as that of 'judge,' or 'squire' in other communities, indicating persons of local consequence."[4]

---

[4] McCrady, *History of South Carolina under the Proprietary Government,* p. 10.

The inviolability of the family relation is another feature of South Carolina civilization. Her people have recognized that the family is the strength of the State. They have done all in their power to uphold its integrity and to minister to its purity and power. There never has been a divorce in South Carolina except during the Reconstruction period after the war between the sections, when the government was in the hands of carpet-baggers and negroes. There is but one case reported in her law books, "and that was during that infamous rule." Some South Carolinians think that this devotion to the purity of the family has been rewarded by many long lines of illustrious men of the same blood.

These principles prevailed to a greater or less degree far beyond the bounds of South Carolina. There have been three great belts of influence reaching across the territory of these United States: One dominated by Massachusetts, one dominated by Virginia, and one dominated by South Carolina. In the days of secession South Carolina was quickly followed by the states of her belt.

In South Carolina itself, these principles had had their source in the low country, which had been settled, and in which civil government had been established long before the upper country was inhabited by white men. Indeed, the upper country, when at length settled by the Scotch-Irish and Englishmen from Virginia, would have welcomed a less "centripetal" government; but hindered in their desires by office holders non-resident in the colony, this, with the other characteristics of the government developed by low country conditions, became a fixed feature of the state as a whole.

Young Benjamin Morgan Palmer grew up in the low country, in the very well-spring of the distinctive features of the South Carolina civilization; and when he said, "I am a South Carolinian, you know," he probably meant that he was a South Carolinian of the low country type; that he had drawn in with the maternal milk not only the great distinctive features of the civilization of the State as a whole but the peculiarities of this primal region of the colony and the State. Hence it is necessary to go somewhat more closely into the mode of life of this particular section.

Born in Charleston, he grew up there, at Dorchester, about twenty miles away near the head of the Ashley river, at Walterboro, which was originally a summer settlement for planters of the Combahee and Ashepoo, and in the neighborhood of McPhersonville, or in that village itself, which is situated about four or five miles from the present railway junction of Yemassee. As the most critical and impressive years of his youth were passed in the McPhersonville neighborhood, and as there he was in the midst of the most typical low country South Carolina life, we must content ourselves with a sketch of this neighborhood.

Geographically [5] this region consisted of peninsulas formed by the rivers Combahee, Pocotaligo, Tullifinny and Coosawhatchie. The topographical features which most impressed the traveler were the salt marshes, toward the coast, sometimes running far back; the frequent rivers, really inlets of the sea; the vast rice plantations, graded and cut into fields by skilled engineers, the back water gathered and husbanded on "reserves" big as the rice-fields themselves, for the watering of the rice fields during certain periods; the numerous causeways across the rice-planting areas; the lands back of the rice fields too high for that industry, and hence devoted to cotton and corn; beyond them the "pine-lands," sandy ridges where the long-leafed pine grew, and the flatness of the whole country.

The region was rich in historical associations. Pocotaligo village, about four miles from McPhersonville, was the scene of the first stage of the terrible massacre which began at daybreak on the 15th of April, 1715, when the Yemassees slaughtered more than ninety persons in that village and on adjacent plantations. The surrounding country was the scene of the Yemassee war which immediately followed, and in which a young stripling named Palmer won honor.

In May, 1779, Moultrie had retreated through this region, before General Prevost. Moultrie had suffered discomfiture in a portion of his force under Colonel John Laurens in the affair of Tullifinny Hill. The British had encamped at Pocotaligo. Here they had erected Fort Balfour, in which patriotic South Carolinians of the neighborhood had been imprisoned. In this general region William Harden, the patriot, and the skilful partisan leader, had accomplished some of his val-

[5] For the sketch of this neighborhood we have received the materials from Prof. Charles Woodward Hutson, College Station, Texas, who was born and bred in the neighborhood himself. We have made free use of his language as well as of his matter.

orous deeds in his country's cause; amongst other things capturing Fort Balfour. Young Benjamin Palmer may have looked on an ancient oak, which was standing at the beginning of the war between the sections, and which stood some paces beyond the little hillock that marked the spot where one of the bastions of the fort had stood. It "was pointed out to younger generations as that in the hollow of which at its base the besieged had stored a cask of gunpowder, on which they were to draw at need when their powder horns should give out." Earlier in the Revolutionary War, a young Tory, Andrew De Vaux, in order to commit his followers irrevocably, had ravaged General Stephen Bull's plantation and burned Sheldon church, in what is now Beaufort county. After brilliant and perilous personal adventures he had risen to the rank of Major in the Royal Militia; and in the days of Harden's exploits De Vaux was making brilliant counter strokes from the Stono to beyond the Georgia line.

As to the living people of the region, by far the most numerous portion was that of the African slaves. While regarded as in some respects the personal property of their masters they were regarded and treated by no means as ordinary chattels. The slave code, Barbadian in its origin, received various amendments till 1740, when it took on the form maintained substantially till the abolition of the institution in 1865. The amendments of 1740 have been summarized as follows by McCrady:[6]

"A penalty of £5 currency was imposed on any person who employed a slave in any work or labor (work for necessary occasions of the family only excepted) on the Lord's Day, commonly called Sunday. The selling of strong liquor to slaves was prohibited. Slaves were to be provided with sufficient clothing, covering, and food, and in case any owner or person in charge of slaves neglected to make such provision the neighboring justice, upon complaint, was required to inquire into the matter, and if the owner or person in charge failed to exculpate himself the justice might make such orders for the relief of the slave as in his discretion he should think fit.

"And because, it was said, by reason of the extent and distance of plantations in the province the inhabitants were far removed from each other, and many cruelties might be committed upon slaves, it was provided that if any slave should suffer in life or limb, or be beaten or abused contrary to the direction of the act, when no white person

[6] McCrady, *South Carolina under the Royal Government*, pp. 230, 231.

was present, or, being present, refused to give evidence, the owner or person in charge of such slave should be deemed to be guilty of the offence, unless he made the contrary appear by good and sufficient evidence, or by his own oath cleared and exculpated himself. This oath was to prevail if clear proof of the offence was not made by at least two witnesses. In case of alleged cruelty to a slave in the absence of white witnesses, the burden of proof was with the person making the charge, while the oath of the party charged might exculpate him unless against the oath of two white witnesses. It was something at least that the owner was called upon to show his innocence. Owners were prohibited from working slaves more than fifteen hours in the twenty-four from the 25th of March to the 25th of September, or more than fourteen hours in the twenty-four from the 25th of September to the 25th of March."

McCrady adds that this slave code was so amended in 1821, "that if anyone should murder a slave he should suffer death without the benefit of the clergy, and if anyone should kill a slave in a sudden heat and passion he should be fined not exceeding $500.00 and be imprisoned not exceeding six months." We shall see that the treatment of the slave was better than the law.

There were grades amongst these negroes, the individual's standing in the social scale being determined in part by the social standing of his master in his sphere, and in part by the native endowments with which he was born, and in part by his occupation. There was a big step between the house servants and those of the fields, brought about by the following causes: The negroes generally were fed on wholesome and nutritious food, suitably but coarsely clothed. They were, in the main, a contented and even a joyous people. But those in domestic service had been selected from the most intelligent, best behaved, and most teachable of all the slaves owned by the master. They were usually the offspring of tribes higher than those that furnished the bulk of imported Africans; and they had, by this time, been in hereditary close contact with ladies and gentlemen long enough to acquire good manners, and in some cases, good morals. They had enjoyed the further advantage over their fellows of going through the annual change of climate and surroundings along with their masters and mistresses. They had grown up the playmates of white children and between them and their owners there was a special warmth of affection bred of kindness and service on the one hand and service on the other.

Above the slaves in social privileges were a class of poor whites, overseers, small mechanics, and the posterity of indentured servants and ex-convicts, human driftwood. This was a small class and from the stabler and more virile elements of this class men were rising to the higher class. Of these poor whites relatively few could vote when elections were held, on account of the property qualifications conditioning the exercise of the privilege of franchise.

Above these were the planters, sprung of good stock, and a stock that had risen superior to all the difficulties incident to settling a new country surrounded by hostile enemies. These low country planters were the posterity of Englishmen, Barbadians, Nova Belgians (as the New Yorkers prior to their conquest by England were called), Huguenots, Irish, Jamaicans, Swiss and Germans. There were intermingled in them the aggressive and persistent energy of the Anglo-Saxon, the shrewdness of the Barbadian, the enduring strength of the Dutchman, and the gentle manners, the gallantry, the frugality and the religious tone of the Huguenots.

The people owning lands in the McPhersonville region were Screvens, McPhersons, Martins, Hutsons, De Saussures, Fullers, Elliotts, Gregories, Mackays, Jenkinses, Heywards, Cuthberts, Maines, Barnwells, Storeys, Stuarts, Middletons, Marions, Giguilliots, De Vaux, and Videaus.

Amongst the planters there *developed* an aristocracy chiefly of wealth and culture. Tradition has done somewhat toward connecting this aristocracy with the European aristocracies, but there seems to have been little connection, as a matter of fact. The South Carolina aristocracy developed under local conditions. The aristocracy of family came after that of wealth, culture and public service.

Notwithstanding the differences in the standings of different citizens of South Carolina, they constituted a people of beautiful manners. As far back as 1770 William Gerrard de Brahan, surveyor for the Southern District of North America, wrote of South Carolina: "A society of men (which in religion, government and negotiation avoids whatever can disturb peace and quietness) will always grow and prosper; so will this city and Province whose inhabitants were from its beginning renowned for concord, compleasance, courteousness, and tenderness toward each other, and more so toward foreigners, without regard or respect for nation or religion." [7]

In colonial days the planters had affected English modes of life. "Their households continued to be organized on the English model," says McCrady, "except in so far as it was modified by the institution of slavery, which modification was chiefly in the number of servants. In every well organized planter's household there were three high positions, the objects of ambition of all the negroes on the plantation. These were the butler, the coachman, and the patroon. The butler was chief of all about the mansion; usually the oldest negro manservant on the premises, his head was often white, the contrast of which with his dark skin was striking, and added much to the dignity which it was always his care and pride to maintain. His manner was founded on that of the best of the society in which his master moved, and withal he possessed much greater ease than is usual in a white man occupying the same position. He became an authority upon matters of table etiquette, and was quick to detect the slightest breach of it. He considered it a part of his duty to advise and lecture the young people of the family upon the subject. He often had entire charge of the pantry and storeroom keys and was usually faithful to his trust. He was somewhat of a judge, too, of the cellar; but there are stories which indicate that it was scarcely safe to allow him free access to its contents. The coachman, to the boys of the family, at least, was scarcely less a character than the butler. He had entire charge of the stable and took the utmost pride in the horsemanship of his young masters, to whom he had given the first lessons in riding. The butler might be the greatest man at home; but he had never the glory of driving the family coach and four down the great "Path" to town and through its streets. The oldest plantations were upon the rivers; a water front, indeed, and a landing were essential to such an establishment, for it must have the periago for plantation purposes, and the trim sloop and large cypress canoes for the master's use. So, beside the master of the horse,—the coachman,—there was a naval officer, too, to each plantation household, and he was the patroon—a name no doubt brought from the West Indies. The patroon had charge of the boats, and the winding of his horn upon the river told the family of the master's coming. He, too, trained the boat hands to the oar and taught them the plaintive, humorous, happy catches which they sang as they bent to the stroke, and for which the mother of the family often strained her ears to catch the first sound which told of the safe return of her dear ones. Each of these head servants had his underlings, over whom he lorded it in imitation of

[7]Quoted in McCrady, *History of South Carolina under the Royal Government,* p. 394.

his master. The house was full, too, of maids and seamstresses of all kinds, who kept the mistress busy, if only to find employment for so many hands. Outside the household the driver was the great man. Under his master's rule he was absolute. He was too great a man to work himself, and if his master was anybody—that is, if the plantation was of respectable size, with a decent number of hands, he must have a horse to ride, for how else could he oversee all of his people? The "driver" was the executive officer. He received his orders from his master, and he carried them out. He did all the punishing. When punishment was necessary, he inflicted it under his master's orders. He was responsible for the administration of the plantation. A plantation was a community in itself. It had its necessary artisans. There must be carpenters, blacksmiths, coopers, tailors, and shoemakers, for there were no ready-made shoes and clothes in those days. Then there was a hospital for the sick and a house for the children while the mothers were at work. All these required thorough organization and complete system. There were no doubt many and great evils inseparable from the institution of slavery, but these were reduced to a minimum on a South Carolina plantation. Generally the slaves were contented and happy, and shared in the prosperity which their labors on the rice fields were bringing to their masters."[8]

The early planters had, in some cases, modeled their homes after London houses, or English country seats; but the climate rendered these unsuitable. They began very soon to build houses so as to secure ventilation and gallery space. Only an occasional planter attempted a pretentious residence. Most of them were content with rather plain story-and-a-half, or two-story houses of any convenient style of architecture. Perhaps the commonest starting plan was that with a room on either side of a central hallway with a staircase running to the floor above. Wings and lean-to sheds were added on demand, convenience and the breezes permitting. Other buildings about "the big house" were the kitchen, the spinning room, the ironing room, the wash house, the dairy, the poultry house, the smoke house where the meats were cured and salted down, sausages hung, and candles made and stored away, the corn house where the distribution of "allowances" was weekly made by the "driver" under the master's superintendence. Beyond these were the stables and the carriage houses, and beyond these, the negro quarters, each cabin having assigned to it a

[8] McCrady, *South Carolina under the Royal Government*, pp. 515, 516, 517.

plot of ground on which the family might raise chickens, or bees, or cultivate a garden for his own use. Amongst the cabins was a house where the children were "minded" when their mothers went to work. There was a hospital for the sick or injured, with a nurse of experience whose labors and skill the "Ole Miss" usually supplemented, and which was visited by the doctor, who was paid so much per year for looking after the health of the whole body of slaves. Beyond all these, again, were the barn and cotton-spinning room, the seed house, the carpenter's shop, blacksmith's forge, and butcher's pen, where black mechanics did the work, sometimes supervised and assisted by a journeyman workman who had been employed for a season. Nearer to the house and flanking the lawn front and back were the flower garden and vegetable garden and the orchards. The master of a large plantation had need of a head for executive ability equal to those of our captains of industry to-day ; and "Ole Miss" needed an equal ability in superintending the work of manufacturing garments for the vast household from crude materials; in storing these against the day of need; in looking after the servants in the mansion, keeping them up to their work, preventing waste and slovenliness; in looking after the health of the whole establishment,—binding, this minute, the lacerated foot of a great man slave, the next visiting a mother that had just borne a child, the next looking after some old fellow with the rheumatism, or the hypochondria; in rearing her own children, teaching them not only the ordinary virtues but how to serve such communities as she served, entertain company with the grace and charm of manner bred of a self-sacrificing spirit, etc.

The plantations in this region were early found to be unhealthful for white people during the summer months. In the early days the planters had resorted, accordingly, to Charleston, to Beaufort, or to other places on the seashore, during the time between the last frost of spring and the first frost of autumn. But in the generation preceding young Palmer's day it had been found that residences a few miles back from the river bottoms, on the low ridges covered by the long-leafed pines, were as healthful as those in Charleston. Thus had Walterboro and McPhersonville and other summer retreats been established. The necessity for this migration from the plantation had its advantages as well as its disadvantages. If the master's absence from the plantation militated against his prosperity, it brought him into close contact with other refined and cultivated men. Nor were the planting interests as materially interfered with, when he moved to the summer settlement, as might be supposed, for "one of the conditions of a site of a summer settlement was that it should be in reach of the plantation, of not less than a day's journey to and from, allowing a sufficient time for a supervision of the place. These summer resorts thus became social centers, collections of people of wealth, and during the summer, of leisure; for it so happened that during the summer there was little to be done on the plantation."

The summer homes were mere camps, small one-story houses with plenty of porch space; as to size, as small as the necessities of the family and guests permitted. They were generally built of undressed lumber. A great continental university cannot be judged by its buildings: these summer settlements were wonderful villages notwithstanding the homely dwellings; the formalities of polite life were observed with scrupulous care.

In these villages would be found one or two churches, a school for boys and a school for girls, taught sometimes by ministers of the gospel, sometimes by life-long teachers, and sometimes by young graduates of colleges and universities, who, after a few terms of teaching, would enter on the profession of law or medicine, or on the vocation of a minister. The school would be kept up the year around, for the sake of the ministers' families and those planters who preferred to keep their children in the village during the winter, under the care of a maiden aunt, or some other female relative, to sending them to a distant school, or providing tutors at home, or making some other shift to school them. Sometimes for the sake of its advantages the planter would keep his whole family in the village throughout the year.

The South Carolina planter was very particular about the education of his family, and particularly his sons. It is probably true that they had as high an average of education as any set of gentlemen in the United States. The planter expected to send his son from the village school to college or university. He might not care to see him become a lawyer, a doctor, or a preacher, but he hoped very earnestly to see him a man of generous education, and ready, after a little special training, for any of the professions. A fair percentage of their sons became graduates. The love of learning in the days of young Palmer was no new thing. While the conditions in South Carolina forbade the growth, in the eighteenth century, of the common school which sprang up in the New England colonies, it may be safely said that in no province was there more provision made by the wealthy for the education of the poor. In his "Retrospect of the Eighteenth Century," Dr. Samuel Miller, of Princeton, expresses the belief that the learned languages, especially the Greek, were less studied in the Eastern States than in the Southern and Middle States. "The reason he assigns is that owing to the superior wealth of the individuals in the latter States, more of their sons were educated in Europe, and brought home with them a more accurate knowledge of the classics." "In a list of Americans admitted as members of the Inns of Court in London in the twenty-five years from 1759 to 1786, recently published, South Carolina contributes more than any other State. Out of one hundred and fourteen names on the list, there are forty-six Carolinians, twenty Virginians, fifteen Marylanders, three Georgians, and one North Carolinian, making eighty-five Southerners, three fourths of the whole."[9] The love of learning which had characterized her people in colonial days remained with her throughout the first half of the nineteenth century.

The contemporaries of young Palmer resorted to the great colleges of New England, to Princeton, to the University of Virginia, the University of Georgia, or to the College of South Carolina, at Columbia, the State's own excellent institution. Their sisters received excellent private teaching, or were placed in good seminaries.

The common love of the South Carolinians for reading is probably evinced in the establishment of a public library in 1698—"the first public library" it is believed, "to be established in America." In young Palmer's time there were many fine private libraries in the State, and many more families possessed quite respectable libraries, the gradual gatherings of generations of readers. "Pope's poems and Fielding's novels sat side by side with Newton's 'Cardiphonia.' Neel's 'History of the Puritans' elbowed Scott's romances."

South Carolinians, like true Englishmen, were devoted to

[9] McCrady, *History of South Carolina under the Royal Government*, pp. 475, 476.

field sports. They rode from their infancy. In the Chickasaws they had a good breed of horses, which was greatly improved by crossing with English blooded horses. Great attention was paid to the breeding of horses; and they were trained to two gaits, walking and cantering. The saddle horses were excellent hunters, and would seldom hesitate to take a six-rail fence at a leap. The boys and girls learned to ride on tackies, which, though small, were active, enduring and easy gaited. The low country was not suited for fox-hunting, it was too cut up with creeks, marshes and swamps. The great sport was deer hunting. The clubs met early in the day. The hounds, usually in charge of a negro, soon found the scent and with full cry began the chase. Their baying was the most exhilarating music to the ears of the huntsman. They knew the country and the habits of the deer and would take their stands at certain places, and the deer, unless brought down at the earlier stands would run the gauntlet of many guns.[10]

To the boys on the plantations the dearest place was the "back-water," the partly artificial reservoir for storing water wherewith to flood the rice fields at stated seasons. Here was his best chance for shooting wild ducks, if he got there just at day dawn on some cold, frosty morning. From its dams, too, under some spreading wild mulberry or dogwood, he could fish to his heart's content, and if the plantation were one of those on salt water, he could fish, or crab, or get raccoon oysters, with the aid of a bait.

The people were as fond of indoor amusements as of field sports. Hence they cultivated music and the knowledge of games of various sorts. These could be indulged in even in the summer homes; and there also, if there was less for the boy in the way of outdoor sports, and more required in the way of dress and attendance on school, he could at least enjoy the cavalcades, "in which there was just as much ceremony in inviting a partner for the ride and sticking faithfully to her side, as if it had been a dance in which the same couple were partners from first to last."

On these cavalcades, on which many matches are said to have been made, and in frequent parties at the different homes the young people found their chief opportunities for intercourse. At the parties, which were regular affairs, there

---

[10] cf. McCrady, *Ibid.*, pp. 517, ff.

was not only the means of gratifying the taste for amusement but that of the palate, though the fare in the summer village could never quite compare with that in the plantation house. To illustrate from the substantials of the feast: in the summer settlement wheat waffles, rice waffles, wheat loaf-bread, rice loaf-bread, biscuits, johnny cakes, muffins, pancakes, domestic fowls, beef, and mutton, vegetables in season, etc., could be commanded; but at the plantation in the winter, in addition to all these, wild turkey, venison, wild duck and the fruit of the sea, for if the master or a son were not good with the gun and rod, there was always a crack shot on the plantation freely supplied with gun and ammunition in order that his master's table might be improved, and more than one successful fisherman. The people generally lived plentifully and well. Theirs was in no sense a somber life.

Political excitement has been a frequent feature of South Carolina. The excitement ran high in young Palmer's day. South Carolina, along with a number of other States, held that the power to levy duties on imports, not with a view to revenue, but to protect and aid particular classes, was not delegated to Congress. An odious, because discriminating, tariff had been borne while it was necessary in order to the payment of of the public debt. But when the debt had been paid and a large surplus was accumulating in the national treasury, the State demanded that the tariff should be conformed to the need for revenue. The demand was refused, the robbery wrought by the protective tariff continued, and continued to exasperate the South. The great leaders in South Carolina, Calhoun, Haynes, McDuffie and others, had recourse to a measure justifiable only on the ground that it was a warning that secession would follow it, if it proved ineffective. "She interposed her prerogative as a sovereign State, to judge, in the last resort, in all questions affecting her own rights, restraining the general government from collecting this revenue within her limits.' It was not ineffective. Congress passed the "Force Bill," clothing the President with the power necessary to enforce the collection, and for this purpose putting at his disposal all the land and naval forces. But for some such instrumentality as that of Mr. Clay, in his famous Compromise Act, which yielded the principle of protection while providing "a gradual reduction of duties, and that at the expiration of ten years, twenty per cent. *ad valorem* should be established as the uniform rate," there had been a collision. While some strong men opposed it, the prevailing sentiment of the people of the State demanded Nullification; and the low country, with the exception of a party in Charleston under the lead of Mr. Petigru, was almost unanimously in favor of Nullification and profoundly convinced of the right of secession. As time wore on they conceived that secession was a duty.

We shall have occasion to note in the sequel that young Palmer was, in the days of his youth, drinking in the views of the great political thinkers of the State.

The moral and religious tone of this region of the low country was excellent during these decades. Horse-racing, gambling and hard drinking had prevailed to a considerable extent in early colonial times. Nor had these habits been uprooted by the preaching of Whitefield, though they had been checked. But providences connected with the Revolutionary War, the work of evangelical ministers of all denominations and particularly the revivals under the Rev. Daniel Baker about 1831, did much to lift up the standard of morality and religion. The communities in which he grew up were Sabbath-observing, condemned worldly amusements, often thought to be entirely compatible with the profession of Christianity, and in general showed a sympathy with a mildly Puritan mode of life.

With this sketch of the environment into which our subject was born and in the midst of which he developed his God-given powers, we pass to the exhibition of his early life.

CHAPTER III.

BOYHOOD AND EARLY YOUTH.

(1818-1832.)

SUMMARY OF HIS INHERITED POWERS, AND OF THE FORCES OF HIS ENVIRONMENT.—CHARLESTON THE PLACE OF HIS BIRTH.—THE HISTORY OF MR. EDWARD PALMER'S FAMILY, 1821-1824, SKETCHED.—REV. EDWARD PALMER'S FAMILY AT DORCHESTER.—AT WALTERBORO.—"BEN PALMER" AS A SCHOOLBOY AT WALTERBORO.—THE PALMER FAMILY AT MCPHERSONVILLE.

THE 25th day of January, 1818, in the home of his parents, Edward and Sarah Bunce Palmer, on Beaufain Street, Charleston, S. C., Benjamin Morgan Palmer was born. The foregoing chapters have made it clear that he was sprung of excellent stock, and born into the midst of a civilization at once unique, commanding and noble. They have made it clear that it is only fair to look to him to manifest the sentiment of devotion to duty for which the early and honest Puritan was so remarkable; to disclose a strong native bent toward culture; to discover vigor of practical as well as intellectual character; to display sweetness of disposition along with virile motives of conduct, and strength of determination; to reveal in himself capacity for breadth of view, generosity in estimating sympathetically, so far as truth allows, diverse systems of philosophy and faith, while at the same time holding, on his own part, a very definite system of philosophy and faith; and to develop somewhat of John Calvin's power to entertain Christian friendship with those between whom and himself there may lie some great differences as to things not absolutely essential. These chapters have also made it clear that we should naturally expect civil and social sentiments colored by the ideals in vogue, not in Ohio, or in New England, or in some European country; but in the State of his nativity and of his moulding. Born and brought up in some other country, he had been somewhat otherwise.

As a matter of fact, he appears to have derived from his mother, and brought into the world at his birth, a penetrating, intense, and powerful intellect and capacities for the formation of a character equal to his intellect in its dignity, intensity, persistence and power. From his father he seems to have received a sense of personal dignity, the tendency to constant courtesy, the spirit of broad charity, and sound common sense. From the Morgans came his aggressiveness and his strong but tempered self reliance.

Thus he begins life, with a certain seriousness and earnestness contributed by the Palmer blood, which "was warranted to go a long way and keep clean and sweet to the end," with the self-reliant aggressiveness of the Morgans, and the intensity, buoyancy and brilliancy of his attracted and attractive mother, Sarah Bunce, who not only put her impress upon him in bearing him, but as we shall see, exerted the chief moulding influence upon him during his youth.

The impress of his mother State upon him has already been affirmed, and certain particulars of it pointed out. In his political views, in his bearing in society, in his breadth of sympathies, in his regard for the family and the home, he was a South Carolinian of the highest type. How large and full and clear was the impress of all that was noble in his environment upon him, will appear more fully in the sequel. For the present it will suffice to have further said: It was inevitable that a youth so impressible and so thoughtful should be affected by his civil and social surroundings. He was under a necessity of nature to note and approve, or disapprove, of that civilization, to condemn it in whole, or in part, or to take it to his heart. He was to be affected by all he met, in some way or in another, and he was to respond actively to every affection. He was not to vegetate; he was to live.

The city in which Benjamin Morgan Palmer was born was a beautiful and cultured city. The Charlestonese prided themselves on the fact that their pronunciation of English was equaled on this side of the Atlantic only in the city of Boston, Mass. It was a place of breadth of sympathies, too. Neither in the State nor in this city, which for a long time had been the colony of South Carolina, had there ever been any considerable prejudice against any man on account of his nationality or religion. The population, while coming from many European, West Indian, and other colonial sources, and containing some unworthy elements, was derived for the most part, from the best of the European peoples,—the English, Scotch, Scotch-Irish, Huguenots, Dutch from New York, and Germans from the Palatinate. These had given character to the city. It was something to be born in such a city, notwithstanding that young Palmer should be carried thence at about the age of six. As the home of his parents prior to his birth and during his early years it would not be without its influence upon himself.

It has been seen that in 1821, his father, under the conviction that he ought to give himself to the Gospel ministry, went to Andover, Mass., in order to furnish himself for that form of service. This step devolved upon Mrs. Palmer the care of four small children, the youngest and puniest of whom was Benjamin Morgan. It was a trying time for both parents. Andover was a long way from Charleston in those days. Any, or all of his family might sicken and die before the father could be informed of their illness. Mr. Palmer as a successful teacher, had been supporting his family in entire comfort. Now the mother would have to be bread winner for the little ones. On taking leave of his children, Mr. Palmer is reported to have long held the frail little Benjamin in his arms, and to have said, "My poor little Benny, I suppose I shall never see you again in this world. You will hardly live to pass your fifth year." Mrs. Palmer and her sister, Mrs. Axson, took a large house in the southern part of Charleston, perhaps on Lamball street; and there kept a small boarding school during the first two years of Mr. Palmer's sojourn in Andover. During this period Mrs. Palmer seems to have kept a few sturdy and reputable young men as boarders also. During 1822 to 1823, the hand of God was sore upon the little family thus orphaned of a father's care. Within a week two fair children were smitten and died, the bright, strong, resourceful young mother, crushed in heart, suffered only less than her far-away husband, who, bereft of his children, felt that he could not assuage the grief of the wife and mother as if at her side. He resolved that the three living members of his family should at once come to Andover to be with him during the remainder of his period of study there.

Accordingly they repaired to Andover and spent there the year 1823 to 1824. There the family kept house; and Mrs. Palmer evinced both her energy, her ability, and her sense of the responsibilities that would devolve upon her as a minister's wife by reading through Locke's "Essay on the Human Understanding," and other useful books. She tried to improve the mind of her oldest child, Sophronia also, by having her read portions of these books, including Locke's. The child was only nine and a half years old; but the mother secured the service without making it an irksome labor to the little girl. She taught her child to think that she could thus help her mother, who would listen to the reading and at the same time perform some domestic labor.

It is worth while to notice again this young matron, slender, and graceful in movement, with a rather lofty and beautifully moulded forehead, penetrating but sweet steel blue eyes, a well shaped nose, a flexible mouth of sufficiently generous proportions, a strong but not a stubborn lower face, and a high purposefulness in all her carriage. She understands and sympathizes with all her children and secures their obedience with tactfulness and ease. The mothering of her children, their noblest development, she makes her high and holy business.

As for young Benjamin, he is disporting himself much as other children between five and six. Soon after their reaching Andover, and while the family was, for about a week, in a boarding house, he is said indeed, to have distinguished himself by rushing one morning into the kitchen and demanding for his breakfast some South Carolina hominy instead of the breakfast dishes common in New England at the time. He loved hoop, ball, and kite; and in the winter to play in the snow with his sister Sophronia, or with her to slide on the ice. They had many experiences which it delighted them greatly to recall in later times: the run of the orchards of considerate neighbors, the roasting of apples on the winter nights. Particularly they never forgot the beautiful wild moss roses which the mother loved so well, and which they would gather for her.

We are not informed of the state of advancement in learning at which this little boy had arrived on leaving New England; but if safe inference may be made from the fact that his sister Sophronia was able to read the New Testament at the age of four; and from the fact that at the age of fourteen he himself was well prepared for college, he had probably made considerable advancement in the rudimentary studies for young children. The same thing may be argued from the intense concern of his mother for her children's progress; and from his devotion to her. It is said that he became her constant companion; and that he would drop his play at any time to go to hear her read or talk, or a little later, to read to her.

Returning to South Carolina in 1824, the Rev. Edward Palmer and his family lived for three years at Dorchester, about eighteen miles from Charleston, in the district of Colleton. Dorchester, now a decadent village, is the principal scene of the romantic tale of the "Partisan," by Simms. In the very heart of the district ennobled by so many gallant episodes of the struggle for independence of Great Britain, it was an ideal place for the development of the historical imagination as well as of the more fundamental tastes for a knowledge of the past. Nor could his gifted mother fail to avail herself of such an occasion. Up to their leaving Dorchester she seems to have been almost his only teacher. In addition to teaching him the rudimental learning usually given boys of his age, she read with him the whole of Shakespeare's plays, Milton's "Paradise Lost," and Scott's novels, thus helping him to that luxuriance, beauty and precision of style for which his own pen was to be remarkable. Moreover, she grounded him deeply in the noblest principles of character and conduct. She, more than any one else, gave the primal shaping to a character which was to develop into unusual splendor and to make him one of the greatest figures of his century.

Two or three incidents related of his childhood, and perhaps to be assigned to the period during which the family was living at Dorchester, would seem to indicate that his mother had her hands full in the effort to bring him up aright. He was undoubtedly a child of strong will and of wilfullness as well. Of one of these incidents he carried to the day of his death a memorial. His father had allowed his faithful horse to graze on the little lawn around the cottage in which he was living. He had warned his son Benjamin to keep away from the animal, but the imp of mischief was incarnated in him; he delighted in creeping up to the animal and startling him with a smart cut, or other means, into a run. Unfortunately, on one occasion he got too near, the horse landed a kick on the face of his tormentor, bruised and cut his lips not a little, and slit one side of a nostril to such an extent that he bore the marks, slightly disfiguring that side of his face, to the day of his death.

We are told again, that the spirit of mischief taking possession of him one morning during family prayers, he slipped out of the house and amused himself by chasing a cat around the yard. In requital he received a sound flogging from his exacting father. The most significant story of the period, however, is the following: A paternal measure, an account of which has not been preserved, had provoked the boy's resentment. Now his father was a man of great neatness and order about his writing as about all his work. Valuable belongings on his writing table were a neat pen-knife for sharpening his quill pens, scissors, paper cutter, etc. It seems that Mr. Palmer valued very particularly these articles. To "pay" his father for the paternal measure just referred to, Benjamin took them and deposited them in a brook hard by. Pretty soon Mr. Palmer missed them, made a search, questioned his household, and amongst the rest Benjamin, who evaded the question for a time and then boldly "lied" about the matter, declaring that he was in no wise chargeable with their misplacement. He joined with apparent sedulousness in the hunt for them. He kept up the pretense for several days. He had chosen to avenge himself on his father and it was hard for him to give over. But the burden was too heavy for so ingenuous a nature. It was his "first lie," or series of lies, for in his old days he said, "I lied straight through for a week." He was all the while most miserable. Child though he was, appetite and sleep were going from him. At the end of the week he rushed one morning into the house, crying, "Where is father?" Receiving the reply, "He is in his study, you must not interrupt him," he exclaimed, "I cannot help it, I must interrupt him;" and rushing in, he confessed the whole matter. When nearing eighty he could say that since that day he did not know that he had ever been guilty of a lie. The loathsomeness of lying was to his nature so appalling that the one experience was too much.

From Dorchester, with its inspiring traditions and its "grand old trees," Mr. Palmer removed with his family to Walterboro in the year 1827. This place had been in the beginning, a summering resort. The planters from about Old Bethel Church on the Edisto, and from the Salkehatchie, had found that there, under the long-leafed pine, they could pass the summer in health. Their houses were plain but comfortable one-story cottages; and their houses had given character to the buildings that were subsequently erected for more permanent occupancy. We may therefore imagine the Palmers moving into a "small one-story cottage," quite low to the ground, for their home in Walterboro. While the dwellings were simple, the place was one of refinement and culture. It was the region of the Glovers, the Hendersons, the Perrys, the Oswalds, the Dents, the Linings, the Frasers, the Parkers, the Fishburnes, the Riverses, the Witsells, and others of good name in South Carolina. It seems to have had its fair proportion of professional gentlemen, for in addition to the ministers of religion and the doctors of physic, tradition tells of the lawyers : J. D. Edwards, D. S. Henderson, J. B. Perry, Solicitor of the Circuit and an eminent legal light, M. E. Carr, O. P. Williams and Carloss Tracy.

In this place the Rev. Edward Palmer and his family continued to live, on this occasion, till about 1832. Mr. Palmer soon became universally and intensely beloved. He was to return to this pastorate again in 1844, there to pass the remainder of his ministerial life, in the greatest honor and affection. The following simple incident, the date of which has not been precisely fixed, indicates somewhat of the regard in which he was held: Some one hazarded a criticism of Mr. Palmer one day, in the presence of an aged parishioner, Mrs. Witsell. Whereupon she broke into ejaculatory thanksgiving to God, explaining that but for the criticism Mr. Palmer would soon have died, since God in his holy Word, had pronounced woe unto him of whom no man spake evil. Mrs. Palmer, in some respects more admired, was only less beloved because by reason of her woman's sphere she was less widely known. It can be said that she made the young people of the town, and especially the girls and young women of her husband's flock, her own. Naturally under such circumstances, in this hospitable region, every door was open to their children, and amongst the rest to Benjamin Morgan. The son of the beloved and honored Christian minister was welcome to the most intimate intercourse with the sons of gentlemen of the highest station, and received at the hands of these gentlemen themselves every proper consideration. As during these years at Walterboro, young Palmer was passing from the age of boyhood to youth, was waking to a manlier life, we must think of him as absorbing much from the society around him. There are not wanting indications that it was in these years that he made the principles of South Carolina civilization tentatively his own.

The country had been wrought up to the nullification measures. The South Carolina principles were at stake. They and the oppressive and "unrighteous tariff" were the staples of conversation. We, indeed, are not told of his study of these principles, but by 1833 he is found defending them bravely. He who knows our subject feels safe in saying that he had given the matter study before taking his stand in regard to it.

These Walterboro years were important not only because of the stimulus to the formation of his views on civil matters, but because he then came, for the first time, under other teachers than his parents. The Hon. Daniel J. Pope, of Columbia, S. C., is our authority for the following account of the most influential teacher under whose influence "Ben Palmer came in this period:" The Rev. J. B. Van Dyck was not a great scholar. He was a rather poor mathematician; a good Latin scholar, but not a first-class Greek scholar. He knew enough to prepare men well for college. While not a great scholar he was a great teacher, he could tell what he knew so as to make a boy understand it. He could, and did, excite the ambition of his boys. Some men have great learning and no power to impart it. Others have no great learning but power to impart all they have, and to stimulate their more gifted pupils to attainments beyond the reach of their own achievements. Mr. Van Dyck belonged to the latter class. Without any extraordinary learning, he had wonderful power of impartation. In addition to the ordinary training of the schoolroom, Mr. Van Dyck established a debating society into which he introduced the boys. He sometimes presided. "While in other schools the boys were playing, in his school they were learning to debate and to speak."

With Mr. Pope, Mr. James Glover, of Walterboro, also, about eighty years of age, agrees as to most of the foregoing account of Mr. Van Dyck. He adds that Mr. Van Dyck was remarkable as a disciplinarian, being rigid to the point of severity.

These old gentlemen unite in affirming that "Ben Palmer" was "a good boy," "played little," and "studied hard," "a model boy." Mr. Pope, who entered the school about the time young Palmer left, says, that "Palmer stood at the very head of this school, had learned all to be taught there by the time he was fourteen, and went at that age "to Amherst thoroughly prepared." Tradition also says that Ben Palmer was the prince of debaters and speakers in that little debating society organized by Mr. Van Dyck. Amongst his schoolmates were Paul A. M. Williams, Laurence Fishburne, Cross-keys Oswald, Benjamin Whaley, and Dr. John O. Gilmer.

The venerable Mr. E. E. Bellinger, Episcopal minister in Walterboro, tells (in 1904) a story of young Palmer's school-days which if it be authentic, betrays on the part of our subject wonderful self-possession. According to Mr. Bellinger, Ben Palmer had gotten into a fight with a larger boy of savage temper, was down, and the boy with a knife drawn was threatening to take his life. Lying on the ground Palmer looked his antagonist in the face and saw his savagery rampant—the fellow was afterwards driven out of his State on account of murder,—and said to him, "Blank, I have but one dollar in the world but if you will spare my life I will give it to you." The savage said, "That is not enough, Ben. You must do more. You have no trouble in reading Greek and Latin; I do, I can hardly read at all. You must read my language lessons from now till the end of the term." The agreement was made, and kept.

In the autumn of 1831 the Rev. Edward Palmer had been induced to accept a call from a Presbyterian church at Stony Creek, in Beaufort District. As he did not move his family until about a year had passed, his son had enjoyed the advantages of the Walterboro Academy during that year without separation from his father's family.

In the summer of 1832, in the fifteenth year of his age, he starts to a Northern college. His experiences there, and in the new home to which his father had removed prior to young Palmer's return "in disgrace," and his subsequent experiences in a Southern university are to be sketched in the ensuing chapter.

CHAPTER IV.

DAYS OF HIS COLLEGE TRAINING.

(1832-1838.)

Goes to Amherst College, in Massachusetts, 1832.—His Career There Till the Spring of 1834.—His Return to South Carolina.—The Home of his Father's Family at this Time.—His Reception by his Parents.—Engaged in Teaching, 1834-1836.—Conversion in 1836, and Union with the Church in McPhersonville.—Enters University of Georgia, January, 1837.—Career in that University till August, 1838.—A Question to be Solved.

At the age of fourteen "Ben Palmer" struck the ordinary observer as undersized; and as probably a youth of no special parts. The man of close observation noted many things in the youngster, however, which attracted attention. Undersized he certainly was; but his movements were graceful as those of a young leopard. From the toes of his pretty little feet to the top of his head he was lithe, supple, elastic, and apparently perfectly healthful. His hands seemed a little less delicately formed than his feet, but were small for a person of his size. If he wanted a trifle in breadth across the shoulders, he enjoyed a compensation for that defect in the depth of his chest. In his face there were warring elements. He was very dark, and had something about his lips (due in part it may be to the kick received from his father's horse), which suggested a highly sensitive and sensuous nature. But there was indomitable strength of will written on his lower jaw, and around that same homely mouth. He had a well-shaped but not large head. His nose was a good one on one side, disfigured slightly by the scar left by the hoof of the horse on the other. In the eyes were features that redeemed and transfigured the face. They always sparkled and changed with the changing thoughts and feelings by which he was possessed; and when he spoke his voice revealed another great attraction. It was a wonderful instrument: it had in it music and laughter, mourning and tears, the thunders of war, and the songs of peace. If he spoke of the waves you could hear their swish in that voice, gentle or swelling as he saw the waves themselves. He thus plainly appeared to be a youth of extraordinary gifts. He himself, it was further noted, had no consciousness of this as yet. He was remarkably free from any self-consciousness. He was, while not forward, easily accessible to his fellows, a remarkably well-bred young fellow.

He is pretty young to start out, all alone, for Amherst, in far-off Massachusetts. But he is of courageous stock; and we may think of his voyage as costing less of anxiety to his parents than most mothers and fathers would feel; and as looking to him as involving no risk in comparison with the ends to be gained by going. One thing tried him—the parting from home and mother. He had been a mother's boy. His disposition seems to have been much like hers. Between them there was a large and rich sympathy. They had had years of communing together of whatsoever things are true, whatsoever things are honest, whatsoever things are just, whatsoever things are pure, whatsoever things are lovely, whatsoever things are of good report.

The Rev. Edward Palmer did not go with his son to Charleston, secure passage with some reliable skipper for him, and see the lad safely aboard for the sail to New York. He did not even ask his elder brother, the Rev. Dr. Benjamin Morgan Palmer, of the "Circular Church" in the city of Charleston, to see his nephew and namesake safely aboard a suitable vessel. The lad was regarded as able to take care of himself. He accordingly went alone from his home in Walterboro to Charleston, provided for his own passage, and boarded his vessel. It would be interesting to know what he saw and heard on the voyage; what questions he put to the skipper and to his fellow-passengers; to know how he felt as the city of Charleston, the place of his birth, the home of his fathers, the capital of his State, faded from his view; and to know what he felt as he watched the rolling billows of the apparently limitless expanse of sea about him, borrowing and adding to their own the varying hues of the vast heavens above him. We may be certain that unusual thoughts and imaginations possessed him; and that had he expressed them, he would have done it in a style at once stately and beautiful, with a kind of high Alpine imagery. For such was his wont. He was of the class of beings who habitually, and of nature, express themselves in lofty and noble terms of sense, who see even commonplace things in their more dignified aspects.

After an uneventful voyage he reached New York, and thence made his way to the picturesque village of Amherst. The village of Amherst was to derive a long growing distinction as the seat of Amherst College. Here, on a hill, off from the forks of the Connecticut, the college had been planted in 1821. It was therefore, a very young college which this young South Carolinian had gone so far to enter. But while young, it had an efficient faculty. It had been founded mainly for the purpose of educating poor and pious young men for the Gospel ministry. There was a large charity fund which paid the tuition fees of a considerable number of students. Perhaps the chief considerations with his parents in making this choice of a college for their son, were the reputation of the place for piety (which stood then in striking contrast, in this respect, to the College of South Carolina), the hope that their son might there be converted and led to dedicate himself to the ministry, and the prospect of relatively small cost in educating him. Amherst was almost matchless at the time for offering literary advantages at little cost. Tuition and room rent could be obtained for $5.25 per term. Table board in a club was to be had at $1.25 per week. The very economical student could get through a year's study on a total expenditure, including that for clothes, of $150.00. There is no reason to suppose that young Palmer was expected to maintain himself on so small a sum; but he was expected to consult economy. His father had but a small salary on which to maintain and educate his family.

"A small group of Southern students nestled like birds in a nest, in that far-off New England clime. Five of the number hailed from Virginia, four from Georgia, and one poor lone speckled bird from South Carolina. The heart lingers a moment over this little coterie, trying to keep itself warm in that cold region by building close together in the bonds of a special friendship. Most of the group rose to eminence in different walks, but chiefly in the service of the church. The names, if given here to the reader, would be found familiar to history, either as Ambassadors at foreign courts, as Chancellors of Universities, or as Ecclesiastics or Divines. It was an uncanny time for Southern men to trim their sails for Northern seas. The Nullification storm had just burst over the country, and was not yet appeased. The abolition fanaticism was rising to the height of its frenzy. The elements of conflict were gathering in the theological world, which a little later resulted in the schism rending the Presbyterian Church asunder. The sky was full of portents, and the air screamed with war cries on every side. The unfortunate South Carolinian, whom fate reserves to record in these pages his own disaster, was too young and unformed in character to steer his bark over such tempestuous billows, and was soon wrecked upon a treacherous reef." [1]

Amongst his fellow students from the South were John Holmes Bocock and Stuart Robinson. Amongst those from the North was Henry Ward Beecher. Friendships more or less strong were formed between "Ben Palmer" and each of these men. Beecher was five years older than Palmer, and a member of a more advanced class. But the youth and the young man were naturally attracted to one another. They were alike in possessing active minds, and facile and powerful speech. They were unlike in that Beecher was the possessor of a vastly more impressive figure, was capable of more sensuous and lurid rhetoric, and could with little reason, or against reason, sweep the average audience with him, while Palmer had always to have reason on his side in order to effective speaking. Palmer had more force with all who thought. He almost never lost command of himself, nor attempted to move without reason at the helm. His speech was more classic, more Demosthenian, more moving to the thoughtful, because in him reason was wedded to feeling and to passion. These two were drawn together also by a common love for the game of chess, a game in which it is said that Mr. Palmer excelled Mr. Beecher.

But if young Palmer formed friendships with men of the Northeast, he found frequent occasions of jars to that friendship. He heard much of the hot-headedness of his section and of his own State in particular, on account of the Nullification measure. He heard the whole South grossly abused on account of her peculiar institution of slavery. He heard the masters and mistresses of slaves vilified as inhuman semi-barbarians. He was not the youth to sit under these slanders in an apathetic, much less in an approving, way. He knew well many large slave holders. He had been a frequent inmate of their homes. He knew the relative happiness and contentment of the slaves. His father had, from the start, been as much a pastor of the slaves as of their masters. He had received more slaves into his churches than whites. More than two hundred and fifty colored members were received into one of his little country churches between 1832 and 1860. Nor was the Rev.

---

[1] From Dr. Palmer's unpublished manuscript on Dr. Stuart Robinson.

Edward Palmer's course exceptional in regard to the slaves. White Christians generally were solicitous, in his region, for the spiritual welfare of their black people. Young Palmer soon became marked as a spokesman for the Southern cause, and was worried not a little by the assaults, in the classroom and on the campus, made upon the land of his birth and rearing. His championship probably provoked repeated assaults. His irritation, thus produced, was not without determining influence in a crisis which was to come in the history of his relations with the faculty.

Meanwhile he had been a good student, and report says that he stood first in his class, notwithstanding his extreme youth. He had completed his first year and gotten about midway of the second, when the crisis in his history as a student in Amherst came.

The Rev. Thomas A. Hoyt, D.D., has left the following account of the occasion of the passage:

"Palmer was attached to a literary society, the members of which were bound by a solemn pledge not to disclose what occurred at its meetings. One of the exercises consisted of the reading by the secretary of anonymous papers which had been deposited in a box at the door. A paper was read at one of the meetings which contained caustic but humorous criticisms of the professors. A divinity student betrayed his fellow-members by informing the Faculty. At the next meeting of the society, an order was read forbidding the exercise, whereupon Palmer, then about sixteen years of age, moved that the paper conveying the order be tabled indefinitely, alleging that the Faculty could not know of the exercises except through the treachery of one of the students, and that it was unworthy of the dignity of the professors to accept perjured testimony as evidence. The president was afraid to put the motion to vote, but two members held him in the chair while the question was put and carried. This transaction was promptly communicated by the same informer to the Faculty.

"That honorable body thereupon attempted discipline for both offenses. In order to discover the author of the obnoxious paper, their plan was to force all who could do so, to swear that they were guiltless; and thus force them by indirection to place the offense at the door of the culprit. A number of high spirited fellows were indignant that they should be thus forced into the role of informers, against their pledge, too, as members of a secret society. The sixteen-year-old Palmer was at their head and their mouthpiece. When summoned into the presence of the Faculty and requested to make his disavowal, he informed that body that he was in honor bound to take no part in disclosing what went on in a society the members of which were each pledged to secrecy. The Faculty insisted that he must tell, declaring that they were as competent to judge of that which was compatible with honor as he was. He refused in absolute terms to comply with their demand. They threatened to expel him should he persist. 'Well, sirs,' said he, 'I will take expulsion at your hands rather than trample upon my sense of honor.' The boy here shows 'the father of the man,' as Dr. Stuart Robinson once remarked, when speaking of the incident. He displayed 'the high qualities of honor and courage which marked his life.' It was some little time before he could leave the town. The Faculty repenting of their severity in dealing with him on account of his youth, and perhaps, on account of the sentiments he had expressed, came to him and would have taken him back; but owing to the irritation he had suffered at the hands of the critics of his State and section and to his dislike of the spirit of the college as illustrated in the occasion of his expulsion, he was determined to leave the institution and to return to his own people. In the whole episode he had behaved like a true son of South Carolina. When one morning, on the top of a stage, he left Amherst, he had good proof that his New England fellow students were generous enough to feel and express their admiration for his course. It is said that 'the entire body of undergraduates assembled and gave him a great ovation, sending him off with ringing cheers.'"

He proceeded to New York, and there engaged passage for Charleston, S. C. While waiting for the sailing of his vessel an incident happened which gave him excruciating misery for about six hours and exerted a life-long influence upon him, inclining him to sympathize with all the stranded sons and daughters of men. Killing time by strolling the streets, he came upon a second-hand book store, entered and looked over the shelves. He discovered a work of value and proposed to buy it. This book store was kept by rascals. Young Palmer had but one bill of currency, a fifty-dollar note. He purchased the book and gave the note in payment, asking for the change. The recipient, leaving his partner in charge, said, "I will go out and get the change." Minutes passed, an hour dragged by; the youth approached the other partner and remarked on the length of time he had to wait for his money; he received the cruel reply that he would never see his money again, that the fellow would not come back. This was to the country-bred youth a staggering blow. He had no other money. He had not yet paid his passage. He did not know what to do. He was afraid to go out in search of a policeman and lodge complaint, lest he himself should be charged with being an impostor. In grim desperation he resolved to stay in that store as long as it should be possible that he might confront the scoundrel upon his return. After six weary hours had passed the man cautiously ventured back to the neighborhood. Circumstances favored Mr. Palmer. While the knave was trying to discover whether the coast was clear of the purchaser, that severely tried young man caught sight of him, dashed upon him, when for very shame the shabby fellow gave up the money.

To his latest day he could never recall this experience without pain. He was ever remarkably ready to respond to all appeals for help made by young men. He often suffered at the hands of the unworthy importunate. He knew it, but would say, "Twelve impostors may hoodwink me, but in the thirteenth man I may aid a person in real need. I will give the money to the thirteen that I may certainly give to him who really needs. I was once in awful straits and if my money had not been returned I had determined to go to some minister of my own church and tell my story and ask him for help. I am behaving now simply as I would have had others behave toward me."

Recovering his money and boarding his ship he reached Charleston, S. C., without other important incident. Thence he made his way to the Pocotaligo Creek and up it to the neighborhood in which his father was now living.

As already narrated Rev. Edward Palmer had in 1831 changed his field of labor from Walterboro to Stony Creek, twenty-five or thirty miles distant. He had not removed from Walterboro, however, till 1832, and perhaps not till after his son had left for Amherst. In the spring of 1834 when "Ben Palmer" was trying to reach his parents, they were living at a country plantation called Laurium, not far from the Stony Creek Church. It will be recalled that the planters whose families worshipped at this church passed their summers at McPhersonville, about seven miles off, on the sand hills and under the long-leafed pines; and that they had a "parsonage" there for their preacher's summer house. They had had a manse near Stony Creek Church for his use in the winter when the most of the planters had their families on the plantations; but the parsonage had been burned and because of the want of a manse they had rented for their pastor's use during the winter of 1833-1834, the plantation house of Laurium. This was a rather imposing house for a minister. The original Laurium house had been of the usual plan, a two-story house, with hall and stairway midway between the two ends, a plain square room on either side of the hall in each story, and broad piazzas on north and south. The preceding owner had added a very long room on each end, the rooms being as long as the breadth of the original house and of the two piazzas, and fashioned in front in octagonal form. They were intended, one as a ball-room and the other as a supper room. The front piazza looked to the north, the back one to the south. It was warm and sunny, with orange trees on either side of the steps.

Ben Palmer had been longing for this home for weeks. Every person he most loved was there. The stern father he admired was there; his two bright and devoted sisters were there; and his younger brother; most of all, his mother, the brilliant, buoyant, pure and noble, his companion, inspiration and mentor was there. He knew that reports from Amherst had outrun him. He did not know how his family would receive him. Laurium did not have a landing on the Pocotaligo, but the boats touched at the adjoining plantation owned by a Mr. Wm. G. Martin, who was an elder or deacon in Stony Creek Church. Ben Palmer left the boat at Mr. Martin's landing, and went to his house as the hour of the little schooner's arrival was late at night. Anticipating some trouble at home, he laid his case before Mr. Martin, who went over and acquainted Mr. and Mrs. Palmer with the fact of their son's arrival at his place. He returned with the message that Benjamin was to come on home.

His welcome under the paternal roof as extended by his father was not warm. Tradition says that Mr. Palmer, having heard the side of the Faculty directly from them, had made up his mind that his son's course could not be justified; that he was greatly mortified at his dismissal from college; felt that his son had sacrificed foolishly capital advantages; and that, as he was himself without private fortune and living on a modest salary, the sacrifice was perhaps an irreparable one. He was fearfully disappointed with the outcome of sending his son, on whom he had set high hopes, to the far-off Northern college. Traditions vary as to the extent of severity which he now displayed. Some say that he forbade his son the house, telling him that he would henceforth have to shift for himself. Others says that he simply expressed plainly his own view of his son's course, suppressed the son's attempted explanation and justification of the course and refused to extend to him the hand of welcome. Whatever the course of the father, it was too severe for such a high-spirited youth, conscious of no grave fault in himself in connection with his expulsion from college. The challenge in his father's conduct and language he was about to accept by leaving home, to begin the future by himself. But he had not reckoned with all his hosts. His mother, of spirit like her boy, and understanding her son to the core, stands near with beating heart, but a masterful grasp of the whole household, and so we may look upon mother and son seated a few minutes later, perhaps in that sunny south porch, with the orange trees on either side of the pathway leading toward the river, talking the whole matter over, and unconsciously growing a deeper sympathy between themselves than ever. Her heart and mind dominate the hour. She understands and sympathizes with the son. She hears the whole story and sees in it as much to admire as to condemn, and perhaps more. She at the same time appreciates fully the father's feelings, and shows the son how natural and inevitable it is that his father should feel so about the matter. There was no great cordiality speedily established between the father and the son. Indeed, it was some years before the estrangement, so engendered, passed entirely away. It did pass entirely away and the father and son became rarely devoted the one to the other. Meanwhile the mother and the wife had ruled both like the queen she was. For her services to him at this time, her son was to bless her memory to the end of his long and most honored life. He would reverently say, "Under God she was at this time my savior," and the thought of her caused many a stirring and eloquent period to roll from his heart and brain, and the performance of many a heroic deed.

The next two or three years young Palmer spent in the work of teaching and private study. He seems to have gone to teaching very soon after his return, in the early spring of 1834, in the family of Mr. Wm. G. Martin, the good man to whom he had gone on leaving the schooner that brought him up the Pocotaligo homeward bound. He next taught during the summer of 1834 the village schoool in McPhersonville in which his father's family and those of his parishioner planters passed their summers. The winter of 1835-1836 he seems to have spent teaching in the family of Mr. Hibbens, at Mt. Pleasant, across the Cooper river from Charleston. He may have taught again in McPhersonville in the summer and autumn of 1836. Tradition says that he was an effective teacher and a determined disciplinarian, that he easily and effectually quelled a somewhat mutinous band of larger boys in the village school that resented his strictness; but reports say also that he was worsted on one occasion by his little sister Sally. It seems that she was a great pet of his; that it was his delight also to lie down and have her rub his head that he might the more easily fall into an after-dinner nap. At the school one day she incurred his official displeasure. He ordered her to take her stand on a high bench in front of the teacher's desk, a kind of punishment he was wont to apply to misdoers. The humiliation was too much for the little miss. Flaring with indignation, she raised her fist aloft and exclaimed, "Yes, sir; you will not have me to rub your head any more when you wish to take a nap;" and bolting for the door, she ran home. What the final upshot of this struggle between authority and wilfulness was, tradition has not reported.

The teaching of the young is a valuable training for men who are to deal with their fellows either as lawyers or ministers. The schoolroom is a fine place in which to study human nature. Providence was training this young man in an excellent school, we may well believe therefore, in these several schoolrooms in which he was trying to teach children and youth. He was at this time, too, taking in more fully the peculiar culture of the country, and unconsciously storing up a great amount of matter which he would afterwards use as illustrative of God's truth from his royal pulpit.

He was now at the age to be invited to the house parties on the plantations. His social standing and his gifts made him welcome everywhere. If the city cousin from Charleston possessed superior polish, he was the youth to note it with discrimination, and to appropriate that which was genuinely elegant, without despising in the least the simpler virtues of his rural neighbors.

He had on these visits, and when residing as a tutor in the families of planters, the best opportunity to acquaint himself with all the methods of that life. And those methods were still so primitive, says Professor Hutson, "that there were many things in the daily life around him to illustrate vividly for young Palmer the scenes of Scripture. There was the plantation mill with its upper and nether mill-stone, the lone grinder at the mill, and the song with which he solaced his labors. There was the threshing-floor of beaten clay where the rice was threshed out by flails swung by sturdy hands. There was the winnowing tower where the rough rice was separated from the chaff. There was the huge wooden mortar wherein with a great wooden pestle the rough rice was beaten clean of its husks. There were the yokes of oxen, the sheep-fold, the lowing cattle driven slowly homeward from pasture to cowpen. There was, too, all that variety and fulness of life which made life on the plantation so much richer than life in the village or town." During a considerable portion of this period, after his return from Amherst, he was the subject of profound religious impressions which at length resulted in his conversion, in the summer of 1836. He had been carefully trained in the knowledge of God's truth. He understood that in taking Christ as his Savior he must take him as Master. Rebellion ran rampant in his heart. He trembled on the brink of infidelity. He has left behind some brief indications as to his experiences at the time as well as to certain circumstances precedent to his conversion.

In his little volume on the "Formation of Character" he gives us a leaf of his own history. He says: [2]

> "When I was seventeen years of age, I was thrown into a large city as much given to gaiety as this, without being subject to any control. I was irreligious, nay, worse than that, I was hostile to religion, in decided hostility to God and the Gospel, in such evil posture that, had I fallen into the hands of scoffers I might have become as infidel as they. Surrounded by companions as unrestrained as myself, most of whom sank into premature graves, through the mercy of God I was saved."

In one of his published sermons,[3] he exclaims:

> "I have no idea that there is one in all this assembly who has ever been, in the worst crisis of his history, the guilty and blasphemous wretch that he was at eighteen years of age who this morning addresses to you the Gospel of the Grace of God."

"The long rankling sense of injustice, as he saw it inflicted by Christian people, set him fearfully against religion," says Dr. R. R. Mallard, so that when grace found him, it found him kicking, like Saul of Tarsus, against the pricks.

---

[2] See pp. 125 and 126. [3] *Sermons,* Vol. I., p. 596.

In an address in memory of Rev. I. S. K. Axson, D.D., pastor of the Independent Presbyterian Church of Savannah, Ga., Dr. Palmer said:

"It is known to but few that the tie which bound the speaker to Dr. Axson was one of grace as well as of nature. There was a spiritual relationship between us in addition to that of kindred and of blood. It happened on this wise. In journeying from Dorchester to Liberty County, his second pastoral charge, his path lay before my father's door. It was my office to light him to his chamber at night; when placing the candle upon his table it was natural to pause a few seconds before parting. He seized the opportunity to address me on the subject of personal religion. There was a persuasiveness in his tone that soothed me as he said: 'My cousin, you are growing up fast to manhood; is it not a good time to give yourself to the Savior, when you are soon to choose the course in life which you shall pursue?' Subdued by his gentleness, I replied: 'Cousin Stockton, I am doubtless regarded by all around me as thoughtless and flippant, because I turn the edge of every appeal with a jest, but I am free to confess to you that for eighteen months I have lived in the bosom of as fierce a storm as ever swept over a human soul.' My friends, I am describing his career, not my own. I may not, therefore, tell the whole story of a heart that trembled on the verge of scoffing and infidelity, conscious of its bitter hatred of God and of divine things. But when this gentle Nathanael said to me, 'Close it up, my cousin, close it up, and be at peace with God,' before reaching the door of his chamber, I took the solemn vow that I would make the salvation of my soul the supreme business of my life, even if it should not be attained until the last hour of a life as long as that of Methuselah. It was long before peace came; for the sea is slow to subside after it has been tossed by a tempest. Six weary months, full of darkness and disappointment, elapsed before the prison door was opened and the captive was free, and the temptation was strong to abandon all in despair but for the solemnity of the form in which the vow was taken. When the peace came, it came to stay, and through five and fifty years it has deepened in the soul to which it came as the balm of heaven. Have I not a commission to be with you to-night and to speak the praise of him who then put his hand upon the burning brand to pluck it from the fire? I believe it was a comfort to him to know the agency he had in saving a great sinner from eternal death, and it is sweet to me to lay this memory as a laurel leaf upon his grave."

We cannot understand from this reference to himself as a great sinner that he was ever addicted to gross sin. It is believed that from a mere human point of view his life would have appeared clean and high. According to the record of the

Stony Creek session book he was admitted to membership in that church July 10, 1836. The scene of admission was the chapel in McPhersonville, in which he was to preach from time to time, and for the last time in April, 1899, when he was to make feeling allusion to this important day in his life's history.

In January, 1837, he renewed his academic studies in the University of Georgia. This institution had been chartered in 1785, but not opened till 1801. During the presidencies of Moses Waddell, D.D. (1819-1829), and of Alonzo Church, D.D. (1829, ff.), it had taken rank with the better colleges of the land. Moreover, and this was no insignificant thing in the eyes of the Palmers, the university and the now pretty little town of Athens, off the shoals of the north fork of the Oconee, amid the foothills of the Blue Ridge, were centers of piety and sound morality as well as of culture. These considerations were leading not a few South Carolina youths to the Georgia school.

We are able to take a view of the Faculty, of the student body, and of young Palmer during this period, January, 1837, to August, 1838, as seen by his roommate for the last session, who is now the Hon. Daniel J. Pope, head law professor in the University of South Carolina. According to Mr. Pope, Dr. Alonzo Church, like a good many able teachers, could not preach, but was a man of great executive abilities and a superb mathematician, but at this time carrying the work of the chair of Ethics and Metaphysics in addition to his executive labors. He had no superior as a manager of young men. He was courtesy and dignity personified. His looks were in his favor: he was about six feet tall, slender and graceful, a brunette, with extraordinarily dark and brilliant eyes, dark hair, a face classical in its modeling and proportions. He was delightful in conversation. He had a delightful voice and lectured to his classes with wonderful ease. He possessed great facility in calling out a discussion of a point on the part of the class and delighted in doing so. He was not a man of wit; but once said a witty thing. A student had gotten hold of his hat and had written in it the word "fool." The doctor picked his hat up, looked at the scrawl with surprise and said: "I do not know who has done it, but some one has written his name in my hat." He made his home educative of our manners. He and his wife, a very handsome woman, were charming socially, and had four beautiful and very charming daughters. They conducted the affairs of the house, and had all the conversational powers of their father. The boys were all in love with them.

All the other professors were able men and very competent teachers. The professor of ancient languages, James P. Waddell, was an excellent classical scholar. William Lehman, in the Chair of Modern Languages, and Dr. Henry Hull in that of Mathematics, were good teachers. Professor James Jackson of the Chairs of Natural Philosophy and Chemistry, was a splendid old fellow, much beloved by the students, "a great Presbyterian, whose face looked every Sunday as if it could not wreathe into a smile at the most beautiful thing in nature or art. He loved a fight and always made the boys tell him fully about every one that occurred." But one of the most remarkable men was Prof. C. F. McKay, Professor of Civil Engineering. He was a great mathematician, an admirable English scholar, and all round, one of the most remarkable men I ever knew.

Among Ben Palmer's schoolmates were men who afterwards were known as Dr. James Jackson, Justice of the Supreme Court; Judge Benjamin P. Pressley, of the Circuit Court of South Carolina; Judge John S. Shorter, of the Superior Court of Alabama; John LeConte, M.D., LL.D., of many distinguished positions, finally President of the University of California; Col. Alexander M. Speer, and Robert Trippe, Justices of Supreme Court, and many others distinguished as professors in universities, colleges, or professional schools, as ministers, physicians, or lawyers.

"Ben Palmer," continues Mr. Pope, "entered the Junior class. I entered the following year. We were from the same general region, knew of one another, and Palmer invited me to be his roommate. Though two years ahead of me in college, he showed for me the greatest consideration and sympathy, putting himself on a level with me. We would converse on all sorts of subjects. His mind was always clear and his use of language very remarkable. Almost as soon as I entered he pursuaded me to join the College Temperance Society. He delivered about this time the finest temperance lecture it has ever been my privilege to hear, though he was at the time only about twenty years old. I was not in his class. I cannot tell you anything of his recitations, but I know he was an elegant Latin scholar, a good Greek scholar, a splendid English scholar, a good mathematician and stood first in all studies. But the place in which I knew him best was the Phi Kappa Society, a debating society which met every Saturday and put in a large part of the day. He was himself wont to regard the training he derived in this society as of the first importance to his subsequent career. Palmer was never absent, and always took part in debate. He was as fluent then as he ever became, as eloquent then as he ever became. I have never seen a youth of his age who could surpass him as a debater. I remember one occasion on which the question was, 'Is Napoleon Bonaparte entitled to be called great?' He took the affirmative, and brought tears to our eyes as he pictured that eagle caged on St. Helena.

"Palmer was always honorable and virtuous. He was a high, clean fellow. He was always in love. He fell very much in love with one of Dr. Church's daughters. But amongst her beaux there was a handsome fellow to whom she had become engaged to be married. Accordingly, when Palmer proposed she declined. Not long after his refusal we were walking together in the woods one afternoon, when reverting to the sore subject, he said, 'Do you think that that man is handsomer than I am?' I was intensely amused; for Ben Palmer, though every inch a gentleman, and a well-groomed one in his appearance, and evidently of great brilliancy and parts to those who knew him, was remarkably homely in the common eye. I said, 'The truth compels me to say that I do think he is handsomer than you, but he has not one tenth of your brains.'

"Palmer was graduated with the first honors, in August, 1838, and on that occasion delivered an exquisite oration."[4]

He ran this distinguished career in the University of Georgia with burdens on his shoulders. He largely supported himself during his entire career in the institution by private labors as a tutor. He served as tutor first in the family of the distinguished lawyer, Mr. Oliver H. Prince, of Athens. He was living in the Prince home, and in charge of the children of Mr. Prince when that gentleman, accompanied by his wife, made the trip to New York, that he might superintend the publishing of the "Digest of the Laws of Georgia" which he had compiled. And when, on their return voyage, the father and mother per-

[4] This account of Mr. Palmer's life at the University of Georgia is largely in the words of the Hon. Daniel Joseph Pope, of Columbia, S. C., taken down as he talked in July, 1904.

ished off the Hatteras coast in the wreck of the steamer *Home,* Mr. Palmer showed the greatest tenderness toward, and exercised the greatest care over, his orphaned charges until they were removed to Macon, Ga., to be with relatives.

His faithfulness and tenderness to the sorrow-stricken children of the Princes, and his qualifications for tutoring, secured an invitation now to become tutor in the family of Mr. and Mrs. Thomas Wiley Baxter. Here he taught Thomas W. Baxter, Jr., afterwards of Atlanta, Ga., Sally Catherine Baxter, who in due time became Mrs. Edgeworth Bird, of Baltimore, and John L. Baxter, who developed into a man of scholarly attainments and note, a physician. He so behaved toward these children as not only to advance them in learning but to gain their fraternal and undying affection. He won the love of the parents as fully as that of the children. This affection he returned, taking Mrs. Baxter into his heart as a kind of second mother to him, and the children as brothers and sisters. For Mrs. Baxter he ever entertained a huge admiration. Hers was a character as "pure and peaceful as ever blessed a home." Years later he said, "Her equable temper, early sweetened by divine grace, breathed around her an atmosphere so sincere, that to be near her was to be *at rest.* Her gentle patience broke the edge of sorrow, leaving it nothing but its pathos. Her step in life was so noiseless that even duty seemed eased of its burden. Her unselfish sympathy plucked the grief from many an aching heart, whilst an unobtrusive charity lighted many a scant home with her beneficence. Neither dazzled by the splendors of fortune, nor daunted by the frowns of adversity, her brave heart preserved an equal trust in the God of her salvation. A sweet and winning piety was hers. It had no glare about it, and was full of meekness and humility; yet it was so pervading it quickened every action and purified every thought, it breathed in every tone and gleamed in every look, rendering her whole life a sweet gospel, full of the savors of Christ.

. . . .

"Precious saint! Across the track of thirty years comes one through this sketch to pour his filial reverence and tears upon your grave. The days of youth are long since passed, when he was a son in her loving home; but the memory of her, who was to him like the sweet mother that first kissed his infant cheek, will ever be as 'ointment poured forth.'"

From the little girl he taught in the Baxters' home, now Mrs. Edgeworth Bird, of Baltimore, Md., we learn that he used, while in college, to have not a little time for social duties, that he wrote regularly for the *Lyceum,* formed by the young ladies of Athens, and to which many of the students were invited; that his papers were full of charming witticisms. She heard him read one of these to a brother of hers, also a university student, for his criticisms. It was headed, "Shall I marry a missionary?" Overhearing it, she laughed out merrily at some of its conceits. Whereupon "he declared that he felt sure his article would at least amuse the ladies, if such a little tot could see anything in it." Mrs. Bird adds, "The girls of Athens were known far and wide for their beauty and the students fully appreciated it."

We learn further from Mrs. Bird, that while he was in college, though a prime favorite socially and leading his class intellectually, he was very faithful to all religious duties. "He had a Sunday school in the country, two miles from town, and in summer's heat and winter's cold was faithful in attendance, generally walking to and from the school." "My father would often say," says Mrs. Bird, "'Ben, order one of the horses, and drive, or ride to your school this afternoon.' With loving thanks, he usually declined, saying the walk would do him good."

At this time he seems to have been, for his years, already an able apologist for Christianity,[5] tactful, resourceful and skilful.

He had found with this noble family a thoroughly congenial home, the memory of which he carried with him as a precious possession to the last.

His life at the University had been one of great success—splendid development and the joy that comes of it. This time he returns to the parental roof with the plaudits of his Faculty, his fellow students and the whole university community following him. At home there was no cold reception awaiting him. But he was conscious of a fight he had to make. To his broadened and broadening view, life's responsibitities were looming large. He had chosen to serve Christ. How was he to serve him?

---

[5] See the article headed The Confessions of a Skeptic, in the *Southwestern Presbyterian,* May 20, 1869.

CHAPTER V.

STUDENT FOR THE MINISTRY IN COLUMBIA SEMINARY.

(January 1, 1839—April, 1841.)

INCLINED TO THE LAW.—DECIDES TO STUDY FOR THE MINISTRY.—ENTERS COLUMBIA SEMINARY, JANUARY, 1839.—THE FACULTY, STUDENTS, AND COURSE OF STUDY AT THE TIME.—HIS CAREER IN THE INSTITUTION.—INFLUENCE OF JAMES HENLEY THORNWELL ON HIM.—THE COMMUNITY AND YOUNG PALMER.—A VACATION INCIDENT.—A SON OF CONSOLATION.—MISS AUGUSTA MCCONNELL.—SEMINARY STUDENT PALMER COURTS HER IN SPITE OF THE POWERS THAT BE.—LEAVES THE SEMINARY WALLS, THE MAN OF PRE-EMINENT PROMISE IN HIS CLASS.

YOUNG Palmer was strongly inclined to the profession of the law. His clear mind, his vigorous powers as a debater, his mastery of the spheres of the pathetic and the sentimental, pointed to the most brilliant possibilities as an advocate. These, together with the very high high order of eloquence which he commanded, suggested a still more splendid career should he, after thorough study of the law, give himself to public life, in the pursuit of statecraft. Hayne and McDuffie, Drayton, and Petigru, Hamilton and Pinckney, and Calhoun, had thrown the sheen of their splendor over this latter sort of course, making it all the more attractive to a young man of such distinguished parts. Moreover, of his young friends in the McPhersonville neighborhood, Wm. F. Hutson, and his cousin Wm. M. Hutson, one of whom was subsequently a brother-in-law to Mr. Palmer, were studying law at the very time that he was at Athens completing his academic studies; and of his friends there, amongst the students, many of the most brilliant had chosen the legal profession, or were so biased in its favor that their choice of it was already practically decided.

But alluring as the legal profession was, it had a rival in his heart, a rival more modest and humble, more certainly knit to narrow worldly circumstances, but very attractive, as concerned primarily with that which is highest as well as most central in man, the moral and spiritual elements of his nature. This was the calling to be a minister of the Christian religion.

We see the love for this sort of work moving him to lecturing in the temperance cause, and to practical Christian work while still a college student. To be an intellectual toiler and to express the results of his toil through speech to his fellows was with him a sort of necessity. To have his heart most fully in his labor it was not less necessary that he should be spending himself to lift man up into a richer character and life; but he had not yet come to the full consciousness that this was so. Hence he had carried these rivals in his heart, from the day he had accepted Christ, perhaps, till he walked forth from his university with her *imprimatur* and her honors upon him.

Some time after August, 1838, he became convinced that the Great Head of the Church had called him to be a preacher of the Gospel of the grace of God.

A tradition long lingered in the seminary which he was soon to enter to this effect: "A temperance meeting was held one evening in a public hall in Columbia, S. C. When the audience assembled there was great disappointment at the absence of some distinguished lecturer, who had been advertised for the occasion. As the situation was becoming painful a gentleman rose to explain and closed by making a call for anyone present who would volunteer to make an address. A young man came forward to relieve the embarrassment. When he finished his remarks everybody was enquiring, Who is this! It came to the ears of some good ladies in the city that the young orator who had spoken was a candidate for the ministry, and on his way to one of the upper districts to teach school in order to pay his way through the Theological Seminary. They told him he must go at once to the seminary and they would pay his way."[1]

In January, 1839, with the purpose of preparing himself for the ministry, he entered Columbia Seminary, an institution which had been put into operation in 1829, at Lexington, Oglethorpe County, Georgia, with the Rev. Thomas Goulding, as Professor of Theology; but which had been moved to Columbia, S. C., in January, 1830; and about a year later to the eligible site it now occupies in the same beautiful city.

The buildings of the institution in 1839 were very far inferior to those which house the institution at present, and

[1] This tradition was furnished by the Rev. Professor W. T. Hall, of Columbia Seminary, and is here repeated in his words.

were, indeed, quite unpretentious, but they were sufficient for the students and the Faculty—the real forces determining the character of an institution.

The professors at the time were the Reverends George Howe, D.D., and A. W. Leland, D.D. Dr. Howe, of New England birth and Puritan ancestry, was a man of imposing personal appearance, an able, learned and accurate teacher whose instructions were greatly valued by his pupils—a man of simple and modest but lofty and beautiful character, whose influence upon his students was very fine. Dr. Leland was a man of fine lineage, and like Dr. Howe, of fine connections, by marriage in the State of South Carolina, though like Howe again, he was of New England birth. According to Dr. Joseph Bardwell,[2] "Dr. Leland was magnificently endowed with natural gifts, both mental and physical. In manly beauty, dignity and grace, he was the admiration, in his youth and early manhood, of all who knew him; and with a mind vigorous and strong, and well stored with knowledge, and an imagination vivid and powerful, coupled with a heart susceptible of the most intense emotion, he could impress all who came within the charmed sphere of his influence. His majestic form, courtly manners, a voice which was harmony itself, and a style cultivated and fervid, made an impression upon those who heard him not soon to be forgotten. As a reader of Scripture and sacred song in public worship, he surpassed in excellence all whom we have ever heard." "He could win the attention and charm the hearers as he read the sacred page with that fitting modulation and emphasis which interpreted it as he read, ere he opened his lips to set forth in his own often eloquent and persuasive words the truth of God."

These two men were then in their prime, Howe being in his thirty-seventh, and Leland in his fifty-first year. While of Northern birth, they were in thorough sympathy with Southern ideals and wedded to the section of their adoption. Later on in their careers, Columbia Seminary was to receive into her faculty men who should add mightily to its efficiency and distinction. But in the days of smaller things Howe and Leland were doing a very valuable work.

There seem to have been about thirty-two students attending the seminary when Mr. Palmer entered; amongst them, J. C.

---

[2] *Semi-centennial of Columbia Seminary*, pp. 207-208.

Brown, H. B. Cunningham, John Jones, T. L. McBryde, William Banks, James R. Gilland, E. F. Rockwell, Neill McKay, James B. Dunwody, W. C. Emerson, George Cooper Gregg, and others whose names have long been held in high honor throughout our Southern country.

As to the course of study pursued by Columbia Seminary at the time, it is enough to say that Dr. Howe had been largely instrumental in planning the curriculum; that he had been educated at Andover, in theology, and that he made the Columbia course the practical equal of the current Andover course; and that he had done his part of the teaching with such distinction that the directors of Union Theological Seminary, in New York City, had, in 1836, called him to the professorship of Sacred Literature in their institution.

Mr. B. M. Palmer was, according to most reliable traditions, a distinguished student in his class, holding the same relative place in this body of men that he had held in his university class. He maintained, also, and probably increased his reputation for eloquence.

Such productions of his pen as have come down from this period seem to indicate very clearly that he not only prepared with great labor and care for all public exercises but that he was laying broad and deep the foundations of theological knowledge. From these may be taken as illustrative a sermon on Rom. 5:19: For as by one man's disobedience many were made sinners, so by the obedience of one shall many be made righteous." The preacher begins by setting forth the connection of his text with the general argument of the epistle; and by marking the stage of the Apostle's reasoning, brings to notice the peculiar aspect which the doctrine assumes in the words of his text. He then declares that in these words "the apostle unfolds briefly but clearly the broad principle upon which is based the whole process of reconciliation with God;" and that the "leading doctrine brought before our notice is that of Justification which is effected by the imputation of the righteousness of Christ;" and that in the explication of this text we are led to consider:

1. What the Scriptural doctrine of imputation is.
2. Upon what general principle it is founded.
3. What is imputed to the sinner in order to his justification.
4. The persons to whom this imputation extends.

In his explication and proof of the answers of these questions he discloses a commanding grasp of the returns that had been rendered by the best theological thought of the past. There is no reference to learned names; there is something better. He has read and assimilated and fused in the crucible of his own thought. The discussion is full, elaborate and able. His style is much like his later style, his periods sonorous and well balanced. In the conclusion he presses four thoughts: (1) "How dire and evil sin is," as this subject shows; (2) "The utter hopelessness of satisfaction by any deeds of the law;" (3) "This doctrine of justification by imputed righteousness affords no shelter for the slothful or stubborn sinner; it is a mere statement of his judicial relations to the law of God;" (4) "This subject exhibits the Christian's security by showing the basis upon which it rests. All his hopes spring from the original covenant of grace which was framed without respect to merit or demerit in himself, and which cannot therefore be contingent."

The whole discussion covers about twenty-eight pages. The pages will average three hundred words to the page. For its delivery seventy minutes would be required at the rate of one hundred and twenty words to the minute. As he was a deliberate speaker, he occupied perhaps one hour and twenty minutes in its delivery.

At the close of the sermon occur the words, "Approved, Feb. 1841." From notes on the cover it is learned that he preached it in Charleston, in the Second Presbyterian Church, April 10, 1841, and in Columbia, First Presbyterian Church, May 9, 1841. He perhaps used it on the occasion in Charleston as a part of trial before his Presbytery, as he was licensed in April of 1841, by the Presbytery of Charleston.

Next to the influence of the Seminary on young Palmer, at this time, must be mentioned that of James Henley Thornwell. In the year 1839, Thornwell was still Professor of Metaphysics in the College of South Carolina, but he frequently filled the pulpit of the First Presbyterian Church of Columbia. During the year 1840 he was pastor of that church. Somewhat as to the influence which Thornwell exerted over him he has himself disclosed as follows:

"It was at this period that the writer's acquaintance with his friend began; though his own position as a divinity student did not warrant the intimacy which was enjoyed a little later, when brought into the relation of a co-presbyter. The impression will never be erased of the first discourse to which he listened, in the year 1839. A thin, spare form, with a slight stoop in the shoulders, stood in the desk, with soft black hair falling obliquely over the forehead, and a small eye, with a wonderful gleam when it was lighted by the inspiration of his theme. The devotional services offered nothing peculiar, beyond a quiet simplicity and reverence. The reading was, perhaps, a trifle monotonous, and the prayer was marked rather by correctness and method, than by fervor or fulness. But from the opening of the discourse, there was a strange fascination, such as had never been exercised by any other speaker. The subject was doctrinal, and Dr. Thornwell, who was born into the ministry at the height of a great controversy, had on, then, the wiry edge of his youth. The first impression made was that of being stunned by a peculiar dogmatism in the statement of what seemed weighty propositions; this was followed by a conscious resistence of the authority which was felt to be a little brow-beating with its positiveness; and then, as link after link was added to the chain of a consistent argument, expressed with that agonistic fervor which belongs to the forum, the effect at the close was to overwhelm and subdue. 'Who is this preacher?' was asked of a neighbor in one of the pauses of the discourse. 'That is Mr. Thornwell; don't you know him?'"[3]

There can be no question that there were great differences between the mental constitutions of these two men. Palmer excelled in his capacities as a word painter and in dealing with the sentimental and pathetic; Thornwell in the power of reasoning, and speculative thought. But there can be as little question that they were enough alike for Thornwell to mould Palmer to a considerable degree. To this influence is perhaps, to be traced the theological type of his preaching that prevailed far along in his life; and to this influence other habits and views which we shall have occasion to note in the sequel. It is hard to estimate the influence of such a tremendous mental and moral force as Thornwell was on a mind and heart so sensitive, responsive and aspiring, so keen, strong and independent as young Palmer's. Thornwell unconsciously became, unawares it may be to Palmer, his model, yet in no cramping way. Palmer's individuality was too strong to follow Thornwell in aught else than what met his judgment's approval.

In addition to the special training which he received in Columbia Seminary, and the highly stimulating influence derived

[3] Palmer, *Life and Letters of James Henley Thornwell,* p. 154.

from Dr. Thornwell, Mr. Palmer profited by the general culture of the people of the community and city. Naturally the homes of the very best people were open to him. He was always scrupulously neat in dress, from his nicely booted foot to the hat that crowned his head. Indeed, there is a tradition that he had had as a youth such a desire for luxurious and showy dressing that it had stood in the way for some time of his deciding for the ministry. Having decided for that calling and thrown to the winds his longing for the more ornate forms and features of dress, he gave to the care of his person and clothing just about the proper attention to make him acceptable to every taste worth considering. His bearing toward all classes commended him again to their good graces. He possessed a large deference for that which is primal and rudimental in man and woman, hence he treated all with respect and consideration; while to virtuous talent he had still larger homage to render. He was easily and naturally at home with all classes of men and women. With women indeed, this homely but elegant and graceful little gentleman was always a prime favorite. He was a born fighter, but he fought so gracefully and with such respect for his adversary that he naturally became to his female friends a sort of knight. His bearing toward them, while restrained, was ever considerate. They had a right to admire his fine speaking eyes, and his grace of body, but were you to listen to them you would imagine that Mr. Benjamin M. Palmer was not a homely little gentleman, but a veritable Apollo in looks, a Mercury in speech, and altogether a sort of incarnation of the angelic, cherubic and seraphic. Some of them might admit that on first sight, indeed, he had not appeared prepossessing; but his speech and manner transformed him.

It was certainly not to his discredit that he again paid for his table board in an excellent family by teaching the younger children of the family. Nor do we think the less of him as we see him in the vacation of 1840 acting as agent for a temperance paper and making temperance addresses and talks on Christianity as opportunity offered. One such glimpse is given us by the Reverend and Venerable R. H. Reid, Reidsville, S. C. He writes: [4]

---

[4] In letter bearing date April 13, 1904.

"The first time I met Dr. Palmer was in 1840. He was a student in Theological Seminary in Columbia, and an agent for the *Temperance Advocate*, published in Columbia. My father, Andrew Reid was an elder in the Good Hope Church, in Anderson County, South Carolina. Palmer called on him and made known his business. He was invited to make his home with us while he canvassed the congregation. He remained over Sabbath and conducted a service, the pastor, Rev. David Humphries, being absent. He made a deep impression on me. I remember his theme distinctly—Blind Bartimaeus,—although more than fifty years have passed since I heard his lecture."

That already at this early age, he had begun to develop as a son of consolation, is shown by the following letter to Mrs. Bazile Lanneau, written upon the occasion of the death of her brother, I. S. K. Palmer, M.D., and of her sister Jane Keith Palmer:

"COLUMBIA, S. C., March 30, 1839.

"Dear Cousin S.———: Although it is delightful for friends and relations to commune together, I almost fear that I will give you more pain than pleasure by writing at this time: for it would be unnatural to write and not to allude to the affliction which has thrown so deep a gloom over our family. How poignant must be your sorrow! I can very easily conceive from the recollection of the anguish which I saw you endure at the time of dear Jane's death; and yet in both cases you cannot sorrow as 'those who have no hope.'

"It is indeed melancholy and even painful to behold the family circle narrowing its limits and approaching as it were annihilation: still this is only one of the illusions of sense. It does not necessarily follow that those whom we bury are dead—for Christians never die; as the poet says, they only 'languish into life.' Were we utterly ignorant of the truths of revelation and possessed only those ideas respecting time and eternity which nature may teach I would unhesitatingly pronounce him most happy who soonest escapes from life and its sorrows. But having the Bible and believing its declarations respecting this world and the next, our views of death must be altered with it. Yet even now there is but one class of persons whose death we can properly bewail, viz: those who are heirs to no hope beyond the grave. Truly I would weep over the tomb of such an one, for he is banished from God, disinherited and dies the second death. But those who in life had been adopted into God's elect family, death is not death to such—dying is but going home—it is a mere transferrence of abode. No doubt, dear Cousin S., you view dear Keith's death in this light: and it affords you sweet comfort. Suppose he had moved to Arkansas, and had there settled: you would have sorrowed at the parting but you would not have grieved and afflicted your soul, 'refusing to be comforted.' Now, where is the difference to you between his going to

Arkansas and his going to heaven, except that you know he is far safer and happier in the latter place? In the former case you would still have regarded him as living, as still a member of the family, as still your brother, but in the latter case he assuredly lives in a higher sense: moreover, if we are the children of God he is still a member of the same family with ourselves—for the Scriptures, speaking of the Lord Jesus Christ, add in a parenthesis this phrase—'of whom the whole family in heaven and earth is named.' Hence it follows that God's family includes not only those who wait around the throne, but also those who upon earth are still struggling with sin—and, dear cousin, the final conclusion to which I would come is this: when our brothers and sisters 'die in the Lord,' we should not think of them as dead but rather as essentially living and that they still *are* (not *were*) our brothers and sisters. The only difference is that they are at home, whereas we are away from home. Yet as we are upon our journey homeward, the day of separation is but short, and we shall all be reunited in one unbroken family in an eternal home, where there shall be no more wandering—no more parting.

"I feel, dear Cousin S., that I do an unnecessary thing when I dwell upon these common, yet never failing, topics of consolation. They have all passed through your mind a hundred times, and have as often brought peace to your troubled heart. Still it is delightful thus to recall and to feed upon the comfort which the Bible affords, and when my thoughts assume this complexion life and all its concerns shrink into their proper compass, and I can realize to some extent that for 'me to live is Christ, but to die is gain.'

"But I must close these hastily written lines. I expect in a few moments to go into the country a short distance to harangue upon temperance, and that I have acquitted myself lamely, attribute partly to the fact that I write amidst company in the very 'strife of tongues.' . . .

"In very great haste, yet with very much affection

"Your cousin, B. M. PALMER."

Benjamin M. Palmer had been accused, while a university student, of always being in love. His removal from the university to the Seminary cloister did not break the force of the proclivity; or if so, it broke it only for a time. Here he found the love of his life. It is necessary to pause at this point for a moment and to trace briefly the source and history of the life that was to flow so richly into his.

Dr. Robert McConnell, of Walthourville, Ga., had married Sarah Ann Walthour, daughter of Mr. Andrew Walthour and his wife, Ann Hoffmire Walthour. To Dr. and Mrs. McConnell two children were born, Mary Augusta, and Blakeley. When his little girl was only four years of age and his little boy only two years old, Dr. McConnell died, leaving their mother a widow of twenty-one years. The young widow remained on her plantation with her children for about four years. Then, desiring to bring them up in an atmosphere of learning and culture, she carried them to Hartford, Conn.; but after a year or so, the little boy was drowned in the Connecticut River. This second bereavement drove Mrs. McConnell back to her Southern home.

In December, 1836, she married as her second husband, Prof. George Howe of Columbia Seminary. She continued the education of her daughter, placing her in the then famous boarding school for young ladies at Barhamville, about five miles from Columbia. It was the custom of "Miss Augusta" to return home every Friday evening and to remain until Monday morning. She was, when Mr. Benjamin Palmer appeared in Columbia, a slender girl of about seventeen summers, good to look at; of medium height; of very fair complexion, possessed a rare combination of very blue eyes and black hair. She was quiet and dignified in manners, but a general favorite, a girl whom all could trust in and depend on; one that could be counted on to show capacity to meet emergencies, too.

Dr. Palmer used to tell the story that before he met "Miss Augusta," a friend from another city who had hoped to woo her for himself wrote to him of his hopes; told him that he was uneasy lest some one else should win the girl of his choice; and begged him to keep an eye on her friends and to warn him if he saw danger ahead. Young Palmer wrote him at once that he would never play spy on any girl, and could not do as asked.

It is supposed that the young seminarian and the fair boarding school miss first met on occasion of one of her weekly visits to the parental roof. The very correspondence he had had about her tended to interest him in her, and as already remarked, it was not hard to interest him in a handsome girl. It is understood that in later years she occasionally admitted that she was really quite desirous to meet Mr. Palmer; that her curiosity had been excited about him by the praises she heard heaped upon him as a student, and a speaker of great eloquence and power, as a man of the most agreeable manners, elegant dress, graceful and courtly carriage. Very soon there was a mutually developing attachment between these two young people.

The course of true love was not to run perfectly smooth in their case. From the moment when Dr. Howe saw that there were signs of a mutual attachment between these two, he combated the cause of the young man with his stepdaughter. He declined to give his consent to an engagement, and forbade their meeting. He had other plans touching his daughter; a future which he believed to be far better for her. He hoped to see her comfortably settled as the wife of some Christian gentleman of means and dignity of circumstance. The pastor's wife must usually look forward to much self-denial, to a lifelong struggle with relative poverty. These young people, however, were quite as determined as Dr. Howe. They chose for themselves, openly met, and continued the exchange of notes all through a two years' engagement. Mr. Palmer would carry Miss McConnell to church, picking her up at a neighbor's; and together they would sit under the very nose of the Reverend guardian as he preached from the sacred desk. Mr. Palmer would carry his *fiancée* back to the neighbor's house; thence she would walk demurely home.

The day was to come when the young man would squarely ask the middle-aged man where the marriage was to take place, informing him quietly that barring divine interference, it certainly would take place. Many a year later when the plaudits were being heaped upon her husband by her stepfather and those who had sided with him, the lips of the girl, now long a wife and mother, would curl a little, and she would say to a neighbor, "Yes, they are proud enough of him now, but once they tried to separate us."

During this period our subject had done at least two things well worth doing: He had given himself to his work of preparation with such diligence and success as to lay broad the foundations of theological knowledge, and had so met all public engagements as to create the highest expectations of his usefulness and success as a preacher; and he had won the love of a virtuous woman, whose price was far above rubies, and who would do him good and not evil all the days of his life.

In the next chapter we shall follow him into, and through his first pastorate, see him take to his little home the girl whose love he had won, and look upon them in their youthful happiness and in the sunrise of his, and their, career.

CHAPTER VI.

PASTOR OF THE FIRST PRESBYTERIAN CHURCH AT SAVANNAH.

(November, 1841—January, 1843.)

Licentiate Palmer Tries his Gifts.—Is Called to the First Presbyterian Church, Savannah, Ga.—Marries Miss McConnell.—Carries Her in a Buggy from Columbia to Savannah.—The Beginning of Their Home-Making.—He had in Savannah a Fine Church for a Young Man of his Parts.—Was Ordained and Installed Pastor, March 6, 1842.—Threw Himself Zealously into his Work.—Prepared his Sermons in a Most Laborious Way.—Was Forced to Change his Methods of Preparation and Delivery.—Consequent Broader Work as a Student.—Did Vigorous Pastoral Work.—Evinced Determination in Dealing with his People.—Did Outside Work.—His Churches Prospered Under his Pastorate.—He was Called to the Pastorate of the First Presbyterian Church of Columbia

MR. BENJAMIN M. PALMER was not one of those candidates who wait for a "suitable place" in which to exercisce their gifts. Having been offered temporary work in Anderson, the county seat of that county in which, a few months before, he had sought subscribers for the *Temperance Advocate* and made temperance addresses and delivered Christian lectures, he repaired to the field as early as the midsummer following the completion of his seminary course. It gave him a place to work and to do the best that was in him under the circumstances; and if the Lord had a more important work for him to do he would be able to find him in his own way and at the right time in the little town of Anderson.

The Rev. R. H. Reid gives us a glimpse of Mr. Palmer's work in Anderson. He says:

"After his licensure, he supplied the church in Anderson for a short while. I was a pupil of Wesley Leverett's famous classical school in that place. There was a protracted meeting in the church conducted by Mr. Palmer. A goodly number confessed Christ and united with the church. I was among the number."

We have proof in these words that he did an important work

in Anderson. Its importance will appear more fully in the sequel.

He was allowed to remain there only three months. As early as October 1, 1841, overtures were made him to become the pastor of the First Church of Savannah, Ga. As Savannah was in a different Presbytery from that to which he belonged, some time was consumed before the call could be formally placed in his hands.

Meanwhile, assured of a modest living for himself and a wife, he returned to Columbia, waited on Dr. Howe, informed him that he and Miss Augusta McConnell proposed an early marriage, but did not know whether they could plan to have it in her mother's home or not. He had come, he said, to Dr. Howe to learn. Good Dr. Howe was a wise man as well as a good one. He had already seen that opposition was useless, and, indeed, he was not certain that the match was so altogether poor after all. Palmer was poor but of vast promise. Dr. Howe assured him most kindly that the marriage could take place nowhere else than in his own home. So the young people were married October 7, 1841; and by the Rev. Professor George Howe.

A few days after the wedding, they made their journey across the country to Savannah in a buggy, presented to them by Dr. Howe as a wedding gift. The trousseaux of the bride and groom and the library with which he was to begin his work in Savannah were all packed into one small trunk, which was strapped on the hinder part of the buggy. He had ten dollars in his pocket. Their leaving Columbia had in it both bitter and sweet. To the lithe, swarth, determined, talented young man it meant less of bitter, though sentiment drew him back to his last and best-beloved *Alma Mater*. To the young girl-bride, it meant more of the bitter. She was parting for the first time from the mother. As they drove the first morning the tears flowed so freely from the young wife's eyes that the husband was disturbed. After a time he felt constrained to say that, if the trial was so great, they had better return to Columbia, and he go on alone to Savannah This startling proposal was just the thing needed to tone up the wifely feeling. That plan looked more dreadful than leaving the mother. Pretty soon smiles chased the tears away.

Well attested tradition says that the pair really enjoyed that trip in the beautiful October weather, through the ever varying vistas of October foliage. It was not yet the age of the Pullman palace car and the Saratoga. It was not even the age of long railways. There was absolutely nothing of the kind between Savannah and Columbia. They did not feel the need of it. He was twenty-three, she was three or four years younger. They were not poor. God had richly endowed them with health and strength, and genius, and energy and character. They went to a sufficient, if modest, living; to a position of honor and esteem which God would enable them to fill. So on over the country roads toward Savannah they drove, close to nature, sympathizing with it, a part of it, close to each other, conscious also of being the children of God. They reached the city safely.

For several months during the first part of the period in Savannah, they boarded in the family of Mr. Joseph Cummings, one of the elders of his church. Then, in view of the expected advent of an important addition to the family, they rented a little cottage, and set up housekeeping in it. It is safe to say that the housekeeping was good, perhaps excellent, from the start. Mrs. Howe had been a housekeeper whose ideal it was to make a home where her husband and children and the passing stranger could find health and comfort flowing daily as from a living well, and in which her husband could do his work unhindered. Mrs. Palmer was afterwards able to do the same sort of housekeeping, and perhaps was thus competent from the start. She possessed one great advantage, however, over the young wives who go to housekeeping to-day; they took with them to that little cottage "Caroline," a young slave woman, who had grown up in the house of Mrs. Palmer's mother. She was about the same age as Mrs. Palmer herself. She became at once their maid of all work. She must have been of capital stuff. She remained with them a faithful and efficient servant not only while negro slavery lasted, but till her mistress had died in 1888, and then continued to live in the broken household till her own death six years later.

Into this little home came to bless it, and through it, thousands of other homes, a little child. He came July 26, 1842, a little hazel-eyed stranger with the imprint of the father strongly upon him. The father has given the following account of the child's arrival and of the emotions with which he was received:

"The morning was opening its eye in the first gray streak upon the horizon, when a faint cry issued from an upper chamber in one of our Southern cities. Instantly the hurried steps were arrested of one pacing uneasily to and fro in the hall beneath. It was a cry which, when once heard, is never forgotten; the low, flat wail of a babe just entering a world to which it is a stranger—the symbol of pain, premonitory of all it must suffer between the cradle and the grave. It fell now, for the first time, upon ears which had ached through the weary night to catch the sound. The long suspense was over; and the deep sympathy which had taken up into the soul the anguish that another felt in the body, gave place to exultation when the great peril was passed. The young father bowed himself on the spot where he stood, and poured out an overcharged heart in grateful praise to Him who had softened the curse to 'woman,' who, 'being deceived was in the trangression,' by the gracious 'Notwithstanding she shall be saved in childbearing, if they continue in faith and charity and holiness with sobriety.'

"Solemn thoughts crowded together in the first parental consciousness; thoughts that deepened in significance afterwards but never are so startling as when they rush upon the soul in the first experience of the new relation. Shall they be embalmed in speech? Thousands in the rehearsal will recall the earliest flush of these emotions.

"'Little miniature of myself—bone and flesh of my own substance—to whom I stand, as the instrumental cause of thy being, a secondary creator!' claiming by equal right the ancestral name, and wresting it from me when I am low in death! Soon to be strong and tall as I—coming each day more into the foreground and pushing me nearer to the edge over which I must topple at the last! Sole occupant then of all my trusts, the mysterious link that binds me to the generations that follow, in whom all my earthly immortality resides; and passing me on as but a figure in the continuous succession! And yet, in all this formidable rivalry, I clasp this first born to my heart and with not the least infusion of jealousy.

"'Little stranger, comest thou to solve or to darken the mystery of marriage? Even at the fountain the stream was parted in two heads in the dualism of sex. Great enigma of nature, lying just at the beginning: man's unity broken by the separateness of woman—yet preserved in her derivation from his side, ideally existing still in him from whom she was taken. The complementary parts are reintegrated into the whole by a mystical union which blends the two spiritually into one. And now the joint life issues in a birth, the child gathers into itself the double being from which it sprung, and diversity returns to the unity whence it emerged. Strange reconciliation of Nature's contradictions—this third, in whom the one and the two are brought together again. Tiny infant as thou art, thou dost yet interpret the symbol of marriage to those who produced thee.

"'An immortal soul, with dormant powers that by and by will compass the universe; now soaring to the copestone of heaven, and measuring the stars; now turning the stone-leaves which beneath the earth record the histories of countless cycles. A soul which will at last strip off the encumbrance of clay, and sweep with exploring wing the vast eternity where God makes His dwelling place and I must stoop beneath this wing and teach its first flight, that will rise higher and higher in the far forever.'

"A soul, alas, born under the curse of sin, through me the guilty channel. And I must stand in the holy priesthood appointed of God, between it and eternal death. My soul must be in its soul's stead, and feel for it the Law's penal frown. My faith must lay her hand upon the covenant, 'I will be a God to thee and to thy seed after thee;' and plead the force of that great instrument with all the agony of human intercession."[1]

The child was called for the father and for his maternal uncle, who as a young lad had perished in the Connecticut River, Benjamin Blakeley. The only son ever born to them, he was not to pass beyond the pale of infancy in this life. But how rich God made them in him for the time! And how important that he who was to deal with the joys and sorrows, the privileges, duties and responsibilities of parenthood, in so influential a way, should have practical experience of the relation himself. We shall see them mourning around the little one's bier in less than two years; but who shall say that his coming was not fraught with consequences sufficient to compensate for all the sorrow?

The First Presbyterian Church of Savannah had been organized in the summer of 1827, of persons who had withdrawn from the Independent Presbyterian Church of that city, fourteen in number. Amongst these had been Lowell Mason, the great composer of sacred music. In organizing, the church had elected Messrs. Lowell Mason, Joseph Cumming and G. G. Faries as elders. The Rev. John Boggs had become stated supply of the church early in 1828, and pastor November 30, 1828, to December 1, 1829. For nearly two years ensuing the church had been without a regular pastor, depending on temporary supplies. In 1831, Rev. Charles Colcock Jones had begun his ministry. After a year and a half of service as pastor,

[1] See the *Broken Home,* pp. 5 to 8.

feeling called to give his time wholly to missionary labors amongst the negroes, Mr. Jones had resigned. Meanwhile he had been instrumental in giving the church an impetus to growth, and in securing the initial steps looking to the erection of a house of worship. Following upon his pastorate had come a series of stated supplies. The next pastorate had been that of Rev. Joseph L. Jones from April 27, 1837, to his death in 1841. The church had thus had a succession of short pastorates, interspersed with stated supplyships. The members were not numerous, but amongst them was not a little stalwart Presbyterian stuff.

While preaching the sermon dedicatory of the present edifice of this church, on the 9th of June, 1872, Benjamin M. Palmer himself described the session of the church as it existed during the period of his pastorate as follows:

"It would require little effort to reproduce the old session of thirty years ago; the faithful body-guard of the young pastor whose inexperience was then first learning how it should 'behave itself in the house and kingdom of God, which is the church of the living God, the pillar and ground of the truth.' Here, just upon the right, sat the patriarchal Maxwell, an Israelite in whom there was no guile; who united the simplicity of the child with the prudence of the sage; in whose fatherly heart the children of sorrow and care ever found shelter, and whose word or smile was a perpetual benediction to the weary and worn. There, in front, and near the middle of the house, was the unbent figure of Joseph Cumming, with the steel-gray eye and compressed lip, the very symbol of decision and power; whose broad intellect measured truth in the grandeur of her proportions, and whose massive will crushed difficulties, as bars of iron are sometimes bent in a giant's grip. A few pews in advance of him was present the honest Crabtree, the frankness of whose nature was like the open sea, with which in earlier days he held communion; positive in his judgment, as those are apt to be whose only education has been hard experience, and whose practical wisdom was gathered in the same school. There, upon the left, sat the John-like Ingersoll, whose gentleness distilled like the dew and softened all about him; whose counsels were always of peace, and whose loving spirit fitted him so early to go up and lie upon the Savior's bosom; whilst a few steps in the rear of him, was the humble and timid Faries, with a gift in prayer that I have never heard equalled since; and a memory so steeped in the language of David and Paul that his petitions at the mercy-seat seemed like the breathings of the Holy Ghost. These it may be proper to distinguished as the 'Overseers' appointed to feed the church of God, purchased with his own blood. But the roll of those who gathered around the sacramental board would sound very like precious names,—as of Richardson, Copp, Ferguson, Sturtevant, Bernard, and others—written in the book of life, and now at the marriage supper of the Lamb in Heaven."[2]

In this church he had a good field for a young minister of his energy and his rich endowment of gifts,—a good field for him notwithstanding his inexperience. It would have proven one of too much work for all save a few young ministers. They would have been reduced to empty talkers, or have been broken in health. He felt the strain of it himself, as will appear; but he had very unusual resources. In one way or another, he could appear before his people three times a week with somewhat worthy of their hearing and heeding.

His ordination and installation as pastor of the church did not take place until he had served the people for several months. They had awaited the convenience of the Presbytery of Georgia, the only Presbytery in the State at the time. On Sabbath morning, March 6, the Presbytery, being in session proceeded to the ordination. By special invitation, the Rev. Edward Palmer, then an Independent Presbyterian minister in South Carolina, had come over to preach the sermon in connection with the ordination of his son. He preached on Ezekiel 30: 7, latter clause: "Therefore, thou shalt bear the word at my mouth and warn them from me." The Rev. Robert Quarterman presided and put the constitutional questions to licentiate and people; and after the ordaining prayer, the Rev. Charles Colcock Jones delivered the charge to the newly ordained and installed bishop, and the Rev. I. S. K. Axson that to the people.

Mr. Palmer threw himself with great zeal into his work. He rejoiced in every part of his labors. Rarely is there found such perfect adaptation to every part of the ministerial work as existed in his case. He delighted in the study of the Bible and the great theologians, and the connected philosophical and psychological subjects. He exulted in preaching. Speech-making was the function to which he had been born. He threw himself into it with joy. The pulpit was his throne and he had been made a king in it by the imposition of the Almighty hand. By his bearing, his tact, unfeigned sympathy, and the confi-

[2] Quoted in the *Historical Sketch* of the First Presbyterian Church, Savannah, Ga., by Wm. Harden, p. 25.

dence and love he inspired, his pastoral work soon came to be a delightful part of his labors.

Nevertheless, his ideals being very high, before a long period had elapsed, he began to feel keenly the burden of preparation for preaching. He himself, in the address *"In Memoriam,* Rev. I. S. K. Axson, D.D.,"[3] which was delivered June 14, 1891, in the Independent Presbyterian Church, of Savannah, Ga., has described and defined in part, just where and how it pressed most heavily, and has told us of the cure to which he was pointed for the uneasiness occasioned by the burden, in the following words:

"There is an experience somewhat dark and painful, which these pastors around me will verify as occurring in the life of every young preacher. It is when he has fairly used up the elementary knowledge which prepared him for entrance upon the sacred office, and he sinks under the oppressive sense of mental exhaustion. He finds himself confronted with responsibilities of which he cannot be divested, except at death, and which he feels wholly incapacitated to fulfill. He has spoken all he ever knew without the hope of another fresh thought as long as he may live. There is for him, apparently, neither retreat nor progress. It was in this trying crisis that the speaker took refuge in the fatherly confidence of Dr. Willard Preston, then in the fifty-seventh year of his age, and not far from the middle of his long pastorate here of four and twenty years. Blessed servant of God, how vividly at this moment do I recall his genial presence, the kindly smile flitting like a wave of sunlight over his placid face, with a gentle humor lurking still in the corner of his eyes! How tenderly he took me to his heart and suffered me to nestle in his bosom! From that hour I have loved him with the reverent affection of a son. Without any show of patronage or of supercilious condescension, he showed how this experience must come sooner or later to every ingenuous student; how this shallowness of present knowledge would whet the appetite for the truth lying in the unfathomed depths yet to be explored; how needful this lesson of humility was to forestall the self-consequence and offensive vanity so apt to be engendered in those whose teachings are accustomed to be received with entire deference by others. Then tearing a leaf from his own record, he exposed the secret of a like humiliation in his earlier years, and, pausing to lay his hand upon the Sacred Book, he pointed to the inexhaustible treasures hid therein, and, as answering to these, he alluded to the depths of Christian experience lying yet undeveloped in my own heart, which would be opened by the Divine Spirit to all the truth contained in the

[3] pp. 6 and 7.

Scriptures themselves. It was another Elisha opening the eyes of the young man to behold the mountain full of horses and chariots of fire round about. From this time forth there lingered no fear of future bankruptcy in the ministry of the Word."

Feeling obliged to study broadly and thoroughly, Mr. Palmer resolved to discard writing his sermons and preaching from manuscript; resolved to prepare the matter with great care and the plans of his discourses and to get the plans well into his memory, but to depend on the inspiration of the moment for language in which to clothe his explicatory thoughts. His natural gifts of speech, inbred correctness as to form, and vigorous training as a debater and orator in every school from the Walterboro Academy to the University of Georgia, came now to his help. He succeeded splendidly in his new departure, whilst most men so young and inexperienced would have failed. His preaching after his new fashion was vastly more acceptable than his former preaching had been. His mental excitement in the pulpit was necessarily greater. Responding to the demand to clothe the skeleton sermon he held in memory in fitting words as delivered, he inevitably underwent the exhilarating labor of recasting as well as reclothing the whole discourse. His exhilaration was imparted to his audience through noble speech, the commerce of his fine eyes, his graceful gestures, and his whole bearing.

Being able to preach after this sort of preparation, he could command the time previously occupied in the laborious writing of his long discourses, in the study of the Scriptures and of such collateral works as he might be specially interested in from time to time.

From a *universal index,* which he apparently began to keep while he was in Savannah, we learn that he was not only reading some of the leading theological reviews and an occasional book of travel and history, but that he was studying certain subjects profoundly, *e. g.,* the evidences of Christianity, the doctrine of justification and of sacrifice, and especially the nature and place of the atonement in the scheme of Christian redemption. He seems to have studied profoundly Witsius, *On the Covenants,* Magee, on the Atonement and Sacrifices, the Works of John Owen and John Howe, Calvin's "Institutes," Dwight's and Dick's Theologies,—not the whole of the works but considerable parts. He seems to have read quite a string of works on "inspiration;" and a considerable number of works on church government, and to have done special reading on the place of children in the church. Kurtz's "History of the Old Covenant" received considerable attention; Boston's "Fourfold State," etc.

This breadth of study as well as thoroughness was of importance in the part he was to play subsequently in very commanding positions. Indeed, it was essential. Mr. Palmer was to serve his church in functions wherein he needed the richest scriptural and theological furnishing as well as all his wonderful oratorical gifts.

Bred up in the home of a pastor of wonderful efficiency, who laid great stress on the importance of the minister's pastoral functions, he naturally threw himself into pastoral work just so far as sickness and other emergencies demanded, and as far as the interests of those committed to his care seemed to him to demand it. He paid many social calls, too, believing that he could thus draw people first to himself and then perhaps, to his Lord. Nevertheless, he was more jealous of the time so spent than he became toward the end of his life, when he could better afford to spend more time outside of the study.

He possessed somewhat of the headiness of youth during this period. From a child he had had a fondness for having his own way. In that he was not, as in some other respects, singular, however. It was soon to become a mark with Mr. Palmer that he could secure his own way with those with whom he had to do by gracious tact. He was rarely to put himself in a position in which he might meet open defiance on the part of a member of a church, or stubborn refusal, or any similarly unpleasant conduct. In his later days he sometimes illustrated what he called his "youthful rashness" in the Savannah pastorate by the following incident: In his church there, there was a member peculiarly gifted in prayer. He had been called upon several times to lead the congregation in prayer and had always done so with evident edification; but at length he suffered, while leading them in their supplications, a sort of stage fright. He subsequently came to Mr. Palmer and asked him not to call on him again, declaring that he could not make the attempt to lead the people thereafter. Mr. Palmer tried to reason with him; and finding that he could do nothing by reason or persuasion, told him that he intended to call on him as before. At an early meeting, perhaps the next one, Mr. Palmer called on him to lead in prayer. There was no response. After a little the pastor repeated his call to the brother to lead the meeting in prayer. There was no response to this second call. After a moment the determined young pastor said: "Brother ———, we shall just sit here till you lead us in prayer." This was too much for the timid but excellent brother appealed to. He led the meeting at once, and in an uplifting prayer; and thenceforth never failed to respond when called upon.

His daring course was followed by good results in this instance. But it is said that when asked in his old age whether he would repeat the process in a similar case, he would smile and say: "No, I think that is a case of God's overruling the rashness of my youth for good. Had the circumstances of God's ordering been different my rashness might have been followed by much evil." The following incident will show that this daring young pastor was, in personal work, a skilful fisherman of men. During the revival to be referred to after a little, a young friend dropped in for a week's sojourn with him in his home. He appeared annoyed at the presence of the revival and would have left but for kindly solicitations to remain. Mr. Palmer did not even ask him to attend church. On the contrary he gave him to understand that he could do as he pleased. The youth, however, chose to attend, having nothing better to do. After a little he developed a restlessness and an irritation of manner.

"Thus," to let Mr. Palmer tell the story in his own words, "matters moved on from day to day, till the Sabbath came and was passed, and on Monday the conflict reached its crisis. I was writing in my study as he came in and sat beside my desk—breaking out, after a little, in the petulant remark: 'You preachers are the most contradictory men in the world; you say, and you unsay, just as it pleases you, without the least pretension to consistency.'

"Somehow I was not surprised at this outbreak; for though no sign of religious feeling had been evinced, there was a restlessness in his manner which satisfied me that he was secretly fighting against the truth. I thought it best to treat the case in an off-hand sort of way, and with seeming indifference so as to cut him off from all opportunity to coquette with the Gospel. Without arresting my pen, I simply answered, 'Well, what now?'

" 'Why, yesterday you said in your sermon that sinners were perfectly helpless in themselves—utterly unable to repent or believe and then turned square round and said that they would all be damned if they did not.'

"'Well, my dear E——, there is no use in our quarreling over this matter; either you can or you cannot. If you can, all I have to say is that I hope you will just go and do it.'

"As I did not raise my eyes from my writing, which was continued as I spoke, I had no means of marking the effect of these words, until, after a moment's silence, with a choking utterance, the reply came back: 'I have been trying my best for three whole days, and cannot.' 'Ah,' said I, laying down the pen; 'that puts a different face upon it; we will go then and tell the difficulty straight out to God.'

"We knelt together and I prayed as though this was the first time in human history that this trouble had ever arisen; that here was a soul in the most desperate extremity, which must believe or perish, and hopelessly unable of itself, to do it; that, consequently it was just the case calling for Divine interposition; and pleading most earnestly for the fulfillment of the Divine promise. Upon rising I offered not one single word of comfort or advice. Youth is seldom disingenuous or stubborn, and the difficulty was recognized as purely practical. So I left my friend in his powerlessness in the hands of God, as the only helper. In a short time he came through the struggle, rejoicing in the hope of eternal life.

. . . .

"The fact simply is, that 'the carnal mind is enmity against God: for it is not subject to the law of God; neither indeed *can* be.' The danger is not so much that the sinner will be crushed into despair by the clear apprehension of this truth, as that he will fail to realize it at all. They wrap themselves in the fatal delusion that they are competent to repent at will, and so they sport with the whole matter as being perfectly under their control. The issue becomes fearfully momentous, as soon as they practically discover that they are, in themselves, utterly without strength, and therefore wholly dependent on the sovereign mercy of God. It is unwise to strip the truth of its apparent sternness by any attempts at metaphysical explanation, or to blunt its edge by offering premature comfort. It is better to deal honestly with it as a tremendous fact, and then leave the awakened sinner face to face with his peril, thrown back in this solemn crisis upon the pledged mercy of God, in Christ. 'Shall I bring to the birth, and not cause to bring forth? saith the Lord.'"[4]

This incident indicates as well as a sermon of the period would do, the kind of a gospel he then held forth, in all its aspects.

He found time to lend a helping hand to the advancement of

---

[4] See *Southwestern Presbyterian,* Thursday, August 5, 1869, under caption, "Practical Uses of the Doctrine of Inability."

religion outside the bounds of his own congregation. During the winter of 1841-1842, a season of revival was enjoyed in the churches of Savannah, beginning in the Independent Presbyterian Church and "chiefly under the preaching of that eminent servant of God, Rev. Dr. Joseph C. Stiles." In this revival all the pastors bore their part; and the young Timothy took his turn with the others at the sacred desk. In the following summer, the pastor of the Independent Presbyterian Church was long absent, owing to sickness, and the pastoral services of Mr. Palmer were given to the people of that church so far as his duty to his own people permitted. In waiting upon their sick and in conducting their weekly prayer-meetings he found some outlet for surplus energies, built them up in their Christian life and knit them to himself, as we shall hereafter see.

During the less than fifteen months of service in the Savannah church, Mr. Palmer had won the love of the people in a remarkable degree. Under his care the church had flourished. Additions had been made to the membership. The church as a whole had been edified. Attention had been called to the church as a congregation where the people were really taught and delightfully taught. They abhorred the thought of giving him up. But that thought was like the ghost of Banquo; it would not down. Other churches were laying eyes on him; and meant to have him if he could be had. Even back in the forties people liked a young preacher that could preach and behave after Palmer's fashion; and the staid old church in the Upper Country capital city of South Carolina, under the eaves of Columbia Seminary, made a successful demand for him. It was a formidable field but a most important one. Those people had had Thornwell as their pastor. He was then frequently heard by them, for as president of South Carolina College he was often accessible to them as pulpit supply when for any cause they had no preacher of their own. He would be an auditor of Palmer's in Columbia. The Columbia congregation almost adored him. But then Palmer could preach to a large resident audience of worthy and influential people, have in his pews the Columbia theological students and teach them, by doing it, how to open God's word to the people; during term time of the college, address in addition, a considerable proportion of college students, amongst whom would be the coming influential men of South Carolina; and whilst the legislature was in session he would have as hearers many of the public men of the entire State. It was a most important post, and the reader can imagine how this call would be pressed in letters from grave professors, legal lights, and other earnest servants of the church, pleading with this young man of just twenty-five to come and fill this great post.

In the next chapter we shall see how he acquitted himself in that place of vantage and responsibility.

CHAPTER VII.

THE PASTOR AT COLUMBIA, S. C.

(January, 1843—October, 1855.)

The Work to Which he Went at Columbia, S. C.—The Zeal with Which he Threw Himself Into his Work.—His Pulpit Ministrations.—His Zeal in the Application of Discipline.—His Labors as a Pastor.—Illustrative Incidents.—The Loss of his Mother.—The Loss of Little Benjamin Blakeley.—His Erection of the Present Noble Church Edifice, the First Presbyterian Church, Columbia.—His Dedicatory Sermon, Showing his Ideals in 1853.—The Results of his Labors in the Growth of his Church.

AS indicated in the previous chapter, when the Rev. Mr. Palmer went to Columbia, he entered a most important field. The members of the State Legislature, and of the courts of justice, the student bodies of the State College and of the Columbia Theological Seminary, during their respective term times, presented severally great opportunities for a wide, pervasive and exceptionally potent influence. In addition to these special opportunities afforded in the Columbia field, there were in the church itself one hundred and sixteen white members and twelve colored members, embracing many families of commanding position and influence in the capital city; which, next to Charleston, was the most important city in the State of South Carolina, and outranked as an educational center even the old mother city on the Cooper and the Ashley. The church was well organized and officered, at least as concerned ruling elders. Amongst the elders when he entered upon the pastorate were such men as William Law—that man of artless simplicity, unaffected humility, unshaken firmness, wonderful guilelessness, strict veracity, spotless honesty, simple and sincere piety, and business abilities, a very great friend of Columbia Seminary; Sidney Crane, the man of unbending integrity, wise counsels, and godly influence; and G. T. Snowden,—the spiritual son of Dr. Romeyn of New York, tutored in the faith by Rev. John Holt Rice, D.D., of Richmond, the man of prayer and works, another friend of Columbia Theological Seminary, a man of theological acumen, a sound Old

School man who magnified the grace of Christ. To the session were added worthy compeers in Mr. James Martin,[1] 1845, Mr. Andrew E. Crawford, 1846, and Professor R. T. Brumby, 1852.

It was his duty to feed this congregation on the Word; and in union with his elders, to guide all its members in their daily living as far as possible in accord with the teachings of the Word; to bring the power of God in discipline to bear upon their lives; and to set the whole force to work for the progress of Christ's kingdom to the end of the world. The responsibilities were huge and Mr. Palmer felt them to be such.

He threw himself with extraordinary zeal into the effort to measure up to the demands of the situation—particularly to the obligation to indoctrinate his people thoroughly, and to secure their disciplinary tuition according to the principles revealed in the word of God. Nor was he dead to his obligation to excite and lead his church into worthy missionary endeavor, as many noble sermons, lectures and addresses on the subject make clear.

His own view of his relations to his new charge as preacher he set forth with elaborate care in his inaugural sermon in the Columbia church, January 29, 1843. He took for his text the words of Balaam, son of Beor, to Balak, Num. 22:38: "And Balaam said unto Balak, Lo, I am come unto thee: have I now any power at all to say any thing? the word that God putteth in my mouth, that shall I speak." After a historical introduction setting forth the circumstances under which the text was originally uttered, the preacher began:

"Beloved brethren and friends, I have selected this passage as peculiarly appropriate to the position which I occupy before you this day. At your own call, in the good providence of God, I appear to you in some sort as the prophet of God. Lo, I am here. And, if I may adopt this expression as my own in reference to my presence before you, with what emphasis may I repeat what follows! Have I now any power at all to say anything? The word that God putteth into my mouth, that shall I speak. It is not my design to run any parallel between the case of Balaam and that of the Gospel minister. God forbid that those who preach salvation through Christ should find their type in this avaricious, ungodly and malevolent prophet. In many

[1] Mr. Martin had served in the church as elder prior to this election, but his relation as elder had terminated on his removal from the place. Having returned he was chosen to the exercises of the functions again.

points they differ widely. He came to curse God's people; they come to bless and comfort. He came at the instigation of the wicked, allured by the prospect of gain; they come at the call of the pious to become the servant of all. He came, Providence allowing and overruling; they come, Providence blessing and commanding. Still the language of the text and the great truth inculcated in the history, are pertinent to our purpose: which is briefly *to show the nature of the ministerial office and the grounds upon which its authority and influence are based."*

Having thus announced his subject, he proceeded to the statement, explication, and argument in support of the following propositions by way of developing it: 1. *That true ministers of the Gospel are specially called to their office by God himself, and their fields of labor specially designated.* 2. *That all true ministerial ability and authority are derived from God.* Having argued these propositions in a very able manner, the preacher closed by reflecting upon the great practical importance of his theme, which discovers to us: (1) The relation which the Gospel minister sustains to God; (2) the relation which he sustains to his people; and (3) the source whence he should desire his encouragement. In Mr. Palmer's view the minister of the Gospel is "a messenger from God to speak only the word that is put into his mouth." He may "not invent or add anything to his message. His sole care must be to inquire what God the Lord will say." Touching his relation to the people, Mr. Palmer holds, that "the pastoral commission is no contract formed merely for the pleasure and amusement of the hearers. The pastor is not called upon to cater to the various tastes which may perchance prevail among his auditors. His duty is to study God's Book, to expound its doctrines, to enforce its precepts, to urge its motives, to present its promises, to recite its warnings, to declare its judgments." In fine, the minister is to look for his encouragement to God rather than to man.

The conception of the ministerial office which he thus set forth was thoroughly Biblical and is worthy of all young ministers' pondering. It was prophetic of the character of his teaching throughout the Columbia pastorate and to the end of life.

He preached on a great range of topics. His aim was to set forth all Biblical truths in their due proportion. There lies before us a huge pile of briefs of sermons, lectures, and series of sermons and lectures, of this period. These have not been arranged in any topical or strictly chronological order. We turn them over and read their titles: "Apologetic Lectures on Christianity," "The Comparative Value of Moral Evidence in Support of Christianity," "The Amount of Moral Evidence in Support of Christianity," "The Father Glorified by the Son," "Folly of Atheism," "Justice of Final Condemnation," "The Gospel, the Power of God," "Sin an Evil and Bitter Thing," "Grace Superabounding," "Opposition Between Law and Grace," "Inward Empire of the Gospel," "Salvation by Hope," "Darkness in the Soul," "If the Foundations be Destroyed, What can the Righteous Do?" "Righteousness and Strength," "Christ in us," "Mortification of Sin," "Bearing the Cross," "Mediatorial Authority of Christ," "Human Apostasy," "Corruption of Mankind," "Man Created in the Image of God," "Practical uses of Predestination," "Sinners Waxing Worse and Worse," "The Inward Witness," "Abounding in the Work of the Lord," "Victory over Death by Christ," "God's Justice and Afflictions," "Death to the Law and by the Law," "Excellency of the Knowledge of Christ," "God's Holiness the Basis of all Worship," "Influence of Christians on Kindred," "Foundation of the Universal Gospel Offer," "Believer's Marriage with Christ Consummated," "Future Punishment," "Brotherly Love," "Antimonianism Latent in Arminianism," "Lectures on the Larger Catechism," "Believer's Witness for God," "Christian Progress," "Spirit of Adoption," "Christ's Constraining Love," "The Lord's Supper an Instituted Ordinance," "God's Presence," "Past Feeling," "The Providence of God," "Predestination Consistent with Free Agency," "The Law a Measure of Sanctification," "Lectures on the Messianic Psalms," "Proofs of the Doctrine of Decrees," "Christ's Life the Life of the Believer," "Sanctification of Christ," "The Transfiguration," "Effects of Repentance," "Men are as they Think," "Crucify the Flesh," "A Series of Lectures to the Young," "Spirituality of Worship," "Alternation of Good and Evil," "Bicentenary of the Westminster Assembly," "Believers the Workmanship of God and Created unto Good Works," "Uses of Affliction," "God's Government over Nations," "Sanctification of the Sabbath," "God's Patience to the Reprobate," "Fatherly Discipline," "Justification and Sanctification," "Spiritual Leanness," "Sinners Self-Destroyed," "Ministers Ambassadors for Christ," "God not the Author of Sin," "Christ the Hope of His Church," "The Impossibility of Salvation by the

Law," "The Doctrine of a Special Providence," "Missionary Lectures," "Office of the Law," "Pleasure in Unrighteousness," "Fear of Death a Bondage," "Christ's Commission to the Church," "Godly Sorrow and the Sorrow of the World," "Universal Salvation Disproved," "Regeneration," "The Son of Man a Savior," "Christians' Witness Against Themselves," "Greatness of Revealed Truth," "The Soul Lost by Attending to Trifles," "The Covenant with Adam," "Deity of Christ," "Duty of Family Instruction," "Duty of the Church to Educate the Ministry," "Infant Baptism Warranted by the Church Charter;" many briefs on phases of prayer, "Grace Sufficient," etc.

During the entire Columbia pastorate his pulpit ministrations were no less remarkable for their fitness to instruct and to edify than to attract and to delight. A born speaker to the people, a well-equipped theologian, commanding largely the treasures of Biblical knowledge, his skill in handling themes and audiences grew with the months. He possessed a growing faculty of clear explication, popular but accurate statement of points, luminous and noble illustrations.

It is interesting to peep into his study and remark his method in the preparation of his sermons. He may be seen after he has made choice of his texts, consulting various translations, and the original itself, and rapidly making up his mind as to their precise meanings. He may be seen to consult a few standard commentaries, but not many; the text itself in its context is the source whence he draws the meaning. He now puts a cigar into his mouth and begins to walk diagonally across his study floor. If you are a close observer, you will already have noted that the furniture in his study is so placed that it gives him one diagonal across the study as a clear path, and that the carpet shows threadbare along that diagonal. He has been making sermons there before. He wears away the threads of the carpet but weaves the threads of mighty discourses in place. Some say he forms polished sentences, sentence by sentence, and files them above his brilliant brown eyes to be called up in order on the near Sabbath. He says he does not, that he "files" away the plan of the discourse in his mind, but that while he thinks through the discourse over and over, he makes no attempt to store the verbiage of the dress of that plan, meaning to body forth his sermon in any words given him at the moment of delivery.

When he came before the people it was generally with a great theme. Most themes from God's word looked big as handled by him; nor did he stint himself as to time in handling them. He preached forty minutes, fifty minutes, sixty minutes, seventy minutes, eighty minutes, ninety minutes, rarely more. His average sermon was perhaps, not under fifty minutes. During a considerable portion of his pastorate in Columbia he preached three times a day, to the same congregation,—in the forenoon, the afternoon and in the evening. This much preaching of this sort shows clearly his zeal to indoctrinate his people. It is a clear proof of his wonderful powers, also. Only a very attractive preacher could have held the same congregation for such a large portion of the successive Lord's days.

In later years he came to look on the effort to hold the third service as largely unprofitable both to congregation and preacher. He was wont to tell a funny story of an experience of his in an afternoon meeting. While preaching one sultry Sunday afternoon he saw that a member of his congregation had been overcome with sleep and was bending forward more and more toward the bench in front; that every nod of the man's head was bringing that organ closer to the back of his neighbor's bench. Trying to preach, he could not avoid calculating the time that must elapse before the sleeper should receive a rude shock. Suddenly the victim of Morpheus gave his head the expected blow,—a rousing one. Startled, he jumped to his feet. Just then a cock, within hearing, gave a lusty crow; and the suddenly awakened man yelled, "Fire, fire!" at the top of his voice. Then looking around, seeing where he was and comprehending the exhibition he had made of himself, he slunk back into his seat.

This was one of the very few instances in which Dr. Palmer was distracted from his theme. Usually nothing diverted him.

If throughout this period Dr. Palmer was energetic in teaching his people, he was no less marked by his loyalty to Christ, the head of the Church, in the application of His power in the sphere of discipline. Mr. Palmer was at the time really as much a believer in the efficacy of discipline and the obligation to its use as John Calvin ever was. The records of the session of his church in Columbia are the sufficient attestation to this. The contingent of colored members furnished occasions of discipline out of all proportion to their numbers; but occasions of discipline were frequently found in the life of the white members of the church. It was faithfully meted out to all members in need of it regardless of condition or color. Excommunication was not infrequent. Suspension was more common. In the records of July 19, 1847, we have a curious memento of a past social institution as well as of his session's consideration in dealing with a negro member. We read:

"A request was presented by Ned, a servant of Mrs. Quigley and a member of this church, that he might be allowed to take a wife in town, notwithstanding his separation from a woman in Fairfield with whom he had heretofore been living. Different members of the session having made diligent enquiries into this case, the following facts appeared: That Ned had never been lawfully married to the woman in Fairfield, though at the time of his joining the church he had regarded her as his wife; that they were now permanently and effectively separated by the wishes of their respective owners; and that the woman had been unfaithful to him. Upon these grounds in regard to which the session had been at pains to gather evidence; and in consideration of the temptation to sin which beset Ned in his single estate, and in consequence of the desire to do right manifested in his taking counsel of the session, it was agreed to grant him the desired permission."

The most interesting disciplinary struggle was that whose history is told in the following excerpts from the sessional records:[2]

"It was brought to the notice of the session that at a public ball given recently in compliment to General Shields,[3] four of the members were in attendance, besides the children of several other members; also at a fair recently held by the order of the Odd Fellows, raffling was countenanced and participated in by several members of the church. The object of this meeting of the session was[4] to confer as to the best method of arresting this comparatively new tide of evil influence setting in upon the church.

[2] From the Records, December 22, 1847.

[3] Soon after the Mexican War General James Shields visited Columbia. The Legislature was in session. The Famous Palmetto Regiment had served in his brigade in the Mexican War; he reported to a full house how nobly they had behaved. Columbia was wild with enthusiasm and gave a big ball for the entertainment of General Shields in which these members of the First Presbyterian Church took part.

[4] The pastor called this meeting.

"It appeared in conversation that considerable diversity of opinion prevailed among the members as to the impropriety of dancing and the sin under certain circumstances, of attending public balls. In view of this fact, and the fact that some of these irregularities, as for instance raffling, have probably been committed thoughtlessly, perhaps ignorantly, it was deemed inexpedient by the session to enter upon any immediate and active course of discipline. A paper was then submitted by the pastor designed as a testimony against these and similar evils which he suggested should be read from the pulpit, as the expression of the views, and an exponent to the church of the course of discipline which would hereafter be pursued by the session. The document being a stringent one, binding the session, hereafter, to a definite procedure, after a long conversation, it was thought best to postpone a decision upon it till Friday night, or in order to allow for due reflection on the part of the session."

From the records, December 24, 1847, it appears that while the session was agreed as to the principles in the testimony Mr. Palmer would utter, "the majority could not agree upon the expediency of reading it in public.

Upon this adverse action by his session, he promptly resigned, giving as his reason that his conscience would not permit him to be the pastor of a dancing church. Such at any rate tradition affirms to have been his course. Whatever the inducement, the session speedily came to his way of thinking as the following from the Records, December 25, 1847, shows:

"The design of this meeting was to reintroduce the subject of the preceding conferences, as it was felt that this matter was left in too indefinite a position, no action being had in the premises.

"It was moved to reconsider the vote passed at the last meeting, setting aside the paper submitted by the pastor designed as a public testimony; which motion prevailed. The paper was then modified and adopted as a public testimony to be read from the pulpit on Sabbath morning and, in its amended form, is as follows:

"According to that Scriptural platform of ecclesiastical order to which we as Presbyterians adhere, the whole government of each particular church is committed to its own particular session. Among the acts, therefore, to which this body is competent, besides the receiving of members and administering the various kinds of discipline, is that of delivering its testimony as a court of Jesus Christ, against such errors in doctrine and practice as are likely to prevail among the people committed to their oversight. If 'damnable heresies' and injurious practices arise, it is not only incumbent on the pastor as a preacher of the Gospel, thus to testify; but since the elders are equally with him Bishops, or Overseers, in the church of God; since they equally hold their commission from the Lord Jesus Christ, and since they exercise joint power with him in the Presbyterate, it is competent to them together with him, in their united capacity as a church court, to give a formal testimony against prevailing errors. Impressed with this view of their power and authority, and fully persuaded that very dangerous practices are beginning to obtain amongst us, the session of this church now raises its voice in solemn warning and remonstrance in reference to matters which they proceed herewith to specify.

"In the first place we testify against the iniquitous practice of raffling at fairs. In relation to fairs themselves we do not feel called upon to give a formal opinion. We cannot but observe, however, that often they are accompanied with such evil doings as to lead us to suspect an inherent vice in this whole system of charity financiering. But *raffling* we are constrained unequivocally to condemn. The lot is a divine institution appointed for the purpose of rendering a divine decision in those cases which men are unable by ordinary methods to resolve. On the part of the creature it is a solemn act of worship, as much so as prayer or praise. It is, moreover, a direct appeal to God as the moral governor of the world, to interpose directly in the manifestation of his will. Obviously, therefore, to use the lot with irreverence or levity is to profane the name and perfections of God. It is plainly just such an offense as cursing and swearing and in direct violation of the third commandment. Nor is there the slightest difference as to the principle, between raffling and gambling; and the identity between them is seen in this, that the sin in both is the same, an irreverent use of the name and attributes of God. This use of the lot, moreover, is not only a profanation of the name of God, it is also a mockery of his government in the thoughtless appeal it makes to the interposition of God. Should idle men challenge responses from the divine oracle in the most frivolous affairs, and in gratification of their mere whims? Of course it follows that church members who countenance raffling by any distinct overt act, as by the sale or purchase of chances, subject themselves to the discipline of the church.

"In the second place, the session delivers its testimony against fashionable worldly amusements, such as dancing parties, balls, the theater, the race course and such like. It may be difficult to draw accurately the line of demarcation between the lawful and unlawful pleasures of the Christian. We believe that this is wisely left in doubt, in order to test the piety and spiritual knowledge of the Lord's people. Yet there is one obvious principle which covers this whole case. Christians are witnesses for God, and among other things they must testify concerning the vanity of this present evil world. But if they participate in the chosen pleasures of the world they do it at the expense of that testimony they must bear for God. The amusements specified above are moreover the acknowledged badges of a worldly profession, in some sort the sacraments of allegiance to him who is the Prince and God of this world. In this view Christians cannot share in the same without in so far forth denying Christ.

"And as no Christian has the right at any time to suppress his righteous testimony, so under no conceivable circumstances is he justified in attendance upon those forbidden amusements.

"The session, too, is constrained to think that promiscuous dancing between the sexes is a practice injurious, and tends to immorality, and should be in every possible way discountenanced. Satisfied of the Scripturalness of these views, the session wishes to be understood that the giving of balls and dancing parties, and attendance upon them, together with the theatre, the opera, and the race course, will be regarded as serious offences against the order and purity of the church, which require the exercise in some one of its forms of a wholesome discipline.

"In the third and last place, the session delivers its most mature and earnest remonstrance to those Christian parents who permit their children, so long as they are minors and under their control, to attend such places of amusement as are prohibited to themselves. It is bitterly to be lamented that the standard of Christian education is so deplorably low; and one aspect of this is the little restraint thrown upon youth as they grow up and plunge into the world. Christian parents should remember that at the baptism of their children they brought themselves under solemn covenant obligations from which no power on earth can divorce, while those children are yet minors. In the judgment of the session, the free indulgence of children when they begin to thirst for those pleasures which their parents as their natural sponsors have forsworn in their behalf is in contravention of the baptismal covenant. And it becomes such indulgent parents to inquire, while they are mourning over the hardness and impenitency of their adult offspring, if this is not righteous retribution of their infidelity to the most stringent oath which ever was imposed upon human beings. We believe that in the overwhelming majority of cases if Christian parents would make a firm stand and make a show of principle, the children would yield their own preferences with greater or less cheerfulness, and thus a check would be opposed to that tide of worldliness and dissipation which sometimes threatens to sweep away all godliness from the land. It therefore becomes the duty of every church session to make diligent inquiry in all those cases where the children, still minors of professing parents, attend balls, dances, theatres and the like. And if such parents have not endeavored to use their influence and authority to restrain their children, but have rather lent their sanction or consent, or connivance, the censures of the church should be dealt to these parents according to the demerits of each case, as though they had personally infringed the law of the church.

"In delivering now these conclusions which they have carefully weighed, the session would most earnestly and affectionately exhort their fellow Christians to remember whose they are and whom they serve,—that being redeemed not with corruptible things as silver and gold, but with the precious blood of Christ, they should glorify God in their bodies and in their spirits which are God's. Let us strive to walk circumspectly, not as fools, but as wise, redeeming the time because the days are evil. Since we profess to be 'children of light,' let us 'have no fellowship with the unfruitful works of darkness, but rather reprove them.' 'Let us walk honestly, as in the day; not in rioting and drunkenness, not in chambering and wantonness, not in strife and envying.' 'But put ye on the Lord Jesus Christ, and make not provision for the flesh to fulfill the lusts thereof.' But rather let us 'live soberly, righteously, and godly,' in this present evil world, 'denying ungodliness and worldly lusts,' looking for and hastening unto the day of God, when the Son of Man shall be revealed to be glorified in his saints.' And to, 'as many as walk according to this rule, peace be on them and mercy and upon the Israel of God. Amen.'"

His session went further, and asked him to preach a sermon on dancing, which sermon after it had been delivered, they had printed.[5] In the course of the episode Mr. Palmer publicly declared that "he would not baptize the children of any parents who taught them to dance."[6] It does not appear that he would have gone to quite such lengths in his later life, nor that he looked upon his views and course as the wisest in every particular; but his general animus remained unchanged.

He seems to have been just as energetic in pastoral work. The very summer preceding his disciplinary struggle, he and his session had divided the church and congregation into wards, each of which was subjected to pastoral visitation by the pastor and one elder working together. Throughout the entire pastorate he found time for many visits that seemed little other than social. They were commonly determined by the ultimate aim to strike a blow for the Master. He paid special attention to the sick, the needy, and all who were presumably open to Christian guidance. Nor did he confine himself to people of his own flock.

The following story of a bit of pastoral work by him in the year 1851 shows somewhat as to the spirit with which he

[5] Related in a letter of Rev. R. H. Reid, dated April 13, 1904.

[6] Letter of Basil Edward Lanneau, dated June 22, 1849.

went about such labors for the Master and somewhat as to his tactfulness. He tells the story himself:

"'Ben,' said my father to me at the breakfast table, the morning after my arrival on one of the visits annually paid to the old homestead, 'do you remember your old schoolmate, H. P.?'

"'Perfectly well,' was the reply; 'it would take more than twenty years to efface the recollection of the most intimate friend of my childhood.'

"'Well,' rejoined he, 'he has one foot in the grave, dying of consumption; and he is such an untamed bear that no one can approach him. Possibly you may gain access on the score of old companionship; who knows what, through God's grace, may be the result of your visit?'

"Let me here introduce to the reader the person concerning whom the above dialogue was held. H. P. was the only son of a widowed mother, whose indulgent love proved unable to cope with the passions of a headstrong and willful boy. Upon approaching manhood he broke away from every source of restraint, and soon lost every trace of virtue. In his swift declension he not only abandoned himself to vice in its lowest associations, but took an insane pleasure in setting public sentiment at defiance, until, for years, he had come to be regarded as an outcast and an outlaw. At the age of thirteen our paths in life diverged, and now, for the first time in twenty years, they crossed again.

"Toward noon, when the morning hours of exhaustion should be over, the writer turned his steps slowly to the house of his invalid friend, upon the skirts of the village. Memory yielded up its stores from the buried past, at every footfall: the lessons conned together under the master's ferrule; and wild and noisy sports at recess, upon the village green; and the playmates of those halcyon days—some of whom, alas, were sleeping beneath the turf, over whose early graves aged mourners had too sadly wept. And now I was soon to look upon the most melancholy wreck of all. But somber as these reflections were, they only half prepared me to greet the specter which slowly glided into the parlor, leaning wearily upon a staff, and sinking, exhausted, even at this effort, upon the sofa by my side.

"'My dear H., it grieves me to the heart to find you thus.'

"'Yes, B———, we have not met for twenty years; and if you had waited a few weeks longer, you must have searched for me in the graveyard of Old Bethel, where the solemn oaks droop with moss over the graves of a century.'

"Reader, I had prayed the Lord to make me wise to win a soul, and I was burdened with my prayer. Laying the hand gently upon his knee, I said, affectionately, 'H., do not be angry with me, for the sake of 'auld lang syne.' Let me tell you what most distresses me; it is that you are half way into eternity and so unready to die.'

"Sepulchral as his own cough was the melancholy response: 'B——, it is of no use to talk to me on the subject of religion; I am a doomed man—as sure of hell as if already shut up in its vault of fire.'

"'Oh! H., my friend, how can you say so?'

"'Because, B———, I am a *drunkard!* and no drunkard shall inherit the kingdom of God.' His eye flashed with an unearthly gleam, as he fiercely continued: 'You do not know what sort of a drunkard I am; I carry my jug to bed with me every night—it takes the place of my wife—and I pull from it so often that it can scarcely be said to be corked at all. If I could only break the bonds of this cruel habit, there might be hope for me; but I have tried, a thousand times, in vain. I am bound, hand and foot, with its accursed chains, and there is nothing left for me but to drink and be damned.'

"Was it said only to the apostles, 'And it shall be given you in that same hour what ye shall speak?' Instantly I replied to this vehement and self-accusing speech: 'H., you entirely mistake the matter. What you need is a Savior to save you from your drunkenness; he shall be called Jesus, because he shall save his people from their sins. The salvation from hell is only the result of this salvation from sin. You must come, dear H., to Jesus, as a drunkard, or not at all.'

"With this, we bowed together in prayer, during which the poor emaciated frame shook with sobs, as though it would fall to pieces with the violence by which it was racked.

"The interview was too exciting to be longer protracted; and during four days the writer was engrossed with a religious meeting then in progress. At its close, and just before returning to his home, he called to take a final farewell of one whom he was sure never to meet again upon earth. The same pale, wan countenance met his view as before, but now lighted up with a strange and happy radiance.

"'B———, a wonderful change has passed over me since you were here, and I do not know what to make of it; it cannot be that I am a converted man?'

"'I should not be in the least surprised, H., to find that you are; but tell me all about it.'

"'Well,' he replied, 'when you went away I prayed God to have mercy upon my poor soul, and all at once the shackles fell off from me and I have been full of peace and joy ever since.' Pausing for a little fuller statement before committing myself to a reply, he resumed:

"'B———, I am a very ignorant man—it is many years since I have been within the walls of a church, and I have forgotten almost everything my pious old mother taught me at her knee. But I want to tell you what I think the Gospel is, and where I am wrong you will correct me.' Promising to be very honest in my criticism, he proceeded: 'I think then that we are all born into the world with wicked hearts, and guilty and condemned from our birth; that Jesus Christ is come into the world to save us, if we will only trust entirely in him—but that *He won't be a half Savior to anybody.* I must not do the best I can and then come to him to complete what remains; but I must come at once, just so, and let him do the whole work, from beginning to end. *He will be a whole Savior, or none.* Is that the Gospel?'

"Grasping his hand in both of mine, I replied in a voice husky with emotion, 'H., if you had been a Doctor of Divinity for fifty years, you could not have put it better;' and kneeling down upon the same spot where we had prayed before, we blessed the God and Father of our Lord Jesus Christ, who, according to his abundant mercy, had begotten him again unto such a lively hope.

"Upon reciting the conversation to my venerable parent, I said: 'With your experience and observation, so much larger than my own, would you not take this to be an illustration of Christ's word, he "that hath heard and hath *learned of the Father,* cometh unto me?"'

"'Yes,' was the reply; 'the natural man receiveth not the things of the Spirit of God: . . . neither can he know them, because they are *spiritually* discerned.'

"I returned to my distant home, rejoicing in the conviction that one who had so clearly grasped the central truth of *a whole Savior,* must be born of God. It was, however, a grateful assurance, to learn that after three months of suffering, which yet were brighter with evidences of grace, my poor friend mounted aloft with rejoicing and song into the rest of the redeemed."[7]

This pastor often had a remarkably masterful way of dealing with men and women, though owing to his courtesy and grace of manner, they seldom found anything to criticise in his bearing. One day a young girl of sixteen came into his study to talk with him about uniting with the church. Apparently he thought he understood her case; and he handed her a slip of paper with a hymn on it which she had never before seen. The hymn began,

"Just as I am without one plea,"

Bidding her read and ponder that hymn, he dismissed her. It proved to be enough.

He habitually discovered extraordinary tact in approaching men on the subject of religion. He habitually kept his head in talking with those in distress, or near to death. The won-

[7] This story was written by Dr. Palmer, and published by the Presbyterian Committee of Publication, Richmond, Va., in tract form.

derful self-command which he showed in the pulpit he manifested everywhere. This did not even forsake him by the bedside of his dying mother.

His mother died in November 1847. He was with her for some days before her death. He wrote an obituary of her which was published in the *Watchman and Observer,* soon after. That obituary gives numerous though veiled references to himself, under the phrases "one of her sons," "an attendant," and the like. His mother had been such a force in his life for good; the picture given of her character, in this obituary, is so much the picture of his own character, as to force, intensity, consecration to duty, and method in its performance, that its reproduction in this memoir is entirely pertinent. The view given of himself as her virtual pastoral guide beside her dying bed suggests that it may be properly presented in connection with this account of his pastoral work. It is as follows:

"The same pious affection which leads us to place the monumental marble over the graves of departed friends, prompts often the desire of sketching for the admiration of others, those living virtues which ever draw forth our own affection. If, too, those who die have 'lived by faith in the Son of God, adorned with charity and zeal' and we have followed them with cautious and timid feet, as far as is permitted to the living, down into 'the valley of the shadow of death;' and have there witnessed the triumph sometimes awarded to believers in their conflict with the last enemy, 'there is added the spiritual desire of reading aloud the lesson of instruction which the grave of a saint affords. It is with this mingled desire of profiting the living, while gratifying the instinct of mere natural affection, the writer presents the following memorial of Mrs. Sarah Palmer, wife of Rev. Edward Palmer, who departed this life at Walterboro,' on the 11th of November, 1847, having nearly completed her 60th year.

"At an early age, just as she was blooming into womanhood, she became the subject of renewing grace under the pastoral influence of the venerable Dr. Ashbel Green, of whom she always spoke with the utmost affection as her spiritual father. A few years after, her elder sister being wedded to the Rev. B. M. (afterwards Dr.) Palmer, she came South and was united in marriage to Mr. Edward Palmer, then residing in the city of Charleston, who still survives to mourn her loss after a union of thirty-six years. Upon her marriage she entered with an ardor characteristic of her family upon all those acts of systematic benevolence which in populous cities bring into exercise the graces of a pious female. In her attention to the wants of the poor, the sick and the orphan, in city missionary operations, in tract distribution, in Sabbath-schools, in every form of pious but unobtrusive labor, she was unwearied. She became thus endeared to a large circle of pious friends from whose affectionate remembrance no length of time ever separated her. Years rolled by and she became the mother of five children, four of them living, when she was called to attest her love to the Savior and his kingdom by a very unusual exercise of patience and of faith. Her husband having become 'a new creature in Christ Jesus' felt himself called to serve God and his generation in the work of the ministry. For this purpose he abandoned a lucrative business and separated himself from the endearments of home for a period of three years, while pursuing the study of divinity in the Theological School at Andover. To some the sacrifice may appear easy, as it was only of personal comfort and domestic enjoyment: but all experience and observation show that far greater resolution is required to wear for years a fretting yoke, and still 'possess the soul in patience,' than to make for once a lofty sacrifice, the pang of which, though severe, is short. For three years did this noble woman nerve her soul to endure a quasi-widowhood, and with painful labor wrought she with her own hands to give her children daily bread. The God of the Covenant, who sustained her in all, was pleased yet to bring her faith to severe test. During this bitter separation, death claimed his tribute of her and chose the two loveliest of her babes. Yet this bereaved mother in loneliness bore her sorrows, and sent no wish after him whose voice could alone cheer, because his heart alone was pierced with like sorrow. The vow of consecration was in her heart, and the same love to God and the souls of men which placed the gift upon the altar, saved her from the sacrilege of recalling it. Through this training she passed to become the pastor's wife, which in due season she was, and the diminished family once more met.

"In this new relation we now contemplate her to the end of life, during twenty-four years of increasing usefulness, happiness and honor. Few persons were better fitted by nature and by grace to fufill the duties of this responsible and difficult station: so adapted was she to all, it would not be easy to decide in which she most excelled. Her singularly active mind made her inventive to do good: what plans she formed, her natural enthusiasm enabled her to prosecute with ardor; and her firm will bore her to the end without failure, almost without fatigue. It were hard to say whether she was most fruitful in planning, most ardent in commencing, or most patient in completing. Affectionate and conversable, she was the confidante of the young; serious and thoughtful, she was the companion of the old; gentle and sympathizing, she was a comfort to the sorrowing; experienced and winning, she assured the timid and resolved the scruples of the desponding. Wholly unselfish, her natural kindness went out in sympathy with all the feelings of the happy; while her depth of soul could always measure the woes of the wretched. Thus rarely endowed, she became pre-eminently 'a mother in Israel,' and the grave must cover many a beating heart before she is forgotten upon earth.

"In her more private and domestic relations she sustained the same high position, of a woman equal to all her trusts. Industrious and thrifty, she turned to the best account a country pastor's narrow stipend. Her practiced and vigilant eye looked through her household, no department escaping her constant supervision. Yet while thus driven by necessity into the detail and drudgery of life, none knew better how to 'redeem the time' for intellectual and spiritual purposes. The habit of early rising gave her an hour before the day began its busy hum, and through the long working hours she would snatch brief intervals for reading. A book was always on her table, and some subjects always on her mind for study and conversation. Thus she became the companion of the husband, sharing his thoughts and studies: and the transient clergyman who passed a night beneath her roof never failed to carry away a deep impression of her intelligence and worth.

"For the office of a mother she displayed a surpassing fitness. Always the teacher of her young children, she had the double faculty of letting herself down into their minds and of feeling a real sympathy with their vivid emotions. So entire was the ascendency she thereby acquired over them that her sons, in all the rudeness of boyhood, never knew the time when they would not gladly exchange the sports and playmates of the field for the quiet conversation of their mother at her work-table. Mingling gentleness with decision, she was able to add guidance to discipline; and seizing those moments when they yielded themselves without prejudice or passion to her influence, her speech distilled upon them like dew upon the mown grass. She never sermonized, but dropping occasional remarks with little apparent design furnished them with maxims suited to all the conditions of life. Let not the reader regard these as mere commonplaces, uttered to fill a period. Who that looks back upon the guilty and critical passages of his life, will not bless God for the gift of a pious mother, feeling that it is her hand that has plucked him from ruin! There are seasons of recklessness in youth when we can place our profane feet upon everything save a mother's love; and a mother's love has often quenched the fire which force and authority would have fanned into a powerful flame. This pious mother met with a pious mother's reward. Of her eight children, four preceded her to the world of bliss above; four wept around her grave, but these four trust in their mother's God, and the two sons preach that Jesus in whom they believe, and whom their mother confessed on her dying bed.

"Following such a Christian through a long life of rare usefulness and high communion with God, we naturally look for an end of peace if not of joy. And surely no hour of her life was more brilliant than that which closed her record upon earth. By a remarkable dispensation of Divine Providence her brother and sister, the Rev. Dr. and Mrs. Palmer, were removed by death within a single week, on the 9th and 16th of October. This double shock, together with the fatigue and excitement attending the funeral of her sister in Charleston, was too much for her feeble and somewhat nervous system. On the 25th of October, the day of her return from her melancholy visit to Charleston, the fatal disease developed itself, which in sixteen day removed her from all sin and care to the rest above. In the commencement of her sickness her hope was somewhat obscured, and she called upon her husband and children to pray that Christ would reveal himself to her, and that she might enjoy the fullest assurance of her acceptance with God. Very soon she said, 'I feel that your prayers have been heard. I am delivered from darkness and see and feel Jesus to be my Savior.' From that moment she rejoiced in an unclouded assurance of hope to the end. As she lay, often apparently asleep and unconscious, her frequent exclamations, 'Wonderful love!' 'Precious salvation!' evinced that her soul was absorbed in adoring views of God's love and mercy in Christ. More than once, speaking of Christ as a complete Savior, she exclaimed: 'What a wretched religion the Unitarian has—he has no God for his Savior!' On one occasion a portion of the 89th Psalm was read to her; she responded with animation to the verses which set forth the perpetuity of God's covenant with his people; and to the person who prayed she remarked, 'I always love to hear you pray, because you dwell so much upon God's covenant—that is my hope.' To this she several times referred, rejoicing that God's love was spontaneous, and his favor not doled out according to the measure of our poor services. When asked if death was at all terrible to her, she replied, 'Not at all so now, but it may be otherwise at the last: pray for special grace in that trying moment.'

"On Sabbath, her husband approached her bed and asked if he should remain with her during the day: 'No,' she answered, 'go and do your Master's work, go and preach.' On the following Sabbath she said to one of her sons who had preached, 'I wish I could have heard you to-day; you preached upon the believer's future likeness to Christ in Heaven.' He replied, 'Mother, you may soon know that mystery fully.' 'Oh, it is a sweet promise,' was her full response. In the evening, the family being alone with her, all her children save one—like herself on a sick bed,—she asked for a hymn to be sung. The words 'Come, Holy Spirit, heavenly dove,' were chosen; it must have been to her like the music of Heaven, for at each line she would exclaim, lifting her hands, 'Oh, how sweet.'

"On Wednesday, the 10th of November, deep gloom settled upon every countenance, for the appointed hour was nigh. She was told, 'You are very low, very near to death'; her calm reply betrayed no surprise: 'I suppose the doctor has done his best.' A few directions were then given to her daughters, and she assumed the posture of one waiting to depart. 'I shall soon be at rest, by the side of dear Mary Jane; how sweet it will be!' As the day rolled on she seemed impatient to be gone: 'Come, Lord Jesus,' 'Why delayeth his chariot?' and such like expressions indicated how her spirit panted after rest. She was asked, 'Why are you anxious to die?' 'It is better to be in heaven.' 'Why do you wish to be in heaven?' 'Because it is a place of holiness; that is the chief attraction.' When the night closed in she said, 'I thought all day the time was about fixed for me to go.' She was asked, what she thought then: her reply was, 'God acts like a sovereign in his own way.' She was reminded that there is an appointed time for man upon the earth: 'Yes,' was her answer, 'and that bound none shall pass.' Being asked if she felt that all was well with her she replied, 'Yes, I am very sure.'

"A few hours after, the last change passed over her previous to death; the glazed eye and heavy respiration betokened its near approach. Her husband took her hand and sought a recognition; but in vain—various questions were put, which showed that every sense was locked up to this world, she knew neither face nor voice of those she loved best on earth. At this moment, an attendant whispered to her those words, 'God is our refuge and strength.' She immediately added, to the joy and wonder of all, 'and a very present help,' the sentence was finished for her, 'in the time of trouble.' Again it was whispered in her ear, 'I have loved thee with an everlasting love:' she rejoined, 'and with loving kindness have I drawn thee.' Desirous of knowing how far she was alive to spiritual things while dead to those of earth, it was whispered to her, 'There is now no condemnation to them which are in Christ Jesus:' with slight verbal inaccuracy she finished the passage 'who walketh not after the flesh but after the spirit.' Finally these words of Paul were repeated, 'I know in whom I have believed': her dying lips concluded the testimony of an assured believer, 'and that he is able to keep that which I have committed to him until that day.' These were her last articulate words. Who can desire a more brilliant end, than to make the last use of the organs of speech in uttering such words pregnant with a calm assurance? Soon after midnight, she slept the sleep which knows no waking. Thus lived and thus died one of the Lord's hidden ones. One grave holds her poor body, but many hearts her memory; and desolate as the home is which she has left, her partner and her children would rather give themselves to so blessed a death, than to mourn for her. She rests, and so shall we, dear reader. May our work be done as well."

Without such a mother Mr. Palmer had not been such a pastor. Perhaps her early death served to accentuate the influence she had so long and so happily exerted over her son.

June 2, 1844, little Benjamin Blakeley, his first born, had been taken away from his earthly home, by the gracious God of the covenant. He wanted a month and twenty-four days of being two years of age.

His father had found in him and the vast responsibilities that came with him, a "new divinity school with richer teachings than that which had trained him and sent" him forth to his life work. "A grand theology was forming itself out of these experiences; where every thought was turned into prayer, and knowledge glided into worship." During twenty months he had indulged in the proud joy of fatherhood, and in pious musings had outlined his son's career, and placed him as his own successor behind the sacred desk. Then through two months he had seen him wither away; for an angel's wing had "touched the babe and dropped into its cradle the call to higher ministries beyond the skies;" and the father had learned other deep lessons in the philosophy which has Jehovah for its author. He had learned, too, the comfort wherewith to comfort others. How many homes in Columbia, and far off New Orleans and elsewhere were to be the better off for that little fellow's mission!

Into the home thus bereft of the dear little boy, there came, while the parents were in Columbia, five little girls, each with her own mission and ministry. Amongst them was one with eyes and coloring much like those of the little brother whom she had lost long before her own birth. When she grew old enough to talk, "her baby accents lisped continually of another world." A score of years later the father recalled these strange words of this babe of three winters:

"When I went to Heaven," she used to say, "I saw a big white gate with a man standing just inside. Before it was a pool of water with a board across it; and the man said, 'Come in, Sissy, but don't fall in.' But I fell in; and he took me out into a room in which there were a great many glory-children, and dressed me in white wings like theirs. Then he took me to see God. I saw a big red pillow with five dots, that God rests on. And, mother, there were two gold rocking chairs for you and father, and five little ones for us children. And, Mauma [her nurse], there was a beautiful white satin dress for you. It felt so smooth; just put your hand on your hair, it felt just like that. I wanted to bring it to you; but when I went to take it, it just slipped away. And now I spend every Sunday in Heaven with God. He puts a ladder for me every Saturday evening, and I go up and come home on Monday." [8]

---

[8] *Broken Home,* p. 57.

When Mr. Palmer went to Columbia he found his congregation worshipping in a barn-like structure of rather modest dimensions. It soon became insufficient for his congregation. Toward the end of his pastorate there, he led his people to erect a new church edifice. In the year 1853, after the usual trials and tribulations of builders, the present edifice was ready for use. It was formally dedicated to the service of God, on Sabbath morning, October 9, 1853, by the pastor; whose theme of discourse on the occasion was, the "Warrant and Nature of Public Service."

The discourse is presented entire, as illustrating his ideals of his own duty as the minister of worship in that church; and as a fine type of the sermon he was aiming to give his people:

John 4: 23, 24.

"THE HOUR COMETH, AND NOW IS, WHEN THE TRUE WORSHIPPERS SHALL WORSHIP THE FATHER IN SPIRIT AND IN TRUTH: FOR THE FATHER SEEKETH SUCH TO WORSHIP HIM. GOD IS A SPIRIT: AND THEY THAT WORSHIP HIM MUST WORSHIP HIM IN SPIRIT AND IN TRUTH."

It is an advantage sometimes accruing from unusual solemnities, that attention is directed to those ordinary rites, which pass current under the sanction of usage and prescription, rather than from an intelligent conviction of their nature and design. Thus, at the threshold of our services to-day, questions break upon us, from the depths of the eternal world, like the surf of the seashore, which gives presage of the boundless and surging ocean. We meet professedly, with public forms, to devote to the service of God this elegant structure, a monument both of the liberality and taste of the congregation by whom it has been reared. But what is meant precisely by this act of dedication? Do we hope, by the incantations of a spiritual magic, to transform this building of stone and mortar into a true and real temple? Can any amount of priestly benedictions put holiness into these beams and timbers? Surely not. Let the wizards peep and mutter as they may, the brick and the marble confess themselves incapable of that holiness which is an attribute of sentient and rational beings only. If, under the Jewish Dispensation, the consecration of particular localities was enjoined, this was due to the typical character of that mysterious economy. Jerusalem and Zion were only because Jehovah chose there for a season to reveal his presence. It was the Shekinah between the Cherubim which made the tabernacle holy. But the tabernacle, with its chambers and its courts, its altars and its ark, its vessels and its veil, was but a type of Christ's humanity, and of the great priestly work to which this was needful. Only until "the fulness of time should come," did it please God to dwell in temples made with hands. Now he dwelleth in the Incarnate Word, which is "the true tabernacle that the Lord pitched, and not man,"—"the greater and more perfect tabernacle, not made with hands,—not of this building." It is, my brethren, a melancholy proof how little we are imbued with the spirit of the Gospel, that good Christians should still "speak half in the speech of Ashdod." A vain superstition still babbles, in the dialect of obsolete Judaism, about temples, and altars, and priests, as though these were anything more than "figures of the truth, for the time then present." As the only Priest known to the Gospel is that High Priest, who by "his own blood entered into the Holy Place, having obtained eternal redemption for us,"—so the only temple now on earth is that which is "builded together for an habitation of God through the spirit," the stones of which are living stones, taken, indeed, from the quarry of corrupt human nature, but polished after the similitude of a palace, in which God dwells by his Spirit. This dedication, then, imparts no sanctity to this material edifice. In the language of another, "No pompous ceremonies, no solemn forms, no magnificent appearances, no gaudy or golden solemnities, can sanctify any place unto God and his worship, or make it more holy than it was before. And though when a commodious building is erected for the worship of God, it is a very decent thing to begin the worship at that place with solemn prayer or addresses to God; yet, all this human prudence, this natural decency, and all these prayers, do not amount to the sanctifying the spot of ground or the building, so as to make it holier than the rest, or put any such holiness upon it as belonged to the Jewish people."[9] Then, "what mean we by this service?" Why this lifting up of our hands, this invocation of the adorable and incomprehensible Trinity, these chants and Psalms of praise? We do but set apart, in solemn phrase, this House to the public worship of Almighty God. A sense of propriety would dictate, on opening a house of worship, that God's blessing should be implored upon all the ordinances to be dispensed therein; and the character of those associations should be declared, which are henceforth to invest the worshipper.

But the antecedent inquiry arises, why should men meet in public assembly to render united homage to the God of Heaven? If, as is often alleged, and in a high sense is most emphatically true, if religion be only the name of man's individual relations to God, lying only between the conscience of the creature and the authority of the Creator, what distinctly is the warrant for these public convocations? Why is it not enough, in the elegant language of Jeremy Taylor, that "every man shall build a chapel in his own breast, and himself be the priest, and his heart the sacrifice, and every foot of glebe he treads on be the altar?" It does not satisfy this inquiry that so it has been

---

[9] Dr. Watts' *"Discourse on the Holiness of Places."*

through all periods of time, and under every dispensation the voice of assembled worshippers has gone up to Heaven, as "the sound of many waters." The universality of this public worship is, indeed, fully attested by the seal of history. If, from the present moment, we ascend, through intervening generations, to apostolic and primitive Christianity, our march will be through assemblies more or less august, till we sit down with the church that was in the house of Philemon or Aquilla. If we cross the line which separates the Christian from the Jewish economy, our feet stand upon the threshold of the synagogue, in which, from the captivity, if not from a remoter age, all the parts of natural worship—prayer, and praise and reading of the Law, were continually performed. With the myriads of Israel again we go up to the holy hill of Zion, where, in the temple of Solomon, or the tabernacle, its pattern, we wait upon those ceremonial and positive institutions which God expressly ordained. Three times a year a nation trod with solemn feet the courts of Jerusalem, and a nation's anthem went up in praise, while a nation's repentance smoked in the blood of unnumbered victims. If again we penetrate the haze which hangs around the Patriarchal Dispensation, when the earth was young, when the ruler was a priest, and the priest a father, we find dim traces of chosen spots honored with the symbols of God's presence, and where lingers faintly the echo of a united worship.[10] So that across the track of sixty centuries, from the moment when we gathered in this assembly to the day when Paul stood on Mars' Hill, and from Peter in the streets of Jerusalem to Noah, a preacher of righteousness to sinners before the flood, the Lord's "faithfulness has always been declared in the congregation of His Saints." But this universality of public worship binds us with the authority of *prescription* only, not of *law.* It proves that some principle exists in man, prompting to these joint acts of worship, but does not declare what that principle is. Nor if it did, would the mere suitableness of this worship, recommending it to such universal consent, be deemed a sufficient basis upon which to rest the duty.

Nor does it satisfy this inquiry to point out the public benefits flowing from the practice. These blessings cannot be exaggerated, though depicted in the deepest colors the most lively fancy shall invent. "Religion," it has been well said, "is the ligature of souls, and the great instrument of the conservation of bodies politic, and is united in a common object, the God of all the world, and is managed by public ministries, by sacrifice, adoration and prayer, in which, with variety of circumstances indeed, but with infinite consent and union of design, all the sons of Adam are taught to worship God,"[11] Science teaches that the harmony of the material universe depends upon one pervading natural law. The power of mutual attraction, which holds together

---

[10] See Blunt's *Coincidences in the Writings of the O. T.*, Part I.

[11] Jeremy Taylor's *Life of Jesus.*, Part I., sec. 7.

two atoms in a lump, holds earth, and all the planets, which in the void immense wheel their course. Whole constellations, too,—"cycle and epicycle, orb in orb," as "with unoffensive pace each spinning sleeps on its soft axle,"—revolve with complex motion round a common center, the *"primum mobile,"* perhaps the august throne on which the Godhead sits. The analogy is perfect. What attraction is to matter, binding the atom to the mass, the planet to the sun, and the constellation to the throne of God, that religion is to soul. Man's responsibility to God gives capacity for obedience to human law. He moves in the narrower sphere of earthly duty, because fastened by a higher tie in a wider and holier relation. While the conscience responds to the challenges of Divine Law, the yoke of authority will be borne under the human. Thus religion is truly the girdle which binds together the complicated interests of society. Public worship nourishes this sentiment precisely in the form which is best suited to immediate application. It is of immense service, at stated seasons, to bring men together in the mass, where they may feel a brotherhood of nature and of race,—where all the artificial distinctions of wealth, position, education and rank, shall for the moment be obliterated,—where each shall feel that "there is one body and one spirit, even as there is one hope of their calling, one Lord, one faith, one baptism, one God and Father of all, who is above all, and through all, and in all." Individual differences are merged, and individual asperities softened, when all look back upon a common ruin, look up to a common Savior, look forward to a common goal, rejoice in the promises of a common covenant, weep tears of a common repentance, and experience the joys of a common pardon. Blot religion from the soul of man, and you have destroyed the cohesion of society; bury the sanctuary in ruin, and you have dashed to pieces the great magnet of earth, which draws all hearts into sympathy and union.

Still less can we overstate the influence of the sanctuary as the educator of mankind. It is God's voice which thunders here, and the human soul must give back the echo. He speaks of law, and, like the needle to the pole, conscience points to duty. He speaks of wrath, each fluttering pulse betrays the fears. He speaks of love, the softened heart gives its wedded vows to him who won it. Under a judicious ministry, who can estimate the slumbering energies aroused, and the mental training which reaches thousands whom scholastic discipline never touched? I speak not, of course, of that fanatical rant, whose ambitious sport it is to lash the soul into a tempest of emotion, leaving only the foam to mark its passage. I speak of that discreet, well proportioned, yet earnest ministry, which feeds the Church of God with wholesome truth,—giving milk to babes, and strong meat to men,—which, not pampering to a taste craving always to be delirious with excitement, chooses to pour a flood of knowledge upon the human mind, and suffers this light of Heaven to draw its own music from the soul on which it beams.[12]

Yet all these advantages, of which only a suggestive hint has been given, do not form the ground of public worship. They fully justify the wisdom which ordained it, and add motives for its due and reverent observance, but they do not furnish the warrant upon which its claims may legally be sustained.

We reach a much higher position when the authority and will of God are distinctly pleaded in its favor. In whatever form this will may be revealed, it silences dispute and rebukes distrust. Whether it be conveyed through the appointment of a weekly Sabbath, upon the lintel of which is inscribed the sentence "the seventh day is the Sabbath of rest, an holy convocation,"—or, in the assurance of extraordinary blessings to such as frequent His courts, as thus, "in all places where I record my name, I will come unto thee and bless thee,"—or, in the more explicit command, "forsake not the assembling of yourselves together, as the manner of some is;" the will of God, clearly known, resolves every scruple and binds the conscience. But the Divine authority, though recognized as ample warrant for the duty, does not forestall investigation, whether in man's essential nature, or in his religious relations, any reasonable ground exists for this practice of public worship. It infers no want of submission to God's absolute authority to trace the obvious reasons of his holy commands, and thus to inflame our admiration of his wisdom and goodness, by discovering the suitableness of his laws, both to our nature and condition.

There are three great principles, from which the institution of stated public worship would seem to flow by necessary deduction. The first is:

I. *That man, endowed with a social nature, cannot attain the perfection which is possible to him, in the privacy and insulation of his own being.* As in worship we have immediate commerce with the Infinite One, it might seem to be a matter of individual concernment merely. But, however true it may be that religion lies only between the man and his Maker, in the sense that God only is Lord and Judge of the conscience, it is not true that religion contemplates man as an insulated being. On the contrary, it penetrates every faculty of his complex nature, and pervades every relation in which he stands. As the moon's motion round the earth does not impede the common and wider motion of both around the sun, so neither does the connection between God and the conscience become less intimate, when the worshipper lifts his voice in the great congregation, than when he breathes his prayer in the whispers of the closet. This "bill of divorcement" which men draw up between the first and second tables of the Decalogue,

---

[12] The celebrated statue of Memnon, in ancient story, was said to utter melodious sounds, when first illuminated by the rising sun.

between their primary and secondary duties, as though the former only fell within the pale of their religion, is the charter of that "filthy Antinomianism" which, in every age, has left its obscene touch upon the Church of God. True religion does not more possess man's nature than it covers man's relations. It is as truly a part of religion to love our neighbor as ourselves, as it is to love the Lord our God with all our heart,—as much a part of religion to "do justly, and to love mercy," as "to walk humbly with our God." The earth's orbit may be around the sun, but the earth's orbit is also among the stars. Man's duty is to know and to obey God, but not the less to serve Him *among men.* True piety is thus an invisible essence, which penetrates the whole character, and relishes the entire life. With supreme love to the Master in our souls, all the hard labor with which we earn our bread in the working forge of life, all the unseen acts of wayside charity,—the morsel of bread to the hungry, the cup of cold water to the thirsty, the tear of Christian sympathy for the mourner,—all these, like the prayers and the alms of Cornelius, come up for a memorial before God; or like the sweet savour which the Lord smelled in the burnt offerings of Noah. If, then, religion though an individual matter strictly, does not *exclude,* but rather, in its comprehensive definition, *embraces* all the social relations of man, surely his worship, which is but the utterance of religion, may be rendered conjointly with others, while yet it ascends from individual souls, sweetly attracted by their Maker's love, as the single flame leaping upwards, and "trembling most when it reaches highest," is yet composed of a thousand blended rays of heat; or as the sun's radiance, which bathes this world in glory, comprises myriads of single beams, each distinct to the eye of God, though blending into common light.

But these remarks do not touch the core of the principle stated above, which was, that man having social endowments and affinities cannot perfect his own nature, in a state of complete seclusion. It is from this postulate that the whole theory of education proceeds, without which it would have neither purpose nor method. It would have no *purpose,* because if man is to live in the seclusion of his own soul, locked up to a transcendental intercourse with his Maker, why not leave him to the impulses received immediately from God, which alone can fit him for that secret communion? It would have no *method,* for no form of education is conceivable which does not draw a man out from the solitude of individual being into correspondence with objects external to himself. Education takes us out of these inner chambers, and ranges with us through the whole domain of nature. We walk among the stars, and call it astronomy; we scrutinize the elements, and call it science; we analyze all the processes of thought and emotion, and call it philosophy; we study the social fabric, with its scale of graduated duties, and call it morality; we combine together the doctrines of Holy Scriptures, and call it theology; we feel their influence upon our own heart and conscience, and call it religion. The whole is education, which leads forth the anchorite from his cell, guides him in these wide excursions through all the provinces of nature and reason, and endows him with a wealth of knowledge, to gather which the whole universe of matter and of mind has been laid under tribute.

So, too, man's social nature lies at the foundation of all development of his faculties. We come into being with a thousand capacities, physical, intellectual and moral, every one of which is dormant, and requires to be developed. The great law seems to pervade the world of rational existence, that moral beings shall live together in society, and their natures be perfected under mutual action and reaction. In all the universe no intelligent being is doomed to a solitary existence, but wherever there is a soul it cries out for fellowship. Angels have society in joy, and devils companionship in woe. The multitude of harpers, whom John saw upon the sea of glass, formed the General Assembly and Church of the First-born in Heaven. The consecrated millions around the Lamb, represented by the four beasts and the four and twenty Elders, in company with angels, swell the chorus of blessing and honor to Him upon the throne. Let it be uttered in the muffled tones of reverential awe, even the mystery of the Godhead teaches the same: since Jehovah, whose greatness is unsearchable, is himself infinitely perfect and ineffably blessed, in the social existence of the Trinity. This analogy, therefore, to which we have discovered no exception, in worlds above or worlds below, would seem to teach that man on earth would not be left to solitary communion with his Maker; but that, in religion, as in all else beside, the social element would have scope in the united worship of the sanctuary. When the sinner is again "renewed after the image of Him who created him," he is not left a lonely orphan, to shape his own character by the power of his own desolate musings; but he is brought into association with others of like precious faith, that by the law of assimilation, and the power of mutual support he may "grow up to the measure of the stature of the fulness of Christ." As a part of this heavenly education, he mingles in those public offices of religion, which profit him, not only by the greater promises of grace annexed to them; but profit him also by "the piety of example, by the communication of counsels, by the awfulness of public observation, and the engagements of holy custom."[13] Thus "the whole body fitly joined together, and compacted by that which every joint supplieth, according to the effectual working in the measure of every part, maketh increase of the body unto the edifying of itself in love."

II. But a second ground, upon which we may rest the institution of public worship, is, that *it is necessary to the Church, as the visible*

[13] Jeremy Taylor's *Life of Jesus,* Part I., sec. 7.

8

kingdom of Christ. It would be superfluous here, to argue the existence of a church visible, as distinguished from that which is invisible. The latter is the Church of the Elect, embracing only the mystical body of Christ, who have "followed him in the regeneration." It is, of course, known infallibly to God only, who are the subjects of this kingdom; and it would require a special revelation, in reference to each, to bring it under human control and government. Besides this kingdom, and to a great extent including it, is another kingdom which is visible, and, as visible, is administered by men. This kingdom is the Church of God on earth. To employ the full definition of Dr. Mason,[14] it is "the aggregate body of those who profess the true religion, all making up but one society, of which the Bible is the statute-book, Jesus Christ the head, and a covenant relation the uniting bond." Now, what is necessary to give *visibility* to this kingdom of Jesus Christ? Obviously, there must be a covenant, or charter, securing the privileges of its subjects, and setting forth the tenure upon which these are held. There must be outward seals, giving legal value to the instrument, the use of which shall involve a solemn assumption of all the duties which are imposed. There must be laws, regulating the conduct of such as desire to be true and loyal subjects, and repressing the rebellion and wickedness of such as are traitorous and false. There must be officers, invested with ministerial power, acting always under the commission of their lawful king. There must be a court from which the symbols of royal power and supremacy may be displayed; and days of interview, when the subject comes into the presence of his monarch to offer up his homage, and to receive the favors which royal clemency or justice may dispense. From her first organization upon earth all these visible marks have been deciphered on the Church of God. Sacrifices were instituted, as the mode by which the worshippers might make an acceptable approach to their king, typical of the great expiation which should be made by the one perfect offering in the end of the world. Priests were ordained to go between the living and the dead, typical of "the only mediator between God and man—the man, Christ Jesus." The temple was erected as the dwelling place of the Divine Majesty, from which all his oracles should issue. Extraordinary prophets were commissioned to make new disclosures of the Monarch's will. Days of convocation were set, when he would display his glory to his subjects, and sacraments were given to seal the bond between himself and them. Great changes have indeed supervened upon that economy since the advent of Christ, but not such as affect the identity of the Church, as a visible Catholic society from the beginning. The sacrifices are withdrawn, but not the great propitiatory oblation in which they were fulfilled. The succession of earthly priests has ceased, only because the great High Priest ever liveth to intercede above. The temple hath not

---

[14] Mason's *Essays on the Church.* No. I.

one stone left upon another, but the true Shekinah dwelleth in Christ, the Word made flesh and dwelling amongst us. The long line of prophets terminates only in that Prophet whom the Lord God was to raise up like to Moses, and their treasured messages are expounded from the Bible by living ministers; while the seals of the covenant have only changed their outward forms. Is it not necessary that there shall be solemn assemblies, in which the laws of this kingdom shall be proclaimed,—when this visible church, with its visible ministry, its visible sacraments, shall also, through a visible worship and visible discipline, commend itself to the love and veneration if its members? The Church, as the visible kingdom of Jesus, has the Sabbath for its court-day, the sanctuary for the King's pavilion, and its instituted worship for the subject's fealty.

But these considerations lead to the third ground, upon which this great institute may be based:

III. *Since, by means of the worship and ordinances of the sanctuary, this kingdom of Christ makes its aggressions upon the surrounding and opposing powers of darkness.* In strict analogy with all other empires, this kingdom rose from small beginnings. It was first set up, with a written constitution, in the family of Abraham; it received a visible expansion in that of Jacob, whose twelve sons were the twelve foundation-stones of the Jewish church. This kingdom, cradled for a season in the fruitful land of Egypt, soon outgrows the limits of the family and tribe, and comes forth a nation. In Canaan, hedged around with peculiar and restrictive ceremonial institutes, it lives without further development till he came, who was the end of all the types. For a season we see it reduced within narrower limits, and must search for it in the house, as in the days of Abraham and Isaac; but it is only to burst forth with a new enlargement, and assume its proper attribute of universality. Now is fulfilled the vision of Daniel, "the little stone cut out without hands shall smite the feet of the great image, and then it becomes a great mountain, and fills the whole earth." From the moment the Church entered into the Christian Dispensation, throwing off the restrictions by which it was swathed in the Jewish, it is confessed to be an *aggressive* kingdom. To its sovereign there is "given dominion and glory and a kingdom that all people, nations and languages, should serve him; his dominion is an everlasting dominion, which shall not pass away, and his kingdom that which shall not be destroyed." The genius of the two Dispensations, the Jewish and the Christian, is strongly expressed in the opposite directions given to both: under the former the language is, go up to Jerusalem; under the latter the language is, go into all the world. In the one, the Church is stationary; moored to the Hill of Zion by peculiar and local rights placed in the center of earth, as at that time known, she throws her light over surrounding nations, and attracts them to her. In the other, all her fastenings cut asunder, she is sent forth upon a great itineracy; no longer stationary, but aggressive, she goes to the nations, who before were commanded to come to her.[15] In the great commission of her Lord, go ye into all the world, and preach the Gospel to every creature, we trace the genius of the New Testament Church. It is no exaggeration of pious zeal, when it is reiterated that the Church of Jesus Christ is essentially a Missionary Church, and her aggressiveness set forth as a capital and distinctive feature.

But not only is this kingdom thus aggressive; its encroachments are made through a peculiar warfare. Its only weapons are persuasion and argument. The arrows that are "sharp in the hearts of the King's enemies" are drawn only from the quiver of eternal truth. The only sword drawn from its sheath is the sword of the spirit, which cutteth to the heart. The only captivity it inflicts is that which "brings every thought into the obedience of Christ." The commission under which its armies go forth to conquest, enjoins that they shall gain their victories simply by teaching all nations, baptizing them in the name of Father, Son and Holy Spirit. And thus the appropriate symbol of this kingdom is that of the angel flying in the midst of Heaven, having the everlasting Gospel to preach unto them that dwell upon the earth. Now, because this kingdom claims to be thus universal and makes its aggressions not by the arm of violence, but by the gracious words of its Lord and Head, therefore these public convocations are required. Wherever its subjects may be scattered, their oath of all allegiance binds them to spread a tent, and invite the nations to a parley. "The great trumpet must be blown, to assemble the outcasts in Egypt, that they may worship the Lord in the Holy Mount." They must take up the song of the angels to the shepherds, and proclaim "the tidings of great joy to all people, that unto them a Savior is born, who is Christ, the Lord." Whatever necessity may have existed in former ages, for the public assembly, it must be a prime feature of the Church in the present economy. Without public proclamation, the Gospel must be stifled in its utterance, and cannot prove itself the power of God, and the wisdom of God unto the salvation of man.

Thus far, my brethren, we have discussed the *warrant* for public worship, which we find to be the will of God expressly revealed to us, having yet a natural foundation in the social constitution of man, pertaining to the Church as the visible kingdom of Christ, and necessary to the aggressions which she is pledged to make against the world of darkness. It will be necessary now to consider the *nature* of this worship, as deducible from the text. The woman of Samaria proposes to

---

[15] See this contrast beautifully presented in a *Missionary Sermon*, one of the earlier performances of Dr. Harris, which made him known to the church at large.

Christ to settle the dispute so jealously maintained between her people and the Jews, whether the worship of God had been appointed on the Hill of Zion, or on Mt. Gerizim, from which of old his blessings had been so solemnly pronounced. To this inquiry Christ replied by showing its utter impertinence. The time had now come when the predicted challenge of Isaiah was to be both explained and fulfilled: "Thus saith the Lord, the Heaven is my throne and the earth is my footstool; where is the House that ye build unto me, and where is the place of my rest? for all these things hath my hand made, and all these things have been, saith the Lord; but to this man will I look, even to him that is poor and of a contrite spirit, and that trembleth at my word." The Dispensation of types is brought to a close. Henceforth, "he that killeth an ox is as if he slew a man; he that sacrificeth a lamb, as if he cut off a dog's neck; he that offereth an oblation, as if he offered swine's blood; he that burneth incense, as if he blessed an idol." Among these vanishing shadows is the gorgeous temple on Mount Moriah. Shall he who "inhabits the praises of eternity," who "fills immensity with his presence," be confined within a material edifice? Behold, the frame of nature is his, and the broad earth his footstool. God is a spirit, infinite, eternal, and unchangeable, without body or parts; it is appropriate therefore, that he be universally worshipped, and with a spiritual homage. The Jewish law was but a "shadow of things to come but the body is of Christ." Since then, Christ, this body, is come, God is to be worshipped, not through the shadow, but in the substance which is Christ. The worship, therefore, which God now accepts, both secret and social, is a worship not restricted to places or to season; it is a worship not ceremonial and typical, but spiritual and internal, the substance and body of which is the truth itself,—the truth known and felt in its power,—the truth as it is in Jesus.

There is obviously the distinction between what is natural and what is ceremonial in public worship: The former having a ground in nature, so that reason itself would enforce it upon the conscience,—the latter deriving its entire claim from the express appointment of God. In the first class will fall such acts as prayer, and praise, and the study of the Word, which, having their ground in reason itself, never can become obsolete with changing dispensations. In the second class will range such symbolical rites as Circumcision or Baptism, the Passover or the Eucharist. For though these symbols may illustrate vital and holy truths, yet the will of God alone can make one symbol more obligatory than another, or indeed bind us to a symbolical worship at all. The Jewish Dispensation was marked by the predominance of the ceremonial over the natural parts in public worship. The courses of the priests, the splendor of their vestments, the variety and number of the sacrifices, the magnificence of the temple, the oblations and incense,—all gave denomination to Judaism, as a system of types and emblems. But under the Christian economy, the natural parts of worship, those having an evident foundation in reason and propriety, and not possessing authority from positive institution alone,—these are brought into bolder relief from the suppression or withdrawal of the symbolical.

This seems to be intimated in the contrast drawn by our Savior, between the typical and the spiritual, in the text: "The hour cometh, when neither in this mountain, nor yet in Jerusalem, shall ye worship the Father; but the true worshippers shall worship the Father in spirit and in truth." Here to worship in the spirit is antithetical to worship ping in Jerusalem, which cannot be explained, unless these terms are the synonyms of a symbolical and a spiritual worship.

This language suggests, too, a certain connection between the *devotions* and the *instructions* of the sanctuary. For though the term truth in the phrase, "in spirit and in truth," does not primarily refer to any dogmatic statements, yet referring to Christ as the substance of the shadowy economy of the temple, it doubtless implies full instruction in all that relates to His person and work. Permit me to dwell with a little minuteness upon what may be termed the Protestant view of public worship, touching the stress which is to be laid upon the office of instruction in the sanctuary. There are three lines of thought which conduct to the inference that formal exposition of truth is a necessary service in the Christian Church. It follows:

I. *From the complete withdrawal of the ancient types.* It is, I conceive, a low and narrow view to take of these, that they were designed as artistic representations, to captivate the senses and delight the imagination. If no inspired interpretation of them had been afforded, drawing out stores of spiritual meaning, it would be more pardonable to speak of them as giving a scenic effect, as it were, dramatizing the worship of God, enlisting the sentiment, and drawing forth the poetry that lurks far down in the nature of every man. The Epistle to the Hebrews is sufficient to overthrow this frigid hypothesis. The Apostle undertakes to unfold the priesthood of Christ, and he does this by simply expounding the import of the tabernacle and its furniture, the priesthood in its courses, the sacrifices and purgations of the old law. We are therefore to regard these types as being really an exhibition of spiritual truths to the Jewish mind,—a sacred hieroglyph, curious enough to provoke inquiry, yet plain enough to be resolved upon investigation. They were indeed a language, peculiar in construction yet pregnant with meaning, if the key were only given to unlock the cypher. It does not concern me now to vent an opinion how far this language was actually interpreted,—whether the pious Jew was permitted to read the high import of these mysterious symbols, or whether, like prophecy, which is a cypher of another kind, the key is reserved till the day of fulfilment. Should I hazard a conjecture upon this collateral point, it would be that types and prophecies both were, in their broad outline, sufficiently understood, at least by the spiritually enlightened,—while yet the details of both were shut up in mystery, and all questions as to the mode and time of fulfilment lost themselves in the uncertainties of conjecture. If, then, these types were a species of language, speaking to the eye, and reaching the reason through the imagination,—if the temple, with its august ceremonies, was but a symbolical painting, somewhat like the sculptured panels and painted walls recently disinterred from the ruins of Nineveh,—then they cannot be withdrawn from a dispensation claiming to be more perfect, without the substitution of a better form of instruction. What this form shall be, is most easily and reasonably determined. In Judaism, Christ was *to come;* his advent was future: In Christianity, Christ *has come;* the event is past. In the one case, the representation of what is future cannot but be symbolic; in the other, the representation of what is past cannot but be historic. In the New Testament Church, therefore, the instruction must consist of plain statements of actual facts—the facts of Christ's life, and the facts of his death—and of didactic expositions of duty founded upon these facts. The change which has taken place is just what we would antecedently expect from the chronology of the two economies. When Christ's advent was future, it was foreshadowed by types and emblems. When Christ did come these types were cancelled, and he is now held forth in the sanctuary as a fact, a substance and a body; and the instructions which are given are instructions concerning a fact; they are plain, literal, historic and didactic.

II. *The same conclusion as to the necessity of formal instruction in the sanctuary follows, from the connection of preaching, with the final spread of Christianity.* "There were great voices in heaven, saying: the kingdoms of this world are become the kingdoms of our Lord, and of his Christ, and he shall reign forever and ever." This is the pæan with which prophecy celebrates the close of this latter age of the Church. But how is this unearthly kingdom to penetrate all earthly kingdoms, and include them? Go preach my Gospel, saith the Lord, for it is by the foolishness of preaching he will save them that believe, and "the foolishness of God is wiser than men." But who shall preach? Even they that are sent. And where shall they preach? What ye have heard in the ear, says Christ, proclaim ye upon the housetops. If what has before been said, respecting the aggressiveness of Christianity be true, and if this universal extension is to be achieved by the simple proclamation of Gospel truths, then the importance of the pulpit cannot be overlooked; and among the appointments of the sanctuary the expositions of Bible truth must be prominent.

III. *But the necessity of instruction in the House of God will appear further from the relation of knowledge to worship.* I am free to admit that the main design of these public assemblies is devotion; yet it cannot be a blind and senseless devotion of the body, without the soul. "God is a spirit,"—and how can he be pleased with what is corporeal? If, for the purpose of instructing men in the higher mysteries of redemption, atonement and pardon, he for a season enjoined bloody sacrifices, it was not because he delighted either in the fat of rams or in the blood of bulls. When he made man in his own image he gave him a thinking soul, and endowed that soul with knowledge and holiness, and the sacrifices acceptable to him are those of a broken and contrite spirit. "To love him with all the heart, and with all the understanding, and with all the soul, and with all the strength, and to love his neighbor as himself, is more than all whole burnt offerings and sacrifices." But how can this devotion be spiritual without the truth? To worship God as a spirit, and with the spirit, there must be knowledge of God, who He is—"infinite, eternal and unchangeable, in His being, wisdom, power, justice, goodness, holiness and truth"—there must be knowledge of God in His relations to us, as our Creator, Ruler and Redeemer—there must be knowledge of His law, setting forth His claims upon our love and service—and there must be knowledge of the way of approach and communion with Him, as it is graphically summed up by Dr. Owen.[16] "This is the general order of Gospel worship, the great rubric of our service. Here, in general, lieth its decency, that it respects the mediation of the Son, through whom we have access, and the supplies and assistance of the Spirit, and a regard unto God as a Father. He that fails in any one of these breaks all order in Gospel worship. This is the great canon, which, if it be neglected, there is no decency in whatever else is done in this way." How, then, can there be true worship without instruction? For these things are known only as God has revealed them and He has written them in a book. Instruction, therefore, is needed in the sanctuary, to afford the materials for devotion; for the knowledge of God and His love supplies the theme of our song.

It strikingly illustrates, too, the wisdom of the Divine arrangements, that in the sanctuary instruction and devotion are so inseparably coupled and the former always in subordination to the latter. If Christianity were taught only in the portico and lyceum, it is hard to see how it should be kept from sliding into a sublime philosophy. But taught in the sanctuary after offices of prayer and praise, and taught as a means to these, it is retained in the heart as religion. The devotions of the sanctuary exercise a secret, but not the less powerful, check upon that spirit of unlicensed speculation, which, in reference to the deity, is always profane; while again, these instructions react powerfully upon the devotion of the worshipper, to enliven and support it. They supply oxygen to the flame, so that the vestal fire burns without extinction upon the altar within.

---

[16] Sermon on Nature and Beauty of Gospel Worship.

It is somewhat a nice point to adjust the instructions and the devotions of the sanctuary so that they shall be mingled in due proportion. Ritualism, on the one hand, so multiplies the offices of prayer and thanksgiving as to thrust aside the exposition of doctrine. Rationalism, on the other hand, spins out discourse till the spirit of devotion is smothered under the weight of human speculations. Romanists, for example, as types of the first, substituting the Church for Christ, and cutting off all access to God save through the priesthood, have no occasion to bring divine truth upon the conscience and heart, and the sermon is ignored. Protestants, on the contrary, who maintain the individual responsibility of men to God, and cannot propose to be proxies for others in this concern, rest upon the truth, as the great medium of spiritual communion with God. In proportion, therefore, as the Protestant spirit prevails, is attention given to the preaching of the Word. The exact measures of the two may not be determined alike by all. But the very genius of Christianity requires that copious instruction shall be given—that this instruction shall hinge upon the vital truths concerning the grace of the Gospel—that it shall be conveyed, not in a dry and scholastic form, but in that practical and experimental form which shall glide most easily into the frames of devotion.

I cannot forbear, even at the hazard of wearying you, from touching upon another feature of Christian worship, clearly implied in the contrasted expressions of the text, viz: *its pre-eminent simplicity.* When Christ says, "the true worshippers shall worship the Father, not in Jerusalem, but in spirit," the antithesis lies not in the language, but in the sentiment. He does not mean to say that spiritual worship could not be rendered at Jerusalem as elsewhere. Jerusalem is here only another name for Judaism,[17] the "Jerusalem which is in bondage with her children;" and to worship in Jerusalem is only the formula for a ceremonial and symbolical service. Here, then, are two facts: First, that the only instance in which God has enjoined a splendid and imposing ritual upon the Church was under a dispensation clearly typical, when the truth was taught by emblems; and Second, that this picturesque and ceremonial service has been unquestionably withdrawn, being supplanted by another that is spritual and simple. As regards the splendor of that ancient service, the following language was uttered by one of the great divines of the seventeenth century:[18] "Mosaical worship, as celebrated in Solomon's temple, outdid all the glory and splendor that ever the world, in any place, in any age, from the foundation of it, ever enjoyed. How glorious was it, when the house of Solomon stood in its greatest order and beauty, all overlaid with gold, thousands of priests and Levites ministering in their orders, with all the most solemn musical instruments that David found out, and the great con-

[17] Brown, on Galatians, p. 235. [18] Dr. Owens' *Discourse on the Nature and Beauty of Gospel Worship.*

gregation assembled, of hundreds of thousands, all singing praises to God! Let any man in his thoughts a little compare the greatest, most solemn, pompous and costly worship that any of the sons of men have in these latter days invented and brought into the Christian Church, with this of the Judaical; take the Cathedral of Peter, in Rome, bring in the Pope and all his cardinals in all their vestments, habiliments and ornaments, fill their choir with the best singers they can get, set out and adorn their images and pictures to the utmost that their treasures and superstitions will reach to, then compare it with Solomon's Temple and the worship thereof, and he shall quickly find that it holds no proportion with it, that it is all a toy, a thing of naught in comparison of it." Yet this splendid, pompous and costly ritual has been cancelled by the same authority which ordained it.[19] After all, it was but a veil which Moses put over his face which the spirit of the Lord hath taken away, that "we all, with open face, beholding as in a glass the glory of the Lord, may be changed into the same image from glory to glory." These were but the elements of the world," under "the bondage" of which the children of God were, "until the time appointed of the Father." The glory of this economy is that it is "the ministration of the Spirit"; who being present, as "the anointing which teacheth the believer, and is truth and is no lie," has forever destroyed that dim, ceremonial service, which, like the shadows of a magic lantern, was only "a figure of the true." To introduce, therefore, pomps and rites into Christian worship with a view to make it impressive and gorgeous, is to Judaize it.[20] If the intention be only to give splendor and dignity to the service, by rights which have no emblematic signification, then it is "a show of wisdom in will-worship." The whole is thereby rendered impertinent and trifling, since the Church never had, even in the days of ceremonial observance, a ritual that was void of significance.

---

[19] "The divine command is the only basis of religious duty; and will-worship of every description has uniformly drawn down the expression of the Divine displeasure. With regard to whatsoever partakes of the essential nature of worship, it may safely be affirmed that what is not commanded is virtually forbidden. This constitutes the broad line of distinction between the worship of faith and the offerings of superstition; the former alone partakes of the character of obedience, being founded upon the knowledge and recognition of the Divine will. Whatsoever is not of faith, whatsoever has not the Divine command as its basis, is not obedience, but sin."—*Conder, on Protestant Non-conformity, p.* 165.

[20] "Idolatry has reference either to the *object* or to the *mode* of religious worship. . . . But idolatrous corruptions of the *mode* of worship are not less at variance with the religious principle. 'The descent of the human mind, from the spirit to the letter, from what is vital and intellectual to what is ritual and external in religion is,' re-

The argument is complete either way. If the ritual be emblematic of truth, then we have gone back to Judaism, reconstructing in part at least, a system that by God's will has "decayed and vanished away;" if it be only sensuous and imaginative, then the arrogance is insufferable, which offers to guard what is confessedly unmeaning, to amuse, as it were, his heavy hours with the gauds and mimicking shows the children love.

If this congregation has erected a building more grand and beautiful in architectural design than that which to-day we have left, it has been done only in the exercise of a lawful taste about a matter in itself morally indifferent. But I would prefer to see it razed to the earth, and its foundation stones be uncovered, than it should be supposed to lend a sanction to that stupid jargon of a so-called ecclesiastical architecture, whose ghostly mutterings have of late, through some Witch of Endor, been pouring in upon us from the dark ages. Be it known unto all men that here is none of "that beauty and glory which carving, and paintings, and embroidered vestures, and musical incantations, and postures of veneration, do give unto divine service."[21] No pealing organ, "through long-drawn aisle, and fretted vault," here "swells the note of praise." No "dim religious light" streams here, through storied panes, to cheat us with its likeness to the twilight hour. Here have we no wooden cross, no altar, no human priest, no emblematic furniture, "no ceremonies, vestments, gestures, ornaments, music, altars, images, paintings, with prescriptions of great bodily veneration."[22] We know but one sacrifice, that which was offered up once for all,—the Lamb of God, slain from the foundation of the world. We know of but one Priest, who with his own blood has entered through the veil into the Holiest, having obtained eternal redemption for us. We know but one temple on earth, that which is made such by the indwelling of the Holy Ghost, the saints of the most high God. We know but one gospel, to wit: "that God is in Christ reconciling the world unto himself, not imputing unto them their trespasses;" and with

---

marks an eloquent writer, 'the true source of idolatry and superstition in all the multifarious forms which they have assumed.' Whatsoever tends to compromise the spiritual for the sensible, whatsoever transfers the attention of the mind from invisible realities to material forms, directly opposes the spirit and tendency of Christianity. All attempts, therefore, to conciliate the homage of the irreligious to Christianity by an accommodation of its principles, its rights or its practical requisitions to the imagination and taste of worldly men, in whatsoever motives they may originate, must be stigmatized as frustrating the primary design of the Gospel and as partaking of the nature of idolatrous corruption of religion."—*Conder, on Protestant Non-conformity,* pp. 20, 21.

[21] Dr. Owens' Discourse, *The Chamber of Imagery.* [22] *Ibid.*

Paul we say, if an angel from heaven preach any other gospel unto us than that we have received, let him be accursed. As for this building, my brethren, beautiful as it may be in our eyes, let it please us to call it only a plain Presbyterian meeting house. The glory we see in it, let it not be the glory of its arches and its timbers,—not the glory of its lofty and graceful spire, pointing ever upwards to that home the pious shall find in the bosom of God; not the glory of this chaste pulpit, with its delicate tracery, and marble whiteness, not the glory found in the eloquence or learning of those who, through generations, shall here proclaim the gospel,—nor yet the glory traced in the wealth and fashion, refinement and social position of those who throng its courts. But let its glory be "the glory of the Lord risen upon it!" Let its glory be the promises of the covenant engraved upon its walls, which are yea and amen in Christ Jesus. Let its glory be found in the purity, soundness and unction, of its pastors,—in the fidelity and watchfulness of its elders,—in the piety and godliness of its members. Let its glory be as a birth-place of souls, where shall always be heard the sobs of awakened penitence, and the songs of new-born love. Let its glory be the spirituality of its worship, its fervent prayers, its adoring praise, and the simplicity and truth of its ordinances and sacraments. Let its glory be the communion of saints, who here have fellowship one with another, and also with the Father, and his Son Jesus Christ. Let its glory be as the resting-place of weary pilgrims, toiling on toward the heavenly city—the emblem of that Church above—

> "Where congregations ne'er break up,
> And Sabbaths never end."

AND NOW, "TO THE ONLY WISE GOD, THE KING, ETERNAL, IMMORTAL AND INVISIBLE,"—TO GOD, "GLORIOUS IN HOLINESS, FEARFUL IN PRAISES, DOING WONDERS,"—TO GOD WHO "IS A SPIRIT, INFINITE, ETERNAL AND UNCHANGEABLE, IN HIS BEING, WISDOM, POWER, JUSTICE, GOODNESS, HOLINESS AND TRUTH,"—TO GOD, THE FATHER ALMIGHTY, THE MAKER OF HEAVEN AND EARTH,—TO GOD THE SON, THE BRIGHTNESS OF THE FATHER'S GLORY, AND EXPRESS IMAGE OF HIS PERSON,—TO GOD THE HOLY GHOST, PROCEEDING FROM THE FATHER AND THE SON,—TO THE SERVICE AND GLORY OF THE ADORABLE AND INCOMPREHENSIBLE TRINITY, WE SOLEMNLY DEDICATE THIS BUILDING, WITH ALL THAT APPERTAINS TO IT. "Lift up your heads, O, ye gates, and be ye lifted up, ye everlasting doors, and the King of glory shall come in. Who is this King of glory? The Lord, strong and mighty, the Lord mighty in battle. Lift up your head, O, ye gates; even lift them up, ye everlasting doors, and the King of glory shall come in. Who is this King of glory? The Lord of Hosts,—he is the King of glory." [23]

---

[23] These concluding sentences formed the closing prayer of the congregation, though incorporated here with the Discourse.

TAKEN AT COLUMBIA, 1854.

"And now, O, Lord God of Israel, which keepest covenant, and showest mercy unto thy servants that walk before thee with all their hearts! Behold the heaven, and the Heaven of heavens cannot contain thee; how much less this house which we have built! Have respect, therefore, to the prayers and supplications of thy servants; let thine eyes be open, and let thine ears be attent unto the prayer that is made in this place! Here choose Zion, and desire it for an habitation. Here abundantly bless her provision, and satisfy her poor with bread! Arise, O, Lord God, unto thy resting-place,—thou, and the ark of thy strength; let thy priests, O, Lord God, be clothed with salvation, and let thy saints shout aloud for joy. Let these walls be called salvation and these gates praise."

Mr. Palmer exercised the greatest care in the reception of persons into the Church. His session demanded of candidates for Church membership, evidence of a real change of heart, and Godliness of life. He and his session were honest, earnest, and thoroughgoing in the application of discipline. Hence the apparent growth of the Church was not rapid. Nevertheless, when he resigned the Columbia Church, in 1855, he left it ninety per cent stronger numerically than when he took it, and still further advanced as an efficient working organization.

CHAPTER VIII.

THE PASTOR AT COLUMBIA, S. C.—Continued.

(January, 1843—October, 1855.)

Served the Church at Large, by Helping to Found and Conduct the Southern Presbyterian Review.—By the Use of His Pen.—Came into Great Demand for Occasional Addresses.—Rendered to Columbia Seminary Varied and Valuable Service.—Made his Home Life Contributory to his Influence for Good: Open to Young People whom He could Help, *e. g.*, to H. R. Reid, Basile Edward Lanneau, *et al.*—The Adviser and Comforter of many of his Brethren on Occasion.—Entertained at his Home many Gentlemen whom He there Bettered.—Calls to Important Posts on Every Side.—Suffered Himself to be Made Professor of Ecclesiastical History in Columbia Seminary.—Mrs. Palmer's Prediction at the Time of his Transfer.—Degree of D.D. Conferred upon Him in 1852.

BETWEEN 1845 and 1847, the desire to have an organ for the thorough, scholarly and unmuzzled discussion of theological and ecclesiastical themes became strong in Columbia. There were giants there, in those days. They had messages from the Lord to their brethren, which they burned to deliver; and they liked not Princeton's disposition to put a gag into their mouths. Accordingly an association of ministers, in the town of Columbia, established that very able periodical, *The Southern Presbyterian Review;* the first issue of which bears the date, June, 1847. This association conducted the *Review* for about a score of years, when the governing body was reorganized on a wider geographical basis and continued the publication of the periodical down to 1885. It was succeeded by the *Southern Presbyterian Quarterly,* which began to appear July, 1887.

The first editors of the *Southern Presbyterian Review* were James Henley Thornwell, George Howe, and Benjamin M. Palmer. There is no reason to doubt that Mr. Palmer gave himself to his editorial work with method, energy and persistence. He thought it no great thing to work fifteen hours out of twenty-four in this period, and perhaps averaged ten hours work a day in his study during his Columbia pastorate. There have come down, amongst his loose papers, lists of subjects carefully framed by his hand, on which he, as editor, wished to have articles from contributors. This suggests that he conducted a share of the correspondence, and probably supervised such articles as he secured, as they were going through the press. An examination of the pages of the *Review* discloses the fact that he contributed, between June, 1847, and the end of his Columbia pastorate articles enough to make an octavo volume of three hundred pages. An examination of the articles gives a new insight into the character, attainments, and prowess of the man.

In the first issue, our young pastor, not yet thirty years old, appears with an article entitled, "The Relation between the Work of Christ and the Condition of the Angelic World." His contention is thus set forth by himself:

"We are persuaded that the scheme of grace revealed in the Bible should be regarded from a far higher point of view than this low earth on which we dwell; that its relations are more vast and extensive than is supposed by those who would confine it to any one district, class, or order of beings. Taking, indeed, the narrowest view of it, it is sublime beyond all human conception. The redemption of a single soul from death, its deliverance from the bondage of sin and the power of Satan, its entire sanctification, and its introduction into heaven, are all events of the most startling and impressive kind. The passage of even one redeemed saint from the deep pit and miry clay of sin to a throne with Christ in his glory, unfolds a history which might command a listening senate of angels. But, if with John, we could behold, in Apocalyptic vision, the one hundred and forty and four thousand, standing with the Lamb on Mount Zion, having his Father's name in their foreheads, their voice as the voice of many waters, and their song that of harpers, harping with their harps: in view of the immense number, each seemingly equally a monument to the mystery of grace, we should confess this is a great salvation, this salvation by the blood of Christ. Yet, this is but a standing point, from which to spring to a higher and more commanding view. We have only to look upon the different orders of worshippers in the heavenly temple and witness the whole hierarchy bending before the throne of the Lamb, to be overwhelmed with the mystery of divine grace. It is not difficult to say why 'the spirits of just men made perfect' should cry day and night, 'Thou are worthy, for thou hast redeemed us by thy blood;' but whence came these,—this innumerable company of angels—these 'flames of fire'—who catch from the redeemed sinner the keynote of praise, and swell the chorus, 'worthy is the Lamb that was slain'?

"The answer to this question brings us to the grave, yet delightful theme, which it is the object of the present article to pursue. It may be expressed in the following proposition:

"'Jesus Christ, by his atonement, has introduced into the moral government of God the *principle of grace,* which avails to the confirmation of beings who are holy, as well as to the redemption of beings who are fallen.'"

In the argument which follows, Mr. Palmer shows familiarity with the best literature on the subject, from the Reformation times down. He discovers an acuteness and subtlety of insight, a reach and vigor of the constructive imagination, an agility, ingenuity, and strength of reasoning power, extraordinary; and he clothes all that he has to say in forms of expression which do indefinite credit to the training his mother had given him in Milton, Shakespeare and the Bible. The imagery is so lofty that it reminds the reader of Milton's; the language is so clear and precise it suggests the student of Shakespeare. As he himself saw that there wanted in his arguments somewhat to establish beyond the possibility of doubt the proposition for which he contended, and, as he explicitly confessed the defect, the reader who is not carried with him in his conclusion, cannot fail to admire greatly this essay.

In the December, 1847, issue of the *Review,* Mr. Palmer enters upon "an examination of the fixed character of the Jew, both intellectual and moral;" and endeavors to discover "the causes which have steeped it in its present mould." He found the most obvious traits of the Hebrew character to be, "its almost superhuman tenacity;" "the singular elasticity of constitution," which enables the Hebrew to recover position of which he has been dispossessed once the dispossessing force has been withdrawn; "their incorrigible worldly-mindedness and consecration to the service of mammon;" "their comparative freedom from the gross vices of other races;" and their intellectual activity and shallowness. He explains the production of these traits in the Hebrew race in an ingenious and able manner, betraying, by the way, no small appreciation of the Jewish people and character. Toward the close of the paper, he declares that "this analysis of the character of the Jews has been made with the practical design of interesting the reader, and inspiring a deep and prayerful regard for" the Jewish people; and presents a number of considerations wherefore

Christians should strive especially for the conversion of this race. He declares:

"Whoever, then, feels a lively sympathy with Christ in his present humiliation and prays to see him Lord of the whole earth, must be ill instructed if he does not feel a corresponding anxiety for the salvation for the House of Israel. It is not improbable that God is now reserving this people for a distinguished service in the way of evangelizing the world. Their complete diffusion over the globe—their comparative isolation among men—the extraordinary enthusiasm and energy of their character, destined to be greater when it shall be toned by truth—their very conversion to Christianity after so many ages of unbelief—all adapt them for extraordinary labor in the missionary service. Perhaps the future history of the church will reveal many a son of Abraham with Abraham's faith, doing the work of Paul, preaching the faith which he once destroyed. And the conversion of the Jews, accomplished in fulfillment of a hundred predictions, will probably be the grand fact argument by which the truth of Christianity, in the latter days, will be attested."

This article is especially interesting in view of the very intimate relations which he sustained throughout most of his later life with the Jews in New Orleans. His interest in the race was long grown; and was explained by his concern for a people so interesting in themselves considered, and by his desire to see them converted to Christianity.

In the issue of March, 1848, of the *Southern Presbyterian Review,* Mr. Palmer appears with an article on "An Inquiry into the Doctrine of Imputed Sin." He espouses the doctrine of immediate imputation; and argues its truth with nicety, elegance and force. In the issue of July, 1849, he appears in a paper headed, "A Plea for Doctrine as the Instrument of Sanctification." The paper was occasioned, as may be inferred pretty safely, by some of his own experience as a preacher, notwithstanding his great popularity. He says:

"That a deeply seated prejudice exists in many parts of the church against the systematic exposition of the doctrines of the Bible, is too obvious a fact to be questioned. It probably falls within the experience of every pastor, to see the gathering frown, the averted shoulder, and the drooping head, as soon as certain doctrines are announced as the theme for discussion. It does not excite our surprise that the world of the ungodly should manifest this displeasure: for the same 'carnal mind' which is enmity against God, is enmity likewise against the truth of God. But that professing Christians should engage in this unholy crusade against doctrinal religion, and that even ministers of the gospel should sigh over the earnest proclamation of its truths, and accuse the faithful witness of 'daubing with untempered mortar,' is certainly a most afflictive and atrocious scandal."

He alleges that this strange phenomenon is explicable, nevertheless; and asserts that in some latent skepticism of the doctrines themselves is the cause; that in others timid concessions to the clamors of the ungodly have had play; that in others the fear of losing church members by the exposition of doctrine prevails; that in others indolence and sluggishness of mind lead them to decry doctrine and to prefer exhortations; and that in others the belief obtains that doctrine is not necessary to sanctification. He next presents five stages into which the ordinary religious progress of Christians may be divided; and shows that doctrine is needed at, and through, every stage in order to progress. In the conclusion occurs the following reference to the standards of his Church as instruments of sanctification:

"Indeed, we utter a long cherished conviction, when we say that, next to the Bible, from which all that relates to God and the soul must be drawn, there are no books we would sooner recommend for an experimental and devotional use than the Calvinistic Standards. We place them in the hands of children and think their office discharged when the 'form of sound words' is transferred to the memory. How few think (to appropriate a child's expression) 'to learn these things by heart.' Many a Christian will devour a whole library of books of devotion and pious biographies, trying to draw on a ready-made experience, as he would a glove, when a better manual of practical religion is almost thumbed out in the hands of his child. Let him put ninety-nine hundredths of these volumes into the fire, and thoroughly digest his Shorter Catechism, and he will come forth a stronger, brighter, happier Christian, and in sooner time, than if he had read the memoirs of all the saints and martyrs from Abel until now. The taste of the Church is so superficial that we should not wonder if the reader is smiling at this as a conceit, rather than a matured conviction of the writer. We would only plead with him for the experiment. Let him take the doctrine which he conceives most remote from practical life, and most hidden among the deep things of God—let him ponder it over till his mind has taken a deep and firm grasp of it—let him trace its relations to other doctrines, and to the whole scheme with which it harmonizes—above all, let him pray over it, until it is so revealed that he feels its power over his own spirit."

In the issue of the same excellent *Review*, for October, 1849, we have, from Mr. Palmer's pen, an article entitled "Church and State." The article discusses with penetration and power the theories as to the proper relation of Church and State, defended, severally, by Bishop Warburton, Dr. Thomas Chalmers, W. E. Gladstone, Esq., Dr. Thomas Arnold, and Baptist W. Noel, M.A. The writer discovers his ability to put his hand on the weak spot in a theory, and to find the joints in the harness of his enemy. Such studies as this show that it was by no accident that Mr. Palmer came to be an acknowledged master of the principles of church government. In the April issue for 1850, Mr. Palmer resumes the discussions of the same general subject, pays his special respects to the theories of Mr. Gladstone and Mr. Coleridge; takes up the five leading arguments by which the advocates of the union of Church and State plead for this union, tears them up by the roots, and effectually disposes of them at the bar of reason. He commends the relation of mutual and helpful independence between Church and State. Dr. Thomas E. Peck, in his "Ecclesiology," chapter xiv., "Other Theories of Church and State," pays to these discussions of young Mr. Palmer a handsome tribute. He forms this chapter in large part by a reduction of Mr. Palmer's presentation of the several theories. He did this apparently without knowing who the author was. The articles were unsigned. The author of the "Ecclesiology" simply refers by volume and pages of the *Review* to the presentations which had pleased him so much.

In the issue of October, 1850, he appeared with a paper entitled "Christianity Vindicated from the Charge of Fanaticism." He found the plan of this paper in the reply of Paul to the Procurator Festus, who had charged the Apostle with being beside himself: "I am not mad, most noble Festus, but speak forth the words of truth and soberness." He first presents a "compendious and portable argument for the truth of Christianity;" and then the sober, sane, balanced view that the Christian takes of things. The production is acute and strong, and, in places, brilliant. In October, 1852, there appeared in the same periodical an article entitled "Baconianism and the Bible." It contained the substance of an address delivered before the literary societies of Davidson College, N. C., August 11, 1852. After a graphic portrayal of the methods and relative fruitlessness of the Greek philosophy, the author sketches the Baconian methods and the beneficent and splendid results flowing from the application of this method. He then proceeds to show why this philosophy should be the philosophy of Protestantism; and that revelation, so far from being hostile to science, contributes a powerful incidental influence in its favor. After a most effective argument he takes the ground that there never could have been a Bacon without the Bible; that Francis Bacon was the offspring of the Reformation which gave the Bible to the world again; and that he did for philosophy what Luther had done for the Bible, bringing out "the older volume of nature" and interpreting its cipher to mankind. In the conclusion, he takes occasion to sound the warning that the philosophy which ignores the Bible and cancels its testimony, is not only baptized into the spirit of infidelity, but "has apostatized from the fundamental articles of the Baconian creed," which forbids the exclusion of a single pertinent fact from its generalizations. We cannot follow the author in an apparently unqualified endorsation of Mr. Locke's philosophy, and in other positions taken by the way; nevertheless he has delighted us with the breadth of his attainments, the vigor of his thought, the force, fire and splendor of his rhetoric, and the strength of his arguments, so that we are in full sympathy with his closing words:

> "This discourse gives in two words—Baconianism and the Bible—a portable argument paralyzing the skeptic with the shock of the torpedo. The Baconian philosophy is the mother of that proud science which sheds such glory upon the age in which we live; and this philosophy, as already shown, has historical and logical connections with the Bible, the charter of our religious hopes. We may rest therefore in the conviction that as the Bible has conferred the largest benefits on philosophy, true science will repay it with the largest gratitude. Kindling her torch at every light between a glowworm and a star, she will read to us 'the silent poem of creation.' She will appear, like an ancient priestess, in the sacred temple of religion; and burn the frankincense of all her discoveries upon the altar of inspired truth. She will assemble the elements and powers of nature in one mighty orchestra, and revelation shall give the keynote of praise, while heaven and earth join in the rehearsal of the grand oratorio."

In January, 1853, "The Claims of the English Language" appeared as the leading article of the *Southern Presbyterian Review* for the month. It was the substance of an address delivered before the literary societies of Oglethorpe University,

Ga., November, 1852. It was a magnificent plea for the study of the English tongue, for the exaltation of the English language to the same preeminence among the languages which those who speak it enjoy among the nations. The advocate had vast stores of pertinent truth which he set forth with marvelous felicity and power. The plea was needed at the time. If republished in pamphlet form and put into the hands of young men entering college to-day, it could hardly fail of doing incalculable good.

In the April issue for 1853, appeared, from his pen, an article on "Mormonism." He had read this as a lecture before the Mercantile Library Association of Charleston, January 26, 1853, and, at their request, published it with such verbal alterations as adapted it to the *Review*. In its preparation he had studied Howard Stansbury's "Exploration and Survey of the Valley of the Great Salt Lake of Utah," a "History of the Mormons, or Latter Day Saints; with Memoirs of the Life and Death of Joseph Smith, the American Mahomet," and Lieut. J. W. Gunnison's "The Mormons, or Latter Day Saints, in the Valley of the Great Salt Lake; a History of Their Rise and Progress, Peculiar Doctrines, Present Conditions and Prospects, Derived from Personal Observations During a Residence Among Them." In the paper he attempts to exhibit Mormonism by running parallels in certain more prominent points with Mohammedanism. The essay was constructed with a philosophic spirit. The reader may not be able to accept the philosophy in every point; but every page provokes thought as well as informs; and every page suggests that its writer was a man of broad philosophic spirit. Let the following excerpt serve as an illustrative proof of the kind of spirit that pervades and informs the article:

"It is never easy to form a correct estimate of religious impostors. The deceit and falsehood which mark their course seem scarcely consistent with the religious sentiment that must underlie the character. The great controversy, for example, whether Mohammed was a fanatic or an impostor, proceeds upon the supposed incompatibility of the two; yet their co-existence is needed to solve the facts of the case. We cannot explain the origin of a religious impostor, without supposing the religious element to be awakened, however it may be afterwards debauched and misdirected. The history of error abundantly shows that the most vicious principles will often mingle with the religious instincts of men, who are driven under this double impulse into the most riotous excesses. The original exciting cause may be slight enough; but the hallucination, once entertained, of miraculous correspondence with heaven, an unscrupulous or ignorant conscience will not long hesitate at fraud in accomplishing the holy mission; and when success shall have consecrated the cheat, the impostor becomes fully ensnared in his own lie, and easily accredits to supernatural revelation the suggestion of his own fancy. Joseph Smith, the founder of the Mormon sect, is dogmatically pronounced an impostor by thousands who do not stop to enquire how far he may also have been an enthusiast; or to solve the query whether it be possible to control the religious convictions of our fellow men, without a previous excitation of our religious nature. The biography of this remarkable person opens with the account of his deep spiritual distress during an exciting religious revival through which he passed while yet a youth. Perplexed in his choice between conflicting sects and creeds, he was for a time in that state of indecision in which multitudes vibrate between superstition and skepticism. While perhaps on the verge of infidelity, he swung to the opposite pole, and conceived the project of founding a church, whose comprehensive creed should harmonize all sects, and swallow up dissent: and this lively suggestion of his own mind a heated imagination may easily have coined into a vision of God. Seven years, however, elapse, before this bold conception embodies itself in a decided scheme. While 'the vision tarries,' the nascent prophet relapses, if the story be true, into the vagrant habits of his early life, which show him to be constitutionally of a deeply superstitious turn. By the aid of seerstones and hazel rods, he had gained no small reputation as a money-digger. Certainly, if he failed to track the secret veins of silver, he did not fail to sound the depths of human credulity. At the end of seven years, he is prepared to enter upon prophetical functions, and announces a new revelation, whose origin forms a curious record in the annals of literary forgery."[1]

No less than three of the articles to which attention has just been called had been prepared first of all to serve as addresses before scholastic or literary bodies. During this period Mr. Palmer came into great demand for occasional addresses. More particularly the demand for this sort of service at his hands came into vogue about 1850. In a letter written by young Basile Edward Lanneau, June 22, 1850, we read:

"The exhibition at Barhamville on Wednesday night was quite brilliant . . . The crowning exercise of the occasion was an address to the graduating class, after they had received their diplomas, by the Rev. B. M. Palmer, whose merits as universal speechmaker are just

[1] See pp. 561, 562.

beginning to be discovered. The object was to delineate the 'perfect woman,' in which he struck all the tones 'from grave to gay,' from lively to severe. It was beautiful, witty and solemn, all by turns, and seems to have given universal satisfaction. The *Telegraph* has requested it for publication, and so a copy may possibly reach you. I hope it did good. 'Cousin Augusta' (Mrs. Palmer) probably sat for the portrait, at least in his mind; and I must do her the justice to say that she is not very far short of the ideal."

Mr. Palmer seems to have made no attempt at keeping a journal. How much of this sort of occasional service he did it is perhaps impossible to discover. But as has been seen, in the year 1852 his address before the literary societies of Davidson College, and that before the literary societies of Oglethorpe University, were so elaborate and able that they were deemed worthy of publication in the *Southern Presbyterian Review.*

Of the impression made by the former of these addresses, the Rev. Professor Wm. T. Hall, of Columbia Seminary, writes:

"The first time I ever saw him was on the rostrum at Davidson College. He delivered as a commencement oration a discourse on 'Baconianism and the Bible.' At first we were not prepossessed. He was rather small, his complexion was dark, his face was dished, his whole appearance was against him. But he had not spoken long until he had full attention. Interest deepened as he proceeded. The interest was genuine, but not painful. We found ourselves carried along by the full tide of the discourse, our vision gradually enlarging, and every faculty enlisted and charmed. The spell of the orator was upon us. Weeks passed before the echoes of that oration ceased to be heard on the college campus."

August 9, 1854, he addressed the literary societies of Erskine College, South Carolina, on "The Love of Truth the Inspiration of the Scholar." In illustrative proof of this simple proposition he pointed in a profoundly philosophical way to the relations sustained by the human mind to the external world; to the repose which belief brings to the human mind, as contrasted with the anguish of doubt; and to the consideration that error is always poison to the mind, while truth is the food upon which it thrives and grows. He followed with a presentation of motives which should urge the student to cultivate the love of truth, closing with a consideration of obstacles which most retard its progress. It is philosophically able and rhetorically brilliant. The style shows that the speaker was not a little under the influence of Mr. Macaulay. The production shows that he had been ploughing in the master thinkers, and more widely still. The reader notes in him "the cormorant appetite with which things most crude and strange have been devoured, and the facility with which these are converted into apt and beautiful illustrations. A child's horn book, or a fairy tale—Cinderella's slippers, or Aladdin's lamp—nothing comes amiss." From his copious reading springs such an affluence of illustration as makes his speeches sparkle with life and beauty. By special request of the faculty and students the address was at once published in pamphlet form.

June 4, 1855, he delivered a discourse, on John 6:68, 69, before the graduating class of the University of North Carolina. In this discourse he ably and eloquently argued the two propositions, viz: I. *That man's religious nature constrains him to find repose in some form of faith and worship.* II. *That the wants of this nature, well understood, are met only in Christianity, as taught in the Gospel.* The next day the members of the graduating class honored themselves by declaring that they were "not contented to have heard once, so learned and masterly a discourse," which had convinced them so thoroughly of the truth of Christianity; and by asking for a copy for publication.

Many addresses less thoroughly elaborated were delivered in the course of the period. Their character may be gathered from the description of one which he delivered at the close of the session of Columbia Seminary in 1852. The Rev. Basile Edward Lanneau describes it in a letter to his parents, bearing the date of July 16, 1852. He says:

"The anniversary of the Society of Enquiry, on Monday evening, was also quite interesting. In Dr. McGill's absence, they fell back on our fluent kinsman, who, with his usual readiness of concoction and utterance, gave us a free and easy, plain and powerful talk on the subject of preaching, the sum of which was, that the preacher was a certain great somebody, with superhuman qualifications, some of which he enumerated. It contained some powerful and stirring thoughts, some perhaps not sufficiently matured, but the more striking and impressive, from the undress in which they appeared."

Columbia Seminary had been struggling with an insufficient endowment, and, in consequence, with an insufficient faculty, from its incipiency up to the year 1855. The institution looked to the pastor of the First Presbyterian Church of Columbia, that one of her sons most honored, for no little incidental service. He helped to raise her endowment that she might command the labor of James Henley Thornwell. That service is described, in part, in the following letter:

"COLUMBIA, S. C., March 24, 1855.

"*To Rev. B. E. Lanneau:*

"DEAR BASILE: It is two weeks to-day since I returned from my journey to the Southwest, and found upon my table your letter together with some forty others. If yours has not been answered before this it is because it could afford to be postponed, while the others had more imperative claims upon my immediate attention.

"You are probably aware that about the 10th of January I started out with Dr. Adger upon an agency in behalf of the Semınary to secure the endowment of a fourth chair; or rather to provide certainly for Dr. Thornwell's support. The history of the effort in Charleston (in which, however, I had no concern, it being conducted entirely by Drs. Adger and Smith) you have doubtless learned through the public prints. About $16,000 was taken up in money and bankable notes, chiefly in the Second Church and in Glebe Street (Church). This, however, includes the $7,500 raised in guarantee of Dr. Thornwell's salary for three years; some portion of which was obtained at Columbia and elsewhere. I then went to Savannah and made a partially successful application there . . . Dr. Adger joined me in a united effort upon Augusta; from which place we moved forward to Montgomery. At this point we separated, I remaining at Montgomery, while he went to Selma. After this we joined forces and made a descent upon Mobile, and then upon New Orleans. In these several places we collected about $12,000, either in money or in notes bearing interest, maturing at specified times and payable in bank. The endowment stands now about $28,000. Edward, my brother, and Miller, of Chester, go out next week upon a joint agency for the same object, to visit the villages and country churches of Alabama. We hope they will return with some $10,000 more. The three churches in Charleston which as yet have done nothing, together with the adjacent islands, will be good probably for $5,000. Then if Columbia and Camden will raise $5,000, in addition, which is not a heavy appraisement, there will remain only some $12,000 to be raised by the rest of Carolina and Georgia. The thing begins to look feasible, and notwithstanding the hard times, we are quietly pushing the endowment forward. The cry of hard times has lost all its terror to Adger and myself; for we have heard it rung in our ears for two months, until we lost all mercy and pushed forward in the very face of bankruptcy and ruin everywhere, and we have both concluded that in spite of the European war and the storms and the pestilence, and more than all, the unnavigable rivers, still the country will hold together long enough for us to endow the Seminary.

"As regards the institution, things remain *'in statu.'* There have been some accessions, and we are all in harness, working with tight traces. Nothing new as to Dr. Thornwell, who still expects to leave the college in December. That, I hope, is now one of Dickens' 'fixed facts.' I have not resigned my pastorship, and probably will not before the fall Presbytery. My long absence has prevented that degree of consultation with the people necessary to so important a step. Besides, I am not unwilling to see further on first, in this whole business.

"I cannot even begin to give you the particulars of my Western trip. It was in many respects very pleasant. I made many new and valued friends, and, I hope, made some capital for the seminary; but among the things most agreeable were two or three surprises. First of all was my meeting with Palmer Pillans, whom I supposed to be in Texas. At Mobile, standing at the church door, I saw a man eyeing me intently as I approached, and though his face was entirely in the bushes, after the fashion of the time, I penetrated the disguise at a glance and recognized Palmer, whom I had not seen since 1836. The pleasure, I believe, was mutual, and I found him the same old fellow that he was when we were boys together. I was greatly pleased, too, with his very pretty wife, whom I would have kissed, pretty cousin as she was, if I had not been afraid of Palmer. At New Orleans, of course, I saw Foster Axson and his sweet little wife, but this was not a surprise as I knew of his location there.

"From New Orleans I ascended the Mississippi, merely to say that I had sailed on the Father of Waters, as high as Vicksburg, and there found to my very great pleasure three families of Bunce cousins—one on my mother's side, and none of whom had I ever before seen. Two hundred and fifty miles of rough staging brought me back to Montgomery. At Liberty I found a religious meeting in progress with some interest, and here I spent three days of extremely delightful and profitable labor. When I left, some thirty persons or more were anxiously enquiring the way of life, and some had already found it.

"I am at home once more and full of work as usual.

"Yours affectionately,

"B. M. PALMER."

During the school year, 1851 to 1852, also, Mr. Palmer had served the seminary, by lecturing on Church History and Church Polity; again, during the session 1853-1854, he had given similar service. In 1854 he was elected as professor for that chair. From that date on to October, 1855, he is to be thought of as filling both posts, his pastorate and professorship. During the session 1854-1855, he is said to have toiled about thirteen hours a day. He kept up his labors through the summer and early autumn of 1855. On the 7th of September, 1855, he writes to Dr. J. B. Adger:

"I am very hard at work on my lectures for the next term; and notwithstanding my numerous drawbacks from job work of different kinds, I hope by October to be sufficiently forwarded, so that with the labors of another term, I shall have covered the whole ground with a set of lectures. It is a very heavy undertaking, however, and I may not quite compass it.

"I must be brief, as I have much to do before going to bed, and I must rise at 5 o'clock in the morning. I cannot stop to confer about various other matters.

"Yours in love,

"B. M. PALMER."

Meanwhile, during these years he had been making his home life contributory to his influence for good. His home was always open to the young people of character and promise. The ties of kinship perhaps were chiefly of force in determniing that the gifted young Basile Edward Lanneau should reside in Mr. Palmer's home, during a portion of his student career in the seminary, and continue to take his meals there during his later residence in the seminary as student, and instructor in Hebrew. On similar grounds might be explained his brother Edward's residing in his home during his seminary career; but there were cases of a different kind. His home and heart were ever open to young men, whom helping, he felt he might also help his Master. Allusion has previously been made to Mr. R. H. Reid. This young man had, while at the famous classical school of Westly Leverette, in Anderson, S. C., come under Mr. Palmer's influence. The latter was at the time a licentiate, just from the seminary. He was already preaching with effect. In the course of his brief service at Anderson he conducted a protracted meeting; a goodly number confessed Christ and united with the church. Young Reid was among the number.

In April, 1843, Mr. Palmer received a letter from Mr. Reid, acquainting him with his desire to study for the ministry and seeking some information as to terms of entrance into the college in Columbia, and some advice as to what was practical for him to undertake. In reply to this Mr. Palmer wrote:

"COLUMBIA, S. C., May 5, 1843.

"DEAR REID: Your letter, dated 22d ult., was received not long since and gave me, I assure you, very great satisfaction. I am glad to be assured by yourself that your religious impressions have not been 'like the morning cloud and the early dew,' and still more that the Spirit of God seems to be drawing you into the holy ministry. It is a noble work, and we are more than repaid for all the self denial and laborious duty which we are called to endure and to perform. I trust that you realize its importance, and the solemn obligations which those assume who enter into it. I am glad also to find that you feel the value of a full course of study. Depend upon it, you will feel it more and more every day of your life, and if you should spend six years or more in study, I do not think you would ever regret it. But I will not stop now to dwell upon general topics, but proceed at once to speak concerning your studies.

"Your ignorance of mathematics will, I fear, be an effectual bar to your admission into the Sophomore class. I had supposed at first that you might enter as far in advance as that, and then you would rise into the Junior class in December, and be only two years and two months in college. But from your account your education hitherto has been unequal, that is, you have been pushed farther in some branches than in others. I send you, in company with this letter, a catalogue of the college, in the latter part of which you will find an account of the studies which are required for admission into the college. In comparing your letter with this catalogue, I imagine that you might enter the Freshman class in October, and rise to Sophomore in December and thus be a little more than three years in college. I presume you are fully prepared for that position as far as your classical and English studies are concerned. You will perceive also that the Freshman class have studied in mathematics Bourdon's Algebra and Legendre's Geometry. By the first of July they will have been pursuing these studies for nine months; the vacation commences in July and they will do nothing till October. Now the question is, can you, by studying very hard on these branches, acquire in *four* months what the class has acquired in *nine* months? Perhaps you may.

"I will try and send you by Mr. Orr, who is now in town, the necessary books, that is, 'Grecian and Roman Antiquities,' 'Bourdon's Algebra,' and 'Legendre's Geometry,' and 'Tytler's History.' If you can, I would advise you to drop your school at once, and devote your whole time to the study of these books. If I were keeping house now, I would urge you to come down at once and live with me and let me assist you in your studies, but as that cannot be, I would recommend to study by yourself as much as you can those branches in which you are deficient. I think that by hard study you might catch up with the class, and thereby save a year in college. . .

"You can do one of these two things, *provided you make up your mind to use great diligence.* You must write to me upon the reception of this letter and tell me what you think of these matters, and now,

Reid, you must put your hand to the plough and must not look back; this course of study will require great patience and unwearied diligence, but remember you do it for the Lord, and that you will have your reward in the end.

"I think you might get some assistance and direction in your mathematical studies. There is Mr. Orr, and young Harrison, now in college, and General Whitman, all of whom can give you advice and direction, if you should become bothered in your studies. I would just ride up to Anderson and apply to some of them; no doubt any one of them will be glad to help a poor fellow over the rough path of learning. That the blessing of God may attend you in your studies is my prayer. Love to your father and mother and brother and all friends.

"Yours most truly,

"B. M. PALMER."

Very soon Mr. Palmer was in possession of a home into which he could take his young friend. He at once wrote, telling Mr. Reid that, if he could raise the other money necessary for his college expenses, his board should cost him nothing. The story may be continued in Mr. Reid's own language:

"The first of October, 1843, found me in Columbia, a member of Dr. Palmer's family. As I had never studied algebra, he advised me to wait till the first of December before I applied for matriculation in college. He taught me one hour a day for two months and I entered the Sophomore class, and for six years I was a member of Dr. Palmer's family. When I graduated from the college, in 1846, I moved to the seminary but still remained a member of Dr. Palmer's family. Parents cannot treat a child with more kindness than I received from Dr. Palmer and his wife. I learned much from him in his table talk.

"I am now (1904) eighty-three years of age. I have come into contact with many men of prominence in my work; but I have never found but one Dr. Palmer,—the prince of preachers, the model Christian gentleman, helpful alike to the rich and poor, whose single aim through a long, laborious life has been the salvation of souls, and the extension of the Redeemer's kingdom."

In helping such youths Mr. Palmer was multiplying his own influence for good. This may be seen by glancing at the results of Mr. R. H. Reid's ministry. After a brief period of service as pastor at Anderson, S. C., Mr. Reid accepted a call to Nazareth Church in the district of Spartanburg and began his long, honorable and largely useful pastorate in that church in January, 1853. Presbyterianism throughout the district received mighty impulses to growth from his labors. In his New Year's sermon in 1857, he brought before his congregation the subject of education. As a result, in October of that year, the cornerstone of the Reidville High Schools, male and female, was laid. These schools have continued for about a half a century a source of incalculable good to all "the region round about." Not only in these ways but in still others did Mr. Reid serve the people of his district. He, and to some extent, Mr. Palmer, in him, served them nobly.

The following letter written, indeed, before Mr. Reid began his work in Spartanburg district, is valuable as showing that Mr. Palmer continued to further his influence over him after he had begun his active work of the ministry, and so to work through him. It is valuable, too, as revealing frankly some traits of Mr. Palmer's own character; and as showing him in an aspect in which he frequently appears in this period, that of an adviser and comforter of his brethren on occasion:

COLUMBIA, May 1, 1850.

"DEAR REID: I acknowledge the receipt of two letters from you, since my last to yourself. The former of these I would have answered immediately, had there been time for you to receive it before the meeting of your Presbytery; the latter has just come to hand. As they both run in much the same strain they may conveniently be answered together.

"I will not disguise from you, my dear fellow, that the tenor of your recent letters has occasioned me some uneasiness. My attachment to you prompts the most earnest wish that you may have an even and pleasant course through life; but that if your lot is to confront trials, that you may pass both bravely and discreetly through them. So far as I am acquainted with your public acts, they are just such as I approve. You did wisely not to yield to the pressure of public opinion, forcing you against your judgment and your conscience into the associations of the day, which wear so many Protean shapes that we scarcely become acquainted with one disguise before it is shifted for another. I concur, too, in the decision not to yield your pulpit and your people on a Sabbath of your appointment, out of mere courtesy to another denomination. The whole arrangement which previously existed was a scandal; and I am glad that you had the firmness to resist at the outset. Your recent refusal also to be ordained except upon the call of the people to settle as their pastor, I highly approve. There are but two offices to which, in accordance with our discipline, it is possible for a minister to be ordained: that of pastor, and that of evangelist. But to ordain *ex professo* for the latter, when everybody knows you are *de facto* the other, strikes me as a sort of pious fraud. The impolicy of this species of Jesuitism is palpable, since no good is proposed to be effected, but the very great evil of discharging churches from the obligations which ought to lie with power upon their consciences. In relation to the postponement of your ordination as pastor, I am glad to be set right by your letter; though Gaillard had previously undeceived me. Your preceding communication merely stated that you had abandoned the expectation of being ordained, without assigning reasons for the change, and indeed, without hinting whether the postponement was for a limited or for an indefinite time. Having no clue of interpretation but the desponding tone of all your recent letters, I conjectured that you were utterly disheartened, or else that some issue had sprung up between the Anderson people and yourself, which had resulted in a separation. I am glad that it is not so; and that you and they are still looking forward at no distant day for the consummation of the pastoral relation.

"I must do you the justice to say that I have had no apprehensions as to the substantial propriety of your actions; I could prophesy, with considerable confidence, upon the rise of every emergency, very much the decision you would finally reach. My anxieties have been rather directed to the state of your own feelings, lest you should work yourself into a morbid state of mind, unfavorable both for action and for deliberation in the midst of pressing difficulties. For some time past, all your letters have been tinged with a gloom which, I think, you should promptly shake off. This is not easy to one of a desponding temperament; especially when, as in your case, the despondency is united with a nervous excitability of the physical man, and a high degree of sensibility in the inner and spiritual man. Yet I do not hesitate to say, that all of your comfort and a large degree of your prospective usefulness, depend upon your controlling these decided tendencies of your character. Why, here you have been fretting yourself into fits because the world is split up into Odd Fellows, Free Masons, Sons of Temperance, *et id omne genus,* and because the Church is half asleep, content to starve their preacher with half an allowance of bread and their own souls with half an allowance of gospel truth. It must be confessed, the case is bad enough to make a good man sigh. But can it be you have forgotten that we have God, and time and truth upon our side, and that we can afford to be patient? We belong to a system which is eternal, and which sweeps in cycles that utterly baffle all human comprehension. 'One day is with the Lord as a thousand years, and a thousand years as one day;' and though this is far from being true of us, it is true of that divine scheme to which we have consecrated our lives, our hearts and our labors. It would be pleasant indeed to be permitted to move the church over an entire semicircle, or some larger segment still; but it is a matter of profound thanksgiving if we are used in pushing it forward but a *single inch.* If God allows ages to elapse in the erection of that splendid temple in which his praise is to be sung through all of a future eternity, it is perhaps enough for you and me to put but a single brick or stone into the glorious structure.

Be sure, that in due season it will go up; and 'the headstone be brought forth with shoutings, grace, grace unto it.' I commend to your notice the thoughts under the second head of a discourse, which I sent you the other day in a number of the *Carolinian,* and which you have doubtless received and read before this time. The great danger to which you are exposed is the same to which I am myself inclined in no small degree: Note that I speak only that which I have myself deeply pondered, and have frequent occasion to recall to my own self-rebuke. It is the danger of impatience under opposition, of being wrought up to such a degree of exasperation, that all prudence and sometimes all firmness are overthrown. What you and I both want are a cool head, a warm heart and a strong will. Survey calmly all the difficulties of your position, decide prayerfully upon the course which you must take in surmounting them, bring your will firmly to bear you on in that chosen course, and then *hold steady,* waiting patiently while God and truth and time carry you to a successful issue. Nothing is gained, but everything is lost, by getting into a fume, working yourself into a holy frenzy. *Be patient;* these obstacles are not to be overcome by a single effort, but by long-continued and faithful resistance. Let us take a lesson from the mariners, who have to shift their sails, and tack from side to side, and learn to drive the vessel on oftentimes in the very eye of the wind. It is a great art that, of managing a head wind so as to sail in spite of it. But haste and flurry never accomplish anything. Napoleon and Cæsar, with all their military skill, would have lost every battle, if they had lost their self-possession, but they kept cool, and conquered. Make up your mind, dear Reid, that you will, God helping, cross the Alps and take Rome. For what purpose, indeed, have we been called to the work of the ministry, but to set crooked places straight? And can we hope to do so without coolness and courage? My son Timothy, 'do thou *endure hardship* as a good soldier of Jesus Christ.' You will live to see a thousand beautiful soap bubbles break themselves against that Rock on which Christ has built his Church. Even 'the gates of hell shall not prevail against it.' 'Consider him that endured such contradiction of sinners against himself, *lest ye be wearied and faint in your minds;* ye have not yet resisted unto blood, striving against sin.' It is well to have zeal, even a 'consuming zeal;' but it is hardly modest to be more zealous than God himself. If he is patient, let us be so; if he waits, we must also; if he tolerates, we can often do nothing more than simply to *protest,* and to wait the divine adjudication of the controversy. Let me cite one more Scripture, pertinent to the matter in hand: 'The servant of the Lord must be gentle unto all men, apt to teach, *patient, in meekness instructing those that oppose themselves;* if peradventure God will give them repentance to the acknowledging of the truth,' etc. There now, I am done. I seated myself with the determination to give you a decent scolding, and I cannot put a better smasher to my last than the above sentiment of the Apostle. I will not apologize for the liberty I take in chastening you after this fashion. You know that with my hatred of the pen I would not take the trouble of writing so long a scold for any whom I slightly regarded. 'Faithful,' you know, 'are the wounds of a friend;' 'let the righteous smite me, it shall be a kindness, and let him reprove me, it shall be an excellent act that shall not break thy head.' . . .

"Brother ——— is now in town making arrangements for his wedding, which takes place on the 7th inst. This match has excited a good deal of remark, as his intended is not only not a pious girl, but one exceedingly gay, fond of dancing, whose only accomplishment is that she can achieve sixteen cotillions in a night. She is said to be very young, and without intelligence, and the spoiled child of indulgent parents, but withal *abundantly rich.* The general impression is that ——— is making a bed in a brierpatch; and he has doubtless injured himself in the estimation of all sober and discreet people.

"By the way, this subject of marriage brings up the curious part of your recent letter in which you seek for whatever I have to offer on this subject. I had a hearty laugh, but have committed it to nobody's confidence but Mrs. Palmer's; whose aid I must require, if I am to provide a wife for you. It is a delicate office; and a man who has risked the responsibility of choosing for himself, would scarcely consent to devolve the same upon any other. You have, however, some precedents for it: the example of the devoted Oberlin, the entranced Tennant, and last, but not least, the famous John Calvin. The young lady in my own church, of whom I once spoke to you, is still single, and though she is poor, she has the intellectual and spiritual endowments to make an active and useful Christian woman, I have but two suggestions on the general subject; for really my creed as to matrimony is exceedingly simple. The first is, commit this selection of a wife to Providence, and wait until you are caught. In matrimony, the fancy of the affections must take the initiative. There is no use of spurring these into action, they act best when they act spontaneously; and while they do not act it will not distress you to live singly. There is no benefit that I know of in loving the abstract passion. Wait until it assumes *the concrete,* and is associated with some object of love. My second suggestion is, do not surrender yourself blindly to the impulses of the taste and heart, but weigh in the balance of a sound judgment the qualities of any who may have caught you by the horns. Piety, prudence and intelligence are the prominent characteristics she should possess. If to these she can add a trace of beauty, that will please the eye; and if a little pelf, that will relieve the purse. But neither of these is indispensable. Considering your peculiarities, good sense and a disposition to look on *the bright side* of things are important traits. Such a wife will attract you to the middle of the house—the safest place, —whereas, you are probably disposed to live either in the garret or the cellar. A good wife is from the Lord: therefore deliver yourself in this to the guiding of his Providence. The great secret of a happy choice may be given in a single sentence: it consists in uniting the taste and the judgment equally in the selection. Let the former be the active power, going forward in the choice; and let the latter be the satisfying power, indorsing or else vetoing, as the case may be. If both are satisfied, there is not much danger of forming a connexion that will be regretted hereafter. But I must close these sentences so imitative of the Proverbs of Solomon. Adieu.

"Most affectionately,

"B. M. PALMER."

"I shall not come to Anderson in May, as you are not to be ordained. I prefer to reserve my visit until such time as that event shall take place. Perhaps I shall hit your marriage at the same time."

Mr. Palmer entertained at his home many persons whom he there bettered; and he met in a social way many more upon whom he put a helpful impress. During his residence in Columbia he was on terms of intimacy with many of the public men of the State, the governors, the judiciary, and the members of the legislatures. On the fly leaf of a volume of Calhoun's works, which may be seen yet amongst Dr. Palmer's books in his old study in the home of Prof. John W. Caldwell, the loiterer reads the inscription:

"Rev. Benjamin M. Palmer, with the respects of J. H. Means." J. H. Means was governor of the State.

During this pastorate Mr. Palmer was a member of a literary society, made up of the most cultivated and refined citizens of the town. In his later life he was often heard to speak of the lavish entertainments given in connection with their meetings. It can hardly be doubted that he was a valued member of this society. Few of his fellows could have equaled him in brilliancy, urbanity and charm of manner.

During his Columbia pastorate Mr. Palmer received numerous calls: He was called to the Second Presbyterian Church, Baltimore, in 1846. He favored accepting the call, but was withstood successfully by his church and congregation before Charleston Presbytery. He was disposed to accept the overtures of the Glebe Street Church, of Charleston, S. C., in 1852, to become its pastor. The session of that church adopted a noble course toward the session of the church in Columbia. The minutes of the latter tell us that, a "courteous letter was received from the session of the Glebe Street Church at Charleston, addressed to the session of this church, informing them of their intention, to apply to Presbytery in order to procure the services of our pastor, the Rev. B. M. Palmer. Said letter was duly considered, without the knowledge and in the absence of the pastor; and the clerk was directed to prepare a reply, setting forth their determined opposition to the prosecution of said call, and the hope that the session of the Glebe Street Church would, at once, arrest, or desist from any further proceedings in the matter."[2] In this same year, 1852, he received a call to Cincinnati. Of circumstances attending this call, Mr. Bazile Edward Lanneau writes to his mother, March 20, 1852:

"The Cincinnatians are very sanguine, but I think he (Mr. Palmer) is now much more staggered by the difficulties in the way and the opposition at home, than he was at first. He made a statement of the posture of affairs to the congregation on Sabbath week, which led to a meeting yesterday for the appointment of a committee to memorialize Presbytery, and the appointment of a commissioner in behalf of the congregation. I do hope that Presbytery will have no hesitation in putting their veto upon it. Dr. Thornwell is strongly opposed to his going, but may be prevented from attending Presbytery, as may also Dr. Leland."

He was called to Philadelphia in the year 1853, and was not a little moved towards accepting that call. He had been a member of the General Assembly sitting in that city in the spring of 1853, was honored by the Assembly and brethren of his faith generally in the city. Hence, perhaps, in part, his inclination to go.[3] In the same year he was elected to the chair of Hebrew in Danville (Ky.) Theological Seminary. This he refused without much difficulty. He never betrays considerable leanings toward the professorial life. In 1854, he was again called to Cincinnati. Mr. Bazile Edward Lanneau writes his mother, January 28, 1854:

"You will, by this time, have heard the news of Cousin Ben's *Cincinnati call,* announced, I see, in the *Watchman and Observer* (Rich-

[2] Records First Presbyterian Church, Columbia, S. C., Jan. 31, 1852.

[3] According to Mr. Alfred Lanneau, Charleston, S. C., the calls for Mr. Palmer's services in the Northern Churches led the Southern commissioners to the Assembly in 1853, in a meeting called for the purpose, to express their unanimous opinion that he should not leave the South.

mond), with (I think) just comment. An emissary arrived last week, followed him to Barnwell and is, I suppose, now on his return. Dr. McGill is at the bottom of it. I have as yet had no opportunity of conversing with him about it, and have no idea how he will regard it. Just now he is more in a condition to be influenced by a call abroad than usual, owing to his feeling of embarrassment in reference to the Seminary. Still I think Cincinnati will scarcely have the attractions, either of inclination or duty, which Philadelphia had, viewed in the radiance of the Assembly of 1853. I do hope Providence will settle him and the Seminary (shall I not say *in* the Seminary?) before long."

This call, from the Central Church of Cincinnati, was presented and urged with great ability by the commissioners from that church, before the Presbytery which met at Orangeburg, S. C., in 1854. The church at Columbia resisted the proposed removal of their pastor, appearing before the Presbytery by a special delegate who fulfilled his trust in a manner highly gratifying to those whom he represented. The discussion, although protracted nearly two days, was conducted with marked courtesy and in a Christian spirit. The result may be learned from the following resolutions which were adopted without a dissenting voice:

"The Presbytery having carefully considered the call of the Central Church of the City of Cincinnati for the services of the Rev. Dr. Palmer and weighed the reasons both for his translation and for his continuance in his present location, do hereby resolve: First, that while we are impressed with the importance of the Central Church in the City of Cincinnati, whose call was so ably urged by the commissioners before us, we feel ourselves unable to place the call of that church in the hands of Dr. Palmer or release him from his present charge with a view of his translation to that church and Presbytery.

"Second, That in coming to that result, we are influenced by no considerations of sectional prejudice. We acknowledge in all its fulness that the church and all her interests are one; but in the Providence of God, our brother is so connected with the great interests of this portion of the church that we regard his continuance here as highly important to the best interests of the Redeemer's kingdom, and our interpretation of the Divine will is in accordance with this belief."

He received calls to several other churches, during his period at Columbia. He received, in 1855, a very important one to New Orleans; but of that somewhat shall be said in the next chapter.

In 1854 Mr. Palmer suffered himself to be made Professor of Ecclesiastical History and Polity in Columbia Seminary.

This made necessary, after a time, his release from his connection with his old charge in Columbia. His church and congregation could not look for help from either Presbytery or Synod for aid to prevent his making this change.

Mrs. Palmer knew her husband well enough to be able to utter a prophecy which was soon fulfilled. To the advocates of his transfer to the professorship she said: "You will soon lose both pastor and professor. Your new made professor must be a pastor; you have, in taking him out of this church, made it inevitable that he shall soon accept a call to another church."

In November, 1852, Oglethorpe University, at Milledgeville, Ga., had conferred on Mr. Palmer the degree of Doctor of Divinity.

CHAPTER IX.

PROFESSOR IN COLUMBIA SEMINARY.

(1854-1856.)

Columbia Seminary in 1855.—Dr. Palmer's Previous Services there as Lecturer and Teacher.—His Years of Professedly Professorial Service.—His Success as a Professor.—The Call from the First Presbyterian Church in New Orleans.—His Conviction that He should be a Pastor and the Grounds for that Conviction.—Leave from Seminary and Synod to go to New Orleans.—Some Incidental Services During this Period: That of Christian Comforter; and the Part He took in the Installation of his Father as Pastor of Stony Creek and Walterboro.— His Transition to a New Sphere.

COLUMBIA SEMINARY had been doing a useful work from the day of her founding. In the year 1854, she had worthy men in her professorate, in Drs. George Howe and A. W. Leland. But she was not measuring up to the demands of her friends. At that epoch there was a general advance in theological education. Princeton, Union Seminary, in Virginia, and Alleghany Seminary, had all been strengthened by the addition to their faculties of men of power. The Danville Seminary, in Kentucky, had been created the year before, with all the intellectual force in its faculty which the West could command. If Columbia was to maintain herself as a competitor of these institutions, it behooved her to equip herself with a full corps of instructors. In the words of Dr. Thornwell, "Things had reached a crisis and something vigorous was to be done, or the seminary virtually abandoned. It was ascertained that if things remained another year as they were, the next session would, in all likelihood, open with the merest handful of students, not more than six or eight. The Board determined to propose a measure which, it was thought, would remove these grounds of complaint. They nominated me for the chair of theology, and Palmer for that of history." This well digested plan of the Board was carried through at the annual meetings of the Synods of South Carolina and Georgia, in November, 1854. During the session of 1853-4, Dr. Palmer had served the seminary as Provisional Instructor in Ecclesiastical History

FIRST PRESBYTERIAN CHURCH, NEW ORLEANS, LA.

and Polity. He had given sufficient promise of distinguished service to the seminary to make some of its friends very anxious lest he should be enticed, before the work of the Board could be ratified, to some other quarter of our Church's territory. The Rev. J. B. Adger seems to have been amongst the anxious ones, as the following letter shows:

"COLUMBIA, S. C., September 4, 1854.

"DEAR BROTHER: Your favor of the 31st of August came to hand by this evening's mail, and spurs my half formed resolution which for days I have entertained of writing you.

"The statement in the *Watchman and Observer,* to which you refer, attracted my attention at the time, as an instance of that idle gossip which creeps into our public journals, and which one knows not how to contradict. I know not who the writer is, but the statement is utterly without foundation so far as respects myself. The allusion must have been to the Augusta call; but that call was declined by me absolutely before the meeting of the Board. I have had no overtures from any quarter since you were in Columbia, and I am meditating no change of field whatever. In regard to Brother Thornwell, I am unable to answer your queries. He has been away since the first of August, and I have received no letter from him. In my late conversation with him, his mind was greatly perplexed. He doubtless has misgivings upon several points connected with the question of his transfer to the Seminary—doubtful whether the number of candidates for the ministry in the South is sufficient to warrant that increase in the Seminary which will justify his removal from the College; and doubtful whether the cheapness of living at Danville as compared with Columbia, will not decide the question with many to go to the former place, who might be expected to come here; and doubtful, in the most favorable circumstances, whether he may not do more for God and the truth in his present position. I think, however, he had not at all drawn back from the ground on which he stood, when you saw him last. During his travels, he has doubtless been thrown amongst those who are warmly attached to him, and who will oppose his resignation of the presidency. What effect, if any, their representations and solicitations may have with him I have no means of knowing. As you say. the suggestion of the Board seems to be the only alternative before the Synod; yet I cannot anticipate its consummation without pain. We give up a great deal in taking Thornwell from the College; and nothing but the sternest necessity justifies the sacrifice; yet that necessity, so far as I can see, does really exist. As to myself, I shall feel thankful to God if He shall turn the mind of the brethren at Synod to the choice of another, as was the case last year. My own judgment and inclination are decidedly against it—much more so than last year. And I do not hesitate to say, if the question was the same as last year, to elect me *alone,* I should instantly refuse to serve. Constituted as the Seminary now is, without an able man in the Theological Chair, I could not entertain the thought for a moment; and if a really able man, say Dr. Thornwell himself, was now the professor of Theology, I should not feel that the Seminary was in such extreme distress as to require on my part the sacrifice of interest, of taste, and of feeling. But it is to secure Brother Thornwell to the Seminary as the teacher of theology, and for this alone, that I have gained my own consent to be wholly passive and allow the Synod to dispose of me as they see fit. If the vote divides upon Brother Thornwell, or he fails to serve, leaving the Seminary as it now stands, I shall not go into the chair of history—for as long as the students are dissatisfied with the instruction received in theology, nothing can raise the institution. If the matter is submitted to me, after all that has occurred, my way is abundantly clear to abide by the office of Pastor—for the way has been as singularly open to me to remain in the pulpit, as it has been closed to my going into a professorship. This fact joined with another that I have a decided love for preaching, and never one antecedent wish to exchange this for any other species of labor, would be conclusive, if I were to trust in my own judgment. I wish the Seminary to prosper—and to this prosperity, the services of Brother Thornwell seem to me to be necessary—and therefore I am willing to occupy the subordinate part which I do in this business. The Seminary being safe, I would be glad if the plan of the Board touching myself should fail. If it succeeds, I shall go into the institution without that glow of feeling which springs from the gratification of one's spontaneous and original choice.

"I am rejoiced to hear the good news concerning Mr, and Mrs. Pelham, and will seek them out very soon. Present me most kindly to your good wife, and believe me

"Your most truly,

"B. M. PALMER."

The foregoing letter makes it clear that its author was being *dragged* off his pulpit throne; that he was unwilling to set his single judgment against that of his brethren; but that all his inclinations and all his motives were toward his teaching from the pulpit men and women in the sap and juice of life, in a wrestle with the world. A little later he wrote again to Mr. Adger, disclosing a similar attitude toward seminary work, a desire to take measures to secure Mr. Adger's election in his place, and disclosing also the heavy burdens he was bearing at the time.

COLUMBIA, S. C., October 13, 1854.

"MY DEAR BROTHER: I do not know why I have taken up the pen, unless it is to exchange salutations with you. Dr. Howe handed me your letter addressed to him, in which you invite an opinion from me respecting the appointment to the Presidency of Davidson College. Briefly, I would say that the College must, I think, ultimately prosper, though for a long time it will be labor under embarrassments. It is an infant institution, has scarcely the furnishing requisite for a college, labors under a low standard of scholarship which the local public opinion too much justifies, and has a corps of teachers scarcely such as you or I would select. The worst of all is an old and open feud between two distinct parties among the trustees and patrons of the college itself. When I add to these things, the trouble and responsibility of managing a body of students, and the necessity of taking the whole institution upon your shoulders, in order to lift it from the dust into something like respectability, I am sure you will not find the situation a sinecure. Nevertheless, I know no man so sure of success in this difficult undertaking as yourself, and I fully justify the wisdom of your appointment. But, my dear brother, if you have the least inclination for scholastic life, why not take the professorship of History in the Seminary? You will be nearer the great heart of the Church, will have associates whom you cherish, and preserve all the ties social, domestic and public which bind you here. As to eyes, you will have to study in either position; and though the range of investigation is certainly wider in the Seminary, yet this is fairly counterbalanced by the greater anxieties of the other position. Anxiety sends the blood to the head full as much as study; and the one place has scarcely the advantage over the other, all things considered, when it comes to eyes. You do not know with what real relief of feeling I would nominate you to Synod in my place. I have not one lurking desire for the chair, and only consented to be passive under the nomination, hoping thereby to secure Brother Thornwell to the Seminary. You will be fully as acceptable to him as myself, and I am sure much more acceptable to the Synod; as I am sure the same feeling exists, as last year, as to my relations to the pulpit. Pray think of this matter; and if possible, do not decide in favor of Davidson till after meeting of Synod.

"I have just returned from the meeting of the Seceder Synod, where Brother Banks and myself were very kindly received; and perhaps as much was accomplished as could be reasonably anticipated at the outset. A similar deputation was appointed to attend our Synod, and a committee raised to confer with any similar committee on our side. I was gratified to find nearly all the leading members anxious for the proposed union; but the body as a whole, and especially the members of the church at large, are scarcely prepared yet for such a result. I hope we will be patient and forbearing, as far as becomes a proper Christian self-respect; and if no more, intercommunion between the two branches will be effected.

"You will be sorry to learn that Dr. Howe is laid up with a serious attack of erysipelas. His face is exceedingly swollen and he suffers greatly. As it is taken promptly in hand, it is hoped he will not be confined long. Dr. Leland still suffers with his arm from the fall, of which you have doubtless heard.

"I have not seen Brother Thornwell for two weeks. He is busy at the College, and I at the Seminary. You do not know how hard I work, ten hours a day, and that scarcely keeps me up with a daily exercise with my classes. I have undertaken the Herculean task of lecturing systematically upon the whole course of Church History in connection with the text-book, in order to give the philosophical and real connections. To one ignorant as myself it is a task scarcely inferior to taking the Alps on my shoulders—Church History in its totality is bigger than the Alps. I am not as much discouraged as yourself in reference to Thornwell's transfer—the opposition in South Carolina Presbytery is more noisy than general, so far as I can learn. Bethel is unanimous, or nearly so—and I hear of no resistance in Harmony except from Brother Coit. The most discouraging feature is, that Brother Thornwell does not himself *particularly* desire the change. He consents, if the Synod so wishes; but that is all. However, I still wish and hope. Brumby's plan of putting *me* into that chair must not be thought of. But my sheet is out. If I am at Synod, I shall lay aside all delicacy, and advocate warmly Thornwell's appointment on grounds I have not yet heard mentioned; and will be most happy if you will consent to be coupled with him in the nomination. With kindest salutations to Mrs. Adger and all of your household, from all here. Most affectionately,

"B. M. PALMER."

Formally elected as professor in 1854, Dr. Palmer most earnestly strove to acquit himself nobly both as pastor and as professor. It has already appeared that his ideals of ministerial duty were very high. His ideals of duty in his professorship were equally lofty. He craved nothing less than philosophical scholarship and the ability to beget it in his students. Tradition says that he had a long working day through this session,—thirteen, fourteen, fifteen hours out of the twenty-four, according to his need. The double burden was too great to be carried according to his ideals; and he came perilously near making shipwreck of his health.

He was a success as a teacher. This is evident from certain remains of his lectures. One of these lectures he published in the *Southern Presbyterian Review,* April, 1856. The subject was, "The Import of Hebrew History." The reader can see in this paper proof of Dr. Palmer's ability to deal with historic movements in a profoundly philosophic way, and in a style, as regards structure and diction, scarcely less splendid then Macaulay's. His abilities as teacher are testified to by many of his students also; from these it is also learned, however, that he did not, in the brief period during which he gave himself to teaching, develop such extraordinary adaptedness to that form of service as to preaching. Thus the Rev. Prof. W. T. Hall, now of Columbia Seminary, who sat as a student under Dr. Palmer during the session of 1855-1856, writes:

"One session hardly affords opportunity for estimating the capacity of a teacher; and a class of juniors may not be the best of judges. Dr. Palmer's own opinion was that his proper sphere was the pulpit: and none of us was disposed to call his opinion in question. Not that he was by any means a failure in the class room; but for the reason that he was a prince in the pulpit. In fact he was easily the best teacher we had until Dr. Thornwell came in, about the middle of the session. We understood that he was offered a chair in Princeton Seminary about the time he left Columbia. There can be no doubt that he would have made a great reputation, and have been a pillar in the Seminary, if he had chosen to devote his life to teaching. In one respect he certainly had no superior. I refer to his personal influence on the students. His Christian character was one of his strong points. I never knew a Christian whose 'walk' was more worthy of the 'vocation.' Students were impressed by the strong, healthy type of his piety; and consulted him in their spiritual conflicts. He was also a model of industry. Report credited him with fifteen hours given to study out of the twenty-four. He was then laying the foundation for his long and successful ministry."

As a teacher he certainly was not wanting in the analytical faculty, nor in the power of luminous statement, nor of logical reasoning, but as a teacher he had less use for some of his preeminent gifts, for he was above all things a wonderful word painter, a past-master in the art of description, and a magician in dealing with the sentiments of the human heart, particularly the pathetic. The seminary professor should never forget that the heart of the student demands his attention as well as the head, but his concern is chiefly with the head; he is to impart knowledge to one already earnestly Christian. He hardly has time or scope for the exercise of the peculiar gifts which made Palmer so easily the master of great popular assemblies, hence Dr. Palmer felt that he was not in his true sphere when in the class room.

In the fall of 1855 his connection with the Presbyterian

Church in Columbia, as pastor, was broken, the people reluctantly giving him up. He continued, at their request, to serve them as stated supply till the end of December, 1855. They would have had him unite with Dr. Thornwell in jointly supplying their pulpit thereafter, but he preferred to wean the people at Columbia from him. As he had to have a preaching place, he complied with the request of the Presbyterian Church at Orangeburg, S. C., to fill their pulpit from Sabbath to Sabbath, during the year 1856.

Meanwhile the First Presbyterian Church of New Orleans had been making powerful efforts to secure him as its pastor. In company with his friend Adger he had, as has been seen, visited New Orleans in the early part of 1855, soliciting subscriptions to endow a chair in Columbia Seminary. The pulpit of the First Church was vacant at that time, Dr. Scott having resigned and removed to San Francisco. On the morning of their first Sunday in the city, Dr. Adger preached to the people of the First Church, and Dr. Palmer, the younger man, at the Prytania Street Church. They exchanged pulpits in the evening. In the interim between morning and evening service, the people who had been in the Prytania Street Church were talking enthusiastically about the little gentleman, the wonderful preacher who had spoken to them. That evening the people of the First Church flocked to hear Dr. Palmer preach; and were captivated by his bearing and eloquent discourse. They were "struck with his graceful action and his beautiful, soul-stirring diction." "The speaker seemed lifted so high by his illustrations, by his grand images" that at times they "feared he would never be able to get down from the heights without a tumble, or at least a stumble;" but he would "come swooping down with all the grace with which he went up" and stand there on the platform a simple, humble man. The matter of his discourse seemed no less excellent, didactically rich and emotionally and spiritually quickening. On the next Sabbath he seems to have preached again to these people, and to have so preached that his message burned itself indelibly into the memories of his hearers. In the month of September following, they gave him a unanimous call to be their pastor. He would gladly have accepted it but was retained by his Presbytery, which resolved, "That after weighing carefully the claims of the First Church of the city of New Orleans, for the pastoral labors of the Rev. B. M. Palmer, D.D., as earnestly and eloquently set forth by their commissioners, who have appeared before this body, we find ourselves unable to place this call in his hands, because Dr. Palmer's labors as professor in the Theological Seminary are indispensable to the prosperity of that institution, and because we must not contravene the wishes, nor defeat the action of the Synod, our higher judicatory, which has unanimously placed him in that office." The commissioners from New Orleans, Messrs. J. M. Picton and J. A. Mabin, at once gave notice of complaint to the Synod, and the next day read a statement of their grounds of complaint, under the following heads:

"*First.* Because the election of Dr. Palmer, by that church and congregation, to become its pastor, was unanimous; their attention being exclusively directed to him through a period of several months.

"*Second.* Because New Orleans is a most important field of labor, eminently requiring the services of Dr. Palmer in it.

"*Third.* Because the interests of our own church would be greatly promoted by the services of Dr. Palmer in that city.

"*Fourth.* Because the interests of the Church of Christ generally require the services of Dr. Palmer in New Orleans.

"*Fifth.* Because a number of members of Evangelical Churches in New Orleans express their earnest wish that Dr. Palmer should labor there.

"*Sixth.* Because the talents and attainments of Dr. Palmer are peculiarly adapted to that place.

"*Seventh.* Because the interests of the Theological Seminary of the Synods of South Carolina and Georgia would not be injured by the removal of Dr. Palmer from the Chair of Church History and Polity, to which he has been elected to become the pastor in New Orleans of said Church and congregation. But on the contrary the said interests would be promoted.

"*Eighth.* Because the arrangements that have been made respecting Dr. Palmer's filling the Chair of Church History and Polity in said Seminary, present no obstacle or impediment to the removal of Dr. Palmer to New Orleans as the pastor aforesaid.

"*Ninth.* Because Dr. Palmer is under no pledge of any kind or nature, either to the Seminary or to its contributors, or others, to prevent his accepting of said call.

"*Tenth.* Because Dr. Palmer considers himself under no pledge of any kind or nature, either to the Seminary or to its contributors, or others, to prevent his acceptance of said call.

"*Eleventh.* Because Dr. Palmer is willing to *accept the said call* to become the pastor of said Church and congregation, from personal observation of that field of labor, and from a strong conviction of his greater adaptedness to the pulpit than to a professor's chair.

"*Twelfth.* Because this call to Dr. Palmer is superior in its claims to any previously presented to him, both on account of the natural affiliations of the Southern and Southwestern States, and on account of the relation of New Orleans to the vast Missionary territory beyond it." [1]

For these reasons, the commissioners prayed the Synod of South Carolina to receive their complaint, and take the constitutional measures to secure the reversal of the decision of the Presbytery of Charleston, complained of.

These commissioners were reinforced in their complaint by a complaint on somewhat similar grounds by those members of the Presbytery, all ruling elders, constituting the minority in opposition to the Presbytery's resolution. When the Synod of South Carolina met, early in November, the complainants were represented by Mr. R. C. Gilchrist, of Charleston, one of those elders. Drs. Howe and Adger represented the Presbytery of Charleston. Much time was given to the discussion, with the result that the Synod refused to sustain the complaint by a vote of sixty-three to nine. South Carolina could not easily give up her Palmer to New Orleans. The First Church of New Orleans had made a determined as well as unanimous call. The result was a staggering refusal.

The people of that church next turned their attention to Rev. Nathan L. Rice, D.D. They gave him a call December 16, 1855. Failing in this direction, and remembering Dr. Palmer's own imperfectly veiled desire to come to them, and learning that other churches were trying to move him from Columbia Seminary, they repeated their call March 16, 1856.

Meanwhile the conviction had been growing in his mind that he should be a pastor and not a seminary professor. The conviction had been growing, too, that his work was in New Orleans. He was fast reaching that state of certainty about the matter that he was prepared to decide the question on his own responsibility, once he had the bare consent of the controlling powers. These assertions are borne out by the following letters; and though the letters contain much matter besides the parts strictly pertinent to the subject under hand, they are presented entire, as bringing forth in salient fashion certain traits of the gentleman whose life and character it is the purpose of this work to portray.

---

[1] *Minutes of Presbytery of Charleston,* Oct., 1855.

"COLUMBIA, S. C., June 1, 1856.

"DEAR BROTHER ADGER: Your reproachful note came to hand last evening, and filled me with surprise. At first I was amused, and thought how admirably you had succeeded in what the children sometimes call 'making-believe.' But a second perusal satisfied me that you were serious; and then I felt a momentary resentment that you should allow yourself to cherish suspicions that were unworthy of you and unjust to me, and at the brusque manner in which you have uttered them. Then I thought, surely it must be only the nervous irritability of a man convalescing, and a return to health will restore his feelings to a normal condition again. There seem to be two counts in the indictment against me: *first,* that I did not answer your letter written some time ago; and *second,* that I have addressed no word of sympathy to you in all the sickness and suffering you have passed through. As to the first, I plead guilty at once; and if you have never without design laid aside the letter of a friend, and postponed a reply till finally it has slipped from your mind, then you may blame me as freely as you desire, and I will meekly bear it as the punishment of my fault. I did receive your letter requesting an account of the *emeute* in the College, which was a long story, and asking some questions about the time of Presbytery's meeting, which I was unable to answer. Being at that time occupied in a vexatious correspondence, I simply put off a reply until a convenient moment. Then came several absences from home at Charleston and Savannah, until it was forgotten. If I had supposed any practical decision of yours was suspended upon an answer, it would have been given as much in the way of business as of friendship—but this I did not realize. I am at best an irregular and delinquent correspondent, and do not even in a twelvemonth write a letter simply of friendship to any one: I have but once written during six months to my father, and that simply to announce the birth of a child. This is the history of that omission: let it be accepted at what it is worth. The point in it valuable to you, is, that it was accidental and undesigned.

"As to the second charge, I have only to say that I did not hear of your sickness until I heard you were better; so that I can scarcely be said to have felt anxious about your condition. Occasionally I heard that you were still improving; and supposed you were a well man long ago. It was not till the other day, upon accidentally meeting with your brother Robert on his return from Pendleton, that I learned the lingering character of your sickness, and that you were still feeble. I had supposed it was an acute attack, which early passed its crisis, placing you very soon beyond the sympathy and condolence of your friends. Now, my brother, all this is a slender basis upon which to erect such a huge superstructure of suspicion and reproach as that of which your imagination has been the architect.

I am prepared then to return categorical answers to your two solemn questions. To the first, 'Have I offended you?' I answer, No, neither by word nor deed. I have never dreamed that you were not entirely my friend; and every gesture and tone of yours I have recognized as those of a kind Christian brother. To the second question, 'Have you forgotten me, and have I become as nothing to you?' I simply reply that outside the circle of my kindred, my heart is knit to no two men in South Carolina as to Thornwell and yourself, linked together as you both are in all my associations, *par nobile fratrum.* And outside of the circle of your kindred, you shall find no one in South Carolina, or out of it, who rises superior to me in the admiration and respect he feels for your talents and for your character, for your qualities both of mind and heart; and no one who exceeds me in that deep and quiet affection which has its root in an unbounded confidence and Christian esteem. And no man has ever defended you with more enthusiasm from the charge of abruptness and dogmatism by adverting to the sterling qualities out of which these appearances seem sometimes to spring. Will this now suffice? Ordinarily, I could not bring myself to say thus much to your face, lest you should denounce me as a toady; but I say it now freely, because the occasion calls for it, and you have challenged it by your interrogatories. It is proof enough of my sincere regard for you, that I have occupied a sheet in my defence; for I do not know a half dozen men in the world to whom I would pen such an exculpatory letter as this. Away then forever with these unpleasant suspicions, which have nothing to rest upon but what is negative; and let the mantle of Charity cover omissions and delinquencies of correspondence—and permit me to feel, as I have always hitherto felt, that you were a friend with whom it was not necessary to stand upon points, but with whom all needful things could be taken for granted.

"As to the New Orleans matter, that will push me over to another sheet: and here I am persuaded is the real ground of your suspicion and doubt of me—since in the renewed negotiations on that subject I have not conferred with you: a shyness, which you have interpreted into alienation. A word on this point. I have conferred neither with you, nor with anyone else, because I already know the contents of your mind and of the minds of all around me on this matter; and there was nothing more to learn—because, I was in full possession of all the points of the case on all sides, and in all aspects of it; and because I felt that at last, in the present posture of things, upon myself alone, upon myself unaided except from above, must rest the entire responsibility and pain of a decision. The time had come to ask counsel alone of God, and to disenthrall myself of those influences arising from private friendship and domestic ease which would only make it more difficult to do right. The time had come for me to confer not with flesh and blood—in spirit at least, to forsake father and mother, wife and children, and to ask God what I should do, with the determination to follow conscience and duty at every sacrifice of feeling that might be involved. To ask counsel of men, at this juncture, would only have been imbecility. Perhaps, too, I have been shy, at this crisis, from a constitutional weakness which makes me shrink from witnessing pain inflicted upon others. I cannot stand by and see a tooth pulled, or a child's gum cut—much less, is it easy to speak the words that grieve and afflict friends whom I love. Then it is that with all my natural communicateness, I shrink instinctively within my shell, and suffer more pain myself in being the occasion of pain and disappointment to others than it is possible for them to feel in the direct experience of the same.

"The rumors that have reached you are correct. I have made up my mind to resign at the approaching meeting of the Board, with a view to accept the New Orleans call, if it shall be placed in my hands by the Presbytery. With the renewal of this call I have had no concern, and was taken as much by surprise as anyone else. Now that it has come, I must meet it. Had I been consulted. I should have resisted and refused all concurrence, as I have done in several other cases since November; feeling bound by my acquiescence in the decision of Synod. The considerations which have controlled my decision are briefly these:

"1. It is clear the Church at large does not acquiesce in my withdrawal from the pulpit. Since November I have been engaged in a laborious and annoying correspondence to frustrate and prevent calls from five churches in as many different cities, and without success in two of the five. What am I to make of these signs of acceptance as a preacher, just at the moment when I am ceasing to be one?

"2. Add to this my own growing conviction that the pastoral work is the work for which alone, I am in a degree, fit; and in which all my tastes, natural and acquired, lie—and that, on the other hand, academic life does not suit me, as I have neither the taste nor the learning for it, and as a professor am only a wretched sham.

"3. The actual and admitted importance of the New Orleans field, in itself considered, and in relation to the outlying territory—and the difficulty in securing a supply of it, arising from the perils and risks incurred through a removal to that city.

"4. The fact that I feel committed in honor, by all that has passed, to go to New Orleans if I leave the Seminary at all, prevents me from considering other overtures; which yet will be pressed, so soon as this is disposed of.

"5. It is certain or nearly so that the Presbytery will put the call into my hand when it shall be prosecuted: and the desire is strongly felt by most of the brethren that they should be relieved from the delicacy of their position by my assumption of the entire responsibility.

"6. The Constitution of the Seminary requiring a six months notice of resignation, I must take the initiative at this meeting of the Board.

"7. It is but right the Electors should have time to think and confer, before they are precipitated upon a ballot for my successor.

"8. I would have preferred to be entirely passive until the Presbytery should have taken action, and with great reluctance do I take a step in advance of their action; but now that the complications of the case, and the interests represented on both sides, require a decision by me, I cannot, consistently with my own repeated declarations nor with the suggestions of my own conscience, decide to remain in the Seminary and to abandon the pastorate. I must therefore decide to go to New Orleans.

"I am deeply convinced of the importance of the Professorship of History in the Seminary; and my own sense of unfitness for its duties is a leading element in my decision—and I am too old to begin at the beginning of an Encyclopædic Department, and go through all the drudgery of microscopic investigation, to be fit for an office which I must vacate by death as soon as the qualifications for it have been attained. I prefer to abide in the work to which I am trained, and in relation to which I have at least measured my strength. Nor am I insensible to the pain I must both give and feel in the rupture of my established and endeared relations, and I dread the months before me, almost as I dread death itself. I am alive to all the risks I incur in going among a strange people, and in stemming other currents of thought and feeling than those I am accustomed to. I have surveyed all the perils as to life of myself and family from an unfriendly climate; and I know nothing in all this but to trust God with an entireness of consecration to his service. I have striven to search my own heart to learn the motives which influence: I am conscious only of a desire to follow God's will, to do good to man, and to glorify Him in whose service I am enlisted. If at last I am mistaken, I can only throw myself for pardon and salvation upon Him who is infinitely merciful through Christ Jesus to the guilty and the erring. I have gone through a sea of mental suffering, such as I never felt before; and it is a comfort to me that 'all things are naked and open to the eyes of Him with whom we have to do.'

"Yours very truly,

"B. M. PALMER."

"I rejoice that you are so rapidly improving, and hope you will soon be perfectly restored. You will, I trust, be able to come down to the Board, the last of June. Salute Mrs. Adger and the children for us all."

"COLUMBIA, S. C., June 10, 1856.

"DEAR BROTHER ADGER: I am glad that the personal portion of my letter to you has proved satisfactory; for it would have distressed me to know that you were permanently estranged, as the loss of your friendship would be to me a sore trial and calamity. Let that then all pass forever.

"As to the protest you have entered on record against my decision in relation to New Orleans, you need be under no apprehension that I will consider it either 'brusque,' 'dogmatic' or 'abrupt.' I understand thoroughly the earnestness of your nature, to which great strength of conviction and tenacity of purpose necessarily belong; and I am very far from taking unkindly any plainness, or even severity of speech, necessary to the articulate utterance of your views. The die is however now cast, and has therefore got beyond the reach of discussion. If the decision is erroneous, no one will pray more fervently than myself that God may yet, in his providence, control and reverse it, or at least overrule it to his own glory. But I have reached it very patiently and painfully; and my mind rests in it with very tolerable satisfaction. If I had been requested to concur in raising the question anew, I would have refused, as I did persistently in every application that has been made since November. Having yielded to the decision of the Synod, I would have no agency in the reopening of the subject. But when it was opened without my concurrence and against my desire, I was compelled to look at it as a new record on a new leaf in the book of Divine Providence. If I have taken a step in advance of the action of the Presbytery, it was with felt and expressed reluctance, as compelled thereto by two complications of the case, and to relieve others of a responsibility which they wished not to assume any longer. I have weighed every step thoughtfully and prayerfully; and my conviction is strong and clear that I ought to be a pastor and not a professor. I have desired and labored to act in the whole case with a good conscience before God and my brethren, and I must bide the judgment of both.

"Let me say distinctly that I neither deny, nor override the rights of the Presbytery. They have full jurisdiction over the case: and if they feel disposed to exercise their power to arrest the call, I shall not murmur, but submit. I shall then have reached the end of my rope in my efforts to follow out what I conceive to be the leadings of Providence, and to act upon the convictions of my own mind.

"A word upon the implied breach of faith to Brother Thornwell. My consent to go into the Seminary with him was given by me without due consideration, and when my own mind had not worked itself out to any clear conviction on the subject. If God, in the unfoldings of his providence, has connected together a chain of events which seems to reprove that decision, and lead me to feel that I have been brought into a false and wrong position, I think the course of true Christian honor is for me to say frankly to him and to you and to all, that I erred, through ignorance and a fallible judgment, in giving that consent, and must retrace my steps. It is not a question simply of personal sacrifice, but of high Christian duty; a question simply of interpretation as to what is the will of Thornwell's Master and my Master. I love Thornwell dearly, and delight to do homage to his genius. I would willingly walk through life under his shadow, and contribute to his usefulness and comfort. But from motives of human friendship, or from a cowardly fear of reproach from mere men like myself, to turn aside from the path of duty and from obedience to God, cannot be thought of, no, not for a moment. I freely admit the possibility of mistake in the determination of duty—but with a conscientious desire to ascertain it, with a careful use of all the means to know it, and with fervent prayer to God for guidance and light, I do not see what remains but to rest in our convictions of duty, as being duty itself.

"But it is tedious to discuss all these things with the pen. I hope you will be sufficiently recovered to attend the meeting of the Board on the 24th inst. and then we can talk it over from the end to the beginning. As long as the matter remains inchoate, Providence can arrest it at any stage; and I am sure that I am willing to be controlled by that high and sovereign Will which I desire above all things to obey.

"With Christian salutations to Mrs. Adger and to all of your household, I am, dear brother,

"Yours as ever,

"B. M. PALMER."

When the Board of Directors of the Seminary met June 24, 1856, they received a letter from Dr. Palmer resigning his professorship, whereupon they adopted the following minute:

"The Board cannot consistently, with a sense of duty, present to the Synod the resignation of the Rev. Dr. Palmer, without expressing its regret that he should feel it his duty to resign his chair in this institution. The interests of the Seminary seem to demand his continuance in his office, and the reasons which he assigns for resigning have all been deliberately considered, both by the Presbytery to which he belongs and by this Synod; and so far from producing in his brethren the conviction entertained by himself, they have had precisely the opposite effect. We believe that he is eminently qualified for the chair, which his letter shows he so highly appreciates, and we cannot but feel that the confidence of the Church in the stability of our plans and the permanence of our measures will be seriously affected, if we permit an arrangement so auspiciously begun to be interrupted before it reaches the point of completion. The Seminary never needed more than at present all that can give it efficiency and vigor. Many of the prominent churches of the South are either vacant or inadequately supplied, and the very pressure upon Dr. Palmer from all quarters for his services, shows the urgency of the call for a thoroughly educated ministry. Our Seminary must be put into a condition with the blessing of God, to supply this demand. This is the place in which Dr. Palmer can most effectually aid in relieving this great destitution. If he is permitted to leave, the insecurity attached to our organization will cripple the Seminary, by sending to other and less fickle institutions the young men who might have been prepared for our own field. The question before the Synod is simply the question concerning the importance of the Seminary. The necessity of its prosperity and success is the necessity of refusing this resignation."[2]

The Board of Directors furthermore resolved to meet at Chesterville, during the next meeting of the Synod of South Carolina, for the purpose of inaugurating Dr. Palmer; and that he "be requested to deliver an address before that body." This seemed to bode ill for his plan to go to New Orleans.

When the Presbytery of Charleston met, instead of doing as he hoped, it referred the question as to whether the call from New Orleans should be put into his hands to the Synod of South Carolina. When the Synod met, a few weeks later, it took up the Reference, spent two afternoon sessions in dealing with it,—hearing pertinent parts of the records and the papers sent by the commissioners of the New Orleans Church, hearing Dr. Palmer himself and speakers in favor of or in opposition to, instructing the Presbytery of Charleston to put the call into his hands. At a late hour, a vote on a resolution instructing the Presbytery "to put the call from the First Presbyterian Church, New Orleans" into his hands, was taken by calling the roll, and resulted as follows: Sixty-seven in the affirmative, and thirty-two in the negative.

On the next day Dr. Palmer, who was Stated Clerk, "offered his resignation of the office, in view of his probable removal," which was accepted. At a later meeting the following minute was unanimously adopted and ordered to be placed upon the records:

"WHEREAS, our beloved brother, the Rev. Dr. Palmer, has felt constrained, by a severe conviction of duty, to resign his professorship in our Seminary, and to transfer his relation to a different Synod, we desire to place upon our Minutes an enduring testimony of our high appreciation of his character and usefulness, and our deep regret at the disruption of the endearing ties which have so long united us, and our ardent wishes and fervent prayers that he may prove a rich and lasting blessing to his future field of labor.

"Deploring, as we must continue to do, the lamented removal of this bright and shining light in which we have so greatly rejoiced, our grief is assuaged by the anticipation of the radiance it will diffuse in that wide and interesting region to which his labors are to be transferred.

"In our separation from a brother so greatly beloved, the members of this body feel painfully the severe bereavement sustained by our Seminary, in the loss of one so richly endowed with those rare and

---

[2] Minutes of the Synod of South Carolina, Appendix pp. 43 and 44.

precious gifts so invaluable to the training of our rising ministry. In this mysterious dispensation, our mourning hearts bow in humble submission to the Divine will.

"As we are well assured that our brother has been governed by a sense of imperative duty in adopting a course which involves so great sacrifices, and causes so much pain to many dear friends, it is incumbent on us to cheer and comfort him in his noble act of self-consecration. We doubt not that he can adopt the sublime language of the Apostle and say, 'None of these things move me, neither count I my life dear unto myself, so that I may finish my course with joy, and the ministry which I have received of the Lord Jesus to testify the Gospel of the grace of God.' Deeply sympathizing with this beloved brother, our hearts should glow with devout gratitude, that one of ourselves, a pupil of our own Seminary, is made capable by grace of so glorious a destiny, is enriched and ennobled with a faith so Apostolic and invincible.

"Convinced, by no doubtful indications, that the Lord hath need of him in another sphere of usefulness, and therefore calls him away, it becomes the duty of this Synod, though with sorrowing hearts, to bid him depart and fulfill this high commission. It is our parting testimony, that he has nobly filled every department of duty and labor in which he has been engaged with us. Long and affectionately shall we remember the energy and efficiency with which he has accomplished his full orbed ministry among ourselves. And now, as he is entering an untried portion of the harvest field, our warmest affections accompany him. In every peril and difficulty, may the angel of the covenant preserve and comfort him! May his life and health be graciously continued for many years; and may his labors be crowned with special manifestations of the Divine favor; so that having served the Church faithfully, and turned many to righteousness, he may shine at last as the stars forever and ever."[3]

Thus nobly did the noble Synod of South Carolina dismiss one of her noblest sons, whom she had so longed to keep, to his great field of the Southwest.

Till December he continued his services in the seminary and in the pulpit in Orangeburg. From the sessional records of his old church in Columbia, it appears that the session, November 17, 1856, "unanimously resolved to request Dr. Palmer to preach a farewell sermon to the congregation the next Sabbath morning."

Meanwhile, during the year 1856, Dr. Palmer had been engaged not only in these professorial and pulpit labors, but had carried on a ministry of consolation unrestricted by the

[3] *Minutes of the Synod of South Carolina*, November, 1856, pp. 34, 35.

limits of any small territory. This is made manifest by such letters as this to the Rev. Bazile E. Lanneau on the death of his father, Bazile Lanneau:

"COLUMBIA, S. C., October 9, 1856.

"DEAR BAZILE: We were much shocked on Monday last upon taking a Charleston paper for Saturday in our hands, to read the notice of your father's death, and the invitation to his funeral. Your note, therefore, of Tuesday did not take us aback by surprise, as it otherwise would have done. I am unable just now to write you as I would like to do, having a painful sore upon one of my writing fingers, almost disabling me from the use of the pen. As soon as I can write freely I will try to pen a letter to your dear mother. At present I can only express the deep sorrow we feel in the bereavement which makes your home so desolate.

"It is no ordinary affliction to lose a father and a husband: bringing along with the loss sustained the untying of one's domestic bonds—and the dissolution of home. Indeed, this loss extends far beyond the family circle; and the whole Christian community of Charleston will gather as mourners by your side and grieve for the loss incurred by the Church of Christ on earth; yet—'Even so, Father, for so it seemed good in thy sight.'

"It would be superfluous to exhort any of you to patience and submission, for I doubt not you have already united in saying, 'The Lord gave and the Lord hath taken away: Blessed be the name of the Lord.' While nature will have her pangs and wring her tribute of tears and grief, you have still so many materials of praise and song that you must mingle thanksgiving and mourning. His pure life, his unstained character, his long devotion to his Master's cause and Church, his pious counsels, and his fervent prayers, his faith and patience and hope—all meeting together in his dying moments: all these will be objects of memory to stay your sorrow and sustain you from despondency and gloom. If, too, the Church below has lost, the Church above has gained. It is only a transfer from one to the other, and the Church is not a loser, though we may miss him much.

"I am glad to hear of your mother's calmness and peace, though it does not surprise. It is what I should expect of her. May the Comforter draw nigh to her and uphold her faith with abounding consolations!

"Affectionately yours,

"B. M. PALMER."

In the course of the year 1856 he took part in the installation of his father as pastor of the Stony Creek Church in Beaufort District. Of the incident he published, in the *Southern Presbyterian,* though not over his own name, a graceful and instructive account which, with one or two unimportant omissions, is subjoined:

"The sermon appointed for the occasion was preached by the Rev. B. M. Palmer, son of the pastor elect; the charge to the pastor was delivered by the Rev. J. L. Kirkpatrick, and that to the people by the Rev. J. L. Girardeau. In addition to these services there was preaching on Friday, Saturday and Monday, which was attended by large and attentive congregations. The exercises were held at McPhersonville, the summer quarters of the congregation, where they have a neat house of worship, a convenient parsonage, schools and other appendages of a pleasant Christian community.

"The Stony Creek Church is one of the oldest and most prosperous of the churches in the seaboard region of our State. Although Presbyterian in its doctrines and internal structure, and supplied by ministers of our communion, it has not, until recently, had any formal connection with any Presbytery.

"About two years ago, overtures were made to it by the Charleston Presbytery to become a component part of that body, which were met and acceded to in a spirit of Christian affection and confidence. Owing to its former position of independence, the above was the first installation service held in the church. The occasion itself was, therefore, one of more than ordinary interest. We trust the impression is altogether favorable.

"At the time the church came into union with the Presbytery, our esteemed brother, the Rev. J. B. Dunwody, was its minister. Soon after, his health having failed, he resigned his charge, and the members of the congregation found their hearts turning with affectionate desire to the Rev. E. Palmer, who had in former times, for a period of thirteen years, served them with great acceptance in the Gospel of their Lord. Him, though now approaching the verge of three score and ten years—an age when most men are unfit for active labor, when most churches shrink from calling a minister, whether fit or unfit for further work—they invited him to return to them, to live with them while life should last, and die and be buried among them when the hour shall come. It was a call he could not resist, and the rare spectacle was presented of a minister, sixty-eight years of age, entering as if anew upon the great work to which a long life had already been laboriously and unremittedly devoted.

"Mr. Palmer, however, retains beyond any man of his age we are acquainted with the vigor and elasticity of body, and the genial warmth and freshness of temperment, that are supposed to belong exclusively to youth. His term of service in the new sphere may yet, through a good providence, exceed that usually allotted to men who enter upon theirs in middle life.

"In consequence of the loss by immigration the congregation of whites is not as large at Stony Creek Church as in former years. There has been, however, a corresponding increase in the number of blacks; and among these the pastor finds a wide field for labor. He loves to preach the blessed Gospel of Christ to these precious souls, who claim and receive a large measure of his time and strength. May his labors for the spiritual welfare of both classes be abundantly successful."

We have now followed our subject through the preliminary and preparatory stages of his life. We have seen him throughout a vigorous and prolonged course of training. He has developed well his brain, tongue, and pen, and all his splendid natural endowments; and so fitted himself to take a great part in the life of a great city and a vast section. He was to become in the new and larger arena not only a great religious leader, but in epochal movements the moral and political mouthpiece of the city, State, and section of his adoption. He was to be the leader of patriots, "the first citizen of Louisiana." He was to be "the public conscience," on moral matters the mouthpiece of God unto vast multitudes even of faiths differing widely from his own. Still he was to tower as a Christian minister higher than in any other role.

CHAPTER X.

THE ANTE-BELLUM PERIOD IN NEW ORLEANS.

(December, 1856—May, 1861.)

The Dr. Palmer of December, 1856.—The New Sphere into which He went: The Southwest; New Orleans; and the First Presbyterian Church.—The Beginnings in His New Pastorate.—His Work as a Preacher and Teacher during this Period.—His Skill in Dealing Individually with Men.—His Work as a Pastor.—Bearing as a Member of the Session.—Care of the Negroes.—Efforts to Secure the Spread of Presbyterianism in the City.—Labors in Behalf of the Church at Large.—Writings.—Occasional Sermons and Addresses.

THE man who left Columbia, S. C., in early December, 1856, to become the pastor of the First Presbyterian Church, was a striking looking man to a close observer. The superficial said, "He is an insignificant looking little fellow." He was rather under medium height, slender, agile as a cat, naturally as graceful as a leopard, simply but elegantly clad from his dainty little foot to the crown of his head. His abundant dark brown hair, cropped just below the ears, was thrown loosely back from no meanly shaped forehead. His piercing hazel eyes twinkled as he gazed penetratingly into your face. His nose was suggestive of discrimination, fastidiousness, and secretiveness; his huge mouth, when still, was clamped by strong jaws; his large lips were very mobile in speech. So strong was his chin that some observers were tempted to call him "dish-faced." He made a strong impression of alertness, and of indefinite reserve power. He made the impression of great kindness of heart and unobtrusive readiness to help his fellow men, whatever their relations.

Even to the shrewd and experienced observer, however, the casket in this case hardly appeared to be an adequate advertisement of the jewel within. The Presbyterians of New Orleans and the Southwest, in getting Dr. Palmer, got one of the first minds, and perhaps the first orator, of his day, in the great communion to which he belonged. They got him in his early prime. He had passed through the period of raw and callow youth in his brief pastorate at Savannah and in the longer one at Columbia. Had he not been assiduous in the cultivation of his talents during those earlier pastorates, he had not been the man he was when he entered New Orleans. Perhaps he had never entered the city into which he now came. But pastorates and professorship had been extended university and seminary courses for him. He had given his splendid natural powers a splendid discipline. He had applied old acquisitions, he had been daily adding new acquisitions to the old, and applying and testing all. He was near to forty, thirty-eight,—but the period of achievement was just to begin.

The commissioners from the First Presbyterian Church in New Orleans had pressed the fact that the great Southwest, of which New Orleans was the metropolis, needed him there. The Southwest did need him. Newly acquired and imperial Texas needed him. The Indian Territory, Arkansas, Louisiana, Mississippi, Alabama and Tennessee needed him in the common beating heart of them all. They were all in the nascent state and needed such a man in New Orleans to help mould their coming civilizations for right and for God. He was wonderfully adapted to serve them in his new post. Aside from his commanding gifts and acquirements, he was a son of that South Carolina who had had so large a hand in mothering all the States just named, and had imposed her views on manners and government, so widely amongst them. When he went to them, he simply went into that greater South Carolina,—went amongst people, who in spite of very considerable differences, were substantially at one with South Carolina in regard to social and civil matters. His great sphere of influence was still within the South Carolina belt. Thus by the South Carolina spirit and character as well as by his singular and extraordinary endowments he was most happily adapted to labor in this quarter.

The State of Louisiana, as indeed some of the others, had not a little in its civilization to differentiate it from that of South Carolina. It had been settled by the French in 1682; and for upwards of four score years the French gave character to its civilization. Between 1762 and 1766 the territory passed to the possession of Spain, much to the chagrin of the colonists. During the last three and a quarter decades of the eighteenth century, Spain was making her contribution to the civilization already established. In 1801 the country was retroceded to France. In 1803 the United States purchased the country, together with the whole vast territory to the northwest and lying westward from the Mississippi River, paying to France eighty millions of francs therefor. Meanwhile immigrants had been coming in from other sources, principally German and American; and after the purchase, Americans from the New England and the Eastern States, and especially from the Southern States flocked into the land. The population became cosmopolitan. The civilizations of the Latin European peoples and of the North Europeans were brought together, and produced a type not exactly paralleled in any of the sister States. The Latin civilization in both French and Spanish forms had been first on the ground and long remained the dominating factor. It furnished the code of laws, a modification and adaptation of the Code Napoleon, which the State has retained and applies down to this day. It furnished the dominant religion also, in Roman Catholicism, which up to the American purchase was the established religion. In these particulars are found differentiating marks of Louisiana civilization; others might be pointed out. The Louisiana type of Romanism had never been fanatical, it is true; the people had opposed, with horror and defiance, the attempt made during the Spanish regime, to institute the Spanish Inquisition amongst them; nor had they been wanting in a more positive sort of liberality. The modified Code Napoleon was a very superior system. The peculiarities of the Louisiana civilization demanded, indeed, of the minister who should go from elsewhere to labor in the Delta State, no small tact and a certain generous breadth of sympathies. These Dr. Palmer possessed in an unusual degree. He inherited them from his mother and from his mother State.

Moreover, in his possession of South Carolina courtesy, the South Carolina sense of honor in its noblest and Christian form, the South Carolina magnification of the rights of the State, and the South Carolina views of slavery, he was peculiarly fitted to accomplish a great work. In Louisiana, with all its peculiarities, he was still within the zone in which South Carolina theories prevailed.

The commercial heart of the Southwest and still more of Louisiana was New Orleans, where the people of his faith had risen and, like the man in the Macedonian vision which Paul saw, had cried, "Come over and help us." This city had been founded in 1718, by Jean Baptiste Lemoyne de Bienville, a French Canadian, Governor of the French colony which in 1699 had been planted by his brother D'Iberville on the shores of the Gulf, along the eastern margin of the Bay of Biloxi.

The colony of Biloxi had grown but slowly. Bienville's new colony had made better progress; and in 1803, when the territory passed into political connection with the United States, its population numbered 10,000, being made up mostly of French Creoles and their slaves. The influx of American immigrants after the Purchase was very great. The dream of LaSalle, that by commanding the Mississippi River Frenchmen might command the commerce of China which he supposed would flow down the newly discovered channel, had been abandoned; but men believed in the vast promise of New Orleans. The Sage of Monticello, had predicted on purchasing Louisiana, that New Orleans would become "not only the greatest commercial city in America, but in the world;" and he gave very good reasons for the prediction. He pointed out, for instance, that it was the natural port of the Mississippi Valley, which he foresaw was to become "the seat of a great and populous empire, and that all the varied products of that valley would find their way to New Orleans by a thousand streams; while in the South lay Mexico, Cuba, and the tropics."[1] The city sat at the gateway of the Continent and seemed the best place to handle the immense trade that must spring up between the Mississippi Valley and the tropics on the one hand, and Europe on the other. Between 1830 and 1840, no other city in the United States kept pace with this one in growth. When the census of 1840 was taken, it was found to be the fourth city in population, exceeded only by New York, Philadelphia and Baltimore. It also stood "fourth amongst all the ports of the world, with only London, Liverpool and New York ahead." It was even ahead of New York in the export of domestic products.

The prosperity of New Orleans, which appeared inevitable in view of her natural advantages received three mighty blows: the building of the Erie Canal which furnished a cheap northern route from the great Northwest to the Eastern markets; the invention by Stephenson of the steam locomotive, and the building of railways, which annihilated the supreme importance of water-ways for commercial purposes; and the war between

---

[1] Norman Walker, in Richtor's *History of New Orleans.*

the sections. This last, coming soon after Dr. Palmer's translation to New Orleans, gave the city a blow so terrific that she had to lay her foundations of business prosperity all over again. The other two forces had been put into operation prior to his call to the city. But their potencies had been fully estimated neither by the people of New Orleans themselves nor by others. If trade with the Northwest had dropped off the trade in the South and Southwest was constantly growing, and so fast that New Orleans became increasingly busy and prosperous. The decade ending at the outbreak of the war saw New Orleans enjoying a vast commercial prosperity, canals and trans-Appalachian railways, nevertheless. More than half the time during this decade, "it exceeded Manhattan in the volume of its exports."

Though too slow in securing railroads, and thus losing the place which, in view of her natural advantages, should have been hers; though suffering and to suffer until Eads should do his work at the mouth of the Mississippi for an exit to the sea of sufficient depth for vessels of the heaviest draught, New Orleans was in 1856 a city of vast power and vaster possibilities and promise. Even if not so great a field as was commonly thought, it was nevertheless a great field, a field of abounding and widening opportunity. In addition to the people of his flock he would there preach for considerable portions of the year to great numbers of planters and merchants from the central and southwestern portions of the great Mississippi Valley. He would preach to travelers and sojourners. His influence would be of the very widest. Loving all men, he would be tactful in dealing with all. To the large Hebrew population he would be as an Hebrew if perchance he might win some to Christ. To the Romanist he would show all the consideration consistent with his calling as a Christian and a minister. Gentle Creole or unwashed Dago, he would win them all by Christian courtesy and beneficence.

Of the church in New Orleans which Dr. Palmer undertook to serve in things spiritual, he has left the following historical account reaching down to the day when he took charge of it:

[2] "It is a little remarkable that the first successful effort to plant

---

[2] This account was read by him at the Semi-Centenary Anniversary of Presbyterianism in New Orleans, November 23, 1873.

Presbyterianism in the city of New Orleans should have originated with the Congregationalists of New England. Near the beginning of the year 1817, the Rev. Elias Cornelius was appointed by the Connecticut Missionary Society to engage in a Missionary tour through the Southwestern States, more especially to visit New Orleans, then containing a population of thirty to thirty-four thousand, and with but one Protestant minister, the Rev. Dr. Hull; to examine into its moral condition, and while preaching the Gospel to many who seldom heard it, to invite the friends of the Congregational or Presbyterian Communion to establish a Church, and to secure an able and faithful pastor. In this tour, Dr. Cornelius acted also as agent for the A. B. C. F. M., to solicit funds for the evangelization of the Indian tribes. In this work he was eminently successful, devoting an entire year to a lengthened tour from Massachusetts to Louisiana, collecting large sums for the American Board, and arrived in New Orleans on the 30th of December, 1817.

"The most important service rendered by Dr. Cornelius, however, was that of introducing the Rev. Sylvester Larned to this field of labor. In passing through New Jersey, on his journey southward, Dr. Cornelius formed the acquaintance of Mr. Larned, then finishing his divinity course at Princeton, and giving, in the reputation acquired as a student, brilliant promise of a successful career as a preacher. The arrangement was there formed between the two, that Mr. Larned should follow Dr. Cornelius to New Orleans, after he should have passed his trials, and should have been admitted to the ministry.

"On the 15th of July, 1817, Mr. Larned was licensed and ordained by the Presbytery of New York. This ordination was clearly to the office of evangelist, which he was in the fullest sense of the word. It appears, too, that the General Assembly of the Presbyterian Church was brought into coöperation with this scheme; from the fact that Drs. Nott and Romeyn were appointed by that body to accompany Mr. Larned to the Southwest. This appointment was not, however, fulfilled, and we find the young evangelist, after a brief visit to his native home, leaving on the 26th of September, and journeying alone to the field where he was to gather the laurels of an unfading reputation, and then to sanctify it by an early death. He reached his destination, after innumerable delays, on the 22nd of January, 1818.

"Through the antecedent preparation of his friend, Dr. Cornelius, who had preceded him exactly three weeks, and still more by his own splendid attractions, overtures were soon made to him for a permanent settlement. Subscriptions were circulated for the building of a church edifice, which by the 5th of April amounted to $16,000. It was proposed, as soon as the subscriptions were completed, to negotiate a loan of $40,000, the estimated cost of a building sixty feet by ninety, with about 2,000 sittings. Considering the infancy of the enterprise, the largeness of these plans betokens great vigor of effort, and the confidence felt of final success in collecting and maintaining a flourishing church. In this costly undertaking, generous assistance was received from the city Council in the grant of two lots of ground, valued at $6,000 and in a subsequent loan of $10,000. In the erection of the building, Mr. Larned's spiritual labors were interrupted during the summer of 1818 by a visit North, for the purpose of soliciting money, and also of purchasing materials for building.

"On the 8th of January, 1819, the cornerstone of the new edifice was laid with imposing ceremonies (and in the presence of an immense throng), on the selected site on St. Charles Street, between Gravier and Union, and on the 4th of July following, was solemnly dedicated to the worship of Almighty God, with a discourse from Psalm 48:9, 'We have thought of thy lovingkindness, O God, in the midst of thy temple,' which will be found the fourth in the series of sermons published in connection with Mr. Larned's 'Memoirs.'

"There are no records from which to learn the spiritual growth of the church during this early period, except that in one of his letters, Mr. Larned speaks of a communion season, about the middle of July, 1820, in which there were forty-two at the table of the Lord, part of whom were, however, Methodists. Mr. Larned's labors were those exclusively of an evangelist; and his brief life was spent in gathering a congregation and building a house of worship. There is no record of his having organized a church according to our ecclesiastical canons, by the election and ordination of ruling elders; and he himself was never installed into the pastoral relation by ecclesiastical authority. It pleased the Great Head of the Church to arrest his labors before they reached this point of consummation. During the month of August, 1820, the scourge which has so often desolated our city made its appearance. On the Sabbath, August 27, he preached from Phil. 1:21: 'For me to live is Christ, and to die is gain:' words alas! prophetic of his speedy call to those mansions 'where all is gain'—forever to the believer. On the following Thursday, August 31st, the very day on which he completed the 24th year of his age, he fell asleep in Jesus, or rather awoke to the glory and joy of his Lord. His remains were consigned to the tomb in Girod Cemetery, with the Episcopal service for the dead rendered by the Rev. Dr. Hull.

"Mr. Larned's successor, after an interval of eighteen months, was the Rev. Theodore Clapp, a native of Massachusetts, and a graduate of Yale College and of the Theological Seminary at Andover. He was licensed by a Congregational Association, October, 1817, and was led providentially to Kentucky, by an engagement as private tutor in a family residing near Lexington, in that State. During the summer of 1821, he spent a few weeks at a watering place in Kentucky and on the Sabbath preached in one of the public rooms of the hotel to the assembled guests. This apparently casual circumstance led to his settlement in New Orleans. Amongst his hearers on that occasion were two gentlemen from our city, trustees of Mr. Larned's Church; who, upon their return home, caused a letter to be written, inviting him to New Orleans. This invitation, at first declined, led to a visit to this city near the close of February, 1822.

"On the third Sabbath after his arrival, he was unanimously chosen to fill the vacant pulpit. Finding the church embarrassed by a debt of $45,000, he naturally hesitated and finally made its liquidation the condition of his acceptance of the call. The method adopted for this purpose, though deemed proper at the time, would now be disallowed by the better educated conscience of the Church. The trustees made application to the Legislature of Louisiana, then in session, for a lottery; which being sold to Yates & McIntyre, of New York, for $25,000, relieved the pressure of debt to that amount. For the remaining $20,000 the building was sold to Judah Touro, Esq., a merchant of wealth, whose magnificent charities have left his name in grateful remembrance to the people of New Orleans. It may be well to state here, though a little in advance of dates, that Mr. Touro held the building to the time of its destruction by fire; allowing the income from pew rents to the use of the minister, and incurring the expense of keeping it in repair. He was Mr. Clapp's personal friend and benefactor throughout life; and when the original building was burnt, and long after it had been carried away from Presbyterianism by Mr. Clapp's secession, Mr. Touro, we believe, built a small chapel for the Unitarian Congregation, until a larger edifice could be erected for their accommodation. Such instances of princely munificence deserve to be engraved on tables of marble. But this is to anticipate.

"The first notice of the organization of this church, as a spiritual body, is in the record of a meeting held for this purpose on the 23rd of November, 1823. Prior to this, the labors of Mr. Larned, extending over a period of two years and seven months, from January 22, 1818, to August 31, 1820; and those of Mr. Clapp over a period of one year and nine months, from March, 1822, to November, 1823, were simply evangelistic. A congregation had been gathered, a house of worship built, the word and sacraments administered, and the materials collected for the spiritual church in the admission of persons to sealing ordinances, all in the exercise of that power which the Scriptures and our Presbyterian Standards assign to the evangelist. The time had now arrived for gathering up the results of these labors in a permanent and organized form.

"On the evening of November 23, 1823, just fifty years ago, at a meeting moderated by Rev. Mr. Clapp, nine males and fifteen females presented credentials of having been admitted to the Sacrament of the Lord's Supper, by Mr. Larned, as follows:

"*Males.*—Alfred Hennen, James Robinson, William Ross, Rob't. H. McNair, Moses Cox, Hugh Farrie, Richard Pearse, John Spittal, John Rollins.

"*Females.*—Phœbe Farrie, Catherine Hearsey, Celeste Hearsey, Dora A. Hearsey, Margaret Agur, Ann Ross, Eliza Hill, Margaret McNair, Sarah Ann Harper, Ann Davison, Stella Mercer, Jane Robinson, Eliza Baldwin, Mary Porter, Eliza Davidson.

"These persons, twenty-four in all, were formed into a church, by the adoption of the Presbyterian Standards in doctrine, government, discipline, and worship, and by a petition to the Presbytery of Mississippi, to be enrolled among the churches under its care, with the style and title of 'The First Presbyterian Church in the City and Parish of New Orleans.' The organization was completed by the election on the same evening of four persons to be ruling elders, viz: William Ross, Moses Cox, James Robinson and Robert H. McNair, who were accordingly ordained and installed on the following Sabbath, November 30, 1823.

"Mr. Clapp's ministry was a troubled one, from suspicions entertained of his doctrinal soundness. From his own statements, as early as 1824 his faith was shaken as to the doctrine of the eternity of future punishment. He pushed his investigations, doubts darkening upon him, through years, until at length he was forced to plant himself in open hostility to the whole Calvinistic Theology. It is not strange that inconsistent and wavering statements of truth should find their way into the ministrations of the pulpit, at the very time his faith was shaken in the tenets which he had subscribed, and when his own mind was working to an entire renunciation of them. A single crack in a bell is sufficient to destroy its tone; and it is not surprising that some of his parishioners should miss that clear ring which the pulpit is expected to give forth. Certain it is, that the repose of the Church was seriously disturbed for years by two parallel prosecutions before the session against two prominent members of the Church, one of them a ruling elder, grounded upon their undisguised dissatisfaction with the minister. In the course of these complicated proceedings, the session, by death and deposition from offices, became reduced below a constitutional quorum; which led in March, 1828, to the election and ordination of five new elders: Alfred Hennen, Joseph A. Maybin, Wm. W. Caldwell, Josiah Crocker and Fabricius Reynolds.

"On the fifth of March, 1830, Mr. Clapp addressed a letter to the Presbytery of Mississippi, in which he says: 'I have not found, and at present despair of finding, any text of Holy Writ to prove unanswerably the distinguishing tenets of Calvinism.' He therefore solicited a dismission from the Presbytery to the Hampshire County Association of Congregational Ministers in the State of Massachusetts. This dismission was refused by the Presbytery, on the ground that it was inconsistent to dismiss, in good standing, to another body one whom they could no longer recognize in their own; and they proceeded to declare Mr. Clapp no longer a member of their body, or a minister in the Presbyterian Church. A letter was also addressed to the church advising them of this action, and declaring the pulpit vacant. No definite action was taken upon this communication of the Presbytery until January, 1831, when the session proposed to take mind of the church, whether to retain Mr. Clapp as their pastor, or to abide by the decision of the Presbytery and to sever that connection. This sifting process was, however, arrested by an exception taken against this action and against the Presbyterian decree upon which it was based. By common consent, the case was carried over the intermediate court immediately to the General Assembly, which body sustained the exception, declaring, 'that as Mr. Clapp had neither been dismissed nor suspended by the Presbytery, he ought to be regarded as a member of that body, and that in the opinion of the Assembly, they have sufficient reasons for proceeding to try him upon the charge of error in doctrine.'

"The case being thus remanded to the Presbytery had to be taken up anew. Meanwhile the agitation in the bosom of the church could not be allayed. On the 13th of January, 1832, fifteen members, including elders McNair and Caldwell, were dismissed at their request, for the purpose of forming another church upon the principles of the doctrine and discipline of the Presbyterian Church. This seceding body worshipped in a warehouse of Mr. Cornelius Paulding, opposite Lafayette Square, on the site covered by the building in which we are now assembled. It enjoyed the services of the Rev. Mr. Harris; but the references to it are scant and after a brief and flickering existence, its elements were reabsorbed into the First Church. Meanwhile the Presbytery concluded its proceedings in the trial of Mr. Clapp, on the 10th of January, 1833; when he was deposed from the office of the ministry, and his relations to the church, which had only been those of a Stated Supply and not of an installed pastor, were finally cancelled. The roll of communicants, just before the secession of 1832, numbered *eighty-nine.*

"Presbyterianism had now to start anew, from a beginning quite as small as at first. The social and amiable qualities of Mr. Clapp endeared him greatly as a man; the large majority of his hearers could not appreciate this clamor about doctrine; and many of the truly pious were slow to credit the extent of his departure from the faith, and were disposed to sympathize with him as one unkindly persecuted. The few, therefore, who came forth, exactly nine, with the two elders, Hennen and Maybin, found themselves in the condition of seceders who were houseless in the streets. Fortunately a spiritual guide was immediately provided. The Rev. Dr. Joel Parker, in the service of the American Home Mission Society, being in the city, was at once solicited to become their Stated Supply. His connection began January 12, 1833, and the little band worshipped alternately with the organism formed a year before under Mr. Harris, in the wareroom on Lafayette Square. These two wings finally coalesced in 1835. In March, 1834, Dr. Parker was unanimously chosen pastor, and on the 27th of April, was duly installed by the Presbytery of Mississippi. During this summer he was absent at the North, collecting funds for building a new House of Worship. Some statements made by him to Northern audiences respecting the religious conditions and necessities of New Orleans were grossly misrepresented in the public prints. A violent excitement was created against him in the city, indignation meetings were held, and he was once or twice burnt in effigy by the population. The storm was met with great firmness and dignity by the church, which rallied around its pastor, produced written evidence that Dr. Parker had been entirely misrepresented, and contended earnestly for the exercise of their own religious rights. In a short time the fierce opposition was quelled, and was eventually lived down.

"Upon the pastor's return in the autumn, worship was resumed in a room on Julia Street, until March 15, 1835, when the basement of the new building on Lafayette Square was first occupied. This edifice, so well remembered by many present, was erected at an original cost, including the site, of $57,616. Subsequently improvements and enlargements were made in 1844, with an additional purchase of ground, amounting to over $17,000 more; making the whole cost of the church, which was destroyed by fire in 1854, $75,000.

"Dr. Parker's connection with the church extended over a period of five years and six months, from January 12, 1833, to June 14, 1838, at which date he left, never to return. The pastoral relation was not, however, dissolved till the spring of 1839. During his pastorship, the church was greatly prospered, having secured a commodious sanctuary, and showing as early as 1836, a church roll numbering 142 communicants. There were two elections of elders: in 1834, Dr. John R. Moore, Frederick R. Southmayd and Truman Parmele being chosen to that office; and in 1838, Stephen Franklin, John S. Walton and James Beattie.

"The next incumbent of the pulpit was the Rev. Dr. John Breckenridge, with whom the church opened negotiations in February, 1839. This gentleman was at the time the Secretary of the Assembly's Board of Foreign Missions. In his letter to the church, dated May, 1839, he consents to serve it in conjunction with his secretaryship, from which his brethren were unwilling to release him, the Board giving him a dispensation of six or seven months for this purpose. These conditions being accepted, Dr. Breckenridge spent the winter of 1839, in New Orlenas; and still again the winter of 1840 till April of 1841. He was called to the eternal rest in August of 1841, retaining in his hand the call of this church as pastor elect. His labors were fragmentary, but efficient; and the church was left to mourn over hopes disappointed in his death.

"The attention of the church was soon turned to Rev. Dr. Wm. A. Scott, of Tuscaloosa, Ala., who was installed as pastor on the 19th of March, 1843, and whose pastoral relation was formally dissolved in

September, 1855. His active connection with the church, however, began and closed earlier than these dates. His term of service as pastor-elect began in the fall of 1842, and his active labors ceased in November, 1854, covering a period of twelve years. Dr. Scott's ministry was exceedingly productive, during which vigorous and constant efforts were made to build up the interests of Presbyterianism in the city. The roll of communicants swelled in 1844 to 439, and before the close of his ministry to 600.

"On the 20th of July, 1845, Dr. J. M. W. Picton and Chas. Gardiner were ordained to the office of ruling elders; and Thomas Bowman and William P. Campbell, to that of deacon. On the 23d of December, 1849, R. B. Shepherd, W. P. Campbell and W. A. Bartlett were ordained to the Eldership; and W. H. Reese, L. L. Brown and James Rainey, to the diaconate; and on the 28th of November, 1852, the Bench of Deacons was increased by the installation of W. C. Black, Robt. A. Grinnan and Simon Devisser—and of J. G. Dunlap on the 23d of January, 1853.

"The church edifice was burnt on the 29th of October, 1854; and it is to the last degree creditable to the congregation that among all the discouragements of a vacant Bishopric and a congregation scattered, it should have proceeded at once to build another of larger proportions and more finished in style. In 1857 the house in which we are now assembled was finished and dedicated to the worship of God. Its cost with all its appointments was about $87,000.

"On the 21st of September, 1854, a call was made out to the Rev. B. M. Palmer, of South Carolina, which upon being presented before his Presbytery and Synod was defeated by the refusal of those bodies to place it in his hands. The call was renewed on the 16th of March, 1856, and prevailed. His labors began early in December of that year, and on the 28th of the same month he was installed by the Presbytery of New Orleans. After a lapse of seventeen years, he is present to-night to read this record of God's exceeding faithfulness and mercy to his redeemed people. It is only proper to add, that the membership of this church, which, after Dr. Scott's withdrawal was thrown down to 350, was carried up in 1861, just before the war, to 531. By the war in 1866, it was again reduced to 436, and now reaches to 648.

"Three successful Mission Schools are sustained and two buildings erected for their accommodation, one of these large and comfortable, at a cost of some $10,000. It is now sustaining a City Missionary, which it has often done in the past, and always with marked results in the extension of the cause so dear to all our hearts."

In the church thus described he began his labors as early as December 9, 1856. On the nineteenth day of the month he was received into the Presbytery of New Orleans. The Presbytery at once arranged for his installation at 3 P.M.,

December 28, 1856. At the installation services the Rev. J. R. Hutchinson, Moderator of the Presbytery, preached from Rom. 11:13, "I magnify mine office," on "The Dignity and Importance of the Ministerial Office," a topic which the candidate for installation was to illustrate in a most remarkable way.

In a few months it was his privilege to preach a sermon dedicatory of the new church building—a most imposing edifice of the Gothic type of architecture, with an audience room capable of seating from fifteen hundred to two thousand people. He made use of the sermon he had preached at the dedication of the church built by him in Columbia; in which he set for himself again, as well as for his people, a high ideal in worship.

Dr. Palmer was now in a new field. It was quite possible for him to relax his efforts in the construction of sermons. He had accumulated a large stock of briefs. We, indeed find that he is not insensible to the fact; find that he uses some of his best old sermons—some of them the products of his youthful labors at Savannah, and more of them made in Columbia; but we find no sign of relaxation, old briefs are reworked, if used, and take nobler forms; and new ones are added to his stores week after week. Some of these new ones he liked very much apparently. When he travelled they went with him; and other congregations than his own heard them. A study of these briefs shows that he continued to preach the Gospel and the whole Gospel; and that, except in one or two instances, he preached nothing but the Gospel.

He had captured the people of his church with his first sermon to them. He speedily and mightily confirmed his dominion over them during the early months of his ministry—a dominion that was to be regal thence to his death and even after his death. As the weeks and months passed, his sphere widened beyond the limits of his own congregation and of his own church. A multitude scattered throughout the city and the sphere of its influence developed an interest in his preaching. This is evidenced by the reproduction of not a few of his sermons in secular newspapers. A portion of the New Orleans press at that date showed a most commendable readiness to open their columns to sermons of a high order of instructiveness. A visit to the New Orleans City Archives and a glance at the great dailies of the years 1857 to 1861 will enable one to read some of Dr. Palmer's sermons in full; and compendious reports of many others. They were not published because they were in any way sensational. They are noble didactic discourses.

His teaching was not confined to preaching on the Sabbath and lecturing on Wednesday evenings to his prayer meeting. On two other week-day evenings he lectured to special classes organized for the study of the Bible.

His individual dealing with those who sought his spiritual counsel was marked by wonderful power of diagnosis, by equally wonderful facility in pointing them to the very truths needed, and by the tactful but courageous and resolute application of the truth. Let an account of his dealing with an inebriate serve to illustrate his skill in dealing with individuals.[3] He told the story as follows, in 1869:

"I was seated one Friday evening in my parlor, enjoying the society of a few friends by the family fire-place, when the door-bell rang, with a hesitating sound, as if touched by a weak or a trembling hand. Obeying the summons myself, without waiting for a servant, the dim light of the street revealed a stranger, who addressed me thus:

"'I presume you are the Rev. ———. If so I would be glad to speak to you alone, in your study.'

"Ushering him upstairs into the little back room, where, each week, the olive oil is beaten for the lamps of the sanctuary, the lighted gas disclosed a form in which it was impossible not to be immediately interested. He was a little above the average height, with a well-knit frame and a graceful carriage, which betrayed him as familiar with good society. A broad forehead—which seemed the more expansive as it merged into a perfectly bald crown—and the clearly cut and compressed lips, were symbols alike of character and intellect. The eye, alas! which should have expressed even more, was blood-shot and streaked with veins, while the entire countenance was haggard and flushed. I had scarcely time for a superficial glance, when he sank upon a chair, and bowed his head between his arms, crossed upon the table, and in that position he sobbed aloud for the space of ten minutes. Satisfied that I was in the presence of a gentleman who would soon be able to assert himself, and direct the interview, I waited patiently for this paroxysm of feeling to pass by, without interposing a word.

"Lifting himself, at length, he turned his face upon mine, and in choice language recited his personal history, substantially as follows:

"'You have before you, sir, a man who has fallen from the highest social position to the lowest degradation. At an early age I was left to the care of a widowed mother, and was reared with all that fond

[3] Dr. Palmer contributed this account to the *Southwestern Presbyterian,* April 29, 1869, but not over his own name.

affection likely to be lavished upon an only child. I was furnished with the advantages of a liberal education, and entered, at my majority, upon the possession of a handsome estate. Prosecuting the study of the law, and admitted to its practice, I was rising gradually in that profession, which promised to reward me with honorable distinction. In due course of time I was united in marriage with a lovely wife, whose intellectual gifts, personal charms, and amiable temper are such as seldom have blessed a human home. And, to crown the whole, I was a professor of religion, and esteemed a worthy member of the Church of God. In the midst of all this earthly prosperity, whilst life was blooming around me like the ancient paradise, I was seized, two years ago, with the insane desire of becoming suddenly rich, and yielded to the temptation of abandoning my profession, in order to speculate in whiskey! Separated by my new calling from the sweet influences of home, and surrounded by the associations which belong to such a traffic, I have fallen a victim to its baneful power, and am now before you a degraded sot! upon the verge of *delirium tremens*. The two weeks that I have spent in your city have been spent in a deep debauch. These two letters [which he took from a side pocket] have been lying, unanswered, all that time; and not till this afternoon have I been sober enough to break the seals, and learn their contents. I have, however, read them over and over again, and you see they are blotted and stained with my tears. I am overwhelmed with remorse; listen to them, and see how they plead with such a wretch as I am!'

"Choking with the emotion which often interrupted the perusal, he then unfolded and read to me the first of these letters; it was from his mother, and a more eloquent and pathetic appeal never flowed, even from a mother's pen. It began with her early widowhood, when 'the strong staff was broken, and the beautiful rod' upon which she had leaned. It told how her bruised affections had gathered around the only child spared to be the comfort of those weary years; and her heart had grown warm with hope as this boy developed into manhood. It described the fulness of her gratitude when these hopes seemed to be realized in the rich promise of his later years, and the proud joy she felt when, in his pride, she clasped a daughter in her arms. It depicted the beauty of his home, where now two prattling babes whispered the name of the absent father. Then came the fearful contrast: how the Tempter entered into this Eden, and with him the blighting of hopes, and the ruin of her son. Upon the back of all this, poured the passionate entreaty—breaking, like a wail, from a dying woman's heart—that the wanderer would come back to the endearments of home, and walk, evermore, in the paths of honor and virtue. The appeal was enough to move a heart of stone. It made me, a stranger, weep; no wonder that he, to whom it was addressed, shook beneath its breath, like a reed before the storm.

"He then opened the second letter. It began: *'My darling husband.'*

Ah! this tenderness of a still loving wife; it cut with an edge keener than that of reproach—to the very core of his remorse. Throwing the sheet upon the table, he covered his face with his hands, and sobbed—without an effort at self-control. It was too much for me, as well as for him, so I put out my hand, gently, to his, and said, 'Put up that letter, Mr. B.; it is from your wife, and let no one come into the sanctuary of that confidence. I was not unwilling to hear the pleadings of your mother—the words of a wife are too sacred.'

"Replacing the letters in his pocket, he turned and said with something like vehemence, 'My dear sir, will you pray for me?' Kneeling down together, I poured forth one of those wrestling prayers in which the argument grows, and the fervor deepens, as we advance, that it would please God to change this remorse into penitence; that the blood of Christ might purge this conscience, groaning under a sense of guilt; that the Holy Spirit might renew and save this poor sinner, upon whom God had so just and perfect a claim. Scarcely had we risen before he cried out, 'Oh! sir, pray for me again!' We knelt a second time; and so a third—and then a fourth—a fifth; when the sixth request came I paused, and said, 'Mr. B., this scene is becoming oppressive; I am afraid that we are in danger of those vain repetitions which the Savior condemns. It is right that we should go to God in prayer, for he is the only source of grace and strength to you in this hard battle with your vices. But we have told it all to God, and now he waits to hear from your own lips what you mean to do.'

"'Do!' said he, 'What can I do?'

"'My friend,' I replied; 'something else is required of you besides prayer; and by the very solemnity of the petitions we have offered here together, I summon you to decide what course you intend to pursue in the future.'

"'Tell me, sir, what I ought to do.'

"'Well, then, in the first place, you must extricate yourself from the accursed business which has been your ruin. Were I you, I would take the hogsheads of liquor you came here to sell, to the levee, and empty them all into the waters of the Mississippi.'

"'Ah, sir, I cannot do that, for I have partners equally implicated in the speculation.'

"Then, at any rate, wash your hands of the whole business, at once; will you do this?'

"'Yes, sir, I will, if I live to see to-morrow's sun.'

"'In the next place,' I resumed; 'go back, at once, to your neglected home, and there, under the sanctity of your widowed mother's prayer, and beneath the softening influences of your wife and babes, foster the purpose of reform. Resume the practice of your noble profession; and throw around yourself all the restraints and obligations of society. Will you do this?'

"'I will, sir,' was the instantaneous response.

"'Once more: I am bound in faithfulness to say to you that I have little confidence in the unaided strength of the human will to break the fetters of such a vice as holds you in its grasp; and none at all in the sinner's ability, without Divine grace, to repent, truly before God. Go, then, in your guilt and helplessness, to him whose promise is, 'though your sins be as scarlet, they shall be white as snow,' and throw yourself upon his mercy, in Christ, for pardon and eternal life.'

"'I can only promise, my dear sir,' was the response, 'to make an honest effort to obey your counsel in respect to this.'

"'What I wish to impress upon you, my friend,' I replied, 'is, that remorse is not repentance, and reformaton is not religion. Renew the covenant which you have broken, with your God, and do not rest until you have a sense of your "acceptance in the beloved."'

"Upon parting with him at the door, I said, 'Mr. B., do not touch a drop to-morrow, and come the next day to hear me preach.'

"On the following Sabbath I looked anxiously around the church for my visitor, in whose welfare I was now deeply interested; and, sure enough, over the gallery, not far from the pulpit, peered the face and head which could not be mistaken. I had found no difficulty in the selection of my theme, for the only dark feature of the conversation above narrated, was the disposition to throw the blame of his fall upon the circumstances which shaped his course. This danger I now sought to disclose, by choosing that passage from James which reads: 'Let no man say, when he is tempted, I am tempted of God; but every man is tempted when he is drawn away of his own lust,' etc. Tracing the genealogy of sin, as here taught, I attempted to show that outward temptations derived their power from the inclinations and state of our own hearts, as congenial therewith; that in every case of transgression, the sinner must assume the blame of his own misconduct; and that any attempt, however disguised, to throw it back upon God, involved the highest absurdity and self-contradiction, and added, immensely, to the guilt. The following day he called at my door to bid me adieu, as he proposed that evening to return to his home in the West, and said, 'You preached that sermon for me, on yesterday.'

"'Yes,' I answered, 'for once in my life I was intensely personal in the pulpit; I had no one in my thoughts but you; I meant every word to be appreciated by you.'

"'I thank you for it,' was the response; 'it was exactly what I needed. I see clearly, now, that I have been the author of my own ruin, and have no one to blame but myself.'

"'Unless you distinctly recognize your own guilt,' I answered, 'you will never deal honestly with God in your repentance. Take your whole burden to him, with perfect assurance that he will never turn the true penitent away, who pleads for mercy in the name of Christ, the Redeemer.'

"Some years elapsed—four of them years of bitter sectional war—

ere I had tidings of the poor returning prodigal. But shortly after my own restoration, from a long exile, to my own charge, a newspaper came to me, which, on being unfolded, contained a beautiful address, delivered at a Sabbath-school anniversary, in the State of ——. The next mail brought me a letter from my lost friend, stating that he had gone back to his home; regained the practice of his legal profession; had sought pardon, and had found peace through the blood of Christ, and was then serving as the superintendent of the Sabbath-school, and as a ruling elder in the House of God. Unfortunately, before this letter could be answered, as my grateful heart prompted, it was mislaid, and the address forever lost. If, by any chance, this sketch should meet his eye, the writer prays that it may be accepted as an invitation to reopen the intercourse so abruptly closed."

Other and equally striking illustrations might be given, of his efficiency in dealing with individuals.[4]

He had not been a great social visitor back in South Carolina. He had been too constantly tense for that. But he had been a good pastor. He had ever been on the alert to seize and to improve a strategic moment. Seasons of joy and particularly seasons of sorrow had not called in vain for his presence and for wise and timely work. To pastoral ministrations in seasons of sorrow, in New Orleans, also, he gave much time and effort. The worse the season of trial for his people the more certain was he to be at hand. He had in him the stuff of which heroes are made and was always ready to go to any bedside where his services were needed, no matter what terrors lurked there. In New Orleans, the flowers bloom as beautifully during the stalking of the pestilence as at any other time; the foliage is as rich and luxuriant, the sky is as bright; and like these other good gifts of Providence, Dr. Palmer was there with all his kindly ministrations.

Yellow fever had prevailed in New Orleans in 1853, 1854, and 1855. During 1853, out of a population of one hundred and fifty-four thousand, seven thousand, eight hundred and forty-nine persons had died of fever, and about twenty-five hundred in each of the two succeeding years. His friends back in South Carolina had held the terror of the scourge over

---

[4] See "A Morbid Experience," *Southwestern Presbyterian,* May 27, 1869.

his head to dissuade him from going to New Orleans. In the distance it did not terrify him. Nor was he terrified by it when it began again to cut down multitudes in the city of his choice. There seem to have been only about two hundred deaths from yellow fever in 1857, but in 1858 there were four thousand, eight hundred and fifty-eight deaths. During this year Dr. Palmer became pastor of people far beyond the pale of his own congregation. Some of the men of the cloth were absent from the city during the awful summer and autumn of 1858. Dr. Palmer being on the ground, in accord with his view that the pastor is needed most just in the hour of stress, pestilence and death, looked after not only his own, but all shepherdless sheep. Indeed, it was his custom, while on his beneficent rounds, ministering to his own people, to enter every house on the way which displayed the sign of fever within; to make his way quietly to the sick room, utter a prayer, offer the consolation of the Gospel, and any other service which it was in his power to give; and then as quietly to leave. A great Jewish Rabbi of New Orleans says: "It was thus that Palmer got the heart as well as the ear of New Orleans. Men could not resist one who gave himself to such ministry as this." This work cost Dr. Palmer not a little as will shortly appear.

It will be recalled that in his earlier charges Dr. Palmer had been a careful member of the session; that he was careful in receiving members into the Church; and resolute in securing the administration of discipline to those deserving of judicial censures. There are not wanting signs that he carried the same theory and the same habits with him into his new field. He had gone into a field which must have suggested changes; but he was no nose of wax. He went about his duties as a ruler in the house and kingdom of God tactfully. While using tact, he neither surrendered, merged, nor concealed his principles. Though desiring to live on the best practicable terms with Roman Catholics—the predominant element in the population of New Orleans—he continued to treat baptism as administered in that communion as invalid. A sessional decision to the effect of its invalidity, embodied in the records, March 4, 1860, may be taken as illustrative of his bearing throughout the period with regard to the principles of Presbyterian government generally.

The spiritual care of the blacks weighed heavily upon Dr. Palmer and his session. In the spring of 1859 the session passed a resolution to secure the permission of the mayor for the regular meeting of a colored congregation in the lecture room of the First Presbyterian Church. Soon after, Rev. B. Wayne was engaged to preach to the "blacks." They were modeling after Dr. Girardeau's Church in Charleston, S. C. Certain worthy and characterful blacks were made leaders of the colored people under the missionary and session. Late in December, 1859, Elder J. A. Maybin was put into the place previously thereto occupied by Mr. Wayne, who had discontinued his services.

Together with his session, Dr. Palmer took measures to secure joint meetings of the sessions of all the Presbyterian churches of the city with the view of conferring and praying for the spread of Presbyterianism throughout the city. In the autumn of 1859 the session is found trying to locate a mission Sunday-school. Such enterprises, as indeed his whole ministry, were to be suspended before much good could be accomplished; but they are valuable as showing the spirit of the man and his co-rulers in the First Presbyterian Church.

Services in behalf of the Church at large constituted a part of his labors from the outset of the New Orleans pastorate. In March, 1857, he was made the examiner of Presbytery in ecclesiastical history and polity, and the sacraments. In 1858 he was appointed by the Synod of Mississippi as a member of its committee to endeavor to secure the establishment in New Orleans of the Southwestern Advisory Committee as a branch of the Board of Domestic Missions. There was sore need of this. The four Southwestern States of Alabama, Mississippi, Louisiana and Texas with an area of 376,637 square miles, and a population of 2,108,502, had then only thirty missionaries, and received from the Board in the Northeast only $8,255, while contributing toward its cause $5,390.50, whereas four Northwestern States, Illinois, Indiana, Iowa and Wisconsin, with an area of 192,052 square miles, and a population of 2,337,491, had one hundred and ninety-eight missionaries, received from the Board $33,192, while contributing only $2,812.15. The brethren in the Southwest rejoiced in the number and success of the missionaries laboring in the Northwest. They understood that the excessive disproportion was due to natural causes, in large measure beyond human control. Dr. Palmer himself, in 1859, pictured the situation in the following terms:

"The West and Northwest are covered with a network of railroads, by which they are easily traversed, bringing their wants under the public eye; while the remoteness and inaccessibility of our territory screen its destitution alike from observation and from Christian sympathy. The poverty of our young ministers, together with the uncertainty of an immediate settlement, operates as a bar to their coming to so distant a region, and leads them to prefer a field lying nearer at hand. The debilitating nature of our climate, added to the perils of acclimation, so prodigiously exaggerated abroad, is an ever-present argument against these tropical regions. Insomuch, too, as the great body of our candidates for the ministry come from the Northern and Middle States, it is, perhaps, natural they should prefer to labor in those parts of the country where all the institutions and usages of society are familiar and congenial. They are also attracted by the promise of larger congregations afforded where the population is more dense; and can, with difficulty, be impressed with the representative character of our small assemblages at the South. It is, moreover, undeniable, and for a lamentation let it be written, that the purely missionary aspect of this field, as embracing a very large number of untutored blacks, is so much overlooked. In seeking a settlement, our young men too generally prefer a field affording more mental stimulus, and turn away from these 'poor who are ever with us,' in their ardor after greater intellectual improvement. All these causes, without dwelling upon others more strictly personal and private, combine to cut off the Southwest from that measure of supply to which it would seem fairly entitled. Upon a candid review of them, we can fully exonerate the officers of the Board, not only from censure, but even from the suspicion of partiality. We are willing to believe the sincerity and depth of their sympathy, while they behold our destitution, which they have not the power to overtake; and we as distinctly foresee that all these difficulties will embarrass any new and local agency that shall go into operation. But were they tenfold greater than they are, it is not possible that those, whose lot Providence has cast within this region, shall sit down and succumb beneath them. We should be recreant to the Church, and to our divine Lord and Master, if, under these circumstances, the question were not raised, What shall we do? Under the pressure of this great necessity, the proposition of a District Committee, with its own Secretary, has been submitted to the Assembly; and should nothing more be achieved by their future labors than to arouse the churches of the Southwest to a more anxious and prayerful contemplation of their duty, and to draw the attention of our rising ministry more largely to this neglected territory, even these results will justify the action of the Assembly in their appointment."

The Assembly of 1859 ordered the establishment of this Committee, an order which was executed in November of that year. Soon thereafter we find that in his church the third

Monday evening of each month is observed as a time for prayer and contributions for domestic missions under the control of the Advisory Committee of the Southwest.

By the Synod which met in January, 1861, he was appointed, along with two other ministers, to prepare a pastoral letter on the subject of Home Missions; with the result that a ringing letter of the sort desired was sent forth.

He was early made Chairman of the Board of Trustees of the Synodical Depository. He was made commissioner to the Assemblies of 1858 and 1859. Thus honors and duties crowded thickly upon him. He took quickly and easily the very first place not only in his city and Presbytery, but in his Synod and in the vast section of the Southwest.

During these years in New Orleans his pen was not altogether idle. It was employed not only in the production of carefully prepared briefs week after week, and of special sermons and lectures, but of occasional review articles. The chief ecclesiastical article was one of ninety-two pages in the *Southern Presbyterian Quarterly,* on "The General Assembly of 1859,"—a very elaborate and able review of the doings of that body. He excites a degree of surprise in the reader, who has been accustomed to associate soundness of doctrine with the name of Dr. Nathan L. Rice, when he teaches that, in the opening sermon, that noted polemic and divine had made a slip as to the nature of the intellectual assent involved in saving faith. Dr. Rice had seemed to make true faith, intellectually considered, to be specifically the same as speculative assent. His critic claims that in accord with evangelical confessions and the Scriptures, "the assent which characterizes true faith is specifically different from the assent of the ungodly, a cognition in which the affection of the heart enters as an essential element; and is not superadded as something separate and distinct;" that it is with the heart that man believeth unto righteousness; and that the immediate ground of cognition is the supernatural illumination of the Spirit. He handles Dr. Rice with the greatest deference but he handles him with no less skill than deference.

He gives a full and critical account of the Assembly's dealing with the various Boards in the Church in 1859, showing that they were criticised as freely as any modern committees are. It has already appeared that the Synod of Mississippi was very desirous of having a branch of the Board of Domestic Missions located in New Orleans. The matter had been pressed before the Assembly of 1858. It was again and successfully advocated before the Assembly of 1859.

The opponents of the measure intimated that the movement originated in sectional design; claimed that it militated against the unity of the effort to evangelize the whole country, and that it rested upon the false assumption that the Board was insufficient to accomplish its work; they stressed the point that the missionary operations depended upon the Presbyteries which could act through a common central agency as well as through agencies near at hand. Dr. Palmer tells us in his review article the substance of his plea for the establishment of the Committee:

"Against these positions, Dr. Palmer averred that this movement did not originate in any sectional design, but was intended merely to lengthen the arm of the Board, so that it might reach over the distant Southwest. The moneys raised would all be acknowledged in the receipts of the Board, and be under their control; though necessarily, for a considerable time, they must be disbursed upon that field. Special reasons might be urged for this arrangement at the Southwest, as the difficulties in the way of evangelizing that region were somewhat peculiar. The country itself was very remote from the center of the Church's operations, and could be reached only after a week's travel. The facilities for communicating with the interior were few, so that its exploration would be a work of toil and time. The population was exceedingly heterogeneous, with a singular admixture of strange and foreign habits. Over a large portion of this region a false and foreign religion still held the dominant sway. In some of these States there were no laws to enforce the observance of the Sabbath; and a Christian public sentiment must, to a large extent, be created. The people of God were few in number; and the wealth of the country, lying chiefly outside of the Church, could only be drawn out by persons known to the givers, and could not be reached by general appeals from Philadelphia. More than all, it was the door opening into a vast outlying territory, extending to the isthmus in one direction, and to the Pacific ocean in the other; a territory which, whether it shall be hereafter incorporated into this Union or not, must be overtaken by the Gospel, and that, too, through our instrumentality, in connection with other branches of the Christian Church. It was of little use for the general Secretary to run down and touch here and there a few points upon the border of this great and destitute missionary region. A district Secretary was needed, who should go patiently to work, explore the whole territory, ascertain its wants, and where missionaries could advantageously be located, raise funds for their support, visit our theological schools. and awaken an interest in the hearts of our candidates for the ministry. By such considerations, showing that the only purpose had in view was to aid the Board of Domestic Missions in that distant and difficult region, and not to impair the unity of the Church, the measure was carried in the Assembly by an overwhelming vote."

One of the most interesting debates in the Assembly of 1859 was precipitated over the Revised Book of Discipline. Dr. Thornwell was the Chairman of the Revision Committee, and delivered one of his lucid and powerful addresses, speaking only to certain general principles embodied in the Revised Book. After reporting this and other speeches *pro* and *con,* Dr. Palmer comments somewhat at length on views embodied in the Revised Book; and amongst others, on the relations of baptized members to the Church. On this subject his reflections were enough like the views subsequently embodied in the Standards of the Southern Presbyterian Church to suggest, what may afterwards appear, that his views were determinative in the framing of those portions of our Standards:

"The second proposition of the Committee, touching the relations of baptized members to the Church, is perhaps the most embarrassed with difficulties, and is the change upon which the Church most anxiously seeks light and guidance. The stringent doctrine advocated by some, that baptized youth, upon arriving at years of discretion, are to be constrained, upon penalty of excommunication, to consummate their union with the Church, we dare to affirm, never can prevail in the Presbyterian Church of this country, simply because the true idea of the Church, as a spiritual body, is more distinctly apprehended here than elsewhere. With all the deference we are accustomed to pay to the mother Church of Scotland and Ireland, in this particular it cannot be denied that the American Church is immeasurably in the advance. She cannot, therefore, stand by the side of a baptized youth and say, with or without the spiritual qualifications you must, under pain of excommunication, seal your connection with the Church by approaching the Lord's table. Nor can she, recognizing the sovereignty of divine grace both as to the time and manner of its bestowal, undertake to limit the probation of such an one; and say, at any one moment, now this matter of your conversion is to be taken into your own hands, and *now* the exhausted patience of the Church refuses any longer to indulge your procrastination. She may, with tears of affection, press upon his conscience the exhortations of God's word, and urge the promises of Jehovah's covenant; but she has no authority from her divine Head to urge him, without the necessary qualifications, to pass into the inner sanctuary; nor yet, if he should refuse to hear, to thrust him out into the court of the Gentiles. From her prevailing practice in this particular, we have no idea that the American Presbyterian Church, with her conception of a spiritual religion, will ever be induced to swerve.

"On the other hand, there is floating in the mind of the Church the impression that our baptized youth are, in such a sense, amenable to the discipline of the Church, that her authority may and should, in some way, be brought to bear upon their lives. How far this discipline should be carried, and in what form it should be administered, are precisely the points which the Church has never settled to her own satisfaction, and it is probably this want of precision and definiteness which has led to almost the universal neglect of all discipline. There is, however, lying in many minds, a painful apprehension that in this neglect the Church is criminal, and multitudes are anxously seeking their way through the difficulties which environ this whole subject. We are persuaded that the shyness of the Church in taking up the Revised Book of Discipline is, to some extent, explained by the embarrassment we have just indicated. On the one hand, not prepared to adopt the rigid discipline based by some upon a strict construction of the phraseology of the present book; on the other hand, not prepared to relax her hold entirely upon her baptized members, the Church considerately pauses to see if there be no *via media* between these extremes. Now, the proposition of the committee, which we understand to be a medium between these conflicting views, seems to us very nearly to meet the difficulty, and we venture modestly to suggest that if the committee, in its further deliberations, will render their middle ground a little more definite and clear, it will go far to harmonize the Church, and prepare the way for a final deliverance upon this subject. We understand their position to be, that while baptized persons are members of the Church, and are under its care and government, they are not proper subjects of *judicial process;* that is to say, discipline may be taken in a wide or in a narrow sense, so that they shall be under it in the one sense and not in the other. Now, if the committee shall be able to define in what form discipline shall be administered without judicial process—how the Church in the exercise of authority may take cognizance of flagrant immoralities in her baptized members, so as to distinguish between them and communicating members, they will succeed in untying the Gordian knot, and the Church will probably come without hesitation to her decision. The difficulty is a real one, to which side soever we choose to turn. The conscience of the Church is sorely tried on the one hand by the discordance between her present neglect of all discipline and the rigid requirements of the existing book; on the other hand, the nature and degree of the government and discipline recognized by the Revised Book, are so undefined as to afford no working rule by which the discretion of the Church can be guided. We greatly fear that the committee may yield to a reaction of feeling, and may expunge all this portion of the revised code. This we would deplore, and respectfully submit, that to remand the Church to the provisions of the old book will not, in the least degree, help the matter, since the difficulty in the recognition and practice of these is fully as great as with the suggestions they have ventured in their revision."

There were several articles produced in the period, some of which will receive incidental notice in the pages to follow.

It was inevitable that he should be called upon for occasional sermons and addresses. One of the ablest and most elegant of these was delivered before the Fayette Female Academy, July 28, 1859, upon "Female Excellence." He pleads for woman's cultivation in the features of *elegance,* of *grace,* of a *richly stored* and *highly trained mind,* of *well regulated affections,* of *sincere piety,* and of *power* to appreciate labor, and to consecrate herself to it. The address was published in pamphlet form by the Trustees of the institution.

By far the most noted occasional sermon of the period was his last "Thanksgiving Sermon," preached in 1860; but of that sermon, its reception, and influence, we shall read in the next chapter.

CHAPTER XI.

ANTE-BELLUM PERIOD IN NEW ORLEANS.—Continued.

December, 1856—May, 1861.)

THE STATE OF THE COUNTRY IN NOVEMBER, 1860.—DR. PALMER'S VIEWS ON THE SUBJECT OF SECESSION.—THE ACTION OF SOUTH CAROLINA, NOVEMBER AND DECEMBER, 1860.—PALMER, A SON OF SOUTH CAROLINA, UNDER THE STRESS OF THE TIMES PREACHES SOUTH CAROLINA POLITICS: HIS FAMOUS THANKSGIVING SERMON.—THE RECEPTION ACCORDED THE SERMON BY HIS AUDIENCE, AND BY THE WIDER PUBLIC.—HIS DOMESTIC HISTORY DURING THIS PERIOD.—HIS LABORS AS A COMFORTER.—HONORS ACCORDED HIM.

THE autumn of 1860 was a critical time in the history of the United States. The country had just passed through its most heated political canvass. A party had ridden into power which, in the belief of Southern men, and of many Northern men as well, threatened the liberties of the people, the stability and even the life, of republican institutions. For decades men had believed in the right of States to secede from the Federal Union upon provocation which they deemed to be adequate. The men of the South, generally, still maintained the right. Dr. Palmer was of this belief.

Being a South Carolinian, the belief came to him as an inheritance; but it had become his also as a student of American history. The political faith which he entertained at this time, he expounded, early in the year 1861, in rejoinder to the somewhat confused teachings of the Rev. Dr. Robt. J. Breckenridge, on secession. After certain preliminaries he said:

"The dispute is whether this sovereignty *(jus summi imperii)* resides in the people as they are, merged into the mass, one undivided whole; or in the people as they were originally formed into colonies, and afterwards into States, combining together for the purposes distinctly set forth in their instruments of Union. Dr. Breckenridge maintains the former thesis; we defend the latter; and in the whole controversy upon the legal right of secession this is the *cardo causae.*

"What, then, is the testimony of history? We find the first Continental Congress, at New York, in 1765, called at the suggestion of the House of Representatives of Massachusetts, and composed of deputies from all the Colonial Assemblies represented therein. We find, in 1773, at the instance of the Virginia House of Burgesses, the different Colonial Assemblies appointing Standing Committees of Correspondence, through whom a confidential communication was kept up between the Colonies. We find the votes in the Continental Congress of 1774, at Philadelphia, cast by Colonies, each being restricted to one only. We find in the celebrated Declaration of Independence, in 1776, 'the Representatives of the United States, in General Congress, assembled,' publishing and declaring 'in the name and by the authority of the people of these Colonies.' We find the Articles of Confederation, matured in 1777, remanded to the local legislatures, and ratified by the several States—by Maryland, not until 1781. The circular in which this form of confederation was submitted, requests the States 'to authorize their delegates in Congress to subscribe the same in behalf of the State,' and solicits the dispassionate attention of the Legislatures of the respective States, under a sense of the difficulty of combining in one general system the various sentiments and interests of a continent divided into so many sovereign and independent communities.[1] We recite these familiar facts to show that during the first period of our history, embracing the revolutionary struggle, the people were accustomed to act, not as an organic whole, but as constituting separate States, and combining for common and specified ends. Indeed, it could not be otherwise. Upon throwing off their allegiance to the British crown, and the sovereignty reverting to themselves, they were not destitute of a political organization through which to act. They had existed as organized, though not independent, communities before. What more natural, in their transition to new political relations, than to stand forth the communities they actually were? As separate Colonies they had been dependencies of the British crown: when that dependence was thrown aside, in whom could the original sovereignty reside, but in the people, who were now no longer Colonies, but States—in which form of existence the people are first represented to our view? The fact that they combined against a common foe, and to secure their independence together, does not impeach their inherent sovereignty. It remains perfectly discretionary with them—that is, with the people, as States—to determine how much of this sovereignty they will retain, and how much they will surrender, in the arrangements afterwards made. In the language of Chief Justice Jay, quoted by Mr. Story, 'thirteen sovereignties were considered as emerging from the principles of the Revolution combined by local convenience and considerations—though they continued to manage their national concerns as *'one people.'* We accordingly reverse Dr. Breckenridge's proposition; we are not 'one Nation divided into many States,' but we are many States uniting to form one nation.

"But let us see how the matter stands from the period of the old Confederation to the adoption of the present Constitution, in 1787.

[1] Story's *History of the Confederation.*

When the former was found to be breaking down from its own imbecility, and the necessity of a more perfect union was becoming apparent, it is curious to see how the pathway was opened through the almost accidental action of State Legislatures. In 1785, commissioners were appointed by the States of Virginia and Maryland to form a scheme for promoting the navigation of the River Potomac and the Chesapeake Bay. As they felt the need of more enlarged powers to provide a local naval force, and the tariff of duties upon imports, this grew into an invitation from Virginia to the other States to hold a convention for the purpose of establishing a general system of commercial relations—and this, at length, at the instance of New York, was enlarged, so as to provide for the revision and reform of the articles of the old Federal Compact. Thus grew up, by successive steps, the Convention which met at Philadelphia in 1787, by which the present Constitution was drafted, submitted to Congress as the common organ of the States, and by it referred for ratification to these States respectively. Here we have the same great principle of the sovereignty of the people, as they are States, clearly recognized. The tentative efforts toward improving the interior commercial relations of the country, are initiated by two State Legislatures; by a third, a Convention of Delegates from all the States is suggested; and the new Constitution is finally debated and ratified by separate Conventions of the people in each—North Carolina withholding her assent till 1789, and Rhode Island till 1790. This historical review seems, to us, conclusive of the point in hand. The people—not as one, but as thirteen—revolt from the English yoke; because only as thirteen, and not as one, did they ever owe allegiance. The people—not as one, but as thirteen—unite to carry on a defensive and successful war; granting to the Continental Congress just the powers they saw fit—neither more nor less—as their common agent. The people—not as one, but as thirteen—prepare and adopt Articles of Confederation, under which they manage their common concerns for seven years. And finally—not as one, but again as thirteen—they frame and adopt a permanent Constitution; under which they have lived for seventy years, and have grown from thirteen to thirty-four. But suppose the two dilatory States, which withheld their assent to the Constitution for two and three years, had withheld it altogether. What then? Why, says Dr. Breckenridge, 'they would have passed by common consent into a new condition, and have become, for the first time, separate sovereignty to any State, 'except as they are *united* States.' How, then, but not separate in the sense of being *distinct*. But he has denied sovereignty to any State, 'except as they are *United* States.' How, then, shall these two States, who, by supposition, refused to be united, become sovereign? 'By common consent,' says Dr. Breckenridge, 'they will pass into that condition.' But on what is this common consent to be based? Why not coerce them into the Union, if the people is one

Nation, and these States are fractions of that Union? Certainly it is just because their refusal to concur would be an exercise of sovereignty, and it must needs be recognized as such. Yet, if the *refusal* to concur would be an act of sovereignty, then, by equality of reason, was their *agreement* to concur an act of sovereignty. In either case, the people of these two States—and so of all the others—were antecedently and distinctively sovereign; and hence, could not owe their sovereignty to the Union which they themselves created. It is reasoning in a circle to say that the States are sovereign only as they are *United* States, when by the force of the term, as well as by the express testimony of history, they are united only by a Union which is created in the exercise of their sovereignty. We commend this fact to the attention of Consolidationists: that two States did, for the term of three years, delay to come into the Union under the Constitution, although they were previously in it under the Confederation. It clearly proves that the people formed the Constitution as States, and not as a consolidated nation. And that these States were not merely election districts, into which the one nation was conveniently distributed—but were organized communities, invested with the highest attributes of sovereignty, which they exercised again and again, by and through their supreme Conventions. If, as States, they could legally refuse to come into the Union, why may they not as legally withdraw from it? Upon the law maxim, '*expressio unius est exclusio alterius,*' this attribute of sovereignty remains, unless in the instrument it can be shown to be explicitly resigned.

"It is plain, then, that before and at the adoption of the Constitution, these States were independent and sovereign. Have they ceased to be such by their assent to that instrument? Or, is the Federal Union simply a covenant between the people of these States for mutual benefits, and under conditions that are distinctly entered into the bond? Let us see. Much stress is laid upon the use of the words, 'the people,' in the preamble of the Constitution—conveying, it is alleged, the idea of an undivided nationality. It is, however, a plain canon of interpretation, that particular terms are to be explained by the context in which they occur. This preamble further states, that 'we, the people,' are 'the people of the United States;' a title evidently intended to embody the history of the formation of the Union as a *congressus* of States, which, by aggregation, make up one people. In proof of this, it is a title simply transferred from the old Confederation, when no one denies that the States were separate and independent. This fact is conclusive. As the Nation is formed by the confluence of States, a periphrastic title is given, which defines the character of this nationality, as not being consolidated, but federated. It is not a little remarkable, that no other title is employed throughout the Constitution but this of 'United States;' the composition of which, historically, describes confederation, and discriminates against consolidation. How does it happen, if the idea of a nation, as composed of individuals, simply districted into States, is the fundamental idea, not only that a baptismal name was withheld which should embody that conception, but that, on the contrary, a composite title was given, which marks precisely the opposite?

"Let us now pass from the vestibule, and examine the framework of the Constitution itself. The first section of Article I. vests the Legislative power in a Congress consisting of two Chambers, a Senate and House of Representatives. In the latter, population is represented. But what population? the people of the Nation as a unit, or the people of the States? Unquestionably, the latter: for Section 4 provides that 'the time, places and manner of holding the election shall be prescribed in each State by the Legislature thereof.' Should a vacancy occur, 'writs of election are to be issued by the executive authority of each State.' Thus the States, individually, direct the election, and count and declare the vote. Plainly, this is done by the States, either as mere election districts, or else as organized communities, in the exercise of a supreme right. In addition to what has already been urged, the fact of apportioning these representatives to the States respectively, according to the population of each, concludes against the theory that the people are fused into the mass, and determines for the idea that, under the Constitution, as before its adoption, the people represented are the people of the States in Congress assembled. In the Senate the case is still clearer, for these States are represented as such, all being placed upon the same footing, the largest having no more power than the least. If you turn to the Executive branch of the Government, the President and Vice President are chosen by the people, indeed, but still by the people as constituting States. The electors must equal in number the representation which the State enjoys in Congress; and they must be chosen in such manner as each State, through its Legislature, shall determine. (Con., Art. II.) Should the election fail with the people, it must go into the Congressional House of Representatives, with the remarkable provision, that the 'vote is there to be taken by States, the representation from each State having one vote.' Why so, if not to forestall the possibility, through the inequality of the States in that chamber, of a President being chosen by a numerical majority merely, without being chosen by a concurrent majority of the States? We submit to the candor of the reader, if these constitutional provisions are not framed upon the conception that the people are contemplated as States, and not as condensed into a nation. If this latter were the fundamental idea, could arrangements be made more effectively to conceal or to cancel it?

"But it is urged that, in the adoption of the Constitution, the States have remitted, in great part, their sovereignty; and have clothed the General Government with supreme authority in the powers they have conferred. 'Congress shall have power,' says the Constitution (Sec. 8, Art. I.) 'to levy and collect taxes, to regulate commerce, to coin money, to declare war, to negotiate peace,' and the like; all which, it is alleged, are the acts of a sovereign. Precisely so: Congress shall have the *executive power;* but the Constitution does not say the *inherent right.* The distinction between these two goes to the bottom of the case, and will clear up much prevalent misconception. The people of the States have not parted with one jot or tittle of their original sovereignty. According to primitive republicanism, it is impossible they should do so. It exists unimpaired, just where it always resided, in the people constituting States. But these States, sustaining many relations to each other and to foreign nations, concur to manage those external matters in common. In their confederation for this purpose, they create an organ common to them all. To that agent they confide certain trusts, which are particularly enumerated; and that it may be competent to discharge the same, they invest it with certain powers, which are carefully defined. They consent to put a certain limitation upon the exercise of their individual sovereignty, so far as to abstain from the functions assigned to this common agent. They come under a mutual pledge to recognize and to sustain this established Constitution, *quoad* its purposes, as the paramount law. But all this by no means implies the delegation of their sovereignty to the general government. Power is often conferred upon municipal corporations to perform certain functions pertaining to sovereignty—as, for example, the power of taxation. But who ever dreamed that these corporations became thus *ipso facto* sovereigns; or that the State, in conferring such charters, remitted any portion of its supremacy? In like manner, the several States, in granting these powers to Congress, granted them in trust, for purposes purely executive: retaining the right inherent in themselves to revoke these powers, and to cancel at will the instrument by which they are conveyed. We confess our inability to understand this doctrine of a double sovereignty: a sovereignty which, while it is delegated to the general government, is nevertheless supreme; and a sovereignty which, while it is retained by the States as a part of their original inheritance, is nevertheless subordinate. The very terms of either proposition appear to be solecisms. Sovereignty, however limited it may be in actual exercise, is simple, and incapable of distribution. It is a still greater contradiction to speak of a sovereign who is under subjection to a superior authority. We can very well understand how several sovereignties shall unite upon schemes which can only be executed by a restraint voluntarily imposed; but not how they shall create a power that is superior to them all. Accordingly, we find the Constitution providing in its very last article for 'the establishment of this Constitution'—not *over,* but *'between*—the States ratifying the same.' The distinction between these two propositions is not metaphysical, but immensely practical and substantive. The first would establish the government of a superior over subjects who obey; the second establishes a common law between equals who recognize and sustain. Still more emphatic is the tenth amendment to the Constitution, which specifies that 'all powers not delegated to the United States are reserved to the States respectively, or to the people.' This betrays the jealousy which watched over the formation of the Union, showing the grant to the general government to be a grant of specified and executive powers, while all the rest remains, by inherent right, with the States in their local and permanent organization, or with the people of those States in their primal and inalienable sovereignty.

"This exposition of the relation of the States to the Federal Union, is confirmed by the debates in the Convention which formed the Constitution, in 1787. Aware of the weakness of the existing Confederation, it is not strange that a party arose desirous of strengthening the central power. It was urged against the new Constitution, that no tribunal was erected to determine controversies which might arise between the States and the Nation. The Supreme Court was restricted in its jurisdiction to causes in law and equity, and could not adjudicate political differences. The proposition was, therefore, submitted to extend its powers, so as to make it the arbiter of all issues that might arise. It did not, however, prevail so as be articulated into the Constitution. Of course, the States were thrown back upon the great principle of international law, that every sovereign must decide for himself in controverted issues, under a sense of responsibility to the opinion of mankind, and the verdict of impartial history. To show still further the relation of the States to the Union, we will cite another fact. Three resolutions were introduced into the Convention, the first declaring 'that a Union of the States *merely federal* will not accomplish the objects proposed by the Articles of Confederation;' the second, 'that no treaty or treaties between the States, as sovereign, will secure the common defence;' the third, 'that a *national* government ought to be established,'[2] etc. The first two resolutions were immediately tabled; the third was adopted; but afterwards, in the course of debate, undue stress being laid upon the word 'national' it was changed into 'the government of the United States.'[3]

"Another method was proposed, to provide for the danger of collision between the Federal and State authorities. The sixth of Governor Randolph's famous fifteen resolutions empowered 'the Federal Executive to call forth the force of the Union against *any member of the Union* failing to fulfill his duties under the articles thereof.'[4] This suggestion utterly failed to secure the assent of the Convention, and the resolution was abridged as to this feature of it. The strongest Centralists in the body, as Mr. Madison and Mr. Hamilton, repudiated the principle, as tantamount to a declaration of war and a dissolution of the Union, and utterly repugnant to the genius and spirit of this Government. We

[2] Elliot's *Debates,* Vol. I., p. 391. [3] *Ibid.,* p. 427. [4] *Ibid.,* p. 144.

cannot burthen this article with the citation of authorities. These general facts are sufficient to show the view taken by the framers of the Constitution, as to the relations between the States and the central authority. They are of no little significance, at a time like this, when so many are clamoring for the coercion of the South, whether it be a *coercion of laws* or a *coercion of arms.* The puerile distinction had not occurred to these wise men of a past age, between coercing a State and the coercion of its citizens alone: a distinction perfectly legitimate, when a State professes to recognize the authority of the Union, and unlawful combinations of individuals exist to resist the same; but a distinction utterly impertinent, when the State asserts her sovereign jurisdiction over her citizens, and disclaims any longer participation in the Federal Union. Manifestly, if a State, while in the Union, may not be coerced by Federal power, without its 'being tantamount to a declaration of war,' then, *ex fortiori,* she may not be coerced when by her sovereign act the bonds have been sundered by which she was held under the compact, and she stands wholly without the pale of the Union.

"The longest argument must have an end. We advert, finally, to the notorious fact, that in the very act of ratifying this Constitution, three States asserted their sovereign right to resume the powers they had delegated. New York declared 'that the powers of government may be reassumed by the people whenever it shall become necessary to their happiness:'[5] and further indicates what people she means, by speaking, in the same connection, of the residuary power and jurisdiction in the people of the State, not granted to the General Government. The delegates from Virginia 'declare and make known, in the name and in the behalf of the people of Virginia, that the powers granted under the Constitution, being derived from the people of the United States, may be resumed by them whensoever the same shall be perverted to their injury and oppression.'[6] In like manner, Rhode Island protests against the remission of her right of resumption. And while the language is not so explicit as that of New York, the meaning is precisely the same; for, as the original grantor of these powers was the people of the States, and not the collective people of the country at large, the former alone had the right to reassume. The other States made no such declarations. Indeed, as the right lay in the very nature and history of the federation, they could be made by these three only in the way of superabundant caution. This right, so solemnly asserted seventy years ago, has been sleeping upon the records of the country. It is now brought into exercise by seven States, and the issue can no longer be blinked. If the insane advice gratuitously tendered in this pamphlet should be followed by the Federal authorities, the war that ensues will be a war of principle as well as of passion: and the South

[5] Elliot's *Debates,* Vol. I., p. 327. [6] *Ibid.*

will know that she is contending against tyranny in theory as well as tyranny in practice.

"It would thus appear the doctrine of withdrawal from the Union is not so novel as it has been supposed by those who scout it as monstrous. Let us see if it has not made its appearance more than once in the history of the country. When Mr. Jefferson was made Secretary of State, after his return from France, he was warmly importuned by Mr. Hamilton to throw his influence in favor of the assumption of the State debts, in order to save the Union from threatened dissolution. 'He,' says Mr. Jefferson, 'painted pathetically the temper into which the legislatures had been wrought; the disgust of those who were called the creditor States; the danger of the *secession* of their members, and the separation of the States;'[7] which was only averted by bringing over two of the Virginia delegation (White and Lee) to support the measure. At a later period, the passage of the Embargo Act, it is well known, inflamed the New England States to the highest degree; so that on the floor of Congress it was declared, 'they were repining for a secession from the Union.' In the Hartford Convention, at which five of the Eastern States were represented, the report which was adopted uses the following language: 'Whenever it shall appear that these causes are radical and permanent, a separation by equitable arrangement will be preferable to an alliance by constraint among nominal friends, but real enemies, inflamed by mutual hatred and jealousy,' etc. Again: 'In cases of deliberate, dangerous and palpable infractions of the Constitution, affecting the sovereignty of a State and the liberties of the people, it is not only the right, but the duty, of such a State to interpose its authority for their protection, in the manner best calculated to secure that end. When emergencies occur which are beyond the reach of the judicial tribunals, or too pressing to admit of the delay incident to their forms, States, which have no common umpire, must be their own judges, and execute their own decisions.' It is a little curious that these avowals of the right of secession should come from the very section which is most chargeable with begetting the present schism: and that the very people now most ready to arm themselves for the coercion of the South could plead for an equitable and peaceful separation, so long as it was meditated by themselves. The infamy attached to the Hartford Convention springs not from their exposition of political doctrine, but from the insufficiency of the cause impelling them to a breach of compact, and from the want of patriotism which could meditate such a step when the country was in the midst of a war with a foreign enemy.

"We have thus argued the legal right of secession, without touching upon its moral aspect. Regarding the Union in the light of a compact, it is not lightly to be broken. Framed for such purposes, and under such circumstances, it was a covenant peculiarly sacred, which could

[7] Irving's *Life of Washington,* Vol. V., p. 61.

not be set aside without guilt somewhere. In this regard, the seceding South is prepared to carry her cause before the world, and before God. When the Union had failed in all the ends for which it was instituted —neither 'establishing justice, insuring domestic tranquillity, promoting the general welfare, nor securing the blessings of liberty;' when these delegated powers were perverted into powers of oppression and injury; when the compact had flagrantly, and with impunity, been broken by the other parties to it, then it became the South to assert her last right, that of a peaceful withdrawal from the partnership. If to her other wrongs this last and most atrocious of them all, an attempt at her forcible subjugation is to be added, then will her defence be as complete as an injured people ever carried over to the judgment of posterity. On this, however, we will not enlarge. It will be seen that, upon the legal aspects of the question, we are at antipodes with the writer, whose essay we have reviewed. He affirms the people to be one, divided into many: we, that they are many, united into one. He ascribes sovereignty to the Union: we, to the States. He regards the Constitution as creating a government which is *over* the States: we regard it as a common law established *between* the States. In his view, 'any attempt to throw off this national allegiance, in any legal, in any constitutional, in any historical light, is pure madness:' in our view, in every legal, constitutional, or historical light, there is no allegiance to be thrown off, and consequently there is no madness in the case. He affirms secession to be rebellion, which must be suppressed at every hazard: we, that it is an inherent right of sovereignty, which cannot be disallowed without an international war. Let the reader put the two into his own scales, and decide for himself." [8]

The people of South Carolina inaugurated the Revolution as early as November 17, 1860. Thenceforward events trod upon the heels of events; and every critical movement made by the people of his old mother State, or of her sister States of like views and sympathies, stirred to its depths the heart of Benjamin M. Palmer. He had throughout his ministerial career, devoted himself with singular assiduity and exclusiveness to his high calling of preaching the Gospel of the Lord Jesus Christ; but he had ever been intensely patriotic. A man of wonderful poise and self-command, he became inwardly agitated. A patriotic fire burned in his bones.

The temptation to utter himself on the great subject of political strife became overwhelming. He came to think he

[8] The article from which this excerpt was taken, appeared in the *Southern Presbyterian Review,* Vol. XIV., pp. 162-175. It came out in April, 1861, but may be safely considered as showing his views in the fall of 1860.

ought to speak on it; to think that it belonged to him as a minister and a divine to do so. Hence the "Thanksgiving Sermon" of November 29, 1860.

The argument of this sermon does not seem, in all points, invincible; but it exercised so vast an influence that it deserves a careful reading not only by every student of Dr. Palmer's life but by everyone who would understand the temper of the Southwest on the eve of the war between the sections. With reference to one of the occasions of strife, at the least, he spoke for the best element in that great section.

The preacher took for his text Psalm 94:20: *"Shall the throne of iniquity have fellowship with thee, which frameth mischief by a law?"* and Obadiah 7: *"All the men of thy confederacy have brought thee even to the border; the men that were at peace with thee have deceived thee, and prevailed against thee; they that ate thy bread have laid a wound under thee; there is none understanding in him."*

He said:

"The voice of the Chief Magistrate has summoned us to-day to the house of prayer. This call, in its annual repetition, may be too often only a solemn state-form; nevertheless it covers a mighty and double truth.

"It recognizes the existence of a personal God whose will shapes the destiny of nations, and that sentiment of religion in man which points to Him as the needle to the pole. Even with those who grope in the twilight of natural religion, natural conscience gives a voice to the dispensations of Providence. If in autumn 'extensive harvests hang their heavy head,' the joyous reaper, 'crowned with the sickle and the wheaten sheaf,' lifts his heart to the 'Father of Lights from whom cometh down every good and perfect gift.' Or, if pestilence and famine waste the earth, even pagan altars smoke with bleeding victims, and costly hecatombs appease the Divine anger which flames out in such dire misfortunes. It is the instinct of man's religious nature, which, among Christians and heathen alike, seeks after God—the natural homage which reason, blinded as it may be, pays to a universal and ruling Providence. All classes bow beneath its spell especially in seasons of gloom, when a nation bends beneath the weight of a general calamity, and a common sorrow falls upon every heart. The hesitating skeptic forgets to weigh his scruples, as the dark shadow passes over him and fills his soul with awe. The dainty philosopher, coolly discoursing of the forces of nature and her uniform laws, abandons, for a time his atheistical speculations, abashed by the proofs of a supreme and personal will.

"Thus the devout followers of Jesus Christ and those who do not rise above the level of mere theisms, are drawn into momentary fellowship; as under the pressure of these inextinguishable convictions they pay a public and united homage to the God of nature and of grace.

"In obedience to this great law of religious feeling, not less than in obedience to the civil ruler who represents this commonwealth in its unity, we are now assembled. Hitherto, on similar occasions, our language has been the language of gratitude and song. 'The voice of rejoicing and salvation was in the tabernacles of the righteous.' Together we praised the Lord 'that our garners were full, affording all manner of store; that our sheep brought forth thousands and ten thousands in our streets; that our oxen were strong to labor, and there was no breaking in nor going out, and no complaining was in our streets.' As we together surveyed the blessings of Providence, the joyful chorus swelled from millions of people, 'Peace be within thy walls and prosperity within thy palaces.' But, to-day, burdened hearts all over this land are brought to the sanctuary of God. We 'see the tents of Cushan in affliction, and the curtains of the land of Midian do tremble.' We have fallen upon times when there are 'signs in the sun, and in the moon, and in the stars; upon the earth distress of nations, with perplexities; the sea and the waves roaring; men's hearts failing them for fear and for looking after those things which are coming' in the near yet gloomy future. Since the words of this proclamation were penned by which we are convened, that which all men dreaded, but against which all men hoped, has been realized; and in the triumph of a sectional majority we are compelled to read the probable doom of our once happy and united Confederacy. It is not to be concealed that we are in the most fearful and perilous crisis which has occurred in our history as a nation. The cords which, during four-fifths of a century, have bound together this growing republic are now strained to their utmost tension: they just need the touch of fire to part asunder forever. Like a ship laboring in the storm and suddenly grounded upon some treacherous shoal—every timber of this vast Confederacy strains and groans under the pressure. Sectional divisions, the jealousy of rival interests, the lust of political power, a bastard ambition which looks to personal aggrandizement rather than to the public weal, a reckless radicalism which seeks for the subversion of all that is ancient and stable, and a furious fanaticism which drives on its ill-considerd conclusions with utter disregard of the evil it engenders—all these combine to create a portentous crisis, the like of which we have never known before, and which puts to a crucifying test the virtue, the patriotism and the piety of the country.

"You, my hearers, who have waited upon my public ministry and have known me in the intimacies of pastoral intercourse, will do me the justice to testify that I have never intermeddled with political questions. Interested as I might be in the progress of events, I have never obtruded, either publicly or privately, my opinions upon any of you;

nor can a single man arise and say that, by word or sign, have I ever sought to warp his sentiments or control his judgment upon any political subject whatsoever. The party questions which have hitherto divided the political world have seemed to me to involve no issue sufficiently momentous to warrant my turning aside, even for a moment, from my chosen calling. In this day of intelligence, I have felt there were thousands around me more competent to instruct in statesmanship; and thus, from considerations of modesty no less than prudence, I have preferred to move among you as a preacher of righteousness belonging to a kingdom not of this world.

"During the heated canvass which has just been brought to so disastrous a close, the seal of a rigid and religious silence has not been broken. I deplored the divisions amongst us as being, to a large extent, impertinent in the solemn crisis which was too evidently impending. Most clearly did it appear to me that but one issue was before us; an issue soon to be presented in a form which would compel the attention. That crisis might make it imperative upon me as a Christian and a divine to speak in language admitting no misconstruction. Until then, aside from the din and strife of parties, I could only mature, with solitary and prayerful thought, the destined utterance. That hour has come. At a juncture so solemn as the present, with the destiny of a great people waiting upon the decision of an hour, it is not lawful to be still. Whoever may have influence to shape public opinion, at such a time must lend it, or prove faithless to a trust as solemn as any to be accounted for at the bar of God.

"Is it immodest in me to assume that I may represent a class whose opinions in such a controversy are of cardinal importance—the class which seeks to ascertain its duty in the light simply of conscience and religion, and which turns to the moralist and the Christian for support and guidance? The question, too, which now places us upon the brink of revolution was in its origin a question of morals and religion. It was debated in ecclesiastical counsels before it entered legislative halls. It has riven asunder the two largest religious communions in the land: and the right determination of this primary question will go far toward fixing the attitude we must assume in the coming struggle. I sincerely pray God that I may be forgiven if I have misapprehended the duty incumbent upon me to-day; for I have ascended this pulpit under the agitation of feeling natural to one who is about to deviate from the settled policy of his public life. It is my purpose—not as your organ, compromitting you, whose opinions are for the most part unknown to me, but on my sole responsibility—to speak upon the one question of the day; and to state the duty which, as I believe, patriotism and religion alike require of us all. I shall aim to speak with a moderation of tone and feeling almost judicial, well befitting the sanctities of the place and the solemnities of the judgment day.

"In determining our duty in this emergency it is necessary that we should first ascertain the nature of the trust providentially committed to us. A nation often has a character as well defined and intense as that of an individual. This depends, of course upon a variety of causes operating through a long period of time. It is due largely to the original traits which distinguish the stock from which it springs, and to the providential training which has formed its education. But, however derived, this individuality of character alone makes any people truly historic, competent to work out its specific mission, and to become a factor in the world's progress. The particular trust assigned to such a people becomes the pledge of the divine protection; and their fidelity to it determines the fate by which it is finally overtaken. What that trust is must be ascertained from the necessities of their position, the institutions which are the outgrowth of their principles and the conflicts through which they preserve their identity and independence. If then the South is such a people, what, at this juncture, is their providential trust? I answer, that it is *to conserve and to perpetuate the institution of domestic slavery as now existing.* It is not necessary here to inquire whether this is precisely the best relation in which the hewer of wood and drawer of water can stand to his employer; although this proposition may perhaps be successfully sustained by those who choose to defend it. Still less are we required, dogmatically, to affirm that it will subsist through all time. Baffled as our wisdom may now be in finding a solution of this intricate social problem, it would nevertheless be the height of arrogance to pronounce what changes may or may not occur in the distant future. In the grand march of events Providence may work out a solution undiscoverable by us. What modifications of soil and climate may hereafter be produced, what consequent changes in the products on which we depend, what political revolutions may occur among the races which are now enacting the great drama of history: all such inquiries are totally irrelevant because no prophetic vision can pierce the darkness of that future. If this question should ever arise, the generation to whom it is remitted will doubtless have the wisdom to meet it, and Providence will furnish the lights in which it is to be resolved. All that we claim for them, for ourselves, is liberty to work out this problem, guided by nature and God, without obtrusive interference from abroad. These great questions of Providence and history must have free scope for their solution; and the race whose fortunes are distinctly implicated in the same is alone authorized, as it is alone competent, to determine them. It is just this impertinence of human legislation, setting bounds to what God alone can regulate, that the South is called this day to resent and resist. The country is convulsed simply because 'the throne of iniquity frameth mischief by a law.' Without, therefore, determining the question of duty for future generations, I simply say, that for us, as now situated, the duty is plain of conserving and transmitting the system of slavery, with the freest scope for its natural development and extension. Let us, my brethren, look our duty in the face. With this institution assigned to our keeping, what reply shall we make to those who say that its days are numbered? My own conviction is, that we should at once lift ourselves, intelligently, to the highest moral ground and proclaim to all the world that we hold this trust from God, and in its occupancy we are prepared to stand or fall as God may appoint. If the critical moment has arrived at which the great issue is joined, let us say that, in the sight of all perils, we will stand by our trust; and God be with the right!

"The argument which enforces the solemnity of this providential trust is simple and condensed. It is bound upon us, then, by the *principle of self-preservation,* that 'first law' which is continually asserting its supremacy over all others. Need I pause to show how this system of servitude underlies and supports our material interests; that our wealth consists in our lands and in the serfs who till them; that from the nature of our products they can only be cultivated by labor which must be controlled in order to be certain; that any other than a tropical race must faint and wither beneath a tropical sun? Need I pause to show how this system is interwoven with our entire social fabric; that these slaves form parts of our households, even as our children; and that, too, through a relationship recognized and sanctioned in the Scriptures of God even as the other? Must I pause to show how it has fashioned our modes of life, and determined all our habits of thought and feeling, and moulded the very type of our civilization? How then can the hand of violence be laid upon it without involving our existence? The so-called free States of this country are working out the social problem under conditions peculiar to themselves. These conditions are sufficiently hard, and their success is too uncertain to excite in us the least jealousy of their lot. With a teeming population, which the soil cannot support; with their wealth depending upon arts, created by artificial wants; with an external friction between the grades of their society; with their labor and their capital grinding against each other like the upper and nether millstones; with labor cheapened and displaced by new mechanical inventions, bursting more asunder the bonds of brotherhood—amid these intricate perils we have ever given them our sympathy and our prayers, and have never sought to weaken the foundations of their social order. God grant them complete success in the solution of all their perplexities! We, too, have our responsibilities and trials; but they are all bound up in this one institution, which has been the object of such unrighteous assault through five and twenty years. If we are true to ourselves we shall, at this critical juncture, stand by it and work out our destiny.

"This duty is bound upon us again *as the constituted guardians of the slaves themselves.* Our lot is not more implicated in theirs, than their lot in ours; in our mutual relations we survive or perish together. The worst foes of the black race are those who have intermeddled on their behalf. We know better than others that every attribute of their character fits them for dependence and servitude. By nature the most affectionate and loyal of all races beneath the sun, they are also the most helpless; and no calamity can befall them greater than the loss of that protection they enjoy under this patriarchal system. Indeed, the experiment has been grandly tried of precipitating them upon freedom which they know not how to enjoy; and the dismal results are before us in statistics that astonish the world. With the fairest portions of the earth in their possession and with the advantage of a long discipline as cultivators of the soil, their constitutional indolence has converted the most beautiful islands of the sea into a howling waste. It is not too much to say that if the South should, at this moment, surrender every slave, the wisdom of the entire world, united in solemn council, could not solve the question of their disposal. Their transportation to Africa, even if it were feasible, would be but the most refined cruelty; they must perish with starvation before they could have time to relapse into their primitive barbarism. Their residence here, in the presence of the vigorous Saxon race, would be but the signal for their rapid extermination before they had time to waste away through listlessness, filth and vice. Freedom would be their doom; and equally from both they call upon us, their providential guardians, to be protected. I know this argument will be scoffed abroad as the hypocritical cover thrown over our own cupidity and selfishness; but every Southern master knows its truth and feels its power. My servant, whether born in my house or bought with my money, stands to me in the relation of a child. Though providentially owing me service, which, providentially, I am bound to exact, he is, nevertheless, my brother and my friend, and I am to him a guardian and a father. He leans upon me for protection, for counsel, and for blessing; and so long as the relation continues, no power but the power of Almighty God shall come between him and me. Were there no argument but this, it binds upon us the providential duty of preserving the relation that we may save him from a doom worse than death.

"It is a duty which we owe, further, *to the civilized world.* It is a remarkable fact that during these thirty years of unceasing warfare against slavery, and while a lying spirit has inflamed the world against us, that world has grown more and more dependent upon it for sustenance and wealth. Every tyro knows that all branches of industry fall back upon the soil. We must come, every one of us, to the bosom of this great mother for nourishment. In the happy partnership which has grown up in providence between the tribes of this confederacy, our industry has been concentrated upon agriculture. To the North we have cheerfully resigned all the profits arising from manufacture and commerce. Those profits they have, for the most part, fairly earned, and we have never begrudged them. We have sent them our sugar and bought it back when refined; we have sent them our cotton and bought it back when spun into thread or woven into cloth. Almost every article we use, from the shoe lachet to the most elaborate and costly article of luxury, they have made and we have bought; and both sections have thriven by the partnership, as no people ever thrived before since the first shining of the sun. So literally true are the words of the text, addressed by Obadiah to Edom, 'All the men of our confederacy, the men that were at peace with us, have eaten our bread at the very time they have deceived and laid a wound under us.' Even beyond this the enriching commerce which has built the splendid cities and marble palaces of England, as well as of America, has been largely established upon the products of our soil; and the blooms upon Southern fields gathered by black hands have fed the spindles and looms of Manchester and Birmingham not less than of Lawrence and Lowell. Strike now a blow at this system of labor and the world itself totters at the stroke. Shall we permit that blow to fall? Do we not owe it to civilized man to stand in the breach and stay the uplifted arm? If the blind Samson lays hold of the pillars which support the arch of the world's industry, how many more will be buried beneath its ruins than the lords of the Philistines? 'Who knoweth whether we are not come to the kingdom for such a time as this.'

"Last of all, in this great struggle, *we defend the cause of God and religion.* The abolition spirit is undeniably atheistic. The demon which erected its throne upon the guillotine in the days of Robespierre and Marat, which abolished the Sabbath and worshipped reason in the person of a harlot, yet survives to work other horrors, of which those of the French Revolution are but the type. Among a people so generally religious as the American, a disguise must be worn; but it is the same old threadbare disguise of the advocacy of human rights. From a thousand Jacobin clubs here, as in France, the decree has gone forth which strikes at God by striking at all subordination and law. Availing itself of the morbid and misdirected sympathies of men, it has entrapped weak consciences in the meshes of its treachery; and now, at last, has seated its high priest upon the throne, clad in the black garments of discord and schism, so symbolic of its ends. Under this suspicious cry of reform, it demands that every evil shall be corrected, or society become a wreck—the sun must be stricken from the heavens, if a spot is found upon his disk. The Most High, knowing his own power, which is infinite, and his own wisdom, which is unfathomable, can afford to be patient. But these self-constituted reformers must quicken the activity of Jehovah or compel his abdication. In their furious haste, they trample upon obligations sacred as any which can bind the conscience. It is time to reproduce the obsolete idea that Providence must govern man, and not that man shall control Providence. In the imperfect state of human society, it pleases God to allow evils which check others that are greater. As in the physical world, objects are moved forward, not by a single force, but by the composition of forces; so in his moral administration, there are checks and balances whose intimate relations are comprehended only by himself. But what reck they of this—these fierce zealots who undertake to drive the chariot of the sun? Working out the single and false idea which rides them like a nightmare, they dash athwart the spheres, utterly disregarding the delicate mechanism of Providence, which moves on, wheels within wheels, with pivots and balances and springs. which the great Designer alone can control. This spirit of atheism, which knows no God who tolerates evil, no Bible which sanctions law, and no conscience that can be bound by oaths and covenants, has selected us for its victims, and slavery for its issue. Its banner-cry rings out already upon the air—'liberty, equality, fraternity,' which simply interpreted mean bondage, confiscation and massacre. With its tricolor waving in the breeze,—it waits to inaugurate its reign of terror. To the South the high position is assigned of defending, before all nations, the cause of all religion and of all truth. In this trust, we are resisting the power which wars against constitutions and laws and compacts, against Sabbaths and sanctuaries, against the family, the State, and the Church; which blasphemously invades the prerogatives of God, and rebukes the Most High for the errors of his administration; which, if it cannot snatch the reign of empire from his grasp, will lay the universe in ruins at his feet. Is it possible that we shall decline the onset?

"This argument, then, which sweeps over the entire circle of our relations, touches the four cardinal points of duty *to ourselves, to our slaves, to the world, and to Almighty God.* It establishes the nature and solemnity of our present trust, to *preserve and transmit our existing system of domestic servitude, with the right, unchallenged by man, to go and root itself wherever Providence and nature may carry it.* This trust we will discharge in the face of the worst possible peril. Though war be the aggregation of all evils, yet should the madness of the hour appeal to the arbitration of the sword, we will not shrink even from the baptism of fire. If modern crusaders stand in serried ranks upon some plain of Esdraelon, there shall we be in defence of our trust. Not till the last man has fallen behind the last rampart, shall it drop from our hands; and then only in surrender to the God who gave it.

"Against this institution a system of aggression has been pursued through the last thirty years. Initiated by a few fanatics, who were at first despised, it has gathered strength from opposition until it has assumed its present gigantic proportions. No man has thoughtfully watched the progress of this controversy without being convinced that the crisis must at length come. Some few, perhaps, have hoped against hope, that the gathering imposthume might be dispersed, and the poison be eliminated from the body politic by healthful remedies. But the delusion has scarcely been cherished by those who have studied the history of fanaticism in its path of blood and fire through the ages of the past. The moment must arrive when the conflict must be joined, and victory decide for one or the other. As it has been a war of legislative tactics, and not of physical force, both parties have been maneuvering for a position; and the embarrassment has been, whilst dodging amidst constitutional forms, to make an issue that should be clear, simple, and tangible. Such an issue is at length presented in the result of the recent Presidential election. Be it observed, too, that it is an issue made by the North, not by the South, upon whom, therefore, must rest the entire guilt of the present disturbance. With a choice between three national candidates, who have more or less divided the votes of the South, the North, with unexampled unanimity, have cast their ballot for a candidate who is sectional, who represents a party that is sectional, and the ground of that sectionalism, prejudice against the established and constitutional rights and immunities and institutions of the South. What does this declare—what can it declare, but that from henceforth this is to be a government of section over section; a government using constitutional forms only to embarrass and divide the section ruled, and as fortresses through whose embrasures the cannon of legislation is to be employed in demolishing the guaranteed institutions of the South? What issue is more direct, concrete, intelligible than this? I thank God that, since the conflict must be joined, the responsibility of this issue rests not with us, who have ever acted upon the defensive; and that it is so disembarrassed and simple that the feeblest mind can understand it.

"The question with the South to-day is not what issue shall *she* make, but how shall she meet that which is prepared for her? Is it possible that we can hesitate longer than a moment? In our natural recoil from the perils of revolution, and with our clinging fondness for the memories of the past, we may perhaps look around for something to soften the asperity of this issue, and for some ground on which we may defer the day of evil, for some hope that the gathering clouds may not burst in fury upon the land.

"It is alleged, for example, that the President elect has been chosen by a fair majority under prescribed forms. But need I say, to those who have read history, that no despotism is more absolute than that of an unprincipled democracy, and no tyranny more galling than that exercised through constitutional formulas? But the plea is idle, when the very question we debate is the perpetuation of that Constitution now converted into an engine of oppression, and the continuance of that union which is henceforth to be our condition of vassalage. I say it with solemnity and pain, this union of our forefathers is already gone. It existed but in mutual confidence, the bonds of which were ruptured in the late election. Though its form should be preserved, it is, in fact, destroyed. We may possibly entertain the project of reconstructing it; but it will be another union, resting upon other than past guarantees. 'In that we say a new covenant we have made the first old, and that which decayeth and waxeth old is ready to vanish away'—'as a vesture it is folded up.' For myself I say that, under the rule which threatens us, I throw off the yoke of this union as readily as did our ancestors the yoke of King George III., and for causes immeasurably stronger than those pleaded in their celebrated declaration.

"It is softly whispered, too, that the successful competitor for the throne protests and avers his purpose to administer the government in a conservative and national spirit. Allowing him all credit for personal integrity in these protestations, he is, in this matter, nearly as impotent for good as he is competent for evil. He is nothing more than a figure upon the political chessboard—whether pawn or knight or king, will hereafter appear—but still a silent figure upon the checkered squares, moved by the hands of an unseen player. That player is the party to which he owes his elevation—a party that has signalized its history by the most unblushing perjuries. What faith can be placed in the protestations of men who openly avow that their consciences are too sublimated to be restrained by the obligation of covenants or by the sanctity of oaths? No: we have seen the trail of the serpent five and twenty years in our Eden; twined now in the branches of the forbidden tree, we feel the pangs of death already begun as its hot breath is upon our cheeks, hissing out the original falsehood, 'Ye shall not surely die.'

"Another suggests that even yet the Electors, alarmed by these demonstrations of the South, may not cast the black ball which dooms their country to the executioner. It is a forlorn hope. Whether we should counsel such a breach of faith in them or take refuge in their treachery—whether such a result would give a President chosen by the people according to the constitution—are points I will not discuss. But that it would prove a cure for any of our ills, who can believe! It is certain that it would, with some show of justice, exasperate a party sufficiently ferocious; that it would doom us to four years of increasing strife and bitterness; and that the crisis must come at last under issues possibly not half so clear as the present. Let us not desire to shift the day of trial by miserable subterfuges of this sort. The issue is upon us; let us meet it like men and end this strife forever.

"But some quietist whispers, yet further, this majority is accidental and has been swelled by accessions of men simply opposed to the existing administration; the party is utterly heterogeneous and must be shivered into fragments by its own success. I confess, frankly, this suggestion has staggered me more than any other, and I sought to take refuge therein. Why should we not wait and see the effect of success itself upon a party whose elements might devour each other in the very distribution of the spoil? Two considerations have dissipated the fallacy before me. The first is, that, however mixed the party, abolitionism is clearly its informing and actuating soul; and fanaticism is a bloodhound that never bolts its track when it has once lapped blood. The elevation of their candidates is far from being the consummation of their aims. It is only the beginning of that consummation; and, if all history be not a lie, there will be cohesion enough till the end of the beginning is reached, and the dreadful banquet of slaughter and ruin shall glut the appetite. The second consideration is a principle which I cannot blink. It is nowhere denied that the first article in the creed of the now dominant party is the restriction of slavery within its present limits. It is distinctly avowed by their organs and in the name of their elected chieftain; as will appear from the following extract from an article written to pacify the South and to reassure its fears: 'There can be no doubt whatever in the mind of any man, that Mr. Lincoln regards slavery as a moral, social and political evil, and that it should be dealt with as such by the Federal Government, in every instance where it is called upon to deal with it at all. On this point there is no room for question—and there need be no misgivings as to his official action. The whole influence of the Executive Department of the Government, while in his hands, will be thrown against the extension of slavery into the new territories of the Union, and the re-opening of the African slave trade. On these points he will make no compromise nor yield one hair's breadth to coercion from any quarter or in any shape. He does not accede to the alleged decision of the Supreme Court, that the Constitution places slaves upon the footing of other property, and protects them as such wherever its jurisdiction extends, nor will he be, in the least degree, governed or controlled by it in his executive action. He will do all in his power, personally and officially, by the direct exercise of the powers of his office, and the indirect influence inseparable from it, to arrest the tendency to make slavery national and perpetual, and to place it in precisely the same position which it held in the early days of the Republic, and in the view of the founders of the Government.'

"Now what enigmas may be couched in this last sentence—the sphinx which uttered them can perhaps resolve; but the sentence in which they occur is as big as the belly of the Trojan horse which laid the city of Priam in ruins.

"These utterances we have heard so long that they fall stale upon the ear; but never before have they had such significance. Hitherto they have come from Jacobin conventicles and pulpits, from the rostrum, from the hustings, and from the halls of our national Congress: but always as the utterances of irresponsible men or associations of men. But now the voice comes from the throne; already, before clad with the sanctities of office, ere the anointing oil is poured upon the monarch's head, the decree has gone forth that the institution of Southern slavery shall be constrained within assigned limits. Though nature and Providence should send forth its branches like the banyan tree, to take root in congenial soil, here is a power superior to both, that says it shall wither and die within its own charmed circle.

"What say you to this, to whom this great providential trust of conserving slavery is assigned? 'Shall the throne of iniquity have fellowship with thee, which frameth mischief by a law?' It is this that makes the crisis. Whether we will or not, this is the historic moment when the fate of this institution hangs suspended in the balance. Decide either way, it is the moment of our destiny—the only thing affected by the decision is the complexion of that destiny. If the South bows before this throne, she accepts the decree of restriction and ultimate extinction, which is made the condition of her homage.

"As it appears to me, the course to be pursued in this emergency is that which has already been inaugurated. Let the people in all the Southern States, in solemn council assembled, reclaim the powers they have delegated. Let those conventions be composed of men whose fidelity has been approved—men who bring the wisdom, experience and firmness of age to support and announce principles which have long been matured. Let these conventions decide firmly and solemnly what they will do with this great trust committed to their hands. Let them pledge each other in sacred covenant, to uphold and perpetuate what they cannot resign without dishonor and palpable ruin. Let them further, take all the necessary steps looking to separate and independent existence; and initiate measures for framing a new and homogeneous confederacy. Thus, prepared for every contingency, let the crisis come. Paradoxical as it may seem, if there be any way to save, or rather to re-construct, the union of our forefathers it is this. Perhaps, at the last moment, the conservative portions of the North may awake to see the abyss into which they are about to plunge. Perchance they may arise and crush out forever the abolition hydra, and cast it into a grave from which there shall never be a resurrection.

"Thus, with restored confidence, we may be rejoined a united and happy people. But, before God, I believe that nothing will effect this but the line of policy which the South has been compelled in self-preservation to adopt. I confess frankly, I am not sanguine that such an auspicious result will be reached. Partly, because I do not see how new guarantees are to be grafted upon the Constitution, nor how, if grafted, they can be more binding than those which have already been trampled under foot; but chiefly, because I do not see how such guarantees can be elicited from the people at the North. It cannot be disguised that almost to a man they are anti-slavery where they are not abolition. A whole generation has been educated to look upon the system with abhorrence as a national blot. They hope, and look, and pray for its extinction within a reasonable time, and cannot be satisfied unless things are seen drawing to that conclusion. We, on the contrary, as its constituted guardians, can demand nothing less than that it should be left open to expansion, subject to no limitations save those imposed by God and nature. I fear the antagonism is too great, and the conscience of both parties too deeply implicated to allow such a composition of the strife. Nevertheless since it is within the range of possibility in the Providence of God, I would not shut out the alternative.

"Should it fail, what remains but that we say to each other, calmly and kindly, what Abraham said to Lot: 'Let there be no strife, I pray thee, between me and thee, and between my herdmen and thy herdmen, for we be brethren: Is not the whole land before thee? Separate thyself, I pray thee, from me . . . if thou wilt take the left hand, then I will go to the right, or if thou depart to the right hand, then I will go to the left.' Thus, if we cannot save the Union, we may save the inestimable blessings it enshrines; if we cannot preserve the vase, we will preserve the precious liquor it contains.

"In all this I speak for the North no less than for the South; for upon our united and determined resistance at this moment depends the salvation of the whole country—in saving ourselves we shall save the North from the ruin she is madly drawing down upon her own head.

"The position of the South is at this moment sublime. If she has grace given her to know her hour she will save herself, the country, and the world. It will involve, indeed, temporary prostration and distress; the dykes of Holland must be cut to save her from the troops of Philip. But I warn my countrymen the historic moment once passed, never returns. If she will arise in her majesty, and speak now as with the voice of one man, she will roll back for all time the curse that is upon her. If she succumbs now, she transmits that curse as an heirloom of posterity. We may, for a generation, enjoy comparative ease, gather up our feet in our beds, and die in peace; but our children will go forth beggared from the homes of their fathers. Fishermen will cast their nets where your proud commercial navy now rides at anchor, and dry them upon the shore now covered with your bales of merchandise. Sapped, circumvented, undermined, the institutions of your soil will be overthrown; and within five and twenty years the history of St. Domingo will be the record of Louisiana. If dead men's bones can tremble, ours will move under the muttered curses of sons and daughters, denouncing the blindness and love of ease which have left them an inheritance of woe.

"I have done my duty under as deep a sense of responsibility to God and man as I have ever felt. Under a full conviction that the salvation of the whole country is depending upon the action of the South, I am impelled to deepen the sentiment of resistance in the Southern mind and to strengthen the current now flowing toward a union of the South in defence of her chartered rights. It is a duty which I shall not be called to repeat, for such awful junctures do not occur twice in a century. Bright and happy days are yet before us; and before another political earthquake shall shake the continent, I hope to be 'where the wicked cease from troubling and where the weary are at rest.'

"It only remains to say, that whatever be the fortunes of the South, I accept them for my own. Born upon her soil, of a father thus born before me—from an ancestry that occupied it while yet it was a part of England's possessions—she is in every sense my mother. I shall die upon her bosom—she shall know no peril, but it is my peril—no conflict, but it is my conflict—and no abyss of ruin, into which I shall not share her fall. May the Lord God cover her head in this her day of battle!"

Says Mr. Wm. O. Rogers,[9] of this "sermon":

"It confirmed and strengthened those who were in doubt; it gave directness and energy to public sentiment—so that perhaps no other public utterance during that trying period of anxiety and hesitancy did so much to bring New Orleans city and the entire State of Louisiana squarely and fully to the side of secession and the Confederacy. The spacious auditorium of the First Presbyterian Church (of New Orleans) was crowded from floor to gallery. Many prominent members of all callings and professions were there. Many were halting between two opinions. New Orleans was a commercial city and had large interests with the North. It was cosmopolitan, and, particularly in its mercantile classes, related in many ways to cities of the North.

"Contrary to his usual custom Dr. Palmer had written his sermon; and read it—slowly, carefully, with constrained voice—without a single gesture, without elevating his voice in any sentence during the hour of its delivery. The solemnity of the audience was very impressive. The calmness of the speaker was the calmness of deep emotion held in check by the solemnity of the occasion. The whole scene was a remarkable tribute to the intellectual and moral powers of the speaker. Sentences like the following, coming from a man so revered and esteemed, fell upon the hearing ear with great power—'to protect and transmit our existing system of domestic servitude with the right, unchanged by man, to go and root itself wherever Providence and nature may carry it. This trust we will discharge in the face of the worst possible peril. Though war be the aggregation of all evils yet should the madness of the hour appeal to the arbitration of the sword, we will not shrink even from the baptism of fire. If modern crusaders stand in serried ranks upon some plain of Esdraelon, there will we be in defence of our trust. Not till the last man has fallen, behind the last rampart,

---

[9] Mr. Wm. O. Rogers, residing at Madison, N. J. in 1904, wrote these words on June 9th of that year, at our solicitation. He was an eye witness and an auditor of that which he describes. He was long a distinguished citizen of New Orleans, a member of Dr. Palmer's church, for many years a member of his session, and a close personal friend, a gentleman of great purity and dignity of character.

shall it drop from our hands, and then only in surrender to the God who gave it.'

. . . .

"It has been my good fortune to hear some of the great pulpit and political orators of my generation, but I cannot recall an occasion when the effect upon the audience was so profound. After the benediction, in solemn silence, no man speaking to his neighbor, the great congregation of serious and thoughtful men and women dispersed; but afterwards the drums beat and the bugles sounded; for New Orleans was shouting for secession."

An editorial in the *Daily Delta,* November 30, 1860, says:

"We will publish in Saturday's *Delta* the Thanksgiving sermon delivered at the First Presbyterian Church yesterday by Dr. Palmer. All who heard that great discourse declare it to be the ablest ever delivered by its accomplished author. The manly and patriotic position taken by Dr. Palmer was such as was expected by those familiar with the frank and decided character of the great divine. Dr. Leacock, of Christ's Church, and the Rev. Mr. Henderson, were as decided as Dr. Palmer in their advocacy of Southern rights, and in their recommendations of resistance to Northern aggressions. The character of these discourses is too important to be disregarded. They are expressions of the profound and universal sentiments of the community—a sentiment which forces itself into notice through every channel, and which is too powerful to be restrained by ordinary forms and conventionalities. Only a pressing sense of duty to the highest interests of that society of which our ministers of religion are in part the recognized guardians, could have compelled this seeming departure from the established customs of the pulpit. In addition to these considerations it must be remembered that the day was not the day devoted by custom or holy ordinance to religious service, but a day set apart by the governor of the State to be observed with reference to our secular condition."

Published on Saturday in the *Delta,* the sermon was republished in the Sunday issue, December 2, 1860. On the first page of this issue appears an article headed, "Dr. Palmer's Sermon on Thanksgiving Day: The Pulpit and the Times." Amongst other things the article says:

"A great political emergency, long predicted by a few, long dreaded yet hoped against by many, and obstinately disbelieved by still more, has come upon us and scattered parties and the devices of politicians as a whirlwind scatters dust and rubbish. At such a time the voice of faction should be hushed. At such a time it is for the patriot, not the partisan, to come to the rescue of his imperiled country. At such a time the political catechism for Southern men is plain and simple: The South, her rights, her homes, her firesides, for life, for death, swear to defend them, whether the sky may become bright or sunless, whether the stars may appear or disappear, whether the gathering storm may roll away or burst in torrents of fire.

"It is in an hour like this that patriotism rises to religion, and religion derives new warmth and vigor from patriotism. That several of our clergymen preached sermons Thanksgiving Day under the influence of such a spirit is no matter of surprise. It would have been surprising rather if they had not done so. Our clergymen, after all, are men and not mere automatic symbols of an abstract creed. It is too late to say that the question of negro slavery, which is made the issue upon which a sectional majority wage an unrelenting war against the South, should be excluded from the Southern pulpit because the pulpit has no business with politics. The moral question of negro slavery had already divided the greatest religious denominations in the Union before the political question of negro slavery began to break up parties and split the Union asunder. The anti-slavery idea began on moral grounds. It allied itself with an anti-Southern party to overcome political obstacles. The combination has thus far triumphed. The Constitution, which was in their way, is dead; the spirit is gone out of it; its corpse is in their possession. The corpse of the South will also be theirs, unless on the 4th of March the South shall lay the corpse of the Union at their feet. Having thus triumphed politically, the anti-slavery idea now resumes its original character as a moral question, and in that form is ready to do the deadly work of sectional despotism. Religion involves morality, and no moral question can justly be excluded from the pulpit. And, therefore, when Dr. Palmer, on Thursday, took up the question between the North and the South, which turns on the anti-slavery idea, and showed that this idea was not only morally false, but was to be used as an instrument for overturning our whole social fabric and plunging us, and all that is dear to us, in an abyss of disgrace and ruin from which the imagination shrinks with terror—when he did this, he acted the part of a clergyman worthy of his calling; he acted the part of a Christian gentleman and scholar, of a Southern patriot, of a frank, earnest, brave, and a high souled man.

"The discourse we refer to was perhaps about two hours long; and a more cogent, exhaustive, logical and impressive production of not greater length we never met with coming either from pulpit or rostrum. It rose far above the conventional forms and phrases of an ordinary sermon. It rose infinitely above the usual thought and rhetoric of a political speech. It was more than eloquent; it was sacramental in its fervor. But the language of praise is out of place in speaking of it. It is above compliment. It was an event of the time passing, and a sign of the time at hand. It will be sure to fire the hearts and stir the souls of Southern men wherever read, while through the glowing words God seems to whisper to them of noble deeds."

In those days there was no *Delta* published on Monday. In Tuesday's *Daily Delta,* December 4, 1860, the sermon appeared again; and amongst the editorial notes, the following:

"*Dr. Palmer's Sermon.*—Scarcely any apology is necessary to be made to our readers on account of the republication of Dr. Palmer's Sermon, which appears, for the third time, in the *Delta* this morning. When we state that we reproduce it in accordance with the urgent request of a large number of our friends, and to supply a demand which seems yet far from exhausted, although the supply from this office alone has exceeded thirty thousand copies, we trust that no further explanation will be required."

Nor must we think of this sermon as accessible only through the columns of the *Delta;* the papers of the city and the State and the Southwest, generally, noticed it and published summaries of it, more or less complete, not a few perhaps, publishing the whole of it. Moreover, on the day of its delivery, the following correspondence touching its publication in a different form took place:

NEW ORLEANS, November 29, 1860.

"REV. AND DEAR SIR: We doubt not that the discourse delivered by you this morning was influenced by a high sense of duty and responsibility. You felt that the times demanded its utterance. Many of us heard it delivered; others have been informed of its tenor. As your fellow citizens, we desire for your own sake that your views may not be misunderstood or misrepresented; for the community's sake, that it may see patently before it an argument squarely up to the occasion; for the nation's sake, that the opinions of a representative man may be read and pondered. We ask you for a copy, that it may be immediately published and widely circulated.

"With sentiments of the highest regard, we remain

"Your fellow citizens and friends,

"William A. Elmore, W. R. Miles, J. J. Michie, J. R. Macmurdo, Thomas E. Adams, B. S. Tappan, R. P. Hunt, H. D. Ogden, A. C. Myers, David Bridges, A. A. Kennett, John A. French, John G. Gaines, William W. King, B. M. Pond, William G. Austin, John Claiborne, W. Rushton, A. C. Hensley, A. R. Ringgold, William Bell, Robert Ward, Thomas Hunton, Charles A. Taylor, Levy Pearce, J. W. Watson, W. Henderson, S. Z. Relf, M. M. Simpson, C. Bell, Thomas Allen Clark.

"Rev. B. M. Palmer, D.D., New Orleans."

"NEW ORLEANS, November 29, 1860.

"*Rev. B. M. Palmer, D.D.*

"DEAR SIR: The undersigned, members of your congregation, believing and sympathizing in the sentiments of your eloquent address, delivered on this, 29th inst., Thanksgiving Day, and that it should be read by every citizen of the United States, beg you to furnish a copy for publication, and oblige,

"Respectfully, your obedient servants,

"H. T. Lonsdale, A. H. Gladden, R. B. Sumner, H. W. Conner, Jr., W. B. Ritchie, Edward Dillon, George O. Sweet, William P. Campbell, Robert A. Grinnan, S. W. Dalton."

"NEW ORLEANS, November 29, 1860.

"To Messrs. H. T. Lonsdale, R. B. Sumner, A. H. Gladden, and others; and to Messrs. W. A. Elmore, W. G. Austin, W. R. Miles, and others:

"GENTLEMEN: That two communications should be received from different sources, requesting my discourse of this day for publication, is sufficient proof that I have spoken to the heart of this community. The sermon is herewith placed at your disposal, with the earnest desire that it may contribute something toward rallying our whole people to the issue that is upon us.

"Respectfully and gratefully yours,

"B. M. PALMER."

Accordingly a handsome pamphlet edition, probably a large one, was also scattered broadcast over the land.

There can be no question that throughout his belt—the South Carolina belt of influence—his "thanksgiving sermon" was generally regarded as correct in its theory of the subject discussed and suited to the crisis of the country; however, much doubt was entertained here and there as to the propriety of a Gospel minister's expressing all these views in God's house.

The divisive consequences which usually flow from political preaching were not wanting. A few of his people broke with him that day, though it came near to breaking their hearts to do it. The time came when the wisdom of his course in preaching that sermon seemed less apparent; indeed, he is said to have repented preaching the discourse, though the day never came when he took an essentially different view of the great subject discussed.

His domestic relations during these years were not without lines of interest. Before the removal of his family to New Orleans he established their home first in a house on the corner of St. Joseph and St. Charles streets. They lived here, however, but one year, moving thence to the corner of Thalia and Prytania streets. In this house they lived for two years. Here in the summer of 1858 the yellow fever found them. Their household, including servants, numbered twelve persons at the time. Out of the twelve, eleven members of the household had the fever. The first to have it was Mrs. Palmer; her case was very bad. About the same time, Mr. Axson, a cousin of Dr. Palmer and at the time a member of the household, was affected with the disorder. Mrs. Palmer and Mr. Axson were scarcely convalescent when the children and the servants were seized by it. Their cases were relatively mild, however. Dr. Palmer was the last of his family to take it. He had been going heroically about, ministering to the sick in his own house and to the sick and dying of the city, with apparent impunity. But, late in October, when all were looking hopefully forward to the coming of the blessed frost and when his friends were beginning to feel that he would pass through the pestilence untouched, he, too, was taken. His case was bad; he was exceedingly ill.

The Old School Assembly of 1858 had met in New Orleans. It was in this home that Dr. Palmer had received and entertained the distinguished men whom that Assembly had brought to his doors: such as A. T. McGill, Cortland Van Rensaelaer, Lewis W. Green, R. J. Breckenridge, Wm. J. Hoge, George Howe, I. S. K. Axson, etc., of the ministers, and elders of scarcely less note.

In 1859, the congregation purchased for a manse the commodious mansion now numbered 1415 Prytania Street (63 old Prytania). Here the family was to live, while in New Orleans, till 1891. The house was an excellent one for its day, three stories, with ceilings of ample pitch, with large rooms, and abundant offices and quarters in the rear for the accommodation of a considerable number of servants. After its further adaptation, in 1866, to Dr. Palmer's needs, by the addition of a study at the side, it was a most desirable domicile and well suited for the uses and character of the most distinguished pastor of his city and his section. The dignity of its spacious parlors and chambers, the solid mahogany staircase and folding doors impress the visitor of to-day.

This house was to be the scene of much happiness, of a high rational and spiritual order. It was to be the scene of much sorrow, which would not, however, be overwhelming. The Palmers were not to sorrow as those who have no hope. One of the daughters was to be married in this house. All of his grandchildren were to be born there. From the same house three of his daughters were to be carried to the grave.

THE PRYTANIA STREET MANSE (1859-1891).

There was a fine side yard with some splendid trees in it, from which, as from all he looked upon in his daily life, Dr. Palmer is said to have drawn some noble illustrations for use in the pulpit.

This house was to be the home not only of his own immediate family but of many others whom he would yearn to help. "He always had some who needed help in his house, boys or girls, young men or young women."

It was his custom to declare that he had left the business of disciplining his children to his wife; that he had made only two attempts at disciplining them and had been forced to conclude that Mrs. Palmer was better adapted to that form of ministry than he was. One of these fruitless attempts was to secure obedience from his little boy, on occasion of an issue's having been made between them. The other was to teach one of his little girls her letters. Mrs. Palmer seems to have been wise and skillful in the management of her children. Her husband felt that he might safely leave the matter in her hands. The relegation of other forms of attention to his children, even to his best beloved, he would never make. He was a most affectionate father; and as interested as affectionate. He counted not his time too valuable to be given in due measure to his children's development.

In 1857, in order to their escaping the scourge of yellow fever, he sent his wife and children back to Columbia to pass the summer. The living children were all girls. They were Sarah Frances, born September 19, 1844; Mary Howe, born September 1, 1847; Augusta Barnard, born June 23, 1849; Kate Gordon, born August 23, 1853; Marion Louisa, born January 10, 1856. Once each week he would write to one of his daughters. He began by writing to the oldest. Between her and himself quite a correspondence developed. All these letters to his children are redolent of the happiest family life. Some of them are valuable not only for the glimpse they afford of that life but for incidental light thrown on other aspects of his life:

"NEW ORLEANS, June 29, 1857.

"MY DEAR FANNY: I do not know whether you will be expecting a letter from father; but I am very sure you will be very glad to receive one, and to know from it how fondly you are remembered and loved. It is a long time since there was an opportunity of writing you, simply because of late we have not been separated; and you are now grown into such a big girl and have so improved yourself by study, that I may write to you very much as I would to mother, without striving after unusual simplicity of style—such as I must use for Mary and Gussie that they may easily understand me.

"It frightens me almost to think how fast you are growing up into a woman. Almost thirteen now! Why we shall only turn round two or three times before you will be a young lady, and I of course must begin to try and feel old. Be assured, my dear daughter, I am not anxious to have it so. If it were possible, I should like to keep you all children for many years just as you are now, so that the house might always be sunny and glad, as you children make it now. But as this cannot be, I am only anxious that you should rapidly improve your mind, and get that knowledge which as a woman you will need, in order to be happy and useful yourself, and that you may be honored and loved by others. Mother writes me that you have commenced your French and drawing. I am glad of it, provided you are not too closely confined. You have been kept very close all winter, and have studied very faithfully at school and I am desirous that you should romp and play, so as to be strong for study next winter. Still, you may learn a little French with ease, so that you and I can follow it up and talk it together, as I am a learner, too. The drawing too will be a pleasant amusement; and will keep alive your talent for that beautiful art. It is my wish, if God spares my life, to make you an accomplished lady, but of course, very much will depend upon you. I am willing to spend money freely for your good; but all the teachers and masters in the world cannot benefit you, unless you put your mind earnestly to it and determine to profit by their instructions. But, my darling, if I am anxious to have you wise and learned, this is nothing to the intense desire I have to see you pious and good. Oh, my daughter, you do not know how many thoughts I have on this subject; and how often and fervently I pray that God would give you a new heart. Do you remember two years ago this very month when you were so ill, how alarmed you were; how you talked with me, and told me you were afraid to die because you felt that you were not ready? I hoped when you got well, that you would remember all this; and that you would be so grateful to God for sparing your life, as to give him your heart at once. But I was disappointed—you got well, and then forgot all these solemn things. I do not know how much you think about your soul, and whether you pray fervently for a new heart. But I am afraid you do not: and you are now two years older, and know more than you did then. If you should be taken sick and die as you are, it would make me miserable the rest of my life; and though you did not know it, it was as much to remove all risk from you (as aught else), that I was willing to send you all from me this summer. I said, who can tell but God will hear my prayer and give her a new heart before next summer, and then I will not fear for my dear child's soul as I do now. Dear, dear Fanny, will you not think about these things—

think what a wicked heart you have—that unless it is changed, you cannot go to heaven—that you may die any moment, and be lost forever? Think, too, how ready Christ is to save you, if you will only go to him —and then delay not—go at once to him, my daughter, and be saved through his grace.

" I have now filled my sheet and must stop, though it is so small that it will not allow a long talk at one time. Tell Grandmother and Grandfather, Emily, Archie and George all 'Howdye' for me, and kiss mother and sisters in my stead. I would be glad if you would write me a letter, even though it should be a great deal shorter than this. Just to hear you say 'dear Father' will do me good in my loneliness. Good-bye.

"Your ever-loving father,

"B. M. PALMER."

"NEW ORLEANS, Saturday, July 4, 1857.

"MY DEAR LITTLE MOLLY: A few days ago I wrote a letter to Sister Fanny: and as Papa loves all his little daughters just alike, he must try to write in turn to each one that is old enough to understand what he says. Dear little Marion, for example, could hardly read a letter. or know its meaning if mother should read it to her; so she will be satisfied if I only send a kiss, which you or Mama may give her for me: only be sure to tell her that it is Papa's kiss, not Mamy's. Sweet Kate, too, cannot read, you know; but she has sense enough to understand every word of a little, wee-wee letter, if mother reads it carefully to her; so, dear little soul, she shall come in for her share after a while. You see that I begin at the top and go down regularly to the bottom. Fanny being the oldest daughter stands at the head of my little class: you come next; and Gussie, because a little younger, comes next to you; and then Katy, last. Marion must be content yet awhile to snug up to Mama's bosom, and enjoy her teat-tie.

"I was sorry, dear sweet Mol, to learn from one of Mother's letters that you were not very well: that poor little head of yours aches oftener than I would have it do—and that little body, too, is so thin and lean. I am afraid it has not juice enough in it. Well, you must eat and play —then you must play and eat—take a plenty of sleep besides: and so by dint of eating, playing and sleeping, you will perhaps grow fat and strong, and be ready for school next winter and bring me such good reports as you did last winter, with ever so many extra credits, and without any checks. Fanny used to be thin and puny, just as you are now; and I hope, by and by, you will change and become hearty and plump, too: all in good time, if we are only patient, and do what is right.

"How does the music come on? Mother has not said a word about that in any of her letters. Sometimes, I fancy the piano is going downstairs; and I stop to listen for the duet:—ah then, it comes back to me, that the little fingers of my two sweet musicians are a thousand miles off, and that no breeze that blows is strong enough to bring so far the delightful notes which I would like so much to hear. Still I hope Grandmother hears them sometimes, and is right glad that she has such little dears by her to love and pet. I take it for granted, you see, that you behave very good, so that Grandmother can pet and love—not exactly take for granted either: because Mother said, in a letter, that the children were behaving very well indeed—and this made me so very happy, that if I could do it, I would hug and kiss you all in turn. It pleases me, too, that in every letter I get Mother has not been obliged to take back her good word, but on the contrary leaves me to believe that all my daughters are pleasant and well-behaved. This makes me glad, and, just a little, proud of my girls, whom I want every body to love. Do you wish to know the secret of being loved? I will tell you, in a little story about Dr. Doddridge's daughter. She was a sweet girl whom everybody fondled and praised. Her father said to her one day, 'Mary, my daughter, why is it that everybody loves you so?' And she answered very quickly, 'I do not know, Papa, unless it is because I love everybody.' Ah! that is the great secret: You love me, and I'll love you—isn't that fair? Remember this now, my pet, all your life: be always kind and loving; and the love of others will always rest upon you, fresh and sweet, like the dew upon a rose-bud. There is one above all others whose love I wish my Mary to enjoy. Can you guess who that is? It is God, my child: I pray to God every day that he would love you. But how can he love you with a proud and wicked heart? Ask him to give you a better heart so that he may love you tenderly: I mean a heart that will love him in return. Would it not be strange if you did not love your father and mother, who have always been so kind to you? But is not God much kinder than they are? Does he not give you everything, even those very parents who cherish you, and those sweet sisters with whom you are so happy all the time? You are old enough now to think about the blessed Savior that died for us; and to pray for a new heart, with which to love him forever. But I must stop now. Kiss Mother for me and all the sisters from Fanny down to Marion, and Grandmother, and all whom you and I love. Good-bye,

"Your loving father,

"B. M. PALMER."

"This is the 4th of July—it is very noisy in the streets. The soldiers are out parading, and one very handsome company has just passed by the door, called the Continentals. Ask Fanny if she can tell who the Continentals were and why people make so much noise on the 4th of July, the men with their cannon, and the boys with crackers? If she cannot, ask Grandfather, and then watch how his big chest will swell as he tells you a long and bright story of the old time when heroes lived. You will read it for yourself, by and by."

"NEW ORLEANS, Monday, July 13, 1857.

"Come here, Katy Darling: and stand by Mother's knee, and with those two bright black eyes see a whole letter written to my little girl, and all of it to herself. What a pity you cannot read it! Then you would snatch it away, and run off into a corner all alone, and nobody, not even Mama, should know a word, until you had drunk all the freshness out of it with those two black eyes. Well, one of these days you will be able to read all the letters that come to you, and to write you own besides—and perhaps one of these days, a long way off I hope, you will get letters from some sweetheart or other, that will read finer than Papa's: and, I guess when that day comes, you will have the reading of those letters all to yourself. But just now, you will be obliged to read this with Mama's eyes, and she will have to tell you all that is in it: and I fancy I can see you now listening and laughing as Mother goes slowly and carefully over these lines.

"I wonder what I can find to write about, that my little Katy will care to hear. Shall I attempt to tell her how much Father loves his darling? I could only say, as you used to say, when you hugged me round my neck, 'with all my heart,' and then you would be apt to answer, 'Oh, Pa! I know all that already: tell me something new. Is there any use to sit down and write a letter to go a great way off, just to tell somebody you love them very much?' Ah! my daughter, when you get bigger you will find out that the oldest things are always the sweetest. Isn't that funny? Yet so it is. Ask Mama if she ever gets tired hearing Father say he loves her, although she has been hearing it almost eighteen years. I reckon if she hears it for eighteen years to come, it will be just as new as ever. So you see, some old things always keep new, and love is one of them. So Father will say it over again, that he loves little Katy darling 'more than tongue can tell,' and he longs to see her, to take her up in his arms, and kiss her; and to hear her sweet merry voice chirping about the house like a canary, only a great deal sweeter and softer. Enough, however, of love for this time!

"Shall I tell you all about my visit over the lake? How I got into a big boat that went puffing and blowing like a great whale through the water?—and came in the evening to a beautiful beach, and went up to a fine house, with a nice plat of green grass stretching out in front? And how I rode on a beautiful horse, and sailed in an elegant boat that swam like a duck, and fished but caught nothing but some miserable good-for-nothing catfish. By the way let me tell you about the horse I rode. He was a great pet of his young master, who taught him to do all sorts of funny things. He would come and eat sugar out of his hand, and then he would lie down upon the grass by him, and if you go up to him and say, 'How d'ye do, Noty,' he will take up his big hoof and put it in your hand as reasonable as any man that wants to shake hands. I never saw such a funny horse but once before: and that one would carry his master's cigar to the kitchen and bring it back lighted for him.

"Maum Maria has just come in to say that I must send her love to Mama and all the children, and to your Maumma and that all the black people send their respects to her besides. Be sure now to deliver this message, as Maria was very particular in giving it to me. Maria takes good care of Father—on Saturday, besides an excellent dinner, she got at market some soft peaches, and a muskmelon for dessert, so that with a plenty of sweet figs and a little milk, I made out capitally. We are very lucky in getting such a cook. Mr. Markham stayed with me last night, and is sitting down at the breakfast table with me. He sends love to everybody, and a special kiss to Katy. Tell Mother that every Sunday night I go up to the Campbells' or Blacks' after preaching, and get a nice plate of clabber and sometimes of peaches and milk. Mrs. Campbell sends her love, and little Palmer is better.

"Good-bye, now, my daughter. Be a good little girl and mind everything Mother and Grandmother say to you. Kiss them both for me, and kiss dear little Marion, and don't let her forget her Papa that she used to love so much.

"Your loving father,

"B. M. PALMER."

"NEW ORLEANS, July 16, 1857.

"MY DEAR FANNY: I received some days ago your sweet letter, for which I owe you many thanks; especially as you wrote of your own accord, and before mine to you had time to come to hand. It is very pleasant to have such mutual recognition, when absent from one another; so that the letters pass each other on the road, showing that without concert, each party is thinking of the other at almost the same moment. There are very few hours of the day when Father's thoughts do not wander off to Columbia, up and down its shady streets, and linger about Grandmother's house, which contains just now all his earthly treasures; and it is very comforting to know that amid all your sports and joys, you send off now and then a stray thought to look me up in these lonely bachelor quarters where I am now, as gloomy as a ship at quarantine.

"I must give you credit, too, for having written a very excellent letter. I read it over and over, with a good deal of satisfaction and pride. The handwriting was uncommonly fine, showing that you will soon, with a little pains, make a capital penwoman: and the style was easy and flowing, so that you will one of these days make a superb letter writer. Do not say Pshaw! to all this: for when we do well, it is right to be praised; and we may take it modestly and be encouraged. By the way, Mrs. Bartlett begs you to write to her. She says, she tried to make you promise to do so, but could not succeed. She will excuse all mistakes; and if you are afraid of making any, you might get Mother to correct your letter and then copy it off. But write to me, my child, if you make a thousand errors; for Father's eye will look very forgivingly upon them for the love which prompts you to write at all, and besides, this is the best way to improve. You would laugh, almost to kill yourself, if you could hear my blunders in French with Mr. Guillet; and yet we rattle on, just as though it was all right. A Frenchman, you know, is too polite to laugh at anybody; and yet I see Mr. Guillet's mustache twitching every now and then, as though it would do him good to take a hearty laugh.

"The mosquitos are beginning to be very bad. Hitherto they have not troubled me much, and I had begun to think they were not worse than in Columbia. But they sting and bite now pretty sharply, and keep my feet in a fever all day long. I am afraid I shall have to take to boots again, which I have pretty well discarded, as they trouble my feet more than hands or face. At night I bid them defiance in my net.

"Tell Mother Tom has gone to a large dinner party to-day, and ask her if she does not think this is a new kink, quite 'a getting up stairs,' or at least high life in the kitchen. She will scold me for being so indulgent; but Tom has really been so well-behaved that I was disposed to grant him this dispensation, and I am a soft body anyhow, that can't say no, perhaps when I ought.

"I hope, dear Fanny, that among you all you will not allow little Marion to forget to say Papa, and that she will not fail to recognize me when I come on. I do miss the dear little toad so much: and fancy sometimes when I come into the room that she is running for my slippers, and seating me in the chair. You cannot imagine how much happiness Mother and I feel in the dear children; and what hopes we have of them, that they will be useful and pious. You must all try not to disappoint us.

"I wish you were here to get some of this good fruit. Everybody is sending me plates of figs, till I am overrun with them; they are the sweetest I ever ate. Maria manages to provide me a muskmelon for my breakfast every morning, and a good plate of soft peaches for my dinner, so that I fare rather luxuriously; but the fruit would be sweeter if shared with those I love. Kiss dear Mother for me and Grandmother, and all the sisters, and tell all the servants 'Howdye,' and love to Emily and the rest. Write again to me and cheer me up.

"Your ever-loving father,

"B. M. PALMER."

"NEW ORLEANS, Wednesday, July 29, 1857.

"MY DEAR DAUGHTER: It was with great delight I broke the seal of your letter written on the 24th, although from the direction on the back I at first supposed it was from your mother. It makes, however, an agreeable variety to receive sometimes a letter from you as well as from her: and you shall not go without your reward for the effort you make toward a correspondence. You shall always have a speedy answer, as often as you may write; if only to convince you how great is the satisfaction I derive from every love note you dispatch to your lonesome father.

"I am sorry to hear that your eye is still painful; and I have already written to your mother that you had better intermit all your studies, until it is entirely well. You must be careful not to try it too much, as this keeps up the irritation and prevents its restoration. It is better that French, drawing and music should all go by the board for a time, than that you should be disabled from all study by a lasting weakness of eyesight. The next five years of your life are of unspeakable importance to you, since they are the years in which you are to obtain your education. What you are to be through life, and indeed what you are to be through all eternity, will depend upon what you shall learn during these five years. I would not, therefore, for a great deal, have any serious obstacle put in your way, as I am ambitious that you shall grow up a very cultivated woman, and be a praise to your parents when they are old. As I have no son, I must make the more of my daughters; and if possible, I would like them to be as learned as I would have striven to make Blakely, if it had pleased God to spare him to us. It will all depend upon yourselves; for I will spare no expense and no labor to secure you the best advantages the country can afford. And I feel the greatest confidence that I shall obtain my reward in seeing all my girls both pious and elegant women; fitted to shine in society, and be abundantly useful and happy in their day.

"I am making some progress in my French, though Mons. Guillet keeps me drilling in the phrases and idioms of the language, and does not yet permit me to read. It will be a help to me, if you should be able to jabber it when we meet; and I think all next winter, we may learn it together. It will be such fun to laugh over our own mistakes; and after a while, we will be able to speak it as correctly as any live Frenchman in New Orleans. If, too, I should conclude to employ a governess, who speaks it well, that will be a great advantage—for she will come to our help whenever we break down. How do you like the idea of a teacher at home, instead of going to school? Would you prefer to have a teacher all to yourself, and arrange your studies according to your own notions? or would you rather go to school, where you can meet with other girls? Everything will depend, I judge, upon the kind of governess we get—but you can form some idea of it, from seeing how it works in Mr. Bryce's family, over the way. Write and tell me what you think about this, for I would like to please you.

"I wish, my dear daughter, that in answering my letter, you had told me about your religious feelings—it would have given you something to write about; and I would have been so glad to know exactly how you feel on that most important of all subjects. Can it be, my darling, that you never think about that soul of yours, which is destined to live forever and ever? that you are not sometimes distressed, when you remember that you are totally unprepared to die; and yet at any moment you may be called away? Oh, do think about this sometimes; and if you ever feel anxious to be saved, do not hide it all up in your heart, as if it was something to be ashamed of. But rather make a friend of your mother and of your father, who desire nothing so much as to see you one of God's children. I cannot tell you how anxious I am about your salvation; how earnestly I long to see you a Christian. Do not put it off, but give yourself over to the Savior, and love and serve him while you are young. Kiss Mother and all the sisters for me, and Grandmother, too—and Emily and all the rest—and believe me

"Your ever-loving father,

"B. M. PALMER."

During this, as during previous periods of his life, he gave himself to the beneficent function of comforting the bereaved, by letters of condolence. A specimen of these is presented in the following, to Mrs. Bazile Lanneau on the death of her son Benjamin Palmer Lanneau:

"NEW ORLEANS, June 16, 1857.

"MY DEAR COUSIN: I have just returned from a hurried visit to Carolina to deposit my family for the summer beyond the range of the epidemic fever of this climate. On passing the depot at Greensboro, Ga., I had a glimpse of Cousin Rebecca, whom Randolph had advised of my movements, and from her I received the first intelligence of the recent heavy affliction which has fallen upon you. Indeed, your cup is full to overflowing; and I cannot forbear taking up the pen if only to utter words of sympathy. Conscience has twinged me more than once for neglecting to write you under the first of your trials; but up to the last moment before leaving Carolina I cherished the hope of running down to Charleston and of mingling my tears with yours at your own fireside. Upon reaching New Orleans I was at once plunged many fathoms deep in a sea of care, and became absorbed in the duties of my first and most trying season in a new field.

"I may, too, as well confess to a peculiar repugnance to letters of condolence, and seldom indite one without a painful sense of mockery. Were not Job's friends less 'miserable comforters' when they sat down with him in the ashes and covered their heads seven days and seven nights—than when their pathetic silence was broken by their long and garrulous discourse? I may perhaps misjudge, having never yet been called to experience that sorrow which cuts down through the soul to the very quick; but it has always seemed to me that in the very first access of severe bereavement before the heart has had time to recover from the first blight of its devastation all sympathy is sheer impertinence and mockery. This intrusion of one's nearest friend would be repelled in the impatient exclamation, 'How long wilt thou not depart from me and let me alone, until I swallow my spittle.'

"It was the possession of this sentiment which has especially restrained me till now. If my pen could only have wept silently with you without mocking you with words its service should not have been withheld. I knew too well the worth of your dear husband—the frank and manly character which won all hearts to him in confidence. I knew too well his worth to you: how much he was the head and center of your home, and the worshipful reverence with which you loved him, through these thirty years, and I said if all the world besides were thrown in could it fill that chasm made in your heart by such a death? I felt not: and therefore I would not break in upon the sanctity of your grief. Nature will have her pangs: and it was better to leave you in the melancholy luxury of solitary sorrow while for a time I should sit down outside the door and pray the Comforter to sustain and cheer you.

"But, my sweet cousin, it has pleased the Lord again to bruise you. Before the tears of your widowhood were dry the fresh tears of a bereaved mother fell fast upon the pale body of your second born. Your afflictions, like your past mercies, come to you in the cluster; their bitter juices you must squeeze and drain to the last drop. How shall earth comfort you now unless it cast forth and restore to you its dead? I can measure your loss thus far to know that a covenant God can alone be your friend now. What can your home henceforth ever be but a broken home, and what can you carry to the grave but a stricken heart bleeding every day in fresh remembrance of your dead? And what can I do for you but weep with you in the church-yard—the only spot where at last all heads shall cease to throb and all hearts cease to break!

"Yet heavy as your double bereavement is, there are surpassing consolations in it, too, which you will soon, if you do not already, appreciate. The husband was spared through all these years till his dependent children are grown into strength to buffet with the world, and the son through short pains, is spared that dying life which his disease would have insured to him. You can look back upon the long life of usefulness in the one—filled with zeal for the Master's glory and with labors for the Church of Christ whose vacant place will long remind the Church how great the loss she, no less than you, has sustained. In the other an early Christian hope has flowered at once into the full enjoyment of heaven. You have the comfort of knowing that neither of them is lost to you, but only saved to you forever. Ah, my cousin, it is the eternal parting that has a sting. If that be spared us surely we can bear the interval of separation when we shall join them to part no more.

"So far, our whole family in all its branches and generations is safely gathered—our parents and children alike, and a blissful meeting awaits us, when they shall welcome us above. And may we not take this in hopeful pledge that so it will continue to be through a long future, our God being the God of our children and of our children's children in all their generations? For my own part I shall never grieve over any of my blood whom God takes to heaven. I did not shed a tear for my mother. I do not think I shall for my father. The one reigning and comforting thought is—that another is safely gathered into rest. But none of these reflections is new to you and I have not designed to play the comforter. 'There is a friend that sticketh closer than a brother' into whose ear I am sure you have poured all your sorrows, and whose tender sympathy sustains you in moments when you droop. The disciples of the Baptist took up his body and buried it, and *'went and told Jesus.'* This is what you have done, and I will not come in with my poor words between you and that friend. I wish you could know how much I have always loved and reverenced you, my dear cousin, that I have never thought of you but it has warmed my heart—how the sight of your patient, cheerful face in the midst of family cares and toils has often given me courage to go out and be a true man in life. If you knew all this you would know how truly I have felt your grief and how gladly I would lighten your burdens.

"God bless you and yours forever more.

"Yours affectionately,

"B. M. PALMER."

The Old School Assembly of 1860 elected Dr. Palmer to the chair of Pastoral Theology and Sacred Rhetoric in Princeton Theological Seminary, giving him two hundred and thirty-seven votes, all the votes cast. This was no small compliment and was probably received as such. But there is no evidence that he gave this call any particular consideration. His mind had been long made up that his place was in the pastorate.

CHAPTER XII.

HIS COURSE DURING THE WAR.

(1861-1865.)

Hard for Southern Clergymen to Steer Clear of Political Preaching in 1861.—Some Political Preaching on Dr. Palmer's Part.—The Political Work of the Old School Assembly of 1861.—The Consequent Action of the Presbytery of New Orleans, Looking to the Establishment of the Presbyterian Church in the Confederate States of America.—In the Augusta Assembly, December, 1861.—His Services to the First Presbyterian Church of New Orleans till April, 1862.—"The Art of Conversation."—Stumping the State of Mississippi, April and May, 1862.—The Fall of New Orleans into the Hands of General B. F. Butler Necessitates Dr. Palmer's making His Home Elsewhere.—At Chattanooga, August, 1862.—At Columbia during Autumn of 1862 and Winter Following.—Eulogy on Thornwell.—Eulogy of General Gregg.—Before the Legislature of Georgia.—Bread Cast upon the Waters Years before Returned. —In the General Assembly of 1863.—With the Army of Tennessee.—Returns Home to Accompany His Oldest Daughter down into the Valley of the Shadow as far as the Living may Go.—In Columbia, Professor of Theology, and the Supply of His Old Church.—Address to General Wade Hampton, "Soldiers of the Legion and Gentlemen of the Army."—Opposed to the Union of His Church and the Synod of the South.—In the Assembly of 1864.--Pastoral Letter to His Flock in New Orleans.—Letter to Miss Anna Jennings.— Letter to Mrs. R.— An Occasion when He Preached with Difficulty.—His Flight from Columbia and Return.—Experiences of His Family during the Burning and Sack of Columbia.—Certain Subordinate Services to the Church during these Years.

THE official discussion of political questions by the clergy had had relatively little place in the South prior to the outbreak of the war between the sections. It had developed no Beechers, no Parkers, and no Cheevers, to disseminate political fads through the medium of their sacred offce. But when, in 1860, the Republic seemed on the eve of destruction, many clergymen, hitherto conservative, deviated from their previous courses, feeling it incumbent on them to express their views on the momentous crisis. The Old School Presbyterian

Church had been marked for its studious avoidance of meddling with the subject of slavery, but it now became prominent for the able political discussions conducted by its clergy. It has before appeared that Dr. Palmer, on Thanksgiving Day, 1860, swayed New Orleans, as had Demosthenes of old the men of Athens. There soon appeared from the pen of Dr. J. H. Thornwell, of South Carolina, what seemed to be an irresistible vindication of the position which had been taken by the South. Dr. Hodge, of Princeton, came out with "a fair and candid" exposition of the Northern side of the question. Then came another effort from the trenchant and versatile pen of Dr. Robert J. Breckenridge.

Under the circumstances we should not be surprised to find Dr. Palmer again dividing his efforts between the preaching of the simple Gospel and the endeavor to solve the problems before his country. This is in fact, what he did.

Thus we find him, Sabbath morning, May 26, 1861, delivering a discourse from his own pulpit, to the Crescent Rifles. His text was Psalm 144: 1: "Blessed be the Lord, my strength, which teacheth my hands to war and my fingers to fight." He began with [1] the story of an ancient castle in which horses and riders fully accoutred stood rooted to the ground under the spell of an enchantment, till the shrill blast of a trumpet disenchanted them, when silence was suddenly changed to the pawing of war steeds and the clangor of arms, as horsemen sprang to the saddle. In this he found a parable of the past and present condition of the country, and passed to the scene immediately before him—the presence, within the house of God, of the flower and pride of the city in military garb, their banners leaning against the consecrated walls, to hear the last words of Christian counsel and receive the last benediction of religion ere they should go forth to the dread encounter. Turning to his text, he vindicated from Scripture and reason the propriety of war in certain circumstances; brought out, in the second place, the principle, that sacrifice and toil are the conditions upon which all earthly blessings are obtained and held, and in the third place, the position that *in the comprehensive government of Jehovah nations have their assigned mission, which they must execute through the conflicts which Providence may ordain for them.*

---

[1] The sermon is found, in full, in the *Sunday Delta,* June 2, 1861.

Endeavoring to discriminate between wars that are relatively criminal and those that are comparatively blameless, he plead that this war, was *"with us,* one of simple defence," that our foes were convicted of guilt before God, *"by the malignant and vindictive spirit" which they breathed in all* their utterances against us, that we were defending our national trust, and great American principle of self-government, and that the issue was *"an issue between religion and atheism;"* the North was crying for "a new Constitution, a new Bible, and a new God."

In conclusion, he urged the soldiers before him to carry along with them a religious conviction of the righteousness of their cause, and to cherish in their hearts a sense of dependence on Almighty God. Finally, he exhorted his hearers to give their hearts to Christ and be prepared for the hour of death and entrance into the world of bliss.

About the same time Dr. Palmer delivered a very eloquent and patriotic exhortation to the Washington Artillery, one of the leading military organizations of New Orleans. He addressed these troops just prior to their marching to the railway station on their departure for the scene of war in Virginia. He spoke from the steps of the beautiful and classic portico of the City Hall. "Besides the military, there were not less than five thousand citizens present on this interesting occasion." The speaker said:

"GENTLEMEN OF THE WASHINGTON ARTILLERY: At the sound of the bugle you are here, within one short hour to bid adieu to cherished homes, and soon to encounter the perils of battle on a distant field. It is fitting that here, in the heart of this great city—here, beneath the shadow of this Hall, over which floats the flag of Louisiana's sovereignty and independence, you should receive a public and a tender farewell. It is fitting that religion herself should with gentle voice whisper her benediction upon your flag and your cause. Soldiers, history reads to us of wars which have been baptized as holy; but she enters upon her records none that is holier than this in which you have embarked. It is a war of defense against wicked and cruel aggression—a war of civilization against a ruthless barbarism which would dishonor the dark ages—a war of religion against a blind and bloody fanaticism. It is a war for your homes and your firesides—for your wives and children—for the land which the Lord has given us for a heritage. It is a war for the maintenance of the broadest principle for which a free people can contend—the right of self-government. Eighty-five years ago our fathers fought in defence of the chartered rights of Englishmen, that taxation and representation are correlative. We, their sons, contend to-day for the great American principle that all just government derives its powers from the will of the governed. It is the corner stone of the great temple which, on this continent, has been reared to civil freedom; and its denial leads, as the events of the past two months have clearly shown, to despotism, the most absolute and intolerable—a despotism more grinding than that of the Turk or Russian, because it is the despotism of the mob, unregulated by principle or precedent, drifting at the will of an unscrupulous and irresponsible majority. The alternative which the North has laid before her people is the subjugation of the South, or what they are pleased to call absolute anarchy. The alternative before us is the independence of the South or a despotism which will put its iron heel upon all that the human heart can hold dear. This mighty issue is to be submitted to the ordeal of battle, with the nations of the earth as spectators, and with the God of heaven as umpire. The theater appointed for the struggle is the soil of Virginia, beneath the shadow of her own Alleghanies. Comprehending the import of this great controversy from the first, Virginia sought to stand between the combatants, and pleaded for such an adjustment as both the civilization and religion of the age demanded. When this became hopeless, obeying the instinct of that nature which has ever made her the Mother of statesmen and of States, she has opened her broad bosom to the blows of a tyrant's hand. Upon such a theater, with such an issue pending before such a tribunal, we have no doubt of the part which will be assigned you to play; and when we hear the thunders of your cannon echoing from the mountain passes of Virginia will understand that you mean, in the language of Cromwell at the Castle of Drogheda, 'to cut this war to the heart.'

"It only remains, soldiers, to invoke the blessing of Almighty God upon your honored flag. It waves in brave hands over the gallant defenders of a holy cause. It will be found in the thickest of the fight, and the principles which it represents you will defend to 'the last of your breath and of your blood.' May victory perch upon its staff in the hour of battle,—and peace—an honorable peace—be wrapped within its folds when you shall return. It is little to say to you that you will be remembered. And should the frequent fate of the soldier befall you in a soldier's death, you shall find your graves in thousands of hearts and the pen of history shall write the story of your martyrdom. Soldiers, farewell! and may the Lord of Hosts be around about you as a wall of fire, and shield your head in the day of battle!"[2]

The preaching of political sermons and the discussion in religious papers of political questions, by Old School divines, was ominous. Some of these divines never so lost their heads

[2] Copied from the *Daily Delta,* New Orleans, May 29, 1861.

as to precipitate their ecclesiastical courts into rendering political decisions. Their indulgence in such discussions, however, was indicative of such a degree of excitement amongst the clergy at large that it was not a wholly unexpected thing that church courts, even certain Old School Presbyterian Church courts, should begin the making of political decisions. But the Old School Assembly of 1861, under the excitement incident to the capture of Fort Sumter, and under popular pressure brought to bear from without on the body, went to an unexpected extreme, in passing the Spring Resolutions; which, according to Dr. Charles Hodge, virtually declared that the allegiance of the whole Presbyterian Church, North, South, East and West, "is due to the United States, anything in the Constitution, ordinances or laws of the several States to the contrary notwithstanding," and not only decides "the political question referred to, but makes that decision a term of membership in our Church," thus usurping the "prerogatives of the Divine Master."

The passage of these resolutions involved a subordination of Church to State, a violation of the Church's Constitution as well as a usurpation of the crown rights of the Redeemer; and a cruel trampling upon the God-given rights of their brethren throughout the whole Southland. Southern Presbyteries began, on the very heels of the Assembly's adjournment, the endeavor to adjust themselves properly to the Assembly which had passed these resolutions.

The Presbytery of New Orleans was not quick to meet. It did convene, however, in *pro re nata* meetings, July 9, 1861, "to receive any newly organized church, and to consider the course pursued by the late General Assembly with matters pertaining thereto; and also to take whatever action might be judged necessary in the premises." Preliminary business having been done, the Presbytery took measures which are recorded as follows:

"The paper adopted by the General Assembly, in view of the state of the country, was then taken up for consideration. It is as follows:

"'Gratefully acknowledging the distinguished bounty and care of Almighty God toward this favored land, and recognizing our obligation to submit to every ordinance of man for the Lord's sake, this General Assembly adopts the following resolutions:

"'*Resolved,* 1. That in view of the present agitated and unhappy condition of our country, the first day of July next is set apart as a day of prayer throughout our bounds; and that on this day ministers and people be called on humbly to confess and bewail our national sins; to offer our thanks to the Father of lights for his abundant and undeserved goodness toward us as a nation; to seek his guidance and blessing upon our rulers and their counsels, as well as on the Congress of the United States about to assemble; and to implore him, in the name of Jesus Christ, the great High Priest of the Christian profession, to turn away his anger from us, and speedily restore to us the blessings of an honorable peace.

"'*Resolved,* 2. That this General Assembly, in the spirit of Christian patriotism which the Scriptures enjoin, and which has always characterized this Church, do hereby acknowledge and declare our obligation to promote and perpetuate, so far as in us lies, the integrity of these United States, to strengthen, uphold, and encourage the Federal Government in the exercise of all its functions under our noble Constitution; and to this Constitution, in all its provisions, requirements, and principles, we profess our unabated loyalty. And to avoid all misconceptions, the Assembly declares that by the terms the 'Federal Government,' as here used, is not meant any particular administration, or the peculiar opinions of any particular party, but that secular administration which, being at any time appointed and inaugurated according to the forms prescribed in the Constitution of the United States, is the visible representative of our national existence.'"[3]

"At the request of the Presbytery the Commissioners presented a statement of the course pursued by the Assembly in connection with the passage of these resolutions.

"Presbytery then went into interlocutory meeting. The roll was called, and each member gave his opinion of the action of the Assembly and of the consequent position and duty of the Presbytery.

"Presbytery then resumed its regular session, and a committee consisting of Messrs. Palmer, McInnis, Henderson, Stringer, and Maybin, was appointed to draft a minute expressing the views of the Presbytery.

"Presbytery then adjourned till 8 p.m. to-morrow.

"Closed with prayer, Wednesday evening."

"Presbytery met according to adjournment, opened with prayer. Present, *Ministers,* B. M. Palmer, S. Woodbridge, H. M. Smith, G. L. Moore, T. R. Markham, J. H Hollander, B Wayne, A. McInnis, U. T. Chamberlain, J. C. Graham, A. S. Johnson; *Elders,* J. A. Maybin, R. C. Latting, F. Stringer, J. D. Henderson, E. Dillon, H. P. Bartlett.

"The minutes of yesterday were read and approved.

"The committee presented the following report which was amended and adopted and is as amended, as follows:

"The committee appointed to draft a minute embodying the views of this Presbytery touching the action of the late General Assembly,

---

[3] *Minutes of the General Assembly,* O. S., 1861, pp. 329, 330.

16

which held its session in the city of Philadelphia in the month of May last, beg leave to submit the following paper:

"The second of the resolutions adopted by the said Assembly aims to bind the whole Presbyterian Church by the authority of its high ecclesiastical court, to promote and perpetuate, as far as in them lies, 'the integrity of these United States, and to strengthen, uphold and encourage the Federal Government in the exercise of all its functions.' This Church is required to profess its unabated loyalty to that central administration, which being at any time appointed and inaugurated according to the terms prescribed in the Constitution of the United States, is the visible representation of our national existence. This extraordinary action was taken in opposition to the notorious fact, that eleven sovereign States had withdrawn from the Federal Union and had established a government of their own; and in opposition to the fact that a large portion of the Church—consisting of ten synods, forty-five presbyteries, 706 ministers, 1089 churches and 75,000 communicants—was embraced within these seceded States; and obliged therefore by their own views of patriotism, and the word of God to support a government entirely distinct from that so arbitrarily patronized by the Assembly.

"The Presbytery can do no less than, solemnly and in the fear of God, protest against this action as being unconstitutional and Erastian to the last degree, since, in undertaking to determine questions of political allegiance, it transcends all the powers granted by the Scriptures to the Church of Christ and the duties which are distinctly enumerated in our form of government; to protest against it also as unchristian and unfair, since advantage was taken of the absence of the great body of the Southern delegates, to consummate an act on which the voice of the whole Church consequently was not heard; to protest against it as tyrannical and oppressive, since it prescribes a political test as a term of ecclesiastical connection, and virtually exscinds those who cannot submit to its arbitrary and unlawful imposition; and finally to protest against it as wicked, since it enjoins that which would be treason against the government under which we live, and which as citizens we cordially and conscientiously support and cherish.

"Since this action places the Southern portion of the Church in a false position before the Church and the world, there should be no delay in recording the protest, and in dissolving, without heat and passion, but with full deliberation, and in the fear of God, the connection hitherto maintained with the General Assembly of the Presbyterian Church in the United States.

"This virtual excision of the Southern Church by the General Assembly, when it shall be accepted and recognized by the different presbyteries, leaves us temporarily in a state of complete disintegration, and the question is at once forced upon our attention, What measure shall be adopted to bring these isolated presbyteries into ecclesiastical union? For this purpose two plans have been proposed in the public prints. The first calls for a general convention of delegates from all the presbyteries, to consider the duty of the Church in the premises, and with power to withdraw in that united form from the Assembly. The second throws this question directly upon the separate presbyteries, who are invited to make provision for an early General Assembly of their own. This latter method commends itself to our judgment as immeasurably the safer and wiser of the two, and for the following reasons:

1. A convention is a body not known to our constitution. It is irresponsible for its action and may, therefore, be dangerous as a precedent.

2. It is unnecessary, as by the system of courts in the Presbyterian Church full provision is made for the mutual consultation and for expressing the visible unity of the Church.

3. There is no party invested with legal authority for calling a convention, and already so many different propositions have been made, as to the time and place for holding the same, that the whole scheme is likely to miscarry for want of concert.

4. As the sitting of this convention is designed to precede the regular meetings of the Presbyteries sufficient time will not be afforded for many of our remote and scattered presbyteries to be represented therein.

5. The action of a convention would not be final but must be referred for ratification to the presbyteries. Whereas the scheme for an assembly would be complete in itself.

We submit therefore the following plan to our sister presbyteries for their consideration:

"That each presbytery for itself and by its own sovereign power, proceed either at a meeting expressly called, or at its fall session, to dissolve its connection with the General Assembly in the United States; and that they appoint commissioners to the General Assembly of the Confederate States of America, to sit in the city of Augusta, Ga., on the 4th day of December, A.D., 1861, or at some other place and time as they shall prefer, that they unite with us in requesting Rev. Drs. J. H. Gray and J. N. Waddell of the Presbytery of Memphis, residing at La Grange, Tenn., to act as a committee, to whom the action of each presbytery shall be reported by the stated clerk of the same as early, if possible, as the 15th of October, and that this committee of commissioners shall be empowered to call a General Assembly at such place and at such time, as shall receive a plurality of votes by the presbyteries; said assembly to be opened with a sermon by the last moderator present, of the Old General Assembly, who shall preside until a new moderator shall have been chosen.

"In conformity with these views be it therefore by this Presbytery:

"*Resolved,* That in view of the unconstitutional, Erastian, tyrannical and virtually exscinding act of the late General Assembly sitting at

Philadelphia in May last, we do hereby with a solemn protest against this act, declare in the fear of God, our connection with the General Assembly of the Presbyterian Church in the United States to be dissolved.

"*Resolved,* That a copy of this action be sent to all the presbyteries within the Confederate States, requesting them, if they concur with us, that they appoint commissioners authorized to organize a General Assembly, to commence its sessions on the 4th day of December next, at 11 A.M. in the First Presbyterian Church, in the city of Augusta, Ga., as a place central, retired, etc.; forwarding due notice of their action to the Committee of Commissioners already designated, and requesting them in due form to give notice of the meeting of the Assembly.

"*Resolved,* That we approve the action taken by Dr. Wilson and the brethren at Columbia, to carry on, *ad interim,* our Foreign Missionary operations, and also the course of the Southwestern Committee of Domestic Missions in assuming, *ad interim,* the independent management of that great interest within our bounds, and we direct the churches under our care to take up and remit their collections for these objects to these committees respectively.

"*Resolved,* That we approve the course of our commissioners to the late General Assembly, believing that they did all that was possible in a body which was in no proper sense a free Assembly.

"Signed—B. M. Palmer, R. McInnis, J. J. Henderson, J. A. Maybin, F. Stringer, Com.

"The ayes and noes were called for on the adoption of this paper, the absent members to have the privilege of recording their votes."

The vote, so far as recorded, was all one way.

From the minutes of the regular fall meeting of the Presbytery of New Orleans, October, 1861, it appears that the body appointed Revs. B. M. Palmer and R. McInnis as principal commissioners, Rev. T. R. Markham and N. P. Chamberlain as alternates; and elders J. A. Maybin and P. Stringer as principal commissioners. W. C. Black and David Hadden as alternates, "to represent it in the General Assembly of the Presbyterian Church in the Confederate States, to be held at Augusta, Ga., Dec. 4, 1861."

It seems that the action of the Presbytery of July 9th had been misunderstood as betraying a disregard for the visible unity of the Church, prejudicing the claims had upon the common property of the whole Church when it was one body, and as annihilating the authority of the Standards of faith and order.

At the fall meeting of the Presbytery, 1861, Dr. B. M.

Palmer submitted a paper which, after amendment, was unanimously adopted. This "Declaratory Act" was as follows:

"WHEREAS, the Presbytery of New Orleans, at a *pro re nata* meeting held in the city of New Orleans, July 9, 1861, did by resolution and for reasons stated therein, cancel its connection with the General Assembly of the Presbyterian Church in the United States of America; and whereas the simple abnegation of the authority of said Assembly unaccompanied with explanation may possibly be misconstrued by some as manifesting a disregard for the visible unity of the Church, or as prejudicing the claims we have upon the common property of the whole Church when it was one body, or as vacating the authority of the Standards of faith and order hitherto recognized, therefore:

"This Presbytery, while not admitting the justice of any of these inferences, yet to satisfy the scruples of others, and in the exercise of superabundant caution makes the following *Declaration* upon these points, *to wit:*

"1. In withdrawing from the jurisdiction of the General Assembly aforesaid, it was not the desire or purpose of this Presbytery to separate itself from sister presbyteries within the limits of the Confederate States, except temporarily, and only in form, and solely with the view of reintegrating in a Southern Assembly which should represent the unity of the Presbyterian Church within our national limits, evidence of which is furnished in the invitation extended to all the presbyteries which are likeminded, to meet on the 4th day of December in the city of Augusta, Ga., for the purpose of organizing such Southern General Assembly.

"2. The Presbytery did not in the passage of said resolution, nor does it now regard its withdrawal from the aforesaid Assembly as affecting in the least degree its synodical relations. On the contrary, since the Assembly grows up through the expansion of the Church by the force of her own inherent life beyond the bounds of a single synod, the only effect of such withdrawal is to cut the connection between these presbyteries of which the Assembly is the ecclesiastical bond. It cannot dissolve the whole interior organization of the Church as held together by presbyteries and synods. In token of this the Stated Clerk is hereby directed to send up as usual the record of this Presbytery, for review to the Synod of Mississippi, at its approaching meeting; and also to lay before that body immediately on its organization, the whole action of the Presbytery, including both the act of *separation,* passed July 9th, and this *Declaratory Act,* now passed, inviting it as the higher court to which this is amenable to declare its judgment upon these proceedings and to make its own deliverances touching the course of the late General Assembly held in May last in the city of Philadelphia.

"3. This Presbytery cannot for a moment conclude that its withdrawal from the General Assembly aforesaid involved in any degree a renunciation of the venerable Standards of the Presbyterian Church, or that it has been since the act of separation without a constitution or a law. On the contrary these Standards having been solemnly subscribed by ministers and elders at their ordination, remain the fundamental law of the Church, and since no alterations nor amendments can be made in the same except by a direct vote of the Presbytery, much less can their authority be entirely vacated without a distinct and formal repudiation. In the stead of which repudiation, it is in the recognition of these Standards as giving the common and public law of the Church, we did and still do propose to unite with our sister presbyteries in constructing a General Assembly as the organ of our visible fellowship and union."

Later in this same month of October, the Synod of Mississippi met in Oakland College, Miss. Dr. Palmer was made moderator. It was found that its other Presbyteries had also taken action "substantially identical" with that of New Orleans Presbytery touching their relations to the old Assembly and to the one to be constituted at Augusta, Ga., December 4, *proximo*. The Synod accordingly declared that all connection theretofore subsisting between it and the General Assembly of the Presbyterian Church in the United States was dissolved; that a similar connection should be formed with the General Assembly of the Presbyterian Church in the Confederate States, as soon as organized; and that in token of this their records should be sent up for the inspection and review of that body.

Similar movements were going on all through the Confederate States. Palmer or no Palmer, some such movements would have taken place. But he seems to have been largely instrumental in determining the precise form which the movements took. The action of his Presbytery of July 9 and 10, to which he gave form, was published abroad and furnished a pattern to the presbyteries generally.

It has been seen that his Presbytery made Dr. Palmer its first commissioner to the Constituting Assembly which met in Augusta, Ga., December 4, 1861. That Assembly numbered not a few men of eminence. Dr. J. H. Thornwell was the man of intellectual preeminence. But Thornwell was not well. The most eloquent speaker in the body was Dr. Palmer. The venerable Dr. Francis McFarland presided until a regular organization could be effected. On his motion Dr. Palmer was unanimously chosen to preach the opening sermon. Dr. Palmer felt the responsibility of the occasion. What was of greater moment, he was prepared to meet it. Endowed with a force and splendor and enthusiasm like Homer's, a fiery and convincing logic, like Paul's, the speaker commanded an eloquence like Edmund Burke's. Habitually an honest and comprehensive student and hence on all occasions a well-furnished preacher, on great occasions he was in possession of the resources and the mettle to respond to the unusual pressure. The present was a great occasion. He pronounced the following discourse:

"FATHERS AND BRETHREN: This Assembly is convened under circumstances of unusual solemnity, and any one of us might well shrink from the responsibility of uttering the first words which are to be spoken here. I see before me venerable men whom the Church of God has honored with the highest mark of her confidence—men venerable for their wisdom, no less than for their age—who should, perhaps, as your organ, speak to-day in the hearing of the nation and of the Church. But a providence which I have had no hand in shaping seems to have devolved upon me this duty as delicate as it is solemn. It only remains for me to bespeak your sympathy, and to implore the divine blessing upon what I may be able to say from the concluding words of the first chapter of Ephesians:

"'And gave Him to be Head over all things to the Church; which is his body, the fulness of him that filleth all in all.' Eph. 1:22, 23.

"You have often admired in the Epistles of Paul the vigor of his inspired and sanctified logic; driving, like a wedge, through the complications of the most perplexed reasoning to its very heart. Not less wonderful is that intellectual comprehensiveness, which, stretching across the breadth of a zone, gathers up all the indirections of his theme, and lays them over upon it in rapid and cumulative utterances—till language begins to break beneath the weight of his thought; and the arguments, set on fire with the ardor of his emotion, reaches the goal a perfect pyramid of flame. The passage just recited is a sufficient example of this rare combination of the discursive with the severely logical in the writings of this great Apostle; for the grand thoughts it presents are nevertheless gathered up by the way, and wrought into the texture of his discourse by incidental allusion. Having first traced the calling and salvation of these Ephesian Christians to its source in the free and gracious love of God, through which they were chosen in Christ; and having unfolded the method of grace, by redemption through his blood, he pauses that he may lift them to some adequate conception of the privileges into which they have been introduced. This, however, he attempts not through cold and didactic exposition, but in the language of prayer, burning throughout with a holy and earnest passion: 'that the eyes of their understanding may be enlightened, to know what is the hope of their calling, what the riches of the glory of their inheritance,' and what the almightiness of the power by which they have been transformed from sinners into saints. Then as if to give some external measure of that power, he points them to the resurrection and exaltation of Christ, in which their own spiritual renovation is implicitly contained. Kindling with the grandeur of his theme growing thus by the accumulation of wayside suggestions, he heaps together in rapid description these phrases burdened with the glory of that Headship which belongs to this risen Savior, and the honors of that Church standing to him in such august relations; till even Paul, with his inspired logic all on fire, can say nothing more than that she is 'His body, the fulness of him that filleth all in all.' The power of human speech is exhausted in this double utterance; and silence lends its emphasis to the unspoken thoughts which no dialect beneath that of the seraphim may express. Who of us, my brethren, has not been stunned by this holy vehemence of Paul, as he piles together his massive words; each bursting with a separate wealth, and revealing the agony of language in uttering the deep things of God? What resource have we, but to halt at the articulations of his text—until, stored with their digressive sweets we return to follow the wheels of his chariot as it bounds along the great highway of his discourse? Such an excursus I now propose to you: for no theme occurs to me more suited to the solemnity of this occasion, than *the supreme dominion to which Christ is exalted as the Head of the Church and the glory of the Church in that relation as being at once his body and his fulness.*

"The testimony of Scripture is given with great largeness to this Headship of Christ. In this immediate connection, Paul affirms that He is 'set at the Father's own right hand in the heavenly places, far above all principality and power, and might and dominion, and every name that is named, not only in this world, but also in that which is to come; and hath put all things under his feet, and gave him to be the head over all things.' Eph. 1 : 20-23. Again, in Philippians: 'wherefore God also hath highly exalted him, and given him a name which is above every name; that at the name of Jesus every knee should bow, of things in heaven and things in earth, and things under the earth, and that every tongue should confess that Jesus Christ is Lord, to the glory of God the Father.' Phil. 2:9-11. What enumeration can be more exhaustive, and what description more minute of the universality and glory of this dominion? In like manner, we read in the prophetic record the testimony of Daniel: 'I saw in the night visions, and behold, one like the Son of man came with the clouds of heaven, and came to the Ancient of days, and they brought him near before him; and there was given him dominion and glory, and a kingdom, that all people, nations and languages should serve him. His dominion is an everlasting dominion, which shall not pass away, and his kingdom that which shall not be destroyed.' Dan. 7: 13, 14. The evangelical Isaiah, too, lifts up the voice of the ancient Church: 'unto us a child is born, unto us a Son is given, and the government shall be upon his shoulders; and his name shall be called Wonderful, Counsellor, the Mighty God, the Everlasting Father, the Prince of Peace. Of the increase of his government and peace, there shall be no end, upon the throne of David and upon his kingdom to order it, and to establish it with judgment and with justice, from henceforth even forever.' Isa. 9:6, 7. Our Lord himself asserts his claim of universal empire and founds upon it the great commission of the Church: 'All power is given unto me in heaven and upon earth—go ye, therefore, and teach all nations.' Matt. 28:18, 19. Finally, the lonely Seer of Patmos turns his telescopic gaze into the heavens, and reveals the Grand Assembly in their solemn worship around the throne, 'and the number of them was ten thousand times ten thousand, and thousands of thousands; and every creature which is in heaven, and on the earth, and under the earth, and such as are in the sea, and all that are in them, heard I saying, Blessing, and honor, and glory, and power, be unto him that sitteth upon the throne, and unto the Lamb forever and ever.' Rev. 5:11, 13. Such is the testimony of prophecy, both as it begins, and as it closes the sacred canon.

"Observe, however, of whom all this is affirmed. It is not alone of the Eternal Word which dwelt in Christ; nor yet alone of the man Jesus, in whom that Word was made flesh—but of the Christ, in whom these two natures meet and are indissolubly united. So that we are compelled to look upon both the terms of His complex person before we can apprehend the nature and the greatness of this supremacy. We shall discover reasons in both for the sublime agency assigned to him as 'the whole creation's Head.' Looking, then, upon the divine side, it is obvious,

"1. *That all the perfections of God are indispensable to the fulfilment of this amazing trust.* Recurring to the passages already quoted, this headship clearly includes universal conservation and rule. The whole administration of Providence and law over matter and over mind is delegated to this Head; who cannot therefore, be a mere creature, lacking the first attributes necessary to the execution of his task. Suppose the universe of matter to be created; yet is it throughout, from the atom to the mass, senseless and inert. The mechanical forces pent up within its gigantic frame slumber in a repose deep as that of death, until evoked and put in play by the operative will of the Great Designer; and the constant pressure of the same external will is the secret power by which the wheels and pistons of the blind machine are driven.

"Proudly as science may descant upon the laws of nature which it is her providence to explore, they are at last but the formulas into which our knowledge, drawn from extended observation, is generalized. It were sad if reason should be deceived by the pompous phraseology, which often serves but as the cover for that ignorance it is too proud to confess. These physical laws are but records of facts inductively classified, not producing causes to which these facts owe existence. They are only statements of the modes through which Nature is seen to work, and not the secret power to which that working is due. Providence stands over against creation thus as its correlate; precisely the same energy being required in *the continuing,* which was first put forth in *the producing.* The agent, then, to whom this administration of Providence is assigned, must possess the attributes of God. His influential presence must pervade all nature, upholding its separate parts, balancing its discordant forces, adjusting in exact proportions its constituent elements, reconstructing it amidst constant change—its omnipotent and supporting Head.

"The same is true in the domain of mind. Myriads of beings, for example, have pressed this globe, each of whom has a history of his own, and each history a separate thread in the great web of Providence. The slenderest of them may not be drawn without a rent in the general tissue. The tiniest babe, that wakes but for a moment to an infant's joy, and then closes its eyes in sleep forever, was born for a purpose, though born but to die. But see these countless units as they are massed together in society, compacted into States, and living under government and law. What complications are here, to be mastered by Him who is placed as Head over all! Alas! the best statesmanship of earth breaks down in the management even of its subdivided trusts. Contingencies it had not the wisdom to foresee, and too stubborn for control, brings its counsels to naught ;and the web so patiently woven by day, is unraveled in the night. What creature, then, may aspire to the premiership of the universe? As the thought ranges upward from the earth through the grand hierarchy of the skies, who among the creatures can take the scale of such an empire, grasp the law which angels and seraphim obey, weave the destinies of all into one historic conclusion, and draw it up finished and entire before the Judgment Throne? Just here, then, in the attributes of his Godhead, we discern the competency of Christ to be the Head over all things; equal to the statesmanship of the universe, in the perfect administration of a perfect law.

"Thus far we have pressed up to the divinity of Christ, but not to his personal distinction in the Godhead as the only begotten of the Father. I remark then, 2. *That this agency is suitably assigned to him as the middle person of the adorable Trinity, by whose immediate efficiency all things were created.* We may not too curiously pry into the mystery of this plural subsistence in the Godhead, revealed to us as the object of faith rather than as the subject of speculation. Unquestionably, God is infinitely blessed and glorious in the ineffable fellowship of these persons as well as in the unity of his being. But as these personal distinctions have their ground in that singleness of nature, they must equally concur in all the external operations of the Deity; and so the

Scriptures variously ascribe the works of creation, providence and grace to each respectively. In this there is no contradiction; since they are assigned comprehensively to all in their unity, and distributively to each in their separateness. However unable we may be to trace the grounds of that distribution, they must be found in the reciprocal relations of those persons in the mystery of the Godhead. Certainly the Scriptures, however they may generally refer the work of creation to God absolute, as clearly assert the special intervention of the second person as its immediate author. John in the opening of his Gospel, declares with emphasis of the Word that 'all things were made by him, and without him was not anything made.' John 1:3. Paul, speaking of the Son whom God 'hath appointed heir of all things,' adds, 'by whom he also made the world.' Heb. 1:2. And in Colossians, 'by him were all things created that are in heaven, and that are in earth, visible and invisible, whether they be thrones or dominions or principalities or powers; all things were created by him and for him —and he is before all things, and by him all things consist.' Col. 1:16, 17. If then in the out working of this mighty plan, the control and government of all created things should be delegated to an agent who must possess the attributes of the Almighty, which of the sacred three may occupy this trust more suitably than He who in the economy of the Godhead executively and directly brought all things into being? Who shall more perfectly grasp the design of creation than He who articulately wrought it out in all its parts? Who shall better gather up all things unto himself as the center and the head, and administer that Providence which is but the continuation of the creative energy which he first put forth?

"Unsearchable as the mystery of God's being doubtless is, three facts are certainly revealed to us: the unity of the Divine essence, a threefold distinction of persons in the same, and a certain order between them by which the second is *from* the first; not posterior in time, but second in the sequence of thought. It would seem to be a consequence of this personal characteristic of the Son, as being *from* the Father, that the total revelation of God, whether by word or work, should be through him. Thus the ground may exist in the eternal relationship of these persons for referring the works of creation, providence and grace, distributively to the first in the way of final authority, and to the second in the way of executive production. The Father who is before all, shall hold in his august keeping, the eternal thought which drafts the mighty plan. The Son, by virtue of his personal distinction as *from* the Father, shall produce the thought, lifting it up from the abyss of the infinite mind and revealing it to the creatures. Thus the Son is also the Word; the one title being descriptive of his personal relation in the Godhead, and the other of his office as the revealer flowing from the same. Hence Christ says: 'No man hath seen the Father, save He which is of God; he hath seen the Father.' John 6:46.

And again the evangelist John affirms, 'no man hath seen God at any time; the only begotten Son which is in the bosom of the Father, he hath declared him.' John 1:18. In like manner, as the Son is from the Father, so in turn the Holy Spirit is from them both; and he who holds the middle place in this sacred triplet looks upon the first for those archetypal thoughts which he shall render into concrete facts, and then upon the third whose concurrent agency shall breathe life and order and beauty into the works of his hands. As therefore in Christ's divinity we discover the resources, so again in his personal distinction as the Son we trace the ultimate reason of this universal Headship.

"But let us turn from thoughts too high for us, to contemplate the *human* aspect of his person. For if the power to wield this empire vests in him as God, no less does the form of that jurisdiction depend upon a true participation in the nature of those to whom he is the Head. I may open this topic in three particulars:

"1. *By his incarnation he has virtually embraced all the grades of being lying between the extremes of the scale.* The peculiar distinction of man is through his mixed composition to be the middle link of the whole creation. As to his body, he is of the earth, earthy; as to his soul, celestial and God-like. How wonderful his bodily organization, of so many parts, and so wisely adjusted! The most singular feature of all being that the presence of an indwelling, actuating soul is the indispensable condition of its physical life. The two are distinct, yet their co-operation necessary. The anatomist can trace the impressions upon the skin with its fine tissues, and the transmission of these along the nerves to the brain, the seat of all sensation. But science will never perfect her methods so as to step from that brain to the mind which uses it as an organ, and thus explain to us the birth of a single thought. By means of the body, the soul comes forth and takes possession of a world which is foreign to itself; and man connects them both by their mysterious union in himself. So far as our knowledge extends, he is the only being who unites these contradictions; thus fitted by his very organization, he was placed by his Maker in Paradise, the head of the lower creation. In token of this supremacy, the beasts receive from him their baptismal names, and express their allegiance to God's vice-regent upon the earth. As the high priest of nature, he must give articulate voice to her silent praise, and gather up in his censer the incense of a universal worship. Such was the glory of man's primeval state: himself a microcosm, summing together in the perfection of his animal frame all the properties of the material creation, and by the union of spirit bridging the awful gulf of separation between the two. Christ now according to Scripture sinks through the entire scale of intelligent beings till he comes to man; 'for verily, he took not on him the nature of angels, but he took on him the seed of Abraham.' Heb. 2:16. The two poles of being are thus brought together in him;

of being, as it is in God, self-existent and eternal, and of being, as it is in man, dependent and derived. In the sweep of his descent he gathers up all the intervening grades, and finds in man at the bottom of the scale a nature which links all the forms of creaturely existence within himself. Thus in the incarnation he lays a broad foundation for his Headship, establishing through it a relation to the creatures by which they may be recapitulated in him as their center and their head.

"2. *The human title of Christ to this Headship is grounded upon that perfect obedience by which he magnified the law.* If we are overwhelmed by the condescension of the Son in stooping to become man, not less amazing is the counterpart to this in the exaltation of man to this universal Headship. The incarnation lays, so to speak, a *physical* basis for this delegated rule, by allying him in nature with the creature; but there must exist some *moral* ground for this apparent inversion, which transfers man from the bottom to the top of the scale.

"All the terms which define a created moral being imply his subjugation under law. The faculties of understanding, conscience and will with which he is endowed must find their scope in relations which are determined and regulated through a law. What the air is to the lungs, the law is to will; it creates the moral atmosphere, through which all the powers of the soul find their activity and play. Even Christ, in the assumption of our nature, was not exempt from this inexorable condition; for 'God sent forth his Son made of a woman, made under the law.' Gal. 4:4. 'Being found in fashion as a man, he became obedient unto death.' Phil. 2:8. How then shall his humanity lift itself above the law, executively to administer it, dispensing on either hand its blessing and its curse? The explanation is immediately furnished in the passage last cited. 'Wherefore God also hath highly exalted him.' Because of this 'obedience unto death, even the death of the cross;' 'a name is given him which is above every name; at which every knee shall bow, of things in heaven and things in earth, and things under the earth.' Phil. 2:9, 10. In no way conceivable shall the man Jesus be lifted to this supremacy, but by rendering a service to the law, commensurate with its dignity, to which this exaltation shall be an equal reward. The mere assumption of humanity by the Logos doubtless invests it with a sublime worth and imparts to the acts done by it an infinite value. But the natural basis thus laid for Headship is quite another thing from the moral reason for appointing it. If, however, the work done by that nature shall be a work of support to the law itself, more conspicuously revealing its majesty and sustaining it against all possible impeachment—if it shall heal the dreadful breach which sin has made, and discovers the love of God in the very assertion of his justice—if, in the language of the prophet, it shall 'magnify the law and make it honorable,' and be a lesson of holiness which the angels themselves shall study: we may then conceive that, to bring out these grand results in more open view, God may place the administration of this law in the hands of that being who has preeminently honored it; and install over the whole creation one who is fitted by his double nature to be its head. Yet the hypothesis I have suggested, is only a faint outline of the work actually achieved by our incarnate Lord. Who can hope to condense into a paragraph the glories of that obedience by which he has forever magnified the law?—an obedience glorious in its perfect voluntariness, not only as being willingly rendered, but as being optional whether it shall be undertaken: an obedience glorious in being distinctly offered to the precept and the penalty —thus covering the whole area of law and exhausting its contents; a characteristic difference between the obedience of Christ and of all other beings throughout the universe: an obedience glorious as shut up within a limit, bounded within a period—so that Christ could testify in the hearing of heaven and earth, 'it is finished;' not like the obedience of mere creatures, ever continuing, but finished and entire; nothing to be added to it—nothing to be taken from it, and borne into the chancery of heaven as the plea for the sinner's discharge: an obedience glorious through the hypostatic union, which brings the splendor of his deity to illuminate the acts of his humanity. If Moses break the tables of stone at the foot of the Mount, behold one greater than Moses descending after him to gather up the broken fragments, cementing them with his blood, and pouring the rays of his divine glory upon the restored tablet, until every letter beams with light above the brightness of the sun. Well may the cherubim bend their gaze between their extended wings upon this repaired law reposing forever within the ark of the covenant. The transcendant worth of this obedience, as sustaining the majesty of God's law and upholding the integrity of the Divine Government, is signalized by placing him who wrought it over the whole creation; and it becomes the title by which this supremacy is held as his mediatorial reward.

"3. *In this Headship are blended the two methods of law and grace, by which God reveals his moral perfections.* Beyond a doubt, the law was the original medium through which God's nature was disclosed to the creature; and it would not be difficult to show that his glory is stamped upon every feature of it. Indeed, springing out from the bosom of his nature, it not only asserts the claims of God and determines the duty of the creature, but it so transcribes and discovers the excellence of the divine Being that the creature's obedience rises at once into the solemnity of worship. For the same reason, the law is generally one throughout the universe. Having its foundation in the nature of one God, it is essentially one over angels and men, modified only in its details to suit the different relations in which these different classes are placed. It is noticeable moreover that this law finds its majesty vindicated in both its grand divisions through the separate destiny assigned to two separate orders of beings: the holy angels, through their constant obedience, historically illustrating the glory of law as found in its precepts; and apostate angels, through constant endurance of its penalty. Such simple provision has God made for securing revenue of praise through the wisdom of his law. Last of all, in compensation of the stupendous service by which its majesty has been upheld, the administration thereof has been committed to the Mediator, and is brought to a conclusion at the Day of Judgment, when he shall sit upon the throne of his glory. Thus by a method of pure law, the sunlight of Jehovah's excellence shines throughout the universe, gathering into focal splendor upon the person of our exalted Savior, the organ by whom it shall be dispensed to the redeemed forever; for it is written of the New Jerusalem, that it had 'no need of the sun, neither of the moon to shine in it, for the glory of God did lighten it, and the Lamb is the light thereof.' Rev. 21 : 23.

"There is reserved, however, a more inferior display of Divine perfections through a *method of grace*. The law discovers God to us in the attributes of wisdom, power, holiness, justice and truth. But how shall Jehovah open to us his infinite heart—disclosing the depths of its tenderness, his boundless compassion, his inconceivable mercy and love? To do this, he must look upon the suffering and loss, and find a surety who shall bear their guilt and die their death under the curse. But where shall this substitute be found? In vain the challenge went forth from the august throne in tones which only the offended law could use, 'Whom shall I send and who shall go for us? Silence reigned throughout the courts of heaven: for none of the sons of the morning might adventure the dreadful perils of such a trust—till a voice sounded forth from the midst of the throne, 'Lo, I come, I delight to do thy will, oh, my God! yea, thy law is within my heart.' Psalm 40 : 7, 8. Bursting from the secret pavilion, the eternal Word leaps forth to execute the stern demand. He unclothes himself of light, and lays aside the garments of praise, and takes upon him the form of a servant, that he may sound the depths of human woe, and pay the costly ransom for a guilty soul. By an obedience grander in its proportions than the aggregate obedience of all the creatures, Christ vindicates the law's injured majesty; whilst through his grace he brings out the tenderest affections of the Father as a God of love. Sublime is that utterance of Scripture, which tells us that God is life; equally sublime the testimony, which tells us he is light; but grander still, in the comprehension of them both, is the revelation which tells us God is *Love*. To enthrone this grace by the side of law as the Queen Majesty, the author of grace is made the administrator of law. As the covering cloud tempered the brightness of God's presence upon the mercy seat, so forever must the law shine out from the mercy in which it is embosomed; that obedience may be sweetened—not only as a debt which conscience pays to duty, but an homage which the heart pays to love. Thus, the two lines of law and grace by which the Divine glory streams forth upon the universe, converge upon the person of

Jesus Christ in the administration of his delegated trust as 'the Head over all things to the Church.'

"I must now turn your thoughts from Christ to his Church, here set forth as his body and fulness, only regretting that I must shut up in simple sentences what deserves expansion through paragraphs.

"The Church, in accordance with a very familiar distinction, may be viewed by us in two aspects. There is the *ideal Church,* conformed to the pattern drafted in the Divine purpose, composed of the elect in all ages, who have been washed, justified and sanctified; and there is the *actual, visible Church,* composed of those who profess faith in the Redeemer, whether they be his or not. These two interpenetrate each other, and are largely identified in the statements of Scripture; and of both, in important though different senses, it may be affirmed they are the fulness of Christ. The former as being,

"1. *The object upon which the fulness of his grace expends itself.* The two you perceive are reciprocal, the fulness and the distribution. Thus the Evangelist says: 'The Word was made flesh and dwelt amongst us, and we behold his glory as the glory of the only begotten of the Father, full of grace and truth; and of his fulness have all we received, and grace for grace.' John 1:14, 16. The same is stated with equal distinctness in Col. 2:9, 10: 'For in him dwelleth all the fulness of the Godhead bodily—and ye are complete in him, which is the Head of all principality and power.' The glory of Christ is not simply in being the architect of grace, by whom it was historically wrought out and engrafted upon law; but in being also the depository of grace—its dispenser no less than its procurer. The two cannot be viewed apart; Christ, the head of all principality and power, and the Church complete in that gracious fulness which he imparts. Hence, true believers in every age have been drawn from all grades of society, under every degree of culture, have been placed under every variety of discipline, subjected to every form of temptation, recovered from every species of sin, and conducted through all the stages of spiritual growth; that through all might be displayed the exceeding riches of Divine grace—grace for all, and according to the varying exigencies of each.

"2. *The Church of the Elect is the body; that is to say, it is the complement of the mystical Christ.* In the Covenant of Redemption, the Father gave to the Son a seed to be redeemed, and constituted him their representative and surety. In all federal transactions the two ideas are conjoined. As in the Covenant of Works, the first Adam cannot be considered in his separate personality, but also as the representative of his natural seed; so in the Covenant of Grace, the second Adam is incomplete except as associated with his spiritual seed. The two terms are united in the very notion of a covenant. In this sense, the Church is preëminently the body and fulness of Christ; and through all time Christ is reproducing himself in his members. While in his immediate person he is exalted at the right hand of the majesty in the heavens, and will never again appear but with his own glory and with the glory of the Father, yet in the Church which is his body he is still 'the man of sorrows and acquainted with grief.' In all the persecutions, afflictions, temptations and distress of his people he renews his own humiliation and the agony of his own conflict with the powers of darkness. This is the ground of our confidence and hope, as we pass beneath the rod and stagger under our cross; that as 'it behooved the great Captain of our salvation to be made perfect through suffering,' so must all members of his body drink of his cup, and be baptized with the baptism with which he was baptized.

"3. *This Church of the Elect is the fulness of Christ, as constituting the reward of his mediatorial work.* Having redeemed them with his own priceless blood, and sanctified them by his own indwelling Spirit, he must, according to the stipulations of the covenant, present them to the Father, 'holy and without blame before him in love.' To this end, he must appear as the resurrection and the life, that they may 'receive the adoption, to wit; the redemption of their bodies.' Amidst the terrors of a burning world, he must sit upon the throne of judgment and pronounce the Father's authoritative benediction, 'come, ye blessed of my Father, inherit the kingdom prepared for you from the foundation of the world.' 'Then cometh the end, when he shall deliver up the kingdom to God, even the Father;' that God, in the supremacy of his law, 'may be all in all.' Having wound up his mediatorial work in this final act of mediatorial authority, and fulfilled all the promises on which the faith of his people ever leans, he presents them to the Father, according to his eternal pledge, a glorious Church, not having spot or wrinkle or any such thing, but holy and without blemish, 'meet for the inheritance of the saints in light.' This Church is then given back into his hands, to be his reward and his rejoicing forevermore. They swell his train, as he ascends a second time through the clouds into the heavens: shouting, as they rise, the triumphant challenge, 'lift up your heads, oh ye gates, and be ye lift up, ye everlasting doors, and the King of glory shall come in.' Psalm 24:7. Gathered at length in 'the General Assembly and Church of the firstborn, which are written in heaven,' they form the nearest circle around the throne, and give the keynote of that song with which the arches of the great temple shall forever ring. Glorious in that righteousness of God which they have received by faith, the saints, like so many crystal pillars, shall surround the Lamb in the midst of the throne; till all heaven becomes bright with the reflected splendors of that wrought righteousness which answers to the holiness of God, expressed through the law. As the great anthem of praise rolls up from the company of the redeemed, the High Priest of the transfigured Church gathers all into his golden censer and waves it before the throne. Thus, in a sublimer sense, the God of Holiness is seen to be 'all in all;' and the Lamb again is seen to be the light of the New Jerusalem. In this final and exhaustive sense, this glorified Church becomes the body of the great Head, 'the fulness of him that filleth all in all.'

"It must not, however, escape us that this spiritual Church has its manifestation here in the Church actual and visible: the incarnation through which it becomes to us a thing tangible and known. In this view, also, Christ is still her Head—and she, his fulness, because—

"1. *In this embodied form Christ is her only King;* enacting by his sole legislation laws for her government—appointing, by his executive authority, officers for her administration—instituting in his priestly jurisdiction the ordinances of her worship—and granting, in the supremacy of his headship, the character by which her immunities and rights are held. In this pure theocracy, the Mediator is King; and all power under him is simply ministerial. By whatever names we choose to designate her earthly guides, their function is simply to expound a written constitution, and to enforce, by spiritual censures, obedience to a spiritual and unseen ruler.

"2. *Because through this visible Church Christ acquires his wider mediatorial authority over the universe.* As mediator, his prime relation is to those whom he comes to reconcile. The plan of grace, though last in development, is first in the Divine thought, the most stupendous of all God's works; and the earth was built but as the stage on which the sublime drama of redemption might be enacted. The whole scheme of nature is therefore subordinated to it: and the administration of Providence is committed to Christ, for the prosecution of that grace which he came to inaugurate. Hence Paul testifies that he is given to be the Head over all things to the Church, 'which is his body;' through her as his fulness he himself 'filleth all in all.'

"3. *Christ, in his precious headship, heals the breach which sin has made between the creatures; and the visible Church, finally embracing all nations within her pale, bodies forth this grand result.* The first transgression not only separated man from God, but seemed forever to have dissolved the brotherhood between the creatures also. From that day till now, the beasts of the field have been in revolt against the dominion of man, and the elements of nature are reclaimed under his control only through the discoveries of science. The one speech of the infant race has been broken into a thousand jarring tongues, and the earth has been covered with violence and blood. But the Reconciler came. Planting his cross as the great magnet of earth, he draws to himself his purchased seed, incorporates them into a society of love, and sends them forth to throw its bands around a shattered world. Prophecy, through her roll, shows in the dim perspective this Church embracing all lands and tongues and tribes within her arms, and 'the kingdoms of this world becoming the kingdoms of our Lord and of his Christ.' The reconciliation ends not here. When this militant Church shall be transfigured in the skies, to her visible worship and fellowship will be added the 'innumerable company of angels' whom sin has never soiled. The sad breach is forever healed, and cherubim and a flaming sword shall no longer guard the way to the tree of life against guilty man. He who has 'made reconciliation for iniquity and brought in everlasting righteousness,' has also 'made an end of sins.' Sin, death and hell are cast into the lake of fire. and the redeemed universe is brought into one under him who is Head over all. Saints and angels shall blend in harmony of praise around his throne, and the schism of sin be cancelled forever in the Church fellowship of heaven.

"Fathers and Brethren, I must not shut down the gate upon the flood of this discourse, without pointing to the consolation for us in this day of darkness and trial, wrapped up in the headship of the adorable Redeemer. *What tenderness it gives to the whole doctrine of Providence!* Once we trembled in our guilt and shame, and could not look upon the angry throne, to us

"A seat of dreadful wrath,
Which shot devouring flame.'

But healing peace flowed into our wounded hearts, as we looked upon 'God in Christ, reconciling the world unto himself.' In like manner the dispensations of Providence seem relentless and stern, as they frown upon us from 'the unknown God;' but the dark clouds are drenched in soft and mellow light, as they are moved by the hands of our 'Immanuel, God with us.' All judgment is committed to the Son of man; can we not trust him, our elder brother, clothed with all our sympathies, who hath borne our griefs and carried our sorrows, and is able to succor in that he himself hath suffered? The name of this precious Jesus broke for us the spell of despair, when in the hour of legal conviction conscience hung up the ghastly catalogue of our sins against the Judgment throne. The name of Jesus will be the last upon our lips, softly whispered by the departing spirit as the last breath wafts it upward to the skies. It will be first upon our lips when the grave shall yield up its dead to meet the Lord in the air. Shall it not be always upon our lips, taking away the bitterness of our private and our public lot; when all these dispensations are read through an exposition of grace, and are seen throughout to be a discipline of love?

"*What safety also to the universe is this headship of Jesus!* He who grasped the idea of creation as it lay a silent thought in the mind of God, can surely work out the eternal purpose in which it was framed. For this very end, he is given to be the Head over all things—that as he is 'before all things,' so 'by him shall all things consist.' The overturnings upon earth make no fissure in the one solemn purpose of the infinite Creator, and no sudden disclosures startle Him into surprise. The shuttle of history moves swiftly and blindly from age to age; but the great web is woven according to the pattern originally designed in the counsel of the Godhead.

"But he is Head over all things to the Church! Whilst, therefore, a purpose of grace remains to be fulfilled in that Church which he has graven on the palms of his hands and wears as a seal upon his heart, so long the world is safe in the keeping of him whose love is stronger than death. The Christian Church is to a Christian nation the ark of Jehovah's covenant; and we are here to-day in sublime faith to bear that ark upon our shoulders in the presence of this infant nation, as she passes under her baptism of blood. Let us gather with reverence around it, and sing with Luther the 46th Psalm: 'God is our refuge and strength, a very present help in time of trouble. Therefore will we not fear, though the earth be removed, and though the mountains be carried into the midst of the sea; though the waters thereof roar and be troubled, though the mountains shake with the swelling thereof, though the kingdoms be moved, and the earth melted—yet the Lord of Hosts is with us, the God of Jacob is our refuge.'

"What glory, too, surrounds the Church; an outer halo, a second rainbow to that which, like an emerald, John saw round the throne! She is the body of Christ, the bride, the Lamb's wife, whose 'beauty' the 'King hath greatly desired.' She is glorious in her 'raiment of needlework,' 'her clothing of wrought gold,' 'the fine linen clean and white, which is the righteousness of saints.' The Church of the living God! and, therefore, herself living by a secret life flowing from him who is life, and bestowed by the indwelling Spirit who is the quickener. The immortal Church of Christ, which survives all change and never knows decay! Alas, the paths of earth are strewn with the wrecks of broken empires, constructed by human wisdom and shattered through human folly and sin. But this Church of the Redeemer moves through them all upon the grand highway of history, and 'flourishes in immortal youth.' She rode upon the billows of a universal deluge, beneath whose gloomy depths lay a doomed and buried world. Patriarchs gathered beneath her shade in the aged and hoary past. Moses pitched her tabernacle upon the sands of the wilderness, and beneath the frowning brows of Sinai. Prophets pointed out her pathway through the uprolling mists of the distant future. Through the unfolding ages she has moved securely on, while disastrous change has ground to powder and scattered to the winds the proudest dynasties of earth. Kings have bound her with fetters of brass; but the fair captive has taken again her harp from the willows, and God has made her walls salvation and her gates praise. Amidst the fires of martyrdom, she has risen younger from the ashes of her own funeral pile. Wooing the nations with her accents of love, she lengthens her cords to gather them into her broad pavilion. And when the whole frame of nature shall be dissolved, she will stand serene above the burning earth, to welcome her descending Lord. Caught up by him into the heavens, she will gather into her communion there all the elder sons of God; still the immortal Church

of the Redeemer, outliving all time and henceforth counting her years upon the dial of eternity!

"Do we understand, Fathers and Brethren, the mission of the Church given us here to execute? It is to lift up throughout the world our testimony for this headship of Christ. The convocation of this Assembly is in part that testimony. But a little while since, it was attempted in the most august court of our Church to place the crown of our Lord upon the head of Cæsar—to bind that body, which is Christ's fulness, to the chariot in which that Cæsar rides. The intervening months have sufficiently discovered the character of that State, under whose yoke this Church was summoned to bow her neck in meek obedience. But in advance of these disclosures, the voice went up throughout our land, of indignant remonstrance against the usurpation, of solemn protest against the sacrilege. And now this Parliament of the Lord's freemen solemnly declares that, by the terms of her great charter, none but Jesus may be the King in Zion. Once more in this distant age and in these ends of the earth, the Church must declare for the supremacy of her Head, and fling out the consecrated ensign with the old inscription, 'for Christ and his crown.'

"Let this testimony be borne upon the winds over the whole earth, that he who is 'Head over all things to the Church,' 'ruleth in the kingdom of men, and giveth it to whomsoever he will,' until all nations are brought to 'praise and extol and honor the King of heaven, all whose works are truth and his ways judgment.' Let us take this young nation now struggling into birth to the altar of God, and seal its loyalty to Christ, in the faith of that benediction which says, 'Blessed is that nation whose God is the Lord.' The footsteps of our King are to be seen in all the grand march of history, which begins and ends in a true theocracy. Our voice is to be the voice of one crying in the wilderness, 'prepare ye the way of the Lord, make straight in the desert a highway for our God:' for he 'will overturn, overturn, overturn, until he come whose right it is'—and, 'the kingdoms of this world shall become the kingdoms of our Lord and of his Christ.'

"Above all, it is ours to bear aloft the Redeemer's cross, and with the finger ever pointing to say, with the Baptist on the banks of Jordan, 'Behold the Lamb of God which taketh away the sin of the world!' May He who wears the crown make us to feel the power of that cross! Brethren, we have to-day been gazing into heaven after our ascending Lord, ascending to his headship and his crown. From his gracious throne he unfolds the sacred parchment on which our charter and commission are engrossed: 'Go ye into all the world and disciple all nations.' With pathetic gesture, he also points over mountains, continents and seas to the 'other sheep which are not of this fold,' wandering upon the bleak heather, under the dark star of some idol god. May the rushing mighty wind of the Pentecostal day fill this house where we are sitting! and may the tongues of fire rest upon each of this

Assembly! Emblem of the power with which the story of suffering love shall subdue an apostate world! Sinking personal ambition, and forgetful of sectional aggrandizement, let us strive to equip the Church with the necessary agencies for the prosecution of her solemn work. Let us build her towers and establish her bulwarks just where the most effective assaults may be made upon the kingdoms of Satan; that 'her righteousness may go forth as brightness and her salvation as a lamp that burneth;' and Zion become 'a crown of glory,' a 'royal diadem in the hand of our God.'"

The preacher was at once chosen as moderator of the Assembly.

The whole of his work in this Assembly seems to have been on the same high level with his sermon. The Assembly indulged in no political decisions and in no political discussions but devoted itself exclusively to the affairs of Christ's kingdom; and even uttered high and memorable testimony concerning the spirituality of the Church.

Returning to New Orleans, Dr. Palmer devoted himself to the performance of his duties as pastor till about the first of April, 1862. Letters from some to whom he ministered during all these months of 1861 and 1862 in New Orleans, show that he continued to be, notwithstanding the tempestuous times and his passionate devotion to the Southern cause, the most helpful of pastors and preachers.

Meanwhile he had found time to prepare a paper on "The Art of Conversation," which appeared in the *Southern Presbyterian Review*, January, 1862,—an article betraying a thorough philosophy of the art and presenting a noble plea for its cultivation as a means of elevating the tone of social intercourse. The production should be published as a brochure and widely circulated.

Early in April, 1862, Dr. Palmer left New Orleans, intending to visit the army of General Albert Sidney Johnston, and later to attend the meeting of the General Assembly of his Church, appointed to convene in Memphis, Tenn. He seems to have been with General Johnston's army immediately before the battle of Shiloh. According to tradition, astride a horse, he delivered a thrilling address to a portion of Johnston's army just before it went into the battle.

In view of the presence of the conflicting armies in the near vicinity of the city of Memphis, and the consequent difficulty and danger of meeting in that place, provision was made that the General Assembly, instead of convening in Memphis, should gather at Montgomery, Ala. Dr. Palmer was his Presbytery's commissioner to the Assembly. It had been his purpose to attend—a purpose which he failed to realize. He found himself pressed by the Governor of Mississippi into the patriotic function of stumping the State with a view to the reconciliation of those disaffected with the Government of the Confederacy at Richmond. Naturally, to the Mississippians insufficient means seemed to have been taken to protect them against the enemy. It was feared that they would be little disposed to co-operate with the Confederacy. Dr. Palmer delivered patriotic addresses at various points and with fine effect. Of his address at Jackson *The Mississippian* says:

"This distinguished orator, philosopher and divine, whose services in the cause of civil and religious liberty have excited the admiration and gratitude of the whole Southern Confederacy, addressed on yesterday one of the largest and most intelligent audiences ever assembled in the Representatives' Hall. It was a most profound, philosophical and exhaustive exposition of the grounds of our defence in the great struggle in progress before the bar of God and in the forum of nations. It covered the whole ground upon which we rest our cause, and challenged the verdict of the world. It was designed to present the argument upon which the Christian moralist and patriot may rely, and upon which we may justify the position assumed by the seceded States. And most triumphantly did he present it. But we shall attempt no analysis of what could in no sense be said to be a political speech, or popular address. It was but giving voice to thought almost too deep for utterance, such as the plummet line of ephemeral politicians, in their discussion of the subject never sounded.

"As his vast audience hung entranced, they knew not which most to admire, the charm of classic imagery, the rich and glowing eloquence which flowed from his lips in words almost divine, the grand and massive proportions of the argument, which challenged conviction and defied criticism, or the catholic spirit of the Christian patriot who confides in the justice of his cause and the justice of his God.

"Dr. Palmer's style of speaking is wholly unlike that of the sensational preachers and orators. There is no straining after effect or display. He has no time to think of the meretricious ornaments of the mere rhetorician. His soul is too deeply imbued with the mighty theme and the mighty thoughts which sway it, to give heed to these things. The weightier matters of the law claim his attention. The graces of oratory and poetry fall in, only because they were born in him. What is said of Lord Brougham may with equal truth be said of Dr. Palmer—'he wields the club of Hercules entwined with roses.'"

The following memento of this trip has been preserved and is a prized possession of Mrs. Gussie Palmer Morris, Mobile, Ala.:

"HEADQUARTERS WESTERN DEPARTMENT,
"QUARTERMASTER'S OFFICE, May 21, 1862.

"CAPT: The commanding General of the Department directs that you furnish a saddle and bridle to the Rev. Dr. Palmer attached to the Washington Artillery of New Orleans.

"Respectfully, your obedient servant,
[4]"GUY G. MCLEAN, *Major and P. Q'r'm.*

"Capt. E. A. Deslinde, A.Q.M., Corinth."

Toward the end of April, 1862, Commodore David G. Farragut's fleet braved the hazards of the Confederate batteries and captured New Orleans. May 1, Butler led his army into the city. Dr. Palmer was looked upon by Union men as an arch rebel and fomenter of treason. His friends advised him not to return. His family were gotten out of the city and into his possession. He carried them, first, to Hazelhurst, Miss.; and in August, to Columbia, S. C., at which place he established them in the home of Mrs. George Howe, Mrs. Palmer's mother.

During the period while his family was at Hazelhurst, Dr. Palmer seems to have again labored with the army of the West, now under Bragg. It was probably near the close of this period that he was disappointed of a congregation to preach to, after having seen a fine one assembled. In view of the alarming conditions then existing throughout the South, the people had been requested to observe a day of fasting and prayer on a certain Thursday a little after the middle of August, 1862. Dr. Palmer being in Chattanooga and stopping at the home of the Rev. T. H. McCallie, D.D., the pastor of the First Presbyterian Church in Chattanooga, was requested to conduct the service. "The house was crowded with citizens and soldiers. Dr. Palmer arose to pray, the audience rising with him and standing; scarcely had he begun to pray when the scream of a shell flying over the church was heard, and the distant boom of a cannon from the opposite side of the Tennessee River. In a moment came another shell screaming and another cannon booming. The soldiers began quietly to withdraw, then the citizens, until presently the church was almost empty, and still the good doctor prayed calmly on. When he had closed his eyes the church was full of people, when he opened them it

[4] It is difficult to discipher this signature.

was on empty pews." "It was an advance of the enemy's cavalry outposts. The party had crept in under Bragg's guard." [5]

Having in the latter part of August established his family in Columbia, S. C., during the fall and winter succeeding he supplied a mission chapel two miles out from the town; and taught in the Seminary during the session 1862-1863, having been offered the professorship made vacant by the death of Dr. James Henley Thornwell, August 1, 1862.

Dr. Palmer delivered a masterly eulogy upon Dr. Thornwell September 17, 1862. Happy the eulogist with such a subject, and happy the subject with such a eulogist. The eulogy was delivered in the First Presbyterian Church of Columbia, at the request of the officers of the church and in the presence of the Board of Directors of the Theological Seminary. It was the germ of the very fine biography of Dr. Thornwell which Dr. Palmer was subsequently to write. Beginning with the thought that we must all reverence great men, he asserts that such an one has passed from their midst, and then draws the following outlines of Thornwell's portrait:

"A man gifted with the highest genius,—not that fatal gift of genius which, without guidance, so often blasts its possessor, its baleful gleam blighting everything pure and true on earth,—but genius disciplined by the severest culture, and harnessing itself to the practical duties of life, until it wrought a work full of blessing and comfort to mankind; a mind which ranged through the broad field of human knowledge, gathered up the fruits of almost universal learning, and wove garlands

[5] This statement was taken in large part from the Manual of the First Presbyterian Church, Chattanooga, Tenn., for the year 1904. But we have ventured to change the date from 1863 to 1862, not without some hesitation since the compilers of that Manual should know the local history and since some little other evidence of probable weight points to the year 1863. Our reasons for making the change of date are (1) that a writer in a Louisville, Ky., paper of 1870 tells the incident and dates its occurrence in 1862; (2) that Dr. John W. Caldwell, son-in-law to Dr. Palmer, and his family say that the incident occurred in 1862, and that Dr. Palmer was not in Chattanooga in August, 1863, a statement confirmed at least with considerable probable force by utterances of Dr. Palmer in his report on his work of that summer, made to the General Assembly of 1864. Should further investigation show that it was delivered in 1863, it will also show, we believe, that it was delivered the last of June or first days of July.

of beauty around discussions the most thorny and abstruse; an intellect steeped in philosophy, which soared upon its eagle wings into the highest regions of speculative thought, then stooped with meek docility and worshipped in childlike faith at the cross of Christ; a man who held communion with all of every age that had eternal thoughts, and then brought the treasures hoarded in the literature of the past, and sanctified them to the uses of practical religion. Yet, a man not coldly great, but who could stoop from lofty contemplation to sport and toy with loving ones around his hearthstone; with a heart warm with the instincts of friendship, so brave, so generous and true that admiration of his genius was lost in affection for the man, and the breath of envy never withered a single leaf of all the honors with which a single generation crowned him. Alas! that death should have power to crush out such a life! Our Chrysostom is no more! The 'Golden Mouth' is sealed up in silence forever!

> "'The chord, the harp's full chord is hushed;
> The voice hath died away,
> Whence music like sweet waters gushed
> But yesterday.'

"The glory of man is as the flowers of grass; 'our fathers, where are they; and the prophets, do they live forever?' The men who with their heroic deeds make history to-day, become its theme and song to-morrow!"

Having dashed this outline on his canvas the speaker went on with telling strokes and deft touches to fill it in, giving one of the most brilliant pieces of literary portraiture in the modern tongues.

December 20, 1862, he pronounced a funeral address over the remains of General Maxey Gregg, also in the Presbyterian Church in Columbia, S. C. The address is fully up to the high level of Dr. Palmer's best work. He was the master of the pathetic and the sentimental. The first paragraph of this address is given because of the light it throws on the conditions within the State and the Confederacy at the time:

"We meet this day in the house of God to mourn—to mourn for ourselves, and for the State, the mother that has borne us all! When death comes in at the window and steals away its victim from some private circle, a whole community will yield obedience to the law of Christian sympathy and weep with those that weep. But to-day the State, like the Spartan mother of old, receives through us one of her noblest sons upon his shield, and pours out her grief upon his venerated form. Alas! Our bereaved mother! How often of late she has strained her dead sons to her bosom, in that last embrace and then turned aside, like Rachel, to weep, 'refusing to be comforted, because they are not!' Where is the family amongst us that does not whisper its secret grief around the evening hearth? And where the village cemetery whose sacred enclosure does not shelter some patriot's grave? Her martyred sons sleep everywhere upon her soil; upon the mountain's grassy slope, beneath the peaceful watching of the silent stars, to where the ocean fingers the earth with its foam, and chants with its deep bass the low, funeral dirge! But here, to-day, in the center of them all, with his sword beneath his head, we bury the gallant chieftain who led the strife in which they bravely fell. What language can rise to the solemn majesty of this assembly, or speak with the pathos which belongs to unuttered sorrow! Were I to follow the impulse of my own heart, I would cover my head, and sit a silent mourner beside that bier, rather than be the voice to utter the wail which now rends every breast throughout this commonwealth."

March 27, 1863, he delivered a discourse before the Legislature of Georgia, on "The Rainbow Round the Throne; or Judgment Tempered with Mercy," Rev. 4:2, 3. The day had been appointed as a day of fasting, humiliation and prayer, by Mr. Jefferson Davis, president of the Confederate States.

Establishing on solid grounds the thesis that there is a union of justice and mercy in God's government of the world,[6] he next raised the question as to whether they could determine "whether the sufferings of our beloved band fell upon it in the way of penal judgment, or of paternal discipline." He asks: "Upon the dark background of the cloud which now hangs so low and drenches it with sorrow and with blood, can we discover the sign of the rainbow, the emblem of mercy and hope?" "To these questions," he says, "I will return the long pondered and deeply cherished convictions of my own heart; and may God help me this day to speak comfortably to Jerusalem, and cry unto her that her warfare is accomplished, that her iniquity is pardoned and that she shall receive of the Lord double for all her sins!" He makes and unfolds with all his fertility of lofty illustration the following points, viz: (1) I recognize in the schism which has rent asunder the American people only a new application of the law by which God has ever governed the world; that of breaking in two a nation which has grown too strong for its virtue, in order to

---

[6] It is disappointing to find that in this argument Dr. Palmer incidentally champions the view that the Civil Government should acknowledge Christ as God of Providence.

its preservation and continuance. (2) We make our appeal to Him who ruled beneath the rainbow, on the ground that, touching this controversy between us and our foes, we are blameless. (Through five and eighty years of our united history we have never broken the covenant sworn for us by our fathers; though a partial and unjust legislation has discriminated against us, turning the products of our fields into their coffers, and draining our wealth to build up the palaces of their merchant princes, etc.) (3) I derive consolation from the marked interpositions of God in our favor, during the present struggle; coupled with his frequent disappointment of some of our reasonable expectations. (4) The North cannot succeed against the South except through the perpetration of a double crime without a parallel in the annals of the race,—the extermination of both the white and the black race upon our soil. (5) Our cause is preëminently the cause of God himself, and every blow struck by us is in defense of his supremacy."

The sermon makes pathetic reading now; but under the magic of his voice and port it could hardly have failed to make heroes of all who heard it. He preferred death to subjugation; and he believed that he and his compatriots were fighting God's battles as well as those of his dear Southland.

The reader will recall that years back Dr. and Mrs. Palmer had shown much kindness to Mr. R. H. Reid, then a College and Seminary student in Columbia. They were now in relatively narrow circumstances. Mr. Reid's people seized the opportunity to do them a kindly service, by making a gift of homespun for clothing. The following letter from Mrs. Palmer both notes the fact and throws a light on their family history which justifies its insertion here:

"BRAMWELL COURTHOUSE, April 18, 1863.

"MY DEAR FRIEND: I am here with Fanny, who is very feeble, hoping that change will improve her health. I intended to have written to you before I left Columbia, begging you to thank the ladies of your congregation who were kind enough to send me the homespun. I can assure you it was a very acceptable present and I have made up the dresses for the three oldest children and they have been very much admired. The children feel quite proud to wear a dress spun and woven in South Carolina and they mean to keep them as mementos of the Civil War.

"I am glad to be able to tell you that Mr. Hutson is in better health than he has been and I hope it will not be long before he is entirely well. They feel the death of their little boy very much.

"I expect to leave this place for Savannah on Monday to spend a week or two. I was obliged to leave the other children and of course I will not stay away any longer than I am obliged to, but I feel it to be my duty to do everything in my power to restore Fanny's health. Sometimes I fear we will not have her long, she looks so very feeble. But I can only leave her in the hands of our Father in heaven who does all for the best.

"If we were keeping house I would insist on your coming down to the Assembly and bringing Mrs. Reid and the children. I sigh to have a home of my own once more.

"Give a great deal of love to Mrs. Reid and kiss the children for me, especially my namesake. I often think of his fat, round face. I will send the likeness you asked for some of these days. I had a good many in New Orleans like the one you saw on the mantelpiece at mother's but they will be of no use now.

"Yours very truly,

"M. A. PALMER."

May, 1863, the General Assembly of our Church met in Columbia, S. C. Dr. Palmer was a member of the body and the man of paramount influence in it. He was the chairman of many important committees and acquitted himself with his usual dignity and ability. To that Assembly came the news of the great Stonewall Jackson's death, of whom "it has been tersely and truthfully and therefore beautifully said, that in the army he was the expression of his country's confidence in God and in itself." Palmer's hand drafted the minute, at once exquisite and noble, which the body adopted on the occasion. He took an earnest hand in the conference held by the Assembly upon the subject of the religious wants of the army. Having offered to do service in the West, on his own charges, if he should be left to some measure of discretion as to the length of time, he was made a Commissioner of the Assembly to the Army of Tennessee. This Assembly also elected Dr. Palmer to fill the chair of Didactic and Polemic Theology, in Columbia Seminary, provisionally, for a year. A party would have elected him without conditions, but he had a body of followers who thought of New Orleans and of his obligation to those people in case the way should be opened for his return. From the reports of the debate on the subject it is clear that some members of the Assembly were not without hope that the Confederate forces would again soon be in possession of the place.

Soon after the adjournment of the Assembly he is found with the Army of Tennessee, busy in the distribution of Christian literature, and in preaching the Gospel to the soldiers. About the first of July he was called home to minister to his eldest daughter, who was fast sinking to the grave.

His letters to her show how much he had hoped of her. He would have seen her developed by the education of a man as well as by that of the most refined woman. But already, ere they had left New Orleans, consumption had begun to prey upon her. While in the public schools of New Orleans she developed this dreadful disease. Coming away from New Orleans, in May, 1862, with a cough, she had grown worse in Hazelhurst, and still worse after their removal to Columbia. The father had been thrown into great mental conflict by his appointment as Commissioner to the Army of Tennessee, by the General Assembly of 1863. On the one hand he had despaired of her recovery; but on the other, he thought it probable that she would linger many months, and accordingly resolved to leave her with her mother and with God. The parting was agonizing to both daughter and father. She uttered only one sentence, "Father, you are going so far; and I am so ill,"—a sentence which was to keep "ringing" in his ears amidst the drums and cannon of the camp, a sentence which occasioned his asking himself daily whether God did indeed require him to thus add to the afflictions of his dying child. He took advantage of "the confusion of the retreat from Shelbyville to run home and look upon the pale face once more." He arrived in the early morning and she was still asleep. Awaking in a few moments, she "burst into tears, and said twice, 'I knew he would come, I knew he would come.' Just as a ray of light illumines a dark room, so this one exclamation revealed to the father what for weeks had been passing in the secret chambers of her soul." It was an exclamation so full of love, so full of trust, that he bowed his head "and wept like a woman." He saw that her end was very near and gave himself to attendance on her till God should take her. On Sabbath evening, July 12, he had a beautiful talk with her about death. She had been a sweet Christian for years. He had felt that she was ready to go, but since her sickness he had not talked to her of her readiness to meet God lest he should tend thereby to defeat her recovery. Now he feels that the end is so near that he must for her own sweet sake, for his and for the mother's, examine her grounds of hope. The conversation may be read in the "Broken Home"[7]—a talk very comforting to both. Four days later she went to heaven; one day and night they watched by the dust so precious in their eyes; and Saturday, July 19, 1863, they laid her down in the beautiful cemetery to sleep until the trumpet's call.

"But the agony," he afterwards wrote, "of turning away, and leaving her alone—leaving her alone whom we had so tenderly cherished, that no wind of heaven blew roughly upon her, this, O God! is known only to Thee and to us. But we have exceeding comfort in this loss. We have no misgivings as to her eternal happiness. She had offered while in life and health the most abundant evidence of a change of heart; and during her long illness, as she had often said, 'This world was dead to her.' The apprehension of death which she expressed arose from constitutional timidity, which was sunk at last in a calm, clear trust in her Redeemer—except as she dreaded its physical pangs, which, thanks to God, she was mercifully spared.

"Besides all this, she has left behind a most precious memory. I cannot say all that I could, lest I should be deemed extravagant; or at least, lie open to the suspicion that, as death throws a halo over the departed, I am under the spell of a fond and delusive affection. Yet I have said of her, long before this sad bereavement, since she was twelve years of age I could find nothing in her to amend. Watching over her with a parent's anxiety to mould her character aright, there was nothing to correct. She has left a memory in which there is nothing we would desire changed; as we travel over it in thought, every spot is green and lovely to the eye. I had learned to reverence her. The attributes which she displayed were so beautiful that I, who sought to shape and guide her aright, was often reproved by virtue superior to mine own. Strange that we did not see through all those years that God was secretly educating her for himself; and when she was ripe, she was plucked to be with him. Her memory is a sweet and an awful thing to us. We think of her not as dead, but as translated to be with Christ. Our lovely flower bloomed awhile on its earthly stem, and then

'She was exhaled—her Creator drew
Her spirit, as the sun the morning dew.'[8]

[7] Pp. 35-38. [8] *Broken Home*, pp. 47-49.

The First Church of Columbia had become vacant in June, 1863, by the resignation of the pastorate by the Rev. F. P. Mullally. Dr. Palmer was asked to supply the church, which he gladly did during such periods as he was in Columbia to the end of the war. The number of new briefs made in these months attest the fact that he still preserved his habits of hard, steady and efficient labor over the Word of God.

When the term-time in Columbia Seminary came to hand, he gave himself also to the performance of his professorial duties and the numerous calls for occasional services which came to him.

"Occupying the chair of Theology only provisionally," he writes, at the close of the session 1863-1864, "I have not felt at liberty to depart from the method of instruction presented by my predecessor—which was to combine the two upper classes, and to carry them over the entire course in two years. During the past two sessions, these classes have been conducted, accordingly, through the whole of Theology, extending the last year, from the beginning to the application of the scheme of Redemption. The leading text-book has been the "Institutes" of Calvin—the students being required to examine, in connection with it, the works of Turretin, of Principal Hill, and of Dick,—and the free use also of Hodge's "Outline of Theology," which has been very profitable in mapping out the special topics for investigation. The manuscript lectures of Dr. Thornwell being fortunately in my possession have also been read to the classes, and enlarged upon in oral explanation. These, with partial lectures of my own, on topics not embraced in the scheme of Dr. Thornwell, have supplemented the course of instruction in this department.

"The lectures delivered last year, on the Evidences, have not been repeated this year, owing simply to the fact, that the Junior Class has, at no period of the year, been exactly organized, and also to the fact that the only permanent member of this class has been disabled by physical infirmity from the full prosecution of his studies. No class, however, has been permitted to leave the Seminary without going carefully through this branch of theological training and the deficiency of the past year may be easily retrieved by a combination of the classes during the next session." [9]

[9] From Dr. Palmer's Report as Professor in Columbia Seminary to the General Assembly, 1864, A.D., p. 299.

In April, 1864, Dr. Palmer was called upon by the ladies of South Carolina to deliver an address of welcome to the "Soldiers of the Legion and Gentlemen of the Army," who, after an absence of three years, had returned to their native State. The address was afterwards published in *The Daily Southern Guardian.* It is an elegant and gracious welcome, accompanied by an attempt at an *expose* of the conditions of American civilization, the meaning of the great struggle in which they were engaged, and the grounds on which the South still had the right to hope for success. It brought with it a confession that he sometimes wished it was his to bear arms. Turning to General Wade Hampton, who sat on the platform with him, he said:

"The day will come when that blade which gleams so brightly by your side in the hour of battle will hang as a relic upon your ancestral walls, and there will come forth some fair haired urchin who, as he takes it down and draws the rusty blade from its scabbard, will say, 'This was the sword with which my great-grandfather passed through many battles of the Revolution of 1860 and '64.' Mark you, he will not call it 'the great rebellion,' as neither you nor I do, but a mighty and stupendous revolution, which gave freedom to our land. At the same time there may be a flaxen haired girl who, as she turns over the old pages of her family history and her eye falls upon the name of 'Hampton,' will call to her remembrance a family tradition, that on a certain April day seventy-five or eighty years ago, her great-grandfather pinned the emblem of South Carolina and the Confederacy as near as he could over General Hampton's heart.

[Suiting the action to the word the speaker advanced to General Hampton, and with a grace that cannot be described in language, attached to his breast an exquisite Palmetto badge interwoven with a miniature Confederate flag. There was scarcely a dry eye in the vast audience, and the brave soldier himself could not restrain the tears, which the act and its associations involuntarily called forth.]

"And now General," resumed Dr. Palmer, "this is a secret which neither you nor your honored lady must ask to be revealed. A daughter of Carolina pins that symbol of the State and of the Confederacy on your heart. I have only to say in the name of the fair lady, see to it that South Carolina and the Confederacy are saved; and [turning to the concourse] I now point you ladies of South Carolina to the Chevalier Bayard of the South—the chivalric knight, 'without fear and without reproach.'"[10]

He had found time, during the early part of the year 1864, also to oppose the union between the Church of which he was such a distinguished representative and the United Synod of the South. It will be recalled that in 1838 a split culminated between the two parties, New and Old School, in the Presbyterian Church in the United States of America. The New School party in that year withdrew and established itself as an independent church. It is a fact that the New School party had embraced many in it who cared little either for a thorough-going Presbyterian polity or for sound Calvinism. The New School party and the New School Church must lie under the charge of latitudinarianism in doctrine and polity. While this must be conceded it is also true that not a few went with the New School party, at the time of the split, who had no considerable sympathy with these forms of laxity. These persons had taken umbrage at the exscinding acts passed by the Assembly of 1837, an Assembly in which an Old School majority and Old School measures prevailed. To put the matter in their own way: they held that "no judicatory of the Church, can *for any cause,* by an act of legislation, constitutionally condemn or exclude from the Church, ministers or private members, without a process of trial, such as is prescribed in the Constitution of the Presbyterian Church." They accordingly went out with the New School men and helped to form the new body.

The New School Church soon developed a strong tendency toward the handling of political questions in its courts. In particular, it developed a strong anti-slavery party, and attempted to discipline Southern slaveholders as such. The result of this departure was the split of 1857-'8, which resulted in the establishment of the Synod of the South. This body was now about to be taken into union with the Presbyterian Church of the Confederate States. It was, in genesis, a portion of the party that had been guilty of the toleration of Hopkinsianism, Taylorism, and other New England theological fads: it had shown indifference to a sound Presbyterian polity. The Synod of the South had never formally repudiated these

[10] Copied from *The Daily Southern Guardian,* Columbia, S. C., June 10, 1864: "Dr. Palmer's Address."

errors up to 1863. Dr. Palmer was fully alive to these and other such uncomfortable facts.

In the year 1863, however, committees had been appointed by the General Assembly of the Presbyterian Church in the Confederate States and the Synod of the South, respectively, to confer as to terms of union. These committees had met and, after conferring jointly had agreed to propose to their respective bodies a "Basis of Union." The "Basis of Union" was published and speedily met the general approval. Dr. Palmer was not so easily satisfied. He regarded, and properly, the exscinding acts as a piece of blessed surgery, necessary to the preservation of Bible Presbyterianism in the great body on which the operations were performed; he had little sympathy with those who, because they had more sorrow for the excision of the offending synods than they had love for the truths of God which these synods were trampling into the mire, went out with them. He knew that the Synod of the South had in it one man of views out of accord with our Confession, that his brethren had elected this man to a chair in the seminary which they proposed to establish, and that, only a year or so before, this man had claimed to have the support of his brethren in some of his non-confessional views.

In the April number of the *Southern Presbyterian Review*, 1864, Dr. Palmer appeared in an article of forty-two pages on "The Proposed Plan of Union between the General Assembly in the Confederate States of America and the United Synod of the South." In the most knightly way he dealt with the defects of the Synod of the South and with the Basis of Union, giving to the latter the most searching and effective criticism which it met with. By skillfully interpreting the "Basis of Union" in the light of published writings of the Rev. Dr. A. H. H. Boyd, of Winchester, Va., the great representative of the New School theology in the Synod of the South, he made it to appear a very doubtful thing.

When the General Assembly convened, in Charlotte, N. C., in May, 1864, Dr. Palmer was a member of the body and along with Dr. Adger, of Columbia, gave expression to his opposition to the movement in the form in which it was being carried on. His speech in opposition was described as "elegant in style and in a good spirit." He began by expressing his admiration of unity, but his conviction that "charity moves on the poles of truth." He asked whether the two bodies were sufficiently agreed as to be able to live together in harmony. He asserted that he did not confide in the United Body, because: (1) They did not at the time of the separation of the Old and New School sympathize with the General Assembly in its efforts to maintain the truth. (2) The testimony concerning them is conflicting. Some assert their soundness; but others with equal positiveness their unsoundness. (3) They seem never to have made a clear and unreserved subscription to the Standards. He doubted, moreover, the constitutional right of the Assembly to take in the body in the way proposed, which would make the "Basis of Union" a part, and a paramount part, of the Standards of the body resulting from the union. He would not express himself as unalterably opposed to it provided safe grounds of union could be found—grounds such as would save our Standards intact.[11]

The truth is that there were three unsound men in the New School body in 1864. One of these, Dr. A. H. H. Boyd, was a man of brains and character. His writings had greatly impressed Dr. Palmer. Had Dr. Boyd been a true representative of his Church in the matter of theology, Dr. Palmer had been right in his attitude. But Dr. Boyd had no following in his theological views, and only two known sympathizers. The Virginia men in the Assembly, with Dr. Dabney in the lead, knew the ministers and elders of the Synod of the South well, the members of that body being found mostly in Virginia, Tennessee and North Mississippi. The project for union after the modifications, the chief of which provided for uniting "on the basis of our existing standards only," carried overwhelmingly.

It is not known that Dr. Palmer ever on the one hand regretted his stand on this important subject, or on the other, ever saw occasion to regret the action of the Church.

To this Assembly Dr. Palmer made a very modest report of his services during the preceding year as Commissioner to the Army of Tennessee.

He said his connection with the army was very brief and as a commissioner amounted to very little; that if he had done any good it was by preaching to the soldiers; that he had preached in all the brigades and nearly all the regiments of one corps of the Army of Tennessee, while it was encamped

[11] *Central Presbyterian,* June 2, 1864, Report of the General Assembly.

around Shelbyville; that when the army fell back to Chattanooga, finding that he could do nothing, he went home just in time to go with a beloved daughter, as far as the living are permitted to go down into the valley and shadow of death; that he had been much impressed by the greatness of the work God was carrying on among our troops; that it had no parallel in the history of the world; and that he regarded it as a special sign hung out from the throne of God, of his favor to our people.

This Assembly made Dr. Palmer Provisional Professor of Didactic and Polemic Theology again for the year 1864-1865.

From the Assembly he returned to Columbia and continued to supply the pulpit of the First Presbyterian Church.

In his absence he yearned for his people in New Orleans, that he might be comforted together with them by the mutual faith of them and him. For fear of increasing their political troubles he long refrained from writing to them; but at length the pent up floods of yearning burst forth in the following letter:

"COLUMBIA, S. C., May 20, 1864.

"To my companions in sorrow and in the fellowship of Jesus, the members of the First Presbyterian Church and Congregation in the City of New Orleans:

"DEARLY BELOVED BRETHREN: Two entire years have elapsed since I departed from you, expecting in three weeks to return to my pastoral work. Some of you will perhaps recall the sadness of my last discourse, just before we sat down together around the table of our dying Lord; for which I was playfully rallied by several, as though I had preached under a heavy presentiment of evil. It was, however, not exactly so. I only knew that the times were exceedingly disjointed, and that I was to be absent for a season. No one could foresee what a day might bring forth: and under this general feeling of uncertainty, I uttered the words which now seem as though they were an unconscious prophecy of a long farewell. How little did I then anticipate the dreadful catastrophe which prevented my return; and which, from that day to this, has cast me forth a wanderer upon the face of the earth! But your lot has been harder even than my own: and often, oh! how often, has my heart yearned to commune with you, and to pour forth the feelings with which it has been burdened! One fear has, however, always restrained me—that of compromising you and of exposing the Church to severer afflictions, if my letters should unfortunately be intercepted. Nothing but this has prevented me from frequently attempting to strengthen your faith in these dark and bitter days, and to bring to those who mourn amongst you the consolations of God.

It has been a great trial to me, to be compelled thus to lock up within my own breast the affection which yearned to flow forth freely to you. But I could not bring myself to run the hazard of increasing your burdens for my own gratification. I am at length weary of forebearing. The fire which has been so long shut up in my bones will burst forth, and I now commit this sheet into the hands of Him who holds even the winds in his fist, praying him to give a safe direction, and to make it only a source of comfort to those to whom it is addressed.

"Whilst denying myself the pleasure of communion with you, I have sought compensation by indulging the visions of fancy which vividly represented scenes once so familiar to me. Sometimes, I surround myself with my books, which again seem to look down, like old and intimate friends, from their cases in my study. Then I transfer myself to the dear old pulpit, which I had learned to reverence, as a king his throne. It has required little imagination to people the pews with their old occupants; and thus to reproduce, one by one, the families of my own happy charge, just as they were accustomed to sit down the long-drawn aisles of that grand and beautiful sanctuary. The dear children of the flock were daguerreotyped before me, exactly as I was wont to see them gathered into classes in the Sabbath-school. When weary of the large assembly, it needed only the waving of the wand to remand all to their several homes: and I would find myself now treading the familiar streets of our city, house after house rising up before the mind just as of yore when my hand was upon each door-bell. The very furniture of a hundred dwellings has revolved before me in the ceaseless panorama—even to the beds beside which I have sat and knelt in my visits as 'a son of consolation' to the sick and dying saint. Thus has memory traveled again and again over the past; and in silent thought, I have held converse with many whom common suffering has drawn nearer than ever to my heart. From these reveries I would be startled by the sickening thought, 'all this is of the past, and the past can never be again;' while this distrust would in its turn be drowned in pleasing anticipations of a happy restoration to you, and fancy has pictured a thousand faces, radiant with patriotic joy, bidding me welcome to church and pulpit, and strange emotions have filled my bosom in thinking of the first sermon I should preach in my own church and to my own people. Thus I have amused the hours of my weary exile, finding in these exhilarating anticipations a prophecy of bright and happy days yet before us. Those days will certainly come: may God keep your faith and mine alive, to watch for the early dawn!

"A kind Providence has directed all my steps since I have been driven from my home. The extreme illness of my wife's mother brought us unexpectedly to Carolina. It pleased God, within two weeks afterward, to remove to heaven my beloved friend and brother, the Rev. Dr. Thornwell, who was buried amidst the deep lamentations of the country and of the Church. His vacant chair in the School of the Prophets was immediately tendered to me; which has, for two years, furnished me with work and with bread. During the past twelvemonth a vacancy having occurred in the pastorate of the Columbia Church, I was summoned by the voice of my old charge to resume the duties of the pulpit. I have accordingly filled to the best of my ability, the double office of a professor and of a pastor: which I shall probably continue to do, provisionally, until the way is open for my return to you. It may not be amiss to state that earnest efforts have been made by my personal friends to induce me to settle again permanently in the land of my birth, rendered now doubly sacred to me as holding in its bosom my precious dead. It has been argued that, after the stupendous changes of the past two years New Orleans can never be to me what it once was, and it has been significantly suggested that possibly I may not hold the same place in your affections as formerly. Of course, as to these things I must remain, for some time, in profoundest ignorance. But my purpose is unalterably formed to decline every proposal from every quarter until I can once more meet with you. The ties which bind me to New Orleans are not only those of affection, but of honor. The present is the hour of trial to you, in which I am incapable of anything that looks like desertion. You are entitled, upon every ground, to the refusal of my future labors. My desire and expectation is to return and gather up the fragments of our scattered congregation, and to share with them the poverty to which we will be reduced together. If it pleases you, I have no wish but to enter with you upon a new career of glorious trial for our blessed Master:—and it must be from your lips I must learn, that God has any other destination for me than to build up our wasted Zion in the midst of yourselves. Until we can meet face to face, I shall continue to hold myself free from all entanglements—leaving the future entirely in the hands of God.

"You have doubtless heard indirectly of the bereavement we have sustained in the death of our eldest daughter. Almost immediately upon leaving New Orleans, the symptoms of her fatal malady began to appear—exciting little apprehension at the first, but eventually producing alarm from the obstinacy with which they refused to yield to the most skilful medical treatment we could procure. At length after many fluctuations protracted through fourteen months, her delicate frame succumbed beneath the insidious destroyer and in July last we laid her precious form beneath the sod, where the quietly flowing waters of the beautiful Saluda chant a perpetual requiem over the dead who sleep in the peaceful cemetery of Elmwood. Ah! there are those among you who know with what an edge a sorrow like this cuts, down to the very quick. It is enough to say that she was very dear, and yet she was taken. 'Even so, Father, for so it seemed good in thy sight!' We bow before that sovereign will, which we would not dispute, even if we could. She has gone up to be with the immortals; and our faith watched her in that splendid flight, till she stood before the throne. We have had no wish to call her back, and have since solaced ourselves with a memory which is as green to us as the Garden of Eden. It is not fit perhaps that I should pour forth in this sheet the private sorrows of a parent's heart: but when I have heard of like afflictions which have befallen you, I have held communion with my own grief, and then have wept for you. Ever and anon the tidings have reached me of the breaches death has made in some of your households. Here a beloved mother has been taken up to her rest in the Savior's bosom; there, a daughter and a sister has dropped out of the family circle; while the echoes of the distant battlefield bring to others the sad report of sons and brothers who sleep forever in the graves of the martyrs. Scarce a family amongst you, that does not whisper its secret grief around the evening hearth; whilst I am denied the poor privilege of mingling my tears with yours, and of lifting the voice of prayer in those dismantled homes! It has been a solace, however, in the solitude of my own sorrow to think of all these distant mourners, and to find my own soul knit to theirs in the grief that has been common to me and to them. 'May the God of all consolation fill us both with peace in believing, that we may abound in hope through the power of the Holy Ghost!'

'It is time, however, to put aside these merely personal allusions. You have been called, beloved friends, to endure heavy and very peculiar trials. It is not prudent, perhaps, to indulge in anything but this most general reference to them. They are such, however, as do not fall once in a century upon any people, and generation may succeed generation before similar sufferings will be experienced again. There is undoubtedly a meaning of most solemn significance in all this, which we must strive to understand. At present, we may not be able fully to do so. Providence is always hard to be interpreted, when we are in the very current of events, drifting and whirling us along too rapidly for the comparison and thought which are necessary to scan the mysterious cipher in which God writes his will upon the page of human history. But an interpretation there is: by and by, when we can look leisurely back upon these tangled and perplexed scenes, we shall better understand that it has been throughout a discipline of *love,* and not of *wrath.* At present, all we can hope to achieve is to have our hearts in proper temper, and with a chastened will to bow before the majesty of him who does his pleasure among the armies in heaven and the inhabitants of earth. This is the first great end of chastisement: when our spirits are humbled and submissive before him, then will come the unsealing of the vision. 'What we know not now, we shall know hereafter.' I have a most profound conviction that God is specially vindicating his own supremacy, as the Ruler among the nations. This conviction fills me with awe. God's footsteps are to be seen in all the grand march of history: but there are special epochs when he discloses his terrible majesty and reveals the title which is written upon his vesture, 'the King of kings and Lord of lords.' We have not yet come to the end of this wonderful drama—but the closing act is not far off which shall give the moral of the whole. We shall then understand what is now partially hidden from our eyes; and will perhaps says, 'true and righteous are thy ways, Lord God Almighty!' We have only to *believe,* and to *wait.* I find myself embarrassed from the necessity imposed upon me of writing obscurely and in parable. But surely, if justice and judgment be the habitation of God's throne, the souls of them that are slain will not cry unheard from under the altar. It is a hard trial of our faith and patience; but, brethren, it were better to die than to lose our confidence in that divine Father who leads us by dark and slippery paths indeed, but always to seats of honor and of bliss. For myself, I have never wavered for an instant, in the trust I have reposed in the God of our salvation. You have only to recall the testimonies which I have delivered to you of old, to know all that I would say to you now.

"But in the midst of these distresses, how precious is the thought that this poor world is not our final home! Its vexations and cares are only the methods by which God trains us for the world of light and love on high. Our school days will soon be over, and we shall escape forever from all this hard, but necessary, discipline. When we stand upon those heavenly heights, we will look back with wonder that we made so much of the sorrow that endureth only for a night. We shall see so much of a Father's love in those very pains which once distressed us, that they will become materials of our song. This shall be our compensation—that for every pang felt on earth, we shall have a new pulse added to our joy. Can we not afford to bear all that sorrow which God so sanctifies and sweetens even here on earth, when we think that it accumulates a store of enjoyment for us in heaven? Oh, the depths of the mystery of grace! which can thus transform our sorrow into joy, and convert our very sobs into hallelujahs of praise! When I think of this, I reverse all my judgments and exclaim, Blessed are they that suffer! Blessed will be they who come out of *great* tribulation! God's own hand will wipe away all their tears, and they will dwell so joyfully in the sunlight of their Father's smile. 'Wherefore, comfort ye one another with these words.'

"But I must hasten to a close. It would be easy to fill this page with individual names to whom I desire to convey my love. They are easily recalled, but it is more prudent to suppress the record. Let each individual whose eye may fall upon these sheets regard them as sent particularly to him and to her. The day, I hope, is not far distant when we may speak face to face. Till then we must learn to 'possess our souls in patience.' Surely after this long and gloomy separation, the Gospel will be both preached and heard as it never was before. I pray God, if I am permitted to return, I may 'come to you in the fulness of the blessing of the Gospel of Christ.' And now, beloved brethren, 'to Him that is able to keep you from falling, and to present you faultless before the presence of his glory with exceeding joy,—to the only wise God our Savior,' I commend you: 'praying night and day exceedingly, that I might see your face and might perfect that which is lacking in your faith, and that God himself and our Father and the Lord Jesus Christ may direct my way unto you!'

"Ever truly yours in the Gospel of Jesus,

"B. M. PALMER."

A characteristic letter of this period is the following to Miss Anna Jennings, granddaughter of Mr. Alfred Hennen, who was a distinguished member of the Louisiana Bar and a very valued member of the session of Dr. Palmer's church in New Orleans:

"COLUMBIA, S. C., July 28, 1864.

"MY DEAR 'DAUGHTER' ANNA: Have I forfeited my right to address you thus by cold neglect? I must remit you for the explanation of all this to the letter I have just written to your mother, so as not to occupy this sheet with a twice-told tale: and now let me kiss those pouting lips, and be forgiven. When, in my first letter, I ventured upon this endearing title, it was not exactly by accident, though the word did leap from my pen without premeditation. Still less was it a trick of rhetoric to catch your ear and thus inveigle you into my confidence. It was, I suspect, simply the inspiration of affectionate sympathy for a dear girl, whose young heart was waking up to the sense of being fatherless. But however it may have been prompted, the adoption has been ratified by your acceptance of it: and from this time henceforth you are to be evermore my *daughter*. Shall I tell you, dearest Anna, how one sentence in your letter thrilled through every fiber of my heart, and made even the marrow of my bones to quiver? It was your tender allusion to my dead Fanny, coupled with a request to be allowed to take her place in my love. Can I then so easily replace my lost one? Now that she has gone up, beyond my reach, above the stars, can I turn those warm affections upon another? It was a very serious question, in answering which the least hypocrisy on my part would be infidelity to you and treason against *her*. I have weighed it well; and I now tell you, my child, to come into my heart and hold a daughter's place. May the God of heaven bless you, and make the thought a solace to you, as it is a comfort to me!

"The metaphysics of this, I suppose, you do not understand: I am not sure that I comprehend it fully myself. I submit, however, the following exposition, for what it is worth. All our earthly relations are sublimed through death. Our loved ones, when they have passed into heaven, sustain a twofold existence to us. In the kingdom of God they appear to us only as 'the angels of God,' redeemed and glorified spirits bending with their crowns before the throne, and far removed out of the circle of the relations which they filled on earth. But they sustain another aspect to us, as memory recalls them in their earthly forms and in their human sympathies. This remembrance, however, is purified through death. The old adage, *'nil de mortuis nisi bonum,'* embodies this idea. Memory presents only the image reflected from the mirror which affection holds up. All that was cheap and common in their character and life is sifted through and drops out of sight; or, to pursue the figure of the image, the glass which reflects it has the peculiar property of absorbing those rays which would discolor, and returns only such as beautify and adorn. Our remembrance is thus a purged and sanctified remembrance—the dead reappear to our thought in their earthly dress, but that dress transformed into a robe of light, and their whole persons gloriously transfigured before our eyes. This beautiful image takes up its abode in our hearts, a most sacred and awful 'Presence,' I have said to your mother; and the affections, which cluster around it, are purer, holier affections than the living ever enjoy. It is love which has undergone a consecration—mingling with reverence, it prostrates itself with a sublime and almost devotional delight before the Memory that is now revealed as the sacred shadow, the umbra, of *the one that was.* You see then, my child, in what sense you can take *her* place in my heart. She, the Memory—the sweet and radiant 'Presence'—must evermore be there, to be cherished with a love spiritual and unearthly—and my chastened heart must ever embrace the thought of her with a strange complex emotion of mingled reverence and affection. But side by side with this spiritualized love, which we give only to the blessed dead, there is room for other loves which are more simply human—and this is the portion for the living. Yes, Anna, with this love I cherish you: and if you will be satisfied with it, I say again, come into my heart, and be my daughter until death. I will put a father's blessing upon your head and shield you with a father's care.

"As the first proof of this, let me ask how you are speeding in your Christian course? Has the blessed hope of acceptance with God ripened into a firm and stable conviction? Does it bring forth the fruits of humility and patience, of faithful obedience to his holy commands, and of joyous communion with your Divine Father through the mediation of his blessed Son? Recognize, in the outstart of your Christian career, the necessity of *earnestness* in serving God. Half the conflicts, and nearly all the spiritual darkness of which most Christians complain, are invited by their sluggishness and indecision. No wonder they are assaulted, so long as they waver upon the border line which separates the two warring kingdoms. Throw then your *whole* soul into the Christian life—mind, heart, will, memory, reason, judgment, fancy, conscience—draw them all up in gallant array and marshal them in solid phalanx. Let the grace of God *rule* in your heart—pervading your entire life—breathing in your conviction—molding your thoughts—and controlling your actions: and so let your piety diffuse its aroma all about you, as the smallest particle of musk will perfume a chamber through a century. Thus you will find your conflicts easy, and your burdens light till you are called Home.

"I must not omit to thank you, my sweet girl, for the draft of your father's will appended to your mother's last letter. It is the most remarkable document I ever read and if published, would be considered by legal men thoroughly unique. It was an exact copy of your noble father himself—just as you have seen in the camera an extended landscape exactly reproduced upon a piece of paper of the breadth of your hand, so the broad surface of that great and noble heart is daguerreotyped here. All the simplicity of his character—his affectionate trustfulness—his strong, direct mind penetrating through perplexities to a single goal—and more than all, his big, generous and cultivated love: every feature that marked the man, is here. We see all of the husband, father, brother, master and friend, at a single view. I do not wonder that you treasure it as a most precious relic; and that your mother especially should bind to her heart this last, full testimony of his appreciation of herself, so well justified by his intimate knowledge of her queenly worth.

"I have only space left to say what great pleasure I have derived from a recent visit of Mr. Smedley; who gave me so many details about you all that could never be written even by the most unflagging correspondent. The rich story of your grandfather, grand in the calmness of a serene old age, baffling the miserable Yankee by asking for the second volume of Kingslake's 'Crimean War,' afforded me the only generous laugh I have had for two years. It was so characteristic; and were I an artist I would surely sketch the scene;[12] the beautiful summer eve—the open verandah—the serene old man, with his venerable locks and benign countenance—the rough, boorish invading soldiers, with thick boots and clanking spurs—the excited and angry females of the house—and then the vacant stare of that insulting clown at the question, 'Can you tell me, sir, if the second volume of Kingslake's "Crimean War" is issued from the press?" Oh, it was a scene for the pencil of a Hogarth! this piece of rainbow spanning a war cloud! and with a sting of sarcasm in it that makes it an illustrative national picture. Dear, brave old man! May God spare his life, till I can grasp his hand, and thank him for his sturdy virtue!

[12]Mr. Alfred Hennen was a great student and reader. While in isolation, on his plantation, during the war, he had been deprived of the privilege of seeing new books. At the time of the incident here referred to the Yankees were devastating his property. But, as the Colonel of the regiment advanced toward him he asked him if "the second volume of Kingslake's 'Crimean War' had been published," unconsciously covering the officer with astonishment and confusion.

"My girls have not been well of late, Mary especially. They have all left me in search of a bracing climate while I tread my mill at home. Good-bye and write soon a forgiving and loving letter. A separate kiss to Alice, Caddy, Cora, and Edith.

"Your father-pastor,

"B. M. PALMER."

The following to another of his parishioners is given in part because it portrays the affliction so prevalent amongst them and amongst all the people of the South in that time of fearful conflict:

"COLUMBIA, S. C., December 22, 1864.

"MY DEAR MRS. R.: I have just heard with inexpressible pain of the death of your dear husband, under circumstances too, of such barbarity, as must greatly aggravate your distress. Having an opportunity to communicate with you through Mrs. ——— I cannot forbear to turn aside and mingle my tears with yours and if I cannot console I may at least enjoy the privilege of participating in your grief. Would to God that I were permitted to sit at your side as in former days when the hand of God was heavy upon you and of drawing consolation together from the sacred Scriptures. But it is idle to indulge in wishes that are so unprofitable; and I must restrict myself to this little sheet only large enough to convey the expression of my warmest sympathy, and too small to contain much that I would utter with a living voice.

"My heart bleeds as I think of your mourning circle. Two sisters bowed together under the sorrow of recent widowhood; each unable to sustain the other because her heart is crushed beneath her own burden while a venerable mother is paralyzed by these successive blows and mourns at once over the loss of four sons. It is a sight to move the heart of the sternest stoic and stirs my heart to its lowest depths. Death is awful when it comes but once over our threshold and the chasm seems dreadful enough when only one beloved form is snatched from our embrace: what must it be when *four* are taken, and two households are left without husband or brother? It is a scene of profounder sorrow than that which moved our Savior when he wept with the two sisters at Bethany, and can you doubt that he looks down with less compassion upon you? Oh! My afflicted friend, turn your eyes to that Jesus, and you will see that he kindly sympathizes in the grief which, for reasons inscrutable to us, he has been pleased to send upon you. I can do nothing more than to point you to Him who 'hath borne our griefs and carried our sorrows,' and assure you that our Redeemer is as compassionate in heaven as when upon earth he wept at the tomb of Lazarus. May he help you with his sufficient grace in this hour more dark and bitter than any other through which you have yet passed. Weep if you will—if you can; for there are some sorrows that are too deep for tears. They drink up the soul and there is no sign which can represent an unutterable woe. Hence I say, weep, if you can. Let the full tide of your grief flow out through the channel of tears. God doth not forbid it. Only do not murmur—justify God in all his ways, like Job; who, you remember in his successive and accumulative bereavements would not 'charge God foolishly' but piously exclaimed 'though He slay me, yet will I *trust* in him.' Seasons of affliction are often seasons of sore temptations, when the Adversary would take advantage of our bruised affections to reproach the God of heaven. Our human hearts, writhing in their anguish, are prone to break out in the impatient question, Why has He done this? Remember the Scripture which says 'What thou knowest not now thou shalt know hereafter.' Be patient until the Revelation of the day of Christ. He shall make these dark dispensations plain to us. We shall then *know;* at present we can only *believe,* but in both let us glorify him, who will not lay upon man more than his right that we should enter into judgment with him.

"You perceive, my dear Mrs. R., that I do not attempt to *comfort* you. The time for that is not come. If I should offer you consolation, it would be like water thrown on heated iron sputtering off and hissing in angry drops. I only weep for you.

"Your greatest comfort now is to be allowed to mourn, and what you need from your friends is only sympathy which means that they suffer with you. We will then sit down with you in the ashes and cover our heads with the mantle and keep silent. When your heart craves for more than this, write me where you are to be found and I will fill a large sheet with what you will then be inclined to read. Just now, I can only press your hand in silent sympathy and lift my voice to our Father in heaven to sustain you in this heavy sorrow, and give your sister and yourself and your dear mother strength to bear all that he inflicts. To God and to the Spirit of his grace I commend you all, praying fervently on your behalf to him who has promised to give the oil of joy for mourning, beauty for ashes, and the garment of praise for the spirit of heaviness.'

"Affectionately your pastor and friend,

"B. M. PALMER."

The whole land had long been a house of mourning; and people were looking to him from every side to minister unto them the consolation of the Gospel. Feeling often the need of comfort himself, he had frequent occasion for the exercise of his wonderful power of self-control in the face of sorrow as bitter as death.

He was singularly tried one February Sabbath, 1865. Just as he was about to enter the pulpit to preach, some one handed him a telegram which announced the death of a prominent young connection of his. The gentleman had been slain in battle the day before, February 10. He was husband to a favorite niece of Dr. Palmer. When the Doctor looked down from the pulpit to a seat nearby, his eyes met the wistful brown eyes of the young wife, who would for an hour listen to what he as God's minister would say, and thenceforth mourn the husband of her youth. Preaching was very hard for him that day in the presence of that young widow unconscious of the blow that had fallen upon her.

A week later Columbia was evacuated, and he in flight. A little later the city was in ashes, and with it all his "private papers, books, and household effects."

Not far from the middle of March three men started from Yorkville, S. C., tramping in the direction of Columbia. They were Mr. Asher D. Cohen, now of Charleston, S. C., Mr. Jas. Wood Davidson, now of Washington, D. C., and Dr. B. M. Palmer. They had simply fallen in together and for a time traveled together. Mr. Cohen tells the story substantially as follows:

Dr. Palmer had some cornbread on which to subsist and I had some fine time-cured Madeira wine. We followed the line of the torn-up railway. Having found an old hand-car we tried to work it and thus increase our rate of travel, but soon gave it up as we lacked the muscle to make that mode of travel a success. The first night we slept on the railway track, making a pillow of one of the rails. The next day we continued our travel, subsisting on the Doctor's cornbread and a little wine. The second night we slept in the same way. The next day we again resumed our journey. Mr. Davidson, I think, left us at Chester. As the night of the third day approached, it began to rain, and I proposed that we should shelter in the piazza of a poor farmhouse. Kilpatrick's men had gone through the neighborhood and our own men also. The people had been well scared. The little home was modest and in poor condition. The little piazza looked out north. It required no little persuasion to get Dr. Palmer to enter the piazza. As I peeped through a crevice in the door to the house, I saw a square room with a staircase on the southern side, leading to the floor above. On the eastern side, in the center, was a large hearth and an old-fashioned fireplace, with a good fire burning in it. I saw an old lady, a countrywoman, in this room. It was getting very disagreeable in the piazza. I knocked and tried to get a response from within. Failing in this, I urged the Doctor that we should enter the room and sit by the fire. He finally consented. As we entered the room, the old lady retreated up the stairs until she reached the top, where she sat down. We deposited our traps, each taking a seat on either side of the fire. It was very evident that the old lady was alarmed. She had suffered much from passers-by shortly before, as we afterwards learned. Our conversation was naturally serious and not of a character to disturb her. We understood the situation well, that is to say, that she looked upon us as suspicious characters. We probably suited our remarks to removing her fears, and letting her know the nature of her visitors. The conversation told. Step by step, with increasing confidence, she descended the stairs. The Doctor kept his eyes on her and she hers on him. At last she was on the same floor with us. The Doctor dropped on his knees and said, "Let us join in evening prayers." I knelt and the old lady fell upon her knees; and then the Doctor, inspired by the situation, offered up a most touching and appropriate prayer, in which he dwelt upon the misfortunes of the war and the trials of the women who were left at home, and their privations. It is needless to say that we were all bathed with tears. It was the most appropriate and eloquent prayer that I ever listened to. The Doctor himself had been touched by the situation; and from the depths of his heart he had endeavored to bring comfort to this poor woman. Her sons were away, in the army. With the rain outside, and the solemn quiet inside, with the tenderness and eloquence of the Doctor, it was a remarkable occasion; and was impressed indelibly upon my memory.

The old lady's fears were dissipated; her heart was softened into kindness. She gave us a comfortable bed to sleep in, and something to eat that was superb in comparison with what we had. She found a stray chicken for our morning's breakfast. We left her with a parting blessing. She sent us on our way with good wishes. We continued our journey down the track toward Columbia till we reached Winnsboro, where the Doctor stopped over Sunday to preach. When we parted he said, "God bless you and good-bye, Mr. Cohen."

When Dr. Palmer, at the earnest solicitation of friends, fled from Columbia, he left his family occupying a house on Laurel Street, opposite the Lecture Room of the First Presbyterian Church, and having with them Mr. Isaac Hutson, a brother-in-law, and his family. On returning to the city, he learned that, after several days of previous shelling the town, the Yankees had entered it Friday, February 17, 1865; that marauding parties and drunken soldiers were soon scattered over the entire city; that Mrs. Palmer requested and soon obtained a guard for her home who endeavored to protect the family from insults and spoliation; that at 6 o'clock in the evening a rocket was sent up, which proved the signal for firing the city; that fire soon started in all directions and that a great portion of the inhabitants, homeless and without protection, were wandering about the streets, exposed to all the unspeakable dangers of the terrible situation. He learned that, at 2 o'clock that night, the family were told to leave their dwelling, as a government factory nearby was to be blown up; that they went into the streets, each one carrying along bundles of clothing, bedding, valuables, anything that might be of use; that they made their way among burning buildings and trees to the house of Dr. Howe, on Blanding street; that in the meantime Mrs. Palmer had been deprived of a box of family silver, which was forcibly snatched from her grasp by a soldier; that Dr. Howe's house, having been several times fired, they left it and spent the remainder of the night in the streets, huddled together around a few bundles which they had been able to retain; that in the morning they returned to Dr. Howe's and had remained there; that, though the night of terrors was past, they did not undress to go to bed for five nights. He learned that, when the army left on Monday, they carried with them all the provisions that had not been destroyed by them; that the people were almost entirely without food. He learned that since the Yankees had left rations had been issued from the common stock which was gotten by putting together the supplies that the few fortunate members of the community were able to save; that Mr. Hutson, his invalid brother-in-law, had gone every day to the depot to obtain the scanty allowance doled out, so much for each member of the family. [13]

Dr. Palmer, finding the condition of things so urgent, went with wagons into the country to obtain provisions for the starving ones. He again resumed his spiritual ministrations

[13] Dr. John W. Caldwell, of New Orleans, has furnished us this account of those last days in Columbia.

also to the devastated church in Columbia; and continued there till the close of the war.

During these years, in addition to the services recounted already in this chapter, he had served his church as chairman of the committee to revise the hymn-book and as one of the most important members of the committee to revise the Book of Church Order.

CHAPTER XIII.

REBUILDING THE BROKEN WALLS.

(1865-1874.)

New Orleans, and the First Presbyterian Church at the Close of the War.—The First Sunday in His Pulpit after His Return to New Orleans.—His Efforts to Rebuild His People:—By Preaching.—By Pastoral Work.—By Putting the People to Work.—Sketch of the Work, 1869-1870, and Later.—Temper toward Other Churches of the same Communion in New Orleans.—Parochial Schools, the Sylvester Larned Institute.—Dr. Palmer's Labors in.—His Aid in the Re-adjustment of the Church at Large to Its New Environment in 1865 and Afterwards.—His Overtures to the Associate Reformed Synod of the South, and to the Cumberland Presbyterians in the Assembly of 1866.—His Services Against Fusion in the Assembly of 1870.—Special Preparation for this Service, Through Studies of Defections of the Church, North, Contributed to the Southwestern Presbyterian of the Summer before.—Other Contributions to the Southwestern Presbyterian.

WHEN the Civil War broke out, New Orleans was one of the greatest ports in the world, and "to all appearance the most prosperous commercial city in America." The year before the war began, the total commerce of the city amounted to $473,290,000. It was the most profitable sort of commerce, too. Consequently, the average wealth of the citizen had become very high. Her merchants, bankers and capitalists were men of great enterprise. Other enterprising cities were not ashamed, therefore, to borrow ideas from New Orleans. Causes were, indeed, at work, such as the choking of the mouths of the Mississippi with sand, the operation of the Erie Canal, and the building and successful operation of transmontane railways, which would have tended to diminish her trade and her prosperity in the course of time; but the war, within the limits of four short years, reduced this prosperous city to ruins, almost annihilated her commerce, occasioned the turning of a considerable part of her trade to other cities, destroyed no small part of it, so that it was necessary to rebuild from the very foundations. Nor were the circumstances under which the rebuilding must be done such as to make the undertaking easy.

After the capture of the city the suspension of commerce and all industries caused a great increase in the number of the poor in New Orleans. These conditions were made worse by the considerable number of negroes who had fled thither to seek safety within the Union lines. In order to feed these bodies of poor, the arbitrary and tyrannical rulers levied assessments on banks, business firms or individuals who had given assistance to the Confederate cause. As time passed the Union men in the city became more and more powerful. Carpetbaggers exercised rule. Even after 1868, when Louisiana became a part of the Union, her troubles the rather increased. Misrule, debt and corruption characterized the time. At length, in 1874, the White League overthrew in a pitched battle the Metropolitan police, in the employ of the Radical party, and the colored militia, numbering three thousand men, and cleared the way for the introduction of a wiser government. The beginning of the Eads jetties about the same time gave new hope and life to the city. When the war closed, in 1865, New Orleans did not present, therefore, such attractions as she had presented in 1856.

If the city had diminished in absolute and relative importance, the First Presbyterian Church had also dwindled in numbers, resources and influence. The church had availed itself of the ministrations of such supplies as it could command under the circumstances. But it came out of the war period with about one hundred and fifty fewer members than were on its rolls in 1860, and these weakened vastly in fortune and otherwise.

Back in South Carolina, Dr. Palmer could conjecture, in the spring of 1865, very accurately the conditions in New Orleans, and her worse conditions to follow, yet he yearned for his people and the remnant of his flock. Accordingly, he appeared in his pulpit as soon as the opening of the way permitted. An editorial note in the *New Orleans Times,* Monday, July 17, 1865, permits the reader to see him on that first appearance after the war, as he was seen by at least one of his hearers:

"Yesterday was quiet and pleasant—a Sabbath of the soul! During the forenoon there was a fine breeze abroad, and a screen of clouds, spread over the face of the sky, tempered the heat, which might other-

attended, particularly the First Presbyterian Church, where Dr. B. M. wise have been oppressive. The churches, we noticed, were very largely Palmer, so famous for his eloquence in other days, held forth as one who had returned from his wanderings to become again a teacher and a guide. It was soon apparent that during his absence the Doctor had lost none of those powers which gave such a charm to his pulpit oratory. He seemed, however, to be more chastened and subdued than he ever was before. With an humbler hope he looked up to the bow of promise which spanned the sky, and with gentler persuasion he called for a renewal of the covenant of grace. He feelingly alluded to the long years of suffering, now so happily closed, and expressed a hope that his own trials and sad experiences would be so far sanctified as to fit him better than ever before for the responsible duties of a Gospel minister. He then told, how in the general affliction, the angel of death had visited his household, and, as he alluded to the sad theme, all hearts were melted and the waters gushed forth from the smitten rock. As for the dead past, he, for one, was anxious to hide it away in the solemn tomb. Henceforth, no word should escape his lips but such as was meet for an humble servant in the temple of his God and King. Wherever called to minister in the land of his birth and of his love, he would emulate the example of Paul the Apostle, by preaching Christ and Him crucified; and his song should be the song of the angels —'Peace on earth, and good will toward men.'

"In the afternoon there was a shower, and at night again all was calm and still."

The responsibilities upon him were now vast. It was his to rebuild his own congregation and membership; and it was his to lead his people, diminished as they were, to give heroic assistance to the weaker bodies of the same communion throughout the city, the State, and the Southwest. Right nobly did he acquit himself of these heavy responsibilities—by his preaching and example, by his pastoral work, and by the organization and stimulation of the rank and file of his people to endeavor on their own part.

His preaching was continued with his old time intellectual vigor, earnestness, eloquence and grace of delivery. It seems to have been characterized by an increased sense of his dependence on the God whose grace is infinite albeit His ways are past finding out. His range of topics was not materially different from that of the first period in New Orleans. He still gave large attention to the Scriptural doctrines of sin, of man's responsibility for sin coupled with his inability to save himself from it, of salvation by grace through Christ Jesus, of the law as a rule of life, and of the Christian's future. The various phases of these great doctrines were presented Sabbath after Sabbath, sometimes in a simple didactic way, and sometimes in an indirect way by polemic attempts against current infidelity concerning any of these Scriptural teachings. As instances of this polemic preaching, an able series of sermons in 1866 on objections to prayer may be referred to. As instances of the simple didactic exposition of Scripture teaching, reference may be made to his series of sermons, delivered on Sabbath nights, 1867, on the Beatitudes, or to the shorter series on various aspects of conscience, preached on certain Sabbath mornings about the same time, or to the series of six sermons on the Parable of the Sower, preached in the year 1874, or to a larger series on the subject of Prayer, preached on Sabbath evenings in 1869-1870. He was, as has appeared before, given to preaching series of sermons. He liked to bring out a theme fully and symmetrically.

In introducing his later series of discourses of Prayer, he told his people that the theme had never been discussed except by homilies and recommendations of the duty of praise and supplication to the Supreme Being; that no extant treatise grappled with the various difficulties which either a weak faith or an arrogant skepticism had thrown around the relations subsisting between the immutable God and the intelligent yet helpless creature man; and that after much reflection and study he had determined, in view of the lack of a complete investigation of the subject of prayer, to prepare and deliver a series of Sabbath evening discourses, that he might leave them some tokens of remembrance when his head should rest on the bosom of the Father.

In addition to the series of many, or several, sermons each, he would very frequently, in treating a great Scriptural theme, devote both morning and evening services to its consideration.

He confined himself rigidly to preaching the Gospel. He understood well how to bring forth its teachings in season. His sermons often show the happiest adaptation to the special circumstances of the people at the time of their delivery. For example, in the late summer and autumn of 1867, when the yellow fever was raging in the city, he is found preaching on such texts as Psalm 23: 4: "Though I walk through the valley of the shadow of death, I will fear no evil: for thou art with me, thy rod and thy staff they comfort me;" Mark

6: 50: "It is I, be not afraid;" 1 Chronicles 21: 13: "Let me fall into the hands of the Lord, for great are his mercies."

The following story, told by Miss Mary Caldwell, of Charleston, S. C., may be taken as showing fairly the degree of influence exerted by Dr. Palmer, at this time, over an audience:

> In the fall of 1866, he went to New York to perform the marriage ceremony for a former beloved parishioner and spiritual child, Miss Anna Jennings. The Sunday after reaching New York, he, together with his traveling companion, went over to Brooklyn to hear Dr. Scott, who had been his predecessor in the First Presbyterian Church in New Orleans. Dr. Scott recognized Dr. Palmer immediately on his entering the church; he betrayed surprise and something akin to chagrin at seeing him there. Turning his eyes from the pew in which Dr. Palmer sat, he was careful not to look that way any more. Nor did he greet Dr. Palmer after the sermon. In a day or two, Dr. Scott wrote him a note saying that *he* would have been glad to have him in his pulpit but had been prevented by the sense he had of his people's impatience with him for his course during the war. The next Sunday they went to Dr. Van Dyke's church. Dr. Van Dyke had arranged for Dr. Palmer to preach for him. He was absent himself. Dr. Palmer began without an introduction. He preached on the Comforter, "I will send you another Comforter," etc. He began in his apparently simple way with sentences, short, clear and crisp. The people were electrified and held as under a spell. That evening the house was crowded. People had gone home from the morning service talking of the modest-looking little gentleman with such command of the teachings of Scripture and such wonderful eloquence in setting the truth forth, whose name nevertheless they could not tell. The sermon in the evening was of equal eloquence. An old veteran of the Northern army inquired who the wonderful preacher was. He finally learned that he was the Rev. B. M. Palmer, of New Orleans, La. "The arch rebel of that name!" he exclaimed. "He preaches like an archangel!"

At this time friends in New York begged Dr. Palmer to establish in that city a Church of the Strangers. Dr. Stuart Robinson plead with him to go. But he said, "Robinson, why don't you go and do that work?" He would preach to his own people in New Orleans.

In 1868, on a visit to South Carolina, he preached twice in the city of Charleston. The following excerpt from *The News and Courier* shows how his preaching was regarded there:

> "The presence of this distinguished divine has created a pleasant excitement in the religious community. He preached twice yesterday—in the morning at the Central Presbyterian Church (Dr. Dana's), and

in the evening at Glebe Street Church (Dr. Girardeau's). He was assisted morning and evening by his venerable father, Rev. Edward Palmer, and on each occasion there was an immense congregation present. All classes of the community, natives and foreigners, Northerners and Southerners, Jews and Gentiles, whites and blacks crowded to hear his far-famed eloquence. In the morning he preached from the text: 'Father, I will,' being the first three words of the twenty-fourth verse of the seventeenth chapter of Saint John. Words fail to describe his eloquence, but its effect upon the audience may be judged from the fact that he compelled their undivided and eager attention for one hour and twenty minutes.

"In the evening he preached from Matthew 27:22: 'What shall I do then with Jesus, who is called Christ?' Readers familiar with the New Testament will recollect that this is the question asked of the Jews by Pontius Pilate when they demanded of him the release of Barabbas. Dr. Palmer used it as the suggestion of a discourse respecting the superior claims of the Christian religion on account of the historic character of Christ. . . The same close attention was paid to the discourse as in the morning. Dr. Palmer is, probably, the ablest pulpit orator in the Southern States, and can have but few if any superiors in the North."

Mr. Alfred Lanneau, also of Charleston, S. C., writing of the latter of these sermons, says:

"He passed rapidly in review the various systems of religion which claimed to rival Christianity. His eloquence was fragrant with the incense of praise to Christ, as he showed the utter failure of them all. Then at the close he suddenly asked, 'But do you retort upon me the question, 'What shall you do with this Jesus who is called the Christ?' Why! I just take him into my heart of hearts; and when weary of sin, temptation and sorrow, to Him who when he was on earth said, 'Come unto me all ye that labor and are heavy laden and I will give you rest'—to Him I would go and laying my head upon his bosom look up with all the love and confidence of a child. The climax was perfect and the effect was intense."

In 1870 the Synod of Mississippi met in Jackson. Dr. Palmer attended. He was appointed, perhaps at his own request, to preach on Sabbath, to the convicts in the State prison. It happened that as the congregation assembled, Dr. T. J. Mitchell, then prison physician, was passing through the chapel on his way to the dispensary. He stopped to ask Judge Thomas J. Wharton, who had accompanied the preacher for the day to the place, "Why they sent such a piney woods specimen of a preacher to preach to the convicts." The Judge, who was Dr. Palmer's host, answered only with a smile. The rest of the story is better told in the words of another: "The hymn was sung, and the preacher opened the Sacred Word and read—as he only can read—a chapter appropriate to the occasion. The Doctor listened, and, forgetting the dispensary, remained through the sermon. Then approaching Judge Wharton, he said, 'Judge, there is only one minister that can read and preach after that fashion. I am prepared to be introduced to Dr. Palmer.' "[1]

If his work as a preacher was with such flattering acceptance, his work as a pastor was not less faithful and efficient. Ever too busy to do much social visiting, he never had too much work of other sorts to prevent genuine, tactful, pastoral visits to those supposed to be ready to receive such visits with profit. In times of sickness he was always attentive. In times of pestilence he was faithful to the point of heroism. The pestilence of yellow fever is a terrible pestilence.

"Yellow fever is not a terrible disease only because of its fatality. In instances of death from most other causes, the victim in the cold embrace of death is kept as long as possible from the coffin and the grave. The friend or relative still loves to gaze with the eyes of affection upon the form, though rigid in death, and on 'the languor of the placid cheek,' though the light of the face be quenched forever; and 'mark the mild, angelic air, the rapture of the repose that's there.'

"Though all hope is lost, yet the fond heart dreads seeing the form taken from the place that is to know it no more.

"With the victim from yellow fever the case, however, is different. As soon as it is decent to do so, the poor unfortunate who has been taken off by the scourge is made ready for interment. There is something so repulsive in the nature of the pestilence itself that even affection does not wish to detain the body from an immediate burial. Even the little infant, that

" 'lovliness in death.
that parts not quite with parting breath,'

when the victim of any other disease, is hurried to the tomb, if stricken down with the horrid pestilence of yellow fever. Thus it is that this disease is terrible apart from its fatality."[2]

Whether the above is a scientifically accurate estimate of

---

[1] L. P., in *Magnolia Gazette*, quoted in *Southwestern Presbyterian*, July 26, 1900.

[2] From *Daily Picayune*, October 6, 1867 (an editorial note).

yellow fever is a question that may be ignored in the study of Dr. Palmer's life. It expresses the current view of the plague and the dread of it. Notwithstanding this view, Dr. Palmer did the work of a pastor faithfully and persistently, in the face of all the repulsiveness and all the danger.

In the following paragraphs may be seen an account from his own pen of a face to face talk in the chamber of pestilence:

"During the epidemic of 1867, a pastor in the city of New Orleans was just leaving his study to attend the funeral of one who had fallen a victim to the pestilence. A crumpled note was placed in his hand requesting him to repair immediately to the couch of a dying stranger. Promising to obey the summons as soon as released from the service then present, within an hour he turned sadly away from the cemetery, where the solemn words, 'dust to dust,' had just been pronounced, to look again upon Death, struggling with his prey, in a retired chamber.

"A single glance revealed the form of an athletic young man, with a broad and noble brow, upon which the seal of the grave was visibly set. Sitting upon the edge of the bed, and taking the sufferer's hand kindly in his own, the preacher said, 'Mr. M., do you know how ill you are?'

"'Yes,' was the quick response; 'I shall soon pass the bourne whence no traveller returns.'

"'Are you, then, prepared to die?'

"'Alas! no, sir,' fell upon the ear like the knell of a lost soul.

"'Will you, then, let me pray for you?' and with the assent given, the knee was bowed before Him who alone has power to save. In two or three terse sentences, uttered with a tremulous emotion, the case of the dying sinner was laid at the mercy-seat.

"The moments were shortening fast; very soon the last sand would disappear from the hour-glass. The conversation was promptly resumed, as follows:

"'Mr. M., I am told you are the son of pious parents, and have been reared in the bosom of the Church; you do not need, therefore, that I should explain to you the way of salvation—for which, indeed, there is now no time. But you know that the Bible says, "God so loved the world that he gave his only begotten Son, that whosoever believeth in him should not perish, but have everlasting life." Only believe *now* in this Savior, and you are saved.'

"'Oh, sir,' was the reply, 'if God will only spare me this once I promise that I will live very differently in the future than I have lived in the past.'

"'My dear friend,' rejoined the minister, 'this is the last device of Satan to destroy your soul. I tell you faithfully, there is no future for you in this world; you are now passing, whilst I speak, through the gateway of Death, and what you do, you must do at once, or be lost forever.'

"To this appeal the only answer was a deep groan, whilst the beads of moisture, gathering upon that ample forehead, and the swollen veins, drawn like a dark seam across it, betokened the anguish of a guilty spirit, shrinking from the presence of an angry God. A few seconds of awful silence intervened; but a last effort must be made to pluck this soul from the lethargy of despair. 'Mr. M., do you remember the story of the penitent thief upon the cross? His time was short, just as yours is; but one brief prayer, not longer than a line, expressed his faith, and was enough. So you see that it is never too late.'

"At this the closed eyes were opened, and the first word of hope fell from the parted lips: *'No, it is not too late; thank God, it is not too late.'*

"'Mr. M.,' said the pastor, 'do you trust now in the Lord Jesus Christ?'

"'Yes, I do. He is my Savior, and I am not afraid to die!' rung out upon the startled listeners, as though a note from the song of the harpers had fallen from heaven into that chamber of death.

"There was another silence of a few seconds—this time a silence of wonder and joy; it was broken by the dying man, as he turned upon his side and whispered to the minister, 'Will you write to my father?'

"'Yes, certainly: but what shall I tell him?'

"'Tell him I have found Jesus, who has pardoned my sins, and I am not afraid to die. He will meet me in heaven.'

"It was his last utterance, for in the next moment the soul, that had passed through this fierce struggle into the second birth, winged its separate flight, and stood before the throne.

The whole interview thus described was shut up within the limits of fifteen minutes, from the moment of entrance into that darkened chamber till the tenantless body lay in its cold sweat, to be shrouded for the tomb.

"Sad, yet sweet, were the pastor's thoughts as he walked to his home, beneath the stars, through the streets of the silent city—thoughts of the vast solemnity and preciousness of his office, as an ambassador for Christ—thoughts of that blessed family covenant by which God remembers the prayers of a believing parent, and looks at the tears in his bottle—sometimes even upon the death-bed of the child—thoughts of that unutterable love which saves, even to the uttermost, and makes it *never too late* to pluck the brand from the burning."[3]

---

[3] This account was published in tract form under the title "Never Too Late" by the Committee of Publication, Richmond, Va. It had been previously published in the *Southwestern Presbyterian,* April 1, 1869.

The following letter illustrates the manner in which he was wont to exercise his functions as pastor, in happier times:

NEW ORLEANS, September 4, 1869.

"*Mr. Charles Bobb:*

"MY DEAR SIR: Ever since your brother united with the Church, I have desired to speak to you on the subject which I doubt not you feel transcends all others in importance. To the present time, however, no fitting opportunity seemed to present itself—and it has occurred to me to avail myself of your absence to address you with the pen.

"I regret that my knowledge of your views and feelings is so slight that I can give no special direction to the arrow that I now place on the string. But even in the dark some things may be safely assumed: among the rest, this: that if there be a Supreme Being in whom we live and move, then He is entitled to our supreme obedience and love. This, you perceive, draws the line between *morality* and *religions,* both of which have their proper spheres, but should never be confounded. It is not enough, that a man should fulfill faithfully all relative duties to his fellow men. There is another Being to whom he owes duties also; and these are supreme love and voluntary obedience. Failing in these, we are precisely as guilty under the first table of the law as we would be under the second, if convicted of robbery or theft.

"Now, my dear sir, the question seems, how do you, and how do I, stand as to this point? There is one unequivocal test. God has made a revelation of himself, more glorious than any other, through his incarnate Son. He commands us to accept that Son as the only Mediator through whom he will communicate with us. Pardon and eternal life are offered as the purchase of his blood. What I want you to notice is, that the command to believe in Jesus Christ as the only Savior of men rests upon the same authority with the command 'thou shalt not kill,' or, 'thou shalt not covet.' If we do not obey all the commands of God, we have not the spirit of true obedience to any; and as long as we withhold our love and our trust from Jesus Christ, we refuse obedience to God, who says, 'this is my beloved Son, hear ye him.'

"I solicit most respectfully your attention, my dear sir, to this 'principal thing.' You have, like myself, reached an age at which the covering is taken off from the delusions of the world. We are no longer children to be deceived by its promises. You have sucked the orange, and know that little remains but the pulp. But if there is a grand *Hereafter,* stretching on beyond the bounds of thought, possibly it may have something in store for an immortal soul, which this material earth is too poor to afford. The inheritance of life and love, purchased for us by the Redeemer, and offered freely to all who will accept it by faith —this, my dear sir, is the prize which I want you to grasp. Holiness forever, after God's image, and perfect fellowship with Him in heaven, this is the state to which I want you to aspire. And it is *all,* ALL found in Christ, at his cross, in the exercise of child-like, trusting faith.

"Pardon now this great liberty which I have taken to which I am emboldened by the conviction that you are too generous to be offended with a well-meant—though it should seem an obtrusion—interest in your eternal welfare. With this apology and with my best wishes for the complete restoration of your health, I commend you, dear sir, to Almighty God and to the Spirit of his grace.

"Respectfully and truly yours,

"B. M. PALMER."

Dr. Palmer was a minister who stuck persistently at his work. Heavy as the burdens were which he carried, he rarely took a vacation. In June, 1867, his session requested him to take a vacation on the ground that his great labors were "endangering his health." As an alternate proposition they suggested that he should drop his Sabbath morning Bible class and his Sabbath evening sermon. A week later he gratefully thanked the session for these kind offers, declared that he did not share their alarm, but that out of deference to their judgment he would merge the male and female Bible classes into a Sunday night expository lecture. During these nine years he seems to have taken only one vacation. To that vacation he was urged in a wonderfully gracious way, and as graciously accepted:

"At a meeting of the members of the First Presbyterian Church and Congregation, held on Sabbath morning, May 28, 1871, at the close of Divine Service, Judge Lee presiding, the following Resolutions were unanimously passed:

"WHEREAS, It has pleased our Great Head to grant to the Church and Congregation for more than fifteen years a pastor who has been unremittingly engaged in ministerial duties, the greater part of that period in immediate pastoral labor and the remainder in toil as arduous, and far more anxious, in fields which for a time demanded his solicitude;

"WHEREAS, During this long period he has been blessed with health and strength for his work, which has prospered in the temporal and spiritual growth of the flock over which the Good Shepherd has made him overseer; and

"WHEREAS, A ministry so unexampled for its usefulness and duration calls from the recipients an expression of thankfulness to their Heavenly Father; and of gratitude and affection to him who has been the instrument of such great good, and of those feelings which the occasion suggests, therefore be it

"*Resolved,* That we render thanks and praises to Almighty God for that good hand which has been stretched out to us during the fifteen years of the present pastorate, leading us through many trials and vicissitudes into a large and wealthy place, and enabling us to exclaim 'that we have a goodly heritage,' and that, therefore, 'we rejoice and are glad.'

"*Resolved,* That it is our happy privilege to testify to the earnest faithfulness and devotion of the Rev. Dr. Palmer, in the work from which he has permitted no temptation to draw him; and to thank him with all our hearts for the instruction which he has given us in his constant pulpit ministrations, for the sympathy and consolation with which he has lightened our homes in prosperity, in despondency, and in sickness; and for those words of loving tenderness which have fallen upon the ear of our loved departed ones. No language that we can command is capable of expressing these thanks; and we pray the Great Giver of all good to bestow upon him and his the blessings which he has so often asked for us and ours at the throne of heavenly grace.

"*Resolved,* That labors so untiring and unremitting compel in us a feeling of anxiety, that the natural wear of human life may be accelerated unless there is a reasonable intermission therefrom.

"*Resolved,* That a solemn sense of duty compels us to ask, that for a brief period, the Rev. Dr. Palmer, will remit his pastoral labors and enjoy a recreation that we firmly believe is needful for the continuance of the health which has so long been a blessing to him and afforded to us such high privileges and comforts, and the Master a laborer in his vineyard of such untiring energy and fidelity.

"*Resolved,* That we tender to Dr. Palmer, and earnestly beseech him to accept a vacation of four months to commence at such a period as may be agreeable to him.

"*Resolved,* That while we have no disposition to impose any restriction or condition upon the enjoyment of this vacation, yet, aware that the reputation for learning, eloquence, ability and pious zeal, which he enjoys, and of which we are justly proud, will induce from many sources, the call upon him for pulpit ministrations, we would most respectfully follow him with a wish, that this vacation may not be invaded otherwise than upon the call of highest duty.

"*Resolved,* That the session be requested to take order for the requisite supply of the pulpit during Dr. Palmer's contemplated absence.

"*Resolved,* That the chairman be requested to communicate to Dr. Palmer these Resolutions; and in such language as he may deem apt, express the earnest wishes of the Church and Congregation in this behalf."

"*Rev. B. M. Palmer:*

"MY DEAR SIR: I esteem it a great pleasure to be the organ of your Church and Congregation in communicating to you the accompanying Resolutions.

"Your congregation appreciating the long and useful service you have rendered them during the many years which have elapsed since your ministration in this city commenced, and the spiritual comfort and consolation they have derived from your wholesome teaching, and from the kindly sympathy you have always extended to them in the hour of trouble; and considering that they have a property in your good health have concluded with entire unanimity, to recommend to you a vacation from labor during the sultry months of the coming season, believing that an occasional season of repose is essential to long continued usefulness and efficiency.

"Trusting that you will see nothing in this arrangement inconsistent with your conceptions of duty, I beg leave, personally and on behalf of your congregation, to tender to you our best wishes for the comfort and happiness of yourself and family during your temporary absence.

"Very respectfully yours,

"J. N. LEE."

"May 29th.

"P. S.—A special fund of $3,000, the voluntary contribution of the members of your congregation, has been placed subject to your order, in the hands of the Treasurer of the Church.

"Yours truly,

"J. N. LEE."

"NEW ORLEANS, LA., June 10, 1871.

"Hon. J. N. Lee.

"MY DEAR SIR: I cannot tell whether I am affected more by the exquisitely tender resolutions adopted by the meeting over which you presided, or by the munificent provision which has been made for carrying out the wishes of the Congregation.

"Indeed, they are but the two parts of one act of supreme goodness; which, however, make a separate appeal to my own gratitude.

"As touching the sum placed at my disposal, I cannot forget that it has been raised at the close of a stringent season, which has been singularly unproductive of wealth to our whole community; nor, that the liberality of the donors has been already severely taxed by drafts necessary to sustain the public enterprises of the Church.

"Both considerations lend an immense emphasis to the act of personal generosity, while they serve to explain that delicacy of feeling which renders the beneficiary of such a bounty somewhat reluctant to avail himself of it.

"In regard to the beautiful Resolutions throbbing in every line with a most generous affection, I can only say that I accept them as a sufficient reward for the labors of a lifetime. I do sincerely bless God that 'He counted me faithful, putting me into the ministry' of his Son: and not less, that he has rendered its service a perfect joy to me for thirty years.

"This, however, has not arisen from any sense of my own merit, but from the wonderful benevolence of every people whom it has been my privilege to serve. In the review of my whole ministry, both here and elsewhere, I feel complacency in but a single fact: that my public teachings have always centered upon the cross of Christ. Though I have not scrupled to employ the aids of philosophy and science, it has been only to illustrate the majesty of that grace which has wrought out a sinner's redemption.

"Yet my heart has often bowed in shame and sorrow before God that the glory of such a theme could not inspire me with a loftier enthusiasm, or fill me with a deeper consciousness of power.

"You will understand then with what sweetness such a testimony comes, as that rendered in these Resolutions, to relieve the sense of grievous imperfection which clings to all the memory of my work. The approval of the good is, in one form, the seal of the Divine acceptance, and for this, I bow my knees in adoring gratitude to the God of all my mercies.

"It has pleased heaven, my dear sir, to grace my life with the sweetest friendships man can possibly know upon earth; while in my official career, I have been permitted to rejoice in many precious tokens of the Divine favor.

"It has made me almost tremble, at times, to think how happy I have been—only thrice in thirty years has grief thrown its dark shadow upon my path—all the rest have been sunlight and peace. Will you permit me to add that, of all this life, the portion which has been spent in this city and among this people—as it has been the most heroic, so it has been the most happy.

"With all the gloom which has shrouded ten out of the fifteen years—with all the burden my soul has carried for a prostrate land and a witnessing Church—the consciousness of rectitude, the pleasure of my sweet work, and the love of my people, have made me happy—as I could be more so only in heaven. And I have no wish dearer to my heart, than to be spared for long usefulness in a Church which, I trust, may bear me in its arms to lay me down in their own tomb at death.

"The indecision I have shown in accepting the large proposal of the Congregation, ought perhaps to be explained. It has arisen from two causes: *First,* life is so short, and the work of God so vast, in such a world as ours, that one would think every inch of time should be spent in active labor. My feeling always has been that nothing short of compulsory illness could excuse a respite from toil—and I could not in conscience allow that plea in the present instance. And, *Secondly,* it seemed to me almost wicked to divert to my personal benefit, funds that were so much needed to build up the spiritual wastes of our land. After anxious reflection, however, I have concluded that it would be ungrateful not to yield to the superb generosity which has been proffered to me with a delicacy and a tenderness absolutely overpowering.

"It might seem obstinate, too, to oppose my judgment to that of others, who may discover traces of physical declension to which I am blind and whose jealous affection would stop the leak in its very beginning.

"I consent, therefore, not without a reluctant admission of its necessity, to be put in thorough repair along with the church building itself—hoping that the autumn will bring the lease for a long term, without the need of paint or varnish.

"I propose, therefore, to leave soon after the next Communion, on the first Sabbath in July, with a portion of my family—two members of which require the change far more than myself.

"I ask that we may be borne upon the prayers of the Church, and that I may be permitted to return in 'the fulness of the blessing of the Gospel of Christ.' My own prayers will be continually offered on behalf of a people who have been especially endeared to me of late, by the magnificent liberality with which they have responded to appeals for carrying on the work of God in this great city, and now doubly bound by so delicate and spontaneous an exhibition of their love to me personally.

"In conclusion, my very dear sir, be pleased to accept individual thanks for the handsome terms in which you have conveyed to me the action of the congregation; which is but an illustration of the elegant courtesy by which you are distinguished, and an outflow of that personal regard which you have always shown to myself.

"In bonds of Christian affection and sincerest gratitude, both to yourself and the constituency which you represent, I remain, dear sir,

"Yours most truly,

"B. M. PALMER."[4]

Three months of this vacation were taken and spent in travel with a precious daughter then in a rapid and fatal decline.

Dr. Palmer believed that it is not the part of a pastor to do all the work of the church. Accordingly, we find that he puts the session and the members to work. The session formally and earnestly invites the students of the Law and Medical schools to attend his church so far as they may desire to do so. Members of the session, so far as their time could be commanded, were put actively to pastoral work. In December, 1866, Dr. Palmer brought to his session's attention "the duty and importance of taking his Sabbath-school directly under its control, and of appointing superintendents to fill vacancies which had recently occurred;" "to all which the session unanimously agreed." A little later male communicants of his church are found banded together in a "brotherhood" for aggressive Christian work in their city. Likewise, also, there was a "sisterhood" formed to further the enterprises of the

[4] The *Southwestern Presbyterian* published this correspondence, June 22, 1871.

"brotherhood" and other missionary endeavors. The "brotherhood" established and built up several flourishing Sunday-schools, at points in the city where there were apparently good openings. All their work was under the control of the session; or, if not so in every case in its organization, it was soon brought not only really but formally under such control.

Believing in the value of a good religious newspaper, the session of Dr. Palmer's church, under his lead, began with the very beginning of the *Southwestern Presbyterian* to subscribe for fifty copies of that excellent paper for distribution amongst the poor of the church.

Good pictures of the church as it lived and labored in the latter portion of this period are found in the eloquent reports made to the Presbytery from year to year. Thus the report for the year ending April, 1870, says:

"*Sixty* persons have been added to the roll of communicants; of whom *thirty-six* have been gathered from the world, by an open profession of faith in Christ. The remaining *twenty-four,* received by letter, exactly balance an equal number dismissed by letter to other churches. To these must be added the names of *ten* others, whom it has pleased the Master to remove from earth, as we hope, to enjoy the joys of heaven. Our communion roll, after placing on the reserved list those for whom we cannot account, numbers *six hundred.*

"During the past year, the officers of this Church, pastor, elders, and deacons, have been at their several posts, and engaged in the duties assigned to each. The Word has been preached with solemnity and constancy, without a single intermission of the services of the sanctuary. The attendance of the congregation has been punctual; except as it has been diminished by the usual absence of many during the summer. Since the autumn the congregation has been more than usually large; swelled by the presence of strangers in the city during the winter. Throughout the entire season the building has been filled, floor and galleries, with serious and attentive hearers; who have given every outward mark of, at least, a general interest in the truths to which they have listened.

"The prayer-meeting on Wednesday night, has been regularly sustained, and the attendance upon it has been uniform and large. The lecture-room, seating two hundred or more persons, is generally full and sometimes crowded. It has taken the form of a prayer-meeting and lecture combined: an informal address being always made by the pastor, while the prayers are offered by the private members promiscuously called to lead in these devotions. Our experience has led to the conclusion that it is better to have one well-sustained meeting of this kind, than to divide them into separate meetings as formerly.

We have gratifying evidence that this social and devotional meeting is highly prized by the pious, who find its exercises highly profitable.

"There are five Sabbath-schools in connection with this Church, all of which are under the acknowledged control of the session. One of these is, of course, the Sabbath-school proper to the Church, embracing our own children and numbering two hundred and three in attendance. The remaining four are mission schools: two of which one of white and the other of colored children, are taught in our own lecture rooms, and number respectively one hundred and thirty-three, and ninety, scholars. Two other mission schools have been gathered in other portions of the city, numbering seventy-five teachers and six-hundred pupils. In connection with the two last, industrial classes have been formed, in which, on Saturday the little girls are taught to sew; and to which none are admitted but such as attend the Sabbath-school. It is an inducement to punctuality and zeal in the Sabbath exercises. The aggregate number in the five schools is one hundred and twenty-five teachers, and one thousand pupils. The fruit of these labors can scarcely be expected to be immediate: yet we have been called to notice with gratitude some clear instances in which the truth has been carried to the home of such as were before ignorant of it, and where its saving power has been felt.

"Probably the most noticeable feature of our religious history, during the year, has been the systematic effort to draw out the dormant energies of our church members in evangelical labors. A little more than a year ago, the male and female members of the Church and congregation were organized into two distinct associations; which have co-operated under the direction of the pastor and session. As the result, two flourishing Sabbath-schools have been gathered, and are now sustained by the active labors chiefly of our young people. A building has been erected, free of debt and costing about $2,000; and incipient steps have been taken for the erection of another. The contributions of these associations have hitherto supported, in great part, one of our ministerial brethren as a city missionary, who is at present laboring at Carrollton. An incidental benefit, of unmistakable value, has been the bringing together our church members, and making them acquainted with each other, thus greatly promoting Christian fellowship. Probably in no other way could we succeed in breaking up that crust which is apt to form over a large congregation; who drift away in their different social circles and are little brought into personal contact. The pleasure derived from this experience has led to another experiment, which also promises to work well. This is simply a social reunion, or levee, held each alternate week; where some one of the congregation throws open the doors of his house to all those who choose to come, between the hours of seven and ten in the evening. In this way, different parties meet, who would otherwise never be thrown together; and the opportunity is afforded to new comers into the Church to form the Christian acquaintance they so much desire. This, however, is but an experiment as yet, the working of which we watch with interest. Hints, too, will probably be suggested of new methods, by which to develop the graces and activities of the Lord's people—an aim which is to be held by us constantly in view.

"In conclusion, the results of a year's toil fall far short of what we desire, and though our faith is sometimes staggered at the disproportion between these and the efforts put forth, still it would be criminal ingratitude not to acknowledge the Divine goodness in what has been experienced. We have only to add that our hearts have been touched with grief by the recent death of Mr. Alfred Hennen, one of the oldest elders, and one of the original founders of this Church. He died in great peace, on the nineteenth of January last, having reached the eighty-fourth year of his age."[5]

From subsequent reports it is learned that the prayer meeting in 1871 was transferred from the lecture-room to the main audience room; that the attendance on that meeting, which "has been termed the electrometer of the Church" had increased in a most surprising way; that it so well filled the body of that large room that it compared favorably with the diminished Sabbath audiences of the summer; that there had been considerable gains in the attendance on the Sabbath-schools; that a second mission school building had been erected during the year, and that when the last payment should have been made, the outlay for the mission enterprises would amount to about $10,000. It is learned that the year ending April, 1872, was, while a year of aggressive effort, and increased attendance on the total of services, a year of discouragement because of the death of so many valued members, people of consecration and abilities, because of the removal from New Orleans of such a large number of his members, and because of the small number of accessions to the church. The year 1872 was the first that Dr. Palmer ever reported to his Presbytery fewer members than he had the year before, but in April, 1872, he had eighteen fewer members than in April, 1871. His church had indeed rapidly decreased in membership during the last three years of the war, but he had not been on the ground. It is also learned, from these reports, that he had no other such discouraging year; that in April, 1874, the session reported *six hundred and fifty* members, his church supporting the Rev.

[5] See Sessional Records, First Presbyterian Church of New Orleans, under date of April 6, 1870.

A. J. Witherspoon as a city missionary, and the venerable elder, Mr. Joseph A. Maybin, in his labors at Carrollton; and that in the several Sunday-schools one hundred and twenty teachers were teaching sixteen hundred and fifty-eight scholars.

He and his session displayed a most generous temper toward the sister Presbyterian congregations in all this aggressive Sunday-school work, encouraging their converts to enter any Presbyterian Church which convenience or duty might dictate. They were laboring for the upbuilding of Presbyterianism at large in the city rather than for the particular organization of the First Church.

It was characteristic of this pastor and session to cultivate, on every side, the friendliest relations with the other churches of the same communion in the city. Dr. Palmer took measures to secure a joint celebration of the Lord's Supper on the first Sabbath of the year 1866. Thenceforth the custom prevailed throughout the period, of the joint communion of all the Presbyterian churches on the first Sabbath of the year. Their sessional records show that the First Church communed not only in the solemnest rite of the Church with these other brethren, but generously helped financially as occasion demanded.

Between 1868 and 1870, the "carpetbag" adventurers coming into power, put some extreme reconstruction measures into force in New Orleans. "One of these measures was rule No. 39, passed by the Board of Education, April 8, 1870, admitting colored pupils to the white schools, in accordance with the law of the 'carpetbag' legislature. This rule aroused the bitterest feelings of opposition in New Orleans, and in spite of the exertions of State Superintendent Conway, who rendered himself obnoxious by his ill-advised efforts, it was found impossible to enforce it. The agitation did not cease until" about "two years later when separate schools were provided for the two races." [6] Meanwhile Mr. William O. Rogers had become the founder of a system of parochial schools for whites, one of which was the Sylvester Larned Institute for girls. Mr. Rogers was a man of ample furnishing for such an enterprise. He was a highly respected member of Dr. Palmer's church. His venture met with hearty support by the Presbyterians of

[6] From Henry Rightor's *Standard History of New Orleans, Louisiana,* p. 240.

the city; and was a great success as long as there seemed to be any sufficient motive for keeping up these parochial schools —that is, till the end of the "carpetbag" government in 1877.

The eight schools thus set agoing were under the care of the several Presbyterian Churches of the city. They enrolled eight hundred pupils the first session. The one assigned originally to the First Church was the high school for girls. During the first session between eighty and ninety pupils attended the institute. During the next session one hundred and sixty pupils attended it; and the trustees of the church were so encouraged by its prospects that they assumed a debt of about $20,000 in order to the purchase of a suitable building in which to house the institution.

There can be little question that Dr. Palmer's labors in the institute, as well as his influence in its behalf, contributed much to its success. The suggestion to establish such schools probably came from him. Once established he gave the one his church specially fathered not a little valuable service. Commencing November 10, 1870, he delivered a set of lectures upon "The Philosophy of History." There were twelve lectures in the course. The briefs of these lectures indicate that he threw himself into this course with all his accustomed energy. His estimate of the mental power of schoolgirls must have been very high if he expected them to carry with them an adequate brief of what he said. Some of these lectures are now sadly antiquated, in view of the discoveries touching the civilizations of the Nile, Euphrates, and Tigris Valleys, made since they were written. Others would be counted very able if published now; but they all speak of the huge energy of the busy pastor who could find time for the wide reading they evince, and of the profound philosophical sagacity of the student who could trace the interconnections of the great events with which he dealt in such an approximately masterful way.

He delivered them to the school in the lecture room of his church. Not only were the students of the school admitted; but the public, by ticket, as far as the space permitted. The lectures were delivered, for the most part, one each week, till toward the end of January, then one in a fortnight.

They were reported and commented on severally in the *New Orleans Picayune* and perhaps in other papers. For example, the *Picayune* of December 14, 1870, says of the fourth lecture:

"When we take into consideration the fact that the Reverend gentleman appears before his audience without a single memorandum, or note, and discourses for an hour and a half without intermission, we are surprised at his clear, powerful and retentive memory, which, grasping the history of a world gradually unfolds it, and by graphic descriptions (interspersing names and dates with wonderful correctness and celerity) lays before his auditors the knowledge contained therein.

"The fourth lecture brought down the history to the period of the exodus of the Hebrews from Egypt. The speaker traced the rise of the Assyrian Empire, which absorbed the Chaldean and sketched its sovereignity over all southwestern Asia; and also that of Egypt from its first settlement till the eighteenth dynasty, including the period of foreign domination when the Shepherd Kings held the land.

"He likewise traced the history of the patriarch Abraham and his successors, and dwelt at length upon the epoch of the rise of the Assyrian Empire, as of one great political change, with which all these movements stood historically connected.

"The lecture was simply a grouping together of the leading historical events, during a period of five hundred years, as these bear upon the general history of the world.

"In the next lecture on Friday evening, December 16th, Dr. Palmer proposes to trace the rise of idolatry in the Asiatic kingdoms, and the different forms it assumed."

According to references in the *Southwestern Presbyterian,* this course of lectures "charmed," "enchanted" and richly instructed his audiences.

By September 1, 1871, the Sylvester Larned Institute seemed to be fairly on its feet. It had been established in quarters specially furnished for it. The session of Dr. Palmer's church was now asked to come to the aid of another parochial school. It was asked to allow the parochial school for boys, under Messrs. Morrison and Roudebush, to occupy the lecture-room of their church, vacated by the institute. In this way his interest in behalf of these schools was still further stimulated.

Dr. Palmer's services were not confined to New Orleans and to Presbyterians there in this period. As a member of the higher courts he rendered distinguished services.

In consequence of the Federal occupation of New Orleans in the spring of 1862, the Presbytery of New Orleans was soon afterwards divided. Till the end of the war it was not possible to hold a reunited meeting of the Presbytery. The fortunes of war had pressed a portion of its members away from their homes. Nor could any communication be held with those that remained. The portion of the Presbytery which was without held regular meetings under the sanction and by the order of the Synod of Mississippi, and was duly represented in the superior courts of the Church. That portion of the Presbytery within the city and in the La Fourche region also held its meetings and took such action from time to time as the order and safety of the churches under its care required. For the first time in more than three years these separated portions met, in October, 1865. The reunited bodies, under Dr. Palmer's lead, admitted the minutes of the two separate bodies to record as giving the full history of the Presbytery without assigning precedence to either body. Further the Presbytery placed itself precisely at the point occupied before the separation of its parts, sustaining the same ecclesiastical relations which it had at the last fall meeting, in 1862, held. Thus was the Presbytery of New Orleans brought to rights, from the action taken by the portion of the body inside New Orleans, March 9, 1864; at which time it had declared itself "free from the jurisdiction and control of any other ecclesiastical body whatsoever," and had assumed the position of an independent presbytery under its old name and style.

As early as February, 1866, Dr. Palmer had organized and applied a plan by which to draw out the liberality of his own people to the utmost in behalf of the Southern Presbyterian Church at large.

The following letter to the Rev. Dr. J. B. Adger, concerned chiefly about the publication and sale of the collected writings of the Rev. Dr. James Henley Thornwell, shows that he was ready to call upon his people not only for the support of the great causes of the Church, but for occasional and special gifts:

"NEW ORLEANS, May 11, 1867.

"DEAR ADGER: Scribner's proposal is not liberal. Baird's is too expensive, and further he does not possess the facilities to push the work into the general market. Robinson's plan is the best for the reason, above all others, that it vests the property in the family; and it would be pleasant to think whatever profits arise from the publication should enure to the benefit of those whom our dear and venerated brother loved best on earth.

"If Robinson, who lives where money is more plentiful, will undertake to raise the half of $2,000, I think we might assume the remainder without undue risk. It is true, we in this city are lying under terrible pressure, from the necessity of raising $60,000 or $70,000 for our own churches here or to lose them altogether; and from the fact that our merchants have been drained to the last cent by advancing to the planters who have been overflowed two successive seasons, and now require to be fed by public beneficence. Still the sponge can be squeezed a little harder; and I am willing to try, after a short breathing spell has been allowed after incessant solicitations of late.

"In this arrangement, however, one thing must be considered. The books must be *circulated,* as well as *printed,* and to this end, the usual channels of trade must be employed. If I remember aright, Robinson, after printing his book in Canada, effected some arrangement with the Appletons by which it was made their interest to push it out into circulation; whilst the connection with the publishers at Toronto secured an agency by which the work was brought before the British public. Something of the same sort will be required in this case.

"As to the arrangement of the volumes, you will have to be guided by the amount of matter and the necessity of imparting something like unity to volumes made up of monographs. For example, the volume on Truth will not be as large as that of the Lectures, unless you swell it to equal size by coupling together all the fugitive papers on moral topics. So the Apochrypha will have to carry along all that he ever wrote on Romanism.

"His Church essays, theological tracts, and literary articles and addresses may fill two volumes, perhaps only one. You will of course be able to decide after closely examining the papers, and estimating their bulk.

"I would say, stereotype as far as you can raise means to do it—then let the proceeds of the sale be reserved for the publication of the rest: after which, all will belong to Mrs. Thornwell and the children—only, do not push this arrangement for their benefit so as to embarrass the first circulation of the work in America and in Europe.

"I do not know to what the project of a Southwest seminary may grow but my impression is that at present it will fail. It is Lyon's hobby, and the Tombeckbee Memorial is only the reflexion of his desire. At the same time, my candid judgment is that the removal of Columbia Seminary (say, to Memphis) would be immeasurably to its interest. If Missouri and Kentucky come to us the case will be stronger. The Synods of South Carolina and Georgia would do well to consider the whole matter seriously. At present I am wholly opposed to the multiplication of our institutions.

"Yours affectionately,

"B. M. PALMER."

Dr. Palmer was a member of the General Assembly of 1866. His greatest service, in that body, was his drafting the following report of the Committee on Foreign Correspondence, in which he leads his Assembly to say graciously to two sister communions, "Come and join us on our platform, by which we must stand:"

"The Committee on Foreign Correspondence would respectfully submit to the Assembly the following minute for its adoption:

"This Assembly has received with the liveliest satisfaction, and reciprocates with the utmost cordiality, the Christian greetings of the Associate Reformed Synod of the South, through its representative, the Rev. H. L. Murphy, and of the General Assembly of the Cumberland Presbyterian Church, through its representative, the Rev. C. A. Davis, D.D. If nothing more were gained by this fraternal correspondence than the expressions before the world of the spiritual unity and fellowship of the Lord's people amidst seeming diversity and separation, the Assembly would for this reason alone desire its continuance. But especially is this interchange to be perpetuated, in the hope that it may lead, at no distant day, to a closer union. These corresponding delegates have both unofficially expressed their conviction that many in their respective communions are ready for this consummation, and this declaration is made in face of the fact that the Associate Reformed Synod at its last session terminated the negotiations for an organic union with this Assembly; and in face of the fact that no overtures for such union have as yet originated in the Assembly of the Cumberland Presbyterian Church. This Assembly would, therefore, seize this opportunity to open its heart, and to put on record a formal deliverance touching this whole matter of consolidation into one body all who can stand together upon the same platform of doctrine and order.

"The spiritual body of Christ is undeniably one, having 'one Lord, one faith, one baptism;' and whilst from the infirmity of our unsanctified nature, differences emerge between those who cannot, upon all points, see eye to eye, yet must this spiritual unity struggle to realize itself, before the world, and bring into visible fellowship and under one discipline all who fundamentally agree, and by subordinating minor differences of opinion to the cardinal doctrines of the Gospel. The High-Priestly prayer of our blessed Redeemer finds a response in every Christian heart—'that they all may be one, as thou, Father, art in me, and I in thee, that they also may be one in us, that the world may believe that thou hast sent me.' It is, however, the mature judgment of the Assembly that this union of true believers, in its outward and visible expression, must begin by approximating those bodies of Christians who agree in their symbols of doctrine and order, and who are separated only by shades of opinion which call for mutual toleration and indulgencies, leaving to the nearer approach of the millennial glory the obliteration of those broader and deeper denominational lines which may still break the visible unity of the Church.

"In practically carrying out this idea, the Assembly, laying aside ecclesiastical etiquette, would affectionately say to their brethren of the Associate Reformed Synod that they may pull the latch string of our dwelling whenever they may choose, and may be incorporated with us upon the simple adoption of our Standards wherever those may happen to differ from their own; and to our brethren of the Cumberland Presbyterian Church, we respectfully suggest whether the time has not come to consider the great importance to the kingdom of our common Master, of their union with us by the adoption of the time-honored Standards to which we adhere.

"This argument, of visibly realizing the spiritual unity of the Lord's people, is enforced by the peculiar circumstances of the times in which we live, and by the nature of the controversies which now agitate the Church. The old conflict for the spirituality and independence of the Church is, to the amazement of many, renewed in our day and upon our own continent. The battle, fought generations ago by the Melvilles, Gillespies and Hendersons, of Scotland, is reopened with singular violence; and the old banner is again floating over us with its historic inscription, 'For Christ's Covenant and Crown.' Upon no one subject is the mind of this Assembly more clearly ascertained—upon no one doctrine is there a more solid or perfect agreement amongst those whom this Assembly represents, than the non-secular and non-political character of the Church of Jesus Christ. Whatever ambiguous or indiscreet expressions may have been extorted under the pressure of extraordinary excitement, from individuals amongst us, the Assembly of this Church deliberately reaffirms the testimony given in the solemn address to the Churches of Jesus Christ throughout the earth, issued in 1861, during its first session in the city of Augusta, and which was pronounced in these words: 'The provinces of Church and State are perfectly distinct, and the one has no right to usurp the jurisdiction of the other. The State is a natural institute, founded in the constitution of man as moral and social, and designed to realize the idea of justice. The Church is a supernatural institute, founded in the fact of redemption, and is designed to realize the idea of grace. It is the society of the redeemed. The State aims at social order, the Church at spiritual holiness. The State looks to the visible and outward; the Church is concerned for the invisible and inward. The badge of the State's authority is the sword, by which it becomes a terror to evil doers and a praise to them that do well; the badge of the Church's authority is the keys, by which it opens and shuts the kingdom of heaven, according as we are believers or impenitent. The power of the Church is exclusively spiritual; that of the State includes the exercise of force. The Constitution of the Church is a Divine Revelation; the Constitution of the State must be determined by human reason and the course of providential events. The Church has no right to construct a government for the State; and the State has no right to frame a creed or polity for the Church. They are as planets moving in different orbits, and unless each is confined to its own track, the consequences may be as disastrous in the moral world as the collision of different spheres in the world of matter.' The early assertion of this radical distinction at the very opening of our history, commits us to the maintenance and defence of the crown rights of the Redeemer, whether, on the one hand, they be usurped by the State, or whether, on the other, they be removed by any portion of God's professing people. Summoned thus in the Providence of God to contend for the same principles for which our martyr fathers of the Scottish Reformation testified even to the death, and which the fathers of the Southern Presbyterian Church labored so earnestly to secure, and rejoiced in having obtained their full recognition by the civil government in America, it would be most happy if all those in the different branches of the Presbyterian family, who are called to renew the protest, could be united in one homogeneous body for the reassertion of Christ's royal supremacy in and over his spiritual kingdom, the Church. The scattered testimony of separate and individual witnesses would deepen in intensity, if gathered into one volume and rolled against those who would place the crown of Jesus upon the head of Cæsar. In view of all which, this Assembly would tender the hand to all who are of like mind with us as to the doctrines of grace, and as to the order and discipline of God's house; that, as one compacted Church, we may oppose a breakwater against the current which is sweeping from its moorings our common Protestantism, until the doctrine of the Church as a free spiritual commonwealth shall regain its ascendency, not only over the Presbyterian, but over the whole American Protestant mind.

"Your committee further recommend that the Rev. Jas. A. Lyon, D.D., with the Rev. J. N. Caruthers as his alternate, be appointed to bear the salutations of this body to the Associate Reformed Synod of the South, at their meeting to be held at Clarksville, Mississippi, on the third Thursday in September, 1867, and that the Rev. T. D. Witherspoon, with the Rev. David A. Cummings as his alternate, be appointed to do the same to the General Assembly of the Cumberland Presbyterian Church, at their meeting to be held at Memphis, Tenn., on the third Thursday of May, 1867. It is further recommended that a committee of five be appointed by this Assembly to confer with any similar committee on the part of the Cumberland Presbyterian Assembly, to ascertain how far the way is prepared for an organic union between the two bodies upon the basis of the Westminster Standards.

"The following preamble and resolutions are also respectfully submitted to the consideration of the Assembly:

"WHEREAS, The General Assembly of our Church did, upon its first organization in 1861, make an explicit declaration, in an address to all the Churches of Jesus Christ throughout the earth, of its sincere desire to hold fellowship, as far as practicable, with all the disciples of our common Lord and Savior in all the world; and

"WHEREAS, We are led to hope that important and happy results may be secured in promoting the great ends of Christian fellowship by the appointment of chosen brethren, whose duty it shall be, as our representatives, to bear true expressions of our views and wishes to such Christians, churches and societies in the Kingdom of Great Britain and Ireland, and, if deemed best, on the Continent of Europe also, as the providence of God may designate, and to explain to them, as opportunity may offer, the character, condition, work and prospects of our beloved Zion; to receive such contributions as may be voluntarily offered in aid to our general schemes of evangelization; therefore

"*Resolved,* That this General Assembly does now appoint the Rev. M. D. Hoge, D.D., Rev. B. M. Palmer, D.D.,[7] and Rev. J. L. Girardeau to this important mission, and earnestly solicit their acceptance of the same.

"*Resolved,* That in view of the privations to which the congregations of these brethren will be subjected during their absence, the Assembly does hereby request their cheerful concurrence in a measure considered by the Church to be one of so much interest, and whose successful prosecution must so greatly depend, under God, upon the peculiar fitness of those to whom it is entrusted.

"*Resolved,* That the Moderator and Stated Clerk be directed to furnish the brethren here appointed with an attested copy of this paper, and with such other testimonials as may be considered proper.

"*Resolved,* That the Executive Committee of Domestic Missions and Publications be directed to make such a provision for the expenses of this mission as may be deemed suitable.

"All of which is respectfully submitted."

Dr. Palmer's labors at the revision of the Hymn Book, protracted now since 1861, came to an end toward the close of 1866. The Assembly of that year instructed its committee to consider, indeed, certain further suggestions; and, if its judgment approved, adopt them; and then to turn the manuscript over to the Committee of Publication to be published. The result of their labors was an excellent book; it served the Church well to the end of the century. To Dr. Palmer's labors is due no small credit for whatsoever of excellence it had.

Dr. Palmer appeared next in the Assembly, when it met at Louisville, in 1870. While there the eyes of a newspaper

[7] The insertion of Dr. Palmer's name in this resolution, was of course by amendment.

man naturally fell upon him. A consequence was this sketch of the New Orleans divine's appearance and character:

"Among the ministers now in Louisville attending the session of the Presbyterian General Assembly, is one having a slight figure and swart complexion, who attracts a degree of attention somewhat out of proportion to his rather unimposing presence and unobtrusive demeanor. One would hardly take this man for a famous divine, and still less for a brilliant orator. He moves quietly about like a shadow, but he is an active religious leader, and close, observant scrutiny will presently detect a certain tone and character in his method of moving and having his being; a certain glow in the eye; a certain restless tremor about the lip; a certain exceptional play about the features which mark the difference between great faculties in a common case and ordinary faculties in a large and showy case, the distinction, in short, between outward port and presence and inward genius. The man is named Palmer and he comes from New Orleans where he is very well known and appreciated."

To the Louisville Assembly of 1870, came the Rev. J. C. Backus, D.D., the Rev. H. J. Van Dyke, D.D., and the Hon. W. E. Dodge, from the General Assembly of the Presbyterian Church of the United States of America. The Old and New School bodies, North, had come together in 1869-'70. They were anxious for the Southern Church to come into their body. Reaffirming the "Concurrent Declaration" of the Old and New School Assemblies, North, 1869, viz.: "That no rule or precedent which does not stand approved by both bodies shall be of any authority in the reunited body, except in so far as such rule or precedent may effect the rights of property founded thereon," they seemed to think they had torn away every bar to the consideration of union. When the representatives of the Assembly, North, had been heard, the paper which they had brought from their body was referred to the "Committee on Foreign Correspondence," of which Dr. Palmer was the chairman, "with instructions to report at the earliest possible time recommending an answer to the proposition" thus made. The majority report of this committee, after a preamble, said:

"Whatever obstructions may exist in the way of cordial intercourse between the two bodies are entirely of a public nature and involve great and fundamental principles. The Southern Presbyterian Church can confidently appeal to all the acts and declarations of all their Assemblies, that no attitude of aggression or hostility has been, or is now, assumed by it toward the Northern Church. And this General Assembly distinctly avows (as it has always believed and declared) that no grievances experienced by us, however real, would justify us in acts of aggression or a spirit of malice or retaliation against any branch of Christ's visible kingdom. We are prepared, therefore, in advance of all discussion, to exercise toward the General Assembly North, and the churches represented therein, such amity as fidelity to our principles could, under any possible circumstances, permit. Under this view, the appointment of a Committee of Conference might seem wholly unnecessary; but, in order to exhibit before the Christian world the spirit of conciliation and kindness to the last degree, this Assembly agrees to appoint a Committee of Conference to meet a similar committee already appointed by the Northern Assembly, with instructions to the same that the difficulties which lie in the way of cordial correspondence between the two bodies must be distinctly met and removed, and which may be comprehensively stated in the following particulars:

"1. Both the wings of the now united Assembly, during their separate existence before the fusion, did fatally complicate themselves with the State in political utterances deliberately pronounced year after year, and which, in our judgment, were a sad betrayal of the cause and kingdom of our common Lord and Head. We believe it to be solemnly incumbent upon the Northern Presbyterian Church, not with reference to us, but before the Christian world and before our divine Master and King, to purge itself of this error, and, by public proclamation of the truth, to place the crown once more upon the head of Jesus Christ as the alone King of Zion; in default of which the Southern Presbyterian Church, which has already suffered much in maintaining the independence and spirituality of the Redeemer's kingdom upon earth, feels constrained to bear public testimony against this defection of our late associates from the truth. Nor can we, by official correspondence even, consent to blunt the edge of this our testimony concerning the very nature and mission of the Church as a purely spiritual body among men.

"2. The union now consummated between the Old and New School Assemblies, North, was accomplished by methods which, in our judgment, involve a total surrender of all the great testimonies of the Church for the fundamental doctrines of grace, at a time when the victory of truth over error hung long in the balance. The United Assembly stands of necessity upon an allowed latitude of interpretation of the Standards, and must come at length to embrace nearly all shades of doctrinal belief. Of those falling testimonies we are now the sole surviving heir, which must lift from the dust and bear to the generation after us. It would be a serious compromise of this sacred trust to enter into public and official fellowship with those repudiating these testimonies; and to do this expressly upon the ground, as stated in the preamble to the overture before us, 'that the terms of reunion between the two branches of the Presbyterian Church at the North, now happily consummated, present an auspicious opportunity for the adjustment of such relations.' To found a correspondence professedly upon this idea would be to endorse that which we thoroughly disapprove.

"3. Some of the members of our own body were but a short time since violently and unconstitutionally expelled from the communion of one branch of the now united Northern Assembly, under ecclesiastical charges which, if true, render them utterly infamous before the Church and the world. It is to the last degree unsatisfactory to construe this offensive legislation obsolete by the mere fusion of that body with another, or through the operation of a faint declaration which was not intended originally to cover this case. This is no mere 'rule' or 'precedent,' but a solemn sentence of outlawry against what is now an important and constituent part of our own body. Every principle of honor and of good faith compels us to say that an unequivocal repudiation of that interpretation of the law under which these men were condemned must be a condition precedent to any official correspondence on our part.

"4. It is well known that similar injurious accusations were preferred against the whole Southern Presbyterian Church, with which the ear of the whole world has been filled. Extending, as these charges do, to heresy and blasphemy, they cannot be quietly ignored by an indirection of any sort. If true, we are not worthy of the 'confidence, respect, Christian honor and love,' which are tendered to us in this overture. If untrue, 'Christian honor and love, manliness and truth,' require them to be openly and squarely withdrawn. So long as they remain upon record, they are an impassable barrier to official intercourse."[8]

These resolutions were adopted by the Assembly, by a vote of eighty-three to seventeen. Those antagonistic to the resolutions, had opposed them on the ground that they sprang "from hatred," and were "an exhibition of a bitter spirit." By implication they made the claim that they themselves were pos-

---

[8] This paper as originally drawn by Dr. Palmer, "simply declined all correspondence for reasons which are assigned." When submitted to the Committee on Correspondence, however, this was deemed unnecessarily harsh. The sentiment prevailed, that courtesy required at least the concession of a committee to confer. As a compromise, this was yielded, and the committee was granted *with instructions*. The change was against the chairman's judgment, and gave to the whole paper an aspect of incongruity under which it has always suffered."—*Dr. Palmer, in the Southwestern Presbyterian, July* 17, 1873. He thought that for the Southern Church to meet and confer with the Northern about the schism, involved an admission of guilt on her part.

sessed of more piety and Christian spirit than those who advocated the resolutions. They condemned the resolutions for making anything of the union of the Old and New School churches, North, as a ground of difference between the Assembly, North, and South, at the present time, since there had been a union between the corresponding bodies, South.

Dr. Palmer took a most effective part in the debate, in the open meetings of the Assembly, in behalf of the resolutions. He can be said fairly to have cut into shavings the arguments of his opponents.[9]

After the taking of the vote, the Committee of Foreign Correspondence was directed to prepare and report a letter, to be addressed to the churches under the care of this Assembly, explanatory of the action of the General Assembly in the paper which it had just adopted. Two days later, Dr. Palmer, from his Committee on Foreign Correspondence, presented the following letter, which was adopted:

"BELOVED BRETHREN: It is alike the privilege and duty of all the courts of the Church, and especially of the General Assembly, as looking forth upon the whole field from the point of highest elevation, occasionally to address the churches under its care upon topics which vitally affect the interests of the entire body. In the discharge of this episcopal function, this General Assembly now addresses you upon a matter of fundamental importance, which has supremely engaged its own attention during its present sessions in the city of Louisville.

"You have been aware for a twelvemonth past of an overture from the Old School Assembly, North, adopted at its sessions in 1869, tendering salutations to us, and expressing the desire of our union with them at no distant day. This overture was virtually superseded by the fusion which subsequently took place between the two great Presbyterian branches, North, into one organization. This united body, sitting contemporaneously with ourselves, in Philadelphia, has passed a resolution appointing a committee of conference to act with a similar committee which they invite us to appoint, who shall jointly discuss the difficulties existing between the two bodies and prepare the way for a permanent and fraternal correspondence. This proposition was conveyed to us by a special delegation, consisting of Rev. Drs. J. C. Backus and H. J. Van Dyke and the Hon. W. E. Dodge, gentlemen of the highest character and personally most acceptable to us, who discharged their delicate mission in a spirit and manner which made the most pleasant impression of their courtesy as well as ability.

[9] The arguments he employed may be seen in the letter to the Church, explanatory of the Assembly's action, given a little below.

"In response to this proposition, this General Assembly has agreed, in the spirit of conciliation and Christian kindness, to appoint the Committee of Conference which was desired, and then, in the form of instructions to the same, has laid down the principles which should control the whole matter, and upon which alone any correspondence on our part would be possible. It may perhaps appear to you, and it will doubtless be so represented by others, that a proposition so simple as that of conference for the adjustment of difficulties, might have been left unembarrassed by any antecedent enunciation of what the Assembly regards as the obstructions to fraternal and official correspondence. It is precisely this which we desire you to understand, as well as the reasons which impelled us to the course we have pursued. The reflective and thoughtful amongst you will at once recognize that, in diplomatic intercourse, the first step is always the most important. It is this that determines all the future and dependent negotiations; and, however unobtrusive the initiatory measure may appear to be, it is often pregnant with concealed results of vast magnitude. This is preëminently true in the case before us. It was incumbent upon us to watch narrowly, lest, in the very opening of negotiations, we might incautiously surrender the principles we hold, which, slipping from our grasp, we might never be able to recover.

"The overture from the Northern Assembly was based upon the fatal assumption that mutual grievances existed, in reference to which it became necessary to arbitrate. This assumption is precisely what we cannot truthfully concede. Our records may be searched in vain for a single act of aggression, or a single unfriendly declaration against the Northern Church. We have assumed no attitude of hostility toward it. In not a single case has there been an attempt to wrest from them their Church property. In not a single case has there been hesitation in receiving their members into our communion upon the face of their credentials, amongst the hundreds who have come to make their home with us since the War. In not one instance has there been exhibited a spirit of retaliation in regard to any of those very measures instituted against ourselves by the Assembly of 1865 and by subsequent Assemblies.

"Whatever obstructions may be in the way of ecclesiastical fellowship were not created by us, and we could not allow ourselves to be placed in the false position, before the world, of parties who had been guilty of wrong to the Northern Church. Having placed nothing in the way of Christian fraternity, there was nothing for us to remove. Whilst, therefore, in Christian courtesy, we were willing to appoint a Committee of Conference, it was necessary to guard against all misconstruction, and misrepresentation by instructing our commissioners to remember this fact, and restricting them to the duty of simply reporting and expounding what we considered indispensable to an honest correspondence, which should not, by its insincerity and hollowness, be an offense to our divine Master.

"Inasmuch as we had never been aggressors against the peace, security and prosperity of the Northern Church, and had not undertaken to approach them with proposals of any sort, Christian candor required us, as the party approached, to state exactly the difficulties which did embarrass the question of correspondence. Without going into much detail or multiplying the specifications, these were summed up under four heads—the significance and importance of which we would have you to appreciate.

"It must be remembered, then, that in 1861 the organization of the Southern Church was compelled by what are known as the 'Spring Resolutions,' which committed the Old School Assembly, with which we were at that time connected, to a particular political theory, and complicated the Church at once with the State. The necessary effect of this political legislation by the Assembly in 1861 was to force the entire Southern constituency out of that connection, who were compelled in their disorganized condition at once to integrate in the Southern Assembly, which was soon afterwards formed. The earliest deliverance of this, our own body, was the assertion of the non-secular and non-political character of the Church, as the kingdom of Jesus Christ, spiritual in its nature and mission, and entirely separate from and independent of the State. And in subsequent deliverances—as those of the Assembly of 1865, at Macon, and the two utterances of the Assembly of 1866, at Memphis, and the formal acceptance of the statement of doctrines and principles of the Synod of Kentucky on this subject, by the Assembly of 1867, at Nashville—the supreme court of the Southern Church has, with singular steadfastness, testified for the same great truth. Upon this very issue we became an organized Church, as distinct from that out of whose bosom we had been thrust by the assertion and operation of the contrary and Erastian doctrine that the Church might rightly intermingle her jurisdiction with that of the Commonwealth. Through several consecutive years, both branches of the now united Assemblies persisted in the utterance of political dogmas, which, whether true or false, they were inhibited by the word of God and by their own statute law from pronouncing in their ecclesiastical chambers. These unlawful utterances remain uncancelled upon the records of both the courts now amalgamated into one. No disavowal of them has been made, as of words inconsiderately uttered in times of high excitement. No counter declaration has been filed, gathering up the sacred truth of God as a new proclamation of the spirituality and independence of that kingdom which is not of this world. The attempt, we are aware, has been made to relieve the pressure of these melancholy facts by faintly retorting the accusation against our own body. But we challenge the world to place the two records side by side, in the severity of contrast. No ingenuity of sophistry can transmute into political dogmas the scant allusions to the historical reality of a great struggle then pending, or the thankful recognition, in the middle of a paragraph, of the unanimity with which an invaded people rose to the defence of their hearthstones and the graves of their dead; or the pastoral councils addressed to the members and youth of our own churches, passing through the temptations and perils of the camp and field; or the half hour spent in prayer for a land bleeding under the iron heel of war; or even the incidental declaration in a narrative, to stand by an institution of the country, a traditional inheritance from our fathers. Even though, from the ambiguity of human language, these chance references may not have been always discreetly expressed, the most that a just criticism could pronounce, is, that they are inconsistent with the judicially pronounced principle upon which the Southern Assembly entered upon its troubled career. And when exaggerated in their largest proportions by all the prejudice of bitter partisanship, they dwindle into motes and specks by the side of those elaborate and colossal deliverances, repeated each year through former committees, and exalted into solemn testimonies co-ordinate with the doctrines of religion and faith, which disfigure the legislation of both the Northern Assemblies through successive years.

"It will thus be seen that in the providence of God the Southern Church has been made a special witness for the crown and kingdom of our Lord, when both were practically disowned; and that upon this very issue she was separated from her old associations. Brought now, through their overture, for the first time face to face with this Northern Church, this mighty principle emerges at once into view. We were cast forth, nine years ago, for this testimony to one of the grand ideas of the Gospel. We must go back with it still upon our lips, and ask those who desire official relations with us, Do we form these relations with a spiritual or with a political Church? We cannot do otherwise without recanting our own words, and endorsing the very error which drove us into ecclesiastical exile. We declare, therefore, that we can hold no official correspondence with the Northern Church, unless the Savior is reinstated in the full acknowledgment of his kingship in his own Church. Called to this testimony, for which we have already suffered the spoiling of our goods, we cannot lay it down at the very moment when that testimony becomes the most significant.

"Again: the overture between us professedly founds upon the happy union just accomplished between the Old and New Schools, North. This is singularly unfortunate; for, in our judgment, the negotiations through which this union was consummated betrayed those sacred testimonies of a former generation, for the most precious and vital of the doctrines of grace. Our difficulty is not the mere fusion of these two Assemblies into one. A similar fusion took place six years ago between ourselves and the United Synod of the South. But the difference between the two cases is wide as the poles. The Synod of the South united with us upon the first interchange of doctrinal views, upon a square acceptance of the Standards, without any metaphysical hair-splitting to find a sense in which to receive them, and without any expunging of whole chapters from the history of the past, with the sacred testimonies with which these are filled. It is not, therefore, the amalgamation of these bodies at the North, simply considered, which embarrasses us; but it is the method by which it was achieved—the acceptance of the Standards in no comprehensible sense, by which the united Assembly becomes a sort of broad Church, giving shelter to every creed lying between the extremes of Arminianism and Pelagianism on the one hand, and of Antinomianism and Fatalism on the other. If correspondence with such a body could be allowed at all, it cannot be based upon a preamble which constructively endorses a recession from the safe landmarks which is to all the lovers of sound Christianity the occasion of grief. We have been constrained, therefore, to fence our commissioners with a caution not to commit us in any degree to that diplomacy by which the union was accomplished, and so to rob us of our birthright in those testimonies, which is all that we brought out with us from that grand old historic Church of the past.

"Again: We require as an indispensable condition to all correspondence, a renunciation of that theory of Church government which practically obliterates the lower courts and destroys the appellate character of the General Assembly, under which that unrighteous decision was reached against the Synods of Kentucky and Missouri. The former of these two bodies, being now a constituent portion of this Assembly, has a just claim upon us for the protection of their good name from the defamation they have experienced as witnesses to the principles which are common to us and them. Not only does good faith require us to keep covenant with those who have entered into union with us, but they are we, and we are they, bound together as witnesses in a common testimony. Fidelity to this testimony demands that those who have been martyrs to our common faith shall be reinstated in their good name before we can fraternally embrace those by whom they are maligned. Upon the principle that the interpretation of the law is the law, it is a simple requisition that this interpretation be disallowed, under which true and faithful men were unconstitutionally condemned.

"The fourth and last condition of this correspondence was the unequivocal retraction of the imputations against ourselves, industriously circulated throughout Christendom. This we would have clearly discriminated from personal resentment, or an unforgiving spirit. It is compelled by a proper sense of self-respect, and a due regard to the honor of our own Church. It is the homage which we are constrained to pay to truth and history. We cannot accept, even by implication, the charges with which the records of both wings of the United Assembly are filled. Extending, as they do, to heresy and blasphemy, they are of the nature of judicial accusations, which must either be sustained or withdrawn. The 'respect, and honor, and Christian love' with which we are approached in this overture are certainly inconsistent with the belief of these grave imputations. If not believed to be true, they should be cancelled, much more for the sake of those who have pronounced them than for ourselves who have so long borne the reproach. However this may be, any form of intercourse, while they remain upon record, would be a tacit acquiescence in the same, and a submission to the dishonor which has been cast upon the name of our people and of our Church.

"The differences betwixt us and the Northern Church are too vast and solemn to allow this question to be determined by any of the baser and meaner passions of human nature. If we know our own hearts, this course is not prompted by feelings of malice or revenge, or that peevish resentment engendered by the irritation of controversy. We trust that Christian magnanimity would enable us to rise above all private wrongs and petty issues, transient as the hour which gives them birth. Our hearts are penetrated with the majesty of the principles which we are called to maintain; and we desire that you should feel yourself consecrated by the high purpose to assert them with us before the world.

"All the great truths of Christianity have had an historical outworking in the midst of human conflict and debate, and by this means they become potential and operative principles, wrought into the very frame and texture of the human soul. In the first centuries of the Christian Church all the great controversies resolved around the relations of the persons of the Godhead, through which the Church wrought out what may be technically called her *theology*. In the age of Augustine and his opposers, the field of conflict was transferred to the nature of man and the condition to which sin had reduced it, through which the Church wrought out what is scientifically termed her *anthropology*. In the great Reformation, when the Church broke away from the bondage of Romish superstition, discussion turned upon the method of grace, and the Gospel as a *plan of salvation* was wrought into the life and consciousness of the Church. But confusion and error still reigned over the minds of men with regard to the true mission and relation of the Church in her corporate character as the spiritual kingdom of the Redeemer upon the earth. The historical development of this is probably the work and the conflict of the present age; and the Protestants of our day are to hold up in the face of derision and scorn the true idea of the Church as the kingdom of the redeemed among men. In the adorable providence of God, our peeled and desolated Church is pushed to the front in this conflict. In the face of those ancient Churches which, in Europe, are still entangled with state alliances, the very foremost of which seem to be slow in grasping the grand conception which the Redeemer's discipline has been so clearly teaching them, and in the face of the Christianity of the Northern section of our own land, which, in the temporary frenzy, as we hope and pray, has resiled from the truth we thought it understood—this suffering Church of ours is called to testify. The pure white banner borne by the Melvilles, the Gillespies and the Hendersons, those noble witnesses of another age, for a pure spiritual Church has fallen into our hands to uphold. Floating from our walls the superb inscription, 'Christ's Crown and Covenant,' rings out the battle cry of that sacramental host which, by protest and reproach, by testimony and suffering, will yet conquer the earth and bring it in submission to the Savior's feet. It is upon the assertion of this great and germinal principle out of which a true *ecclesiology* is yet to spring, this Assembly desires to place herself and you. The royalty of the thought will render you too kingly in all your purposes and desires ever to debase this testimony by yielding to the lower resentments of an unsanctified heart in the proclamation of your testimony.

"These are the convictions which rule our decision in relation to correspondence with the Northern Church. Their offense with us is that we would not yield to the mistaken conscience which permitted them to bind the Church of our divine Lord to the wheels of Cæsar's chariot. We cannot surrender this testimony for the privilege of sitting within their halls. Regarding them as still parts of the visible Catholic Church, notwithstanding their defection on this point, we place them where we place all other denominations whom we recognize, though differing from us. Wishing them prosperity and peace, so far as they labor to win souls to Christ, we feel it a higher duty and a grander privilege to testify for our Master's kingship in his Church, than to enjoy all the ecclesiastical fellowship which is to be purchased at the expense of conscience and of truth.

"It may seem to some of you that any hesitancy on our part to enter into correspondence with any Church is out of accord with the spirit of the times, which finds expression in formal protestations of amity and unity between all evangelical Christians. But a little reflection will make it manifest that this want of accord is only apparent, not real, so far as relates to any unity which is founded on a common reverence for the truth of Christ. For in every case of separation between brethren of the same Church on account of errors held, or supposed to be held, on the one side, and the purpose to testify against the same on the other, a formal recognition of each other may be incompatible with the very end held in view in the separation. It may involve an utter obscuration of the testimony of the witnesses. Thus, it will be remembered, there was no official correspondence between the two bodies into which our Church divided in 1837-'38 for the space of twenty-five years; though each held official correspondence with other bodies even less near to them in doctrine and order. Nor indeed was such correspondence even proposed until it was suggested as a preliminary to organic reunion. The Christian instincts of both bodies suggested that such correspondence must involve the inconsistency, on the part of each, of standing apart from the other, while under not only the same articles of faith, but the same constitution—each bearing witness against the other while affecting relations of unity.

"In the spirit, therefore, of these councils, we commend you, brethren in the Lord, to Him that is able to keep you from falling, and to comfort you with all the joys of his salvation."

Though put forth as the work of a committee, this letter was, substantially, Dr. Palmer's own in matter and form. Not stickling for the observance of small parliamentary rules, he was a great presbyter, comprehending fully the grand principles of the polity of his Church, and ready to lay himself out to see them applied in its history. He was capable of rendering eminent services without apparent effort. Other services were rendered by him in the Assembly of 1870, and with his accustomed grace and efficiency; but his greatest services were in the production of the two papers just quoted: To determine the precise form of the reception to be accorded by the Assembly, South, to the overtures from the reunited Assembly, North, called for a peculiar combination of tact, and honest and steadfast adherence to the truth not easily found. Dr. Palmer possessed this combination in the highest degree. He understood the differences thoroughly; and in the Providence of God he had been specially prepared for just such a task.

Beginning with the issue of August 19, 1869, a series of seventeen elaborate articles, on the "Reunion Overture of the Northern General Assembly to the Southern Presbyterian Church," had appeared in the *Southwestern Presbyterian.* They were signed "Presbyter." They were from Dr. Palmer's pen. The writer objected to union in any form with the Northern Assembly because that body *"has involved itself in criminal errors touching the kingly office of Christ; ignoring, persistently, His spiritual kingdom, the Church—betraying her spirituality and independence, and perverting the power of the keys to uphold the State, and introducing terms of ecclesiastical communion, unwarranted by Holy Scripture, and contradictory to the commands of Christ."* Through six articles of considerable length he carries the reader, piling high the proofs of this grave charge. In doing this he took up the Minutes of the Old School Assemblies, in order, from 1861 to 1865. His manner of presenting this proof may be best learned by the study of a sample. Accordingly, here follows the first of two articles on "The Assembly of 1865:"

"When the tribe of Benjamin had been nearly exterminated, we are told in the Book of Judges that 'all the people came to the House of God, and abode there till even, before God, and lifted up their voice, and wept sore, and said, O Lord God of Israel, why is this come to pass in Israel, that there should be to-day one tribe lacking in Israel?' This beautiful precedent we might have expected the Presbyterian Church to follow when it met in solemn Assembly, at the city of Pittsburg, in May, 1865. It was shortly after the surrender of the Southern forces, and the termination of hostilities; and the poor South lay panting and bleeding under the heel of the conqueror. The warpath of a victorious army—cut through the heart of her territory—smoked with the ruins of sacked cities and burning homes. Hungry and spent, feeble women and starving children lined this path of war, picking up the grains of corn which had fallen from the horses' mouths during a night's bivouac; and our famished soldiery sprang from the arms they had stacked, to ask their former foes for bread. Perhaps the warrior justified these severities upon the plea of Cromwell, when he put to death the garrison at Drogheda, that it was necessary, to 'cut the Irish war to the heart.' But now that it is all done, surely the children of Israel will 'repent them for Benjamin, their brother.' Sorrow will darken the face, and tears will moisten the cheeks of this venerable council, at Pittsburg, that a tribe should be lacking in Israel. Alas! Nothing is seen but the flush of fierce exultation in the hour of triumph; not a whisper is heard, but of vindictive retribution! Who will not exclaim, with David, 'Let us fall, now, into the hands of the Lord, for his mercies are great; and let us not fall into the hands of man?' It is impossible now to say what would have been the result, if a generous reconciliation had been tendered in the hour of broken-heartedness, as we sat upon the ruins of all our hopes. If the overture of 1869 had been the overture of 1865, there had been fewer difficulties to surmount, and an easier return to the bosom that had not ceased to love. But the spirit of peace did not waft his wing over that haughty council. Had he been frightened away by the discordant sounds of the four preceding conventions? Certain it is, the water-spout of political fury, which had been gathering through four years of strife, burst, in the first hour of peace, in a deluge of wrath, on the Southern Church.

"In support of this allegation we quote from a Minute adopted as follows:

"'WHEREAS, During the existence of the great rebellion, which has disturbed the peace, and threatened the life, of the nation, a large number of the Presbyteries and Synods of the Southern States, whose names are on the roll of the General Assembly as constituent parts of this body, have organized an Assembly, denominated, 'the General Assembly of the Confederate States of America,' in order to render their aid in that attempt to establish, by means of the rebellion, a separate national existence, and 'to conserve and perpetuate the system of slavery;' therefore,

"'*Resolved,* That this Assembly regards the civil rebellion for the perpetuation of negro slavery as a great crime, both against our national government and against God; and the secession of those Presbyteries and Synods from the Presbyterian Church, under such circumstances, and for such reasons, as unwarranted, schismatical and unconstitutional.

"'*Resolved,* 2, That the General Assembly does not intend to abandon the territory in which those churches are formed, or to compromise the rights of any of the Church Courts, or ministers, or ruling elders and private members belonging to them, who are loyal to the government of the United States, and to the Presbyterian Church. On the contrary, this Assembly will recognize such loyal persons as constituting the churches, Presbyteries and Synods, in all the bounds of the schism, and will use earnest endeavors to restore and revive all such Churches, and Church Courts.

"'*Resolved,* 3, The Assembly hereby declares that it will reorganize, as the church, the members of any church within the bounds of the schism who are loyal to the government of the United States of America, and whose views are in harmony with the doctrines of the Confession of Faith, and with the several testimonies of the Presbyterian Church on the subject of domestic slavery,' etc.

"We forbear citing the remainder of this lengthy paper, in which provision is made in detail for giving efficiency to the principles above enunciated. But we may quote, in this precise connection, a portion of the instructions given to their Board of Domestic Missions, as found in the two following resolutions:

"'*Resolved,* 3, That the General Assembly direct the Board of Domestic Missions to take prompt and efficient measures to restore and build up the Presbyterian congregations in the Southern States of this Union, by the appointment and support of prudent and devoted missionaries.

"'*Resolved,* 4, That none be appointed but those who give satisfactory evidence of their loyalty to the National Government; and that they are in cordial sympathy with the General Assembly of the Presbyterian Church in the United States of America in her testimony on doctrine, loyalty and freedom.'

"The aspersions against the Southern Church, in the foregoing extracts, we reserve for special consideration hereafter. We are, at present, establishing the charge of an unlawful complicity with the State, on the part of the Northern Church.

"It will be observed how exactly this Assembly adopts the policy of the government. As the one decides that the States must all remain in the Union, even if they are to be pinned there with the bayonet, so the other decrees all the Southern Presbyteries and Synods to be 'unconstitutionally and schismatically' withdrawn from the Assembly's jurisdiction. As the State claims the right to coerce the seceded States back into the Union, so the Church will coerce the schismatical Presbyteries back into their old ecclesiastical fellowship. And precisely the same measures of reconstruction are proposed in the Church, which have worked so awkwardly in the State, viz.: A wholesale disfranchisement of all who are suspected of disloyalty, and the erection of petty minorities in churches and Church courts into churches and courts in whom all the rights and franchises of a true succession are to vest.

"It will be observed, again, with what vigor the Assembly addresses itself to the task of sowing discord and creating schism in the bosom of the Southern Church, by the 'appointment and support of devoted missionaries,' who, like the carpet-bag politicians in the State, shall swoop down upon the prey, fanning the flame of discontent, if haply, it should anywhere burst forth; and offering every species of ecclesiastical bribes to the minorities whom they shall induce to secede. We are not without practical proof of the methods by which this fraternal scheme of disintegration was to be worked. For example, in the case at this moment pending, of the Church at Jacksonville, Fla., where the property is wrested by a minority, and held in the grasp —by the way, of the very Central Presbytery of Philadelphia, with whom this late overture of re-union originated—and which, at the very moment it extends with one hand these fraternal salutations, holds with the other the property of a Southern Church, wrested from it by the very process initiated by this Assembly of 1865 upon which we are now commenting. And if this scheme of disintegration did not generally succeed 'within the bounds of the schism,' the failure is due to the wonderful unanimity of our own people, presenting so few fissures in which to drive the wedge of division and strife.

"It will be further noted how uniformly a profession of loyalty to the government is made the test of adhesion to the Assembly and the distinguishing qualification of their agents who are to be employed in this work of ecclesiastical reconstruction, and finally, how these political utterances are exalted to the nature of 'testimonies;' and how, in these testimonies, 'loyalty' and 'freedom' are co-ordinated with 'doctrine' and 'the Confession of Faith'—the same emphasis being placed upon both. Nay, so far is this carried, that these testimonies on 'loyalty' and 'freedom' are to be received *ex animo,* just like the doctrines of our religious creed. Inquisition is made into the secret heart, whose hidden 'sympathies' must all be in harmony with these deliverances. Orthodoxy, piety, general fitness for the work of preaching the Gospel are all of them to be set aside, if 'satisfactory evidence is not given' upon this new and purely political test of 'loyalty to the National Government!' However discreetly in silence a godly minister may seal his lips upon these disputed points of allegiance and human rights, he is proscribed in the ecclesiastical Star Chamber, at Philadelphia, from which the commissions are issued to the evangelists of the Church, unless his concealed *sympathies* should be in conformity with the new standard erected.

"But, the brevity of a newspaper article forbids expansion. We must be content with barely writing out the facts themselves, upon which the reader must make his own reflections. We pass on, then, to the action taken by this Assembly on the overture from the Presbytery of California, inquiring 'what course ought to be taken in admitting to this body ministers who are suspected of disloyalty to the Government of the United States?'

"From the answer it would seem that a needless alarm had seized the body, lest there should be a general rush of the eight hundred ministers in the South into its embrace, against which invasion the doors must be closed in season. We give only what is necessary to enable the reader to understand the spirit of this paper:

"'III. It is hereby ordered that all our Presbyteries examine every minister applying for admission, from any Presbytery or other ecclesiastical body, in the Southern States, on the following points:

"'1. Whether he has, in any way, directly or indirectly, of his own free will and consent, or without external constraint, been concerned at any time in aiding or countenancing the rebellion and the war which has been waged against the United States; and if it be found, by his own confession, or from sufficient testimony, that he has been so concerned, that he be required to confess and forsake his sin in this regard before he shall be received.

"'2. Whether he holds that the system of negro slavery in the South is a divine institution; and that it is 'the peculiar mission of the Southern Church to conserve the institution of slavery as there maintained;' and if it be found that he holds either of these doctrines, that he be not received without renouncing and forsaking these errors.

"'IV. This injunction to Presbyteries is, in like manner, applicable to Synods; and it is hereby ordered that upon the application of any Presbytery, etc., such Synod shall examine all the members of said Presbytery on the points above named, etc.

"'V. Church sessions are also ordered to examine all applicants for church membership, by persons from the Southern States, or who have been living in the South since the rebellion, concerning their conduct and principles, on the points above specified; and if it be found that, of their own free will, they have taken up arms against the United States, or that they hold slavery to be an ordinance of God, such persons shall not be admitted into the communion of the Church till they give evidence of repentance for their sin, and renounce their error.'

"We shall recur hereafter to this paper and render our own opinion, and those of our people, on some of its allegations, which may turn out a rather different version from that which these translators have given. We are dealing now simply with the politics of this doctrine and the spirit which it breathes toward the Southern Church. Here, then, precisely at the close of the war, before we had time to view our altered condition, and to look the question of future duty in the face, this venerable Assembly closes down upon us as rebels in the Church, no less than in the State, to whom a due punishment must be meted out. Instead of an overture saluting us as brethren in Christ, we are denounced as rebels and schismatics. Instead of the sweet wish that 'we may again be united in one great organization,' the door is slammed rudely and violently against any return, and then locked, bolted and barred by imposed conditions, which the venerable body knew could never be complied with, through all time.

"Although the Presbyterian Church at the South was thoroughly organized with a complete scale of Courts, this Assembly claims jurisdiction over her whole territory; proceeds in an effort to disintegrate her; then appoints measures of reconstruction from the chaos which is to be wrought; and winds up with a bill of attainder, which, if it could only take effect, would deprive all the ministers and churches of the Southern Assembly of every ecclesiastical franchise. Singularly enough, too, the charges preferred do not touch one of the doctrines of grace, but are based upon subjects on which human opinion has, through all ages, been the most divided, and lying exclusively within the sphere of the State: the nature and limitation of civil allegiance, and the doctrine of natural rights. Thus, with entire consistency, the Northern Assembly follows the established precedents of its previous legislation, and stamps its own character as rather a political than an ecclesiastical body."

His second objection to union in any form was based upon "*the flagrant violations of the constitution in the Assembly's treatment of the signers of the Declaration and Testimony;* destroying all confidence in its interpretation of the only instrument which serves as a bond of union between the members of the same ecclesiastical organization. This point he argued most ably in three articles.

His third objection was based "*on the slanders deliberately uttered against the Southern Presbyterian Church, and remaining still uncancelled upon the records of the Assembly, which now proposes this overture for union.*" He denounced as slanderous: "1. *The charge that the Southern Assembly was organized in the interest, and to subserve the ends of the Confederate Government.* 2. *The charge that the Southern Church, in separating from the Northern, was guilty of unwarranted schism.* 3. *That the Southern Church had changed its ground on the subject of slavery, so as to hold opinions that were heretical and blasphemous."* His refutation of these charges is about as nearly perfect as a refutation could be. It is full, expressed in five articles of considerable length, able and thorough, leaving little to be desired.

His fourth ground of objection to the union with the Northern Church was *"founded upon the consolidation, now almost accomplished, between the two wings of the Northern Church, the Old School and the New."* In this connection he shows that the United Church came together on a Latitudinarian and comprehensive basis; that in regard to the polity of the Church the Old School had conceded almost every point of difference to the New School; and that the Old School had cancelled all her peculiar testimonies concerning doctrine.

Finally, he urged powerfully, against the proposed reunion with the Northern Church, that the utter ruin of *the Presbyterian cause at the South would eventually ensue.*

There had been a call for the republication of these articles in pamphlet form, from different parts of the Church, in response to which they had been republished, in January, 1870, in the form desired—an edition of twenty-five hundred copies, each an octavo of eighty-seven pages. These scattered over the Church had done somewhat to prepare the mind of the Church for the work of the Assembly.

He seems to have received hearty thanks and congratulations on his course in regard to fusion. He writes, July 21, 1870, to Dr. John B. Adger:

> "In regard to the action of our Assembly at Louisville, I am in the receipt of letters from all parts of the Church expressing the warmest approval." He adds: "After a good deal of reflection, I am satisfied this action is not only right as to substance, but wise as to its form. Notwithstanding the dissent of a few, I am clear that the appointment of a committee, dry so, as Dr. Brown contends for, would have yielded the whole case upon its principles. It would have sent distrust and anxiety through our whole Church; and would have resulted within a year in the organization of a distinct party for reunion at all hazards."

The following letter shows that he was reluctant to restate once more the arguments against fusion, as early as the fall of 1870:

"NEW ORLEANS, LA., November 8, 1870.

"Rev. Dr. J. B. Adger:

"DEAR BROTHER: I have just returned from Synod, and find your letter upon my desk. As to the article you desire for the *Review* I am not strongly impressed with the importance of it. The whole subject has been thoroughly discussed, and except as a mere resume of the argument, preserved in a form somewhat more paramount than either the newspaper or the pamphlet, I see no call for the article in question.

"Admitting, however, its necessity, I think it will come with better grace from any other pen than mine. Being so much implicated in the decision of the last Assembly, as to the form in which it was rendered, it might be construed in the light, somewhat, of a personal defense; and the article would have less weight, in coming from one whose position compelled him to be biased, in a review which ought to be calm and candid.

"I dislike to seem disobliging, and would waive my judgment if necessary. But either yourself or Woodrow or Wilson can write the article—and from either of you, it would be more acceptable than from myself.

"You are very kind to offer me the chance of replication to the personal assault of the *Princeton Review;* but I have got clean past any sensibility in such matters; and am callous to all such criticism, as an alligator would be to the sportive assault of a parcel of boys.

"If I felt that my pen could do a real service in this particular case, I would cheerfully comply, and upon purely public grounds.

"I have $50.00 for Mrs. Thornwell. Where is she now—and how can I most safely remit to her?

"Affectionately yours,

"B. M. PALMER."

Presbyterians in the Southwest had long felt the need of a denominational organ of local publication. An attempt had been made with the *Presbyterian Index,* at Mobile. That failing, a most successful effort was made at New Orleans in 1869, the Trustees of the *Depository,* which had been established sixteen years before, undertaking to publish the paper known as the *Southwestern Presbyterian,* with Dr. Henry M. Smith as editor.

Dr. Palmer was a member of the Board which published the paper, and a constant and highly valued contributor.

The first issue contains a keen critique on the "Fanaticism of the World." In each of the next four issues he had an article on Foreign Missions, the first three polemical, directed against the principal objections to the work of Foreign Missions; such as "That the enterprise is chimerical," "That the

Church has enough to do at home," and "That the heathen stand an even chance with ourselves to be saved, without the Gospel." The last article considers the grounds on which the great and solemn obligation to missions rests. Immediately following these came several exquisite sketches "From a Pastor's Portfolio," in which Dr. Palmer presents to his readers a series of pastoral experiences, sketched in a most charming way, and quite equal to the best of the Rev. Elihu Spencer's. Several of these have already been given the reader in presenting Dr. Palmer's pastoral labors in the several periods of his life up to the present.[12]

One of these papers is headed, "The Young Student," and is as follows:

"It was the month of June, and the rays of the golden sun glanced from the bosom of the broad Mississippi, as from a burnished mirror. Seated just within the saloon of the elegant steamer, where the eye was screened from the dazzling brilliancy without, whilst it feasted upon the shifting scenery of the distant bank, the writer surrendered himself to those dreamy meditations which so often hang like a soft mist around the mind of a traveler. His reverie was soon broken by a young man, who drew up his chair, and modestly opened the following conversation:

"'I trust, sir, that you will not consider me obtrusive in introducing myself as a student of the University, whose commencement exercises you have just attended, and, as one of the audience, which listened to your stirring defense of Christianity.'

"'On the contrary,' I replied, 'I am entirely disengaged, and have a recollection of my own college life fresh enough to secure the warmest interest in every young student I may chance to meet.'

"'Well, sir, I find my mind laboring under many difficulties on the subject of religion; and if I can persuade you that I am not actuated by a captious spirit, but by a sincere desire to know the truth, I would like to set them before you, under the conviction that you will be able to resolve them, if anyone can.'

"Assuring him that I would listen with the utmost candor, I begged that he would free himself of all restraint, and speak everything that was in his thought.

"'I have often desired such an opportunity as this,' he replied; 'but have always been afraid to express my doubts to those who could

---

[10] There were thirteen of the papers. *From Pastor's Portfolio.* They began with the issue of April 11, 1869 and ran till about the first of August *proximo.* The materials wrought up in these sketches were drawn from all parts of his previous pastoral life.

best relieve them, lest I should be written down as a free-thinker, and forfeit the esteem of those whom I revere.'

"'In this suspicion you greatly wrong us, my young friend. Ministers of the Gospel have wrestled with too many doubts, in reaching their convictions, not to sympathize with the early struggles with others in the search after truth. Doubt,' I continued, 'is but the hunger of the mind, the starting point of all inquiry; and you remember, doubtless, that splendid passage of Sir William Hamilton, in which he defines the relation of honest doubt to all knowledge?'

"A smile of grateful confidence played upon the ingenuous countenance before me. He had encountered no professional dogmatism, such as he had hinted at in his preliminary protest; and I felt that I had secured a pledge of his candor—so important, if disputation is to be carried to any positive result. This point gained, I invited the statement of his difficulties.

"'Oh!' said he, 'the Bible is so full of mysteries, which I cannot comprehend.'

"'Granted;' was the reply; 'but what of that?'

"'Why, it does not seem reasonable, to me, that I should be required to believe what I do not understand.'

"'My young friend,' I said; 'will you stick to that?'

"This challenge brought up the discussion at a round turn. He paused for a moment, as though measuring the sweep of the admission, and a little suspicious of some discomfiture lying in ambush.

"'Why do you hesitate?' I resumed; 'you have stated the principle in broad terms, as universal in its application. If sound in one department of inquiry, it must be equally so in every other; else, it is wholly without value as a critical test.'

"'I cannot see,' said he at length, 'but that it is a just canon; I will stick to it, wherever it may lead.'

"'This skirmishing is not without its use,' I added; 'for unless we settle principles at the outset there is nothing to which we can refer as the arbiter between us.' Taking, then a letter from my pocket: 'Will you write upon the back of this, with your pencil, the fraction 1-3, and give me its value in decimals?'

He jotted down upon the blank envelope a string of .333, quite across its length. 'Have you exhausted that fraction?' I asked.

"'No,' was the reply.

"'Well, go on until you do exhaust it.'

"'It is of no use; for the exact value will not be expressed though I should extend this line of figures to the North Pole.'

"'And yet you tell me that every additional figure brings you one step nearer to that value?'

"'Certainly!'

"'Well, my friend, if there is one conclusion plainer than another, it is that, if at each step I get nearer to an object, I have only to go on until I reach it.'

"'But, my dear sir, that is the doctrine of 'the Infinite Series' which mathematics demonstrates goes on and never ceases.'

"'Precisely so,' I replied; 'and I firmly believe it. But what becomes of your fundamental principle of refusing to believe what you cannot comprehend?'

"He was evidently stunned by the unexpected retort, drawn, as it was, from the very science which professes to rest upon absolute demonstration, and claims to be certain of its conclusions. 'You are not staggered,' I continued, 'at the Infinite in mathematics; why should you be scandalized at the Infinite in God?'

"As my antagonist remained silent, it was not necessary to press the illustration—which some of my readers will perceive to be exactly similar to those employed by Dr. Mason, in his admirable brochure, entitled 'The Young Traveler.' 'But,' said I, 'let us subject your favorite canon to another test. What is this which I toss in my hand?'

"'A gold pencil,' was the answer.

"'And the point with which it writes?'

"'Why, that is lead.'

"'Very well. Now tell me, what is gold? and, what is lead? and what is it that makes the one differ from the other?'

"He enumerated, with entire accuracy, the different properties of the two metals, and then paused. 'So far, so good,' I rejoined; 'you have described the special qualities of the two, by which they may be distinguished. You have told me, in other words, a good deal *about* them both—perhaps all that can be known, but you have not yet stated what either exactly is. You are too much of a scholar to confound the *accidents* with the *essence*. I wish to learn what that is in both these metals, which underlies their respective properties, and which makes the one not to be the other. You call it *substance;* but what is substance, but the unknown and incomprehensible *something* in which outward and inscrutable qualities inhere, and which renders what we behold a true entity?'

"'All our knowledge of matter,' he replied, 'is relative; that is to say, we know its properties, and the laws or conditions under which they are manifested. But the essence of things transcends our knowledge, and must be assumed as a final fact, attested by the existence of the qualities which must belong to some substance, as the ground of their being.'

"'All that I can readily receive; but how you can do it, my young friend, in the face of your original principle, which rejects the incomprehensible as an object of faith, I can scarcely reconcile with logical consistency.'

"'I am perfectly satisfied,' the student frankly replied; 'and I thank you for rending the skepticism in which I was entangled.'

"'And yet do you perceive that I have not solved any one of your many difficulties?'

"'You have done more, sir; in showing the falsity of the principle upon which they all rested, I see clearly that the same difficulties meet me in the sphere of the natural as of the supernatural; and that I must either discard my infallible test, or plunge into universal doubt and unbelief.'

"'Precisely the point to which I desired to lead you,' I replied. 'The fact is, the supernatural touches you everywhere; you cannot move a dozen paces in any path of science before you bring up against the unknown; and all the inductive sciences really found at last, upon faith. Facts, not yet understood, are accepted simply as facts, each upon its own testimony. We, then, classify and compare, ascending from the lower generalization to the higher, until we eliminate the grand formula, or law, under which they are produced. Lay down, however, the canon, at the outset, that we may not believe what we do not comprehend, and the very basis is destroyed upon which your whole induction rests.'

"'That is transparently true in physical science,' he rejoined.

"'Much more then must the principle be false in religion,' I added; 'where the subjects presented to our view are, in their very nature, transcendental. Whoever undertakes to carry it out, consistently, will find himself master of a very short creed. The doctrine of the Trinity is discarded because we cannot understand how God can be both one and three—as though these two propositions were affirmed of the Divine Being in precisely the same sense. Thus the mystery of the incarnation is abandoned because we cannot comprehend how the two poles of being shall be united in the same person, without mixture or confusion. But not to insist upon these higher mysteries, who ever conceived, rightly, of God's absolute eternity—without successions of time, but an eternal and present *now?* Who can explain how God *knows?* which is not by passing from mere premises to conclusions, as with us, but by one infinite, all-embracing thought; so that, by one movement of the magician's wand, God and nature both disappear, and leave you and me in a universe that is blank. The principle, therefore, with which you started, must be discarded, or you are left a prey to absolute pyrrhonism.'

"'I see it! I see it!' responded my young friend; 'and I shall turn, now, with more docility to the teachings of Scripture, where God has been pleased to record his testimony of the supernatural.'

"'And may God give you the true wisdom, that you may know Him who is the Eternal Life.' was the benediction under which this interesting dialogue was closed."

This series was followed by a paper advocating the founding of a great Southern Presbyterian University. In this paper he showed how large and open a field for such a university there was by reason of the overthrow of the State and denominational colleges and universities, through the war and reconstruction. He urged that Presbyterians must not prove faithless to their ancient educational renown, that they must become again educators, and that, realizing the practical demands of science and advancing knowledge, they must abandon the plan of each Synod's having its own small college and must have one great Presbyterian University for the whole South. Then came the seventeen articles opposing fusion with the Assembly, North. These were followed by two brief papers on "Parleying with Temptation," and, "Accepted in the Beloved." Then came a most instructive and edifying series of nine papers expository of the Beatitudes. These expositions are as profound as they are simple.

His contributions to the *Southwestern* during the first year of its course would have made an octavo volume of two hundred pages. His series on "The Beatitudes" had run over into the second volume of the paper. These were followed by nearly a score of other papers, four of which were on subjects of prayer, four on "Christian Paradoxes," rich bits of practical exposition; but the contributions to the *Southwestern,* February, 1870, to February, 1871, did not amount to one-fourth the mass of those he had provided the year before. This falling off, is perhaps explained by his having to prepare his lectures on the philosophy of history for the Sylvester Larned Institute during the fall and winter of 1870 to 1871. Owing to the necessity under which he labored, of traveling with a beloved daughter who was nearing the grave, in the summer of 1871, and owing to her death, his pen remained comparatively unused during the year 1871 to 1872. We have, however, a few days after her death a significant paper on "Temptation in Sorrow" in which the Christian philosopher appears. This was followed, two months later, by a new and improved edition of his previously published papers on the Paradoxes. In the fourth volume of the *Southwestern Presbyterian* are about a dozen articles from his pen; of a devotional, expository, and practical character, for the most part. In the fifth volume, Dr. Palmer's work is more conspicuous. He writes on, "I go to prepare a place for you," "The Remorse of Judas and the Repentance of Peter," "The Suicide of Judas." The

Northern Assembly began, again, in the spring of 1873 its attempt to draw the Southern Church into itself. It declared that in accordance with a resolution unanimously adopted by the two bodies then constituting the reunited Church, all action touching the brethren of the Southern Presbyterian Church, and the brethren of the Old School Synod of Missouri had been since the reunion, and was then, null and void. Expressing its confidence in the Christian character of the Southern brethren, it affirmed its belief that the barriers of separation would be removed on more intimate communion. With regard to the relation of Church to State the Assembly deemed it "sufficient to call attention to" certain principles and statements found in the Confession of Faith and the Form of Government. Dr. Palmer presents his views on this renewed overture in four issues of the *Southwestern,* beginning June 12, 1873. In the first of these articles, having quoted in full the paper, of the Northern Assembly, looking to reconciliation, he begins:

"However we may regret the continued agitation of a subject, which we had supposed fairly put to rest, it is again thrust upon the attention of our people and must be again looked fully in the face. It is a comfort, however, that the proposition was not sprung upon our Assembly, by reason of its early adjournment, and that we have an entire year to consider it thoroughly; from which we hope this good to result, that the Church will be prepared to render its decision promptly, without the intervention of committees or conferences, against which we will deliver ourselves more distinctly by-and-by. We embrace now this first opportunity, when our columns are free from the proceedings of our own Assembly, to examine the claims of this new 'Olive Branch.'

"1. This proposition is identical with that which was submitted to our Assembly at Louisville in 1870, and which was by it rejected. The language used then was as follows:

"'*Resolved,* That with a view to the furtherance of the object contemplated in the appointment of said committee (of conference) this Assembly hereby reaffirms the concurrent declaration of the two Assemblies (Old and New School) which met in the city of New York last year, viz: That no rule or precedent which does not stand approved by both bodies shall be of any authority in the re-united body, except in so far as such rule or precedent may affect the rights of property founded thereon.'

"Under this purely constructive cancellation of former deliverances against us, by the operation of a declaration which had no reference to us when it was first made, but was simply part of the negotiation then pending between the Old and New Schools, we were invited in 1870 to consider our grievances healed. Is the proposition different on May 21, 1873? Mark the language: 'That in accordance with a resolution unanimously adopted by each of the two bodies now constituting the reunited Assembly, all action touching, etc., *has been since the reunion null and void* and therefore of no binding effect and not to be pleaded as a precedent in the future.' It is the old 'concurrent declaration' basis over again, nothing more, nothing less. Has anything occurred to make that satisfactory in 1873 which was rejected as quibbling and evasive in 1870?

"There is a curious history about the paper on which we are now commenting. Some few weeks ago, the draft of an overture to be submitted to the Northern Assembly was prepared, it is said, between Drs. Brooks and Niccolls, the representatives of the contending parties in Missouri, and was extensively circulated amongst our ministers as a preliminary test of its acceptableness. The resemblance of this overture to that which was actually adopted by the Assembly, plainly shows it to have been the basis upon which the latter was framed; and yet upon this particular point, its language has been most materially modified. The original draft, to which Dr. Brooks is understood to have given his assent, requires the Northern Church to declare of its offensive legislation against us that *'it be, and the same hereby is, declared null and void.'* Here, then, a direct legislative enactment is proposed annulling and cancelling the past. But this is studiously altered into a mere declaration that it has always *been null and void since the reunion;* and by the mere force of a resolution seeking to bring the Old and New Schools together, and which never had any other than an *ex post facto* application to ourselves. What does this cautious change in the language of the original overture mean, but that the Assembly does not intend to be understood as *repealing* any of its former offensive legislation, but only as consenting to its becoming *obsolete?*

"Any lingering doubt on this point will be removed by the following remarks of Dr. Niccolls, the chief mover of the measure, and the only speaker who is reported as advocating its passage. He says: 'These resolutions bear on the future prosperity of our Church. I would not have anything done to humiliate this Church, and *we make no confession or apology,* but we simply want our brethren to understand there is no brand resting on them. When we deal with our fellow men, we must deal with them as equals. All our brethren want to know is, that there is nothing standing on the records against them. The two Assemblies, at their union in 1871 (?) [1869] made this declaration, and *we to-day take no new action, but simply reaffirm the old.'*

"Our objection to this basis of union is to-day exactly what it was three years ago, that it *prevaricates.* It *dead-letters,* whilst it refuses to *disown*. We confess our utter inability to comprehend the state of mind and heart which such a course reveals. During a period of five years the records of the Northern Assembly teem with the most atrocious slanders against us, in the form of solemn testimonies delivered in the fear of God against enormous wickedness. Now if those allegations were true when uttered, they are true still; for we declare that we have not changed our opinions and convictions in the least degree, nor in a single particular. Nay, if guilty under these charges in 1865, when they were heaped the most bitterly upon us, we are more guilty now by reason of persistency in what Northern Christians so intemperately denounced. Here then is the embarrassing dilemma in which the Baltimore Assembly places itself; if these things affirmed of us be true, how can they consent to hold them as *obsolete;* if they are not true, how can they be held back from openly *retracting* them? This is the view that is the most painful to us; this want of manliness in standing by their own convictions, or that feebleness of convictions, which makes truth and honor mere matters of diplomacy and convenience. We cannot understand how a thing *is,* and yet *is not,* at the same moment; we cannot learn how to *say* and to *unsay,* in the same breath. This is our trouble in the matter of fusion with the Northern Church; and the objection holds good against fraternal correspondence as well as against organic union, so long as these terrible charges are not distinctly withdrawn. It is a mere evasion to say they are no longer insisted upon. This Assembly has by the very alteration of the original draft of their own paper plainly declared, that they take nothing back We repeat, with the profoundest sorrow at the necessity which compels it, that it is a prevarication to 'declare confidence in the Christian character of these brethren,' while 'these brethren' are stamped upon their records as heretics, blasphemers, traitors,—published industriously as such throughout the world until the hearts of all Christendom are turned away from us,—and a steady refusal is maintained to express even so much as regret for it all. The longer this matter is agitated in its present form, the deeper becomes our distrust of a body which sinks candor, honesty and Christian manliness in the effort to 'palter in a double sense,' and after the maxim of Talleyrand uses words for no other purpose than to conceal thought.

"So far as the basis proposed for fellowship and future union, it is precisely what we have already considered and rejected. We believe the Southern Church stands more firmly upon the action taken in Louisville, in 1870, than she did when that action was first proclaimed. We have other objections to urge against the new 'Olive Branch,' which we must reserve for the present."

In the next two papers he stresses the following points: 1. The inconsistency between the high professions of this overture, and the history of the Northern Church in wresting from us our property and fomenting divisions amongst our people. 2. The unsatisfactory character of the overture as testimony to the spiritual character of the Church. 3. The false principles and false facts contained in the overture. Possessed of a copy of the paper drafted, on request, by Dr. Brooks of the Old School Synod of Missouri, and presented to the Northern Assembly to be passed as an overture which would meet the approbation of the Southern Church, Dr. Palmer showed what the Northern Assembly would not do as well as what it would do; particularly, that instead of a clear, definite, and manly reaffirmation of the spirituality of the Church, and the headship of King Jesus therein, the Assembly deemed it "*sufficient to call attention to the following principles and statements,*" in the standards. The principles were indeed there, but the Northern Church had been trampling on them since 1861 till year of grace, 1873. Under the head of *false principles and false facts,* he exposes a number of sophisms, and some popular idols. For example, the Northern Assembly had spoken of "divisions" as a matter to be deplored—which duty and fidelity to the Lord required to be healed—and this, too, as necessary to a practical manifestation of our oneness in Christ. Over against this he poured himself out in a torrent of fiery reasoning. He will not have it that his Church is schismatical simply because she is not ready to dump herself onto the Northern heap.. In this connection he says:

"Our mature conviction is that the reckless desire throughout Christendom to blot out all lines of separation, and to roll up all the branches of the Church into one imperial organization, has grown into a heresy which requires to be combated. Unification is not unity, which is often destroyed when the union is accomplished. The unity which is sought to be realized in our day is a different thing from that which the Bible enjoins—which is, 'the unity of the Spirit in the bonds of peace.' This is far different from the unity of imperialism, the unity of external organization. It is not prompted by the ambition to create a national Church, which by its mere bulk shall be a power in the land, able to cope with rival organizations in the influence they exert upon the politics of a country. It is a unity founded upon justice, which the Northern Church denies to us—and upon truth, which the Northern Church steadily obscures. It is a unity of faith—distinctly opposed to the Broad Churchism which quietly ignores doctrinal soundness, and merges into one general negation the most discordant creeds. In a word, comprehension is not unity.

He thinks that there are ample reasons why the Southern Presbyterian Church should maintain her own independent existence. In a subsequent article he argues the competence of the reunited Northern Church to repeal the evil legislation of the Old and New School bodies down to the time of the Union, notwithstanding their assertions to the contrary.

At least fifteen other articles in Volume V of the *Southwestern Presbyterian* are from his facile, elegant and able pen. The most of them were intended to quicken and stir the spiritual life of the people. Toward the close of this volume we come upon the beginning of a most helpful series, which runs over into Volume VI. The series begins with an exposition of the words "God setteth the solitary in families." There are eight papers in the series. In them he attempts to analyze the several relations of the family, "to trace throughout the delegated authority by which it is constituted the model of the State;" to show "in the subordination of its various parts how the great principles of law and government are illustrated, and how these are carried over, in the gradual expansion of the family into all the ramifications of the most diffused society."

This series was followed at once by another series, of five papers, in which we have a presentation of the unfolding of the family as the primary germ, into the Church. As shall hereafter appear, out of these two series was to grow a book.

CHAPTER XIV.

REBUILDING THE WALLS—Continued.

(1865-1874.)

Occasional Addresses and Sermons.—A Good Turn to Columbia Seminary.—Begins the Labor of Preparing and Bringing Out the Biography of James Henley Thornwell.—Letters of Friendship and Pastoral Concern.—Letters to His Sister Sophronia.—Letter to Colonel Hutson.—Tribute to Mrs. Hutson.—The Death of His Daughters, Kate Gordon and Marion Louisa.—The Marriage of His Daughter, Gussie Barnard.—Interest in the Establishment of a University for the South-east.—His Call to the Chancellorship of the University.—Held in New Orleans.

THE demand for occasional addresses and sermons continued to be great throughout this period. No history of Dr. Palmer's life could be regarded as even approximately adequate that failed at least to refer to some of these discourses.

Mr. Alfred Hennen, the patriarch of the New Orleans Bar, at the time, a charter member of, and one of the two oldest ruling elders in, the First Presbyterian Church, a most admirable gentleman, a scholar and a Christian, died January 19, 1870. Soon thereafter Dr. Palmer was asked to deliver in connection with Mr. Hennen's death, an address on "Christianity and Law; or the Claims of Religion on the Legal Profession." After a glowing tribute to Mr. Hennen, he presented a masterful argument for Christianity, founded upon its wonderful affinity with human jurisprudence. The address was received with high favor. The following members of the bar, Messrs. C. Roselius, Wm. W. King, John Finney, Thos. J. Semmes, Robt. Mott, and B. R. Forman, requested its publication "believing it well calculated to elevate the character of the profession."

The death of Gen. Robt. E. Lee was an occasion of universal grief throughout the South. On the evening of October 18, 1870, New Orleans gathered at the St. Charles Theatre. Eulogies were delivered by the Hon. Wm. Burwell, Hon. Thos. J. Semmes and Dr. Palmer. The whole brilliant inside of the great building was covered with broad folds of black and white. The house was jammed, all standing places taken, and multitudes not able to enter. Mr. C. A. Johnson served as president of the gathering, having with him, seated on the stage, perhaps three hundred and fifty vice presidents, including representatives from every prominent family in the city. Noble eulogies were pronounced by Mr. Burwell and by Mr. Semmes. The address of the latter was so fine that some of Dr. Palmer's friends awaited his exordium with a degree of nervousness. Their nervousness was not justified. The minister took the audience to yet higher ground. His address was almost entirely *impromptu,* but he understood the demands of the occasion and met them. He spoke for his city, his State, and for the whole Southland.

After some preliminaries he said:

"It would be a somewhat singular subject of speculation to discover how it is that national character so often remarkably expresses itself in single individuals who are born as representatives of a class. It is wonderful, for it has been the remark of ages, how the great are born in clusters—sometimes, indeed, one star shining with solitary splendor in the firmament above, but generally gathered in grand constellations, filling the sky with glory. What is that combination of influences, partly physical, partly intellectual, but somewhat more moral, which should make a particular country productive of men great over all others on earth and to all ages of time?

"Ancient Greece, with her indented coast inviting to maritime adventures, from her earliest period was the mother of heroes in war, of poets in song, of sculptors and artists, and stands up after the lapse of centuries, the educator of mankind, living in the grandeur of her works, and in the immortal productions of minds which modern civilization with all its cultivation and refinement and science has never surpassed and scarcely equalled.

"And why in the three hundred years of American history it should be given to the Old Dominion to be the grand mother, not only of States, but of the men by whom States and empires are formed, it might be curious were it possible for us to enquire. Unquestionably, Mr. President, there is in this problem the element of race, for he is blind to all the truths of history, to all the revelations of the past, who does not recognize a select race as we recognize a select individual of a race, to make all history; but pretermitting all speculation of that sort, when Virginia unfolds the scroll of her immortal sons—not because illustrious men did not precede him gathering in constellations and clusters, but because the name shines out through those constellations and clusters in all its peerless grandeur—we read the name of George Washington. [Applause.]

"And then, Mr. President, after the interval of three-quarters of a century, when your jealous eye has ranged down the record and traced the names that history will never let die, you come to the name —the only name in all the annals of history that can be named in the perilous connection — of Robert E. Lee [applause] — the second Washington. [Applause.] Well may old Virginia be proud of her twin sons. [Applause.] Born almost a century apart, but shining like those binary stars which open their glory and shed their splendor on the darkness of the world, sir, it is not an artifice of rhetoric which suggests this parallel between two great names in American history; for the suggestion springs spontaneously to every mind, and men scarcely speak of Lee without thinking of a mysterious connection that binds the two together.

"They were alike in the presage of their early history—the history of their boyhood. Both earnest, grave, studious—born alike in that peculiar purity which belongs only to a noble boy, and which makes him a brave and noble man filling the page of a history spotless until closed in death; alike in that commanding presence which seems to be the signature of heaven sometimes placed on a great soul when to that soul is given a fit dwelling place; alike in that noble carriage and commanding dignity—exercising a mesmeric influence, and a hidden power which could not be repressed, upon all who came within its charm; alike in the remarkable combination and symmetry of their intellectual attributes, all brought up to the same equal level, no faculty of the mind overlapping any other—all so equal, so well developed, the judgment, the reason, the memory, the fancy, that you are almost disposed to deny them greatness, because no single attribute of the mind was projected upon itself—just as objects appear sometimes smaller to the eye from the exact symmetry and beauty of their proportions; alike, above all in that soul greatness, that Christian virtue, to which so beautiful a tribute has been rendered by my friend whose high privilege it was to be a compeer and comrade with the immortal dead, although in another department and sphere: and yet, Mr. President, in their external fortune so strangely dissimilar—the one the representative and the agent of a stupendous revolution, which it pleased heaven to bless, and give birth to one of the mightiest nations on the globe; the other the representative and agent of a similar revolution, upon which it pleased high heaven to throw the darkness of its frown, so that bearing upon his generous heart the weight of this crushed cause, he was at length overwhelmed. And the nation whom he led in battle gathers with spontaneity of grief over all this land, which is plowed with graves and reddened with blood, and the tears of a widowed nation in her bereavement are shed over his honored grave. [Applause.]

"But these crude suggestions, which fall almost impromptu from my lips, suggest that which I desire to offer before this audience to-night. I accept Robert E. Lee as the true type of the American man, and the Southern gentleman. [Applause.] A brilliant English writer has well remarked with a touch of sound philosophy, that when a nation has rushed upon its fate, the whole force of the national life will sometimes shoot up in one grand character, like the aloe which blooms at the end of a hundred years, shooting up in one single spike of glory, and then expiring. [Applause.] And wherever philosophy, refinement and culture have gone upon the globe, it is possible to place the finger upon individual men who are the exemplars of a nation's character, those typical forms under which others less noble, less expanded, have manifested themselves.

"That gentle, that perfect moderation, that self-command which enabled him to be so self-possessed amidst the most trying difficulties of his public career, a refinement almost such as that which marks the character of the purest woman, were blended in him with that massive strength, that mighty endurance, that consistency and power which gave him and the people whom he led such momentum under the disadvantages of the struggle through which he passed.

"Born from the general level of American society, blood of a noble ancestry flowed in his veins, and he was a type of the race from which he sprang. Such was the grandeur and urbaneness of his manner, the dignity and majesty of his carriage, that his only peer in social life could be found in courts and among those educated amidst the refinements of courts and thrones. In that regard there was something beautiful and appropriate that he should become in the later years of his life the educator of the young. Sir, it is a cause for mourning before high heaven to-night, that he was not spared thirty years to educate a generation for the time that is to come; for as in the days when the red banner streamed over the land, the South sent their sons to fight under his flag and beneath the wave of his sword, these sons have been sent again to sit at his feet when he was the disciple of the Muses and the teacher of philosophy. [Applause.] Oh, that he might have brought his more than regal character, his majestic frame, all his intellectual and moral endowments, to the task of fitting those that should come to the crisis of the future, to take the mantle that has fallen from his shoulders and bear it to the generations that are unborn.

"General Lee I accept as the representative of his people, and of the temper with which this whole Southland entered into that gigantic, that prolonged, and that disastrous struggle which has closed, but closed as to us, in grief. Sir, they wrong us who say that the South was ever impatient to rupture the bonds of the American Union. The War of 1776, which, sir, has no more yet a written history than has the War of 1861 to 1865 [applause], tells us that it was this Southland that wrought the Revolution of 1776. [Applause.] We were the heirs of all the glory of that immortal struggle. It was purchased with our blood, with the blood of our fathers, which yet flows in these veins, and which we desire to transmit, pure and consecrated, to the sons that are born to our loins. [Applause.] The traditions of the past sixty years were a portion of our heritage, and it never was easy for any great heart and reflective mind even to seem to part with that heritage to enter upon the perilous effort of establishing a new nationality.

Mr. President, it was my privilege once to be thrilled with a short speech, uttered by one of the noblest names clustering upon the roll of South Carolina—for, sir, South Carolina was Virginia's sister, and South Carolina stood by Virginia in the old struggle as Virginia stood by South Carolina in the new [applause], and the little State, small as Greece, barren in resources but great in the grandeur of the men, in their gigantic proportions, whom she, like Virginia, was permitted to produce—I heard, sir, one of South Carolina's noblest sons speak once thus: 'I walked through the Tower of London, that grand repository where are gathered the memorials of England's martial prowess, and when the guide, in the pride of his English heart pointed to the spoils of war, collected through centuries of the past, said this speaker, lifting himself upon tiptoe that he might reach to his greatest height, I said, "You cannot point to one single trophy from my people, or my country though England engaged in two disastrous wars with her."' [Applause.] Sir, this was the sentiment. We loved every inch of American soil, and loved every part of that canvas [pointing to the Stars and Stripes above him] which as a symbol of power and authority, floated from the spires and from the mastheads of our vessels; and it was after the anguish of a woman in birth that this land which now lies in her sorrow and ruin took upon herself that great peril; but it is all emblematized in the regret experienced by him whose praises are upon our lips, and who, like the English Nelson, recognized duty engraved in letters of light as the only ensign he could follow, and who, tearing away from all the associations of his early life, and abandoning the reputation gained in the old service, made up his mind to embark in the new, and with that modesty and that firmness, belonging only to the truly great, expressed his willingness to live and die in any position assigned to him.

"And, I accept this noble chieftain equally as the representative of this Southland in the spirit of his retirement from struggle. It could not escape any speaker upon this platform to allude to the dignity of that retirement—how from the moment he surrendered, he withdrew from observation, holding aloof from all political complications, and devoting his entire energies to the great work he had undertaken to discharge. In this he represents the true attitude of the South since the close of the war—an attitude of quiet submission to the conquering power, and of obedience to all exactions—but without resiling from those great principles which were embalmed in the struggle, and which, as the convictions of a lifetime, no honest mind could release. [Applause.]

"All over this land of ours there are men like Lee—not as great, not as symmetrical in the development of character, not as grand in the proportions which they have reached, but who, like him, are sleeping upon memories that are holy as death—[applause]—and who, amidst all reproach, appeal to the future, and to the tribunal of history, when she shall render her final verdict in reference to the struggle closed, for the vindication of the people embarked in that struggle. [Applause.] We are silent, resigned, obedient, and thoughtful, sleeping upon solemn memories, Mr. President; but as said by the poet preacher in the Good Book, 'I sleep, but my heart waketh,' looking upon the future that is to come, and powerless in everything except to pray to Almighty God who rules the destinies of nations, that those who have the power may at least have the grace given them to preserve the constitutional principles which we have endeavored to maintain. [Applause.] And, sir, were it my privilege to speak in the hearing of the entire nation, I would utter with the profoundest emphasis this pregnant truth: That no people ever traversed those moral ideas which underlie its character, its constitution, its institutions and its laws, that did not in the end perish in disaster, in shame and in dishonor. [Applause.] Whatever be the glory, the material civilization of which such a nation may boast, it still holds true that the truth is immortal, and that ideas rule the world. [Applause.]

"And now, I have but a single word to say, and that is that the grave of this noble hero is bedewed with the most tender and sacred tears ever shed upon a human tomb.

"I was thinking in my study this afternoon, striving to strike out something I might utter on this platform, and this parallel between the first Washington and the second occurred to me. I asked my own heart the question, Would you not accept the fame, and the glory, and the career of Robert E. Lee just as soon as accept the glory and career of the immortal man who was his predecessor? [Applause.] Sir, there is a pathos in fallen fortunes which stirs the sensibilities and touches the very fountain of human feeling. I am not sure that at this moment Napoleon, the enforced guest of the Prussion king, is not grander than when he ascended the throne of France. There is a grandeur in misfortune, when that misfortune is borne by a noble heart with the strength of will to endure, and endure without complaining or breaking. Perhaps I slip easily into this train of remarks, for it is my peculiar office to speak of that chastening with which a gracious Providence visits men on this earth, and by which he prepares them for heaven hereafter; and what is true of individuals in a state of adversity is true of nations when clothed in sorrow. Sir, the men in these galleries that once wore the gray are here to-night that they may bend the knee in reverence at the grave of him whose voice and hand they obeyed amidst the storms of battle; the young widow, who but as yesterday, leant upon the arm of her soldier husband, but now clasps wildly to her breast the young child that never beheld its father's face, comes here to shed her tears over this grave to-night; and the aged matron, with the tears streaming from her eyes as she recalls the unforgotten dead, lying on the plains of Gettysburg, or the heights of Fredericksburg [applause], now to-night, joins in our dirge over him, who was that son's chieftain and counselor and friend.

"A whole nation has risen up in the spontaneity of its grief to render the tribute of its love. Sir, there is a unity in the grapes when they grow together in the clusters upon the vine, and holding the bunch in your hand you speak of it as one; but there is another unity when you throw these grapes into the wine press, and the feet of those that bruise these grapes trample them almost profanely beneath their feet together in the communion of pure wine: and such is the union and communion of hearts that have been fused by tribulation and sorrow, and that meet together in the true feeling of an honest grief to express the homage of their affection, as well as to render a tribute of praise to him upon whose face we shall never look until on that immortal day we shall behold it transfigured before the Throne of God. [Applause.]"[1]

February 16, 1872, Dr. Palmer delivered a lecture before the Historical Society of New Orleans, on the "Tribunal of History," an able piece of work in which he shows that truth will out. It was intended to comfort as well as to instruct; to give courage as well as to inform. He says:

"In the gloom that hangs about us there is a prevailing tendency to spurn the testimony of all human records. We are in a condition to see how history is manufactured for a purpose; how an impudent partisanship manipulates the facts; how the truth we personally know is suppressed; how gross fictions are stereotyped by endless repetition; how the brand of injurious epithets is freely used to stamp falsehood with the seal of truth; and how misrepresentation and calumny

---

[1] Reported in *Southern Presbyterian,* October 27, 1870, p. 3.

are stuffed into books which circulate round the globe and preoccupy the minds of men. Is it strange if some should morbidly infer that all history is but a romance at best, if it be not also a libel and a slander? To which we reply, that falsify the record of particular and isolated facts as men may, there is a residuum of truth which cannot be destroyed, and which shall be the basis of a safe appeal to the judgment of an impartial posterity. Throw into the region of fable all the achievements of Semiramis and Sesostris, still Assyrian and Egyptian histories will survive, which in the aggregate we are able to measure, and whose precise value we can determine. History delves amidst the ruins of Nineveh and Persepolis, walks around the hanging gardens of Babylon, surveys the temples and tombs and pyramids of Egypt, calculates the physical force which lay in all those ancient despotisms, and then renders her decree. It is, that this long succession of gigantic empires simply held the world until the light of freedom could break from the West—until, out of the bosom of a better civilization, philosophy and science should rescue it from the dominion of a superstitious and fantastic imagination. It points the wholesome moral, that of all things on earth nothing is weaker than force; and in its calm judicial tone, pronounces the most withering sarcasm upon the ambitions and achievements of the sword."

June 9, 1872, he delivered a great discourse at the dedication of the new church edifice of the First Presbyterian Church, Savannah, Ga., his theme being "Christ the Builder of the Church." The discourse was delivered without manuscript, according to the preacher's habit. The people wished the sermon printed in pamphlet form. About six weeks later the busy pastor in New Orleans finds time to reproduce the "line of thought."

June 15, 1872, he delivered an address on the One Hundredth Anniversary of the Organization of the Nazareth Church and Congregation in Spartanburg, S. C. The address is a truly magnificent sermon on Ephesians 3: 20, 21, his subject being; "The Glory Which the Infinite and Blessed God Secures to Himself Through His Immortal Church." The people having heard wished a copy of the sermon, which he writes out and mails to them the 20th of August, proximo.

Meanwhile, June 27, 1872, he had delivered a memorable address on, "The Present Crisis and Its Issue," at Washington and Lee University, Lexington, Va.

Dr. Palmer began this oration in his usual modest conversational tone: "History breaks into epochs which constitute its natural boundaries, just as rivers and mountains define the limits of countries upon our globe. Annalists, therefore, who seek to partition it by centuries, are as foolish as geographers would be in making parallels of latitude the lines of separation between provinces upon their maps." Presently he possessed his hearers of a clear conception of what he meant by "epoch." He pointed to two classes of epochs, one relating to universal, the other to particular, history; and was saying: "To this latter class of epochs lying in the range of particular rather than general history, I desire now, gentlemen of the University, to solicit your attention. That they are critical periods, is plain from the fact that they are periods of transition. The navigation is always dangerous through the narrow straits which connect two open seas. And the grave question arises, how a people brought to the end of a given cycle, may safely tide over the bar, and find the deeper sea-room lying beyond. The question is a most practical one to us upon this continent, to-day; for it involves the possibility of a great people 'slouching down on the wrong side of its crisis;' which a moderate share of virtue would enable it to turn with safety and honor."

The speaker declared that there were at least two canons which experience had furnished, bearing upon this issue, viz.: "*That no people has long kept its place in history after traversing the fundamental principles upon which the national character has been formed;*" and "*that in passing successfully through any crisis, a people must possess elasticity enough to adapt themselves to new conditions, and thus to meet the issues of another cycle.*" Having nobly unfolded and illustrated each of these canons, he passed to "The consideration of what we should endeavor to retain from the past and what we should cheerfully surrender to the future." In this connection he made and pressed the following suggestions

"1. *Before all others, is the problem of race,* in adjusting the relations between two distinct peoples that must occupy the same soil. It is idle to blink it, for it stares us in the face wherever we turn: and the timidity or sensitiveness which shrinks from its discussion, is equally unwise and unsafe; for the country needs to know the comprehensive principles which will compel its settlement. Under the old regime, the relation betwixt the two was exceedingly simple, because it was domestic. The bonds were those of guardianship and control on the one side, of dependence and service on the other. All this is now changed, and the two races are equal before the law. The suddenness of this translation, without any educational preparation for the new position, was a tremendous experiment. It furnishes no mean illustration of the heroic boldness of American legislation; and its early and successful solution will afford the most conspicuous proof of the vigor of the national life. My own conviction is, that it is far too delicate and difficult a problem to be solved by empirical legislation—either by the State, on its political side, or by the Church, on its ecclesiastical. It must be patiently wrought out in the shape which an infinitely wise Providence shall direct—and it needs the element of time, with its silent but supreme assimilating and conciliatory influence. But so far as I can understand the teachings of history, there is one underlying principle which must control the question. It is indispensable that the purity of race shall be preserved on either side; for it is the condition of life to the one, as much as to the other. The argument for this I base upon the declared policy of the Divine Administration from the days of Noah until now. The sacred writings clearly teach that, to prevent the amazing wickedness which brought upon the earth the purgation of the Deluge, God saw fit to break the human family into sections. He separated them by destroying the unity of speech; then by the actual dispersion, appointing the bounds of their habitation, to which they were conducted by the mysterious guidance of his will. The first pronounced insurrection against his supremacy, was the attempt by Nimrod to oppose and defeat this policy; and the successive efforts of all the great kingdoms to achieve universal conquest have been but the continuation of that primary rebellion—always attended by the same overwhelming failure that marked the first. Among the methods of fixed separation between these original groups, was the discrimination effected by certain physical characteristics, so early introduced that no records of tradition or of stone assign their commencement; and so broadly marked in their respective types, as to lead a class of physiologists to deny the unity of human origin. I certainly believe them to be mistaken in this conclusion, and firmly hold to the inspired testimony that 'God hath made of one blood all nations of men, for to dwell on all the face of the earth.' But there is no escape from the corresponding testimony, biblical and historical, that the human family, originally one, has been divided into certain large groups, for the purpose of being kept historically distinct. And all attempts, in every age of the world, and from whatever motives, whether of ambitious dominion or of an infidel humanitarianism, to force these together, are identical in aim and parallel in guilt with the usurpation and insurrection of the first Nimrod.

"However true that the specific varieties within these groups may safely intermingle and cross each other, the record of four thousand years confirms the fact, that there can be no large or permanent commixture of these great social zones, without ruin: and that ruin as complete as can be conceived, since it extends to the entire physical, intellectual and moral natures. Why, just follow the history of colonization by the Anglo-Saxon and Latin races, respectively. The former, distinguished by what I may be permitted to term the instinct of race, has steadfastly refused to debase its blood by such admixture: and over all the world, in all latitudes, their colonies have thriven. England, for example, besides the glory of giving birth to such a nation as our own, boasts to-day of her immense dependencies amid the snows of Canada and the jungles of India. On the other hand, the latter, with a feebler pride of race, has blended with every people, and filled the earth with a mixed breed—the most emasculated to be found upon the globe, incapable of maintaining a stable government anywhere, or of developing the resources of the lands they burden with their presence.

"In carrying over this doctrine to the solution of our own problem, I have no opinions to conceal. What I 'proclaim upon the housetop' to-day, I have uniformly 'spoken in the closet' to the representatives of the black race, as I have had opportunity. I have said to them—and to their credit be it testified, the proposition has generally been accepted as the council of wisdom—if you are to be a historic people, you must work out your own destiny upon your own foundation. You gain nothing by a parasitic clinging to the white race; and immeasurably less, by trying to jostle them out of place. If you have no power of development from within, you lack the first quality of a historic race, and must, sooner or later, go to the wall. I have said to them, I deny nothing to you which, with our positions reversed, I would not refuse to myself. Were I a black man, I should plead for a pure black race, as, being a white man, I claim it for the white race; and should only ask the opportunity for it to work out its mission. This it is at once the duty and the desire of our people to afford. Accepting squarely, as the terms of national pacifications, the Negro's emancipation and his political status, however hastily or unwisely conferred, along with these franchises should go the privileges of education and culture. But let these stand upon their own footing. The true policy of both races is, that they shall stand apart in their own social grade, in their own schools, in their own ecclesiastical organizations, under their own teachers and guides: but with all the kindness and helpful co-operation to which the old relations between the races, and their present dependence on each other would naturally predispose. As to all the details of the problem, they will find an adjustment through the gradual changes of time, in the exercise of practical Anglo-Saxon sense, and under the direction of a wise Providence which still binds the destinies of the two together.

"2. The problems in a nation's career are never single. *This changed relation of the two races draws after it the whole labor question.* I do not here refer to the insufficiency of labor for the country's wants, nor yet to the inadequate control over that which exists. Both these must be remanded to the science of political economy, to be resolved by the quiet application of its fixed laws. The allusion is rather to the new condition of things, exacting a personal devotion to labor, rather than a mere superintendency of it as wrought by others. Undoubtedly the old system of large baronial estates must yield to that of small proprietorship, filling the country with a denser population, and inducing a sharper competition, out of which only the more energetic and thrifty will emerge into success. The dainty descendants, who might have been content to repose upon the laurels of an honorable ancestry, find themselves suddenly thrown into the position of those ancestors themselves, and called to the high office of being the founders of families in their turn. In all this there is nothing for a wise man to regret; for it is far more honorable to be an integer in the social arithmetic than to range in the line of decimals into which a noble lineage must eventually thin out.

"The diversity of pursuits in the development of our mineral wealth, and the branches of mechanical industry to which this will give rise, will open the door to activity and enterprise for our ambitious youth, who must enter with ardor the new fields of toil, or find themselves rooted out by hardy adventurers from abroad, reaping the ample rewards and filling the social niche they will then have fairly earned. The instinctive wisdom of our people has already foreseen the peril; and in the enlarged curriculum of this institution, and in the simultaneous adjustment of all our colleges to fit our young men for the practical businesses of life, we discover the provision to meet the exigencies of our new position. A healthy sentiment is thus created, which we must at once formulate into a doctrine; that as an advanced civilization creates new wants and multiplies forms of industry, so no species of labor is disreputable whose products swell the volume of that civilization, and cement more firmly the parts of the social fabric. The usages and habits which formed around the old state of things, should gracefully yield to those which necessity enforces in the new. A proper elasticity of character, adapting us to the change, will bound us over the crisis, and carry us forward to new and better destinies.

"3. *In this connection, a caveat must be entered against that coarse and selfish utilitarianism which measures all things only by a material standard.* This is the peril which I most dread in the impending crisis; that in the friction of these competitive industries, the fine sense of honor which formed the beautiful enamel of Southern character may be rubbed away, to be followed by the swift decay of virtue, of which it was at once the protection and the ornament. Materialism, sitting in the schools and speaking through the forms of philosophy, is not perhaps much to be dreaded. It is too monstrous to be believed. It shocks our moral convictions, and startles the pride of self-love, to be told that thought is only a secretion of the brain—that the rapture of joy and the pathos of grief are only currents of electricity along the tissues of the body. We can safely leave this to the instinct of human scorn, which resents as an insult such a libel upon our nature. But the spirit of materialism, infused into all the transactions of business and common life, is the Angel of Pestilence dropping the seeds of death from its black wing wherever it sweeps. It is this subtle and dangerous spirit which is at the bottom of that fearful demoralization that has spread like a leprosy over the land. It is rapidly displacing legitimate commerce by the silent invasion of its fixed laws, rendering the individual trader helpless in the grasp of a powerful combination controlling the market by irregular and unnatural methods, and making it to depend upon the interest and caprice of large capitalists. It is corrupting public justice through venal juries, no longer impartially selected, but chosen from the hangers on of courts, whose sole subsistence is the bribe of the wealthy litigant. It is filling the noble profession of the law with mendicant attorneys, prostituting the solemn priesthood of their office by opening the subterfuges of legal chicanery to villany and fraud. It invades even the sanctity of the bench, and overwhelms judicial integrity by the pressure of political and commercial combinations. It is converting public office from a ministry of responsibility and trust to a place of emolument, where the perquisites to be enjoyed outweigh the duties to be performed. And worse than all, it is sapping the truthfulness, the honesty and honor of private life, and silently destroying the moral bonds by which society is held together. Through all its grades, from the highest to the lowest, every man is striving to outstrip his neighbor in the possession and exhibition of wealth; and the most sacred claims of love, and all the sweet charities and refinements of social life are sacrificed upon the altar of universal greed.

"Few, perhaps, suspect the deep and hidden sources from which this foul idolatry draws its inspiration. A virgin continent in the possession of the most aggressive race upon the globe; its rich and varied soil, to reward the labors of agriculture; its stores of mineral wealth, to throw a charm around even the grime and toil of the miner; its vast opportunities of commerce, lying between two great oceans, with an extended coast line upon both, and traversed through its whole extent by broad, navigable streams—the tide of immigration bringing to its shores the thews and muscle necessary for its rapid development: all combine to stimulate the spirit of acquisition in our people, and lead them to exaggerate material prosperity as the chief good in life.

"Paradoxical, too, as it may appear, the influence of our democratic institutions bears strongly in the same direction. For whilst all stand professedly upon one general level, the only recognized distinction is that of wealth, which is, therefore, the more intensely coveted as the only badge of pre-eminence. The suddenness with which a few shoot up from the depths of obscurity and poverty, and the obsequiousness which bows down in worship of this rapidly acquired wealth, intoxicate and render men delirious in its pursuit. The most vulgar of all aristocracies is thus created, entrance into which is open equally to all, and stimulates an ambition at once the most groveling in its character and the most debasing in its influence.

"Strangely, too, the very science of the age lends its aid both to increase and to sanctify this gross materialism. It is distinguished, not only by the comprehensiveness of its range, but even more by the steady application of its discoveries to the arts of practical life. It penetrates deeper into the mysterious mechanism of nature, interprets its more complex laws, and involves its more hidden forces; but not content with these achievements, it harnesses them all in the service of man as agents to execute his will. It tunnels our mountains, spans our rivers, weaves the network of travel over the face of the earth, lays its wires beneath the ocean's bed, over which the nations whisper diplomatic and commercial secrets across a hemisphere. Not only so—it bakes and brews, it stitches and weaves, and through its witty inventions, relieves the drudgery of domestic toil. But the effect of all is to intensify the lust of acquisition, until it becomes a supreme passion, which it even ennobles by the splendors of that science with which it is associated, and by which it is indirectly fed. A nation's glory comes to be placed in its railroads and factories, its populous cities and gorgeous palaces, its extensive commerce and accumulated capital. An external and material prosperity is made the measure of national greatness, when the country may be rotting to its foundation in dishonesty and crime; private virtue, the public faith, even liberty itself, being sacrificed to purchase grandeur and power.

"It would be an immense protection against these debasing tendencies if, amid the exactions of our new position, we could carry over those gentlemanly instincts which have hitherto characterized our people. In employing this unusual term, I do not mean that dainty mannerism which puts on the air, without the quality, of the gentleman. But I refer to that exquisite education of the conscience which makes duty and benevolence the habit of the soul; that fastidious honor which cannot, even in thought, condescend to meanness; that lofty self-respect which will observe the proprieties and practice the virtues of life, with the readiness of impulse; that nobleness of principle which makes it as easy to be brave and true as it is to breathe; that instinct of rectitude which shrinks from the false and the base as from the contamination of the plague. It would be a rare combination this, of courtly honor with the hardness of toil. But if labor is ennobled when wrought by the hands of a freeman, how much more when associated with the dignity of the gentleman?

"Let us guard, then, with the jealousy of genuine alarm, against that despicable spirit of utilitarianism which, like a hucksterer in the shambles, is always haggling with truth about her price. She is immeasurably more precious in herself than in all the uses to which men may put her. Truth, integrity and honor are the highest attributes of any people, and the enjoyment of regulated freedom, under a wise and constitutional government, is its noblest privilege and reward.

"4. Coupled with this, *we must retain from the past that individuality of character which makes a man a solid unit in society.* This attribute has with us been largely the product of circumstances. An agricultural people, living apart from one another, every man in the center of a given circle of dependence for whom he was called to think and plan, there was nourished a personal independence which we cannot afford to lose. On the contrary, in a crowded population, men are cheapened in value, like the leaves in a forest. The individual comes to be little more than a single brick in a blank wall, answering only to so many square inches of a common surface. Through a perpetual commingling, thought ceases to be a fresh production of the mind, and there is substituted for it a public opinion which is caught and given back, just as one breathes in and breathes out a common atmosphere. This explains the amazing rapidity with which the wildest heresies are propagated amongst the masses, whose multiplied voices are but the reverberations of a single sound which echo prolongs. It explains the caprice with which hosannas are turned into execrations at the bidding of demagogues, who are 'the pest of republics as courtiers are of monarchies.' It explains the sadder fact, how the few who do think are browbeaten and crushed, and yield up their convictions and conscience, to be trampled in the dust by the buffaloes of the herd, as they snuff the air and scour the plain.

"This is one of the chief perils of the Republic. For as the people are the fountain of power, they must, in the elective franchise, coalesce in a joint expression of will: and as with the increase of population, the drill of party becomes more and more rigid, the sense of personal responsibility becomes more obscure, and the exercise of it more difficult. You will not understand me as advocating that impracticable individualism which splits upon hairs into a thousand schisms, but that honesty of mind which will lead every man to contribute his quota to a true public sentiment, of which his conscience will not be ashamed. For, depend upon it, with the extinction of this individual responsibility, there is no longer the possibility of virtue. In the massive language of Mr. Webster, 'a sense of duty pursues us ever;

it is omnipresent, like the Deity.' If the sense of it be lost within the soul, there is the rejection of the Divine control; and the nation slides down the steep declension into moral decay and death.

"5. *Finally, we must carry over to the future a patriotism that is born of adversity and trial, more intense and purer than in the prosperous and joyful past.* Love of country is inextinguishable, because it is filial. It ranks with that we owe to the parents who begot us, and have given to us their image and their name. But I plead for it not upon the cold footing of duty, but as a precious sentiment of the heart. As a principle, it strikes its root far down into the conscience; but its bloom must expand into a holy passion, and its fruit ripen into acts of enduring service for the public weal. The best affections of the soul are those which strengthen under trial. The alloy of selfishness burns away in the crucible, and the pure love comes forth with a power of endurance which nothing can exhaust. It is thus we bear up each other under the discipline of life; not through the compulsion of necessity, nor the cold obligation of duty, but with a warm devotion which finds its joy in those ministries of love. A genuine patriotism is not that which shouts itself hoarse amid holiday celebrations; but when the country groans in the anguish of a great crisis, waits upon its destiny, though it be that of the tomb. And this land of ours, furrowed by so many graves and overshadowed with such solemn memories, calls for a consecration of the heart which shall be equal to its grief. The patriotism which these days demand must refine itself into martyrdom. It must suffer as well as act. Strong in the consciousness of rectitude, it must nerve itself to endure contradiction and scorn. If need be, it must weep at the burial of civil liberty; and wait with the heroism of hope for its certain resurrection. Such a spirit will wear out the longest tyranny, and assist at the coronation of a brighter destiny.

"Young gentlemen of the University, I have delivered the message with which I felt myself charged. I have not been able to address you with the fopperies of rhetoric. I have done you the higher honor of supposing you capable of sympathizing with the deep emotions of my own heart. When your note of invitation reached me some months ago, it touched me with the solemnity of a call from the grave. I felt, as I turned my steps hither, that I was making a pilgrimage to my country's shrine. I should be permitted to stand uncovered at the tomb of the immortal chief who sleeps in such grand repose beneath the academic shades where he found rest after heroic toils. Should I look upon it as the emblem of my country's death? Or should I prophesy beside it the birth of a new career? Memories holy as death have been throwing their shadow upon my spirit; and I have spoken in the interest of country, of duty, and of truth. The dim forms of Washington and of Lee—twin names upon American History, as well as upon your own walls—appear before me the Rhadamanthus and the Minos, who shall pronounce judgment upon every sentiment uttered here. If aught said by me should draw the frown of their disapproval, may the Angel of Pity drop a tear and blot it out forever! Standing upon the soil which gave birth to a Washington, a Madison, a Jefferson, a Henry, a Randolph, a Marshall, a Jackson and a Lee; and lifting the scroll which hangs, around the ensign of my native State, the names of Pinckney, Laurens, Rutledge, Lowndes, McDuffie, Hayne, Calhoun—I summon their immortal shades around his tomb whom a nation has so lately mourned. In their dread presence I solemnly declare that the principles of our Fathers are our principles to-day; and that the stones upon which the temple of American liberty was first built are the only stones upon which it shall ever be able to stand. And you, gentlemen, representing the young thought and hope which must shortly deal with these mighty issues, I swear each one of you by an oath more solemn than that of Hannibal, not that you will destroy Rome, but that you will save Carthage. I charge you, if this great Republic like a gallant ship must drive upon the breakers, that you be upon the deck, and with suspended breath await the shock—perchance she will survive it—but if she sink beneath the destiny which has devoured other great kingdoms of the past, that you save from the melancholy wreck our ancestral faith, and work out yet upon this continent the problem of a free, constitutional and popular government. And may the God of destinies give you a good issue!"

It was a characteristic of this gifted man, that, when speaking at his best, he seemed to clothe himself in splendor, that beauty and majesty became his; and that, in consequence, he often produced a powerful revulsion in his auditors' personal estimate of himself. He produced such a revulsion of judgment and sentiment in his highly cultured audience that day at Lexington. Amongst the distinguished men on the platform from which he spoke were Mr. John Randolph Tucker and Commodore Matthew Fontaine Maury. "When Dr. Palmer began to speak Commodore Maury turned to Mr. Tucker and remarked, 'He is the ugliest man I ever saw, sir.' After Dr. Palmer had been speaking about ten minutes, Commodore Maury remarked to Mr. Tucker again, 'He is getting better looking, sir.' When the address was about two-thirds through, Commodore Maury, who had for some time been unable to sit quietly in his seat but had been unconsciously twisting and turning about as the result of his almost uncontrollable emotions, turned to Mr. Tucker and said, 'He is the handsomest man I ever saw, sir.' "

The Rev. Dr. S. C. Chester, who tells the story as given above, adds that "These three remarks exactly describe the situation as it impressed a great many other people for Dr. Palmer, who was not by any means an imposing man in his appearance when he was sitting or standing without saying anything, was literally transfigured in appearance when he became warmed up in the delivery of his address. Another incident showing the spell which he threw over the audience that day was that at a certain point in his address he stepped forward and made quite a stumble, his feet missing the edge of the upper platform upon which he thought he was going to step. He recovered himself, however, without making any break whatever in the flow of his speech and there were many people who scarcely saw what had happened so intent were they on listening to his address.[2]

Many stories somewhat similar to the foregoing but difficult to verify, are related of the transfiguring power of his eloquence. Once men had seen him, and heard him, delivering mighty discourse, the swarthy little gentleman of modest demeanor, misshapen lips, heavy eyebrows but penetrating kindly brown eyes, was clothed upon with attributes of high sort—the vital, the magnetic, the gracious, the commanding, the irresistible. The sheen of the regal master of assemblies came upon him.

In March, 1873, Dr. Palmer was invited to go to Austin, Texas, to deliver an address in connection with the laying of the corner stone of the Southern Free Presbyterian Church. He went, and found himself pressed into numerous services besides. At Houston, Texas, he preached the 12th inst., in the large Methodist Church, to a crowded house. Reaching Austin the afternoon of the 13th, he preached in the large Baptist Church, which was filled to overflowing. The Legislature, being in session, "in anticipation of his coming had appointed their two chaplains as a committee" to wait upon him with a request to visit them, and open their session with prayer. This request he complied with the next morning. In the even-

[2] Dr. Chester was a member of the graduating class of the Washington and Lee University at that commencement and as such occupied a position on the platform. He observed the conversation between Messrs. Tucker and Maury, but could not hear it. He subsequently learned what he has repeated, through "reliable authority;" he thinks, through Dr. J. L. Kirkpatrick.

ing he preached in the Cumberland Church, which was filled, persons standing in the doors and windows throughout the services. On the 16th inst. the laying of the corner stone took place, when he made an address of an hour and five minutes, in the open air to a great crowd—embracing the governor, the chief State and city officers, the members of the Legislature and a host of representative citizens,—an address of great eloquence, with which his audience was pleased as well as edified. On the next day, which was Sunday, he preached, morning and evening, in the House of Representatives, they having offered their chamber for the purpose, to audiences of a thousand people each. Monday morning he left for New Orleans, but was caught in Galveston, and made to deliver an address before the Galveston Bible Society, which provoked the following reflection by the *News* of that city:

"Men who do not themselves 'attend church,' make a great mistake in undervaluing the influence and power of the sacred desk. Even when represented by mediocre and otherwise obscure men, its power is immense.

"This influence is based upon the speculative habit of the human intellect demanding the representation and discussion of metaphysical truth, as well as by the instinctive desire to learn of the supernatural, the rudiments of which each one feels in his own immortal hopes and fears. Religion is necessary, and he who ignores the fact or who sneers at its existence, belittles himself in the light of all ages, and is rebuked by the concurrent opinion of the best and ablest men of all classes and races of mankind.

"We were made aware of the practical existence of this fact on the evening of the 18th inst., upon the occasion of the anniversary of the Galveston Bible Society, by the very remarkable address delivered by the Rev. Dr. Palmer, of New Orleans.

"Many years had elapsed since the voice of this distinguished Christian orator had fallen on our ears. It was once our good fortune, in our collegiate life, to sit habitually under the preaching of Dr. Palmer, then in the flush of his early prime. He then gave evidence of those brilliant and logical powers which since have made him the worthy successor in the Presbyterian Church of that prince of metaphysical orators, the lamented Thornwell. It was with eagerness that we listened to him again after so long an interval—an interval which has touched his hair with frost.

"Although unprepared, speaking entirely *ex tempore,* before a strange audience and on a grand theme, which even tempted so rich a mind to undue discursiveness—we mentally exclaimed as he finished, *'Ex pede*

Herculem!' His hand had not forgot its cunning, nor had time deprived him of one element of his peculiar power.

"Such men as Dr. Palmer are at once the ornaments of the section in which they dwell, and the conservators of principle, of noble manhood and pure religion. The large audience that listened spellbound by the masterly exposition of the character of the Divine Book will attest the genuineness and nobility of his impassioned proof of the true unity of Christians of every name, upon the broad and deep basis of the Bible.

"These wide and liberal views commended themselves with power to the representatives of, probably, every church in the city, as the sacred orator illustrated the subjective oneness of Christian belief, amid all the objective diversity of name and denomination.

"One was at a loss in listening whether to admire the elevated range of thought and sentiment, the splendor of diction in which they were conveyed, or the affluence of mental wealth poured out as easily and copiously as the birds sing, or the waves roll.

"No one could hear such a discourse without being better for it, mentally, morally and socially.

"We have able and devoted ministers amongst us, and they, of all, will esteem the tribute we would pay to this great divine—providentially with us upon a passing occasion—as just and merited.

"Were all our pulpits filled with such men as Palmer, we would hear less of the 'Gospel of hate;' less of that fatal venality which has flooded our land, and has made our national Legislature a den of thieves."

On occasion of the Semi-Centennary Anniversary of his own church, November 23, 1873, he read an able historical paper on "Origin and Growth of Presbyterianism in the City of New Orleans."

The following letters show that Dr. Palmer continued to serve Columbia Seminary as he found opportunity; that he, in the latter portion of this period, was expending vast toil in the preparation of the noble biography of Dr. Thornwell, and seeking the means of publishing it; and that he was, while looking with dread toward the issue of the meeting soon to be held in Baltimore between the Committees of Conference appointed by the Northern Church and his own, arming himself to fight there for the truth as he saw it:

"NEW ORLEANS, LA., July 8, 1872.

"Rev. Dr. J. B. Adger:

"MY DEAR BROTHER:—I remit to-day to Rev. Dr. Howe $4,247—to be added to the endowment of the Seminary, after deducting $500 to be placed in your hands—in fulfillment of some pledges made to you by Mr. John McKowen, of Jackson, La., now deceased. You of course understand for what purpose this latter amount is given—though unknown either to myself or to Mr. James King, who is the personal friend who has had this money in trust. Mr. McKowen left the remainder to be employed for the Church, as Mr. King and myself might agree upon: and we both concur in giving it to the Seminary.

"I have not yet had time to examine the papers of Dr. Thornwell, but will do so presently, and will write you in reference to them. The Latin inscription, if any is used, I must leave to yourself and Dr. Howe. He has a little book of such inscriptions, from which something appropriate might be selected.

"Yours truly,

"B. M. PALMER."

"NEW ORLEANS, LA., December 4, 1872.

"Rev. Dr. J. B. Adger:

"MY DEAR BROTHER: Yours of the 23d ult., together with the package sent by the express, is at hand. I have hardly yet set fairly to work upon the biography. There was a hideous gap of the first twenty years of Thornwell's life, covering the important, because forming, period of boyhood and youth. This necessitated a large correspondence with parties that might be able to supply the deficiency. I have been rewarded, however, with quite a number of papers, though some important ones have not yet come to hand. All this of course has taken time, and as the trouble lay at the very threshold of the work, it was impossible to make a beginning. With the materials thus gathered, I hope to cover the break without any marked chasm in the narrative.

"I would be glad to have all the waste matter that you do not work up amongst the published monographs from his pen. There is no telling how much might be culled, to illustrate the formation of his character and development of his genius.

"In regard to his original letters addressed to Dr. Breckinridge, fearing that a sudden call might be made for them by those who are preparing the memoirs of Dr. Breckinridge, I have had them all copied, and can, therefore, surrender the originals at any moment, upon call. I was resolved not to be put at disadvantage in respect to that correspondence. The letters of Dr. Breckinridge himself are of course our property and can be held. I wish you would push up McMaster—but perhaps I had better write him myself. Pelham has never replied to my letter, and he ought to be able to furnish material on the point which I suggested to him, which is the extent and thoroughness of Dr. Thornwell's classical knowledge, and the proof of it which he must certainly have. I would be glad if you would prick him with an ox goad, until he discharges an obvious duty to one who was his friend, kinsman by marriage, and perhaps to some extent a patron also.

"I am glad of the good fortune of the Seminary, and hope that the legacy may turn out to be valuable. I really do not know its amount, nor how soon it will become available.

"I have not yet seen the two additional volumes of the 'Collected Works,' but will have them soon. Witherspoon is coming here to reside as an evangelist in our city, supported by my Church. As soon as he arrives, I have no doubt he will take an interest in the canvass of our city for the same.

"You have seen Robinson's defense of the Revised Book, of course. I have written him my thanks for the lucid manner in which he has put forth the main facts, and urging him to give a wide distribution of his argument, in pamphlet form, throughout the Church.

"As to the marble slab, I do not feel the force of your objection about the setting of a precedent. Every case must stand upon its bottom. The chief difficulty, I think, is, that you have no good chapel in the Seminary to place it. Why would it not be a proper thing to put it in the Columbia Church, with which he was so long identified, and in whose service he almost died?

"I have sent you, of course, copies of both my discourses, in Savannah and at Nazareth: hope that they reached you safely.

"Dr. Wilson's visit was very profitable to our people, and personally to myself and family a great refreshment. He made friends here, as he does everywhere, by the granite honesty of his character.

"Sorrow continues its dark shadow upon our home, where another voice will soon be silent. Pray for us that we may be able to be still, as we see our darling, our youngest born, melt daily before our eyes like 'a snowflake upon the river.'

"Yours in love and toil,

"B. M. PALMER."

"NEW ORLEANS, LA., December 3, 1874.

"MY DEAR DR. ADGER: I cannot tell from the tenor of your last, whether it was written in reply to the suggestions I made in a recent letter, or not: though I rather conclude that this was scarcely received by you. If so, you will probably write me again, now that it has come into your hands.

"What do you say to printing the first edition of the Life *without stereotyping?* It will save that much of the expense. If another edition should not be called for, this will suffice—with that much money saved. If another should be called for, it is likely that some improvements may be made. Other facts may be brought to light by the publication, not now known, but which will be communicated. In which case, it may be stereotyped. I simply throw out the suggestion for what it is worth, and without seriously committing myself to it.

"In our interview, we failed to settle the title page, although I had it written. What do you think of this? 'The Life and Letters of James Henley Thornwell, D.D., LL.D., ex-President of the South Carolina College; late Professor of Theology in the Theological Seminary at Columbia, S. C., by B. M. Palmer, D.D., LL.D., pastor of First Presbyterian Church, New Orleans, La."

"I am much inclined to drop my own title, being much ashamed of the last, which I do not deserve. But I don't know what to do with it. Will it answer to drop it, without giving offense to those who conferred it? If the omission of it should be noticed, will I not be jumping out of the frying pan into the fire?

"I have also a Prefatory Note, simply making acknowledgment by name to those who have aided in supplying the materials. This, on second thought, I prefer to omit, and let the book go out in its simplicity, and tell its own story. If this volume is published alone, by all means let the political articles of Dr. Thornwell go in the appendix. In that case you must furnish them—and perhaps also his letters to Governor Manning on education, though that is not material and may be reserved.

"Answer the suggestions of my previous letter, and if I must confer with publishers, during my trip next month, let me know what terms you would be satisfied with. You know I am not sharp in business matters, and might make a poor bargain. I wish you could spare the time and money to go on yourself and attend to this matter. We might time it so as to act together. I must be in Baltimore on the 7th of January, and in New York on the 15th. Between the two dates, I may be able to stop in Philadelphia. In haste,

"Yours as ever,

"B. M. PALMER."

"P. S.: I will say hereafter what I will do toward writing for the Review, when I shall know whom you have gained over to your plan as contributors. I like the arrangement, if it can be carried out.

"As to my reviewing the four volumes which are out, there is this objection—it will look too much like working in a ring. It ought to be done by some one who is more of an outsider. Suppose you let it rest, till the Biography is out—and then let us get Robinson to write a review of all. The Life will bring out all the Polemics, and justify him in signalizing them, with which he is in full sympathy—and the Theology and Philosophy will be furnished by the other volumes—and the Polemics, too, for that matter. If you agree to this, I can almost engage Robinson to undertake it.

"Yours, 'P.'"

"NEW ORLEANS, LA., December 14, 1874.

"MY DEAR BROTHER ADGER: I did not respond to the forebodings of your former letter, simply because I did not wish to strengthen them by my own. It takes from our courage to look too much at what we fear; and we shall have need of all our moral force, to meet what is before us in the fortunes of our Church. So long as we live, we must be actors; and with me, it is fatal to effort to lose hope entirely and drift into a morbid state of feeling. Fortunately, time is an important element in human affairs, and mighty reactions sometimes take place—and God loves His Church. Anyhow, should the worst come, we must be found in our place to deliver the final protest, and trust to the resurrection of truth after it is slain.

"I frankly own to you that I often anticipate that I may die alone, outside of the Presbyterian Church. By which I do not mean that I shall cease to be a Presbyterian, but that the Church will drift away from me and leave me stranded on the beach. Only the forlorn hope is left, that some others will be of like mind and the loneliness may not be complete. I am looking with dread to the coming Conference at Baltimore. Will you begin to pray for me on the 7th of January, that I may do what I can to prevent the catastrophe?

"I cannot keep down the feeling, that somehow the fate of our Church is wrapped up in that interview. The disintegrating process, I fear, is begun: and if that Conference goes wrong, the first step will be taken toward final fusion, and nothing will be left to some of us but a feeble schism. But a truce to all this! I will restrain tears till they must be shed.

"As to Thornwell's works, I agree to your plan as perhaps the best. If the fifth volume cannot be produced now, we must try to carry out your idea of a special fund to cheapen the entire sale. At this moment, nothing can be done here, for everything is at sea with us. But later, things may not be so dark—and a well concerted and united effort may be successful.

"Can you not go to the next Assembly? A more important and critical meeting will not occur soon. If you cannot go, see that a true, and if possible a strong man is sent.

"Do not forget that I leave home on the 4th of January—and all that you have to say about the Memoirs must reach me before that. If you have occasion to address me in Baltimore, direct your letters to care of Mrs. S. C. Bird, No. 40, Mt. Vernon Place, Baltimore.

"I have some things to say to you in relation to the Review, but must lay it over until I return from the North. Have just received the last number. I have only read Cozby's article, which is conclusive and admirable. I will only add, that it seems to me the time has come for an elaborate and temperate *rediscussion* of the old issues in which we could largely reproduce both Breckinridge and Thornwell, in the way of profuse quotation and ample references. It is on this point, in a form more enlarged than is here stated, that I would like to exchange views with you. In haste and late at night,

"Yours in trust and love,

"B. M. PALMER."

Extant letters make it clear that he was much consulted and deferred to. They make it clear also that he was a man of the tenderest and strongest friendships. The following series of letters to one of his spiritual daughters is presented, to show how affectionately he followed those who had once been members of his flock, how he sympathized thoroughly with them in all their changing circumstances; how he strove to ennoble their ideals; how gracious he was when preaching in this private way; and how he loved his poor downtrodden South with a true patriot's heart. There are some remarks about the North that seem harsh until it is remembered that these letters were written during the period of military rule and re-destruction:

"NEW ORLEANS, March 30, 1866.

"MY DAUGHTER ANNA: It is a long time since my pen has traced this address; not of course that you have been forgotten, but simply that no special occasion has occurred for writing. Expecting every week to welcome you to the city, it was natural to postpone intercourse until there could be a readier instrument than the pen. Besides this, our dear Alice has sprung forward with a peculiar claim upon my notice—and the few letters I could write were shaped for her guidance, in this the most critical period of her young life. But I hope that the ties of sisterhood are close enough between you two to make you sharers in all that so nearly concerns you both, as you both are sharers in that strong affection which prompts my letters. I would like it understood that you stand now so *together* in my thoughts, like binary stars, that when I write to one I write also to the other. You are both dear to me, for your parents' sake, and for your own; and now that you have alike chosen Christ as your friend, I will reverently add that you are dearer still for His sake, whom we now together love.

"I shall never forget, my precious Anna, how affectionately you came in the hour of my sorrow, and nestled in the *vacant* place. Death had smitten two homes: you wanted a father, and I, a daughter, and so the pillar of stone was raised in memorial of the covenant between us. These are all precious and peculiar ties, sanctified by all that is holy in grief and sweetened by all that is dear to memory. There is an alcove in my heart which is all your own, and these blessings and prayers shall ever shower upon your head.

"Alice will tell you of my chagrin at your coquetry with me, and how, too, writing pretty notes that you were to be in the city within a week, and then whisking off with a full head of steam to bustling New York—leaving only a poor good-bye, which I am to digest with a sorrowful appetite, even while the iron horse is snorting in the pride of the speed with which he is hurrying you away. Pretty girls, both of you, to treat your father so! sending him off into his solitary study to count the weeks upon his fingers between April and October. Well, this suggests the only condition upon which I can forgive you—which is, that you watch carefully those little hearts and make no provision for an absence beyond October. I am just jealous enough to scan everyone who looks lovingly upon you—not selfish enough to lock you up in a tower, like Danaus of old—but sufficiently so to prohibit the bans which do not promise you a *Southern* home. New York may have you for a summer, provided it will paint your cheeks with the bloom of health, and send you dancing back with elastic steps—but New York cannot have you for good. Do you understand, then, that paternal authority is firm on that point? Love any good fellow that will not take you from us—but I am getting old now and cannot afford to be stripped bare of those who have crept in and nestled in my heart. I shall be green with jealousy of those Northern beaux, till you come back; so, 'an thou lovest me,' let not one of them come nearer to you than the edge of your widest hoops. I hope your trip will do you great good. You will of course visit glorious Niagara—jot down your thoughts and send them to me, if it does not make you, as it made me, so drunk with wonder and praise that I preferred to worship amid its thunders, than to write sonnets upon its rainbow and its spray. Take a good look at the golden splendor of the hollow North (I speak of course of the people and not of the land which the Lord has made beautiful and wasted it upon them) and then come back with a deeper love for the simpler South, where at least honesty and truth have a home.

"But I must silence my garrulous pen, lest I swell my package to congressional bulk. This is enough to convey messages of love. Write me occasionally, if the whirl and bustle of that great world ever allows you a moment's quiet leisure—and believe me ever truly and affectionately, Your pastor and father-friend,

"B. M. PALMER."

"NEW ORLEANS, May 16, 1866.

"MY DEAR ANNA: Your letter of April 30 came to hand a few days since, and needed no apology for its length. The best letter is that which contains the simple outpouring of feeling and thought, such as would spring to utterance in the freedom and abandon of conversation. No matter if it does ramble from topic to topic. This license of gossip is the privilege of fireside chat, and is the charm of correspondence. Never fear, then, to give your pen all the liberty of the tongue, for which at best it is only the sorry substitute. You have, however, this large advantage, that you are in the midst of new and exciting scenes, with a thousand subjects on which to descant; whilst I must go down into my own breast, and fill my sheet with such poor thoughts as I may find hung up all grim and rusty upon its walls.

"The country in which you now are I remember as exquisitely beautiful. The scenery of the Hudson once entranced me, as I saw it quietly sleeping under a soft May moon; and the memory of it is like a delicious dream. But alas! such a chasm now yawns between that people and our own, that I have not the joy I once had in recalling its loveliness. It belongs now to strangers, like the Alps of the Switzer or the beautiful Rhine of the German. I do not envy its possessors; but sadly wish they were more worthy of the gifts of a munificent Providence. Perhaps, however, I should be better employed in praying that God would render my own people more grateful for the blessings that still lurk under our heavy afflictions. Our poor South! how dear she is to us now that she sits a desolate widow upon the ashes of what was once her home! All scarred and battered as she is, with the cruel furrows of war traced all over her broad bosom, I would not exchange her for the brightest and wealthiest land upon which the sun shines. Dear, old mother! Affliction makes her surprisingly beautiful now in her weeds of mourning—and I cling to her in her tears, as I never did in the days of her laughter and pride. May my heart never taste again the sweetness of joy, if I esteem not her reproach above all the treasures of Egypt! Does not the sight of all the gaudy magnificence you now behold cause you to turn with a new love to your poor, sorrowing land? I know it does. Continue to cherish your own simple South in your heart. It is her boast that her daughters have been truest in the hour of disaster and defeat—let nothing come between her and you. You see, I am half fearful of trusting you so far away. The dread haunts me like a spectre, that in the whirl of a new, bewildering joy, as you gape upon what must appear a world of enchantment, some sleek magician of the North will persuade you that you are necessary to the completeness of the picture. I am willing the Yankee should have his Hudson, but not my Anna. It is better for you to come back and take hold of one of these armless sleeves about our streets, and bless one of our own weather-beaten boys that stood for truth, for honor and for right, till truth and right were trampled down together in the dust. Come back, and live like a true heroine amidst those who are learning how to suffer; and be buried, when you die, beneath the cypress which waves over your country's grave—but a truce to all this. I intended to be playful, and lo! I am as sad as a funeral. What was meant to be a song has slipped into a dirge.

"I am not sorry that just at this period of life you have the opportunity of looking upon the opulence and splendor of the North: and would be still more pleased if you could get an *inside* view of all this magnificence, and see how much of it is Petroleum Shoddy. . . . But whether or no you shall gain this interior view, you will come back having learned one valuable lesson—that all this vanity and pomp do not constitute happiness, the elements of which must be sought in our own virtue, piety and intelligence. History honors Cincinnatus at his plow more than Heliogabalus amidst the splendors of a dissolute court. As long as you remember those who have been to you the types of proper manhood, you cannot but look with a lofty disdain upon all who have the grimace without the inspiration of the sibyl. A just comparison will always distinguish between gold and pinchbeck. It is the mind and heart which make the man a king; and these always transform a cottage into a palace.

"The strong desire you express for the salvation of your unconverted relatives is worthy of commendation, and reminds me of what is reported of the celebrated Melancthon, who in the fervor of his early zeal thought he had only to tell his fellow men of Jesus Christ and they would embrace Him. It required much disappointment to wring at last the testimony, that 'the old devil was too strong for young Melancthon.' Alas! my child, you can scarcely realize the strength of those fetters which bind men in worldliness, skepticism and sin. We are often shut up to this as our last and only resource—to live religion out in its power before the eyes of such, and to bear their case in mighty intercessions before God with whom is 'the residue of the Spirit.' Description and argument are nearly useless against those who are cased in prejudice and unbelief. But the argument of a holy life is the most irresistible of all—and if you can succeed in laying them down well before God in prayer, it will be hard for them to resist the conviction which His grace may implant. I cannot enter upon this large topic here—it would expand into a sermon. Only this I will add: never be discouraged about the salvation of any soul for whom you feel a spiritual interest to pray, and remember that it is a grave responsibility to assume, that of a Mediator with God in this business of prayer. It pledges you to constancy and faith—to earnest wrestling and vehemence of desire—the putting of your soul in that other's stead, and praying as for the life of your own soul. Along with this, strive to exemplify God's grace in your life and carriage, so that the power of your principles may be recognized and confessed. Affect nothing—avoid cant, of all things the most distasteful to men of sense—be simple, childlike—honest, artless in your Christian utterances—not preaching up your religion ostentatiously, on the one hand, nor foolishly ashamed of it on the other.

"I have spun out a letter almost as long as your own—for I could not think of your mother's going directly from New Orleans, without embracing the opportunity of sending you my salutations.

"I sincerely hope this summer will be one of uninterrupted enjoyment, and hope your future memories of it will be unalloyed with regrets. We shall all be glad when you return in the autumn, especially as you will then reside in the city, where we can often see you. Until then I commit you to the guardian care of our Heavenly Father, whose eye never closes and whose promise never slumbers for those who trust in Him with an absolute faith.

"Ever truly and affectionately yours in the Gospel of our blessed Lord, B. M. PALMER."

"NEW ORLEANS, August 24, 1866.

"MY DEAR ANNA: Your intelligence did not wholly surprise me; although the completeness of it, '*totus atque teres,*' (you know Latin enough to justify this scrap of quotation) did a little startle me. It is not at all wonderful that you should be loved, nor that you should be wooed and won: and if you had only written that you were engaged, and that marriage lay off in the dim distance, I should have accepted the information with a perfect '*nil admirari*' look. I do not know that it would have caused even the slightest perceptible arch of the eyebrows. But it was a staggering blow to be told of the thirteenth prox., and off to Europe to 'do up' the old world, all in one breath. Oh, Anna, if it did not involve the parting with you! that is the thorn beneath the rose. But it is just so all through this poor life: Somebody must enjoy the rose, and somebody else must take the thorn. By and by, and in a brighter world, there will be no thorns; but it cannot be so here. A truce to reflections like these—they are selfish. They will creep upon you in silent, twilight hours, of their own motion, without suggestion from others—and as they come trooping along, the sad associates of your new found joy, will throw a thin shadow over the happiness which would else be complete. My child, there is no perfect joy on earth, and you will have a keen reminder of this when the parting kiss of the old, true friends who have loved you from the cradle calls out the tears from eyes that are now dancing with the delight of love and hope. Never mind, those who take the thorn will pour their priceless benedictions upon your bridal wreath, and convert them into prayers to our Heavenly Father to make the benedictions real by making them His own. God bless you, my daughter! for this new love must not cut the cords which in the past bound you to us. Your ———— (let the dash suggest the word it would just now make you blush to repeat) must consent to your remaining forever my dear daughter Anna.

"I am not sorry that you are to marry. With such a wealth of love as your broad, warm heart contains, it would be an injury and a wrong to you not to fill all the relations which call for love. I accept all you tell me of Mr. Carter—and from other sources I hear that he is all the word gentleman implies. Knit to the man who is worthy of you, and with a true love between you, life will be brighter and happier to the end. I say it deliberately and upon knowledge, that a true marriage multiplies the joys of a life a thousand fold—and that despite all the sacrifices and sorrows that may be incident thereto. Take the joy with a grateful heart, renewing the consecration of yourself to our loving Redeemer, and trust Him for grace to bear every bitterness which His holy will may hereafter allot for your discipline. But I have not time, at this late hour, Saturday night, to write you all I desire. I thank you for the strong wish that you express that I should solemnize the marriage—I take it as a mark of your affection. It was not until to-day I could see my way clear to decide to come—and have both written and telegraphed to Mr. Carter to that effect. I will leave on the third and be in New York on the seventh. I can reserve all my good advice for an hour's talk that you will give me, so there is less need of making a preach in this brief letter. With many wishes and prayers for your future happiness,

"I am as ever affectionately yours,

"B. M. PALMER."

"Thank your mother for her letter, which I need not answer just now."

"NEW ORLEANS, November 6, 1866.

"How shall I begin my letter? If I write, My Dear Mrs. Carter, that style of address seems to hold you at arm's length and does not sound like the oldtime; and if I say, My Dearest Anna, that seems to invade the peculiar privileges of your excellent husband, who may now claim this language as belonging only to himself. Shall I solve the perplexity by eschewing every prefix of every sort? But then, as sure as the world, my pen will slide, before I get through, as if by force of habit, into some expression of endearment. We may as well settle this matter at once—that if you are encompassed with the new blown dignities of a wife, you are still to remain my daughter as of yore; and Mr. Carter will not be jealous of this assumption, nor of any affection which an adopted father may feel entitled to cherish. As we grow old (I mean this only for myself), we are unwilling to change any of our relationships and I cannot consent to put you off upon the crowded platform of common friendships, merely because you have fallen into another's possession. I would much rather take him in, than to let you out.

"I owe you many thanks for your kind remembrance, amidst the varied pleasures of a bridal tour. It would not have been strange if all your thoughts had been absorbed by the new friends you have been called to make. Nor should I have felt myself in the least slighted, if the earliest recollection of me had been awakened across the sea, when the first spell of home-sickness had brought thronging memories upon you 'feelingly and fast.' It is the more pleasant, therefore, to know that I had not to wait for any such hour of darkness; but that in the brightest sunshine of your joy, with the voice of bridal congratulations still ringing upon the ear, your loving heart turned, by its own polarity, to those who long ago learned to whisper benedictions upon your head. God bless you, my child, and may your life be a perpetual song! Ah! has the preacher been betrayed into a sentiment contradictory to any formula of faith? Surely not. There is no music without the blending of notes, that to an untutored ear might appear intended discord. And so your life may be a song—a solemn and delightful chant, even though sorrow may now and then send forth its wail to mingle with the lighter notes of mirth and gladness. Young as you are, you have had some experience of this. The winter winds no less than the summer air, may sweep over the Aeolian harp and awake its music. The low, deep moans which went up to heaven amidst the pines of Eureka, when grief held your heart in its crushing grasp, did they not enter into your 'Psalm of life' as truly as now the more cheery warblings of your married joy? Yes, it is so: the believer's life is an anthem, whose music God and the angels hear—and, however diversified by pain and pleasure, those very discords of our experience blend into holy song as they float away beyond the stars and chime in with the melody of heaven.

"It is in this superior, Christian sense I pray God to set you to music. Our Father loves you too well not to purify you by sorrow: and he began early to strike those bass strings of your harp—now his hand sweeps, with surprising skill the firm chords of joy and love. But if your heart be only in tune, whether one or all be struck, you will always be music, and your life a psalm. But I have spun this allegory far enough.

"So your mother is to come home childless! I have half threatened not to condole with her. Did I not know how perplexed she really is, and that her heart's desire is to do the very best for her children, I should quarrel with her outright for leaving those poor girls away off there in the cold—and to tell the sad truth, I cannot get grace enough to love the people who are to profit by her patronage—and I do so want our poor South to cling together in this day of bitter adversity. But then, I shall be obliged to relent when she comes and tells me all the domestic reasons for this arrangement—and have made up my mind to pity her just a little for her loneliness, even though I may wish to scold just a little too. As for you, little scapegrace, you are quite out of reach with the roll of the great sea between us: and if I should storm at your desertion, you would quietly wrap yourself in your own great happiness, and smile, as one smiles in bed at the gusty night outside. I am sorry that I cannot have things as I wish—

but ah! have I not been sufficiently taught it is not best that I should? Do not be afraid. This is not another text for a homily, though it is my trade; let me only say peace, peace to my weary heart—things will be as I wish, bye and bye, when I can see them in God's light. Just now the earth is very dark, and I thank God that I have faith, when I cannot have knowledge. I ought not to throw my shade over your sunlight. It is very selfish, but oh! Anna, I am sometimes very sad. The loss of my dear Fanny, and the deeper loss of my country—it costs me an effort to throw off the double pressure. Yet it is all right, and I kiss the hand which has smitten. I have not always the strength to shake off the dew from my wings and rise with the carol of the lark towards heaven. I would be glad sometimes to fold those wings under the shadow of God's throne—but not yet, the Master says. I must beat the air longer yet in a world that seems for us to be filled only with bitterness and wrath and clamor and all uncharitableness. But I feel that I am growing mellow under it all, like a hard apple that will not soften except under blows. Forgive this dash of melancholy, and pass on to the next page.

"You are in Europe, the land of history—yourself bright and happy in the first gushings of that strange, strong joy which most fills a woman's heart—with almost the lightness of a fairy's step you will move rapidly through a world of enchantments, as Europe's great panorama unrolls itself before your eye. You will tread upon the dust of kings, and moralize over the graves of perished empires. Rome's old grandeur will strike you all the more impressively from its contrast with the rags and wretchedness of what is now Italy. The frivolous splendor of the French capital will flaunt its ribands and ribaldry before your eyes. Germany dreaming its mystical philosophy amidst the pipes and tobacco of learned professors, or dancing in short petticoats and redolent of lager; Switzerland great in the creative grandeur which formed her mountains and glaciers, and greater still in her proud Alpine independence, too poor perhaps to be coveted by envious kings; England, too, mighty in her constitution and her commerce, with a nobility which even the worst agrarian might reverence, and a peasantry that even the proudest aristocrat might honor—and with a history instinct with liberty and enshrined in glory; Old Scotland, with heath and moor sanctified by religion and traditionary legend; and perhaps, beautiful Greece, with her columns and temples, with her poetic mythologies—Greece that ought perhaps to be viewed only in the moonlight of her own great past: all these you will see, while history and song will repeat the story of the ages gone and be your teachers as you tread the mighty pathway over which the civilized and the savage have chased and scourged each other. It is a bright day for you, Anna: and I hope you have left behind you at home the old album all blotted with tears and stained with grief. I think of you only as opening a new fresh record, to be filled with happier experiences, and crowded with bright and joyous memories which you will bring back with you from the old world. But don't stay too long, and carry Christ and the hopes of heaven in your heart, wherever you go—and return with a warm love for the land of your birth, whom it is a greater delight to honor and to serve now that she is smitten to the dust than when like a queen she clothed the nations of the earth.

"Yesterday was our communion Sabbath, when we had a few precious additions to our roll. Your venerable grandfather made his first appearance, since his return, with his white locks which always remind me of Solomon's 'crown of glory' when the hoary head is found in the way of righteousness. In a few days, I shall leave for Memphis, to attend the General Assembly—and write this late at night and in great haste, to be sure you will have a word of greeting soon after your arrival in England.

"Please commend me gracefully to your husband, and charge him anew to take the best care of you, if he does not expect to be held to a strict responsibility on his return to America—and say to him how much I thank him in advance for the books of which you speak, and of which I have only as yet the knowledge you gave. With much love, and with prayers for your highest happiness here and forever,

"I am ever truly yours,

"B. M. PALMER."

"NEW ORLEANS, May 1, 1867.

"MY DEAR DAUGHTER ANNA: It will never do for your mother to go to you from my very door without sending at least a line of salutation, if only to convince you how affectionately you are remembered, and how much we are inclined to complain of that wide waste of water that separates you from us. Ah! just see what mischief you have wrought! Not content yourself with getting as far off as you well can, you must entice your mother away to another continent, to stay ever so long: while we, poor souls, must sit down and suck our thumbs in this wretched, dismantled country, with utter discontent at fortunes which we have no power to control. Well, there is at least a proud satisfaction in bearing the affliction which is common to us all, right here when the bitterness of it is tasted every hour, for even martyrdom has its sweets.

"The European trip, with the prospect of which I have been amusing myself all the winter, is finally abandoned. If it were lawful for me to consult only my own pleasure, I have no doubt I would have enjoyed it greatly: but I had no fair excuse to undertake the voyage. The little correspondence with parties abroad made it plain that no public benefit would accrue to our Southern Church by executing the mission entrusted to us by our Assembly—and I have not the private plea of needing the recreation of a trans-Atlantic tour. So I have not the pleasure, which at one time I anticipated, of accompanying your mother and sisters, and of receiving at your hands an English welcome to English soil. It would have been delightful to travel with such companions, and with the expectation of such a greeting in the land of my forefathers—but Providence has ordained a disappointment, and we are happiest, at least, in the way of duty. I shall, however, follow your mother in thought at least, and picture the gladness and enthusiasm of your meeting. If there be anything which will complete the circle of your hopes and joys, it will be the pleasure of your dear mother, and the participation by Alice in all the delights of your European tour. It is not necessary for me to say how truly I wish for you all the realization of the pleasure which the sight of all that is historic and grand in the old world must impart to those who are so competent to appreciate and enjoy it all. May our kind and loving Father above shield you from aught that would throw a shadow upon plans so bright.

"You will have all the news from New Orleans detailed orally with so much fulness, that it would be impertinent to engross any of it upon paper. We are jogging along—still under military rule, with no early or solid prospect of release; the only comfort that nobody can take us out of God's hands—and when His purposes, as yet unknown to us, are fully accomplished, He can restrain the wrath which seems bent upon working our ruin.

"I had hoped, dearest Anna, to have written you several sheets full of pleasant talk, but with my usual procrastination, have put it off till the very day of your mother's departure and now there is not time. Please remember that hitherto I have been hearing of you through your mother's correspondence, but that now I shall be dependent upon letters direct from yourself. Drop a line now and then, when the spirit moves, and I will try to answer, notwithstanding the bad credit which I have as a correspondent. My best regards to your excellent husband, of whom I am reminded every day as I consult the valuable books he was so kind as to send me at parting.

"Yours ever in Christian love,

"B. M. PALMER."

"NEW ORLEANS, June 20, 1868.

"Mr. Thos. L. Carter.

"MY DEAR SIR: I have seldom been more completely surprised than upon breaking the seal of your letter, dated Louisville. I had only two days before dispatched a long letter to Mrs. Jennings, containing messages to Anna and yourself—and here you are on this side of the water, almost within earshot. If I could have anticipated the pleasure of meeting you in Baltimore, this would have turned the weights in the scale, for I hung in doubt some time whether to go there or not. My good people gave me leave of absence in May to go to see my venerable father, whom I had not visited since 1863, with *carte blanche* to remain away as long as I pleased. So I could easily have taken a week longer for the Baltimore trip. But as I had no particular business there beyond the mere pleasure of looking in upon our Assembly there in session, I decided to return home as soon as my filial mission to South Carolina was accomplished. To have known that I would meet you in Baltimore, which would have been to see my darling Anna, by proxy, would have been a motive for reversing that decision, much greater than the feather's weight which often turns the scale in cases of doubt. However, I have missed that pleasure now; and there is no use in pouring forth useless regrets about it. I suppose there is no hope of seeing your household, until they have got their fill of Europe, and begin to feel the pangs of homesickness. As you plan a brief sojourn in Switzerland, it is to be hoped that you will feel the contagion of that nostalgia which is said to hang around the mountains of that beautiful country, and which makes one sick unto death with the desire to return to one's native land. But alas! our country is so big, and our people so nomadic, that the feeling of country is scarcely concentrated enough to produce this wholesome disease in an American.

"Yet tell them all, when you get back to Europe, that we, who are not intoxicated with the witcheries of foreign travel, miss them here; and long to see their vacant places filled again as in days of yore. We stand on the shore with eyes strained with expectation, and with arms of open and cordial welcome. The laggard hours will spin their flight; only do not get weaned from a land trebly dear to the patriot heart for the sorrows with which she is baptized. The heel of proscription is upon her broad bosom yet: but God alone knows how we love even the scars which to other eyes besides our own seem to mar her beauty. The soil of the South is just as dear to us, as the *cause* which has sanctified it with blood.

"I need not tell you, my dear friend, how truly I mourn with you in the loss of your little Anna—for the full expression of this was given in the letter to the mother, to which you have referred. But the bud so early broken off from the earthly stem has opened in the Paradise above—and the Redeemer needs just such flowers to breathe their fragrance in the beautiful gardens He has prepared. 'Yet a little while,' said our Savior on earth—a word which, to the pious mourner, has so often spanned the abyss of the grave, until he too shall 'cross the river and sit beneath the trees.'

"Give much love, when you return, to Anna and the three girls, whom I love with a co-ordinate affection—and to Mrs. Jennings, all that respectful affection which belongs to her great worth, and which is reciprocally due to her partial kindness for me. I long to have you here: for I do not expect even death to break the bonds which unite my heart with theirs. Mrs. Palmer and my daughters join me in their Christian salutations. Yours evermore,

"B. M. PALMER."

"NEW ORLEANS, LA., January 4, 1869.

"MY DEAR ANNA: First of all, let me wish you 'a Happy New Year'—to yourself and all your home circle. I breathe this wish from the depths of the heart. How swiftly the years chase each other! Do you not begin to find it so? It is only in childhood that time seems to move with laggard steps; because childhood looks with such undefined longings to the independence and freedom with which life appears to be crowded when we become men and women and escape forever, as we suppose, the tyranny of our masters. But when we would arrest time in its too rapid flight and hold longer possession of our joys, it takes ample reprisals for the contemptuousness of our youth, and speeds all the faster for the wish that would restrain it. You will be astonished to find how few years it will take to place you exactly where your mother stands—and then to look back, the present will appear but as a brief yesterday. Well, as the milestones fly past us on the highway of life, they also mark our approach to a brighter world.

"'Where life is not a breath,
Nor life's affections transient fire,
Whose sparks fly upward and expire.'

"And now let this clean page be consecrated to congratulations of another sort. I heard yesterday, at church, from your Cousin Anna, that a second babe sleeps upon your breast. My child, I wish you joy. I know exactly how you received this gift at your Heavenly Father's hand; how you said in your heart, 'this shall comfort me instead of the other.' Why, this is human experience from the days of the first family sorrow felt on earth: 'and she shall bear a son, and call his name, Seth; for God, said she, hath appointed me another seed instead of Abel, whom Cain slew.' What infinite pathos in those simple words of early history! We look through them down into the deep of the first mother's heart. We see all that unutterable anguish, which even Scripture does not attempt to describe, over that first death in our poor world that has seen so many since—how the first mother writhed in her sorrow in that first parental bereavement, and laid the remembrance of her martyred son down in the bottom of her soul as though it was a treasured joy. And now that another is born, it is the first restored to her embrace—a happy resurrection of the dead Abel, and she called him Seth, the 'appointed;' embalming in this significant name the joy that came back into her heart out of the grave in which a mother's love had been buried for a season. Thousands have passed through this experience since Eve: for example, you and I. Perhaps you know how my own firstborn slept, and we were childless—and then another came, whom we took and kissed, and were comforted. So, perhaps, I understand all about that moderated joy with which you placed this second babe over upon your heart, which still holds in it the little grave of the first. It is a joy, the full pulse of which you distinctly feel; but how much more quiet a joy than the first! shaded by the remembrance of another gone, which you would not put from you if you could. The sweet sanctity of the tomb throws its mellowing influence upon you; and the smile, with which you greeted this little stranger, had in it the pathos of a tear, through which it shone with a subdued and tender gladness. I am not afraid that you will pronounce this sentimental. There is a touch of nature in us all; and one heart can hold up the mirror to all other hearts—and Eve with her Seth is the type of all mothers who have received their second over the grave of the first.

"It will be curious to you to contrast, if you have not already done so, these two natural experiences of yours—to remember the exultation with which you welcomed the firstborn, and the somewhat proud satisfaction you felt in completing the circle of domestic relations as mother no less than wife—to recall the fond imaginings which instantly began to picture the future when she should be grown, unapprised of the terrible contingencies which even in the cradle snap the threads which our fancy is so busily weaving. But now with a joy as deep, but less exulting—with a gratitude that is far lowlier, you receive this boy: feeling, as you could not fully comprehend before, the uncertain tenure of all earthly blessings—conceding God's property in this as you did not realize it in that, and accepting the new gift much more fully as a trust to be rendered back one day, and for aught you know, too soon. In a word, Anna, it is now the chastened love of a heart that has known sorrow. I remember once to have stood upon Mt. Yonck [?] and to have looked out upon a wild but gorgeous landscape. There was one feature in it, fleeting as a moment, that has been the vision of a lifetime. One little cloud, thin and transparent as a bridal veil, hung over me in the sky, and threw the most delicate of all shadows upon the deep green of a meadow at the mountain's base. I have never seen such a shadow since; but to have seen it once was to remember it forever. It was a shadow that was not shade, but light. As though the sun looked through a veil of finest tissue for the purpose of softening his own garish splendor, and the light he cast through it was so sweet because it was so subdued. Just such a shadow as this I have felt often in life. It is when the heart's warm love shone through the remembrance of some sanctified sorrow, and rested with a mellow and chastened light upon the green pastures of life. Such is your love to-day, as a mother's heart gives it forth in smiles resting upon the face of your sleeping babe—a love that has moisture in it, as it glimmers through the memory which is full of tears.

"This time it is a son! What solemn responsibilities cluster around that word! This boy-babe is after a while to be a man. Can you tell what a vast intellect may be slumbering within that little head? Who knows but that the fate of an empire may be wrapped in the folds of his career? Those little hands may wield the destiny of this great Republic—and that tiny voice may sway the councils of a nation; who knows! That little heart, it may be a volcano of passions, to be belched forth in smoke and fire upon a devastated earth—or it may be the well-spring of a mighty stream of beneficence to refresh and fertilize the world. Which shall it be? Do not stagger, nor be affrighted, when I answer that under God all depends upon the mother. A fearful trust is reposed in you, my daughter, in this boy's birth; for of a truth, in time and in the great hereafter, he will be just what you shall make him. It is too late to shrink back in terror. He is yours; and the great God, who gave him to you, says, 'Take this child and nurse it for me, and I will give thee thy wages.' Mark the terms of the contract, for therein lies the trust, and the comfort too. *'Nurse it for me'* —that is the trust: 'and I will give thee *thy wages'*—this is the assurance. Both are bound together. If you nurse it for God, you shall have ample recompense. Like the blessed Mary, take this word and 'ponder it in your heart'—it will strengthen you to pour forth many a prayer, which perhaps in the day of future temptation will interpose a shield between your erring boy and the red anger of God: and to weave around him such an influence as will shape his character for life and make him all that the holiest mother would have her son to be. Believe it firmly, that if you nurse him for God, you shall have your wages, and then take up your trust with a brave heart and bear it bravely in faith, until your little one shall bless you, as I do this night bless the memory of my dead mother who has been these twenty years in heaven. God, who makes our strength equal to our duty, makes also our comforts equal to our responsibilities. But let this page conclude this homily. A letter is not exactly the place for a sermon, which I will reserve till you can hear it from the old pulpit on Lafayette Square.

"This letter ought to be a long one for I am in debt for that you wrote me from Dinan, I believe it was. It would not have been delayed thus long, but you were so constantly on the wing that I could not be sure where to strike you in your flight. Indeed, I am far from sure that either your mother or yourself have received all the letters I have sent. I am so glad that in your youth you and Alice enjoy the rare privilege of seeing the old world with all its memories of the past. These sights will form a part of your education, and be woven into the very fabric of your minds. As for me, I never expect to see them at all—and if I should, they would never be incorporated, as with you, in the very substance of my being. Life is shortening too fast with such a day laborer as I have been, to allow the thought of such a luxury as a European tour. I must hasten to gather up the ends of a too imperfect work, that it may not go up to the judgment a poor, raveled, and slovenly service as it looks to me now. When I weigh anchor and set sail from these shores, it will be to explore the antiquities of that older world that lies beyond the stars—and my largest and proudest wish is for a clear head and a sound frame to work on till the grand summons pealing from the skies to leave the mattock and the spade and rise amid the angels. The joy of life to me now is its toil.

"So you must see and enjoy for me; and keep your enthusiasm fresh to pour it all out in story, when you come back. Tell Alice that I shall expect to find her expanded into a large hearted woman—with all her sensibilities quickened and her tastes refined, ready to take hold of life with an earnest aim and to be a blessing to us all. Caddy and Cora, too, will have grown almost into women, having to learn the names of the old faces and places over again. God bless them all, with your dear mother! from whom as well as from yourself I hope to hear the details of the newcomer, what dimples in the cheeks and exactly how he holds the great toe of either foot.

"I have snatched off these lines, as you can see from the lumbering periods, with an impatient pen that will not wait for thoughts to crystallize. As they are, let them go—if only to bear a message of love and congratulations in the new joys that have broken in upon the gloom of past bereavement. My best love to your husband, whom I have not specially named only because he has been bound up in my thoughts, as he is bound up with you in the parental relation to the young stranger. With kindness and kisses to all, I am as ever,

"Affectionately yours,

"B. M. PALMER."

"NEW ORLEANS, LA., December 26, 1874.

"MY DEAR ———: Your letter is just at hand, and fills me with surprise and sadness. I had heard that Mr. ——— had met with losses, but did not dream of their being of such extent as to reduce you to such plans as you are now meditating.

"As I expect to be in New York on the fifteenth of January, I would prefer putting off any reply to your letter till I can see you face to face. This delay, however, might not be seasonable, and I will therefore write you with entire frankness. In the first place, you ought not to decide upon the course which you propose, without the knowledge and sanction of your husband: partly, because he is your head and his will must be your law—and partly, because you might fearfully wound his pride and self-respect. To me, were I in his place, such a proposition would be extremely painful—unless the necessity for it were extreme and uncontrollable. It may be right for you to cast about and revolve various measures of relief; but you should conclude nothing without his entire approval and consent.

"In the second place, are not your hands full in the education and care of your children—drawing more and more upon your time and services, as they grow older? It may be well for you to consider whether what you lose in this direction may not be more than you would gain in the other. Only the sternest necessity should jostle a mother out of her peculiar place as the guide and nurse of her own offspring.

"In the third place, can you not aid your husband as much by a system of retrenchment and economy, as by earning with him a common support? There is no *eclat* in this, I grant; but there may be a superior heroism. Consider this well before you decide. For until you have exhausted all the resources that may lie hid in a close economy, you are hardly justified in the effort you are thinking of. I hope things are not going to remain as dark as they are at present with you. Mr. ——— will, I trust, regain his feet. Be tender of him in this sad depression, and act under his counsel and advice in all matters.

"But your resolution is a noble one, as soon as *the necessity of the case shall fully justify it.* Of that I cannot judge, without a fuller knowledge of the circumstances; and about that I will talk with you, *if you desire.* I need not say that I will do my utmost to aid you in your plans, if they shall hereafter be carried out, and will take great pleasure in commending you others.

"I can think of no place more suitable than another in which to begin the experiment. You will find the ground preoccupied almost everywhere, and that your school will have to be built up gradually on its own reputation. Two years ago, there was a great want for such a school at Austin, Texas, but whether it has been supplied since, I do not know. I can make inquiries for you, when the time shall come.

"With much love for you, ————, and with much sorrow that this care is laid upon your heart, I yet know that you will prove equal to all the emergencies of your lot—and you have a dear Father above who will not suffer you and yours to suffer. Much love to your mother and sisters and to your little ones.

"Affectionately and truly yours,

"B. M. PALMER."

The following letters to Mrs. W. F. Hutson constitute a fair sample of his correspondence with those knit closely to himself through the ties of blood as well as of grace:

NEW ORLEANS, LA., December 18, 1872.

"MY DEAR SISTER: How long is it since I wrote you last? I fear you will reply, that the memory of man runneth not thereto. Well, I have my good cap on to-night; for I have just written a letter to Sallie, in whose books I am down as deep a debtor as in yours. But in penning this to you I am only fulfilling a purpose formed when Charley passed through our city on his way to Baton Rouge. I was both surprised and pained to hear from him your continued indisposition, having supposed you completely restored from the attack of last spring. These warning notes of sickness fall upon us now like sentinel cries from just across the border. The two worlds do lie at last so close. We ought at least to feel it, seeing how easy it has been for those of our own household to step over the line. Two dear daughters have melted like the snow right before our eyes; and now a third is wasting away, and we are powerless to hold her. I did not use to feel that sickness meant much—only a little sympathy and a little physic—but now it means, to us at least, the long good-bye.

"I do not want to make you sad—certainly not to send this letter as the raven croaking over your door. I only mean, dear Sophie, that the shadow is upon my own house, and it gets darker and darker every day. Our poor Marion is doomed. It is idle now to listen to the whisper of hope. All summer long she has held the disease so well at bay, neither gaining nor losing, that we began to think of possibilities. Perhaps it was not the real consumption, but something else; or perhaps youth might triumph over disease. But all this is past, now. The handwriting is too plain, in which the sentence of God's decree is written: and in that sick chamber there is the awful stillness of those who bow before the Supreme Will and await its execution.

"But I will not burden your heart with our sorrows. We know exactly all the bitterness of the cup, from which we have drunk so often, and are perhaps a little steadier for the experience. Still God is amazingly good. Our timid Kate did not flinch a hair in the struggle, but went to sleep upon the bosom of the Promiser like an infant. And Marion talks of the mighty issue before her as quietly as though it were only going from the parlor below to the chamber upstairs. It teaches me whole volumes of theology—these tender, timid girls treading upon the fears of death and the solemnities of the tomb as if they were roses strewn upon their bridal path. I never knew before how strong grace is, nor how easy it is for faith to walk upon the sea. My dead children have been my teachers, and I bow with awe before them. We try to drop out of sight the years they miss spending on earth, and to think of the everlasting mansion which is to come so soon. Sometimes I feel as though I could touch the eternal walls, they are so near; and then again, bereavement yawns before us like a vast abyss. Pray for us that we may bear ourselves aright under this continued discipline. Especially pray for my poor wife, upon whose face the lines of sorrow are being deeply chiseled. You can feel for a mother.

"I was sorry not to have seen you last June, when I was in Carolina. But I was upon the utmost stretch to overtake appointments very distant in space, but almost abreast in time. Besides, you had not then returned to Orangeburg, from the Island.

"Charley is doing well in Baton Rouge. But we are in such a fearful muddle politically, that I fear the University and every other interest in Louisiana will soon be prostrate. There never was a grosser outrage upon the liberties of the people—and if it is sustained by the judiciary and executive at Washington, he must be blind not to see that the grave of the whole country is dug, for the North as well as the South.

"Give much love from us all to William, and to both the girls.

"Hope you received two discourses recently sent you in pamphlet.

"Your affectionate brother,

"BENJ. M. PALMER."

NEW ORLEANS, LA., February 18, 1873.

MY DEAR SISTER: I wrote a long letter to father a few days after our recent bereavement, giving a detailed account of Marion's death, and requested him, after reading it, to enclose it to you, with instructions that it be forwarded also to Sally. Before this it has doubtless come into your hands; and you will readily comprehend why I should desire to abridge the pain of dwelling upon a scene so full of sadness to us. Indeed, I was not adequate to the task of repeating the story; and I am glad now to assume that you know all the particulars.

"Your welcome letter has been received; and the sympathy which it breathes has been a great refreshment to our hearts. This last blow has not been heavier than the others, but it has come upon the top of them. There is a cumulative force in sorrow; and the weight of past grief has been replaced upon us, in this, and a most distressing sense of loss and of disappointment, in being deprived of so many of our fold. We are a little calmer now—but I never expect the shadow to be lifted from our path, whilst we sojourn below. Of course, it is all supremely right; and we do bow before the Infinite Will which has ordained it all. This alone is a vast support. Then, we cannot but adore the grace which has taken away the sting and the curse, in the case of all the four who have gone up to the Savior's bosom. As long ago as the death of our dear mother, I was so penetrated with the glory shed upon her dying hours, that I felt that I would scarcely allow myself to grieve for the departure of any whom I loved, could I be equally satisfied of their ascension to heaven. God has been exceedingly good to all the branches of our family circle, in bringing them all into his kingdom, and in removing none from earth who have not given evidence of their preparation for the change. The assurance of this in the case of our dead children does more than comfort—it fills me with praise. Though their early life has been short, it has not been without profit. We ought to bless Him who lent them to us so long, and that they have all of them been a joy and a delight to our hearts. They are gone—but have left a memory in which there is nothing we would like to blot out. I feel that it is a great privilege to have begotten children who swell the number of the redeemed in heaven. The interval between this world and that seems so short, that I can easily anticipate the reunion above. In addition, I can see, as I look back, that there was a special lesson taught in each bereavement which the Holy Spirit has sealed on my heart, and which I have carried along with me in my whole ministry. It is certain that we learn a great deal through the affections: and if it pleases God thus to sanctify these sorrows, I cannot fail to accept the loving discipline which is made so profitable to my own soul, and perhaps also to the souls of many others to whom I am called to minister.

"Nevertheless, dear sister, I am very weak, and this affliction has plunged us all into the depths. Never think of us but with silent prayer that the God of Grace may strengthen and sanctify us more and more. We never so much needed Divine consolation and support—and I am thankful to say, neither of the two has been entirely withheld.

"I am sorry to write you in these general terms. But I cannot begin to unfold the thousand thoughts that crowd upon me. I can only touch their skirt, and leave you to fill up the rude outline, from your own knowledge of the Spirit's dealing with the hearts of Christians.

"Give much love from us all to William and Emily—and though I am such a poor correspondent, believe still that I cherish a brother's love always for you. Ever yours affectionately,

"B. M. PALMER."

The following letter explains itself:

"NEW ORLEANS, LA., May 30, 1873.

"MY DEAR WILLIAM: The sad news of your letter, this day received, has fallen upon me like a bolt from a clear sky. It is true, that Emily and Frances, in recent letters to Gussie, spoke of their mother's sickness, and of her attack as being similar to that of last year. Perhaps this helped to lull all suspicion to sleep. Certainly I dreamed of nothing so serious as this; and though I read it as plain as can be, 'She died in five and a half hours,' I cannot put it as a fact into me. I shall not be able to realize it all until I visit you again in your desolate home, and see for myself that she is not there. Oh, my brother, I pity you! As for her, there is nothing dreadful in it. Abundantly prepared through grace for her change, it was for her only a translation. We can in the unselfishness of love, wish her joy in the immortal ascension. But the loss, the grief, is to us that remain; especially upon you does the blow fall, in its most cruel force. The union of almost forty years is dissolved in a moment, and I know that it has been one of more than usual confidence and love. Your children, too, all married and away from your roof, I look in upon those lonely chambers with a heart profoundly sad for you. But why say all this? Alas! what can even a brother's sympathy avail in an hour when even the solid earth itself seems to be slipping from beneath your feet? May God help you to bear it! First sustaining and then comforting with those rich and beautiful hopes that lie along before you, in the land across the flood. My dear William, we can afford to be patient and brave, for a long and happy past is behind us, beyond the reach of all contingencies—and the future is short, until we, too, touch the shores where our loved ones are gone. In all my own sorrows, I am unspeakably grateful for a past which must ever be mine, while memory endures—a past like your own, lighted up with joys whose brightness can never fade. All my dead are where I shall shortly find them, in the blessed reunion of the ransomed forever. Oh, how safe our treasures are—and all of the eternity in which to recover and enjoy them. 'We are conquerors, and more than conquerors, through Him that loved us.' Sorrow and death are subdued and made the ministers of our true and lasting joy.

"But I wish I could have seen my sister once more upon earth—and could I have foreseen this, I would have left all, to stand by her dying bed. I grew up under her shadow—young enough to revere her as the elder sister, but old enough, even in boyhood, to be her companion. Of late years we have been separated, and the occasional and brief intercourse, thrown in at such long intervals, was more a mockery than a satisfaction. But since your letter has been received, I have lived over a long life in a few hours—and the long buried past has yielded up a thousand precious reminiscences of her that was so dear to you and me. A pure, precious, guileless spirit has passed away from us—but leaving a track of memory behind it that is fragrant and sweet. Her fresh mind and overflowing heart gave out to us a life upon which the dew has ever rested, and in its dewy freshness it will remain with us until we meet her above.

"All join me in love to you and to the girls; it was providential that they were with their mother. I will write Charlie as you desire.

"Yours most affectionately and in the sympathy of a personal sorrow,

"B. M. PALMER."

The brother could not let this sister pass away without laying a flower on her new-made grave. Hence there appeared in the Southern Presbyterian, some weeks later, this unsigned

"TRIBUTE TO THE MEMORY OF MRS. S. L. HUTSON."

"Our blessed Redeemer has sanctified everything which he hath touched, even death. Though it rob us of much that we have loved, it returns them to our thoughts so beautifully transfigured that affection is changed into a strange and worshipful reverence. Who that has ever mourned has not rejoiced in this compensation, when his dead come back to him with every wrinkle smoothed out of the character, so transformed by the beautifying touch of death that love feeds upon the image dwelling like a sacred presence in the soul? Most sweet prophecy of the resurrection which God has embedded in the affections of our nature! None can wholly die out of our love. They float down to us from beyond the stars, reinvested with the familiar body, clothed with the old relations, and blending again with us in the current of life; yet so much more beautiful than before, as those who have been communing with angels and with God. Cold reason may stagger at the metaphysics of the doctrine; but is there no presage of the resurrection in this power of love to glorify the image which memory reproduces? The wounded heart finds it transformed already into what it shall be. The dead have risen and returned to us, and we hold communion with them, based upon suggestions of the earthly past, but with a love spiritual and akin to heaven. There are those, too, in whom Divine grace has so wrought out its own ideal that death has nought to do but to put on them the robes of light and bear them up to the bosom of God. One wishes no change in the memory, only that it be encircled with the halo of the glory that is beyond. Such was she to whose surpassing worth this tribute is paid by one who loved her well.

"Mrs. Sophronia L. Hutson was the oldest surviving child of the Rev. Edward Palmer, the venerable patriarch of the Synod of South Carolina, who, under the weight of more than eighty years, still leads the flock to which he ministered half a century ago, and gathers in his arms the children's children of the children whom he then baptized. May God deal tenderly with his dear old servant, and ordain this to be the last sorrow under which his great and brave heart may be called to bow. The blessed mother that bore her has walked the streets in the city of God these five and twenty years, and the two have greeted each other and reknit their love already before the throne.

"Mrs. Hutson was born in the city of Charleston on the 27th of July, 1814. In 1829, at the early age of fifteen years, she united, on profession of her faith, with the Presbyterian Church at Walterboro, Colleton District, S. C., then, as now, under her father's pastoral charge; and on the 11th of February, 1836, she was married to Col. W. Ferguson Hutson, then of Beaufort District, S. C. This union was dissolved after seven and thirty years by her own death, at Orangeburg, on the 24th of May, 1873. She was the mother of ten children—three of whom alone survive—one son and two daughters—all of whom are married. These, with the smitten husband, and four grandchildren, too young to appreciate their loss, are all of her immediate household to weep in sad submission over the grave which hides her cherished form. An aged father, one sister, and two brothers, come forth in sorrow from the home in which she was born; while in her husband's house there is a mother, with sisters and brothers, who loved her as one of their own blood; and a wide, wide circle of relatives and friends gathers in from every side, as sincere a company of mourners as ever kept the funeral watch or wept beside the open grave. For all along and between the hard dates given above, there lay such a loving life that those could but feel the wrench who were called to part with the joy of it.

"She was the type of her sex in the perfect *womanliness* of her nature. This word exactly defines her character, and its expansion would be the exposition of all her virtues. It made her what she was in all the relations of wife and mother, daughter, sister, and friend, with the truest strength lying in the bosom of softness. Her inward graces found a symbol in the outward presence. With unusual symmetry of form, preserved even to the verge of age; with a dignity of carriage that never stiffened into stateliness nor slouched into negligence; with a face which rippled under every gentle emotion; an eye that could easily sparkle into mirth or droop beneath a tear; a silver voice that breathed music into speech or upon its birdlike notes bore aloft the songs of the sanctuary above the chorus of the multitude—she possessed just that beauty which springs from *completeness,* the combination of many parts to form the harmonious whole. This was, however, but the rich setting to the richer jewel within. Inheriting a vigorous and clear intellect, which was developed by the highest education in her day; with a taste for reading, which kept her abreast the varied literature of the age; with that feminine power of absorbing knowledge from intercourse with some of the best thinkers of her native State—she had the culture that fitted her to shine in every circle through which she moved. The piquant freshness of thoughts invested this knowledge, when reproduced, with an originality which was all her own. She passed it through the mint of her own mind, and the coinage stamped it as only hers. Her practical judgment was that which belongs particularly to woman. It does not weigh differences and strike the equation, but penetrates with a vision of its own, and instantly perceives the right, the convenient, and the true; while with her an educated conscience safely applied the rules needed for human guidance with the precision and certainty of the highest moral instinct.

"Her temper was genial and cheery. It was her happiness through life to have a heart satisfied with love. Her contentment, therefore, shone through the discipline of sorrow as the sun through the mists of the morning. With a nature so mellow, she was able to stand the severe tests of a woman's strength, which we take to be the power of penetrating and pervading every being with whom she comes in contact. It is a divine gift which makes every woman strong on whom it is bestowed, and Mrs. Hutson possessed it in the largest measure. Few could so let herself down into the heart of childhood, enabling her to make the Sabbath 'a loving day' to others besides her own household, and causing her influence to leaven the society in which she moved. A sort of magnetic power belonged to her of interpenetrating others, which made her the stay of the weak and the joy of the strong. Let him who knew her earliest on earth draw the portrait, in antithesis, worthy of the pen of Addison: 'She was so mild in disposition and yet so decided in character, so affectionate in heart and yet so firm in purpose, so courteous in manner and yet so determined in action, that she gained, without the expense of trouble, the good-will of all.'

> "'None that knew her can ever forget
> Those thousand decencies that daily flowed
> From all her words and actions.'

"As a Christian, her record is her life. Springing from a parentage of faith running back upon the line of the covenant for more than two hundred years without a break, it was not strange that she passed into God's kingdom in the dew of her youth. And thus early renewed, it is easy to see how her character should have crystallized as it did. Her piety was sincere; it breathed itself into every word and every deed. Too refined and delicate to obtrude upon others the sacred experiences of her soul, the silent testimony she bore to the riches of divine grace could only be gathered from her humble but consistent walk before the world. As disease invaded her frame, her face looked more fondly upward and took in the rest that awaited her. The closing sentence in one of her last letters was: 'The time seems so short for us all, that I hope we shall all soon dwell in eternal oneness.' And when the end came suddenly upon her, there were no painful questionings. With characteristic simplicity, she looked with an eye of love upon the earth she was leaving, and with an eye of faith upon the heaven to which she was hastening, and sweetly said: 'I am sorry to part with you and the children, but I am safe in Jesus' arms.' Though death broke in abruptly at the last, when hope was brightening for her recovery, there was no surprise.

> "'To her it was not more than the sudden lifting of a latch,
> Nought but a step into the open air out of a tent
> Already luminous with light that shines through its transparent folds.'"

Dr. Palmer's family history during this period was one over which shadows hung, darkening twice to death. His fourth daughter, "Kate Gordon," of singular attractiveness from birth, with her large, dark brown eyes, "full of lustre," yet "liquid and soft," had grown into a physically elegant and beautiful if fragile young woman. Developed by mental and moral training into a woman of sweet, gracious, unobtrusive manner, also, albeit one of independent thought, she fell a victim of consumption and faded away. Her trouble began with "a hard bronchial cough" in the autumn of 1870. It could not be overcome, even with the aid of the best medical skill. Her father spent the summer of 1871, in traveling with her in the vain hope of restoring her health. October 23, 1871, after certain preliminary and suggestive conversations, he concluded that he must inform his precious invalid of her actual condition. He tells the story himself in the following words:

"The stern duty was laid upon the father to cut away all ground of hope from his darling child, and open to her the certainty of her approaching doom. It required nerve, and all nature shrank from the discharge of so painful an office. Would she be able to bear it? Evidently she had rallied to hope upon the supposition that her disease was not wholly incurable. With the extinction of all hope would there not ensue an immediate collapse? And what if terror and alarm should seize upon a timid spirit, and his words hasten the dreaded catastrophe? Thoughts like these flitted, like birds of evil omen, through the mind. It was as though the patriarchal Abraham must lift the sacrificial knife over the beloved Isaac again. Yet the poor girl must not be suffered to make the dreadful plunge wholly in the dark. Even love, the highest Christian love, pleaded that she might at least be allowed to 'gather up her feet in her bed,' ere she left us. Breaking his ground cautiously, he asked: 'Kate, do you know how sick you really are? And do you not sometimes think that it is impossible for you to recover?' 'No, I do not feel that I am so very sick—if I could only eat —that is my trouble.' 'But, my daughter, do you not see that *that* is a part of your disease, and the very worst part of it, too?' She was silent, and he continued: 'My darling, it is best that you should know the whole truth about yourself. It is now certain that you have consumption. Hitherto your lungs have been in the state of what the doctors call consolidation, or hardening; now they are beginning to break down, and will go entirely in course of time. You may linger a good while, as many do, or you may be taken away at almost any moment. Tell me, my daughter, does this alarm you?—are you afraid to die?' With a superb courage, without the moistening of an eye, or the quivering of a muscle, she heard her doom, and folding her hands upon her breast, simply said: 'I am ready.' 'Is your hope fixed simply upon Christ as your Redeemer, my child?' 'Yes, I have nothing else to trust to but that,' was the reply that closed the interview. It would have been comforting to lengthen it, to have drawn her out in the details of Christian experience; but in compassion this was spared. Even this brief conversation was at the expense of much suffering from unutterable exhaustion, and the incessant cough which every utterance only irritated and increased. In the evening of the same day she repeated to Marion the substance of what had been said as to her physical condition, and added, 'But I am so weak that I cannot talk—father is going to have prayer with me.'

"They watched beside her couch the three or four days she was yet spared to them. Saturday, October 30, 1871, they laid her to rest in Lafayette Cemetery.

"The setting sun looked through the autumn air,
  The rich October, through its tincture brown,
O'er tree and bower; we were gathered where
  Affection lays the lost and cherished down.
I stood, with many others, on that eve;
  But nineteen years of life the one had known
Whom we had met to bury—and to grieve
  That one so young and good so soon had gone.
The father and the mother came to part
  Forever with the one they'd cherished long;
And looking on his brow I saw his heart
  With sorrow conquered, yet in faith was strong.
A grand and mighty spirit, such as his,
  Feels sorrow deeply; mind his pulses warm—
Like the unsounded depths of the abyss,
  It suffers in its stillness, 'neath the storm.
There is no struggle in the books of time
  Like that which dares even at death's portals grim,
To bury such, yet say with faith sublime,
  'E'en though He slay me yet will I trust him.'
We are all tested in the things we teach,
  As our strength—'tis thus our toil must soar,
And life is awful and has thoughts that reach
  Through death for the hereafter to explore.
For death's enlargement and unsetting light
  Must bathe the soul in splendor ere it plume
Its might to catch the reason of the blight
  That we call Death and hide within the tomb.
Was not her life—not for herself—but others lent,
  As a sweet solace, as a polished gem,

Rich in itself, whose mingling lustre blent
  Complete the structure of some diadem?
O'er whitened tombs the votive flowers lay,
  And cold, gray death, as life's great fact, accept.
Be up and doing while 'tis called to-day,
  Hope's rainbow arches o'er the dead we've wept,
The warm and loving instincts of each life,
  The rich embodiments of heart and soul,
Though earth and time are marching in their strife
  O'er prostrate homes, yet still their God's their goal." [3]

He was a most affectionate and devoted father. While it was fresh in his mind, he wrote down every precious word of these last days of his darling; and prepared a sketch of her life and character that he might thus keep her memory exact and vivid. Providence had designed that in doing so he should prepare a work that would carry comfort to many stricken hearts. The account is full of human love and human grief and full of love to the Giver of children and of grace.

Back into the harness from this grief he sprang at once; and went on speaking for God and for his fellow men, writing for God and for his fellow men, and living for them. Men wondered at his self-control; for few saw self-control as a Christian virtue as he did; and few took in how altogether real heaven was to him and his house.

Eighteen months had scarcely passed, when his youngest daughter, Marion Louisa, was taken down with pneumonia. She had been the family pet, delicate all her life, one of the most amiable and virtuous of children, sanctified as he believed from the womb. It was now his lot and the lot of his beloved wife to look for the third time on a grown child wasting away in their sight and to feel their utter powerlessness to arrest the process.

Pneumonia ran into consumption of the lungs. On the first of February, 1873, as the day was rising to its noon she was taken from them. About a fortnight later he wrote to Mrs. Sallie Baxter Bird:

"NEW ORLEANS, LA., February 19, 1873.

"MY DEAR SISTER: So you, too, have a burden to bear, and have just skirted the edge of a great sorrow? I thank God on your behalf. Having just drained this very cup, we know its bitterness, and can the better rejoice in your exemption. Most fervently do we hope and

---

[3] Signed, G. K. W. New Orleans, La.

pray that you may be spared our anguish. Ah! you have endured the supreme sorrow, in which all others are engulfed. I feel that you can teach us all that is meant in the words, suffering, patience, submission—for in the comparison, ours though heavy are light. Now that I have taken the pen, I scarcely know what to write. Shall I tell you of our child? Alas, the words, that would appear to you so full of exaggeration, would fail to present all her goodness, as we know it. The obituary gave you a faint, but true, sketch. I would only mar the picture by enlarging it. Could she be anything but dear to us—so sweet, so gentle, so unobtrusive, so obedient, so affectionate? Her devotion to her mother swelled into positive worship. Then she was our youngest—for seventeen years, the pet of the entire household—handled the more tenderly, because from infancy so delicate that we feared every rough wind would blow the flower to pieces. We find, too, there is a cumulative power in sorrow. The old wounds were not healed—we thought they were—are they ever anything but simply closed? and how little it takes to tear the slender covering away, and to renew the past distress! It seems now, just as though all three had lain down together, and that a sudden desolation had blotted out our home. Do you remember those touching lines of Jean Ingelow? They keep ringing in my ears, and I find myself crooning the melancholy ditty, on my pillow at night:

"'I had a nestful once of my own;
Ah! happy, happy I!
Right dearly I loved them; but when they were grown,
They spread out their wings to fly.
Oh! one after one, they flew away
Far up to the heavenly blue:
To the better country, the upper day,
And—I wish I was going too.

"'I pray you, what is the nest to me,
My empty nest?
Can I call that home where my nest was set,
Now all its hope hath failed?
Nay, but the land where my nestlings be,
There is the home where my thoughts are sent,
The only home for me—ah, me!'

"The last three lines are full of solace. Sometimes, the dangerous thought shoots through me, like an arrow from the enemy, you have begotten children for nought—for what purpose have they lived, except to die? And it is answered by the sweet assurance that they are all in heaven. Yes, it is something to have borne and nursed them for God: that they swell the glorious company of the Redeemed—that heaven is enriched by their accession, and the Church of the Firstborn rolls up a stronger praise through their added voices. We scarcely have a family now on earth—the table looks so scant with only two, where five used to gather: but then, the family in heaven! and the sea that rolls its flood between, that used to look so wide and stormy, has dwarfed to a thread, and it is so easy to cross it. To us it appears thus—just to shake out the sail, and a single cupfull of breeze wafts us over: it is just a pant, a gasp—and all is past.

"I ought perhaps to tell you, that it pleased God to put in the bottom of this cup one very bitter drop. Marion had suffered much, more than the others—and her emaciation was so extreme, that only by padding her all about with great care could we prevent the wasted limbs from wearing through the skin. Only one prayer was left us, that God would grant the weary child an easy release at the last. And she was so good—so like Lydia, whose heart the Lord opened—so early did she come into the kingdom, and with so little of struggle with sin—so meek and patient in her long illness—never by word or tone indicating restiveness—but constantly thanking us for every attention, even a glass of water—that perhaps we had got to think her entitled to that slight alleviation at the end. She was lying on her side, and the breath was shortening—it looked so peaceful, that I placed my hand on my wife's shoulder and said, 'God has heard our prayer—in a few minutes it will be over,' when just then she moved her head and turned upon her back. The movement was fatal: one short cough, and the fearful rattle of the clotted phlegm—the poor child was strangling: I sprang on the bed, lifted the living skeleton to a sitting posture—there was just one clutch of those long, bony fingers at the neck of the dress—one look of despairing appeal at each of us out of those patient, blue eyes—and my child was suffocated in my arms! Oh, my sister, it nearly killed us. Thank God, it was short—hardly more than a minute: but it has bowed us down before the sovereignty of Him who denied our prayer, and did not spare her! I feel, as I write, that I am in the presence of an awful mystery: that death should be permitted to riot in his triumph over that poor wasted frame—leaping upon it like an enraged giant, and with ruffian violence wrenching away that young life, just as she was meekly yielding it up—and throwing upon us that great anguish, which as a fierce remembrance burns into our very bones! If I use the language of passion, it is not that of resentment. God knows that we bow before Him even in this, and say, 'Thy will be done!' But, what does it teach—what great lesson does our loving Father mean us to gather up and treasure, in this apparent, and unspeakably painful, harshness to us and to her? I will tell you the conviction, which the Holy Spirit seems to be impressing more and more upon my own heart. I have never had before such an overwhelming sense of the testimonial character of human suffering, and of the awful holiness of God as the particular fact to which the witness is borne. Surely it is right—nay, it is *supremely* right—that God should exhibit, in the very bosom of His grace, His dreadful displeasure against sin. You perceive that I go behind all secondary causes for the origin of suffering. However it may be brought about through fixed and necessary laws, the moral ground of it is to be found in the fact that we are sinners. The curse —the curse—that terrible word which is written as the superscription over a doomed world—rests upon us, and we suffer. When God, therefore, interposes with grace, and turns this curse into discipline, giving us in sorrow and anguish, not the punishment, but the correction of our sin, He is thereby proclaiming His dreadful holiness. He does it, in those whom most conspicuously He saves, that the world may understand that He saves as a holy God. Are we not in danger, while contemplating His infinite compassion and love, of lowering our views?[4] . . .

Still later he wrote:

"NEW ORLEANS, LA., April 15, 1873.

"MY DEAR SISTER SALLIE: The human heart is very deep. In prosperity, the sun shines into it; and, as in a well, there is an eye twinkling on the surface that you think is shallow perhaps. But when sorrow comes, how far the leaded line goes down and finds no bottom! It is just here that the creature comes nearest to the infinite which is in God. The mind is capable, I know, of great adventures. Thoughts shoot forth with an immense spring, and traverse all nature and all space: but you can see and feel its boundaries. There are not only limits to its excursions, but limits which we can in some degree assign. But the *Heart!* Do its outgoings ever pause until they rest upon God? How these affections deepen every day! And when the loved ones cross the flood, do they not carry our heart with them? Can distance, or death, break the cord which has power to stretch over all abysses, and hold them still to us as our own? Did you ever put together the threefold description of God, in the Bible? God is *light;* how grand! God is *life;* this is sublime. But you do not reach the climax until you read that God is *love*. Here is the sum of the other two. Love comprehends them both, for love is light and life. That one soft word which makes all the joy of this poor earth, exhausts all that we can tell or think of God. When we have said this, we have said all. And now when he gave us these, our hearts, he made us most like himself; and so he has endowed them with a power of expansion which makes them spread beyond all the measurements of time, far out into the vast and immeasurable eternity—and so they travel on and up, over and over the highest steeps in that great Beyond, until

[4] The remainder of this letter has not come into our possession.

they touch and rest upon the Infinite, Uncreated, Eternal Love, which is God himself. But could we know it without sorrow? Cannot you and I say, that till sorrow came—and the sorrow too that touches eternity—we did not know how deep our nature was? Oh, blessed discipline of sorrow, that widened us out beyond all this world, clear over into that which is above the stars! Sweet death! That has lost all power to divide, but only joins the next to this: just like the ocean which parts the continents, and yet is the highway by which we go from this to that! Sorrow has been profitable to me, little sister; and I must praise it and the hand that sent it. I have had a heap of joy in my time; and joy as pure and varied as ever fell to the lot of man—the joys of thought and of high reason—the joy of reputation and of man's praise—and above all, the joys of a sweet home. But joy at last is only the eye on the surface of the well; twinkling and bright, but on the surface still. It did not penetrate, like sorrow. It did not search into the dark places of the soul—it did not sanctify love, like sorrow. The hard freeze of your Northern winter makes the earth ring like a piece of iron, for a time; but the frost is searching down many feet below—it mulches the earth and makes it friable—and then spring comes with its thaw, and the green carpets the soil that was before so frozen and hard. What sweet flowers bloom over the heart which sorrow has searched and crumpled a little, although hardened and stiffened at first! Take up then your old sorrow, which, like mine, stretches over the wild, bleak sea which parts you from your lifelong love. And take up your new sorrow, as it presses upon the mother's heart by the sick bed of her suffering child. Draw the curtains and shut out the broad glare of the mocking sun—and there in the mellow shadow kiss your griefs over and over again, which have taught you what power there is in you to love God, and the triumphs which the heart achieves over the death that cannot tear from us those whom memory holds in embrace.

"I have had a hard struggle. We men do not excel in the passive virtue. We can do easier than we can bear. Your sex has quicker sensibilities, and perhaps feel a keener torture than we are capable of appreciating. But you have a compensation in a nature that is more yielding. You submit better than we. I can see it in my wife and daughters. I had to wrestle with myself. And then I had not the privilege of retirement. Right out before the world's great stare, I must stand up and speak for God's right to use the rod: and then come down from all those grave words to 'pour out my soul in me' before God, in my study—to put a bridle upon grief before others, and then to utter such moans in secret as come only from a wounded spirit. It is over now: 'the Lord gave, and the Lord hath taken away—*blessed* be the name of the Lord.' But if you do not know from experience how hard it is to turn anguish into worship, I cannot tell you, nor could

Job. But you *do* know it: for the sorrow has gone deeper into you than into me—and I believe that you have been as much taught of God. Yet a little while, and we shall have 'the singing for the sighing'—a little while! It is the watch word upon the lips of all the redeemed.

"It is very sweet in you to contrive such pleasant plans for our dear Gussie. But she has plans of her own that will prevent compliance with your kind suggestions. She is just about to make the great venture of life, as you and I did long ago in the days of youthful hopes. Well, with all the grief that has been born of it, we do not regret it. The joy and the sorrow have together formed the two arms of the shears, with which God has cut out the pattern of the character we shall wear forever. Let us hope the same for her. She is worthy of a good fate and will win it, I believe. She has all those womanly qualities which render your sex the guardian and the joy of ours, and constitute you the pivot on which all human society turns. She marries a poor man, who has not the leisure nor the means even for a bridal trip—or I would send them on to you. But God often makes the poor rich in the smallness of their desires—and it is so with them. Mr. Colcock is a young man of excellent points; and will, I hope, make her happy. If a woman's *heart* be satisfied, that is the *all*.

"I am delighted to hear such good news of Mr. Machen. Give them both my heartiest congratulations, in this new and spiritual tie that binds them together, and for both worlds.

"If Saida will receive a kiss from me, and perhaps she will not object, so long as you are my proxy, tell her how I am waiting and praying to hear that she consecrates her convalescence to the great Father who has brought her through so much, and has spared her. And tell her that no consecration will answer, short of the full and clear vow to take up and wear before the world the Savior's redeeming name. May the Spirit enable her to do this soon, with an intelligent and comfortable persuasion that she is indeed 'in Him that is true!'

"With kindest love to her and to her husband and to Edge—and with all that you want from us all, to yourself,

"I am, as ever, yours,

"B. M. PALMER."

In May, 1873, another important event in his family history occurred. The third daughter, Miss Gussie, was united in marriage to Mr. Daniel D. Colcock, with whose family Dr. and Mrs. Palmer had long been acquainted as one of the most honorable in South Carolina. This event took place while their grief for Marion's death still sat heavily upon them. The universal esteem and affection manifested by his people for the daughter and the honor shown her family on the occasion was all that man could give towards a solace.

During these years Dr. Palmer was solicited more than once by people living elsewhere than in New Orleans to change his field of labor, or at least to consider a call to another field. For a long time he was proof against all such appeals. Some of his reasons for preferring New Orleans appear in the following letters to Mrs. Bird, who, as Sallie Baxter, of Athens, Ga., had been the child friend of his young manhood:

"NEW ORLEANS, LA., July 8, 1870.

"MY DEAR MRS. BIRD: Your letter, directed to me at Louisville, came safely to hand; but found me so employed with important matters then before the Assembly, as to preclude the attention which it challenged. Immediately upon the rising of that body, I was hurried off to Missouri to fulfill a series of public engagements, which for the time being occupied all my thoughts. Upon my return home, which was not till the very end of June, I was at once taken up with a communion season, and with discharging a heavy correspondence accumulated during so long an absence. I had not quite got through the pile before your second letter was received—as though chiding me for neglect of one whom I so dearly love. I am at pains to detail all this to you; for an old, constant friendship, such as ours, demands to be kept free from the least suspicion of indifference. I value your esteem too much to imperil its preservation by forgetfulness—and am measuring that period in life, when memory brightens up in its recollections of the past and revels in the recovered joys and associations of youth.

"On one account, I do not regret the delay that has occurred: since it has enabled the good people of your church in Baltimore to consummate their arrangements, without complicating them by any reference to myself. I fully appreciate your kindness in so earnestly wishing to draw me to Baltimore—and can so far reciprocate it as truthfully to say, there is nobody on this wide earth to whom I would be so happy to sustain the relation of a living pastor as yourself. But I am afraid that in order to this, you will have to come to New Orleans to live—except so far as these sweet pastoral duties can be discharged through the pen, which is but a poor substitute for the daily and fresh intercourse between those who are in personal contact.

"The fact is, so far as anything can be fixed in this world of ceaseless change, I may be considered established here for life. In the first place, there is an immense loss in the exchange of fields, by any pastor who is successful at all. There is the loss, for example, of that peculiar hold upon the confidence and love which is only acquired in seasons of trial and bereavements; and in the course of years, a large proportion of one's flock is bound to him by this peculiar tie. There is the loss of that special interest which springs from his having bound parties together in marriage, and afterwards administered baptism to their children. In a very few years, a whole generation grows up who transfer all the veneration of childhood to the judgment of maturer years. There should be large advantages gained by the exchange, to compensate for the surrender of so many associations which cluster around the old pastor, and, to some extent, make up for the abatement of his natural vigor.

"In the second place, my field of usefulness here does not yield to any other in the whole country. There is not a single pulpit, even in the great city of New York, which stretches its individual influence over so wide a territory as my own. It is the representative pulpit of our Church in this great valley of the West. Every Sabbath, during eight months of the year, from three to five hundred strangers wait upon my ministrations, gathered from the Lakes to the Gulf: so that I am largely a missionary, with this peculiarity that this portion of my audience revolves around me, instead of my itinerating to find them. It was in view of this, that I did not hesitate to decline, before the War, an earnest call to the Church in New York, now supplied by Dr. Hall (formerly Dr. Alexander's).

"In the third place, my family and myself have passed safely through the perils of the yellow fever; whilst my removal would necessarily subject another to all the risks of acclimation. And, lastly, I am bound up, I think, in the affection and esteem of my people. They support me liberally—anticipate every wish—come up bravely to every public enterprise to which I desire them to rally and in every possible way demonstrate their confidence in me as a leader, as well as their attachment to me as a man. It would take a great deal to separate me from them, so long as there is evidence that I am useful to them. And I have a theory that a minister who has passed the age of forty (I am fifty-two) rarely possesses the power of knitting strongly to a new charge.

"The only point that remains to be disposed of, is that on which you chiefly insist—the consideration of climate and health. And I suppose you will regard it a strange paradox when I say there is scarcely a spot on the globe with half the attractions of our climate—the winters always open, soft and bland, with scarcely a trace of rigor—the summers, long, but balmy, full of refreshing breezes, exquisite nights—the spot where people often come to be cool and enjoy the luxury of summer life. The mosquitoes are domestic and tame, behave quietly all day, active and stirring only at night, when we put them at defiance with our nets. As to health, bating the yellow fever, which we have all had, and therefore dread it no longer, New Orleans is just the healthiest spot in creation—where folks live the longest, and, when they do sicken, die the quickest. Even Baltimore can hardly make a showing of so many and such capital advantages as these.

"You see, therefore, how fortunate it was that my name was not brought up before the electors of your Church: for had they been pleased to unite upon me, it could only have ended in disappointment at the last. I shall be truly sorry if it turns out that the election they did make is unfortunate. As to that, let us all hope for the best; but it would not have been possible for me to come to their relief. You must try to uphold your new pastor to the utmost, and with your social gifts you can be invaluable to him. But if he should fall too far below your ideal, so that as we say out here—you cannot 'cotton' to him: why, then, eke out the deficiency by turning to your life-long friend, the almost son of your dear, grand old mother.

"In the spirit of emphasis of this last uttered sentiment, let me now say to my little sister Sallie, with what extreme pleasure I traced the cheerful, almost buoyant, lines of her last letter. I thank God, if time, the great consoler, has lightened the pressure of the dreadful grief which at first wrung such bitter wailings from a crushed heart. I have no doubt it is still there, with its great roots sunk down into the bottom of a soul that has no power of forgetting. I have no doubt that the sorrow comes back often, with its solemn tide flooding the heart anew. But then, it is a great gain, when that sorrow has its ebb, too. It is a great matter to find there is a let-up to the grief, a moment to breathe and take heart, in the intermission of the pressure which was before so constant and so heavy. It is well when we can arrest the communings with memories of what is gone; and turn once more with a healthy desire to the joys and the duties which a merciful God has still spared to us. It pleases me to hear my Bird sing again, with somewhat of the old glee which used to sparkle in her tones. Will you let me justify this a little? You remember, when the wave first broke over you, how I wrote and justified your grief? I believe in all the true instincts of nature—and therefore I said, open the gates of your heart and let the deep wail of a real grief flow out. Who should forbid you, in such an hour, the secret luxury of woe; when the only homage which love can pay to the dead is the anguish of a breaking heart? You remember, too, that when the second bereavement came, and you knelt by a mother's grave, I said love demands that you should take her place and be your mother to those who look up to you, as you looked up to her. Both these words did you good; and now I write, that a true nature will rise at length, even from such sorrow as your own to a subdued but real enjoyment of life again. It is a sickly religion and a false philosophy which teach otherwise. It is no treason against the allegiance we owe the dead, that we consent to be happy once more. It springs from no decay of the sensibilities, that we lean upon all this love that is left to us.

"My bereavements have not been comparable with yours; still they were and *are* keenly felt. But I am continually surprised to find how I am able to gather all these tender and tearful memories about me, in the consciousness that in the bosom of them all I am more deeply, yet more serenely, happy than I even was before.

"It seems a violent contradiction. But there is happiness in submission to God's blessed will—in the subdued tone which grief lends to the character. There is a sanctifying virtue in sorrow, which brings us into closer sympathy with our transfigured ones who are with the Lord. It seems as though the rest into which they have entered had thrown a soft shadow upon our own life, tranquilizing those cares which formerly chafed us. We are drawn up on a higher plane, and are nearer the blessedness of those who have gone before us. Our dead are with us; and their memory becomes personal, dwelling like a sacred presence in the soul—but the communion with these is so unfleshly, so holy, that it does not dash the earthly comfort coming up from the earthly love to those below. There is true nature in all this, and therefore a profound philosophy, of which these suggestions give but the vaguest hint. My end is answered, if you should be encouraged to cultivate all the joy you can feel in life—with the clear perception of its perfect harmony with all the devotion you desire to cherish toward the memories that are so unspeakably precious to you. It is thus God fits us for duty, and sanctifies to us the discipline of his hand.

"Please remember me to your children, whom I wish I knew—and both of whom I hope may be given you in the Lord. I have scribbled a long letter, which I trust may provoke a reply, if it does not weary you by its prosiness. Mrs. Palmer and the girls all join me in much love.

Your affectionate friend,

"B. M. PALMER."

"NEW ORLEANS, May 8, 1871.

"MY DEAR MRS. BIRD: I confess to a great disappointment that you will not be able to meet me at Athens in July, next. Not that I expected it with the extreme of confidence; for I knew it was for you a movement in the wrong direction, at that season of the year. Still it was cherished among the hopes that might be realized—and I was not aware how strong the hold was upon me, until your letter compelled me to relinquish the expectation. Indeed, Athens will not be Athens to me without the Baxters—and I begin to anticipate that my visit will be fraught with as much pain as pleasure.

"We sincerely appreciate, while running in the usual routine of life, what great changes time and death have made in the circle of those we love. Memory brings up images of the past—and we are not prepared for the vacant spaces to be encountered upon the canvas. How vividly that past will be recalled, the past of three and thirty years ago! Your father's form is as distinctly before my eye at this moment as it was then; and your precious mother, whom I have been permitted more than once to see since, is daguerreotyped upon my memory forever. Her quiet laugh, the most perfect index of her whole character, full of gentle humor and so self-contained, rings upon my ears yet. I do not know that I shall care to go to the old homestead; if I do, it will be due to the strange fascination with which our previous thoughts cling to whatever is somber in experience. But I shut down upon musings of this sort, or I shall provoke in you the melancholy I do not wish to feel myself too soon.

"In regard to the New York call, about which you so earnestly enquire, you know full as much as I do myself. If there is anything in it at all, it has been studiously concealed from me. The rumor has arisen, I apprehend, out of some correspondence held with me last winter, which some gossiping reporter has got hold of when out of date, and has rushed into print with it as a sensational item. There are parties, however, in New York, desirous of organizing a Presbyterian Church in connection with the Southern Assembly; partly out of sympathy with us, and partly out of dissatisfaction with the fusion of the two wings (Old and New School) of the Northern Church, in which they think, justly, the past solemn testimonies of the Church against doctrinal error have been compromised. These persons opened a correspondence with me, proposing to rent a public hall if I would come on and spend six or eight Sabbaths, with a view to rally those who might favor the movement, and try the strength of the party. This measure did not commend itself to my judgment: first, because the temporary assemblage of a crowd is easy enough in any great city, and would not be a test of the matter in question; second, because the movement would instantly collapse, if some one was not provided to take it up when initiated, and a failure would prejudice any future effort in the same direction; third, I clearly foresaw that I would, if successful, be thrown into an awkward dilemma either to kill the enterprise by withdrawing, or else to break faith with my people here, who naturally would not be willing to spare me for such a service without a guarantee of my return. I therefore declined the proposition; and this terminated the whole affair, so far as I am concerned. There has been no communication with me since; and if anything is lying back, I do not know of it. I suspect the whole story you have heard is that old matter refreshed. I have only space to kiss my hand and say good-bye. God bless you and your children, and fill you with peace! Write me often.

"Ever affectionately yours,

"B. M. PALMER."

It has already appeared that, in 1869, Dr. Palmer advocated the establishment of a Presbyterian University for the Southwest. He wrote, December 13, 1872, to Dr. Stuart Robinson, of Louisville, Ky.:

"It would have been a relief to me to have had a three hours' conference with you upon various matters of public interest, especially in reference to our educational policy. I was sorry that you in Kentucky took that shoot in building up a college for yourselves; and thus continuing the old policy of synodical colleges which has been so unfortunate in the past. It makes it so much more difficult to secure that coöperation without which no institution can be reared such as the age and the progress of education demand. But it is useless to discuss this matter here; perhaps it is too late in point of time. You might have secured the entire Southwest in the movement. I almost despair on the whole subject. Certainly our hold on the education of the country is gone with the reinauguration of the old policy of a college in every synod."

The subject became one of increasing interest throughout that vast region. After a few years of agitation, a result was the organization of the Southwestern Presbyterian University, under directors chosen by the Synods of Arkansas, Alabama, Memphis, Mississippi, Nashville and Texas. The directors, of whom Dr. Palmer was one, met in January, 1874, determined the name and nature of the institution, took certain preliminary steps looking to the election of a body of professors, and drew up a memorial to the Session of the First Presbyterian Church, of New Orleans, urging the brethren of that Church to give their consent to Dr. Palmer's acceptance of the office of Financial Agent of the Board for six months.

The following is the memorial:

"MEMPHIS, TENN., January 15, 1874.

"*To the Session of the First Presbyterian Church, New Orleans, La.:*

"HONORED AND DEAR BRETHREN: At a meeting of the Directory of the Southwestern Presbyterian University, held in this city on the 13th, 14th and 15th days of this month, the initial measures for the organization of the Institution, and for giving it shape, were taken. Among the first, and most important of these measures, was the appointment of an Executive Agency for the purpose of securing the requisite endowment for the support of the University. We need not say to you, that until this primary and essential object is rendered certain, the existence of the institution is impossible save in theory, and its success an end that cannot be accomplished. Another preliminary remark growing out of this, is that the enterprise of endowing such an institution is among the most difficult of all objects *at any time,* and this difficulty is greatly enhanced by the stringency of the financial condition of the country.

"Appropriate means for raising the endowment seemed to us so rarely available as to require great faith and earnest prayer to God for direction in the search for these means. As the most effective of these means we regard the selection of and sending out into the field of the suitable man to act as our agent in raising funds. Men enough were to be found who would go; but to the anxious and earnest inquiry of this Board, 'Who is the proper man?'—there came no satisfactory answer—until in this emergency, the providence of God, as we surely believe, and humbly trust, turned the attention of the Board to the beloved and honored brother who has so long and so acceptably, and with such eminent success, served you and the Church you represent, as pastor. We pray you be not startled, or shocked, at the idea, until you shall have heard us through.

"Unanimous as was this choice, there was not a member of this directory who did not entertain the most exalted conception of the pre-eminent sacredness of the pastoral relation; nor was the thought for a moment indulged of a dissolution of the relation. The very facts, that Dr. Palmer was pastor of the large and important First Church of New Orleans, and bound to you by the tenderest and strongest ties; that the Church was known and honored all through the borders of our Southern Zion, as one that wielded a vast influence for good, not locally only, but abroad as well, in the kingdom of our Savior; that the combined efforts of this pastor and his church were exerting an influence so powerful and favorable upon the cause of truth; and that this power was still moving with undiminished and increasing success—these facts, we say, tended to prevent, and did seem to forbid any of us looking for a moment in that direction.

"But when, to the surprise of us all, the name of this beloved brother was uttered in this connection, and our thoughts were turned to him, two suggestions in quick succession entered our minds:

"1. This is the finger of God's providence—this is the voice of God's Spirit; for man would not have devised the plan.

"2. This is the man, above all others, preëminently fitted for this work. Allow us then to say a word or two on some remaining points:

"1. The Directory most respectfully presents to you the earnest request that you make us the loan of the personal services of your pastor for the term of six months, that for such space of time he may act as our agent in raising an endowment for this Institution. We ask it as a loan; we hope to be able, at the termination of this service, to release him, and to restore him to his own work with you, with fitness for it undiminished, and with the love, admiration and gratitude of all his brethren of the Southwestern Church, if possible, enhanced. Of course, we pledge ourselves to furnish to him the same support pecuniarily which he receives from you, during the continuance of his service as our agent.

"2. We are very well aware that nothing in this paragraph is, of itself, an adequate motive to influence you in responding favorably to our request, and we add, therefore, that, appreciating (as we do most fully appreciate) the great sacrifice you would make in granting our request, we appeal to the higher consideration that you will, thereby, be doing service to the cause of Christ, the value of which cannot be conceived or expressed.

"In connection with this last topic, we beg to present you some considerations in their nature calculated to enforce it:

"1. The Institution we desire to establish, under the auspices of the Synods of Alabama, Arkansas, Memphis, Mississippi, Nashville and Texas (to which number we have strong hopes of being enabled, erelong, to add the Synod of Kentucky), is based upon an intellectual training of the most exalted standard, and a moral training having for its basis the Word of God.

"2. It is our purpose to raise, at the earliest possible period, an endowment fund of at least $500,000.

"3. This Institution is an absolute necessity to the Church. All institutions endowed by the State are degenerating into mere political engines; with no security against the infidel and materialistic teachings of this age, since the Church, and the religion of Jesus Christ as such, are utterly ignored; so that we are forced, in self-defense, to inaugurate this enterprise.

"4. It is of the last importance that, in the presentation of this cause, in the process of raising funds, a successful beginning should be made, for two reasons: (1) A failure at the outset may prove failure to our future; (2) A success at first may render it much easier for a succeeding agent to proceed with the work.

"5. The obstacles which are foreseen in our future progress, among which we suppose the pecuniary straitness of the times to be chief—satisfy us that no less a man—no other man than Dr. Palmer can be looked to as likely to make this beginning a success.

"6. To close this line of thought, we declare it is our firm conviction that he possesses every needed qualification to secure success. Familiar with all the elements of a grand institution such as we design, possessing the lips of persuasive eloquence, the enthusiasm of an ardent love for the cause, with a fame already coextensive with the limits of the nation, with the love and confidence of this entire people concentrated upon him, his influence, under God's blessing, we honestly believe, will ensure success.

"With these words of fraternal respect and Christian love—with the highest appreciation, on the one hand, of the sacrifice we ask you to make, and, on the other hand, taking into view the magnitude of the interests of the kingdom of Christ, involved in the establishment of the Southwestern Presbyterian University, we submit our case to your candid, prayerful consideration, praying that grace, mercy, and peace from God, our Father, and from the Lord Jesus Christ, our Savior, may be abundantly multiplied unto you evermore!

"Signed in behalf, and by order of the Directory,

"THOS. R. WELCH, *Vice President of the Directory,*

"B. M. ESTES, *Secretary of Board.*"

To this the Session responded:

"SESSION ROOMS, FIRST PRESBYTERIAN CHURCH,

"NEW ORLEANS, January 28, 1874.

"*Rev. Jno. N. Waddell, D.D., LL.D., Chancellor University of Mississippi, Oxford, Miss.:*

"DEAR SIR: The communication of your Board of Trustees of the Southwestern University, addressed to the Session of the First Presbyterian Church of New Orleans, was received in due course of mail; at an early date Session was convened to consider the same; and, as Secretary of Session, I have the honor to make known to your Board its conclusions.

"Session was not insensible to the importance of the enterprise your Board has on foot, both in respect to the education of the rising generation, and its bearings, in the future, upon the prosperity and extension of the Presbyterian Church in the Southwest: That if the Presbyterian Church expects to retain her vantage ground, earned long since by her prominence in and her devotion to all educational schemes, she must bestir herself and come up to the work demanded by the times, else other Christian denominations will leave her in the background; that the work now assigned to her in the order of importance is, first, the endowment of a University for the Southwest, and that everything contributing to that end ought to be dear to each and every heart. Such being the views of Session, with its sympathies in favor of your enterprise, it was anxious to know its duty and to perform it promptly. But in its deliberations upon the proposition of your Board to lend the services of the pastor of our Church for six months to aid in bringing before the public mind the University project with the view of creating an interest in its success that would be sure to ripen into the fruit of a liberal endowment, without which it would be seriously cramped in its operations, Session was forced to the conviction that it had not the power to separate the pastor, for so long a period, from his charge; that it could only be done by the congregation, where the authority resided. Nor was it deemed expedient to convene the congregation to lay your letter before them, as it could not be expected of a large body to act with perfect unanimity on such a subject; hence Session was compelled to decline your proposition, which it did in the following manner:

"*Resolved,* That the request of the Board of Trustees of the Southwestern University, as presented in their communication of the 15th inst., be respectfully declined, the matter therein contained not coming within the scope of Session's authority.

"The next thing to be considered was, how can Session aid your Board in this the hour of its feeble beginnings, so that no flagging shall rest upon its efforts? for it was admitted that a prominence must be given to the enterprise in order to interest the public mind up to the giving point which should be commensurate with your wants and which could only be met in an endowment fund of $500,000. Seeing that it had deprived you of your main agency in accomplishing such large results, how could the difficulty be overcome? These were considerations that did not admit of easy solution, until it was suggested that Session had the right to vacate the pulpit during the summer months, for purposes of recreation to the pastor of the Church, and that it could place in his hands leave of absence for the months of July, August and September, which, in the judgment of Session, was time ample to admit of more than an ordinary canvass of the entire field which your Board desired to have made. This it consented to do, and in this manner: Session can aid you, if not to the extent desired, at least enough for the sowing of a goodly number of seeds which under a judicious cultivation will yield an abundant harvest. Session will provide for the salary of our pastor during his temporary absence. With great respect,

"Your obedient, etc.,

"(Signed) WM. C. BLACK, *Clerk of Session.*"

Dr. Palmer's Session, Church and Presbytery were soon asked to make a much larger sacrifice than this. These Directors of the Southwestern Presbyterian University were led to think that he was the fittest man not only to raise the endowment but to establish the character of the University as a literary institution. At their May meeting, 1874, they elected him to the Chancellorship. He thoroughly believed in the importance of the projected institution; and, notwithstanding his strong personal preference for the pulpit to every other sphere of labor, he conditionally accepted the post. Almost at once he sent the following letter to his Session:

"NEW ORLEANS, LA., May 23, 1874.

"*To the Session of the First Presbyterian Church, New Orleans, La.:*

"DEAR BRETHREN: We have been associated through a period of

eighteen years; and it is with profound sadness I now lay before you a communication which will probably give you pain.

"You are aware of the effort, made within the past two years, to unite the synods of the Southwest in the support of one institution of learning for this Mississippi Valley. The proposition when first made by the Synod of Nashville to that of Mississippi received my earnest support—under a conviction that Presbyterians could not hold their ground in the matter of education without just such combination as this. But I never anticipated taking any other part in the enterprise, than such as would be perfectly consistent with my duties as the pastor of a Church. In the late meeting of the directors, however, I was caught in one of those swift currents which sometimes set in and sweep a man from the convictions of a lifetime. Indeed, I went up in my innocence to Memphis with a wholly different plan for the organization of the supposed University: when to my confusion and surprise, I found the Board already possessed with the determination to identify me fully with the endowment and organization of the institution.

"After much prayer and anxious thought I have concluded it to be my duty to accept that position, which will involve of course the dissolution of my pastoral relation with this Church.

"I have maturely weighed all the considerations which you would perhaps urge against this decision. It may not be amiss briefly to recapitulate them: For example: 1. That in the judgment of the Church at large, such gifts as I possess, both natural and acquired, lie in the direction of the pulpit. 2. The rupture of very tender ties, in separating from a people whom I greatly love, and who have evinced their affection by acts of kindness repeated through many years. 3. The extreme difficulty of settling upon another pastor, who will meet all the exigencies of the position—and who must undergo the perils of acclimation which I have surmounted. 4. The condition of the Church encumbered with debt—and the temptation to many to flake off during an interregnum, and to attach themselves elsewhere. 5. A removal from a community in which I have a recognized position of influence and usefulness. 6. The utter distastefulness of the duties to which I am first summoned, and the possible risk of failure in accomplishing the work assigned. 7. The hazard of attempting an entirely new role, at an age when habits of thought and feeling have been perfectly formed. 8. The breaking up of a pleasant home, and abandoning a handsome income for one that is much smaller and perhaps at first insecure.

"This list might be extended; but the above enumeration will suffice for one side of the question:

"On the other side it may be urged: 1. That the success of this scheme, or some equivalent, is indispensable to the life and growth of the Presbyterian Church in the Southwest. 2. That the undertaking is Herculean in this period of general prostration and distress—requiring the most efficient agency for its successful prosecution. 3. That I am called to it by the voice of six synods through their representatives —who with manifest reluctance and against their antecedent judgment, unite to urge its acceptance under the pressure of what they conceive a great emergency. 4. That failure to accomplish what has been projected and so publicly proclaimed would cover the Presbyterian name with dishonor, and be a demonstration of our weakness, from which my loyalty to the kingdom of the Master obstinately recoils. 5. The very sacrifices which are involved are such as often mark the path of duty to one who sincerely seeks only to know where it lies.

"I will not dwell upon minor considerations, which, though they occur as elements in this decision, have little independent weight. Indeed, I can say with entire truthfulness that, if the University were an existing fact, if, with only half an endowment, it were in actual operation, equipped with its corps of instructors—I would not entertain the proposition for a moment, to abandon a pastoral charge to preside over it. The question submitted to me is wholly different from this: it is whether I will shrink from any sacrifice, under God, to *create* the institution? and I find it easier to reply to this challenge, since under every conceivable view of the work imposed it calls for complete self-abnegation on my part.

"I feel bound in honor, at the earliest moment my own mind is ascertained, to reveal it first to you. Up to this moment I am uncommitted. No one outside of my immediate family has heard a word from me on the subject. It will be for you now to take it under advisement, with the assurance that I will do all in my power to aid you in the premises. My request is that you will in due time and form lay this matter before the congregation, that they may decide upon uniting with me in an application to the Presbytery of New Orleans to dissolve my pastoral connection with them.

"With a burdened heart, your brother in the Lord,

"B. M. PALMER."

"P. S.: The Board at its late meeting directed the Executive Committee to address a memorial to the Church and also to the Presbytery, on this subject."

The Session made repeated efforts to induce Dr. Palmer to change his mind. After two sessional meetings spent in conference on the subject, he still clung to his decision. The Session then urged him not to close the matter at once but to take time to think over again, the whole subject of the changes involved. Four days later he sent the following letter:

"NEW ORLEANS, LA., May 30, 1874.

"To the Session of the First Presbyterian Church, New Orleans, La.:

"BELOVED BRETHREN: I am unable to withdraw my letter of resignation, as you request; simply because my mind remains unchanged as to the supreme importance of the University movement—which, with all deference to your judgment, does not seem to me to be fully considered by you.

"I see no course to be pursued now, but to let the case go before the Presbytery of New Orleans; which, as a Constitutional Court, will be bound to look at both sides of the question, and whose decision either way will be final with me.

"I need not reiterate to you that I have no personal wishes in the matter, beyond the simple desire to ascertain the will of God in the disposal of my future labors.

"Praying for the Divine direction and blessing upon your counsels, I remain as ever,

"Yours affectionately in Christ,

"B. M. PALMER."

To this the Session replied:

"SESSION ROOMS, FIRST PRESBYTERIAN CHURCH,
"NEW ORLEANS, LA., May 31, 1874.

"Rev. B. M. Palmer, D.D., LL.D.

"REV. AND DEAR BROTHER: Session received your letter of yesterday's date and was pained to learn that your convictions were such as to render you 'unable' to withdraw your resignation, as had been requested.

"This course necessitates action on the part of Session which it had hoped to avoid, as it could only lead to pain and sorrow on the one side or the other, probably to both, for separation from your pastoral charge can only be viewed by Session and the congregation in the light of a great sorrow.

"And now, my dear pastor, as the organ of Session it becomes my duty to say to you that with great earnestness members of Session have sought to be guided in their deliberations by the Holy Spirit, so that no conclusions should be reached in the case presented by you except such as should be in accord with His mind; and if Session shall fail in its course, based as it is upon its convictions of duty, to satisfy you as to the course you should adopt, under the guidance of the same Spirit, He, the Great Head of the Church, will decide all differences betwixt us, according to the counsel of His own will.

"The conclusions reached by Session were few and simple, such as —it could not accept your resignation if it desired, having no authority to do so; nor could it be done by the congregation; nor could Session and the congregation join you in a petition to Presbytery to dissolve the pastoral tie subsisting between you and them, for this would be contrary to all their convictions of duty, and, therefore, such action on their part would involve a moral wrong.

"Whatever may be the course you shall take to dissolve the pastoral tie now existing between you and the members of the First Presbyterian Church, *Session will do nothing to aid you in it,* believing as it firmly does that the Master has not called them to such a work. Session is thankful to God for having kept you 'lo, these many years in these ends of the earth' to labor in His cause in building up the Redeemer's kingdom amongst men. If in this our reward has been greater than our merit, and if, we having failed to profit as we ought by your ministrations of the word, He now intends to move you to other fields of labor, our hearts and our prayers shall follow you, and our testimony shall always be, 'His will is our will, for His ways are not as our ways, nor His thoughts as our thoughts.'

"May the Great God guide you in all you shall do, is our prayer. With sentiments of great esteem,

"Your brother in Christ,
"(Signed) WM. C. BLACK, *Clerk of Session.*"

Their beloved pastor, without their aid, proceeded to take the steps to secure the separation, which they would in no wise aid, as the following shows:

"NEW ORLEANS, LA., June 8, 1874.

"*To Session of the First Presbyterian Church, New Orleans, La.:*

"DEAR BRETHREN: In compliance with the request of two ministers and two elders a *pro re nata* meeting of the Presbytery of New Orleans is hereby called in the lecture room of the First Presbyterian Church, New Orleans, on Friday, June 19, at 8 o'clock p.m., to consider the application of the Rev. B. M. Palmer, D.D., for the dissolution of his pastoral relations with the First Presbyterian Church, New Orleans.

"In absence of the Moderator,
"WILLIAM FLINN, *Stated Clerk.*"

The Session appointed an able member to represent it in this called meeting. The Presbytery cited the congregation to appear and set forth reasons against granting the request of their pastor, if so disposed. Sunday, the 21st, the congregation held a meeting and adopted the following paper:

"WHEREAS, The Church and congregation have at the close of the morning services been cited by the Presbytery of New Orleans to show cause on Tuesday next, the 23rd inst., in this house (if any they have) why the pastoral relation existing between Rev. Dr. B. M. Palmer and the Church should not be dissolved; and, whereas, the period for the return of the citation is short of what in the judgment of some is the requirement of the form of government of the Presbyterian Church, yet as there is a large attendance, probably larger than could be obtained by further delay, and as the subject has engaged the attention of the congregation for nearly or quite a month and the interests of pastor and people and the cause of religion in our bounds demand a speedy settlement; and the congregation now present is unanimous in its views; be it,

"*Resolved*, 1. That all objection (if any exist) as to the citation and return is waived.

"2. That the following persons, members of the congregation, viz.: J. N. Lee, J. A. Maybin, Wm. C. Black, J. D. Hill, G. O. Sweet, I. C. Morris and James Rainey be appointed commissioners on the part of the congregation to appear and answer the citation aforesaid.

3. That said commissioners be instructed to represent to the Presbytery the great unwillingness of this Church and congregation to allow of the dissolution proposed.

"4. That reposing entire confidence in the said commissioners no further instructions are given; but they are requested to inform the Presbytery that the unanimous opinion of this Church and congregation is that the work and field now assigned to Dr. Palmer far transcends in importance to the interests of the cause of Christ, the secular employment to which it is proposed to transfer him. That nearly eighteen years of ministerial labors in our midst have satisfied all, that Dr. Palmer's judgment at the beginning as to his relative qualifications for the office assumed and that of a professor in the ancient School of Theology at Columbia was right: and we have never ceased to rejoice in the persistent effort of the fathers of this Church which induced his translation. That it is mortifying to us as a people and against our just sense of the fitness of things, that after these years of intercourse and confidence and love a new field lower in the plane of spiritual activity than Columbia should be even thought of to which to translate him. That the post of preacher in this metropolitan pulpit has in the opinion of this Church and congregation not diminished in importance to the interests of religion in this region since 1856; but on the contrary increased.

"5. That the peculiar circumstances of our people generally claim for us the sympathy and confidence of all Christians, and, therefore, we deplore any action which may result in a diminution of the power and influence of the existing ministry in this city."

June 23d, the Presbytery convened. The following memorial of the Board of Directors of the University was read:

"MEMPHIS, May 18, 1874.

"*To the Presbytery of New Orleans:*

"REVEREND AND DEAR BRETHREN: The Directory of the Southwestern Presbyterian University, by a unanimous vote, did call into their service Rev. Dr. B. M. Palmer, as Chancellor of the University, and Financial Agent, and instructed their Executive Committee to prepare and forward to the First Presbyterian Church of New Orleans, of which he is pastor, and to the Presbytery of New Orleans, of which he is a member, a memorial setting forth the views they entertain of this subject, together with the reasons upon which their action is based.

"1. Importance of the enterprise. This cannot well be overestimated. All over this land the institutions for the education of our young men are struggling for existence, and the antagonistic forces which necessitate the struggle are the poverty of the people on the one hand, which prevents them from establishing the needed institutions, and the insane demand for social equality which presses upon State institutions, and thereby keeps the public mind in a state of feverish apprehension in regard to them, and prevents their patronizing them. It is, therefore, a necessity for the Church to inaugurate a larger and more extended scheme, whereby the resources of a greater number of our people may be brought together and concentrated in one grand institution which shall meet the educational wants of the Presbyterian people of the Southwest, and over which they can exercise a controlling influence, without ever being subjected to the impertinent interference of politicians, or the intrusion of unwelcome patronage. There is, in our judgment, no method whereby the desired ends in view can be secured save by the immediate establishment of one university for the Presbyterians of the Southwest.

"2. The means necessary to the success of the enterprise: We need not state to your enlightened body what these are, but we refer to this subject to present our views as to the extent of the demands and necessities of such an institution. The time has been, in the history of our country, when an endowment of a much less amount would have sufficed to establish a college or university, ample in its dimensions for the wants of the country. The curriculum of study was comparatively limited, the progress of science was respectable, but by no means extensive; the apparatus, museums, collections and appointments of this day's institutions would not have been considered necessary to adorn the institutions, and illustrate the teachings of that day, and our Presbyterian educators were then very nearly alone in the occupancy of the field.

"Now all this changed. The demand of this age is emphatically for the higher education. The vast enlargement of the area over which science has spread her operations; and the achievements and conquests of scholars in the domain of intellect and discovery; the entrance into the great sphere of efforts of so many other competitors for the prize of high attainment in practical education; the boastful arrogance of infidel institutions require and imperatively demand vast endowments in order to place our institutions upon a foundation adequate to meet the various issues of the times, and maintain our traditional pre-eminence as the educators of the land. No one community can come up to the measure of this great need. Six great Synods, therefore, propose to do this, and through a directory chosen by them they now call upon the people to furnish these means. Not less than half a million will warrant even a beginning; and to this we must add, year by year, as the Lord shall help us, until a sum shall be obtained equal to that on which the greatest and best universities of this broad land are now operating. The means—the material aid and comfort—without which we shall fail in the plan—consists of a large endowment in money, to come from the people themselves.

"3. How to obtain these means. This will never be done by appeals in eloquent language, through the press. It is idle to speak of such expedients as our main reliance. This is important. The pulpit, the press, and all other expedients together will be needed, as co-operative agencies, and it will require the combination of all to bring to bear favorably the interest and zeal of our people. But we mainly rely upon the blessing of God accompanying the personal efforts of the best man in all our connection, who shall go forth as the agent and present himself to all our people as the representative embodiment of the enterprise, authorized to set forth the nature, the necessity, the advantages, and the wants of our University; and by persevering earnestly, by persuasive appeals, by burning zeal, and eloquent words and exhortations to stir the profoundest depths of the hearts of the members of our churches, as well as those of outside friends of sound learning and solid education. We want such a man; we must have him if we can obtain him.

"4. Where is the man, and who is he? He is of your number, the honored pastor of your chief Church, a prominent member of your own body, Dr. B. M. Palmer. We ask you for him. We appeal to your love for Christ's cause, and point you to a wider field for the exercise of his God-given powers; we ask you to repress the suggestions of a blind partiality which would retain him in your connection, and curtail his influence and usefulness in a sphere too narrow, and we would urge you nobly, and generously to give him up to the service of *all the churches,* and not to *one only,* however great, and beloved—to the service of *all the presbyteries,* and not *one only,* however influential, and important its standing and position. We wish a permanent dissolution of the pastoral relation, which you alone can grant. We do not make him Financial Agent only, but to give dignity, prestige and authority to his efforts in this behalf, we have made him Chancellor; and by taking this high ground, at once show our own earnestness and our high appreciation of this beloved brother's eminent fitness for this work.

"May the common Father of us all guide you in your deliberations, and lead you to the proper decision!

"THOS. R. WELCH, *Vice President of Directory.*
"B. M. ESTES, *Secretary of the Board.*"

After this memorial had been heard, Rev. J. B. Shearer, D.D., was invited to present the subject in behalf of the University, which he did in an able and eloquent address which was listened to with profound attention. He was followed by Dr. Palmer, who gave a brief but exceedingly interesting statement of the steps by which he had been led to feel that he could not shrink from the responsibility laid upon him by the unanimous call of the Directory. With all his preferences for the pastoral work, he was entirely willing to accept the labors of the new position should it be necessary to the life of the institution; on the other hand, should Presbytery decide against dissolving the pastoral relation, he would cheerfully accept the result. He submitted the question to the decision of Presbytery.

The Commissioners from the First Church asked for time to enable them to prepare the reply. Whereupon the Presbytery adjourned to meet on the evening of the 27th inst.

At the time set, the Presbytery convened, heard an address full of feeling and impressiveness from the venerable elder, Mr. J. A. Maybin, and a very able paper of the Commissioners, through their chairman, Hon. J. N. Lee. After which the Presbytery, in the exercise of its episcopal oversight, endeavored to decide on public grounds the whole case brought before it. By a very large majority it refused to dissolve the pastoral relations and to let him pass to the service of the University.

As soon as the vote was taken, the Doctor announced his cordial acquiescence.

At an adjourned meeting on Sabbath, June 28th, the congregation passed certain resolutions expressive of their gratitude to God for the aversion of the threatened calamity of the loss of their pastor, their happiness that in the month of agitation just closed no bad feeling had been engendered, their continued devotion to their pastor, etc. They, also, resolved, "That it is the duty of this Church and congregation to show our gratitude to our dear Savior for the renewed favor he has bestowed on us in continuing our beloved pastor to break the bread of life to us, by a more devoted consecration of ourselves to his service; and that the more devoted that consecration shall be, the better shall we show thereby our appreciation of his divine favor to us."

Dr. Palmer made the following reply to these resolutions:

"NEW ORLEANS, July 5, 1874.

"To the Congregation of the First Presbyterian Church, New Orleans:

"BELOVED BRETHREN: It is proper that I should, in some form, acknowledge the resolutions adopted by you, at an adjourned meeting held on last Sabbath, and transmitted to me by the Secretary. I embrace, therefore, this first public opportunity of saying, that they have filled my heart with a new sense of gratitude to God; not only for the expressions of personal confidence and love which they contain —but even more for the pious recognition of God's own hand, in all the events which have agitated us. Undoubtedly, the pastoral relation has been subjected, in this case, to a most violent strain; and the result is a beautiful illustration of the resistance it is capable of enduring, without a rupture.

"Instrumentally, this is due to a twofold conviction: on your part, the conviction that I duly appreciated all your past kindness—kindness shown in anticipating wants before they had a chance to arise, and in promoting my usefulness both at home and abroad; on my part, the conviction that you were entirely persuaded of the honesty of my desire to serve and to do God's will in the premises—and that I was suffering the greater pain, of giving pain to those I loved. There was no misunderstanding, on either side: and the preservation of confidence was the conservation of love.

"It is no grief to me to be remanded to the work which has been the joy of my life; nor to be spared the anguish of sundering ties which have made my residence in this city so sincerely happy. Let us both return at once to the old condition of security and repose—but stimulated to more zeal, and imploring a larger blessing upon the relation which has been preserved unbroken.

"Affectionately, yours in the Lord,

"B. M. PALMER."

In the letter subjoined, Dr. Palmer summarized the whole struggle:

"NEW ORLEANS, LA., July 6, 1874.

"Rev. Dr. Robinson, Louisville, Ky.

"MY DEAR BROTHER:

. . . .

"In reference to the University, I cannot explain matters fully without covering too much paper. A complete union of the South and Southwest in a broad educational movement, has been long lying upon my heart. But the proposition that I should head the enterprise was sprung upon me suddenly, and crossed all the notions I had entertained of my life work. But upon reflection I did not feel that I could blow upon it in its very inception. I, therefore, accepted the position, notwithstanding the first duties were so entirely distasteful. But the announcement blew up all sorts of a storm down here, and the whole city came down upon me, together with the congregation. After refusing to withdraw my letter of resignation the Session declined to lay it before the congregation and stubbornly refused to take a single step until they should be compelled by presbyterial citation. The onus of convening the Presbytery was thus thrown wholly upon me, and placed me in the most direct antagonism to my own people. The case was fully and ably argued before the Presbytery, and their decision you know. Throughout, my position was painful in the extreme, for I was obliged again and again to resist the effort to make it out a case of reference; and the Presbytery was obliged to take its own responsibility in the decision. I believe that I succeeded in holding myself honestly to the University and to the position of acceptance, but in doing so, of course strained my own relations to my own people to the utmost. It is wonderful they were not ruptured; but I believe my place is firmer here than before. Indeed, apart from the sorrow that the University scheme should be embarrassed at this crisis, it is no grief to me to be remanded to the work which has been the joy of my life; and to be spared the anguish of separation from a charge which I have the best reason to love, and wish to serve.

"I must accept the conclusion as from the Lord, and feel great peace in the assurance that I stood ready before Him to do His will in all things, and to serve His cause and kingdom in any form of labor He should appoint. But all the future of our educational schemes we will talk over in September.

"I write in haste and late at night,

"Ever affectionately yours,

"B. M. PALMER."

The pastoral relation, which was near to being severed, was continued more sweetly, if possible, than before. We shall see him in his palmiest days in the period now to engage the attention.

TAKEN ABOUT 1875.

CHAPTER XV.

AT THE SUMMIT OF HIS POWERS AND PRODUCTIVITY.

(1875-1888.)

A Wonderful Preacher.—Some Characterizations of Him in the Pulpit.—A Faithful Pastor.—A Partial Summary of His Achievements in New Orleans During the First Twenty-five Years.—Call to the Presbyterian Church in Columbia, S. C., and to the Chair of Pastoral Theology in the Columbia Seminary.—History of His New Orleans Charge in this Period.—The Session.—Service in Other Courts.—An Advocate of the Co-operative Alliance with the Dutch Reformed Church.—Agitator in Behalf of Sabbath Observance.—Reaching Forth the Hand to the Old Catholics.—Continues His Opposition to "Fraternal Relations."—Opposes "Organic Union."—Opposition to Our Church's Going into the Pan-Presbyterian Alliance.—Letter to Dr. Stuart Robinson.

DR. PALMER was now at the very zenith of his powers as a preacher. He had exercised his great faculties actively and according to well-considered laws ever since he had consecrated himself to God's service in the ministry of the Gospel of His Son. He had crossed the threshold of his forty-first year growing. He crosses, not far along in the period now before us, his sixtieth year line, without the slightest indication of decadence; he crosses it growing. He was better fitted for preaching during these fourteen years than he had ever been before. In addition to the maturity of mind he had all the interpreting force that comes of schooling in sorrows. He was competent now in very deed to be a master of assemblies.

His self-possession in the pulpit was phenomenal. His people had signal illustrations of it from time to time. On one Sunday night not far from the beginning of this period,[1] "Dr. Palmer was preaching in his pulpit in his usual style, a colored woman, in the gallery, following his discourse with great apparent interest. Suddenly, during the earnest and solemn appeal, this woman threw up her hands above her head, and shouted, 'Glory, glory, glory, hallelujah!' It was an un-

[1] This incident may have occurred in the preceding period.

looked for interruption, and some of the members of the church made toward her, with the intention of removing her from the building; but Dr. Palmer, looking up toward her, said, very firmly: 'Be quiet; don't do that again;' and directing the gentlemen not to trouble her, quietly proceeded with his sermon."

Far toward the end of our present period, one Sunday night in the winter of 1886, as he was preaching to a large audience, the congregation was suddenly startled by the sound of a voice, loud and musical, breaking in upon the preacher's words. It proceeded from a lady who had risen in one of the pews; she sang in a high key, with power and accuracy, the first strain of the Aria from Handel's Messiah, "I know that my Redeemer liveth." Everyone turned to find out the source of the interruption. Dr. Palmer looked at her and said to her in a peremptory way: "That will do; sit down now." She sat down, and the Doctor went on as though nothing had occurred.[2]

With his intellectual, moral and spiritual furnishing were united a great variety of other gifts and acquirements, including a magnificent voice, easily managed, seeming never to grow old, capable of expressing every kind, and every degree, of sentiment; genius in action and bearing; and a superb diction.

The matter of his preaching was rich, full, and as varied as he saw the needs of his people. He aimed at the inculcation of the word of God in the whole length and breadth of its Calvinistic interpretation. Beginning in August, 1875, some of his sermons, one sermon each Sabbath, were taken by a phonographer, written and submitted to him for revision and then published. They were sold at twenty cents a number. This series was kept up for fifty-two weeks. The same enterprising phonographer continued the publication through a second year; and lowered his price to ten cents a number, so liberally did his people and others buy them. In the year 1883, a similar attempt was made and conducted for a good many weeks. Besides, many sermons found their way into the newspapers.

A study of these sermons, and the briefs which have never been published, shows that, on rare occasions, he was inaccurate in thought, or wanting in grasp; and that very rarely he betrayed clearly, though not offensively, a consciousness of his great reputation. But they also show that he possessed an

---

[2] These incidents were furnished by Dr. John W. Caldwell.

amazing mastery of Scripture—of the *ipsissima verba* of Scripture, so that he could quote from almost any part of it at will; that he possessed a masterful grasp of the Christian system as set forth in the Westminster Standards; and that in expounding the truth of any one text he was wont to regard it in its place as a part of that great system; that he was a noble and fearless expounder of the law, a most persuasive preacher of the Gospel, a man of ability to construe Bible teaching in easily intelligible terms of current common life, of infinite breadth and variety of illustration and argument, with a genius for planning discourses, whether in simple or complex fashion so as to exhaust the meaning of his text. He was as fond of series of sermons as ever. For example, April 1, 1877, he preached on "Truth, the Law of the Intellect;" April 8, on "Justice, the Law of the Conscience;" April 15, on "Love, the Law of the Heart;" April 22, on "Obedience, the Law of the Will." Between January 27, and April 28, 1878, he delivered ten lectures on the first twenty-three verses of the Eleventh Chapter of Hebrews. Between October 22, 1882, and January 7, 1883, he gave twelve lectures on the first six chapters of the Book of Acts. He was, as appears from all these sermons, a man of splendid pictorial powers, and an almost absolute master of the pathetic.

He rarely, he almost never, wrote a sermon prior to its first delivery. Thereafter when asked to do so, he would, sometimes, reduce a sermon to written form. His manner of preparation continued to be to form an outline more or less full, usually rather full when time permitted; and then, walking the diagonal in his study to think it through and through. When he came to the pulpit, he came with neither scrap nor line, and gave re-birth to his thought with all spontaneity and freshness.

The impression made, during this period, upon his auditors by Dr. Palmer as a minister of worship may be conveniently set forth by calling some of those who heard him to the witness stand. The Rev. Wm. Frost Bishop wrote, February 11, 1885, from New Orleans, to the *St. Louis Presbyterian:*

"Sunday morning, upon entering the Church, I found it crowded to the very door. Approaching the sexton or usher, I said: 'Please give me a good seat: I am a stranger here.'

"To this he replied: 'No seats are left, except the chairs in front of the pulpit, and they are for gentlemen accompanied by ladies. You had better go into the gallery.'

"Finding all seats in the gallery occupied, I walked boldly forward and seated myself on the steps in the left gallery and within sixty feet of the speaker.

"Dr. Palmer was reading an account of our Lord's passion, as given in John's Gospel at the eighteenth chapter.

"There was a peculiar tenderness in his voice, and I was early persuaded that the preacher had been in the sick room a great deal during the past week, or else in the house of affliction.

"In the prayer which followed the reading, he prayed very beautifully, and touchingly for one of his flock, 'smitten with a disease from which there was no earthly escape.'

"He offered special petitions that she might be reconciled to the Divine will and made ready for the change. Nor did he forget the little children, who should lose by this providence a mother's care. There was something deeply touching in his allusion to these little ones.

"While the collection was being taken up, I looked around the audience. There were over one thousand five hundred persons present.

"Dr. Palmer announced the following as his text: 'The cup which my Father gave me, shall I not drink it?" John 18: 11. He wore a vest cut very low, exposing a great deal of white linen, and the coat was left unbuttoned. His enunciation was distinct and his delivery deliberate. This calmness of manner continued till the chariot wheels took fire toward the close of the sermon, which lasted an hour and ten minutes.

"The great preacher began his sermon in the simplest manner possible, describing the closing conflict of our Lord's life, with occasional flashes of interpretation which showed that he had studied the context carefully and also that a storm of eloquence was gathering.

"About the close of his introduction, a passing band of music so filled the house with its din and noise that the speaker's voice was scarcely audible. This lasted for a minute or more, but Dr. Palmer did not seem to notice it. The audience, too, behaved remarkably well.

"The subject was treated first in reference to Christ, the motives which lay back of his submission, such as the cup coming from the Father and none else—its being a cup and therefore a *limited* measure of suffering—its being a token of a covenant relation—the suffering being the vestibule of the glory which should follow. These and like considerations were presented with great power. He also unfolded for us the pregnant comment of Dean Alford, that 'the cup here spoken of had allusion, no doubt, to the cup of the Lord's Supper.' The old economy, with the paschal lamb, died in the act of giving life to the new dispensation of the Christian Sacrament.

"The second application of the subject was to the sufferings of believers. The great preacher had not proceeded far with this theme when I perceived that he was moving upon what a certain poet has termed 'the unknown seas of feeling' in my heart. I tried to show myself a man and keep my handkerchief in my pocket—but it was no use. The man who sat next to me was rough and unlettered—a man of the world. He found it convenient, just at this time, to brush his rough hand over his eyes, in order to see better. I looked down upon the one thousand people beneath me, and they reminded me of 'the tops of mulberry trees' when the wind is shaking them. The men were shielding their faces with their palm leaf fans, while their wives made public use of the handkerchief. It was the most *effective* eloquence I had ever known. A pew in the center of the Church arrested my attention. At either end were the parents, now melted under the eloquent and powerful description of the sufferings of the human heart. Between them were three sweet children, with nicely dressed hair and broad, white collars, turned down over their nicely-fitting jackets. One was writing upon the fan which he held in his lap; another was toying with a bit of string, while the third was softly slumbering, with its head in its mother's lap. How suggestive and how touching! How it carried me back to the sunny days of childhood! I have no doubt that those little ones thought the sermon long and uninteresting, but their parents were feeding upon the manna of the Gospel and gaining strength for the battle of life.

"I have no words to tell you of the soaring thoughts which marked the close of Dr. Palmer's sermon, in which a comparison was instituted between philosophy and religion. There was the unction of Spurgeon with the eloquence of Beecher.

"Walking away with the preacher and his family from the Church, I ventured to ask why the speaker had chosen the theme of suffering for such an audience of strangers and men of the world. The reply was, 'I have reached the conviction that the best way to reach the unregenerate is to show him what Christianity is able to do for the believer.'"

Of the next Sunday's services, Dr. Bishop writes:

"A thing happened on this great day—the famous *Mardi Gras* Sunday, which carnival by the way he was accustomed to call a 'carnival of pasteboard and tinsel'—a thing happened which was remarkable in every way. It was well that his pulpit was of marble and firmly anchored to the floor, for it had that day to sustain a greater weight than that of the big pulpit Bible.

"He was preaching from the passage in Matthew which tells of the prophecy of 'Jeremy the Prophet' and the thirty pieces of silver paid for the 'potter's field' (Matt. 27: 9). Amid breathless silence he startled his audience by announcing that no such passage as that quoted by

Matthew and ascribed to Jeremiah, nor any passage similar to it, is found in Jeremiah or was ever found there. Here was a difficulty. Were the Scriptures trustworthy? He stated the point with great force. Worse yet, he found the quotation and read it from Zechariah 11: 12. This simply made bad matters worse. Matthew had said the prophecy was in Jeremiah. It was not. In addition to this, it never could have been at any time in Jeremiah, for it was found actually to be a quotation from Zechariah. The suspense was painful, the congregation suffering. After a slight pause the speaker said: 'We shall have to go a little deeper, my brethren, than the surface, in order to know the mind of the Spirit of God, the author of these Scriptures.' And, then, by an exegesis both skilful and brilliant, as well as satisfactory, he found the *original* prophecy, not in Zechariah but in Jeremiah, as Matthew had said, the key of the whole passage in dispute being given in Jeremiah 32: 6, 8. His vindication of Matthew was triumphant, and the effect upon the audience—after its painful suspense —was electrical.

"At this point the strange incident happened. Taking advantage of the victory he had just won upon the field of exegesis, the sympathy of the people being now with him in thorough appreciation, Dr. Palmer was delivering an apostrophe to heaven, praising God with every fibre of his being for the inestimable gift of an inerrant Scripture, and not only praising God but triumphing in the fact of such a gift. I sat just behind him in the pulpit. When he began the apostrophe, his face was toward the South, the main audience to his left and the pulpit desk just at his back. His hands at the start were stretched to heaven, and his head thrown back. As the eloquent language of adoration and eulogy poured from his lips, his body leaned back more and more upon the marble pulpit behind him till at length first his shoulders and then the weight of his entire body rested upon the pulpit, and his arms fully extended toward heaven and his feet scarcely touching the floor. Was there ever such an attitude in the pulpit! The reading desk was low, reaching to the small of the back, the Bible itself yielding as a pillow support to his head. Yet, the pose was graceful, and the prostration backwards was begun, continued and ended without the slightest offence to good taste. But, surely, no one except Dr. Palmer could have done it."

Some months farther along in the period, we have from the pen of a gifted correspondent of the Louisville *Courier-Journal* a still greater tribute to the power of our subject, when on his pulpit throne:

"NEW ORLEANS, January 22.—At New Orleans lives and ministers one of the greatest divines of his time. His eloquence is an era in pulpit oratory; and, here, is almost wasting, as it were, a stream that should refresh and invigorate the nation. His pulpit ministrations are a school to which theological students might well resort, both to be enlightened by Scriptural exegesis, and to learn 'action and utterance' untaught in books. For this noble orator suggests that the Horatian utterance as to the poet may be applied, with a little change of application, to the orator: *"Orator nascitur, non fit."* I do not know whether he went through the laborious training of voice and gesture that Demosthenes, Bolingbroke, Mansfield, and Chatham did, or whether he at all drilled himself in the technique of the rhetoric school. But I do know that I never saw such amplitude, roundness, finish and felicity of action as I have seen in him. No mood or mode of utterance but finds aptness, grace, apparently unstudied ease of gesture as its concomitant. From the action to comport with the acumen that analyzes and elucidates (with the 'dry light' of nicest ratiocination) the most abstruse topic, to that which is adapted to the most soaring and impassioned flight—all is harmonious. He never 'saws the air with his hand,' never 'tears a passion to tatters.' His action is never feeble, commonplace, inapt, inane, overdone, ungraceful. Except to a watchful artist, it would never distract or consciously delight, separately from the thought; for action is subordinated to utterance, intended to support and enforce it. The truly sympathetic auditor never sees any rhetoric in the man.

"If Demosthenes' definition of eloquence, 'Action, action, action,' be true, then is Rev. B. M. Palmer, D.D., a great orator; for 'action' informs and possesses him. If Cicero's definition be true, *'Sapientia copiose loquens,'* he is a great orator, for he is wise, and discourses at length. Not that his sermons are too long—he speaks generally in morning service about an hour—but his breadth of view generally lays bare the marrow of his theme. Col. Wm. Preston Johnston, the polished and erudite president of Tulane University here—himself a scholar, author and student—told me, in conversation about Dr. Palmer, that he intended to construct some Greek word which should express a feature of oratory that Dr. Palmer had added to its large field, so largely had the latter expanded its grand domain by his superb gifts and his glorious innovations.

"But, let us look a little more minutely at the *armamentaria coeli* this wonderful divine possesses. He is a very ripe scholar, and keeps conversant with the rich old tongues of Greek and Rome. And he not only has the key to, but has explored and possessed the treasures of these languages. While he is never pedantic, his erudition is ever and anon cropping out in illustration, comparison, in comment on the force and meaning of words in Scripture. The literature of these languages has left its humanizing stamp upon his thought and speech. I think, too, he is a Hebrew scholar, but of this I cannot judge. In ecclesiastical lore he is well versed, and has drunk deeply of the wells of the Holy Fathers.

"With the classics of English literature it is impossible to doubt his conversancy. He has read and remembers Hooker, Barrow, Jeremy Taylor, Milton, Shakespeare. With the English text of the Holy Bible he is very familiar. And from that 'pure well of English undefiled' he often enforces his thoughts in most fitting and forcible quotation. He is a great logician, too; and while hardly ever reasoning with the formulas of the art, his cogent and crushing argumentation shows this phase of intellectual equipment. Never a formal and avowed controversialist against modern heresy and the rampant rationalism of the day, he hits them some tremendous and trenchant 'side blows,' as he digresses for a moment to commend the solaces of and solidity of the Christian religion, or warns his hearers against the emptiness, fallacies and seductions of modern unbelief.

"He seems in the very zenith of his intellectual powers, with ripe judgment, a warming, but not dominating imagination; an exquisite taste and vast stores of erudition. His imagery is apt, original, very illustrative and enforcing, at times sublime, seeming spontaneous, and he works his bold and burning metaphors into the very texture of his style. His diction is never labored, often very nervous, often elegant, oftener sublime. His sentences seem unstudied. There is a little antithesis or epigram. Never mechanical system or measured cadences. The all-pervading air of sincerity prevents the suspicion (or soon dispossesses one of it) of display. Self is utterly wanting. The Gospel is the overshadowing, burning theme.

"With the largest capabilities for sentence building, word painting, diction embossing, there is no hint, nor suggestion of phrase mongering. At times, when one yearns for a word or two of glowing color (which he could easily utter), or a touch of rhythm to periods (which his melodic mind could bestow, and his mellow organ deliciously voice), he nobly disdains the opportunity, retreats from the temptation to tickle the ear and taste, and projects the Gospel, and hides himself behind the cross. Here his noble self-abnegation is most striking, for instead of glorifying himself he glorifies God. This absence of claptrap, to the true Christian, has, however, a higher effect than the highest art. but is in the very highest and best spirit of art, as it is in the highest spirit of a Christian.

"I have heard many pulpit orators whose best utterances fly around the head, but come not near the heart. But there are none of the devices and artifices of rhetoric; no clap-trap, rhodomontade or period rounding in Dr. Palmer's sermons. Amplitude of survey, acumen, cogency of reasoning, force of phrase and statement, lucidity of enunciation, harmonious proportion of treatment, resistance of digression and discursiveness, the capability of throwing away unnecessary ideas —all mark his sermons.

"Then he is utterly free from bigotry—unsectarian, catholic in spirit, and a man of most fervent piety, blameless life, an endeared pastor.

"So much for some traits of the moral and intellectual side. But we have seen many scholars, logicians, eminent divines in piety and pastorship who were prosy and droning in the pulpit. They could rend infidelity, could pin heterodoxy to contempt by an epigram; knew roots to the bottom; but one could hardly keep awake while they preached. We pity anyone who can sleep within sound of Dr. Palmer's voice. His voice is large, yet flexible; mellow, yet penetrating and sonorous, with a roundness and smoothness remarkable in one of such power. His whispers (when he whispers), can be heard anywhere in the large auditorium where he preaches. When in his leonine mood his voice swells and thunders until 'earth and air seem loud.' Its inflections and cadences are very rich and varied; terrible and harsh in warning of divine wrath; soft and tender and wooing in invitation to acceptance of Divine mercy; triumphal, soaring and mighty in adoration. His features are very flexible and have a wonderful scope of play—his face rippling and fluid with expression. At times there seems an aureole about his head like the glory the old masters painted about the faces of their saints. Then a supernal light invests his features, and he seems almost all ensouled. The place to see him, at such supreme moments, is in the gallery. With head thrown back until you would think he must fall, with almost transfigured face, uplifted hands and pealing voice, he is one of the most sublime and enthralling spectacles of earth.

"His felicity, force, originality and polished grace of action I have spoken of briefly. The finicality and coxcombry of the mere elocutionist, the hollow and ostentatious charlantry of the mere rhetorician are ever absent. But his action, in aptness, amplitude and, what I would term a glorious felicity, is past description and enumeration. And yet, so subordinated and adjusted is it to support and enforce thought, that the most bold and original action is hardly noticed, consciously. I have seen him perpetrate feats and gestures that, dissociated from the utterances, would seem grotesque. His spell must be upon you for such to be tolerated. This shows the charm of his eloquence.

"Under the inspirations of the moment, he 'snatches a grace beyond the reach of art,' and as I have said rhetoric has, in his cadences and gestures, a vast field from which to gather treasures.

"In thinking of Dr. Palmer's style, I have been, almost without effort, comparing him with great pulpit orators I have heard, and with descriptions of great public and forensic orators. In throes and almost convulsions of vehemence, in his rapt moods, I am reminded of descriptions of Charles James Fox. but only as to the torrent of feeling possessing the latter, for he had 'broken sentences, ungainly gestures,' as well as the 'choking of his voice,' 'his sudden starts of passion,' and 'the absolute scream with which he delivered his vehement passages.' There are no 'broken sentences,' 'ungainly gestures,' in Dr. Palmer's oratory. And if, at times, there is 'the choking of his voice,' it is in the sublimity of 'the mating mood,' when drowned in tears, floods of pathos deluge the hearts of hearers.

"I call to mind characteristics of Chatham, the transcendant mien, the trumpet voice, the flashing eye and far-reaching glance, the mighty commanding gesture, the glorious bursts, so enthrilling, the tremendous union of fire and reason—when, as a great writer says of him: 'All went together, conviction and persuasion, intellect and feeling, like chain-shot.' I have got past the age of easy illusions, and spells and influences denying analysis. Therefore, when enchained and entranced, I know there must be a mighty magic at work. Until personal intercourse dispelled the impression, I thought Dr. Palmer a man of great stature, whereas he is rather under medium height. But, so majestic and august is his port in the pulpit, in his swelling scenes, that I thought him as lofty in stature, almost, as in mood.

"And I have heard from most dispassionate judges that Dr. Palmer excels any living pulpit orator of English tongue. I know not his style in earlier days, but in the past two years, when I have heard him very frequently, he is prone to what Shakespeare terms those sublime

"'Tempests, torrents and whirlwinds of passion.'

"His style in these most impassioned flights is an

"'Eagle's flight, forth and right on.'

"He is possessed by these red-hot moods, and pours floods and torrents of molten eloquence upon his auditors as though he were a cataract of holy fire. He is then Titanic and absolutely enthralling, and seems almost like a divine energy incarnate. A transcendent light irradiates his countenance. A holy vehemence seizes his frame and convulses him with its transports. His voice peals and soars like some supernal sounds. His frame seems to dilate to superhuman proportions. He lifts his sympathetic auditor, in a spell of devout entrancement, through flights of exultation to thrilled and almost breathless listfulness. At such times he seems most worthy of all men, in any earthly action, of that passage in 'Hamlet' in Shakespeare's apostrophe to man:

"'In action, how like a God.'[3]

He continued throughout this period, as he had shown himself before, one of the best of pastors. His life was ever full

---

[3] Signed M. B. H.

of care for his flock. It was his wont to stir up the stronger members to look to the comfort and well-being of the weak. In practical beneficence he himself set the example. Of his own money he gave to the needy, often too freely; he has been known to send the comfortable chairs from his own study to the chambers of frail old people in reduced circumstances. He was neither too great nor too busy to think of serving God's little ones in such wise.

"Always a pastor he looked particularly after his flock in times of storm and trial. For example, when the yellow fever broke into an epidemic in the year 1878, he was absent from his field. But he went straightway back. He writes to his 'dear sister,' Mrs. Edgeworth Bird:

"The summer of '78 was a dreadful summer. We were having a high time at the Virginia Springs with some old friends whom we have known almost as long as we have known you, and loved almost as much, when we were hurried home to witness nothing but sickness and death for months together. The worst personally to us was, that we had to bring our motherless pet right into the jaws of the pestilence—perhaps to close her little eyes in the long sleep, with the agonizing sense of our own responsible agency in the dreadful exposure of the helpless innocent so dependent upon our care.[4] It required some nerve; but the nerve did not belong to me. I pleaded with the grandmother to remain in Tennessee, as the keeper of the young life. But the logic was short which cut through the knot. 'You are obliged to return to New Orleans, and, therefore, I must go; therefore, must she.' Oh, these *quiet* women, like your own dear mother, how they always have their own way! Within ten days, the little darling went down under the plague, and God in his mercy spared her to us. This was the baptism of trial which awaited us on our arrival; and then God's restoring grace, in giving back to us our babe, gave me strength to go through the rest. You will form some idea of the trial, when I state that during three months, I paid each day from thirty to fifty visits, praying at the bedside of the sick, comforting the bereaved, and burying the dead; and that, too, without intermitting the worship of the Sabbath or even the prayer meeting in the week."[5]

He served as pastor to many beyond the bounds of his own communion. A case of this kind is referred to in the subjoined letter:

---

[4] A remarkable feature of the pestilence of the summer of 1878, was its fatality among children, the proportion of children under ten, to adults dying, running as high as seven to ten.

[5] From letter dated October 8, 1879.

"HOTEL GERARD, 123 W. 44th St.

"MY DEAR MRS. CALDWELL: My sympathy is so deep that I risk intruding upon your grief to express my regret for the death of our great and good soldier of Christ who has gone to his reward. About a year before my husband died he became very restless and announced his intention to go to New Orleans. We had several guests in the house and I suggested his waiting until Monday, but he said decidedly, 'I want to go to-day.' It was Saturday. He came back on Monday evening very calm and cheerful. In a day or two he said, 'I went to commune with Dr. Palmer, and it has done me a world of good.' I asked him if Dr. Palmer would accept an Episcopalian at his communion table. He answered, 'Dr. Palmer would never break a bruised reed.' Something had disquieted him greatly and he went to Dr. Palmer for comfort. When your great and dear father did me the honor to call when I was last in New Orleans I meant to have told him this, but as is usual with me on such precious occasions a stranger interrupted the conversation and Dr. Palmer left. I think he was the only man with a great reputation and large following of whom I never heard an evil word; and a proud privilege is yours to be his child.

"That our merciful Father may send his Comforter to you is the prayer of

"Yours with deepest sympathy,

"V. JEFFERSON DAVIS.

"June 3, 1902."

Along with a recapitulation of his labors and achievements generally, we have a further glimpse of his pastoral toils, in a letter written by his venerable father to Mrs. I. M. Hutson:

"NEW ORLEANS, January, 1882.

"MY DEAR DAUGHTER: I promised in my last to give you some items of your brother's Herculean labors, in his own circle, which may be interesting to you, as they are certainly honorable to him. You may detect a good deal of pride in me, as to this matter—but I hope, mingled with that, you may allow a due measure of holy gratitude to the Bestower of the gifts upon him, by which he was enabled to accomplish so much, and lay it all at the feet of the blessed Master.

"The last Sabbath of the outgoing year was his church silver wedding day—completing twenty-five years of ministerial labor in the city of New Orleans, and in the First Presbyterian Church in the place. It happily occurred to him to investigate his church records, in order to get at the fruits or results of the labors of a quarter of a century—a thing he had never before attempted to accurately ascertain. During that period there had been received into the communion of the church about seventeen hundred individuals, or, on an average, sixty-one or sixty-two persons each year, sometimes more, and at other times less. The number of baptisms, together with that of marriages, deaths, funerals, etc., he could not accurately articulate; but of course they were in union with, if not in number, greater than the admission of members. He then showed me the list of families which he had annually to visit, some once, twice, or more, according to providential dispensations, and the number amounted to three hundred and forty, so that on his visiting days, which were usually the first four days after each Sabbath, he had to pay from three to ten daily calls in order to meet the demands. Then add to them the numerous private visits in his study, many of which, very naturally, were of an important character, and you have a survey of what the cost ot time, labor and thought must be, and that without cessation.

"One is ready to ask, Where is his time for *study?* Oh! It is in this view, and under these circumstances that the *peculiar gifts* of Providence become manifest. He is able to do a great deal in a comparatively little time. His brain-work is as rapid as a railroad engine, and as bright and clear as a sunbeam, and his *memory* as retentive and faithful as a well-regulated clock — God's gifts, I have remarked. Now think of the expanding outer circle, called *here and there,* by *night* and by *day*—with *friends* and with *strangers,* in *high places* and in *low,* for *this thing* and *that thing* and the *other thing*—and you have the sum total of his stupendous work. I stand amazed at the amount; and yet I have said nothing of two sermons each Sabbath and two weekly evening services. What shall we say but that God gives him the strength, the ability, and the grace to endure and perform it all. Let *Him,* the *Giver,* have all the glory. . . ."

In the spring of 1881, the Board of Directors of Columbia Seminary elected Dr. Palmer to the Chair of Pastoral Theology. The Assembly of that year heartily endorsed the election, while refusing to express a hope that Dr. Palmer would see fit to leave New Orleans for Columbia, S. C. The church at Columbia had also called him to serve them as pastor, that church and Seminary working in unison to capture him. He seems to have given the call careful and faithful consideration. But June 12, he announced to his congregation that he had decided to decline the call to Columbia. He and his friends in the Southwest and in other parts of the Church, thought that his opportunities for usefulness were greater where he was, and that the interests of the Church at large demanded that he should stay there. Certainly he was doing a great work in New Orleans.

His church, it is true, did not seem to grow fast in numbers.

The roll of communicants numbered six hundred and fifty-eight, in 1875. It was reported as containing six hundred and thirty-five in 1888. The total of children in Sunday-schools in 1875, is given as one thousand six hundred and nine; the total in 1888, was eight hundred and eight. Business reverses had been felt by many of his members about 1880; and the church which had found it so easy to raise money for its enterprises found itself burdened to carry on some of these undertakings. In consequence, the Sylvester Larned Institute property was sold in the summer of 1881. But he had no just ground in all these things for discouragement. Had he and his session preferred, they might have boasted, in 1888, a communicant roll of seven hundred and seventy; they preferred to reckon as members only those on the ground, for whom they were able to account. Moreover, the population was in part shifting. If his numbers did not considerably increase, the cause was not that he did not receive members on profession and by letter; but that there were frequent removals from his flock to other parts of the country, and many deaths. A colony had been sent off, too, to establish the Carrollton Church early in 1880-5. The great decrease in the roll of children in the Sunday-schools, explained in part by the abandonment of one point where they were hopeless of final results, and by giving up control of the little school that had been conducted at Carrollton, left in the thinned ranks scholars of a much higher level and worth; the good work was carried on all the more vigorously with the remnant. The business reverses and the loss of consecrated, wealthy members, were repaired as the years went by. The yearly contributions of his church to all causes would perhaps average $20,000, throughout the period. One year it ran up to $33,881.

"If he and his noble session mourned the inroads of worldliness into his flock—especially 'amongst the more fashionable females'—the prayer meeting, 'the thermometer of spiritual life in a congregation,' was thronged to the capacity of the lecture room, by his own members and by strangers. He had great audiences to preach to, composed in part of his own people and in part of sojourners who wished to hear him break the bread of life. The exposition year was a year of vast audiences for him. In the Records of the Session, April 1, 1885, we read, 'Since the opening of the Exposition in our city, the church building has been thronged much beyond its seating capacity, by an audience of strangers exceedingly respectful and reverential. It has been a rare opportunity for sowing the seed of the Word broadcast over the whole country, which will doubtless yield its harvest in eternity.' "

The session of Dr. Palmer's church continued a noble session. Exercising much care in the reception of members into the church, they were called on to apply severe judicial discipline in relatively few cases. Some such cases are recorded in their minutes. For certain of their members, not guilty of offences in the technical sense, they were sorely exercised. Over and over they deplore the fact that, in their pleasure loving city, professors of Christianity are under so many temptations to "conform to the world in some things greatly to be regretted;" declaring that the only "remedy is to be found in deepening the religious experience, and in educating the conscience to appreciate more clearly the distinction which should lie between the Church and the world:" and that "until this can be accomplished, external discipline would prove only divisive and harmful, tearing up the wheat along with the tares."

The session lost some of its most valuable members: Mr. Joseph A. Maybin, May 14, 1876, of whom his pastor said, "I have never known anywhere on the face of this earth an elder who could approach Mr. Maybin in the zeal, in the constancy, in the fidelity, in the patience, with which he did the work of an elder in visiting the flock of God and being a shepherd in the household of faith;" Mr. Wm. C. Black, November 30, 1879, a man of the most robust Christian and Calvinistic faith, into whose virtues the strength of the Divine life had been infused, whom Providence and Grace had wrought together to make a pillar in the house of God and in society in general; and Mr. Wm. Allen Bartlett, March 23, 1882, the sympathetic friend of the poor and the sorrowing, the aggressively active agitator for the cause of his Master. These removals left but five ruling elders in the year 1882, viz.: E. S. Keep, J. P. Hardie, T. G. Richardson, W. F. Ogden, and J. B. Woods. But at the beginning of the new year the Presbyterate was again strengthened by the election of Messrs. W. T. Hardie, T. J. McMillan, John J. Barr, and L. T. Turner.

A great leader in his own local church and session, he was

not less a leader in the several courts above, viz.: the Presbytery, the Synod, and the General Assembly, in which last body he sat in the years 1875, 1881 and 1887. Ever modest, his efficiency in counsel and cogency in debate were such that his brethren would have him to the front. Nay, he was himself eager to take a hand when possible without unseemly obtrusiveness; delighting to quicken and empower the aggressive movements of the Church against the world and zealously guarding the Church that she might not further contaminate herself by compositions with the world.

The correspondence with the Dutch Reformed Church, which was begun by our own body, in 1871, for "the cultivation of a mutual sympathy and brotherly love," ripened. In 1873 a committee, of which Dr. Palmer was a most important member, was appointed to prepare a plan of "co-operative alliance." He reported the perfected plan to the Assembly of 1875, which adopted it. This plan embraced features of co-operation in publication, home missions, foreign missions, and education.

He was ready for co-operation on a wider scale than this where it involved no subordination of principle. This is proven by his headship of the Sabbath Observance League of New Orleans.

To the preservation of the Sabbath he gave much thought and energy. He maintained that the obligation to observe the Sabbath is perpetual and universal, resting on man as man, and extending to all generations and all classes. He contended that this view flows from the following facts: "1. That it was appointed by Divine authority at the beginning of time; 2. That it was given to the first man, in whom, as their natural root and covenant head, the whole race was comprehensively included and putatively existed; 3. That it was sanctified and blessed by Jehovah, as the emblem of that rest which the holy should enjoy forever; 4. That it was the memorial of the Creator's work, in which all mankind are through all ages equally interested; 5. That it was perpetuated through all the dispensations of the Church, and through all the changes in her outward economy; 6. That it is incorporated in the moral law, in the bosom of precepts, every one of which is universal in its obligation upon the race; 7. That the Divine testimony to its continual obligation becomes more full and solemn as Divine revelation increases in volume and bulk; 8. That in the last dispensation of all it is made the attesting seal of that salvation by grace, in which every sinner upon the earth is equally concerned." He believed that on the Sabbath "man, as at the beginning" should bring "his whole being and time as an offering to God; just as in his charities he" should consecrate "all his possessions to the Giver from whom they were received."

He lamented bitterly that this obligation does not receive a universal response; and that in our age the Sabbath is assailed not only by its old-time foes of infidelity and cupidity, but these reinforced by the growing prevalence of the "Continental views," a "leprous taint" affecting public opinion; and by "a far more subtle and potent influence," "the complex and materialistic character of our civilization," illustrated in "the system of railroads and telegraphic communication, which has revolutionized the old modes of commercial business," and which has spread like a vast network over the continent, North, South, East and West.

Upon the practical question: What should the Church do under the circumstances? he gave a two-fold answer: *First,* Within her own sphere the Church should: 1. As a faithful witness for the truth of God, hold aloft, without the least abatement of its rigor, the law of God, and bear a constant testimony against the sin of Sabbath-breaking; 2. "With the watchful eye of a mother inspect the conduct of her children," striving "to quicken the conscience so that it shall have nice perceptions of Christian duty and assist by her counsels in resolving questions of doubt." "In all manifest and flagrant breaches of the Sabbath by such as profess the religion of Christ," the Church should in the exercise of patient and loving disciples, wield the "authority which the Lord hath given her for edification and not for destruction." *Second,* The Church should bring her influence to bear on the secular authorities, not by demanding, in her organized capacity, Sabbath legislation. The Church's battles are to be fought not with the weapons of Caesar but of Christ. The State, if it be pleased to make Sabbath legislation, must do it on different grounds from those on which the Church is bound to ground the rights of Sabbath observance. "If the Church as such appears on the arena and carries the cause through her influence and government, then the door is open to wider evils than this from which she seeks to escape. The line between the civil and the ecclesiastical jurisdictions is obliterated." "But what she cannot undertake in her organized form she may accomplish through her members as citizens of the Commonwealth. They may combine as individuals to any extent; and as component parts of the State, they may plead for the Sabbath upon any grounds which the State shall feel itself competent to admit, and upon the validity of which it may be able to pronounce." These views in substance he agitated before his Presbytery, and Synod, and, through his Presbytery, laid them before the Assembly's committee.[6] He secured the passage of resolutions bearing not on their own members only, but enjoining that every "effort should be made by official correspondence and private intercourse, to bring all branches of the Church into line, for the common defence and perpetuation of the Sabbath."

In accord with the resolutions, he and his fellow presbyters, in the city of New Orleans, invited to a conference on the subject representatives of the different forms of religious belief obtaining in that cosmopolitan city. "The response to the invitations was general and cordial. There were representatives of the Romish Church appointed by the Archbishop; and a prominent Jewish Rabbi also took part in the proceedings." A platform was agreed upon, which was supposed fairly to represent the moral sentiments of the community, and which they hoped would rally the better classes of the whole community to the support of the movement.[7]

From this time on, for years, he was the virtual head of this league. There was nothing meanly narrow in him. He was too true a Presbyterian. If he had decided and clean cut views as to what his own Church should hold he always coupled with that a readiness to acknowledge all that was good in men of other faiths and to cowork with them for any common end.

To many it would seem rather incongruous that Dr. Palmer's Presbytery should be addressed by a representative of the Old Catholic movement. This, nevertheless, happened in 1879. By the Presbytery's invitation Father Vaudry addressed it on the Old Catholic movement, of which he was a representative. The Presbytery was careful to set forth its view that the movement

[6] See Minutes of Synod of Mississippi, 1881; and of Presbytery of New Orleans, 1881, 1882.

[7] The Constitution of this "Lord's Day League" may be seen in the *Southwestern Presbyterian*, April 20, 1882, p. 5.

was defective in that it protested against corruptions in discipline rather than against more radical errors in the Romish Church; but it felt that the movement was in the right direction, and should be encouraged. Under such convictions and satisfied of his purity of life and honesty of purpose, the Presbytery extended to Mr. Vaudry "the hand of encouragement and hope, praying that in his important and difficult mission he may be upheld and guarded by the power and the wisdom from above."

These and other such services, which he, as a representative of the Church in wider spheres, performed, seemed wholly consonant with his character, which was thoroughly amiable, kind and Christian. Other struggles which he waged, to some even of his admirers, have seemed discordant with that character. A friend of his, a distinguished Jewish Rabbi, says, however, that they were not discordant; that the explanation of his character and life is to be found in his devotion to righteousness, and that in these efforts under contemplation "Palmer was just simply following the right as he saw things."

Of these efforts, one was the vigilant and ever-ready opposition to the establishment of "official correspondence" with the Northern Presbyterian Church, on any such terms as the Southern Church was able to secure from the Northern. His life cannot be reproduced without a sketch of the struggle that went on between the two Churches and, at length, within the Southern Church itself. Such a sketch he himself published in the *Southern Presbyterian Review* for April, 1883. In it his own history, in connection with the subject, is involved, for, as he was heard to say, in debating a kindred subject, four years later, he was "connected with this matter from the start." This now, is the history of the struggle, given at the cost of some brief partial repetitions, over the establishment of fraternal relations as he saw it, viz.:

"The original policy of the Northern Church toward the Southern was not that of *conciliation*, but of *conquest*. When their Assembly convened at Pittsburg in May, 1865, the war had terminated in the surrender at Appomattox, and the South lay prostrate under the heel of the conqueror. Not a tear of pity was shed over her alleged errors, such as a suffering Savior wept over sinning Jerusalem. It was not the hour for mercy, but for unrelenting justice; and with a firm hand was it meted out by that haughty council. It began by declaring the secession of those Presbyteries and Synods which now constitute the

Southern General Assembly to be 'unwarranted, schismatical, and unconstitutional.' It announced its purpose 'not to abandon the territory in which those churches are formed, or to compromise the rights of any of the Church courts, or ministers, ruling elders, and private members belonging to them, who are loyal to the government of the United States, and to the Presbyterian Church.' On the contrary, it determined to 'recognize, *as the Church,* the members of any church within the bounds of the schism who are loyal,' etc., etc. To give effect to these declarations, 'the Board of Domestic Missions was directed to take prompt and efficient measures to restore and build up the Presbyterian congregations in the Southern States of this Union, by the appointment and support of prudent and devoted missionaries,' care being taken that 'none be appointed but those who give satisfactory evidence of their loyalty,' and the like.

"It is not necessary to draw the reader's attention to this un-Christian attempt to sow the seeds of discord and strife amongst a people sufficiently burdened with sorrow of another kind. Nor will we dwell upon particular illustrations of the zeal with which these measures were carried out, in cases which can easily enough be cited. All this is past, now, and let it be remembered only so far as it reveals the spirit in which the Southern Church was first approached by those who soon became so anxious for the fraternal embrace. Fidelity to history requires, however, one further illustration of this domineering spirit to be given. Lest the eight hundred ministers of the South, together with their churches, should rush too suddenly into her bosom, this cautious Assembly duly enacts that every minister from any Presbytery in the South, and every private member from any Southern church, seeking admission into their fold, shall be examined as to his opinion and conduct during the rebellion; and if a participant therein, shall 'be required to confess and forsake his sin in this regard.' Flushed with the triumph of their arms, the Northern Church had no other thought than to dragoon their brethren at the South into abject ecclesiastical submission.

"It gives us no pleasure to recur to this period of intense sectional bitterness; nor would we do so except to point a warning. The Northern Church proposed nothing then but to *absorb* the Southern; it proposes to itself nothing but that now. Whatever may be the faults of that people, they possess one quality of the virtuous man which Horace describes in the words, '*Tenax propositi.*' They never give up what they once undertake. If it cannot be accomplished in one way, it will be in another. In our negotiations with them on this subject of fraternal relations, if we recede from our testimony by the breadth of a hair, their purpose of absorption will be accomplished finally, and it will be the absorption of conquest.

"This condition of things continued three years, from 1865 to 1868, during which time it became apparent that force accomplished nothing. With all their efforts at disintegration the wedge could be driven in nowhere, and the Southern Church became more and more compact under the pressure. Whether the failure of this coercive policy led to its abandonment, or whether in the interval passion had subsided and Christian sentiments began to resume their sway, in 1868 more gentle measures were inaugurated. The knowledge of this change was communicated to us through a paper adopted in 1869, the preamble of which reads thus: 'Whereas, The last General Assembly' (of course, that of 1868) 'acknowledged the separate and independent existence of the Presbyterian Church in the Southern States, and enjoined upon all subordinate courts so to treat it; thus according to its ministers and members the privilege of admission to our body upon the same terms which are extended to ministers and members of other branches of the Presbyterian Church in this country,' etc.

"The two bodies were, by this action, put upon a more friendly footing than before, and the way was now open for a more perfect adjustment of differences. Accordingly, the resolution following the above recited preamble proceeds to convey to our body the Christian salutations of the Assembly of 1869, and to 'give expression to its sentiments of fraternity and fellowship;' and, after a compact argument addressed to that point, expressed 'the desire that the day may not be distant when we may be united in one great organization that shall cover our whole land and embrace all branches of the Presbyterian Church.' The reader will not fail to notice the distinctness with which the absorption of the Southern church is here proposed, in the most blissful forgetfulness that their entire record, bristling with accusations and slanders, formed a *chevaux de frise* from which the most impetuous cavalry charge would be repulsed.

"This paper did not reach the Southern Assembly until 1870, during the sessions at Louisville. It was accompanied with another overture adopted at Philadelphia in 1870, which was borne to us by a delegation appointed for the purpose. The latter paper, after reaffirming the pacific sentiments of its predecessor, goes beyond it in the recognition of difficulties in the way of reconciliation, and proposing a practical method for their removal. It will be remembered that in the negotiations which resulted in bringing the Old and New School bodies together at the North, the most troublesome obstruction was found to exist in certain testimonies and deliverances fulminated in the past by the one against the other. The problem was how to get these out of the way without a flat retraction. They were at length simply dead-lettered in the following concurrent declaration from both the parties: 'That no rule or precedent which does not stand approved by both bodies shall be of any authority in the reunited body, except in so far as such rule or precedent may affect the rights of property founded thereon.' It is reported that when this cunning declaration was framed, an astute ecclesiastic pointed out the use to which it might be put in healing the breach with the South. At any rate, it was gravely proposed by the Northern Assembly at Philadelphia, and elaborately pressed by the worthy delegates at Louisville, that we should come in through this hole in the wall, through which, like Ezekiel of old, they had brought out so much of the stuff in their house; and among the rest, why not constructively all the utterances so offensive to the Southern Church?

"We have noted the change of base in the Northern Church from 1865 to 1870; what, in the meantime, has been the attitude of the Southern body on this question of fraternity? In 1861, when the Southern Assembly was first organized, its position was defined in these words: 'We desire to cultivate peace and charity with our fellow Christians throughout the world. We invite to ecclesiastical communion all who maintain our principles of faith and order.' In 1865, at the close of the war, the following language is used, and the spirit of which should be placed in contrast with that of the Northern Assembly in the same year: 'It may be proper at this point to declare concerning other churches in the most explicit manner, that in the true idea of 'the communion of the saints,' we would willingly hold fellowship with all who love our Lord Jesus in sincerity; and especially do we signify to all bodies, ministers, and people of the Presbyterian Church, struggling to maintain the true principles of the same time honored Confession, our desire to establish the most intimate relations with them which may be found mutually edifying and for the glory of God.' The active hostility of the Northern Church in this very year 1865, which has been already described, imposed upon the Southern body the duty of preserving a calm and dignified silence. This remained unbroken until she was approached by the other party in 1870 with an overture of peace. The following bold proclamation was made in that year: 'The Southern Presbyterian Church can confidently appeal to all the acts and declarations of all their Assemblies, that no attitude of aggression or hostility has been, or is now, assumed by it toward the Northern Church. And this General Assembly distinctly avows that no grievance experienced by us, however real, would justify us in acts of aggression, or a spirit of malice or retaliation, against any branch of Christ's visible kingdom. We are prepared, therefore, in advance of all discussion, to exercise toward the General Assembly, North, and the churches represented therein, such amity as fidelity to our principles could, under any possible circumstances, permit.' It must not be allowed to escape notice that from the time of her organization in 1861 to the first advance made to her in 1870, a period of nine years, the Southern Church remained quiet and passive under grievous wrongs. She would indulge in no recriminations; but as the party aggrieved, she was restrained by a sense of self-respect from any approach to the other side. This is emphasized here, as indicating a fixed policy marked out on principle for herself by the Southern Church.

"To the proposition for appointing a Committee of Conference to meet a similar committee from the Northern side, a favorable answer was returned. Such a committee was raised, 'with instructions that the difficulties in the way of cordial correspondence between the two bodies must be distinctly met and removed.' To leave no doubt as to the nature of these difficulties, they were articulately stated under four heads: 1. The political deliverances of both wings of the Northern Assembly, against which the Southern Church felt constrained to bear testimony; 2. The union betweeen the Old and New School organizations, North, effected by methods which involved the surrender of past testimonies for the truth; 3. The unconstitutional legislation by which the Declaration and Testimony men of Missouri and Kentucky had been expelled from the Northern Church; 4. The injurious accusations against the Southern Church which had filled the ears of the world. It only remains to be added, that when this action was reported to the Assembly at Philadelphia, 'the further consideration of the subject was postponed, and their committee discharged,' on the alleged ground that all the questions at issue had been prejudged by us. Thus ended the first chapter of this diplomatic history.

"Negotiations were not resumed until 1874, and then simultaneously by both the estranged parties. The Southern Assembly of that year was overtured on the subject by two of its Presbyteries; one of which specially desired the appointment of a Committee of Conference, without instructions of any kind. A paper was also received from the Northern Assembly, adopted in 1873, deploring the existing division, and announcing the appointment of a Conference Committee on their part. To this the Southern Assembly made response by raising a committee untrammeled by instructions; and the two committees met shortly after in the famous Baltimore Conference. This overture of the Northern Assembly should not be dismissed without a brief statement of its contents, which were somewhat remarkable. It declared all former action of the Old and New School wings of their body, touching the Southern Church, to be null and void since their reunion, and of no effect as a precedent in the future. It expressed confidence in the orthodoxy and piety of the Southern Church, and, as an offset to their political deliverances, made liberal quotations from the Standards as to the relation which the Church sustains to the State. It is not probable that these general protestations had much influence in determining the action of our own body; for, in a vigorous protest against this action, it was shown (1) that the measures declared null and void had been enforced only the year before in the Walnut Street

Church case; (2) that the slanderous charges against the character and motives of our ministers and people remained still without retraction; and (3) that the Northern Assembly had always professed to acknowledge the spirituality and independence of the Church during the very period they were trampling these sacred privileges in the dust.

"We are brought now to the conference of the two committees in the city of Baltimore, in January, 1875, and reported in May following to the respective Assemblies. It was opened with a proposal from the Northern side, to 'recommend the interchange of delegates, thus recognizing each other as corresponding bodies,' to which it was replied by the Southern committee, that they had been appointed to confer about the removal of the causes which had hitherto prevented such interchange, which were then distinctly stated under two general heads—*unjust and injurious accusations*, and *the course pursued in regard to Church property*. The second of these topics was never reached, the Conference having broken down upon the first. The failure is easily explained. The Northern committee insisted that all the accusations and imputations complained of had been canceled in the concurrent declaration which had been already quoted, 'that no rule or precedent which does not stand approved by both bodies, shall be of any authority in the reunited body,' etc. The Southern side objected that this was an arrangement to facilitate the union of the Old and New School bodies, North, and had originally no reference to the Southern Church; that it was an indirection at best, and failed to meet the issue betwixt themselves and us in an honest and manly way; and that it could not, by its own terms, go back of the year in which it was adopted, and did not therefore touch our grievances at all. In declining this settlement of the case, the Southern committee proceeded to say: 'If your Assembly could see its way clear to say in a few plain words to this effect, that these obnoxious things were said and done in times of great excitement, that they are to be regretted, and that now, in a calm review, the imputations cast upon the Southern Church are disapproved, that would end the difficulty at once.' This suggestion was peremptorily declined, and the Conference was dissolved without coming to any agreement.

"The only matter of any present importance in the proceedings of the Baltimore Conference is the alleged elimination of the political utterances by the Northern Assembly from the grounds of offense and complaint. With reference, therefore, to what we shall hereafter say upon this point, it is necessary to give here the text of their action: 'It is suitable to represent freely and fully to the brethren of your Committee that this kind of political action, begun in 1861 and carried on in successive Assemblies through 1866, constitutes at once a most weighty grievance to us, because much of it was aimed at our people; and constitutes also a serious hindrance to establishing fraternal relations, because they are lamentable departures from some of the fundamental principles laid down in those noble Standards, which, as you truly observe, we hold in common.' Then follow a few specifications in which this offense was committed. A little later, these additional words were employed: 'It is at this point that reference is made to your political enactments and opinions, partly because much of it was aimed at our own people, and all of it was enacted while that Assembly still held us on their roll as a part of their own body. But we have not said that we refuse fraternal relations for these causes, or that they are an insuperable obstacle. We say that they constitute a serious hindrance. By this statement we abide.' The reader will please to note the form and the extent to which this grievous politication of the Northern Church is waived as a barrier to fraternal intercourse. We shall have use for it in the sequel.

"The records of the Southern Assembly for the year 1876 contain but two references to this particular subject. The Presbytery of St. Louis having sent up an overture requesting some action in regard to fraternal relations with the Northern General Assembly, in order to remove misapprehensions as to the true position of our Church, the following resolution was adopted: 'That the action of the Baltimore Conference, approved by the Assembly at St. Louis, explains with sufficient clearness the position of our Church. But inasmuch as it is represented by the overture, misapprehension exists in the minds of some of our people as to the spirit of this action, in order to show our disposition to remove on our part real or seeming hindrances to friendly feeling the Assembly explicitly declares, that while condemning certain acts and deliverances of the Northern General Assembly, no acts or deliverances of the Southern General Assemblies are to be construed or admitted as impugning in any way the Christian character of the Northern General Assembly, or of the historical bodies of which it is the successor.' A double use was made of this resolution, in sending it to the Northern Assembly at Brooklyn, N. Y., in answer to a telegram received from that body 'expressing its hearty and united wishes for the establishment of cordial correspondence,' and 'reiterating its cordial desire to establish fraternal relations on terms of perfect equality and reciprocity, as soon as it is agreeable to their brethren to respond to this assurance by a similar expression.'

"It will be observed, that with all these reiterated proffers of amity and intercourse, not a word is said, nor a step taken, to remove the causes of alienation so distinctly brought to view in the Baltimore Conference. Nothing remained, therefore, for the Southern Assembly but to reply, 'We are ready most cordially to enter on fraternal relations with your body on any terms honorable to both parties;' and with this was sent, in further explanation, the answer to the overture from the St. Louis Presbytery, which has already been recited.

"In 1877 the subject was brought up in the Southern Assembly by a communication from the Northern, which returned, *in ipsissimis verbis,* the declaration sent to them by us the preceding year, as taken from the answer to the St. Louis Presbytery. The reply to this equivocal trifling was conveyed in the following language: 'That we cannot regard this communication as satisfactory, because we can discover in it no reference whatever to the first and main part of the paper adopted by our Assembly at Savannah, and communicated to the Brooklyn Assembly. This Assembly can add nothing on this subject to the action of the Assembly at St. Louis adopting the basis proposed by our Committee of Conference at Baltimore, and reaffirmed by the Assembly at Savannah. If our Northern brethren can meet us on these terms, which truth and righteousness seem to us to require, then we are ready to establish such relations with them during the present sessions of the Assembly.'

"Thus far in these negotiations, so persistent had been the refusal of the Northern body to consider the basis of the Baltimore platform that a protest was entered against the action of the New Orleans Assembly, on the ground that 'it is inconsistent with self-respect to press this ultimatum after its distinct and repeated declinatures by the Northern Assembly.'

"During the years 1878, 1879, 1880, and 1881, the discussion was revived in no form; but Christian salutations were exchanged between the two bodies in their annual convocations. In 1882 the subject was reopened, with perhaps greater vigor from having slept so long and peacefully. It was brought up before the Assembly at Atlanta, by overtures from the four Presbyteries, desiring the establishment of fraternal relations with the Northern Assembly, by sending forthwith a delegation to that body, in session at Springfield, Ill. A proposition so definite and conclusive was bound to excite a lively discussion; and after a tangled debate, the following paper was adopted: 'In order to remove all difficulties in the way of that full and formal correspondence which, on our part, we are prepared to accept, we adopt the following minute: That while receding from no principle, we do hereby declare our regret for, and withdrawal of, all expressions of our Assembly which may be regarded as reflecting upon, or offensive to, the General Assembly of the Presbyterian Church in the United States of America.

"'*Resolved,* That a copy of this paper be sent by telegraph to the General Assembly now in session at Springfield, Ill., for their prayerful consideration, and, *mutatis mutandis,* for their reciprocal concurrence, as affording a basis for the exchange of delegates forthwith.'

"The Northern Assembly, upon receiving this message, immediately telegraphed back their adoption of this paper, without the alteration of a letter or a point; and by this identity of action, the two bodies were permitted to rejoice in the supposed termination of this unhappy dispute. Alas, that so brilliant a prospect should be again darkened with clouds! In a short time came a private telegram from the Moderator of the Northern council, conveying a resolution adopted to this effect: 'That in the action now being taken, we disclaim any reference to the action of preceding Assemblies concerning loyalty and rebellion, but we refer only to those concerning schism, heresy, and blasphemy;' whereupon a telegram of inquiry is sent from Atlanta, couched in these rather undiplomatic words: 'If the action of your Assembly, telegraphed by your Moderator to our Moderator, does not modify the concurrent resolution adopted by your Assembly to ours, we are prepared to send delegates forthwith.' To which the following answer was received: 'The action referred to does not modify, but it explains, the concurrent resolution; and the explanation is on the face of the action. There is nothing behind it or between the lines.' The final action of the Atlanta Assembly was to 'declare its entire satisfaction with the full and explicit terms in which the General Assembly of the Presbyterian Church in the United States of America has expressed its "reciprocal concurrence" in the paper transmitted to said Assembly on fraternal correspondence.' Delegates were accordingly appointed to bear the greetings of our body to the other at their meeting in May, 1883.

"From this history briefly, but sufficiently, sketched, we deduce the points to which the attention of the reader is respectfully solicited.

"1. The conciliatory and Christian attitude of the Southern Presbyterian Church throughout this painful controversy is most conspicuous. At the period of organization in 1861, amidst the agonies of a Civil War, she stretched forth her hand in 'peace and charity' to the whole Christian world. In 1865, at the very moment when excommunication and proscription were decreed as 'the portion of her cup,' she desired 'fellowship with all who love the Lord Jesus,' and to 'establish the most intimate relations with all the branches of the Presbyterian Church.' In 1870 she responded to the first request for a conference with the other side, and made a frank statement of the difficulties to be removed. In 1874 she consented to renew negotiations for peace, after they had been abruptly broken off by the other side, and withheld instructions to her agents which, in the former instance, had given offense. In 1875, reducing the causes of estrangement to their minimum, that is, to the injurious accusations against her good name, so considerate was she of the feelings of the other party, as to make allowance for the excitement and heat of the times when these things were said and done, and to suggest this as a ground upon which they might, without humiliation, be withdrawn. In 1876, she not only reiterated her 'desire for fraternal relations upon terms honorable to both parties,' but actually led the way in removing all obstacles by purging her own records of what had been excepted against by the opposition. We have reserved the statement of this interesting fact for insertion here. Whilst the pride and dignity of the Northern Church refused even to look upon the blots which defaced their legislation during four years, the Southern Church, upon a simple intimation that one of her utterances had excited unfavorable criticism, appointed in 1875 a committee to examine her entire records, with the view of discovering and correcting anything inconsistent with her declared principles or with the Standards. This Committee reported in 1876 the following, which was adopted: 'Inasmuch as some incidental expressions, uttered in times of great public excitement, are found upon our records, and have been pointed out in the report of the committee, which seem to be ambiguous or inconsistent with the above declarations and others of like import, this Assembly does hereby disavow them wherever found, and does not recognize such as forming any part of the well-considered authoritative teaching or testimony of our Church.' Through consecutive years, down to 1882, the same attitude of Christian readiness to adjust all differences is consistently maintained; until wearied out with the unwillingness of the other side to attempt the solution of the difficulty, she herself, at the last Assembly in Atlanta, takes the initiative, and proposes a resolution, which, if adopted by both parties, will cut the knot and let them both out of the trouble.

"All this is in brilliant contrast with the course of the Northern Church, which commenced with open hostility and acts of aggression, then proposed a conference for the adjustment of differences, from which she backed down as soon as those differences were honestly stated. When the conference was finally held, she peremptorily declined the mildest terms of reconciliation which honor and truth would allow to be offered — proposing on her part only to dead-letter, and that by an obscure indirection, charges which honesty and candor required her openly to withdraw; and finally allowed herself to be outstripped in magnanimity, by receiving the tender of reconciliation which she ought to have made; the acceptance of which is traversed by a back-handed retraction of one half of what is professedly conceded. We present this contrast in no boastful or self-righteeous spirit, as though we had not much ourselves to confess and bewail before Almighty God; but because the strong inclination, manifested in some quarters to close this dispute on any terms, springs possibly from the apprehension that we are held guilty before the world of an unamiable and unforgiving spirit. If our record could be placed fully before the Christian public, we should be sure of a hearty acquittal of this charge. It is a comfort to know that the records of both parties lie open before the omniscient Judge, by whose verdict of unerring justice we are willing to abide. Meanwhile, we would be glad to have our own people so familiar with their own history as to be led by no maudlin sentiment to overthrow truth in the attempt to secure peace.

"2. It is apparent, from the preceding history, that the Atlanta Assembly has not only departed from, but has reversed, the position of the Southern Church, upon this subject of fraternal relations. From the beginning the attitude of the Southern Church has been that of quiet expectation of approach from the other side. It was the only attitude consistent with self-respect. At two epochs, at her organization and again at the close of the war, she had extended the hand of fellowship especially to the Presbyterian household of faith. She was met from the Northern Church by a decree of outlawry and confiscation. What could she do but retire within her own borders, and preserve her dignity by entire silence and reserve? She was thus quiet and passive from 1865 to 1870. When delegates appeared from the other side with a proposal for conference, they were received with marked courtesy; but at the same time the difficulties in the way of perfect amity were fully disclosed. The attitude was that of a party which was sought, and which responded to overtures made by another. So that for four years longer, from 1870 to 1874, the Southern Church still felt 'her strength was to sit still.' After the conference at Baltimore, she put forth her ultimatum, and stood by it from 1875 to 1882, to this effect: 'As soon as, by a few plain words, these hard accusations, uttered in times of great excitement, are withdrawn, we are ready to establish a cordial correspondence.' We are not discussing the wisdom or the propriety of this position. The only object is to show, from the form of the proposition, that the responsibility was thrown upon the Northern Church to take the next step. The language of our Church has always been, 'whatever obstructions may be in the way of ecclesiastical fellowship, were not created by us; we cannot allow ourselves to be placed in the false position before the world of parties who had been guilty of wrong to the Northern Church. Having placed nothing in the way of Christian fraternity, there is nothing for us to remove.' Such was her language in 1870; and her practice, through all the years from 1865 to 1882 has been consistent with it. From first to last, her attitude has been that of anxiety to be at peace, but waiting for the offender to remove the obstructions which he had put in the way.

"From this fixed policy, adopted deliberately and upon principle, there is not a single deviation until the last Atlanta Assembly reversed the position of the parties and made the Southern Church the suitor of the Northern. By taking the initiative, and hypothetically placing herself by the side of the aggressor, and making the same confession, she hoped to coax the apology from the other side which would fulfill the conditions which her honor required. Nothing is presented here to the reader but the historical fact that the action at Atlanta was revolutionary. The carefully considered policy adhered to through seventeen years, and sanctioned by the endorsement of seventeen consecutive Assemblies, is suddenly abandoned and reversed. The Church is no longer standing upon the ground she had deliberately chosen, but is drifting at sea, upon an expedient which may prove to have neither rudder nor keel. It was a very grave responsibility for any Assembly to assume—a responsibility more clearly seen and more deeply felt by the members of that venerable court since its adjournment, than during the confusion and darkness of an exciting debate. We will not perplex this issue by discussing the constitutional right of the Assembly to assume this power; but was it safe to encounter the risks which have been subsequently shown to be involved? It may be replied, that four Presbyteries clamored for a change in our relations to the Northern Church. There were sixty-two Presbyteries which were silent; and the overwhelming presumption was that the policy of seventeen years and of seventeen Assemblies was the policy which the Church would prefer. Was it, therefore, morally right for one Assembly, in the hurry of a few days, to unsettle the established policy of our entire previous history, without first ascertaining the mind of the Church? Was it fraternal, nay, was it in any sense fair, to spring such a movement upon the Assembly, carry it through with a rush, and commit the whole Church to a policy which cannot afterwards be discussed upon its merits? As the case now stands, the question comes up in the form, Can the Atlanta action be arrested? Many, who deplore that action as unwise, feel that the thing is done, and cannot be undone. Others, who equally bewail the mistake which has been made, are unwilling to antagonize the highest Church court, and thus to weaken all Church authority. Others, again, weary of the continual agitation, have withheld from further participation in it, leaving matters to take whatever shape others may determine. Thus, by different routes, men reach the same conclusion, and an accidental majority is created, which does not reflect the true mind of the Church. Is any course fair which leads to such complications? Is it strange that a deep dissatisfaction is pervading the Church, and setting not a few to think what further limitations can be placed upon the power of a court which enable a single Assembly by a *coup d'etat* to capture the Church? But this is rather more than we undertook to say under this head. Our only object was to show that the Atlanta Assembly has changed the entire policy of the Church and reversed the position of the parties in this controversy, and that we no longer stand upon the ground occupied through the whole of our previous career.

"This is not all. The Atlanta Assembly has, in the resolution adopted by it and sent to the Northern Assembly for its concurrent adoption, conceded what we have hitherto steadfastly refused to acknowledge as true. Our declaration in 1870, was, 'Our records may be searched in vain for a single act of aggression, or a single unfriendly declaration against the Northern Church.' Still later, in 1876, lest any accidental word of asperity should have crept in since, it was declared that in condemning certain acts and deliverances of the Northern Assembly, nothing was to be construed as reflecting upon the religious character of that body. Special pains were taken, therefore, to cancel voluntarily and beforehand any chance expression that might be offensive. In view of these well-known facts, what right had the Assembly of 1882 to 'declare their regret for and withdrawal of all expressions of our Assembly which may be regarded as reflecting upon, or offensive to, the General Assembly of the Presbyterian Church in the United States of America?' We anticipate the reply: This statement was drawn in accordance with the code of honor acknowledged even by worldly men, in order to save the *amour propre* of the other party, and render it easier for him to make an acknowledgment which means more for him than for us. Is it strange, then, that the other party, finding themselves caught in a diplomatic snare, should retort severely as they did, by a recalcitrant resolution, which in turn put the sting upon us? Human nature being open to just such resentments, it was most natural for a wary antagonist to take this sort of reprisal; and we are not sure but the Atlanta Assembly richly deserved to feel the recoil of their own gun. We are of those who do not believe much in diplomacy in the affairs of Christ's kingdom and amongst His people. But the question for the reader to ask in this connection is, Who gave the Atlanta Assembly the right to confess to the Northern Church what the Southern Church had over and again denied to be true? With all our veneration for the courts of the Church, we feel that this august body will find it difficult to withdraw its shoulders from a responsibility to which it will be held by the verdict of time.

"3. We proceed to show that the treaty of peace concluded between the two Assemblies in May last violates the conditions laid down in the Baltimore Conference—in substance, if not absolutely in form. In this utterance, we grapple with the position deemed impregnable by the advocates of this pacification. Their line of defence is, that the Northern Assembly, having conceded all that the Southern Church laid down in its ultimatum when it sanctioned the proceedings of the Baltimore Conference, no alternative is left us but to accept the disclaimer which is made, and to put the offence out of sight forever. This would certainly be true, if the action of the Springfield Assembly had terminated with the adoption, *simpliciter,* of what is designated as the 'concurrent resolution.' We have criticised the Atlanta Assembly for thus formulating the terms by which our grievances should be redressed, and thereby reversing the position in which the two parties stood. But it cannot be denied that the proposed action went to the bottom of all the accusations against us, and made an honorable and satisfactory adjustment of the dispute. Had the 'concurrent resolution' been adopted alone, not a whisper of objection would have been heard throughout the South. The reconciliation would have been accepted as frank, manly, and Christian—obliterating every trace of the old feud, and rendering the sentiment of our people towards their brethren at the North cordial and grateful. But, as the reader well knows, this was not the action taken by the Assembly at Springfield. The 'concurrent resolution' was not adopted until a rider was fastened upon it which changed its whole aspect as a measure of pacification. The Herrick Johnson resolution, as it is commonly distinguished—which was deemed of such importance that it was passed by the body before the main resolution, which it was intended to qualify—formerly sets forth that, in declaring 'their regret for, and withdrawal of, all expressions of their Assembly which may be regarded as reflecting upon or offensive to the Southern Assembly,' no reference is made to 'the acts concerning loyalty and rebellion, but only to those concerning schism, heresy, and blasphemy.' This is not the action proposed by our Assembly to theirs for concurrent adoption, but one wholly different.

"But, it is replied, the Northern Assembly has explicitly affirmed that this rider fastened upon the main resolution, 'does not modify it, but only explains it;' and that we are obliged, by common courtesy, to accept the interpretation they put upon their own act, and of course the disclaimer which this includes. It is impossible for us, however, to abdicate the exercise of our own judgment and reason, and believe that a paper is not modified when it *is* modified. Men of the world may accept a disclaimer which they know to be false and absurd, since the code of honor is framed only to stop a quarrel, and not to regulate the subsequent intercourse of the parties. But Christians profess to base their action upon truth and righteousness; this pacification is intended to bring the parties into bounds of amity and fellowship. How, then, can we ground a reconciliation upon an equivocal agreement which is construed differently between the parties? Is it satisfactory to say to the one litigant, You must in courtesy accept the interpretation of your contestant, though your own judgment is clear that he is mistaken? For our part, we are heartily tired of all this legislation which 'palters in a double sense;' which blows hot and cold with the same breath; which says and doesn't say, in the same words; which dead-letters where it ought to retract; which seeks its end by indirection, rather than by open declarations; which is diplomatic, when it should be candid. A reconciliation which rests upon subtle constructions and hair-line discriminations is not worth the p per upon which the agreement is executed. The friendship which deserves the name must be frank, open and sincere. Everything short of this is hypocrisy before God.

"But the Herrick Johnson resolution, it is rejoined, did nothing more than take out of the category of things withdrawn the original political deliverances of the Northern Assembly during and immediately after the war. And since all this political legislation is waived by the Baltimore Conference as a barrier to fraternal relations, the action taken by both Assemblies is in agreement with the terms we ourselves have offered, and we are bound by our antecedent pledge to abide by the treaty thus made. Grant, says the Atlanta advocates, that the rider does modify 'the Concurrent Resolution', to which it was attached, it does not contravene the platform upon which the Southern Church has stood since 1875; and, therefore, should not arrest the correspondence between the two bodies. The Northern Assembly say they may not have done the beautiful and clean thing by us, and we may mourn that they have shown themselves incapable of a grand magnanimity; still, as they have come up to our proffered ultimatum, our own truth and honor are involved in the acceptance of the result. Of course, if all this be so, there is not a word further to be said; we have simply 'sworn to our own hurt,' and must keep the oath.

"Is it true, however, that peace has been concluded upon the terms embraced in the Baltimore platform? Let us look again at the text which we have already engrossed, and see what the committee did actually say: 'This kind of political action, begun in 1861, and carried on in successive Assemblies through 1866, constitutes at once *a most weighty grievance to us,* because much of it was aimed at our people; and constitutes also *a serious hindrance to establishing fraternal relations,* because they are lamentable departures from some of the principles laid down in those noble Standards,' etc. 'But *we have not said that we refuse fraternal relations for these causes, or that they are an insuperable obstacle; we say they constitute a serious hindrance,* and by this statement we abide.' We have italicized the points in this declaration to which we wish to give emphasis. It is admitted freely that the past politication of the Northern Church is not interposed, since the Baltimore Conference, as a bar to intercourse. It was 'a weighty grievance' and 'a serious hindrance to fraternal relations,' which the Southern Committee at Baltimore found it 'difficult to surmount,' but on the ground that we are not held as endorsing the errors of those religious bodies with which correspondence is held, this politication in the past was not construed as 'an insuperable obstacle.' To the same effect, the Atlanta Assembly inserted in their 'Concurrent Resolution' a limiting clause—'without receding from any principle'—which was intended to reserve to both the parties their conscientious convictions of truth and duty, so that neither the one nor the other should be called to the surrender of any principle. But if 'a serious hindrance' in the past is waived by us, does this give the offender the right to dig up that 'hindrance' out of the past and put it into the very articles of agreement upon which the reconciliation is to rest? We ask the reader to mark the distinction which we draw. The political deliverances from 1861 to 1866 are not urged as a bar to peace; but it is another thing to put forward the right thus to politicate as a claim, the recognition of which is made the condition precedent of the reconciliation. Is this an exaggerated statement of the case? The South says to the North, 'Will you, without receding from any principle, withdraw what in your records reflects upon us?' 'Yes,' replies the North, 'everything except what we said against you as rebels and traitors; we cannot touch those utterances without giving up our right to have made them.' If peace is concluded upon these terms, is not this right acknowledged? And was this the thing which was waived by the Baltimore Conference? The South says to the North, 'Hold what political opinions you please, and bind your testimonies upon your head as a crown of glory, so far as we are concerned; for we ask you to recede from no principle.' 'Ah, yes,' replies the North, 'but that is not enough; it must be entered into the bond between us that these political utterances should have been made, without the recognition of which we will take back nothing.' This is the significance of the Herrick Johnson Resolution; and it is a new offence against the Southern Church, re-enacting in cold blood all the violences and maledictions of years of intense excitement, rolling them up in one bolus which must be swallowed and inwardly digested as the condition of fraternity. Has the Southern Church since 1875 interpreted the Baltimore ultimatum as meaning this? The Herrick Johnson Resolution unquestionably means something. It was not needed as protection against the surrender of any of their honest convictions, the Concurrent Resolution itself affording the necessary guarantee in the reservation of every principle held sacred by both the parties. In the way of explanatory legislation it is wholly superogatory, as much so as would be a duplicate nose upon a man's face. What, then, was its purport and design? We can see no other end than to insert in the body of the treaty between the two parties a recognition of the propriety of all the political affirmations of the Northern Church during the war. We may be willing to waive those utterances in the past as a bar to fellowship, when we are not willing to acknowledge their fitness and propriety, or to embody them in our articles of agreement as one of the conditions of reconciliation. It is insisted, therefore, that the late pacification is not based upon the Baltimore platform; but, on the contrary, in spirit, if not in the letter itself, contravenes all its positions.

"To condense the argument in a nutshell: the Concurrent Resolution, on which it was proposed to base the reconciliation, exactly embodied the Baltimore proposition. It may be paraphrased thus: While receding from no principle, we will not urge your past politication as 'an insuperable obstacle' to fraternal intercourse, 'serious hindrance,' though it be; and we will withdraw any offensive language we may have employed in relation to it. The Northern Assembly, in its rider to this Concurrent Resolution, palpably spurns the Baltimore platform and practically says, We will do all in our power to make the obstacle insuperable by reaffirming the grievances and compelling your recognition and assent.

"4. In establishing official correspondence (we like this term better as being more discriminating than fraternal relations, which really have existed ever since 1868)—in establishing official correspondence upon the present basis, we have taken a position which will in due time necessitate organic union. The Southern brethren who oppose our views say constantly, 'Your contention against the political action of the Northern Church is perfectly valid as against all incorporation with that body, but is not valid against formal intercourse with them as a separate organization.' They say further, 'Whilst we favor the latter, we are at one with you when it comes to the defeat of the former.' But what, dear brethren, if it should then be too late? What if the waters, trickling through the concession we have made in establishing fraternity, should have swept away our entire embankment, and we find ourselves at the mercy of the flood? What, in short, if the very ground beneath our feet should have dropped away, and left us standing upon nothing? When our brethren declare they are as much opposed as ourselves to union with the Northern Church, we believe it fully as to the vast majority of them. Otherwise, we would not take the trouble to pen these lines. But there is a logic in history quite as compulsory as that of the subtlest dialectic. A false step in action, as well as in reasoning, will lead to consequences, however remote, which are inevitable. Our brethren may not wish to go into union; but into union they will go by a fatal necessity, because they have unwittingly given away the only ground upon which resistance could be successfully made.

"What, then, is the distinctive feature which separates us from the Northern Church? We profess to hold the same symbols of faith and order; our creed, our government, our worship is the same; why, then, should we not be brought under the same ecclesiastical jurisdiction? It is only partially satisfactory to reply that such an arrangement would be inconvenient, as making the body too large to be handled. The Presbyterian system is too elastic, in its gradation of courts, to succumb under any practical difficulty of this sort. The true and sufficient answer is, that the two bodies are not at one as to the relations subsisting between the Church and the State. This is the differentiating feature which compels the one to be separate from the other. Observe, too, that it does not come up an abstract dogma, a merely speculative truth. In the providence of God, the Southern wing of the Presbyterian Church was compelled to take issue with the

Northern upon this question. It was the wedge driven in by other hands than ours to divide the Church. Without any will or wish of our own, we were forced into an attitude of protest against this defection from our common Standards. Of all things on earth, the Northern Church is the most anxious to rid themselves of this protest. They would rather do it by absorbing us, since our mere existence, as a separate Church, is an outstanding and visible testimony against them. But if this cannot be accomplished, the next expedient will be to muzzle the protest which they cannot suppress—to spike the cannon which they have not been able to capture.

"The Baltimore Conference went very far in weakening that protest when it consented to waive the past politication of the Northern Church as a bar to official correspondence. But when we have gone a great deal beyond this, in allowing these political declarations to be imported into the treaty between us, as in part the basis of the reconciliation, what then becomes of our testimony against these political utterances? When organic union becomes the subject of discussion, as it surely must, will we be able to urge their past political action as an objection? The immediate answer will be, 'Your plea is barred by the treaty of 1882; in express terms we affirmed our right to have uttered those decrees; and you responded by a resolution declaring "entire satisfaction with the full and explicit terms in which we expressed our reciprocal concurrences."' What can we reply to this? In establishing fraternal relations, the Northern Assembly openly placed her whole political action in our path as the steps by which we might ascend and stand with them on their platform. In recognizing these deliverances on loyalty and rebellion, imported bodily into the treaty of peace by the Herrick Johnson Resolution, we have abandoned our testimony against politics in the Church courts, and have forfeited the right to plead it as a bar to organic union. The historic ground upon which the Southern Church was organized in 1861, and upon which she has stood ever since, was ceded by treaty in 1882, and she will find it difficult to show cause to the world why she should longer exist. This is the logic of fraternal relations upon the Atlanta basis. Upon the line of this policy, we must as certainly crumble into the Northern Church at last, as a bank of sand is washed away by the constant action of water. When we become weary of this friction, then, just as we have become weary of the friction now, the Northern Assembly will resume its action in 1874 in some grand affirmation of the spiritual nature of the Church as the kingdom of Christ, and in its entire separation from, and independence of, the State; and will then turn to us and ask, 'What do you want more orthodox than this new proclamation of Christ's supremacy?' Will we point to the blemishes upon their records from 1861 to 1866? The withering response will be, You disabled your own testimony by the written agreement of 1882, and it is beyond your power to enable it any more. Having admitted the claims set up in the Herrick Johnson Resolution, by which the 'Concurrent Resolution' was *'explained'* to us, we have no longer the right to take issue with the Northern Church upon its mingling of politics with religion. This ground of separation being swept away from our feet, nothing will remain to us but to settle down quietly into her bosom. We are thus emphatic in setting forth the logical consequences of our present position, in the hope our Church will retrace her steps before it is too late and find her anchorage upon her historic testimony as before.

"It is greatly to be wished that the Southern Presbyterian Church would gravely consider the danger of her present situation. Very many of her ministers and members are deeply wounded and grieved. They find the Northern Assembly rising up in cold blood, and absolutely without provocation, throwing anew into their face the taunt of disloyalty and rebellion. The charge is simply absurd in view of the fact that the Federal Government abandoned it with the acknowledgment that the indictment could not be sustained in any court under the Constitution. We would not, therefore, care for the silly allegation of it in the Herrick Johnson Resolution as passed by the Springfield Assembly, if it had not been accepted by our own Supreme Court at Atlanta. It is this which has driven the iron so deep into the soul, and bowed down so many with humiliation and sorrow. We are of those who think rebellion is a crime; and could we believe ourselves guilty of it, we would repent in sackcloth and ashes all our days; and to have the charge even constructively recognized by our own mother, this pains like the killing of a nerve. What lasting injury this unwise attempt at pacification has inflicted upon the Southern Church, time only can disclose. Even though it should not lead to the absorption so much dreaded, its present effect has been to sow distrust and alienation between brethren who honored each other with a supreme affection, and to weaken confidence in the stability of the Church herself and of the principles which she avows. The hollow fraternity with outside parties is dearly purchased with the uneasiness and sorrow and pain it has produced within.[8] In view of all which we think it incumbent upon the next Assembly to represent frankly to the Assembly, North, that the present settlement is unsatisfactory from the failure on their part to return an untrameled adoption of the Concurrent Resolution."

The time never came when he approved of the Atlanta basis

[8] What is more disastrous still, by an arbitrary and ruthless exercise of power the Assembly has already antagonized the Presbyteries to itself—a conflict between the courts of the Church which has only to become chronic to issue in entire disintegration. Yet the fearful peril must be encountered, in order to escape the opposite danger of an oppressive despotism.

for the establishment of "official correspondence" between the two churches. Nor was he at pains to conceal his sentiments; as the Augusta Assembly of 1886, before which he delivered a great speech on "The Church a Spiritual Kingdom," learned, in the course of that address; and as numerous proofs make manifest; e. g., this letter to the Rev. A. C. Hopkins, D.D., of Charlestown, W. Va.:

"NEW ORLEANS, LA., June 16, 1886.

"MY DEAR DR. HOPKINS: Your welcome letter of the first awaited my return from the Commencement at Clarksville, Tenn., and was a great refreshment to my spirit. 'Fraternal relations' were not established in the clean way, by the Atlanta Assembly; so that I have never felt since that we stood on solid ground. It was, therefore, under some oppression of heart I spoke at Augusta—not only upon that point, but also upon the matter of Lay-Evangelism. I was greatly relieved on both points by the number of the younger members of the Assembly, who came to me with the assurance that they stood squarely and firmly upon the principles I announced. It has given me more hope for our future than I had dared to cherish. Many thanks to you for the cordial endorsement of your letter: and still more for the personal consideration which prompted you to give me this drop of comfort. If we could only have a let-up from the ceaseless agitation of all manner of subjects; less tinkering at our Book of Order—less discussion of revolutionary measures of Church organization—and a total stop of this importation of scientific theories into our theology. But we must abide in our lot, and push the Master's work on, as best we can under these hindrances.

"Permit me to close, dear brother, with the expression of the wish that we could have the rich pleasure of a visit from you some day. The chamber is always ready for you, and the pulpit.

"Yours in Christian love,

"B. M. PALMER."

The question of "Fraternal Relations" once settled, the party in the Church that had been agitating for closer relations began to agitate for "Organic Union" with the Northern Church. This Dr. Palmer deprecated for still more imperative reasons than obtained in the case of "Fraternal Relations." The Assembly of 1887 was asked, through certain overtures, to institute measures looking to the establishment of "closer relations." Dr. Palmer was a member of that Assembly and made, perhaps, the most telling speech in opposition to every device to loosen the Church from her moorings. Like many great men, he found himself, when the vote was taken, in the minority. That minority was, however, not done fighting. They got together and appointed a committee to prepare an open letter to the Church at large. Dr. Palmer was made the chairman of that very able committee. The points of the open letter are the points of his speech put into written style and more carefully substantiated. Here is the letter:

"*To the Members of the Southern Presbyterian Church:*

"At the recent meeting of the Southern General Assembly held in St. Louis, overtures were presented from the Synods of Missouri, Arkansas, Alabama, and the Presbyteries of St. John, Upper Missouri, Chesapeake, Missouri, Holston, Indian, East Alabama, and Dallas, favoring closer relations with the Northern branch of the Presbyterian Church. These overtures were immediately referred to a special committee, composed of members drawn from all the Synods, which resulted in the return of two conflicting reports for the consideration of the Assembly. The majority report, signed by sixteen names, is in these words:

"'*Whereas,* The Synods of Missouri, Arkansas and Alabama, embracing fifteen Presbyteries, have taken action favoring reunion of some kind between the two Churches; and

"'WHEREAS, Subsequent thereto eight Presbyteries, to-wit: St. John, Upper Missouri, Chesapeake, Missouri, Holston, Indian, East Alabama and Dallas, have manifested special interest in the matter by overtures or resolutions, favoring closer relations between the two Churches; while from only five Presbyteries have come any expressions of dissent and that chiefly against organic union; therefore,

"'Your committee recommend that a committee of five ministers and five ruling elders, with the Moderator of this Assembly added thereto as ex-officio chairman, be appointed by the present Moderator of this Assembly to confer with any like committee that the other Assembly may appoint, concerning the whole subject of organic union, co-operative union, and any other relation between the two Assemblies, and said committee be directed to report the result of the joint conference to the General Assembly at its meeting in May, 1888, for approval or disapproval. And that the committee be instructed to take and maintain the following positions:

"'1. The mere acceptance of the common Standards of our Church, Confession of Faith, Shorter and Larger Catechisms, does not in our minds form a sufficient basis of union; but the acceptance of that peculiar interpretation of our Standards which affirms and emphasizes the purely spiritual nature of Christ's kingdom and forbids her legislating upon political and civil matters, is the only true basis of union.

"'2. And further, we insist that the colored brethren within our bounds shall be organized into separate congregations, Presbyteries and Synods.'

"The Minority Report, signed by nine of the committee, reads as follows:

" 'The undersigned members of your Special Committee appointed to examine and report upon the papers and overtures submitted to the General Assembly on the question of organic and co-operative union with the Presbyterian Church in the United States of America, are of the opinion that the difficulties in the way are so numerous, and of so serious a nature, that they cannot be removed.

" 'They arise mainly out of the fact that the two Churches are not agreed in matters of either *principle* or *polity.* The plea that the two have the same "Confession of Faith," may be fully met by the simple statement that all Evangelical Denominations have the same Protestant Bible. But the difference in the one case, as in the other, arises out of the interpretation of the teaching of the two Books. So the separate existence of the Southern Church is as much demanded because of the widely different interpretation of the language of that Confession of Faith in matters both of *doctrine* and *government,* as the separate existence of other denominations of Christians is demanded, because they are not sufficiently agreed in their essential tenets to constitute one organic body.

" 'No suggestion has been made, or, in the opinion of those signing this paper, can be made, for the removal of this most serious obstacle which meets us at the very opening of this question.

" 'To unite, or attempt to unite, the two Churches on any compromise of these fundamental differences, or upon any general statements, such as the reception of the Standards "pure and simple," would "serve only to bring together those who could not act in harmony, and would perpetuate strife and alienation."

" 'These conclusions have been reached by us after a full and careful examination of the whole question in the light of all the papers submitted for our consideration. The discussion of the question for some time past, both North and South, has made it equally manifest that the further agitation of this question would hinder the progress, weaken the efficiency, and endanger the unity of our Church.'

"The two papers were jointly considered in the discussion which followed, all the points involved in either being handled without restriction. The wide range of this debate brought the whole subject of union between the two Churches under review, to be discussed upon its merits simply and without being entangled with minor issues. At a later stage a substitute was offered for both reports, and was adopted by a vote of eighty against fifty-seven. We give the text of this substitute:

" 'WHEREAS, A number of overtures in reference to closer relations to the Presbyterian Church in the United States of America have come up to this Assembly; and

"WHEREAS, The General Assembly of the Presbyterian Church in the United States of America has just adopted the deliverance of the two Synods of Missouri on the spirituality of the Church; and

"'WHEREAS, The two Assemblies ought to labor together for the accomplishment of the great object they have in view, if they are sufficiently agreed in their principles to make them more efficient for their work united than they now are divided; and

"'WHEREAS, The recent action of the General Assembly of the Presbyterian Church of the United States of America, apparently different from their former action, as to the spirituality of the Church, makes the impression on the minds of many of our people that one obstacle to closer relations to that Church has been, or soon may be, removed; therefore,

"'*Resolved,* That a committee of four ministers and four ruling elders, together with the Moderator, be appointed to meet with a similar committee of the General Assembly of the Presbyterian Church in the United States of America, if such a committee shall be appointed, for the sole purpose of inquiring into and ascertaining the facts as to the point above mentioned, and as to the position that Assembly proposes to maintain as to colored churches, ecclesiastical boards, and any other subjects now regarded as obstacles in the way of united effort for the propagation of the Gospel, and report these facts to the next General Assembly for such action as they may warrant.'

"Their names being on the record of ayes and noes, the minority do not care to enter a formal protest against the policy pursued; but in a conference held by some fifty of their number it was resolved to set forth the grounds of their opposition in an open letter to the Churches, in which there should be a calm restatement of all the issues involved in this controversy. This delicate task was assigned to a committee of eight, as follows: B. M. Palmer, R. L. Dabney, R. K. Smoot, J. L. Girardeau, C. R. Vaughan, ministers; and C. F. Collier, Judge Armstrong, W. L. T. Prince, elders. This brief history forms a proper introduction to the statement, which follows, of the reasons why so large a portion of the Church, as represented in the late Assembly, stands unalterably opposed to the fusion of the two bodies and to all steps leading in that direction.

"1. We allege the original ground of separation existing still in full force, which in 1861 compelled the withdrawal of the Southern Synods and the formation of another Assembly, to-wit: the right claimed and exercised by the Northern Church to intermeddle with questions of State policy lying outside of ecclesiastical jurisdiction. In sustaining this charge, it is not necessary to cite all the political deliverances of the Northern Assembly during the four years of the late Civil War, from 1861 to 1865. For the sake of brevity, we sink all these in the first—known as the famous 'Spring Resolution'—adopted in 1861 by a vote of one hundred and fifty-four against sixty-six. It reads as follows: [See page 240 of this volume for these resolutions.]

"Here, then, is an interpretation of our Civil Constitution, as formal and precise as though it had emanated from the Supreme Court of the United States. Not only so, it undertakes to decide a question left open by the framers of the Constitution, and upon which the statesmen of this country have been divided ever since the foundation of the Republic. It is of no consequence, in this controversy, whether this is a true decision or not. Our contention is that an Ecclesiastical Court was incompetent to entertain the subject, especially in view of the fact that the Church is defined in our Standards as 'a government in the hands of Church officers, distinct from the Civil Magistrate.' (Conf. 30: 1.) Still more expressly is it declared, 'these Assemblies (Congregational, Presbyterial and Synodical) ought not to possess any civil jurisdiction, nor inflict any civil penalties. Their power is wholly moral or spiritual, and that only ministerial and declarative' (Form of Government, Chapter 8: 2). As though the Church was not sufficiently separated in her spiritual jurisdiction from the State, she is sternly restrained within her appropriate sphere, in this language of inhibition: 'Synods and Councils are to handle or conclude nothing but that which is ecclesiastical, and are not to intermeddle with civil affairs which concern the Commonwealth' (Conf., Ch. 31: 4). In the face, however, of these explicit statements rigidly defining the nature and functions of the Church, the Northern Assembly in 1861 undertook to determine the vexed question, the fearful legacy left through the indecision of our forefathers, whether the allegiance of the citizen was primarily due to the State or to the Central authority. Against this palpable invasion of the province of the State a protest, signed by the venerable Dr. Chas. Hodge and forty-five others, testifies in the following nervous style: 'The General Assembly in thus deciding a political question, and in making that decision practically a condition of membership of the Church, has, in our judgment, violated the Constitution of the Church, and usurped the prerogative of its Divine Master.'

"Of course, all this political legislation by the Northern Church is now obsolete, the occasion which called it forth having passed away. But the principle remains, upon which it was based; and upon which we are as necessarily separated from their communion, as when we were forcibly ejected in 1861. Northern Presbyterians by no means deny the spiritual nature of Christ's kingdom, as an abstract doctrine. They will subscribe the declarations of our common Standards upon that point, as readily as ever they did. If necessary, they would not hesitate to renew their testimony in as many fresh deliverances as the exigency may demand—which was actually done, it will be remembered, by their late Assembly at Omaha. The difference between them and ourselves lies not in subscribing opposing Standards of faith, but in interpreting the same Standards. It is not for an instant to be suggested that intelligent Christian men would deliberately fly in the face of the solemn covenant by which they are held together, with the avowed purpose of tramping their professed convictions beneath their feet. It is claimed and honestly believed by our brethren at the North that, in the great crisis then upon the country, the Church was imperatively summoned to the defense and support of the State. A higher law suspended the operation of the lower, rendering consistent with the spirit of the Standards the political legislation which trampled upon the letter. Not only during that period of intense excitement, but in the afterthought of five and twenty years which have since elapsed, this interference in matters of State policy has been defended as just and proper; and these political utterances have been, and still are, enshrined in her archives as precious testimonies of that 'spirit of Christian patriotism which the Scriptures enjoin, and which have always characterized this Church.' There is no partisan exaggeration in the statement that the right to utter these pronunciamentos is still maintained in the Northern Church. In all the conferences between the two bodies since 1870, there has been no recession from their original position; and as late as 1882, when 'Fraternal Relations' were formally declared between the two Assemblies, it was openly proclaimed that only the charges of heresy, blasphemy, etc., were withdrawn; while all the fulminations of the Presbyterian Vatican are still hurled against what they are still pleased to denounce as the 'Rebellion.'

'We wish it to be clearly seen that the Southern Church is separated from the Northern by no lingering resentment of the war; but by a principle for which, in the providence of God, she was solemnly appointed as the witness. Her testimony has been silently delivered, simply through her separate existence; and this renewed agitation may be divinely ordered, to recall her attention to the sacred function which she must continue to discharge. We at the South understand the Church to be restrained by her organic law from intermeddling with the affairs of Caesar's household—that when she is defined in the Scriptures as 'the kingdom not of this world,' she has other and higher functions than those assigned to the State—that as a non-secular and non-political body, the line is to be clearly drawn between herself and the Commonwealth, which no sophistry shall be allowed to obscure. They at the North, on the other hand, accept the general truth as to the spiritual nature and functions of the Church with a wide margin of interpretation; so that whenever politics shall rise into the sphere of morals, it is brought fairly within her jurisdiction. It does not seem to occur to them that every question which touches man in his social relations has necessarily a moral side; and that the principle avowed by them obliterates every line of demarcation, and sweeps everything into the domain of the Church. This then is the first barrier to union between the two bodies. The instant it is accomplished, we surrender the testimony we have been called to bear as to the true nature of Christ's kingdom upon earth; we concede the right claimed by the Northern Church to determine our political relations; we abandon a principle hitherto held sacred by our people. As a mere fraction of the body into which we have been absorbed, our feeble protests will be unavailing to arrest the tide of political legislation upon which the Church must necessarily embark; until a new secession shall disturb the peace, and liberate our conscience from a bondage too oppressive to be endured. If any should regard this danger as imaginary, under the impression that public sentiment at the North has undergone a wholesome change in this respect, it will not be difficult to adduce a chain of political decisions running through recent years, and terminating with the action of the last Assembly at Omaha in committing the Church to Prohibition as a political measure to be grafted upon the Civil Constitution. This action taken by the very Assembly which was protesting its belief in the spiritual character of the Church shows conspicuously how easy it is through the moral side of politics to interpret away the salutary restrictions of the Standards. What resistance could we make to reckless legislation of this sort, in a minority of one to five in the united body? And how long would the Christian conscience of our people be able to abide this constant evasion of our organic law, before declaring their freedom in a new exile from the house of their fathers?

"2. It should not be overlooked that the body into which we are desired to fuse is not the same from which we were separated five and twenty years ago. The incorporation of the New School wing, effected in 1869 and 1870, has not only doubled its size, but has introduced elements so different as to render it prudent to enquire into the doctrinal basis upon which we will be expected to stand. Lest this language should seem to betray an unworthy suspicion, it will be necessary to recall somewhat the history of the past.

"It is sad to reflect how often the truth of God has been betrayed by those especially set for its defense. The pride of human speculation has overborne the reverent study of the Word and obscured, if not perverted, its teachings. Seasons of defection, sometimes of open apostasy, occur at different epochs and in different portions of the Church, in which the truth has again and again suffered a partial or a total eclipse. In the early part of the present century, a protracted struggle took place in the Presbyterian Church for the preservation of the doctrines of grace which were being undermined through a subtle method of interpretation. The principles of Church order and government were also contravened; and the Church was so overlaid by agencies foreign to her system, that in her organized form she was in great danger of being throttled in the unnatural embrace. This conflict, it need scarcely be said, terminated in the disruption of the Church in 1837-8. One week before the meeting of the General Assembly in the former of these two years, a Convention of Old School men was held in the city of Philadelphia, presided over by the Rev. Dr. Baxter, of Virginia. A memorial went up from this Convention to the General Assembly, and was adopted by them, in which testimony was borne against certain doctrinal errors declared to be then rife in the Presbyterian Church. To this solemn indictment in sixteen distinct specifications, the New School members of the body felt called upon to make reply in order to purge themselves of participation in the same. The replication was, however, so unsatisfactory on many of the points, that on motion of the Rev. Dr. Plumer their protest was admitted to record without answer, among other reasons, because 'the character of the paper rendered another disposition of it proper and necessary.' This was followed by a resolution, 'that duly certified copies of this paper be sent to the respective Presbyteries to which the signers of the Protest belonged, calling their attention to the developments of theological views contained in it, and enjoining on them to enquire into the soundness of the faith of those who have ventured to make so strange avowals as some of these are.' Our narrow limits will not allow the incorporation of the original documents, which are lengthy on both sides; but they are of easy access in the published Minutes of the General Assembly of 1837, and may also be found fully engrossed in the revised edition of Baird's 'Digest'—which we happen to have at hand, and is upon the shelf of almost every minister's library in the land. This general reference is sufficient for our purpose, which is to show that serious doctrinal differences existed between the Old School and New School, which could not be adjusted; and which caused the Church, in that eventful year, to be rent asunder, the two sections walking apart during a period of thirty years.

"If it be asked how such a flood of errors should be let loose in the Presbyterian Church, whose doctrinal symbols are so full and so exact as apparently to leave no room for ambiguity anywhere, the answer is ready. It had become fashionable in those days of lax theology to subscribe these sacred symbols 'for substance' only. Instead of the hearty acceptance of them in their plain English meaning, there was a 'paltering in a double sense.' The slippery phrase, 'for substance of doctrine,' like 'the moral side of politics' in our time, enabled those who so desired to play fast and loose with the Standards of faith—introducing a metaphysical jugglery by which, whilst remaining in outward seeming, they vanish into airy nothingness without sense or sound. Delphic oracles, which echoed on the secret wish of those by whom they were consulted, had no power to utter God's truth with which they were no longer inspired.

"But what have these troubles of fifty years ago to do with our fusion into the Northern Church of 1887? Why, just this: That if we find the Old School and the New School now together, who were separated by doctrinal differences fifty years ago, it is natural to inquire how they came together: especially if, as a party to the same union, we are to stand upon the basis of doctrine which they have established. Unfortunately, just here our perplexity begins. The core of the controversy in 1837 was the sense in which the Standards of Faith were to be received. Obviously if all parties subscribed the Confession *ex animo,* in the obvious meaning of the language employed, there could be no difference between them: they would be in perfect agreement upon the terms in which they understand the truth to be delivered in the sacred Scriptures. But the difficulty was that the Old School demanded reception of the formulas of faith in the precise terms in which they were rendered; whilst the New School demanded liberty, so that under a general adherence to these venerated symbols a wide latitude should be allowed in their explication. In this state of case, there could be no settlement of the issues between them, because there was no umpire to whom they could be referred. Of course, nothing remained for them but to part as Abraham and Lot did, one going to the right and the other to the left. Now so far as we can see it is precisely upon the same lax subscription of the Standards the two parties have agreed to come together—delivering both over to a loose and uncertain theology, and laying the foundation for another schism in the future; or, what is worse, creating a sort of 'Broad Church' with its 'liberal Christianity' admitting every shade of opinion, and surrendering the truth to be slaughtered by all her foes.

"The negotiation between the parties was opened in 1866, by the Old School Assembly expressing its 'desire for reunion with the other branch of the Presbyterian Church at the earliest time consistent with agreement in doctrine, order and polity, on the basis of our common Standards.' Accordingly committees of Conference were appointed by both, who continued their labors through 1867 and 1868, striving to find a sense in which they can agree to accept the Westminster Standards. In both these years they send up reports to their respective Assemblies, which were, however, unacceptable on the one side or the other. At first, the sense defined was to be 'the fair historical sense, as it is accepted by the two bodies in opposition to Antinomianism and Fatalism on the one hand, and to Arminianism and Pelagianism on the other.' Then, the 'Confession is to be received in its proper historical

—that is, the Calvinistic or Reformed—sense;' whilst the 'various methods of viewing, stating, explaining and illustrating the doctrines of the Confession, which do not impair the integrity of the Reformed or the Calvinistic system, are to be as freely allowed in the United Church, as they have hitherto been allowed in the separate Churches.' In all these conferences the strange absurdity does not seem to have struck the contending parties, of accepting Standards which are not a final authority; nor the still stranger absurdity of setting the Church adrift upon the wide sea of ecclesiastical history, to find in Calvinistic or Reformed utterances a standard for the Standards. One would suppose it far easier to get directly at the meaning of an outspoken instrument, like the Confession of Faith, with its terse dogmatic statements, than to gather up the voices scattered through all the centuries.

"When compromise had failed to adjust its scales to the nicety of expression required in the case, nothing was left but to accept the Standards *simpliciter,* without any sense upon which the contestants could agree. What can this mean, after two years' haggling over the matter, but that the point is waived; and that both parties shall go their way, and fix the sense exactly as it pleases either? But this precisely was what each did before the disruption; and the Northern Church stands to-day, in the matter of subscription to the Standards, just where she stood in 1837 when the Old and New Schools parted from each other in bitter strife.

"The sad story is not yet completely rehearsed. The doctrinal basis was accompanied with a number of 'Concurrent Declarations,' to be adopted by both the parties, settling certain details of the Covenant between them. We pass over several which invite our criticism, in order to fix attention upon two especially germane to the point now before us. They are as follows:

" 'The publications of the Board of Publication (O. S.) and of the Publication Committee (N. S.) should continue to be issued as at present; leaving it to the Board of Publication of the United Church to revise these issues, and perfect a catalogue of the United Church, so as to exclude invidious references to past controversies.' Again: 'And no rule or precedent which does not stand approved by both the bodies should be of any authority, until re-established in the united body; except in so far as such rule or precedent may affect the rights of property founded thereon.'

"We group together these expunging 'Declarations,' because they sweep the field of the past clean to the very horizon. What becomes of all the acts and testimonies of the Old School body in the great semi-Pelagian controversy of 1837? Under the first, every book and tract issued by the board in defense or explanation of Old School positions, as a witness for the doctrines of grace, must be expurgated so as to exclude anything which might be construed as offensive to the other party. And if the last 'Declaration' be pressed to its ultimate reach, it surely cuts through even to the 'exscinding acts' themselves, and to the famous 'Act and Testimony;' and potentially repeals every deliverance of the Old School Church up to the genesis of the schism. What is this but a neat surgical operation, by which three and thirty years are cut out from the history and life of the Church, bringing the two edges of the wound together for adhesion? The obvious design is to place the United Church of 1869 in immediate connection with the United Church of 1836, dropping out the intervening period with all the various and solemn transactions with which it is filled. Are we prepared for the surrender of all these testimonies of those venerable councils in which we ourselves sat more than thirty years ago, when a disguised Pelagianism sought to root out the cross of Christ from the earth? For this reason alone, if for no other, the Presbyterian Church of the South must refuse to enter into an alliance which exposes her, in the future, to all the perils of a loose theology creeping in through an uncertain subscription of the Standards of Faith.

"It may be asked whether our own Church is not involved in the same condemnation, through her previous union in 1864 with 'the New School Synod of the South.' There are several points of difference between the two cases: (1) The 'Synod of the South' was never suspected of doctrinal unsoundness, except as to one or two of its members. These alleged errors prevailed rather in the Northern section of our country, and had scarcely invaded the Southern. The 'Synod of the South' was led into connection with the New School party chiefly through opposition to the 'exscinding acts' of 1837 as being, in their judgment, unconstitutional; and was forced eventually to separate itself, and form an independent organization. (2) A single conference between them and us was sufficient to evince an entire agreement upon points of doctrine. (3) The union was effected at once upon an *ex animo* reception of the Standards, without any antecedent effort to find a 'sense' in which the two could agree. We incline to think that this element in our body will be as slow as any other to consent to fusion with the now united Northern Church.

"III. It is necessary to remind our brethren of a matter which may perhaps have slipped somewhat from their memory: to-wit, the solemn covenant made with the Synod of Kentucky, in relation to their 'Declaration and Testimony' when it entered into union with the Southern Church. This may require to be illuminated a little from the history of the past.

"It was not possible for the Northern Church so fatally to complicate herself with the State, without earnest opposition from many who still prize her spirituality and independence, as one of the doctrines of their ancient faith. The vigorous protest of Dr. Chas. Hodge and others in 1861 died away in decreasing echoes, as the war spirit became more rampant; until the proscriptive edicts of the Pittsburg Assembly in 1865 aroused the slumbering dissent to utter its remonstrances in tones that could no longer be smothered. A solemn 'Declaration and Testimony' was drawn up against the entire political action of the five Assemblies from 1861 to 1865 inclusive. In fourteen specifications they recapitulate the errors into which the Church had fallen; testifying against the same (1) 'because they are contrary to the Word of God, and subversive of its inspiration and authority;' (2) 'because they are contrary to the doctrine of the Presbyterian Church, as taught in her Confession, Catechisms and Constitutions;' (3) 'because they tend to obliterate all the lines of separation between the civil and ecclesiastical powers—to confound their jurisdiction—to identify them with each other, and so destroy the freedom of both;' (4) 'because they have brought the ministry, and ordinances of religion, and the authority of the Church, into public disrepute;' (5) 'because they tend to keep up strife and alienation among brethren of a common faith;' (6) 'because they are schismatical.'

"We cite the language thus far, in order to show the spirit of a famous document which, covering twenty pages of print, is too lengthy to be here engrossed. This appeal to the conscience of the Church, instead of bringing her back to the old paths, irritated the Assembly of 1866 to the adoption of retaliatory measures. We cannot pause to enumerate the various and grievous usurpations of authority by this misguided Assembly, in which they trampled not only the Constitution of the Church in the dust, but violated every principle of justice and law as between man and man. The older ministers in our body are familiar with the facts to which we here allude; the younger may find the record in the published minutes of the body in which they were enacted. It may amaze them to discover how the foundations of representative governments were removed, in the displacement of Commissioners whose title was clear and undisputed as that of any other member of the body; how the forms of judicial progress were overridden by undertaking to manage an essentially judicial case by purely legislative methods; how ministers and elders were enjoined the exercise of the necessary functions of their office, whilst without trial they were recognized as presbyters in the Church; how the authority of the Assembly was stretched over persons and subjects not within its jurisdiction; and how finally Presbyteries were dissolved *ipso facto* by a contingent legislation, which by a self-acting power makes the unfortunate court guilty of *felo de se*. The result of this passionate legislation was to rend the two Synods of Missouri and Kentucky, each into two parts, creating thus another schism in the house of God.

"We are brought now to the point where all this bears upon ourselves. In 1867 this excluded portion of the Synod of Kentucky appeared through its commissioners before the Southern Assembly in Nashville, presenting a letter covering fifteen printed pages in the Appendix to our Minutes of that year. It is a historical document of great value, setting forth the doctrines and principles which the Declaration and Testimony party in Kentucky—and we may add, in Missouri—had so vigorously and righteously maintained through these years of conflict. This full statement of fundamental principles was prepared by the Synod and sent to us, 'to stand as their testimony for the truth and order of Christ's house, and to be substantially the basis of a covenant upon which the Synod of Kentucky may form an organic union with the General Assembly of the Presbyterian Church in the United States.' Their object will be more clearly seen in the following quotations from that important instrument:

"'We deem it scarcely necessary, fathers and brethren, . . . to assure you that it is not because of any distrust of your faithfulness to those doctrines and principles that we have thought of this method of forming an organic union with you on the basis of a solemn covenant agreement to maintain the doctrines and constitutional principles set forth in this paper. . . . We deem it but a proper attestation of our earnestness and sincerity in bearing this testimony, to claim for it a record and acknowledgment as a part of the acts and monuments whereby, historically, the Church interprets its Standards. Nor do we doubt for a moment that on solemn consideration of the signs of the times, and of the Erastian tendencies of our Presbyterianism both in the United States and in Great Britain, you will gladly embrace the opportunity by so peculiar an occasion to join with us, should a union be formed, in a solemn covenanted testimonial to the truths for which in common we have been "contending earnestly as the faith once delivered to the saints" and to erect in the historical records of the Church a monument which shall at once declare to those that come after us our appreciation of the inestimable value of these principles as the bulwark of the Christian liberty wherewith Christ sets his people free.'

"The closing sentence of the letter is in these words:

"'The Synod feels unwilling to enter into organic union with any large and powerful organization again without some such guarantee to its churches and people against troubles in future, similar to those just passed through.'

"Our Assembly responded to this overture in the following terms:

"'The Assembly feels free solemnly to assure the Synod of Kentucky not only of our cordial approval of, and sincere concurrence substantially in, the Synod's statement of doctrine and constitutional principles, as contained under the four heads of the third division of their letter, but of our sincere joy to find our brethren of Kentucky so ready to unite with us in solemn covenant, with a view, among other things, to the advancement and maintenance of these doctrines as against the apparent Erastian tendencies of our American Protestantism.'

"Then follows a resolution:

"'That the letter of the Synod of Kentucky be admitted to record, as they suggest, as a part of the historical acts and monuments of the Church, by publishing it in the Appendix to the Minutes of the Assembly.'

"The argument from these premises will be alike brief and pointed. Here is a portion of our constituency which exactly twenty years ago entered into union with us, on the basis of a solemn contract. The Synod of Kentucky made it a condition precedent of this union that we should covenant to maintain the doctrines and principles of their Declaration and Testimony, and admit it to record as being identical with those for which we ourselves had been contending—and thus it should be acknowledged as a part of the acts and monuments whereby, historically, the Church interprets its Standards. They demand this as a guarantee of their own safety, that they might not in the future be delivered over to the perils from which they had just escaped. This guarantee we gave; and so far endorsed their principles as to adopt them in our records as our own. If now it be proposed to transfer this Synod—and we may add the Synod of Missouri, which came into union with us shortly after—to the very body from which they had been expelled, it becomes us to examine critically that we may not be guilty of a breach of covenant. Has then the Northern Church, during the one and twenty years which have elapsed since these indignities were put upon our Kentucky and Missouri brethren, given any evidence of regret for the same? Have they taken a single step towards repairing the breach made by themselves in their own Constitution? When in 1864, in the State of Missouri, the celebrated 'Rosecrans Order,' placed a sentinel at the door of that Synod to administer a civil oath to its members as a qualification for admission, has the Northern Assembly ever put forth any declaration of the supremacy of the Church within her own jurisdiction; thus repairing any dislocation of their system through the rudeness of war? If not, how can we now transfer to that body these Synods, who came to us demanding a guarantee that they would never be betrayed into the sorrows and conflicts through which they had just passed?

"Even though these Synods should, in the lapse of time, grow indifferent to these afflictive memories and so consent to the transfer in question, have not we solemnly pledged ourselves to the maintenance of the principles of the 'Declaration and Testimony,' by incorporating it among our own 'acts and monuments?' Can we, under the obligations of this covenant with the Synod of Kentucky, ourselves unite with the Northern Church, until they have made matters straight with that Synod by repudiating the usurpation under which it has been wronged? In a word, do the advocates of fusion, as a measure of peace between us and the Northern branch, perceive the old wounds they are ripping open and the endless controversies into which they are plunging the very parties whom they seek to reconcile?

"IV. An insuperable barrier to union with the Northern Church is the race problem, which the presence of the Negro in such numbers at the South forces us to consider. Let us examine it, uninfluenced by sentiment upon the one hand or by prejudice on the other. It cannot be denied that God has divided the human race into several distinct groups, for the sake of keeping them apart. When the promise was given to Noah that the world should not be again destroyed with a flood, it became necessary to restrain the wickedness of man that it should not rise to the same height as in the ante-Diluvian period. Hence the unity of human speech was broken, and 'so the Lord scattered them abroad from thence upon the face of all the earth.' Now co-ordinate with this 'confusion of tongues,' we find these groups distinguished by certain physical characteristics—and that, too, as far back as history carries us. We are not warranted in affirming that this differentiation through color and otherwise was accomplished at the same time, and as part of the same process, with the 'confusion of tongues;' but since the distinction exists from a period in the past of which history takes no note, and since science fails to trace the natural causes by which it could be produced, the inference is justified which regards it as fixed by the hand of Jehovah himself. At any rate, all the attempts to restore the original unity of the race by the amalgamation of these severed parts have been providentially and signally rebuked. In all instances where the Caucasian stock has crossed with the others—as when the Latin families, with a feebler instinct of race, have intermingled with the people whom they found in Mexico and in portions of South America--the result has been the production of a stock inferior in quality to both the factors which sunk their superior virtues in an emasculated progeny. Largely to this cause is due the failure of these Latin families to hold the colonies which they have established in different parts of the world; and which have, one by one, slipped from their hands into the possession of others. The Anglo-Saxon stock, on the contrary, through all time jealous of its purity of blood and refusing to debase it by intermingling with inferior races, has preserved its power and to this day dominates vast empires in which it has planted its banners. These are stubborn facts lying upon the face of history, open to the inspection of all who will studiously consider their import.

"Upon no point are the Southern people more sensitive, to no danger are they more alive, than this of the amalgamation of the two races thrown so closely together and threatening the deterioration of both. This is the peril which confronts us in the proposal to re-integrate in the Northern Church as being one of the early steps leading surely to that final result. The North is not embarrassed with this negro problem; so few of this race are found in any of their communities, that they may be assumed into social relations without disturbance of society at large. The infusion of two or three drops of ink into a tumbler of water will not discolor it; and in Northern circles, the Negro is an inappreciable factor. He may appear here and there, an occasional Presbyter in their ecclesiastical courts, and be found now and then a commissioner in their General Assembly, but he is practically lost in the large body of the other race, and shorn of importance except where a sentimental and purely fictitious distinction lifts him into momentary prominence. There is no danger that the Church at large will be ruled by a Negro majority, fastening their crude superstitions and fantastic usages upon those so far superior to them in intelligence and virtue. With us at the South, the conditions are different: the Negroes exist side by side with us in almost equal numbers, and the relation to obtain between us becomes a vital question. A policy which would be safe at the North, would be ruinous at the South. A Negro Presbyter associated with us, here and there, would be as inappreciable in a Southern as in a Northern Presbytery. But it is easy to see how, with a view to ecclesiastical subjugation, Negro churches could be multiplied of infinitesimal proportions, packing our courts with Presbyters of that race to whom the entire Church would be in hopeless subjection. In addition to this ecclesiastical peril, there is another which is social. How can the two races be brought together in nearly equal numbers in those confidential and sacred relations which belong to the ministry of the Word, without entailing that personal intimacy between ministers and people which must end in the general amalgamation of discordant races? We simply hint at evils which we do not desire to discuss in detail: the mere suggestion of them will put the readers of this paper upon their own line of reflection, filling out the argument to its due proportion.

"Nor can we think of any device by which we may be preserved from these dangers, in the bosom of the Northern Church. If we fall upon the expedient of Provincial Assemblies ascending to a national Assembly representing them all, this last must be a true court of the Church and have final jurisdiction over the courts below it. All questions, therefore, arising out of our connection with this race will be brought under the review and control of our Northern brethren; so that the autonomy of the Provincial Assembly, which was expected to exempt us from their supervision, will be found unavailing; unless we throw such restrictions around that highest court as shall deprive it of all its true nature as a court and make it a mere excrescence upon our system.

"It will doubtless be asked if we cannot confide in the Christian character of our brethren at the North, who surely possess intelligence enough to see these perils as clearly as ourselves, and whose piety will insure a due sympathy in the same. To this challenge we reply with perfect candor. There are thousands of beloved and honored brethren in the Northern Church, in whose considerate piety we can confide to the last degree. If we had to deal only with them, all these troubles had long since been adjusted upon principles of righteousness and truth. Unfortunately, however, behind these wise and safe men there is a wild and unmanageable constituency, which sleeps in calm repose until an occasion suddenly calls out all their fanaticism and fury. We cannot shut our eyes to the fact that on the subject of the Negro the mass of the Northern people has been going wild for half a century; and, therefore, to-day, when the Negro is in a position to be more an element of disturbance than ever, this is the one subject which we cannot trust the Northern Church to discuss for us, or to legislate upon. Simple prudence advises us to keep this matter in our own hands, under a sense of responsibility only to Him before whose throne we bow with adoring and yet loving awe. We know the Negro, and he knows us. There is not one of that race who does not confide in the unswerving truthfulness with which we have always dealt with him; and to-day the word of a Southern man goes further with him than the word of any other man. He knows that the Christian people of the South wish him well in the attitude in which he stands before the world. We desire his advance in sound education, and in the knowledge of all those arts and industries by which he can be rendered happy and prosperous in this life. Above all, he knows that we desire his spiritual welfare. At the first, we hoped to hold him in connection with us in our churches, as in the old-time we were accustomed to worship together in the House of God. We were slow in coming to this ground when, under the race instinct, he demanded a church and ministry of his own; and now, there is no sacrifice of toil or of means which the Southern Presbyterian Church will not gladly make, to bring the race to which he belongs to be 'joint heirs with us' among the sons of God. And we are convinced that the policy of a separate Church organization, which the Negro was the first to demand, is the only policy which is practical or possible in the relation which the two races now hold to each other.

"There are numerous other objections to union with the Northern branch of the Presbyterian Church, which we had intended to group under a distinct head: such as the use of 'Boards' which we have cast aside, and thus got rid of a tedious and most unprofitable controversy; the different view of the eldership prevailing in the two bodies, rotary in the one and permanent in the other, admitted to the Moderator's office in the one and excluded in the other; the different Books of Church Order, under which the two bodies are administered;

the disposition at the North to multiply guilds within the Church, and leagues without, for the accomplishment of special ends which are all within the scope of the Church's own agency; the woman's rights crusade which disturbs the repose of the North and from which we are comparatively free: these, with others which might be named, will present to many minds practical difficulties rendering the union in question a doubtful blessing, even if it could be obtained. The length, however, which this letter has already reached, debars the prosecution of these topics. We are willing to rest our opposition to the proposed fusion upon the four grounds already elaborated in this paper. They present difficulties, not of mere policy, but of enduring principles—of principles which outlive the mere historic occasion which first called for their outward expression, and which demand a new advocacy in those moments when they are most in danger of being forgotten.

"These views we present respectfully to our brethren, in the hope that they will avail among other influences in preventing either the disintegration or the disruption of our beloved Church."

Dr. Palmer believed that he was simply doing a plain duty in thus opposing "closer relations" with the Presbyterian Church, North.

There was another movement [9] which he in like manner unsuccessfully opposed; but opposed on principle. The grounds of his opposition he brought out in a speech against the movement, in the Assembly at St. Louis in 1875. The speech as reported in the *Southwestern Presbyterian*, June 24, 1875, is, the preliminary remarks omitted:

"Moderator, the Presbyterian Church in this country has always suffered whenever she has departed by the breadth of a hair from her recognized principles. She never has entered into compromises with Congregationalism, or gone into the support of voluntary associations of any sort, without suffering in the end. Here, then, is the first objection which I raise—that you are creating a power, as Colonel Ogden has so eloquently stated, and which, therefore, I need not repeat. *You are creating a power.* It may content itself with recommendation; but still it will stand up as the apex of the great Presbyterian cone. The decisions and utterances of that body will be regarded as the enunciation of the Presbyterian sentiment of the world, and its utterances will be *pro tanto* decisions. They will, in the force which they will gather around them, overbear the opinions, judgments and utterances of the particular Presbyterian Assemblies of the particular countries where they are held. The very argument used in this As-

[9] That which resulted in the foundation of the Pan-Presbyterian Alliance.

sembly that we must 'come into line' will continue to prevail—that we must keep in line, that we must not break away from the path marked out by this great council which represents the thought and sentiment of the whole Presbyterian world. Sir, it is too great a power to be irresponsible. I am afraid of it. I tell you, Moderator, I am afraid of it, and my only hope is that before it shall be able to do any serious detriment to the Church of God, it will break down by its own weight and become disintegrated. If it does not, I tell you that it will become, in the end, a great, irresponsible, infallible Presbyterian Pope, and there will be no power in any Presbyterian Assembly to stand in her place, to lift up her voice and measure strength with that 'creature' which aggregates all the elements of Presbyterian power throughout the world, and which is not held in check by one solitary restraint which we can impose upon it.

"I have another objection, sir; and I will endeavor to be brief. What kind of Presbyterianism are you going to put in this General Council at the apex of the cone? Mark you, sir, each constituent factor that goes into the composition of that body must necessarily concede something which is peculiar to itself. And when you have aggregated all these concessions which are made by all the constituent factors in that body, you get a Presbyterianism of the lowest conceivable type—a Presbyterianism the least positive in the assertion of our principles—a Presbyterianism which, through concessions here, concessions there, and concessions everywhere, will be denuded of its power. Such will be the Presbyterianism which is to utter the Presbyterian sentiment of the world and to overbear our testimonies which will then become feeble as lifted against theirs.

"Let me illustrate; and I do it without any offence. Here is the Presbyterianism in Europe which is linked with the State. Is it possible that we can go into that general council with these Presbyterian bodies which are identified with the State, and lift up the testimony which you have uttered this very evening in the paper, unanimously adopted, in which we declare, in the most emphatic terms, the non-secular, non-political character of the Church? I tell my excellent brother, Dr. Robinson, by whose side I have been laboring all my life in defense of these principles and contending for the non-political character of the Church, that, if he should go under the appointment of this Assembly and stand upon that floor, he will find his hands tied and his tongue paralyzed as to any utterance which he shall dare to make in that body in reference to the principles which God specially calls us to uphold and to proclaim. I use this only in illustration, to show that the Presbyterianism of that general council will be the most degraded Presbyterianism the world knows, and is bound to be so by the operation of natural principles. It will be a Presbyterianism created by concessions on every hand. And, Moderator, I would not have a

Presbyterian people of that sort. If we are to have a council, let it be a council that grows up in the form of a legitimate Assembly, where there is no contravention of the spirit and principles of our government and order.

"With reference to this point, before I part with it I desire to say a word in regard to this matter of 'Isolation'—not going into detail, but taking it up comprehensively. Moderator, I have lived simply, in my sphere and according to the measure of my poor ability, to propagate in the Church, with which I am connected, the purest Presbyterianism that I know. I hope that I will not startle my brethren here when I say that, from the moment of the Reformation, when the Church emerged from the bondage of Popery, for three hundred years, Presbyterianism has never had, anywhere upon the face of the globe, an opportunity fairly and fully to work out its principles. In Europe, in this country, in that country and in the other country, she has been trammeled by her connection with the State. In foreign countries she has been under bondage and despotism, enduring persecution from the State. There was a grand opportunity given to the Presbyterian Church, when it was transferred from European shores and stood upon this virgin continent, to work out untrammeled the principles of a pure and perfect Presbyterianism; but, alas! under the same infatuation which I fear is overbearing this Assembly we went into an alliance with Congregationalism and Independency; and to this very hour our principles and our practice are, to a large degree, tainted with the influence which was exerted upon us by and through that alliance. Sir, I do not speak it egotistically, or with complacency in reference to this dear Church of ours, which in the wise and blessed and loving providence of God is an *ecclesia pressa*—but, believing that this isolated Church of ours is, in the sublime providence of God, placed in exactly the same position to work out a pure Presbyterianism, I consecrate my life to that; I am content with the sphere of the Southern Presbyterian Church. I have no ambition to walk the streets of Edinburgh, or to preach to the congregations in Scotland, if I must do so at the sacrifice of appearing as a delegate upon the floor of such an Ecumenical Council as this paper proposes. No, sir, the remainder of this life will be consecrated in the fear of God to the development, the perpetuation and exposition of the principles of Presbyterianism as I understand them, as they are summarily expressed in our Standards; and I am unwilling to run any ventures by which this Presbyterianism, which I desire to be more perfect in this Church of ours, shall be strangled.

"I do believe, Mr. Moderator, that my excellent brother, Dr. Robinson, is making the saddest mistake of his life in giving his adhesion to this movement, and that he will find himself, from this period to the end of his days (unless he shall be led by considerations such as I am now suggesting, somewhat to review and perhaps reverse his decision) crippled and trammeled in the very work to which I know his conscience and his heart are pledged. I want to save him from that mistake. I want to save this dear Church of ours, the only home on earth that I know, from being entangled in alliances which will cripple her efficiency and power. Be it so, Moderator, that like the Waldenses, we are the conies upon the tops of the mountains, hanging to the ledges of the rock with our feeble feet; let us in our feebleness, in our isolation (still in that isolation the object of universal contemplation) work out our destiny until the Lord pushes us to the front to do the great work in propagating our principles to the end of the earth. Here, in the corners of the world, let a pure Presbyterianism find a refuge—a Presbyterianism that I believe is on the eve of being strangled in the Northern Church, that cannot successfully, under present arrangements, be worked out elsewhere anywhere on the globe but here. Let us, in our isolation, in our obscurity, upon this plane, work out our mission, and the Lord will give us all the prominence that we deserve and all that we desire; and we shall speak out from this obscurity, from the chambers in which the Lord God has placed us for a time to hide us, a voice that will peal over the earth and whose echoes will ring until that trumpet sounds which shall wake the dead to judgment!

"I have a third objection, which I will simply state, and then close, thanking the Assembly for their kind attention to what I have said. Moderator, there has been a quiet change made in this paper from the original draft, which is somewhat suggestive. In the form in which it first came out, there were fifteen specifications which are now (boiled down) to five, and I see that there have been dropped out of the specifications one or two of the things which excited my greatest alarm. But even in this brief statement of the objects which that Council will pursue, I can see intimations of exceeding danger. Why, sir, at first it was proposed that they should undertake to protect the feeble, and push forward the cause of civil freedom throughout the world, to speak to the Sultan of Turkey and to the Emperor of Russia. That is not articulately mentioned here, but the very fact that it was suggested at the beginning shows that it is lying as a reserve thought in the mind. It is said here that this General Council is to take up the whole matter of 'Temperance,' and the whole matter of managing our religious interests in our crowded cities. You will find the very work which the Master has committed to his Church in her organized form, assumed by this irresponsible and voluntary Association, which is not a court and which therefore has no right to intrude upon the province of the Church in directing her as to how she is to manage these mighty issues.

"Sir, I close with the statement of my apprehension. I did not wish to make this speech. It has been pressed out of me with great sorrow and with great pain. I had hoped that my brethren would have accepted the proposition which would have estopped this discussion, and simply raised a committee to inquire into the expediency of going into this thing, bringing into the next Assembly a learned, elaborate paper in which the whole matter would be discussed from top to bottom, for that Assembly to decide as to the position our Church should take in reference to this movement. In the progress of a year, developments might be made. This preliminary conference would meet and draft a Constitution, and we would see how the thing stood. At the end of the year, perhaps, some of these difficulties might be met. Who knows but when that Council meets, that this very principle with which I started in the beginning might be raised—that if we are to go into this thing, we are to go into it as a court, a General Assembly for the whole world. What I wanted, was to pause without committing our own Church to one side of the question or to the other; and I did not desire that there should be any debate in reference to it at all. But the debate has come; and now, what is the result? What will these brethren gain by pressing this matter to a vote which will strip it of effect? You cannot get. in this body, anything like a unanimous vote, or a vote even approaching unanimity. The proposition may even be rejected. I do not know on which side the majority of this Assembly will stand, but you are going to have a split vote, and a vote, therefore, which, if carried only by a technical majority, will not express the true sentiment of the Church—not such a vote as that by which you ought to carry your Church into a policy so vast and attended by such important results as this. I would be glad if, as the final result of this discussion, the Assembly should determine simply to raise a committee to consider the expediency of the whole movement and report to the next Assembly, not such as that proposed by my friend, Dr. Robinson, which is to go into a correspondence, and thus commit us to the thing about the expediency of which we are to inquire."

We have further evidence of his profound and universal concern for the welfare of his communion at large in this letter, viz.:

"NEW ORLEANS, LA., Nov. 25, 1875.

"My dear Robinson: I have been intending, ever since your return from Europe, to write you a line of congratulation. For, while I differ from you upon the mission which carried you there, I can truly rejoice in all the good you may have accomplished, or even attempted, and still more in the kind Providence which watched over all your steps and brought you home in safety.

"I take up the pen, however, at this time for a definite object. You have doubtless been directly conferred with in reference to 'the new departure' taken by the *Southern Presbyterian Review,* at Columbia. Adger writes me that the brethren at Hampden-Sydney, Va., have ageed to unite with those at Columbia, as co-editors. It is proposed further, that a few others shall be solicited to pledge at least one article a year; and amongst those, I understand that you and myself and Girardeau and Miller of Charlotte are placed. I presume therefore that some correspondence has been had with you on this subject. I take it for granted, too, that you will cordially co-operate in this effort to place the *Review* upon a broader foundation, and to make it eminently worthy of the patronage of the Church.

"My purpose in this writing is to recall to your remembrance a conversation we had together, when I was last at your house. I ventured to suggest, and I understood you as concurring with it, that a syllabus of topics should be carefully drawn up, covering a wide field of thought, and such as would be peculiarly suited to the conditions of the Church; and that these should be distributed amongst those who could best handle them, securing thereby a continuous discussion, and that not specially polemic, of the great principles which we desire to see prevail in the Church.

"In preparing Thornwell's life for the press, I have been greatly convinced of one practical error which he and Dr. R. J. Breckinridge committed. It was that they sprung grave issues upon the Church, calling for *immediate* legislative action. The result was that, on each separate point—Boards, the elder question, the quorum question, *et al.*—they were floored, in the outset, by an adverse decision. The Church had not been prepared for these issues by antecedent discussion; voted blindly and wrongly; and these able men were placed at disadvantage in all the discussions afterwards, in that their opposition seemed to be a fractious one.

"I am pretty sure that you agree with me in thinking that, taking the whole country through, the Church tends to drift away from the Standards, both of Doctrine and Order. These great principles require to be fundamentally discussed again; and we now have a grand opportunity of doing it. We have an organ already established, just suited for the purpose, and we have the writers, if they can only be combined.

"If I have your sympathy in what I have written, which I do not doubt, as you see from the perfect freedom with which I pen these lines, will you not assist with your suggestions, in getting up this schedule? It need not be perfect at first; and I would like it broad and comprehensive, so as to cover all kinds of error that we ought to combat. For your convenience I will sketch *tentatively,* on a separate sheet, some subjects that occur to me. Will you give your opinion of them, by just drawing your pen through such as you think had better be dropped; and then add as many more topics as may occur to your own fertile brain?

"Adger highly approves the thought and begs to confer with you about it, as it has been already a subject of conversation between us.

"Yours as ever, in the Gospel of the Kingdom,

"B. M. PALMER."

Many other important services the Church received at his hands, as his continued labors on the revision of the Book of Church Order till the adoption of the Revised Book in 1879, the preparation and publication of the "Life and Letters of Dr. Thornwell," the production of a volume entitled "The Family in Its Civil and Church Aspects," addresses and essays, etc. But of these and other things in the succeeding chapter.

CHAPTER XVI.

AT THE SUMMIT OF HIS POWERS AND PRODUCTIVITY.

Continued.

(1875-1888.)

PRODUCTIONS OF HIS PEN: "LIFE AND LETTERS OF JAMES HENLEY THORNWELL, D.D., LL.D.," AND THE WAY IN WHICH IT WAS RECEIVED; "THE FAMILY IN ITS CIVIL AND CHURCHLY ASPECTS." REVIEW ARTICLES AND NEWSPAPER CONTRIBUTIONS.—LAGS IN WRITING THE LIFE OF DR. STUART ROBINSON.—OCCASIONAL DISCOURSES: ON "PERSECUTION OF JEWS IN RUSSIA," 1882; ON "RABBI GUTHEIM;" ON "THE CHURCH A SPIRITUAL KINGDOM."—THE SYLVESTER LARNED INSTITUTE, AND HIS WORK IN IT.—PASTORAL LETTERS: TO MRS. LONSDALE, TO CAPTAIN MACFIE, TO MRS. MACFIE, TO MRS. ANDERSON.—LETTER TO REV. W. C. CLARK.—LETTERS TO MRS. BIRD, AND TO MRS. ROBERT C. SHOEMAKER.—LETTER TO HIS FATHER.—HIS FATHER'S LAST LETTER TO HIM.—THE WAY IN WHICH HE REGARDED HIS FATHER'S DEATH.—HIS DOMESTIC HISTORY.—THE PHYSICALLY STRONG MEMBER OF HIS FAMILY; GIVES UP THE TOBACCO HABIT; FALL AT STAUNTON, VA.; DEATH OF GUSSIE PALMER COLCOCK.

THE "Life and Letters of Thornwell" were ready for the press about the beginning of the year 1875. There was difficulty, however, in finding a publisher. Dr. Palmer approached firm after firm in the North only to be refused. February 24, 1875, he writes to Dr. J. B. Adger: "The difficulties attending Southern authorship have impressed me with a new sense of the importance of our Board or Committee of Publication." March 5, 1875, he wrote, again, to Dr. Adger: "I see no resource but in Baird's offer [1] to publish by subscription. I will write to him, but not commit myself until I hear from you. On this account please answer as speedily as possible, and give your views fully. We are nothing to the North; and it is very clear to me that we must develop our own publishing interest."

He and his friends instituted vigorous and effective methods

[1] Dr. E. T. Baird was at that time Secretary of the Committee of Publication, Richmond, Va.

to gather subscribers. They soon secured a large list and in early December, 1876, the volume was issued.

For the production of this work Dr. Palmer possessed the amplest qualifications. For twenty years he had been intimately associated with Dr. Thornwell. They were then both laboring together in the same town, "and the utmost freedom and cordiality of intercourse existed between them." Their friendship was fervent. Palmer knew Thornwell in the intimacies of his home life—enjoyed his "bosom friendship;" and he knew him as a fellow presbyter on the floors of Presbytery, and Synod, and Assembly. He was gifted with the capacities to appreciate and to reproduce his life. He had that degree of sympathy with his subject without which a good biography cannot be written. He was at the same time a man of judicial and impartial temper.

He had a noble subject. It was his to tell how genius rose superior to obstacles, "how Divine grace prepared and trained it for the sublime mission of subsequent life," how it shone in sunshine and shadow. It was his to sketch the historic arena on which Thornwell ran his career, and show how his life was interwoven with the life of his age, how he was affected by it, and it by him. He did all in a most masterful way.

The literary style of the work demands the highest praise. It has been well said, that, "No reader can fail to be struck by the rhythmical flow and musical cadence of the sentences, the graceful elegance of expression, the copiousness and yet appropriateness and vigor of diction, the graphic vividness of portraiture, and the transparent clearness and masterly ability of didactic statement and exposition which characterize the book."

The "Life and Letters" received universal and unstinted praise throughout the South—praise which he felt he hardly deserved but which occasioned thanks to God as he writes in this letter to Mrs. Edgeworth Bird:

"NEW ORLEANS, LA., March 9, 1876.

"MY DEAR SISTER SALLIE: It is worth the labor of writing a book to receive such an overflowing letter as that which I have just perused from your pen. Really, I must accept these encomiums as the reflection of your own goodness simply. It would be an inordinate self-love that could construe them as a testimony to one's own merit. It is the privilege of friendship to look through magnifying glasses; and I escape from a sense of shame only by remembering that you read my book through the strong lens of your own partiality.

"Still I will not deny that your praise gives me pleasure. In one respect I am like the friend whose character I have portrayed—not that I would in any other particular 'compare my little Mantua with his great Rome.' The genuine praise of friends, in whose sincerity we fully confide, ought to please. It is a healthy tonic to a healthful spirit. To the general applause of the world I am about as indifferent as I am to its censure—and it must be a shallow person who can be intoxicated by the one or greatly depressed by the other.

"You are kind enough to think me in no danger of being 'spoiled.' My precious sister, there is one most effective preventive. Do you not suppose that a truly earnest nature must always fall so far below his own ideal, as to forestall self-complacency? And the interval which lies between the desire and the achievement must always fill the soul with a sense of failure. It may not be safe to generalize too far. But I can truthfully say that I never have laid my hand upon a single performance of my own, with the feeling that it was a success. Often, often, when congratulations have been poured into my ear the inward mortification has been so great that I could creep through a keyhole. In the wonder they excite I simply yield myself in gratitude to God, and in thankfulness to the human kindness which is willing to accept what appears to me so worthless.

"Much of this, perhaps, is due to the fact that I commenced my public life by the side of the greatest intellects in the Church—and continued to be associated with them long enough to be impressed with the disparity betwixt me and them. To some extent this did not serve as a stimulus. My own ambition became chilled in the shadow of their superiority. The standard of excellence was so lofty as to appal rather than to encourage. And I have been painfully conscious, all through life, of undeveloped power—and shall go to the grave with the feeling that I have never achieved all of which I was really capable. This is the mortifying part—the recognition of the melancholy fact as a proof of inherent weakness. But the moral effect has been salutary, in the repression of vainglory and of pride. I must, however, arrest this train of thought lest you discover in the self-depreciation itself the evidence of too much self-love. Yet, it lets you down a little deeper into my experience than you have ever before explored.

"In regard to the 'Life of Dr. Thornwell"—if I have comparatively succeeded, it is because I always love hard; and in this case my heart held the pen—diffusing a glow over the composition which the head alone could not have imparted. It is an immense satisfaction, that the work has received the cordial approval of Dr. Thornwell's own personal friends. I undertook the task with trepidation, knowing how difficult it would be to meet the expectations of those whose love for him was so ardent, and whose admiration of his genius was so intense. If these are satisfied, I shall not be disturbed by the criticism of others upon it as a work of art. He was as good as he was great; and I shall rejoice if I have been able to place him in the affections of the Lord's people somewhat as he lies in my own.

"You are equally kind in what you say of my sermons—and you have said the best when you speak of them as doing you good. Only bear in mind that they are not put forth as models, in any sense. They are rather the rough, unpolished utterances of an off-hand speaker. As literary productions, they would be better if I myself wrote them out. They are, however, taken by a reporter from my lips in the pulpit, and though revised by me before publication it is not possible to remove the imperfections which cleave to extemporaneous addresses. The only gain is that they retain a little of the glow and passion which belongs to the forum, and which the coldness of the closet would not perhaps impart. They are, however, an exact reproduction of my constant preaching. I have reason to know that they are increasingly sought after and appreciated by parties at a distance who cannot sit under my ministry—and may thus extend my usefulness.

"Ever affectionately yours,

"B. M. Palmer."

In 1876 Dr. Palmer put through the press another volume. It was entitled, "The Family in Its Civil and Churchly Aspects." The volume was a small one, of two hundred and ninety-one pages. It had its origin in a series of articles, originally published in the columns of the *Southwestern Presbyterian,* and to which reference was made in a preceding chapter. Judicious friends, upon reading these articles, had suggested that they should be published in a somewhat enlarged and more permanent form. One of the masterful minds of the Church says that this little book is the "ablest thing that Dr. Palmer ever wrote." He is pleased with its succinct brevity, coupled with the lucid exhibition of the principles involved.

In the eight chapters which constitute the First Part, the gist of the author's teaching is that "the family is really the model State;" that "it is not simply a device for the propagation and maintenance of the species," but that "it is a strongly compacted government;" that in it, "the nature of law is punctually expounded by the actual enforcement of it;" that "its lessons of obedience are learned in the absolute subordination of the part to the whole;" that "the great principles are unfolded upon which all human government rests, and society is created in germ;" that in its development through the patriarchal and national stages, the simple law of the household expands through all the ramifications of the commonwealth; and that "a true statesmanship must glean its great and essential principles from the subordination first established in the family;" that "the nearer a government is conformed to this ideal, in the distribution of power and in the combination of influences by which society shall be controlled, the more perfect will it be, both in its conception and administration," that "the type of all obedience is to be found in the homes where we are born;" moreover, that "man needs to be *moulded* as well as to be *controlled;*" that "the family is a school of education as well as an empire of law;" and that its "superlative value is found in the combination of influence with authority, under which men are trained to the obedience which requires to be enforced." Similarly he shows that the family is the natural germ, so far as one is to be found of the Church.

Among his contributions to current publications are three able articles in the *Southern Presbyterian Review,* one being an old-fashioned review of Dabney's "The Sensualistic Philosophy of the Nineteenth Century Considered," which appeared in the July issue for 1876; another being an able discussion of "Lay Evangelism and the Young Men's Christian Association," which appeared in the issue for 1878; the third being the history of establishment of "Fraternal Relations" and condemnation thereof; with which the reader has already become acquainted; and a thoughtful article on the "Grounds of Certitude in Religious Beliefs," in the *Presbyterian Quarterly*, for July, 1887. Dr. Palmer condemned roundly "lay evangelism" and with it the development of the evangelistic feature of the Young Men's Christian Association, as attacks on the rights of the Head of the Church, and something of which Christians will repent in days to come.

As he had been greatly interested in the founding of the *Southwestern Presbyterian,* so he was interested in its maintenance; and gave to its very able editor, the Rev. H. M. Smith, D.D., not a little help, in the form of contributions to its columns, and otherwise. For example he expounded the Sabbath-school lessons, from the Book of Acts, for the first six months of the year 1883; and during September and October, 1886, from the Gospel of John. He contributed also many short articles on devotional and practical topics and a polemic now and then, as occasion seemed to demand. His tributes to deceased persons, supplied to the columns of this paper, if collected and republished in book form, would make quite a volume. Some of these tributes are very beautiful.

Early in October, 1881, he went to Louisville, Ky., to look for the last time on the face of Stuart Robinson, and to lay upon his bier a beautiful chaplet. After the repeated solicitations of Mrs. Robinson, and upon her assurance that all the necessary material was at hand and would be furnished, he undertook to prepare a life of Dr. Robinson. When the material came to hand he seems to have been somewhat disappointed in its character; nevertheless, he set to work upon it, sorting, arranging and writing. This he seems to have continued at intervals from 1883 to 1888. In 1888 Mrs. Palmer died; early in 1889 he himself was taken ill and for several years labored under the necessity of taking great care of himself. At this juncture he became convinced that he ought not to attempt to carry any unnecessary burdens, and feeling that the most difficult part of the work had been completed, he forwarded his manuscript—about one hundred and forty-five typewritten pages—and all the matter that had been sent to him, with the request that Mrs. Robinson should secure someone else to finish the work, which he felt compelled, in justice to his Church, to lay down.

It is probable that to few men in the whole Southland has fallen the lot to make so many special addresses and discourses. His high ideals, broad sympathies, wide generalizations of truth, ability to give solid, timely and pertinent instruction, coupled with graciousness of manner, grace of port, and vigorous, chaste, and splendid diction, made him everywhere sought as commencement orator, anniversary orator, dedication orator, funeral orator, etc.

Not even a catalogue of these special addresses shall be, here, attempted; but attention must be drawn to one or two as illustrating some aspects of Dr. Palmer's character in a new or more striking light. In 1882, the Jews were suffering bitter persecutions at the hands of the Russians. Indignation was stirring, it must be believed, wherever a thorough-going Christian civilization obtained. In Louisiana indignation against the wrongdoers and sympathy for the oppressed found practical expression, in the offer of a home to the wronged. At a public meeting in New Orleans, held for the purpose of crystallizing the sentiment, Dr. Palmer was one of the speakers; and so spake that the Hebrews of that city, already his admirers, loved him thenceforth with peculiar affection. Tradition, floating amongst New Orleans Hebrews, says that Dr. Palmer for once seemed restless till his time should come to speak, tapping his little foot impatiently with his cane; and that when introduced he sprang forward with a bound and began:

"When you and I have read in the public press accounts of these outrages upon the Jews in Russia, the eye instinctively has ranged up the column to the top, to read the date, lest perchance we had stumbled upon some torn chronicle of the Dark Ages. And when you read of them as perpetrated in April, May, June, and August of 1881, your spontaneous impulse is to meet in this hall to-night and roll up your indignant protest against wrongs which appear so unnatural.

"If, fellow-citizens, you have not learned the story in secret, I must say that there is no form of language in which it can properly be uttered before a public assembly. It would be easy to lay the grievance before you in bulk—to tell how three million of people have been overwhelmed by the fury of a lawless and frenzied mob; how in one thousand six hundred towns and villages they have been rendered homeless; how whole streets have been pillaged and fired; how hundreds of thousands have been reduced to beggary and want; how property to the amount of eighty million dollars has been wantonly destroyed or stolen. But these details would not inflame your resentment as the nameless atrocities perpetrated against women and children, the mere mention of which, if it were possible, would cause every ear in this house to tingle.

"These outrages have been extenuated as the work only of an insurrectionary and violent mob, for which neither the Russian government nor nation should be held responsible. But the evidence is too full that the unhappy Jews were quietly surrendered to the maddened populace who were led to believe that the constituted authorities were in perfect sympathy with these lawless proceedings. No arm of protection was extended by the law; instead of which the very police and soldiery abused their trust and aided in the slaughter and pillage.

"I know not how it may strike the minds of others; but in my judgment the cowardliness of the persecution deepens the stain of its guilt; cruelty appears worse when it is joined with treachery and meanness; and for the Russian government to skulk behind an irresponsible mob and to throw the blame upon those whom it should have controlled, is a feature of the case which justifies the cultivated resentment of the world. But it will be asked, Of what avail is this remonstrance from a distant province of a distant continent? Let it be answered broadly that in the department of morals no question is settled upon the grounds of utility. When this wail comes across the sea it is right that the human heart should give its response, and demand the maintenance of justice and truth. And since the authors of these wrongs wear the Christian name and profess the Christian faith, we cannot purge ourselves of seeming complicity in these horrible transactions except by rendering a protest in the most nervous language which a righteous indignation can employ.

"But these words of remonstrance will not be without their effect. Ideas at last rule the world. The true monarchs of earth are not the sceptered kings upon thrones, but the men of patient thought, who embalm great principles in immortal words and send them ringing around the globe; and if our voice to-night should be but the echo of an echo, let it swell the reverberation until it fills the dome of Heaven.

"Those have read history to little purpose who have not learned that the weakest thing on earth is that which men call force; and Russia, trembling at the mouth of a volcano, is the last empire of Europe that can afford to stand against the moral sentiment of the world. Never in the past has any empire been upheld by the power of the sword; but in the height of their prosperity they have crumbled like a bank of sand beneath the waves that wash them from their base. In this age of universal commerce, when the highways of intercourse and travel cover the globe like a network, no nation can insulate itself and be independent of a common law which governs the world. And Russia, despotic and proud as she may be, will yet bow before its silent and commanding influence.

"I beg leave to enforce this sentiment uttered by the preceding speaker, that this voice of remonstrance must come up from American soil. From its earliest history America has been the refuge of the oppressed; and the first settlers upon her shores were those who sought in her wild forests freedom to worship God. The great sentiment engraved upon the corner stone of our civil government, is man's inalienable right to life, liberty and the pursuit of happiness. When, therefore, the Russian Minister of State, with cruel taunt, points to its western border and says that it is open for the Jew to go, let us point to the open port of our eastern border, and say, that they are all open for the Jew to come. Never while this continent lifts itself above the sea let it be anything else than the asylum of the oppressed, or its voice ever speak except in defense of justice, liberty and truth.

"I somewhat fear that I may offend against the proprieties of this occasion if I utter the sentiment which lies deepest in my heart. Yet I cannot be just to conscience in its entire suppression. I do, for one, feel for this persecuted people because they are Jews. I read in history that they were chosen four thousand years ago to be God's particular people; I read that during one thousand five hundred years to them was given 'the adoption, and the glory, and the covenants, and the giving of the law, and the service of God, and the promises.'

"Their sacred books are in part my sacred books, and through their hands I derive that religion which is the ground of my hope beyond the grave. For more than two thousand years their history has been one of unspeakable pathos. Whenever persecution bursts upon the Jew there would I be at his side—an Hebrew of the Hebrews—to suffer and to do. If we cannot stay the hand of persecution abroad, let us welcome them to our homes and our bosoms here, and roll up such a sentiment in favor of civil and religious freedom on this new continent that it shall never be darkened with the stain which rests upon the old."

It is said that as he uttered his peroration the Hebrews in the audience went wild in applause. In this connection attention should be called also to a lecture delivered before the Hebrew Association of New Orleans, on *the political significance of the Hebrew Commonwealth, the part it was called to perform in the historical drama of its own times*—a richly suggestive and informing production, but specially worthy of notice here as an indication of his attitude toward the Hebrew people and their veneration for him. A still more remarkable illustration of mutual regard occurred June 8, 1886. On that day was buried all that was mortal of James K. Gutheim, the Senior Rabbi, of the Hebrew Community of New Orleans. For thirty years he had been their spokesman. He had been the leader of the Reformed Judaism of the South, he had been public spirited, genial in his manners, and had so lived as to have won the esteem of the entire community. The funeral ceremonies were representative in their character. Rabbi Leucht delivered a eulogy; Rabbis from other parts of the South conducted other parts of the service. The services at the Synagogue were closed with an address by Dr. Palmer, "in which as a Christian he laid a Christian's garland of respect and sympathy upon the bier of the Hebrew teacher." [2]

This touching and beautiful tribute to Rabbi Gutheim drew all Hebrews closer to the great preacher. His additional manifestations of sympathy to the immediate family of the Rabbi were received in the most appreciative spirit. This was

---

[2] *Southwestern Presbyterian,* June 17, 1886.

evidenced, a few days later, by the gift, from the late Rabbi's library, of a handsome volume containing the Lord's Prayer in one hundred languages and by the following letter:

"NEW ORLEANS, June 19, 1886.

"The Rev. B. M. Palmer, D.D.

"REV. AND DEAR SIR: Mother begs that you will accept this volume as a memento of my lamented father, and her devoted husband. During his life, it was the centerpiece of our parlor table, and voicing forth in a hundred different tongues the simplest, grandest prayer of the later testament, shows perhaps better than all else, that catholicity of spirit —embracing all that was true, beautiful and good—which, animating his every action in life, was the inspiration of the unusual honors accorded him at his death. As you feelingly suggest, my dear sir, the grand demonstration at the obsequies of my father will ever remain to us a source of honest pride—a heritage richer by far than any material wealth he could have left us—the heritage of an unsullied name and a life of positive goodness. Among the many testimonials of esteem and respect to the memory of my dear father that we have received since his death, none have so much touched the depths of our sorrow as the eloquent tribute paid by you in public, and your tender, soulful letter of condolence to my bereaved mother. Knowing the high esteem, respect and appreciation he bore you during his life, and conscious of that invisible bond of sympathy that always unites the truly good and great, we assure you, dear sir, that we prize above all else, as a memento of the late sad occasion, the letter to which you so expressly subscribe yourself my 'father's friend.' That we also may render ourselves worthy of being embraced by such a friendship will be the life endeavor of my dear mother and

"Yours in all sincerity,

"MEYER GUTHEIM."

From the time of the establishment of Tulane University in 1884, Dr. Palmer was almost always called upon to take some part in its public exercises; and made several appropriate and impressive addresses in connection with them. While the Exposition was going on in New Orleans, he was asked to address a great Negro assemblage in the grounds, on the day devoted to that race. He delivered a thoroughly characteristic discourse, stressing the obligation to preserve the races in their purity, and to build up character; and pointing out the conditions of safe and successful character building. He developed his views faithfully and strongly but with a spirit so manifestly kind that no offence was taken at the plainest things said.

The most distinguished occasion on which he was invited to deliver an address during these years was the Quarter-Centennial of the Organization of the Southern Assembly, in 1861. His subject on the occasion was, "The Church a Spiritual Kingdom." He developed it with beauty and power, and emphasized the holding aloft of this principle as the great special mission of our own denomination, which she could not fail in without incurring a stupendous guilt.

The Sylvester Larned Institute continued its career till about 1881, when, owing to the financial stringency under which his people were suffering, and to the improved conditions of the public schools, it was thought best not to endeavor to carry the enterprise longer. Meanwhile Dr. Palmer had been giving not a little dignity to the institution by the lectures which he delivered before it from time to time. He seems to have framed two new courses of lectures for it between 1875 and 1880, viz.: a course on "Evidences of Christianity," and a course on the "Canon of Sacred Scripture." The course on the *Evidences* is embraced in eighteen lectures. In the first lecture we have an argument for the being of God. Then follow lectures on *Atheism, Pantheism, Materialism,* respectively. The fifth lecture is on the *Necessity and Reasonableness of Revelation;* the sixth on *What Constitutes a Revelation,* the seventh on *Objections to Inspiration.* In the eighth lecture we have the evidences of Christianity from *Miracles;* in the ninth, *Objections to Miracles;* in the tenth, *Prophecy,* in the eleventh, *Classification of Prophecies;* in the twelfth, *Early Preparation of Christianity.* The remaining lectures bring out the *internal evidences* of Christianity. The outlines show that the lecturer commands the conservative arguments to the full; and that he might have ably filled a chair of didactic theology.

Though always calling himself a poor correspondent and often accused of being such by his friends, he wrote a great many letters with a pastoral purpose. He never ceased in heart to be pastor to people who had once belonged to his fold, and in times of stress and storm to them, he would write. To his brother ministers in trouble, also, he was wont to send letters of consolation and advice. Some examples of these are now presented:

This is to a widowed mother who has just lost an only son:

"NEW ORLEANS, LA., March 23, 1876.

"MY DEAR MRS. LONSDALE: A new sorrow has fallen upon you. It strikes upon a different spot from the other, and perhaps you are almost as sore. I do not intend any comparison; for every relation in life has its own characteristic; every affection, its own tenderness; and every sorrow, its own peculiar edge. Each bereavement cuts its way down to the quick—and the suffering, though diversified in form, has precisely the same throb in the depths of the soul. And then, is there not a return of the old grief, as it rises up to meet the new? How strangely they blend into one! And we scarcely know which pang is the sharpest. That is my experience. I know nothing of the deadening sensibility under repeated blows. To me, it is rather the cumulative power of grief, and the irritation of sensibility—which trembles like a nerve at every new touch. The bruised affections lie so still, that we think them healed—till a new sorrow touches us, and they flutter as a wounded bird that tries in vain to take the wing again.

"Therefore it is that I have pitied you so much—and said often to myself, 'Poor Helen! It is the mother's heart which is pierced now, but that is the heart of a *widowed* mother—and she weeps, too, for an only son! How often you have looked into the face of your boy, and said, 'This shall comfort me in the stead of the other!' As his traits began to unfold, in which you thought you could discover the germs of a noble character, sorrow gave place to honest pride. Maternal solicitude watched every development; and a strong joy took possession of you, as you cast the horoscope of his manhood and saw him standing before you such a man as your father. But now this blessed office of moulding him into what he should become is vacated; and you sit upon the wreck of the brightest hopes that could fill a mother's heart!

"Perhaps this is not the way to comfort you. Yet it is good sometimes to exasperate the grief, and then to open all the valves to let the imprisoned feeling escape. I wish you were here. Words are so cold and hard that one hates to use them. I would rather sit beside you, with a sad countenance and with that deep silence which tells better than speech how much I feel for you and with you. I would tell you to weep your fill of tears. Nature must have her tribute, and it is best to pay it. God has not made it a sin to mourn. Alas! it is the only way we can show our love to our dead. They are beyond the reach of tender ministries. We can only sit down and weep, because they are not. There is nothing more heartless than the platitudes of premature consolation. I offer you none. Enjoy the secret luxury of grief. Let the pent-up love flow out in cries for your boy. Somehow, there is a mysterious comfort that springs up in the mourning itself. I suppose it is the love indulging itself in the very sense of our own loss. The heart feels that it is rendering its homage to those who are gone, in feeling so bitterly that they *are* gone. Let me then sit down with you in the ashes, and cover my head with your mantle. I will put my soul in your soul's stead, and feel your wrench as if it were my own. Ah, little sister, do I not know all about a parent's grief breaking forth over a child's coffin? I have had six; only one is left. Five times I have drained the cup which God now puts to your lips, and the bitter taste is with me yet.

"But, in all this mourning, do not murmur. I am sure, you will not. 'The secret of the Lord is with them that fear him'—and I am persuaded, you have found that secret out. God makes no mistakes. He could easily show you that even this sorrow is sent in love—in love to you, and to your boy as well. Just lay him down in the arms of your great Father—and in all the soreness of your spirit, say, The Lord gave—the Lord hath taken—blessed, in either case, be the name of the Lord. I cannot roll away the 'clouds and darkness' that are round about him—but this is certain, 'What thou knowest not now, thou shalt know hereafter'—and this means that you will *approve* as well as *know*. Oh, it is a grand triumph of faith to be able to justify God in our own thoughts, even where all is dark. 'I opened not my mouth,' says David, 'because *thou* didst it.'

"When I read in Hebrews and Galatians the hearty commendations upon Abraham's faith in offering up his only son, Isaac, it occurs to me that the form of sacrifice is not so peculiar to him as it seems. Think, my sorrowing child, if you are not called to do the same. In the full, free consent which, in your submission and faith, you give to little Henry's removal, is it not Abraham's act over again? Be like Abraham, then, and stagger not through unbelief. Lay that which is most precious upon the altar before God—and feel that the Saviour has a use for him in Heaven, which you and I do not comprehend—and 'loose him and let him go.'

"I have not begun to say what I want. But if I go on, I will spoil a letter by writing you a sermon.

"The Lord bless you with such a sense of his love as shall make this darkness light to you! With much affection,

"Ever yours, B. M. PALMER."

"My best love to your sister, Grace—and kisses to Helen."

The following note is to Capt. J. P. Macfie, of Columbia, S. C., of whom Dr. Palmer said after his death: "James has never ceased to be my ideal young man."

"NEW ORLEANS, LA., February 28, 1884.

"DEAR MACFIE: I have just returned home after three weeks, absence and learned for the first time your narrow escape from death by the falling of a tree. I cannot forbear sending you this line of congratulation for this marvelous deliverance. You know what right I have to feel an interest in whatever concerns your welfare. My acquaintance with you all began in January, 1839, when your sisters and yourself were little children.

"Not long after I became your mother's pastor, and saw you and them grow up to maturity. A Christian friendship, which has lasted without a jar through six and forty years deserves to be reckoned a life-time friendship; and as we grow older, our hearts turn most fondly to the friends of our early youth. My love for your venerable mother and for all her children has not abated during my long residence in this distant city; and I beg you to receive this letter in evidence of the fact.

"Grant me then the privilege of this ancient friendship to say, that in this wonderful escape from sudden death you have received a call of love from Heaven, to give the Saviour your heart.

"You come, my dear friend, of a pious ancestry, and many prayers are recorded in God's book of remembrances on your behalf. Has not the time come for them to be ansewerd? It will not do for such an one as you, with all the responsibilities of a Christian baptism and education, to pass by all the offers of grace; and now that God has touched you with his own hand in this solemn providence, I lift up my poor voice to entreat you now to grasp the gracious hand stretched out to you in the offer of reconciliation and peace. May God bless you with his salvation in glory!

"Your most sincere friend,

"B. M. PALMER."

This is to Mrs. Macfie [3] on the death of her youngest daughter, Catherine Macfie Lomax.

"NEW ORLEANS, LA., June 13, 1884.

"MY DEAR MRS. MACFIE: Ever since your last sorrow I have been intending to write you the expression of our sincere sympathy. But frequent absences from home, and the accumulation of cares upon every return to my duties, have hitherto prevented. A sorrow of this kind, however, is lasting; and there is no danger that my letter will come any too late, with its balm of Christian consolation.

"How strange, that the same event should be at once the subject of congratulation and condolence! Here is your dear Kitty, for instance, fragile from her birth, threatened with an early dissolution through her whole married life, whom you have been holding at arm's length always to place her in the Divine bosom forever—how much longer has she been lent to you, than you once dared to hope for? Then, this frail daughter has been spared to do a full life work, as wife and

[3] Mother of the gentleman addressed in the foregoing.

mother. She has lived to bless another human home, and to leave behind her those of her own loins who will 'rise up and call her blessed.' It will be found in Heaven to be no small joy, to have lived a life of blessing upon earth—crowned with the fulness of reward above. In addition to all, you have the testimony of her triumphant death. Does it occur to you, to remember that this high privilege is often denied to the most eminent saints? The disease is sometimes of a kind to becloud the mind, or they are drugged into stupor, or they die suddenly, or in the exercise of his own sovereignty God withholds those lively manifestations granted to others. It is therefore matter of grateful praise, when a life of faith is crowned with a holy triumph at its close. Such I have understood was the end of your Kitty; and these are themes of praise on your part and of congratulation on mine.

"But on the earthward side, how much there is both dark and bitter! We are depressed by the unnaturalness of burying those whose hands, we think, should close our eyes and lay our bodies in the tomb. Then, too, at your advanced age, there is no retreat into other affections and relations, so as to take off the edge of bereavement. We have got through life, and the only future is that which opens beyond the grave. Perhaps, in the after reflection the hope of speedy reunion may afford a sweet solace; but in the first access of the sorrow, we are exposed broadside to the blow, and are for the moment prostrated by its force.

"All sorrow is bitter, that it may serve the ends of gracious discipline, and it seems to me that our first strength to bear it is found in the spirit of complete submission. In this we lean upon our Father's will, which is of course to lean upon his strength.

"But why tell all this, to one so long taught in the Saviour's school? The discipline of grace has long since enabled you to say, 'The Lord gave and the Lord hath taken away, blessed be the name of the Lord.' We are dull pupils of the Holy Ghost, if we have not long ago recognized that He who lays our loved ones in His bosom, makes no mistake as to the way or time of doing it. God be praised, that in this affliction there is nothing but loving-kindness to you, and to her whose loss you mourn. You recall the line of the hymn,

"'And we are to the margin come;'

isn't that enough? When so soon, in the mansion above you are to greet her again, with an earthly love all glorified in the superior love for your Saviour, what matters this dash of sorrow rolling at your feet almost in the moment of your own ascension? Let us accept our privilege of taking only happy views of our religion. The cloud, so dark to the Egyptians, was luminous with the glory of Jehovah's presence to the Israelites; so is the Covenant cloud to us.

"Ever yours,

"B. M. PALMER."

"Mrs. Palmer and Mary, who is with us, all send love to all with you."

The following was to Mrs. Mary I. Anderson, sister to Mr. Wm. C. Black, who had been for a long time one of his most valued elders:

"NEW ORLEANS, LA., April 23, 1885.

"MY DEAR MRS. ANDERSON: In a letter received from Mrs. Black a few days since, casual mention is made of your failing strength and health. At your age, this can only mean the 'dissolving the earthly house of this tabernacle'—the loosening of the pins which hold together its timbers, preparatory to the removal of the whole structure. You see how fearlessly I plunge into the recognition of what so many dread to contemplate. To you, I know, there is little of sadness in these premonitions; for assuredly you 'have a building of God, an house not made with hands, eternal in the Heavens.' It would surprise me very much to hear anything else from your lips but the declaration of Paul, that you 'earnestly desire to be clothed upon with your house which is from Heaven.' I wish I had space to expound the whole of this wonderful passage in Corinthians. I can only add that, in reading the sixth and eighth verses, you must supply the rendering 'at home' consistently throughout. It adds to the emphasis and beauty of the passage to read—'whilst we are at home in the body, we are away from the home of the Lord;' 'willing rather to be from the home of the body, and to be at home with the Lord.' Yes, 'dying is but going home.' 'Father, I will that those whom thou hast given me be with me where I am, that they may behold my glory.' 'It doth not yet appear what we shall be; but we know that when he shall appear, we shall be like him; for we shall see him as he is.' Would it not be unutterably sad to remain always here in the body, and away from the home in glory, where we shall be changed into our Saviour's image from glory to glory?

"To the old, moreover, the ties which bind them in earlier life to earth have been sundered one by one, so that it is easier to mount upward to the eternal heights. This has been very closely brought to us in the recent departure of Mrs. Palmer's mother, who last week, at the age of eighty-two, fell asleep in her Savior's arms. We could not mourn her; it was so much better for her to exchange the loneliness of her sorrowing widowhood for the society of Heaven, and all the infirmities of increasing age for immortal youth, that it would have

32

been the acme of selfishness to hold her back even in the vain wishes of our heart. And so, my dear sister, I have nothing but congratulations for you that you are nearing that shore, whose dim outlines you have hitherto been able to discern by faith. I am able to picture you, in my thought, lying in the sweetness of perfect submission in the hands of your heavenly Father, saying, 'If I live, I live unto the Lord; if I die, I die unto the Lord; so that living or dying, I am still the Lord's.'

"I am glad that I have the privilege of knowing you on earth—that I have so often seen your gleaming eyes looking up to mine in the pulpit, as you were drinking the consolation of God's holy word; and I cherish the hope of sitting down with you upon the mount of God in some future happy day, and of turning all these memories of earthly privilege into songs of adoring praise before the throne.

"I pray God that your life may run clear to its last drop—that the Comforter may be with you affording you the sweetest experience of grace—and that your last testimony for our dear Lord may encourage those of us who remain to press forward to the same goal, in the assurance of the same blessed hope to the end. With the sincerest affection,

"I am yours most truly,

"B. M. PALMER."

To a young brother pondering one of the first and most important problems of his early ministry he sent this letter which, "proved very helpful" to him:

"NEW ORLEANS, LA., September 17, 1875.

"Rev. W. C. Clark, Pass Christian, Miss.:

"MY DEAR BROTHER: In reply to your letter, received to-day, I have to say, in the first place, that the question of accepting or declining the call which has been made out to you is one which you alone can settle. It is just the responsibility which meets every young minister at the outset of his career, and where foreign advice is of very little assistance. It has to be fairly encountered, laying the case before God in earnest prayer, and must be decided in the light of those impressions which are then left on the mind—and which may fairly be construed as the intimation of the Divine Spirit. Human considerations of expediency form no Guide to duty here. We are as truly assigned to our fields of labor by our Great Head, as we are by Him called into the ministry—and the Holy Ghost directs in the one case, as in the other. Our business, therefore, is simply to find out the Master's will. It is not whether the field is large or small, prominent or retired, easy or difficult, pleasant or irksome, well-paid or scant in support: but simply whether it is the flock over which the Holy Ghost has appointed us. It will be an amazing support and comfort to you through life, to take this high view of the matter—placing yourself at the absolute disposal of the Lord Jesus, and dismissing forever all those perplexing considerations of policy, with which we are so often troubled.

"If I am right in this presentation of the case, all that you have to do is to review the whole train of Providences by which you have been led to your present position, then to take the mattter at once and sincerely to God in prayer; and you will find the case deciding itself, by the force of such impressions borne in upon you, you know not how, as will render you easy and satisfied in mind.

"There is one thing, however, which may not have occurred to you, and which may be an important element in your decision. It is the doubt whether the Presbytery will think of ordaining you, except as a pastor. I have no right to pronounce as to this—only that we have had rather a sore experience in ordaining men *sine titulo,* which will make the body a little cautious: and with a call in your hands, I more than doubt the competency of the court to do it.

"Whether Presbytery can or will supplement the salary for a minister on that coast will depend on several things. It cannot be answered now. But whether the salary will be sufficient for you by and by, is a matter that belongs to the future. Your duty relates to the present; when you overtake the future, you will have materials for your decision—and God's Providence and Spirit will make all things plain to you at the proper time. With the light that is before you, decide what you ought to do now—even if all should be broken up six months hence. It is the only safe rule to go by—for who has wisdom to forecast the possibilities that lie ahead of him?

"Yours truly,

"B. M. PALMER."

This busy man continued to find no little time for letters of simple friendship. Of these some specimens are given. The first two are to his lifelong friend, Mrs. Edgeworth Bird:

"NEW ORLEANS, LA., October 29, 1876.

"MY DEAR SISTER SALLIE: It was right sisterly of you to let me know what is probably yet a family secret: but really one can hardly decide whether to reply to *you* in the tone of congratulation or condolence. It would be easy enough to determine, if this were addressed to Edge. But a parent has, at such a time so much to give up, that the sorrow will run its dark thread along with the bright silver thread of joy. And the worst is, that the sorrow is all directly our own, while the joy is indirect and ours only by sympathy. Your love for your boy compels you to be glad in what makes him so happy—but clearly your letter is pitched upon a minor key, and a subdued moan trembles along the chords. It is entirely natural—especially with a mother—and towards an only son—around whom a widowed heart has learned to twine even those affections which belonged once to another. I fancy that I understand the case. You must give up the ownership: but then that is all absolutely—so let me comfort you with a little philosophy. Consider that in surrendering the proprietorship, you do not exactly abandon the possession—nor do you abdicate your supremacy. I must help Edge to pluck just that thorn out of your heart. You will always be his *mother:* and don't *you* know above most women, that we never have but one mother—and that a thousand husbands, or a thousand wives, or a thousand children, will never jostle her out of place? No: the very reverse of this. Edge will prize you a thousand fold more through his wife—she being such as you describe. Nothing deepens the soul like the power of loving—and the more the objects are multiplied and diversified, the more is the capacity enlarged. You will pardon me for adding, that no man knows the priceless purity of woman until he marries. All his conceptions of the sex are ennobled by his closer knowledge of one, and a man has a truer and higher appreciation of mother and sister who has been taught by a wife what are the superior qualities of a true woman's nature.

"Above all, there is the most perfect coördination in all the relationships of life—and each has its own type of love. A woman does not love her husband, as she loves her parents—and yet it might be difficult for her to say which is the stronger of the two. You never loved Saida or Edge, exactly as you loved your mother—and yet are they not all equally real? The fact is, all these manners of love lie coiled up together in the human heart with the most perfect harmony between them. Hence you must always have that supreme place in the affection of your son, which belongs to a mother—and when his head is as gray as mine is getting to be, he will still say 'my mother' with as much tenderness and reverence in his tone as he does to-day.

"Tell him for me that I wish him joy. Having pushed through five and thirty years of married life, and tasted no little of the sorrows which spring from it, I can say that he who findeth a good wife, findeth favor of the Lord. May heaven bless him in his choice, and cause him to rejoice in the possession of the prize, as did his father before him rejoice in the love of his mother!

"I send you my sermons still. Do you receive them? Three have been forwarded of the second series—the fourth will follow in a day or two.

"We are well—have recently visited our only child in Tennessee. She and hers are also well, and happy. Gussie's little babe grows charmingly, and is a wellspring of comfort and joy to us. Her father, too, is perfectly recovered, which is a special subject of gratitude and praise to God.

"With kindest love from us both to dear Saida and husband, to Edge and your own precious self, I am as ever,

"Yours,

"B. M. PALMER."

"NEW ORLEANS, LA., May 8, 1880.

"MY DEAR SISTER SALLIE: In the left hand drawer of my desk lies an unanswered letter of yours, of so ancient a date that I am ashamed to mention it. A sluggish correspondent, you will ejaculate, hardly worth the trouble of such frequent forgiveness: but one who loves none the less, for all he is so delinquent. But if I do not bring up arrears at once, you will be off somewhere in your summer flight and I will not know where to strike you upon the wing.

"You were kind enough to say that you would pardon all neglect, if I would only write a letter of sympathy to your distressed sister at Macon. I should not have required this stimulus, had I dreamed that any words of mine could lighten her sorrow. Indeed, I left Baltimore last October with the full purpose to attempt the delicate task as soon as I should reach home. But as the days sped by, the fear of obtruding upon the sanctity of their grief grew upon me, until at length the opportunity seemed to be lost in the postponement. Immediately, however, upon your intimation that such a letter would be welcome, I sat down and penned such consolations as more than once had soothed my own heart. Still, I know that time is the great consoler, beveling off the edge of bereavement so that it does not cut and tear under every remembrance—drying up the tears which blind us at first to the halo with which grace surrounds it. Ere this, I doubt not, a sanctified memory of so much Christian loveliness brings to them an exceeding refreshment—and that the departed daughter and wife reappears and dwells in their thoughts as a glorified presence. But ah, how long the scales go up and down, in which we strive to weigh the gain to the dead against the loss to the living! Let us bless that helpful grace that enables us at last to settle into an unselfish and holy fellowship with their supreme joy.

"We have had the great pleasure of Mary's society, with that of her children, for two months this winter. The climate in Clarksville is vigorous: and as she is not robust, we think it prudent for her to avoid the breaking up of the season in February and March. She has, however, returned to her home, leaving our house less bright than it was. We have the hope that they will all come back to us in June, when the college exercises are over. You will think it strange that New Orleans should be selected as a summer resort. But if we escape the visitation of fever, there is no better summer climate on the Continent than just here—and if the epidemic should break out, a run of twenty-four hours bears them to their home in Tennessee. We are gloating over this prospect of a family reunion.

"I leave on the 11th inst. for Louisville, Ky., to make an address on the 16th at the anniversary of the American Bible Society—which they have got on wheels, trundling it out of New York. From Louisville I go to Charleston, to attend the General Assembly—thence back to Clarksville, to be at the commencement of our University. Altogether, I shall be three weeks from home. I find I must break off abruptly—a public engagement on hand: and if I do not mail this to-day, it will not go at all.

"I think often of your pleasant home, and that choice circle of friends around you in Baltimore. God has taken much from you: but He has left you much—two such children, with their expanding households—and all with you, baby and all, to love and fondle every hour—and above all, a bright sunny heart in your own bosom, which makes you a joy and a blessing to everybody. God bless you and yours evermore! Mrs. Palmer joins in love to all.

"Affectionately,

"B. M. PALMER."

The following are to Mrs. R. C. Shoemaker, Wilkes-Barre, Pa.:

"NEW ORLEANS, LA., July 15, 1885.

"MY DEAR MRS. SHOEMAKER: In response to your kind note of the eighth, addressed to Mrs. Palmer, I drop this line to say that, should the city continue as healthy as it now is I propose to start by the 3rd of August to fulfill several engagements. First, to lecture at Monteagle, near Nashville, on the 6th, then to preach a dedication sermon at Henderson, Ky., on the 9th. I hope then to come on by way of Pittsburg to Wilkes-Barre, to enjoy a day or two with you and with your sister. It will prove a brief visit, however; as I must be at Coopertown, N. Y., on the 20th, and want to take Albany en route. If I cannot accomplish all this in the time mentioned, I must modify the plan a little: but I will try and fetch a compass, so as to fulfil my long promised visit to the sweet homes at Wilkes-Barre. . . .

"With kindest remembrance to Hetty and to Mr. Shoemaker, without omitting Mr. and Mrs. Hunt, I remain in haste,

"Yours most affectionately,

"B. M. PALMER."

"NEW ORLEANS, LA., September 2, 1885.

"MY DEAR HELEN: It does not seem right to address a grave and reverend matron by her name as a girl. But you have so ordered it, in the fulness of your affection, and must, therefore, mediate between Mr. Shoemaker and myself. I confess that, lacking in respect as it sounds, the familiar title brings me nearer to the associations of the past, and is by so much the more pleasant address.

"I am constrained to write a due acknowledgment of the enjoyment I had in your sweet home. How could it be otherwise? Outside, was the loveliest country upon which the eye can hope to rest: inside was the warmest welcome a poor sinner ever received from a generous friendship which overlooked all ill desert. In the more quiet happiness of my home, I still feel the exhilaration of that visit, and hope to be the better for it in the years to come. Is it not a part of true theology, as well as of true religion, that enjoyment as much as suffering goes into Christian experience? For are they not both elements entering into our Father's discipline? Hath He not 'set the one over against the other,' in His wise guidance of His children through the treacheries of this world to their rest above?

"It was a great refreshment to see dear Grace and yourself both so happy, in such delightful surroundings which God in His love has put as an offset to the deep sorrows by which you especially have been chastened. Henceforth, it will require little effort of the imagination to bring you all before the eye—around the hospitable board, enjoying the amiable thrusts of the teasing husband and the still more amiable endurance of the quiet wife: (poor creatures who are called to bear so much from their cruel tyrants, perhaps because they know so well how to secure their revenges when they get the tormentor alone by himself). All this remains to memory, with laughing Hetty perplexed to choose between the antiquated beaux assigned to her. And then, the lovely drives through the historic valley over which Campbell has thrown the glamour of his bewitching verse: and the deep, black mine of which poetic inspiration never dreamed, throwing up its grimy heaps as the special features of the landscape, and showing how man's impertinence strives to smutch the fair face of beautiful Wyoming. Long these visions will float before me, as I recall the pleasures of my late delightful trip.

"How are you progressing with your book on the 'Traditions of the Mine?' Is the first broad outline struck out as yet? Take your time about it, only be sure to make it racy and full of that Divine wisdom which a pious heart can tuck in the folds of any narrative on earth. But I have another suggestion which will touch you nearer than the other. I thought of it on my journey homeward, as one you would do well to execute without delay; and which no one but yourself can accomplish. It is to write a full, yes, even a little embellished, account of your little Henry—with all the evidence you may have of his early piety, and especially his remarkable death scene. Then weave in all the letters in your possession, showing the stimulus of his legacy upon others. The story may be longer or shorter, according as it may grow upon your hands. It will do good in a twofold way: first, as rebutting the scepticism existing upon the possibility of child piety; second, as evincing the part which children may have in the extension of Christ's kingdom, and the importance of training them to this work.

"But good-bye. I have only time to write this large—God be with you. Love and kisses for Hetty; and as much for Mr. Shoemaker, if he were only a girl. With much affection,

"Yours ever,

"B. M. PALMER."

"NEW ORLEANS, LA., December 26, 1885.

"MY DEAR HELEN: I will drop all conventionalism at once and address you by your girlhood name, which your good husband must forgive, for the sake of 'auld lang syne.'

"I am glad now that, with my usual dilatoriness, I did not answer immediately your kind letter of November 23, since the arrival of your Christmas remembrance of us has brought us under additional obligations. The box, containing both the card and the match box, came to hand safely and in good season to convey the salutations they were intended to transmit. The card was beautiful, and somewhat unique in its design, and the verses exceedingly appropriate: but the match box 'took the cake,' as the souvenir of your region and of my expedition with you into the coal mine last summer. It will overtop all the bric-a-brac of the season, because it measures more in its suggestion of the past, but not forgotten, pleasures.

"It is no small proof of God's goodness that he so wonderfully fills up the crevices of life with these unexpected delights. Just when and where we are not looking for it, some flower blooms in our path upon which the perfume of a life friendship seems to be consecrated. I knew, for instance, that I was going to have a nice time at your home when I was wending my way thither last August: but I did not realize how sweet it was, until memory gathered up all Mr. Shoemaker's whole-hearted hospitality and Hetty's and your own affectionate kindnesses. And when all is supplemented with the recollection of equal enjoyments in Grace's lovely home, I begin to esteem the way our Heavenly Father has of insinuating happiness into us, as through the pores of our natures. And then I think what it will be in heaven, where not a thread of all this will be wanting to complete the texture of our bliss—and the whole glorified, by being seen and enjoyed over again in the light and love of our Father's presence there.

"I begin to think, dear Helen, that it is a mistake to suppose that our happiness diminishes as we grow older. If we lose those delights which spring from anticipation, we are entitled to those which depend upon memory; and certainly hope grows brighter, as we approach the dawn of the great day when all that we have ever dreamed is to be fulfilled. What I desire to impress upon your heart, is that as I grow older the friendships of other days roll over me with inexpressible sweetness. The chambers of imagery become filled with the presence of departed ones, whom I am swiftly overtaking in my own descent into the vale of years. I wonder often whether I am peculiar in this, because so many have been transferred from my own fireside to the bright beyond. At any rate they are not dead to me, but warm with the life that is eternal and with the love which can never die from the heart that has once felt its power.

"But I must stop this strain of moralizing or I will run over upon another sheet. Give a kiss to Hetty for me, and my best salutation to your excellent husband; whom, by the way, I failed to thank for his very kind letter—none the less appreciated, however, for that. Carry over to the house at Wilkes-Barre all that is written in this; and believe me lovingly yours,

"B. M. PALMER."

"NEW ORLEANS, LA., May 16, 1887.

"MY DEAR MRS. SHOEMAKER: On Saturday (14th) a mysterious box was landed at my door, without note of introduction from any quarter. On being opened, it disclosed a collection of beautiful specimens of coal, etc., with impressions of leaves and flowers as they were imbedded in the coal formations. Amongst other treasures were a beautiful Easter gift book to Mrs. Palmer, and a little box containing a gem of iron-pyrites set in coal for myself. If you had studied a week for a keepsake most acceptable to this household, you could not have hit upon anything more gracious. Our boys, Mary's sons, inherit from their father decided scientific tastes: and some time ago began collecting geologic and mineral specimens, and have already a considerable juvenile cabinet. They pounced at once upon the treasures in your box and begged lustily to be allowed to appropriate them all. You have greatly enriched them, and the specimens will abide in the house, a constant reminder of your thoughtful regard for us.

"I can do nothing more than make this hasty acknowledgment of your kindness, as I leave in two or three hours for our General Assembly at St. Louis. But I could not postpone this note of thanks till my return, lest we should be thought irresponsive to your goodness. You will be sorry to hear that Mrs. Palmer has been seriously sick the past month, confined three weeks to her bed; is only barely convalescent even now. It was a gastric trouble, always so hard to subdue and control.

"With sincere affection from us all to those of your household, and of your sister's as well,

"I am, as ever, most truly yours,

"B. M. PALMER."

"NEW ORLEANS, LA., December 24, 1888.

"MY DEAR MRS. SHOEMAKER: We are again debtors to you for kind remembrance. It is, at this time, peculiarly grateful—as cool water to the parched lips of a fevered patient. Our Christmas will prove a season of sadness, though we strive to break the gloom for our children. The dark places will be theirs in turn: I would not cloud their young years with a premature sadness.

"Accept our thanks, chiefest of all, for thinking of us; and then for the gifts which are the tokens of it. The cup sent to me will be pleasantly associated with my visit to your delightful rural home. As I sit at my table I shall call up the picture of your table, with Mr. Shoemaker and his genial humor at one end, with dear Hetty at his side the butt of his affectionate jokes, except when the shafts glanced straight across the plates and struck the amiable lady presiding over the tea tray. You see the picture is vividly photographed upon the memory; so that I shall drink my coffee always under the twinkle of your loving eye. The little book also sent, brings up an incident, a little tender just now, which I ought to relate. Last year, if you can recall it, you sent to my dear wife a beautiful little book, richly illustrated, entitled, 'Grandma's Attic Treasures.' Well, I was the first to read it, and I read it aloud to the assembled household. It was deemed a rich treat to the rest of the party, to see me choke at all the tender portions of the story. Mrs. Palmer always amused herself at my inability to read the pathetic without overflowing a little at the eyes. Whether she accounted it a mark of weakness, or relished it as a sign of gentleness, I know not: but I hope never to reach that degree of hardness, as never to yield at the touch of gentleness. She who is gone was a beautiful example of strength springing out of the bosom of softness.

"Mary begs me to return her grateful acknowledgment of the token of remembrance sent to her, which is exceedingly neat as well as useful.

"Will you be kind enough to say to your sister, Grace, that we received the picture of her boy, Lea, through Mrs. Pagaud? It was late in being delivered, in consequence of some trouble in Mrs. Pagaud's sphere preoccupying her mind; and was not received at the time I wrote to her in reply to her letter of sympathy. What a large boy he has grown to be, and how he preserves the likeness to himself. He will prove a treasure to her during all his youth, and I hope a great comfort when he shall have reached manhood. Please give to her and to her husband my warmest love, with a thousand wishes for their continued prosperity and happiness.

"And now, dear Helen (if you will allow me to go back to the days of your girlhood, and take you up in all the associations of your entire life), God bless you, with all whom you love on earth! God has given you much to be thankful for, and I doubt not your heart abounds in praise. Oh, let us try to look for the eternal home over which hangs no dread that it will one day be broken up. Love to Hetty and to all.

"Affectionately yours,

"B. M. PALMER."

To Mrs. Edgeworth Bird, on occasion of her son's being made an elder in his church:

"NEW ORLEANS, LA., December 15, 1888.

"MY DEAR SISTER SALLIE: Yours of the 9th came duly to hand, but I have had no leisure to reply until this moment. The Apostle of love writes, 'I have no greater joy than to hear that my children walk in truth;' this 'your joy is, therefore, fulfilled.' It is a splendid record of Edgeworth, which is given in your letter. That he should be pressed, against his own protest, into an office so sacred as that of 'ruler in the house of God'—and that the choice should be unanimous in so large a congregation, is a testimonial of his worth which you may justly rejoice over as his crown and your own. It is a grave trust placed in his hands. Tell him for me, as you tender my congratulations, that he will find the duties imposed both a profit and a pleasure, just in proportion as he has singleness of heart in their discharge. The back look upon life across the track of seventy years, is apt to be intensely serious. My only regret is that I was not more absorbed in my work, and more diligent in its prosecution, that I might carry more fruit with me into the heavenly kingdom. The snares in the present day are very numerous and treacherous. And they come from every side. They seduce into skepticism, or a half-hearted acceptance of the truth, from a false and pretentious science, from a bold, over-confident philosophy, from society with its increasing blandishments; so that it is not easy to keep the eye perfectly single, and the walk perfectly steady to the end.

"The lifelong love I have cherished for yourself shall be a love for your children: and I will earnestly supplicate the God of all grace to endue Edgeworth plentifully with his Spirit, and cause him to be an exceptionally faithful steward in the trust committed to his hands.

"I have not much to say about ourselves. We continue in usual health, with the exception of colds which are somewhat epidemic with us here. Mary carries a sad heart beneath a sad countenance; and she has reason, for she has lost one of the best and purest of mothers. Still, we lie in the hands of a Covenant God; and 'though He slay us, we will trust Him.' I am thankful there is no bitterness in our grief —great soreness, but no repining.

"As for myself, I perceive as I never knew before—with the intellect perhaps, but not so vividly through the affections—that God's largest, richest, sweetest revelations of Himself come through clouds and darkness which shut out the earth. It was when Moses was taken into the cloud from which shot devouring flame, that he spake with God face to face. And was it not through the appalling darkness which overhung Calvary, that His saving love cut its way down to earth and redeemed our guilty race? So, He has brought down His thick cloud which darkened our home, covering me in it that I might be alone with Him as never before, and behold His glory.

"Good-bye. God bless you and yours, and bring us all together in the upper kingdom. Ever yours, "B. M. PALMER."

To his venerable father on his ninety-first birthday, he had written:

"NEW ORLEANS, LA., December 25, 1878.

"MY VENERABLE AND PRECIOUS FATHER: I write you simply a note of congratulation and love on this your birthday, which puts you, I believe, in your ninety-first year. According to human arithmetic, how near you are to immortal youth! And what a clear, bright day has your life been, on the earth! A few private sorrows have thrown a momentary mist over the face of the sun—but with what a blessed light it has shined upon others, at least, if not upon yourself. It has been a long life, undimmed by a single reproach—as it seems to us, not obscured by a single mistake—a life never embittered by human enmities—as judged by any earthly standard, a life of rare gentleness and humility, of singular consecration to duty, of transparent sincerity and religious devotion, a whole burnt offering of service and of sacrifice to God, and to man.

"Pardon me, my Father: I have too much reverence for God's sacred truth to shock you with any extravagances of speech—or to imply that you do not require, like the rest of us, the dear atoning blood to cleanse you from unrighteousness before God. Rather, it is because you have been able through Divine grace to 'adorn the Gospel'—and, through a long life of most conspicuous consistency, to reveal the virtues of a sanctified nature: it is this which compels this outburst of admiring joy from your poor son, who has only the grace to venerate that which he cannot equally exemplify. When was there a time in all your long career, that men did not put the crown of their reverence upon your head? and a reverence, too, not stately and stiff, as being only rendered by the judgment and conscience—but reverence shading off into love, warm, deep and personal, making it as well the homage of the heart. Do you wonder then that your children rise up around you, in your old age, and 'call you blessed?' Feeling its influence in the shaping of their own character and destiny, they rejoice in the beauty of your life's sunset, even more than in the glory of its noonday brightness. The sun will set with you in its drapery of crimson and gold, hiding itself for a little behind the stars, and rising again in the Eternal Day. Death will touch you with its gentle sleep and its terrors be lost in the translation to the home of the Redeemed: and we, who survive, will gaze upon you in the immortal ascension: and cry as the prophet to Elijah, my Father, 'my Father, the chariot of Israel and the horsemen thereof.' Let the tears and benedictions of your children rest upon you, beloved and honored Father; and let your blessing be their legacy!

"I am still alone—though Augusta will be with me a week hence. With Christmas wishes to all of Sarah's household, I am as ever,

"Your dutiful son, "B. M. PALMER."

To his daughter, Mrs. Hutson, the venerable father handed this letter to read, with eyes suffused with tears, and said: "What a letter for a father to receive from a son, and such a son. I prize it above all the gold that could be given.[4] And *this* from Benjamin." With deep humility he spoke of his unworthiness of such great praise. "God has honored me by making me the father of such a son," he remarked.

The following is the last letter Dr. Palmer ever received from his father:

"BARNWELL, September 30, 1882.

"MY DEAR BENJAMIN: Yours of 22d inst. received, and I take the opportunity of replying while I feel able—for there are times when I have neither the disposition nor the ability to take pen in hand. I have just passed through a periodical attack of the disease I had while with you—the rigors of which have not been so trying and overpowering as at first, nevertheless render respiration quite difficult and painful. I have been unable to preach for the last four Sabbaths—and while not confined to either chamber, or dwelling, yet enjoining upon me prudence and rest. I had been making preparation for attendance at Presbytery, at Walterboro—on next Wednesday, October 4, but have to abandon the project altogether. The disappointment is great, as I had promised myself a pleasant visit to my old home and people, the latter of whom had expressed a warm desire to have me spend a month or more with them.

"When relieved, I am able to take short walks—but have to observe great caution, so as not to overtax my strength. I think it will prove a lifetime affliction with me—the length and endurance of which are known only to Him, who orders all things according to His sovereign and righteous will.

"My great aim, now is—or [and?] should be, to look to, and prepare for—the solemn end—praying that at the (last) 'evening time there may be *light*'—special *heavenly light:* and happy am I in the thought that in this particular my own loving and loved son is uniting with me.

"I will not speak of my feelings, for they vary with varying circumstances—but with a dying saint, of whose demise, I have just read, and who was able to utter (from paralysis) only the single word '*Bring*'—and having shaken her head, as a refusal, when different objects and persons were presented, still crying—'*Bring*'—looking

[4] He had received on his ninety-first birthday a purse of ninety-one gold dollars.

steadfastly at the sacred Cross—finally—with one spasmodic effort cried—

"'Bring forth the royal Diadem,
And crown Him—Lord of all.'

So, would I keep the *blessed Savior*—the great—*'All in All'* continually in view—while with dear old Mrs. Singleton, of Dorchester, on her deathbed—requesting a hymn to be sung—and on being asked her choice—replied—'Oh, sing *Show Pity, Lord'*—I would have added to it —*'Oh, Lord, forgive.'*

"Oh, may the rainbow of the Covenant be then in full view—casting its beauteous rays, over the pillow of death.

"All here send love to the New Orleans happy home.

"Your ever affectionate and thankful

"FATHER."

"You will see, and—I think, agree with me, that a visit to you, happy as it would make me, is among the improbabilities, or I should rather say, the impossibilities this fall—the future is to us locked up, and we must wait its advent."

This letter should have been dated the 29th, instead of the 30th. Mr. Edward Palmer went to his room, partly to write it, about 11 o'clock a.m. of that day. Before 1 o'clock of the same day, his daughter found him sitting in his chair "wholly insensible from paralysis." He was restored to semi-consciousness, recognized in a dazed and bewildered way those about his bed; and, September 30, at 11 o'clock a.m., passed gently into the rest of the redeemed.

The manner in which the subject of this memoir received the death of his father is indicated in the following letter to Mrs. Bird:

"NEW ORLEANS, November 8, 1882.

"MY DEAR SISTER SALLIE: It was kind in you to write so prompt an expression of sympathy, upon receiving the account of my father's death. But it may surprise you to know that it is not the cause to me of much sadness. Ever since his illness at my house last winter, my greatest anxiety has been lest, from his astonishing vitality, he might live too long for his own comfort. It was so apparent that he must undergo great distress, if that should be the case; and that the trouble would increase with every month that should be added to his years. Thus, I have been more than prepared to acquiesce in the wisdom and mercy of his early translation. His life had been so long, so honored, so useful, and in the main so happy, that I felt there was nothing left to be desired for him but simple euthanasia: and my prayer was that the silver cord might be gently loosed at the end.

My heart goes forth in grateful praise to our Divine Father, that his beautiful life was permitted to round itself off in a sort of poetical termination—a long and blessed life dropping at last into gentle sleep.

"Death, of course, is always sad to those who survive, in that it puts a final arrest upon all that intercouse which is so sweet between those who love. But every personal and selfish thought is swallowed up in the joy of his immortal ascension. I know there was great rejoicing in one of the 'many mansions,' on that Sabbath eve when we were saying 'dust to dust' here below. I felt like kissing the brow of my mother, these thirty-five years gone, upon the happy reunion; and wondered what questions my own sweet girls would be asking of the dear old grandsire. Do you not think that these broken threads are taken up and woven into a brighter tapestry in the depths beyond the stars? As with your dear mother, so with my reverend father, their memory remains a perpetual benediction upon us. But enough.

"I do not know that I should have answered your letter so promptly, except that I wished to tell you of a painful accident with my dear wife. You know what a partiality she has for falling down stairways. The other day she was out shopping: and in descending from the second floor in one of our stores, her heel caught in the turn of the stair, and she was thrown head foremost down the rest of the descent. Unfortunately, she did not escape as well as at your house. Besides a violent contusion of the head just above the eye, the force of the fall, together with her weight, was such as to break her wrist. For two days she suffered much pain. Since then she has been comfortable; and is now moving about the house, with her arm in a sling. She has borne the accident, as she has done all her trials, with that quiet heroism which is peculiarly her own. We are both of us most grateful to God for His preserving mercy which did not suffer a worse thing to befall.

"We are truly sorry to hear of Mrs. Machen's sickness—please convey to her our sympathy and earnest wish that she may soon regain all her health and strength. Life is but a checker-board: and the figures stand now upon the black squares and now upon the white, as they move through the game. But the time for true life, that is all ahead; and we shall take hold of it by and by.

"With ever so much love from wife and me, not forgetting your own Saida and Edgeworth, and the little ones of both.

"Yours most truly,

"B. M. PALMER."

The visitor to Live Oak Cemetery, at Walterboro, S. C., may read on the monument of the Rev. Edward Palmer the following Latin epitaph, appropriated to the purpose by his gifted son:

"VIXISTI, GENITOR, BENE AC BEATE,
NEC PAUPER, NEQUE DIVES, ERUDITUS
SATIS, ET SATIS ELOQUENS, VALENTE
SEMPER CORPORE, MENTE SANA, AMICIS
JUCUNDUS, PIETATE SINGULARE."

In his domestic history, Dr. Palmer was the one healthful member of his family. No amount of work seemed to oppress him. He had, indeed, a struggle over tobacco, which he abandoned about 1876. Dr. Thornwell had taught him to smoke in the days when they were together in Columbia. Dr. Palmer had become a hard smoker. He smoked very fine cigars. It took him but a little time to consume a box. His whole nervous system became more or less "deranged." For nights together he would be unable to sleep. He resolutely discontinued his use of the weed with the result that in the course of some months his excessive nervousness left him.

"During the meeting of the Assembly in Staunton. while endeavoring to make his way to his stopping place, after night and alone, he fell into an open sewer, and suffered not a little from the bruises received. He found much to be thankful for, however, in the circumstance that he was not more seriously injured, seeing that the sewer was deep and ugly.

"Speaking generally, throughout the period he had in his body an excellent servant."

February 12, 1875, at the residence of her father, Mrs. Gussie Palmer Colcock died of consumption. She had been wasting away for months, ere the end came. She had been a young woman of singular sweetness and strength of character. She had been endowed with rare gifts of mind as well as of heart. She had been broadly and generously cultivated, and had, for several years, been her father's chief mental companion. Her going rendered their home chill and dark for a time, notwithstanding she had left a sweet little babe in her place.

On the afternoon of a beautiful Sabbath, amidst a vast concourse they "put her to sleep by the side of Marion and Kate." Then, sitting down in the twilight in their "dismantled home" the parents "thought of the 'mansions' above already furnished with the household waiting to greet" them on the threshold when they, too, should be called.

On the next Sunday he preached on the words, "What I do thou knowest not now, but thou shalt know hereafter." In the course of his sermon he "recited a few lines with a pathos that could only come from a heart nearly breaking with unutterable anguish:" [5]

"I had a nest full once of my own, ah! happy I,
Right dearly I loved them, but grown, they spread out their wings to fly.
Oh! one after one they flew away, far up into the heavenly blue,
To the upper country, the better day, and I wish I was going there, too."

His sense of loss seemed for some weeks to grow upon him. To his friend, Dr. J. B. Adger, he writes, February 24, 1875:

"I will not say a word as to our own sorrow, except that the weight of four graves lie upon us at once, and this last bereavement leaves us almost stripped and bare. Nothing but a conviction of God's gracious sovereignty, and the immense love He has shown to us in them all, keep us from sinking beneath the pressure. We do not repine; but it is very hard to lift ourselves up, and I am almost without strength to take up even my necessary duties. May God help us to carry ourselves patiently, and to His glory!"

To Mrs. Edgeworth Bird he writes a fortnight later:

"NEW ORLEANS, LA., March 10, 1875.

"MY DEAR SISTER SALLIE: My letters to you must come burdened with sorrow—and, do you know, one of my strongest temptations is to throw my pen into the fire and if I dared, to seal my lips in perpetual silence? Ah! How can I write, or speak, when every tone must sadden other hearts and throw upon them the shadow of our grief! Shall I confess to this great weakness? But I would feel it an immense relief, just to hide away from the sight of man and to bear *alone,* the burden of these four graves, which lie heavier upon my bosom than upon my dead. For the first time in all my life, I find my public work to be oppressive. I do not understand it. Is it only a severe temptation of the great Adversary, who would tie me in the meshes of his own web, or make me an unwilling worker for my God? Or is it a sin of this poor guilty heart, that cherishes a secret repining against a discipline that is most holy and just? Or, is it only the weakness of the flesh giving away for a little, under repeated blows that have broken the elasticity of the spirit? *You* know all about this natural recoil from the life around you, in the hour of bitter bereavement; but perhaps you can little comprehend how hard it is, with all the strength and hope crushed out within you, to stand up calm and unmoved before men, and do full justice to God in the vindication of His justice and of His truth. Oh, what would I not give just now, for a little retirement—to be by myself with God for a little while

[5] Letter of G. W. Beattie to Dr. Palmer, November 27, 1888.

and to be spared the necessity of any intellectual effort. Yet it would be wrong, and perhaps injurious. God knows best—and so, with the heavy sleet storming upon my heart, I must move about and speak cheerfully, as though nothing was the matter with me at all.

"Unquestionably, this last sorrow is the heaviest of them all; in part, just because it is the last and gathers into itself the pangs of those that went before—in part, because it leaves us almost entirely bereft. *One* only of our six is left; and she, alas! lives away from us in a distant State; so that, but for the little babe, the dead mother's legacy to us, we would be as bare as when we began life, three and thirty years ago. Think of us with pity; only the dry sapless trunk of the family tree, without a branch or a leaf, save one poor little green bough shooting out feebly from the top! Such is the wreck of what was, not long since, as bright and happy a home as could be found in this sinful world! This is the dark side of the Pillar of Cloud, which is guiding us through the desert. Sometimes, faith creeps feebly round to the side that is *bright;* for you know that all of God's clouds have a heavenward, as well as an earthward look—and then the thought is comforting that Jesus is furnishing our 'mansion' above, with the household waiting to greet us, on the threshold, when we shall be called in our turn. What a pity that faith is not always steady and bright! But one swings so, from faith to sense again and all is dark as before. Don't you comprehend this paradox, too—this double experience of conflicting emotions, so that in the midst of God's sweet consolations, and while the heart is mellow with gratitude and love, it yet manages somehow to ache all over with the pain and the *freeze* of the bitter loss? What a riddle is man! And when the Gospel comes in to set the crazy machinery all right, the mysterious blending of nature and grace reaches new puzzles for you, until it begins to be a comfort that God at least understands us, if we do not ourselves: and then we fall back upon Him, for the help we do much need!

"Gussie was a very dear child to me; I will not say a favorite, because they all had their individual characteristics, and the place which each held in our affections was distinctly marked and unchallenged by any other.

"But this daughter developed from early childhood a force of character that was, to me, singularly attractive. There was about her a freshness of thought, a frankness of heart, a degree of self-abnegation that postponed her own pleasure to the enjoyment of others; and withal, a measure of quiet determination which assured you, there was nothing that was commonplace and purely negative in her gentleness. She had no personal beauty—less indeed than others of the household: but there was a singular reflection of serene sweetness, and such a sense of what we call character in her face, that one found repose in her. At least I did so and always felt that she would mature, if long life were granted, into one of those womanly women that our sex loves so fondly. These expectations were in course of being realized most fully. There never was a young woman more universally beloved by all who knew her. She fascinated even strangers—not by her brilliancy, but by the womanly grace and sweetness which would have made her in time a good deal like your dear old mother, 'a mother in Israel' whom everybody *could* trust and *must* love.

"She lived longer, too, than the others and did not marry so very early. Hence she was, through a number of years, my companion in study; and I look back with wonder at the wide range of our reading together—in history, literature, science and philosophy. Her modesty never betrayed the extent of her culture. Perhaps no one knew it but myself; yet she was familiar with authors and with systems of philosophy, ancient and modern, that even college graduates would not be ashamed to confess their ignorance of. Do you wonder that I mourn for one whose tastes were like my own, and whom I had so carefully and so fondly trained to be a thoughtful and educated woman? But she is gone, and there is nothing left but the memory of a beautiful dream.

"Let me, however, tell you of her end. It was *peace*—peace majestic, yet serene, like the peace of a gorgeous summer sunset. I reached home on the 26th of January and I saw at a glance, that her end was near. All reserve was broken through at once between us. I revealed to her her true situation and we conversed often and freely to the last. There was just one final struggle with the instinct and love of life—'She was *so* happy,' she said. It lasted but for a day and the victory was complete. I know from the great force and decision of her character, that it was final—from that moment as she repeatedly told me, not a shadow of doubt rested upon her hope in Christ. At times, her thin, wan face was radiant like that of Stephen. But there was no rapture, no ecstasy, only full and perfect peace and so she slept herself, without a movement or a sigh, into the Savior's embrace in heaven.

"All is comfort as to her—that is, whenever we escape from the intolerable anguish of our own loss, so as to sympathize fully in her gain. But—it nearly kills me to give her up. I wish that I could look less longingly on the path of her ascension. I do not say 'Come back to me, my child;' but I cannot say—'Go, my child and be with Jesus,' as much, or as freely as I would like. Pray for us, that God would help us to be strong—especially for me—for my dear wife bears up beautifully, with her quiet, gentle ways—while I—I am almost broken down.

"Love to all with you from us both.

"Affectionately yours,

"B. M. PALMER."

The following letters show that he was soon on his feet again; and championing the ways of Divine providence:

"NEW ORLEANS, LA., June 10, 1875.

"MY DEAR SISTER SALLIE: A thousand thanks to you for the overflowing sympathy of your sweet letter; which would prove a good text for a long discourse, if I wrote but half the thoughts which are rushing in upon me. Ah! this unconquerable propensity to ask the "*Why*" of God's mysterious discipline! Let me touch first of all upon this; with suggestions that may help you as they have helped me, if ever the dark sorrows should gather upon your path again. It was a wonderful experiment—speaking after the manner of men—when God created a being like the angels and like man, and endowed him with the property of *will*. The creation of myriads of worlds was as nothing to the creation of a soul in His own image, with the mighty prerogatives of thought, of emotion, of choice, of decision—of *will*. Look at the hazard of it. What if this being in the spontaneity of these powers should lift up that will against the will of the Supreme! Ah! my sister, what is the melancholy record as to both angels and men! The omnipotent Jehovah places no arrest upon the freest exercise of the created will—it was a part of His majestic plan to let it swing with entire freedom in the autonomy of those natures which He had formed: and the result was open insurrection against His authority. Shall God allow Himself to be dethroned? The whole history of His government is but the action of the Supreme will over and upon the unfettered will of His creatures. It is will asserting itself against will, from first to last. Do you not see the imperious necessity that God should guard, with extremest jealousy, His own supremacy? He does not retire our will, nor bind it; but He shows His to be the will that ought to rule, and to which the created will must bend. Man's first probation turned simply on this: whether he would spontaneously bow, in the highest exercise of his own will, to the will of the Supreme. The test of obedience was in a matter itself wholly indifferent, in order that the reason of the obedience might lie only in the Divine command. For the same reason God will not, and ought not, in every instance, give the explanation of His Providential Dispensations. There may exist certain larger principles, whose wise application may go far to afford the solution: or the explanation may come afterwards, either here or hereafter, when the ends of discipline have been accomplished. But our submission, like our obedience, must rest alone upon His rightful supremacy, or else God vacates His throne to the creature. If we must first know the 'Why,' then submission and obedience shift their ground. resting upon our approval of what God decrees—and we become His judges. No! No! it is better as it is: with a large and generous confidence in God Himself, to accept His wisdom and justice and goodness as final in every case—and to say with David, 'I opened not my mouth *because Thou didst it.*'

"This principle, you will think with me, goes to the root of the matter; but it is not entirely exhaustive. This Christian life of ours is purely disciplinary—the only word that unlocks the mysteries of Providence. And hence it is suspended wholly upon *faith.* If God explained Himself at every step, He would contravene the fundamental law of the economy under which we are here placed. We would not then *believe,* but *know*—and our whole spiritual education would be arrested. Consider it closely, and you will perceive that no other principle but that of faith would meet the conditions of our existence in this world, not only because the things which fall in the sphere of religion are in their nature transcendental, beyond the discovery of reason, and resting solely upon Revelation, but for the deeper fact that man's sin began in unbelief and distrust of God, and, therefore, our way out of the ruin must be by the exercise of that very faith or trust which man originally withheld. The Gospel is a remedy, and the character of the remedy is always determined by the disease. We fell by the transgression of our Head—we are saved by the obedience of another Head: law is magnified, precisely where it was dishonored. So Adam doubted God's wisdom and goodness in the first prohibition, because jealous of his Creator, and thought His restraint unkind. All sin continues in the same distrust of God; disbelieving the sincerity of His holiness, of His justice, of His power, and of His love. The necessary condition of salvation is faith *replaced,* where it had been withdrawn. Hence this command, believe on the Lord Jesus Christ, is not arbitrary but indispensable. The whole Christian life must also run upon that same line of unreserved trust, until we reach heaven, where we at length strike the region of knowledge. Yet we perversely confound the two spheres, and want to *know* where God summons us only to *believe.* For this reason, God surrounds His dealings with the darkness of mystery. Did it ever occur to you that, in our submission to the Divine will simply as such, we exercise only that kind of faith in which we repose upon Christ Jesus for salvation? Ought it to be more difficult in the one case than in the other? It is the way the blessed Lord educates His children. The lessons are sometimes very hard and difficult; but then, it is not the easy lessons that develop the pupil and make the strong thinker. So in the School of Grace: We must sometimes weep over the book, and learn under the master's ferule, if we ever attain to ripe scholarship.

"And just here, take a spring with me into the upper world. Do you or I know what God is training us for, in the great beyond? Is it a just conception of heaven, to think that we shall sit idly upon 'a damp cloud' and sing psalms forever? Have these immortal minds been trained on earth to have larger thoughts; and have such deep affections, as you and I are conscious of, been stirred to their awful depths, for *nothing?* Oh, no! There will be space for these high activities, when they shall be quickened to the utmost by the presence of God. There are sublime missions for us in heaven—a great work to do for God—holy ministries to be discharged—running out along the lines of that immeasurable eternity—and for these God is mysteriously educating us. In this earthly gymnasium He is developing our strength, and making us great heroes for the service that is to be wrought by and by, when we are abreast of the angels and take up the work of eternity. Do you wonder that He should stretch our sinews, till they almost crack? How can it be otherwise? It is the way in which athletes are trained: and so, God puts faith and hope and patience and submission and obedience and love to the torture, that through the torture we may be 'strong in the Lord and in the power of His might.' Dr. Axson said truly, 'we shall know hereafter.' We must wait for it—and when we come to the blessed, individual service which is to be ours when the angels shall be astonished at our promotion, we will justify the training which made us competent to assume it. Till then we must justify it, and God in it, through humble, confiding faith.

"May I venture upon a third sheet? for I have not yet touched the sentence in your letter which thrilled me most. You write, 'there is much in your precious letter which comforts me for you; but I am disturbed as to *my own acceptance* of what has come to you.' And again, 'never in all my life has my faith been so staggered, as by the repeated blows which have so nearly crushed your dear wife and yourself.' 'I wondered and marvelled and almost rebelled against what (God forgive me) seemed almost a pitiless, cruel affliction.' I quote thus largely these suggestive sentences, because I have much to say in the honor of my dear Lord and Master. . . . God bless you for the blessed sympathy they pour into our broken hearts! Yet with all the wealth of gratitude which reciprocates the love, I must take exception with you.

"I must not let you think of me, as you do; it would be a dreadful hypocrisy. I am nothing on earth but a poor, wretched sinner, with only God's rich, free, sovereign grace betwixt him and the hell he deserves. Even though permitted to preach that Gospel so precious for the salvation it brings to me, a Gospel sweeter and sweeter to me every day I live, yet through it all a poor, sinning man still, and still and still! A sinner, battling all my life against the sins I loathe! contending with a rugged, imperious temper—with ambition and self-seeking and vanity—ah, much worse, with so much that is vile in thought and desire and affection! I cannot uncover it all to you—only to God, whose love can forgive it all. Has He then been 'pitiless' in the afflictions He has sent? It is of His mercy, that I am not consumed in His wrath. Had every pleasure been a pain, and every joy a sorrow, I would be obliged to say, He has not rewarded me as my iniquities have deserved. No, He has been good to me all my days—and my very griefs have shown to me how good He is, by the very contrast with the awful wrath He might have dispensed. I could never have appreciated the amazing stretch of His mercy, but for those chastisements which He has shown to be corrective and not penal. You must praise Him with me, that He has dealt with me only in the severity of His grace, and not in the visitations of judicial displeasure. Think of what all sin calls for in the exercise of retributive justice, and then help me to say that 'the Lord is merciful and gracious, and abundant in goodness and truth.' I should hate myself with a hatred that is vengeful, if I harbored any thought of Him but that He is full of pity in all these sorrows. *Your faith must not be staggered.* If you knew me as I know myself, you would see more than reason for all the blows, and for blows a thousand fold heavier than have fallen upon me. Let the blessed God be then fully vindicated in your thought, now and evermore.

"My dear sister, even you wrote 'God forgive me,' in a parenthesis. Do you know what I thought about that? Oh, how many feelings we have, which cannot bear to be put into words. As long as they lie untranslated, in the depths of the soul, we do not realize how terrible they are. But when brought to the surface, and looked at in bodily shape such as words give, we recoil from them with affright. You recognized it in this case. But in how many instances do these feelings lie in concealment, known only to Him who searches the heart and reveals the unspoken things! And what a view does this open to us of His compassion and grace, in not laying these injuries to our charge! I am afraid we often hurt His feelings, when we least suspect it: and if He were not God, infinite in His forbearance, He would hardly keep company with us for a single day. 'Oh, praise the Lord, for His marvelous goodness to the children of men!'

"I have not quite done. It seems a strange thing to you, that God should so heavily bruise one who tries to serve Him. A word about that. Have you never observed how often God most heavily afflicts those whom He loves best? It is often brought up, as one of the mysteries. There is one principle which explains it, and I did not learn it till lately. When my poor Marion died—our baby—our pet—she who carried the innocency of an infant up to budding womanhood—so guileless and pure, that we always thought of her as sanctified from her birth: there she lay on her bed, a breathing skeleton, with the loose flesh lapping over her thin bones like an unfitting garment—and God permitted death to leap upon her like a beast of prey, and *strangle* her last breath. Oh, agony is a weak word to express what we felt then: and to this moment, I cannot see those long fingers of hers grasping in despair the white throat without tears pouring like rain down my cheeks: but I know that God was righteous in all His ways, and had a just reason even for this, though I knew it not. At length, He spoke to me out of the bosom of His cloud. His words were 'the great and dreadful God,' 'glorious in holiness!' Since then I have known more than I did before of the awfulness of God in His unspeakable holiness.

"Is there not danger lest His amazing condescension to us sinners should lower our conception of His majesty? When we find Him so ready to forgive, is there no danger that we shall think it a small thing? And is it not right that He should be at pains to display His matchless purity, in the very bosom of His grace? Therefore, He selects those whom He loves, and shows that He hates the sin which yet He freely forgives. As though He should say to us, 'You cannot doubt this man's acceptance with me—he knows that I have saved him—and you all know that I love him tenderly—on this account then he is the best subject through whom to reveal the fact that I am none the less holy because I am gracious—just because you can make no mistake as to this man, and will be obliged to read my meaning aright, I will lay upon him such sorrows as shall be for astonishment, that all may know the God who saves from sin is the God who 'cannot look upon sin with allowance.' Some to whom I have expressed this thought regard the idea of vicarious suffering for the instruction of others a little extravagant. But I cannot doubt its truth, in that the Lord has taught it to me. I thank Him for the lesson. I never felt His holiness to be so real before; and it deepens everything, my love, my obedience, my submission and my worship.

"You are in your old home, where the 'memories' throng upon you 'feelingly and fast.' I wish I was with you a little while, that you might unburthen the melancholy pleasures of the soul—'the memories of joys that are past, pleasing but sad, to the soul!' But then the solitude is sweeter to you, than any companionship but that of which the sacred spot is full. God bless you in the tender reminiscences! But look *upward,* still—beyond the white spots that fleck the sky—through the blue, look and look: there is nothing to hinder sight, only until it is lost in heaven and in God!

"Mrs. Palmer is away from me, but I have sent her your letter. She is in Clarksville, Tenn., with Mary—who has been with us since January, but had at last to return to her husband. She has not well recovered, and her mother felt constrained to be with her, our only child.

"Mary has a little son, of two months—named after myself. She has now three sweet children. Gussie's little babe is teething, and at times a trifle puny. We have changed her name, to that of the mother.

You see 'how large a letter I have written with my own hand.' Answer it, if only a note, before you leave Sparta.

"Ever truly yours,

"B. M. PALMER."

"NEW ORLEANS, LA., June 28, 1875.

"MY DEAR SISTER SALLIE: I must take you on the wing, I suppose, if I answer your letter which came to hand to-day. Before this reaches you, you will probably have left Sparta for Baltimore. I, therefore, direct to the old address.

"I do not know whether there was a subtle satire in your characterizing my long epistle, as a *sermon;* though its length, if not its tone, may have merited that designation. But if you approved its sentiments, that is enough; whether it 'turned out,' as Burns says, 'a sang' or 'a sermon.' You did not suppose, however, for a moment, that a single word of it was written in the spirit of reproach to yourself. Some expressions in your last—in which you speak of 'retracting' the utterances of the first, and of 'bowing your head in confusion'—render me a trifle nervous, lest my words may not have been chosen with delicacy. But, like yourself, I write rapidly and without revision, under the inspiration of the moment—and might thus easily lay myself open to this charge. Yet I need not say to you, how perfectly I understood all you wrote to be a passionate and loving sympathy with our successive and dark sorrows. I wished in reply only to express my earnest conviction of *God's integrity*—nay, rather of the hidden mystery of His infinitely *wise* love—in all His chastening of us. That was all. As for you, beloved, your heart was always right before Him. You did not doubt His goodness; you simply could not see it—and hence the recoil of your tender sensibilities from the severe suffering of those you love. How happy for us, that our God knows us altogether; and that He is able to discriminate as to our emotions, in a way that we dare not attempt for ourselves! It is wonderful, God's generosity in the interpretation of our mixed human affections. Do you remember how sweetly Jesus apologized for His disciples, when they slept in the garden? 'The spirit is willing—the flesh is weak'—and yet Jesus was truthful—He could and did distinguish between the fault of the heart and the infirmity of the body. And so with us; in our wild questionings, when under the pressure of sorrow the pendulum swings from complete submission, on the one side, to an almost complaining and resentful insurrection on the other—oh, think you, the loving Master does not lay His hand upon the quivering heart in pity when He stills its throbbing? Nay, sister, out of the depths let us look up to Him as 'abundant in goodness and truth'—out of *all* the depths, let us look up: for there are depths in the awful mysteries of life, where the understanding sees no lighter depths in our unutterable sorrows, when the thick gloom gathers over the throne of infinite love itself—depths upon depths in our sin, to which only a Divine pardon could look down—out of them all let us look up to Him who does all things well, in doing all things after the counsel of His own will. I bless Him every day from a full heart, that in all His heavy discipline He has never left my dear wife or myself to utter a whisper of complaint, or to harbor a suspicion of His goodness. Whether there be light enough to see Him or not, we praise Him because He is worthy to be praised.

"Mrs. Palmer is still away from me, with Mary in Clarksville—the parental instinct swallowing up all, and making every sacrifice easy. This explains why she does not join in messages of love to yourself and Saida and Edge. May God bless you with a sense of love which, because it is His own, is sweeter even than what you missed in your Sparta home—tender memories of the past. How they are sanctified to us and bear fruit in heaven. Thus it is, the earth itself is transfigured and glorified.

"Your ever true friend and brother,

"B. M. PALMER."

Notwithstanding the sorrows that had come to it, the Palmer home life was remarkable for the beauty of it, for the geniality and simplicity of the hospitality, for the power commanded by both host and hostess to make their guests feel perfectly at ease and to do so without taxing themselves. They impressed all comers with their "gentle kindness, simple and sweet manners, unaffected piety and Christian courtesy." "One thing," says the Rev. Dr. Richard McIlwaine, "I can never forget, is their family prayers after breakfast, while sitting at the table, where all the members of the household, colored as well as white, sat together in earnest and interested listening to the word of God and joined together devoutly in prayer. As I saw the negro butler, who had waited on the table, after handing the Bible to Dr. Palmer, take his seat, and at the same time, two old colored mammas, richly turbaned in brilliant scarfs, as was common in ante-bellum days, walk reverently in and assume their places, it brought vividly before me the scenes of my childhood and youth, when in my father's house and in other Christian families in Virginia (such scenes were an every day occurrence."

In the spring of 1888 the Rev. J. L. Stuart and Mrs. Stuart paid Dr. Palmer a visit. Mrs. Stuart has never forgotten his kindness to her little Robbie, then about five years old, and his efforts to entertain him. She recalls a "pretty picture of the grand old preacher down on the floor with the little boy, showing him how to build a house with the blocks he had brought out to please him;" another, "of the child sitting on his knee, a delighted listener to the story the dear old man was telling in his inimitable way;" and "still another little play on words with the child: 'Robbie, your father has gone to Red Stick to-day.' No, sir, I heard him say he was going to 'Baton Rouge,' replies the child. Back and forth it was between them, 'Red Stick' and 'Baton Rouge,' for some time until they agreed that it was all the same in reality." She adds: "I mention these incidents to show the tender side of his nature as I saw it in the home. 'Thy gentleness hath made me great,' was the thought impressed on my mind at this time. This seems quite in contrast to the reputation he had in some quarters as a war horse, a fighting man."

After 1884 his family was increased by the return of Dr. and Mrs. John W. Caldwell and their children from Clarksville, Tenn., to New Orleans, Dr. Caldwell having been made Curator of Tulane University. They lived with Dr. and Mrs. Palmer and added much to the brightness of their home.

He needed them sorely, toward the end of 1888, for he then sustained the greatest loss of all. He tells us of the loss in the following letter to Mrs. Mary Jane Macfie McMaster:

"NEW ORLEANS, LA., November 17, 1888.

"MY DEAR MRS. MCMASTER: Your affectionate telegram, received so early after our great sorrow, touched us deeply. It tasted like the old wine stored away thirty years ago in the cellar of memory. Your household is nearly all that remains of that old flock to whom I had the privilege of ministering in 'the long, long ago' and when you lifted up your voice to soothe and bless, I felt as though the whole living assembly rose from the tomb to pronounce their benediction. God bless you, and keep this grief far from your happy home.

"I can do little more than simply acknowledge your act of love. The blow that has fallen is so heavy and so sudden, that we have not recovered from the daze and bewilderment. The history of the case may, however, be outlined briefly, thus: Eighteen months ago, my darling was attacked with a violent form of gastritis; and from May to October it was doubtful whether she could weather the storm. After this, for an entire year she was on the ascending grade, recovering her energy and spirits, though not her flesh nor her strength. We were buoyant with hope that her trouble, so held in abeyance, would yield her to us with care for a long time to come. Unexpectedly it recurred with extreme violence on the 8th inst., baffling all efforts to control it. Still we apprehended no immediate danger; but were sad at the prospect of months of suffering probably before her. On Monday night, the 12th, she was restless and greatly distressed, which we attributed to nervousness induced by quinine, but which we now understand as proceeding frcm failing action of the heart. About four o'clock Tuesday morning she seemed to be in a state of collapse. which yielded kindly to restoratives, but the reaction soon ceased—and the end came on with haste. She suddenly exclaimed, 'Lift me up;' then turning her eye upon me, added, 'I believe I am dying.' Sooner than I can describe it, she turned upon me again her eye, now dilated to its fullest expansion, and with that mysterious far-off look which appears as though it were the first sight of the unseen world, she breathed out her spirit without a sigh or a struggle. The heart suddenly failed and she was gone.

"My friend, I cannot tell you what a wrench this is. She was everything to me and to this house; with her quiet force she ruled this home, its center and its stem. But thanks to God we are leaning with a subdued and tender trust upon His loving kindness. I was never so conscious of being near to Him, my precious Savior and friend. Give much love to your mother and all within your enclosure. Do me the favor to show this to George and Annie Howe, and then forward it to dear Mrs. Peck. It will save me the painful repetition of the story.

"Affectionately yours,

"B. M. PALMER."

Dying on November 13, Mrs. Palmer was buried on the 14th, amidst a great concourse of sorrowing and sympathizing friends. The crowd was composed of Protestants, Roman Catholics, Jews, of white and black, rich and poor. The Episcopal bishop and every resident Protestant minister were there. The Rabbis, Drs. Leucht and Hellar, were there. Before the Sabbath approached his elders went to Dr. Palmer and begged him not to attempt to fill his pulpit on that day; but the wounded veteran said: "I will preach, *Deo volente*. I have been telling men how Christians should bear even such bereavements. I must illustrate my preaching by setting an example," and preach he did, to a crowded house. He chose for his text Lamentations 3:28: *"He sitteth alone and keepeth silence because he hath borne it upon him."* Tradition says that his subject was, "Christian Fortitude." It says that in developing his theme he at one point carried his hearers through successive abysses of suffering, speaking of suffering from business reverses, suffering from the loss of dear friends, suffering from the loss of brothers and sisters, suffering from the loss of parents, suffering from the loss of children, and, finally of that suffering that comes of the sharp blade's "cleaving through the dual entity of marriage, with but the one-half left to live and mourn." He made no allusion to his own experience at all. One of his elders in describing the scene said: "The congregation was weeping, but the dear old gentleman, never shed a tear. I never saw him shed a tear. I don't reckon he could shed tears. All his tears were in his voice."

No doubt there were tears in his voice that day for there were tears in his heart and his wonderful voice naturally carried every faintest feature of his affections and passions. But the good elder who had heard him preach for years was mistaken about his being a tearless man. The pulpit was not his place to weep. He was exerting his iron will to control himself as he had exerted it for forty-five years under other circumstances.

At the evening service he preached a sermon in a series he was at the time giving on the life of Christ. Thus he went on for weeks with his regular work.

Between whiles he uttered his praises of his "other self," his grief for her loss, and his sense of God's grace through it all, as in this letter:

"NEW ORLEANS, LA., November 27, 1888.

"MY DEAR MRS. SHOEMAKER: No words of sympathy could be sweeter than those which come from Wilkes-Barre, in our deep sorrow. Can we tell how great it is? Who knows better than those who have passed through it, how much it overpasses all other bereavements in life? And you knew my precious wife, with her sterling qualities which made her the center and joy of her home. With a quiet force so peculiarly her own, she controlled all about her without even the show of resistance: and yet herself so loyal to every interest and relation in life, that she conquered in the very act of yielding. The very soul of gentleness, she had the secret of power—the sacred power of unselfish devotion and love.

"The demonstration of affection on the part of all here at home, both within and without the Church, has been universal: and it has been no small comfort to me to see how much she was loved for *herself*. It was her habit to say, 'Yes, the people are all very kind, but it is all for you.' So willing was she, in unaffected humility, to shine in a reflected light. Since her departure, I have so wished she could know the place she had in the hearts of the ladies in her religious and social circle: and who can say that she does not? For who can unfold the mysteries that lie along the narrow border between the two worlds. Enough for us to know that she is caught up into the presence of her Lord, and 'beholds His glory.' It was a grand reception when she was met by those who had gone before, trooping down to meet her at the gates of pearl and giving glad welcome into the mansion prepared for us all (I hope) in the better land.

"It is not to all, dear Helen, I would venture to speak of the amazing consolations we enjoy in this awful bereavement. The untaught world might possibly flout the mysteries of grace, so often revealed to God's people in their darkest gloom. My dread of this special grief has been, through life, excessive. It has always seemed the one sorrow that human nature could not bear; and I have looked upon those who have lived through it with a sort of wonder. Now this insupportable grief has been given to me, *and I live.* In the bosom of a great anguish, with all the hunger of heart for her who is my other self, I have never before been so conscious of nearness to my Savior or of the tenderness of His love, as in this hour of need. He has put me 'in the cleft of the rock, in the secret place of the stairs,' where I have 'seen His countenance and heard His voice.'

"Give much love to all.

"Affectionately,

"B. M. PALMER."

He wrote to Dr. Theodore L. Cuyler:

"Truly my sorrow is a sorrow wholly by itself. What is to be done with a love which belongs only to one, when that one is gone and cannot take it up?[6] It cannot perish, for it has become a part of my own being. What shall we do with a lost love which wanders like a ghost through all the chambers of the soul only to feel how empty they are? I have about me, blessed be God! a dear daughter and grandchildren; but I cannot divide this love among them, for it is incapable of distribution. What remains but to send it upward until it finds her to whom it belongs by right of concentration through more than forty years?

"I will not speak, my brother, of my pain—let that be; it is the discipline of love, having its fruit in what is to be. But I will tell you how a gracious Father fills this cloud with Himself—and covering me in it, takes me into His pavilion. It is not what I would have chosen; but in this dark cloud I know better what it is to be alone with Him; and how it is best sometimes to put out the earthly lights, that even the sweetest earthly love may not come between Him and me. It is the old experience of love breaking through the darkness as it did long ago through the terrors of Sinai and the more appalling gloom of Calvary. I have this to thank Him for, the greatest of all His mercies, and then for this, that He gave her to me so long. The memories of

[6] *Recollections of a Long Life,* by Theodore L. Cuyler, D.D., LL.D., pp. 222, 223.

almost half a century encircle me as a rainbow. I can feed upon them through the remainder of a short, sad life, and after that can carry them up to heaven with me and pour them into song forever. If the strings of the harp are being stretched to a greater tension, it is that the praise may hereafter rise to higher and sweeter notes before His throne—as we bow together *there*."

Meanwhile, his friends, the children of God, of many names, had been raining in upon him letters of condolence. They came from every quarter of this land, and some came from abroad. This outburst of sympathy did him good, which he gratefully acknowledged, saying: "True, human sympathy touches but the edge of the wound which only the great Healer can cure. But the same impotent spirit which cried out "miserable comforters are ye all," was soon forced to utter the wail, "Have pity on me, have pity, O ye my friends, for the hand of God hath touched me." These letters came by the score and score. The following are presented as types:

"COLUMBIA, S. C., November 15, 1888.

"MY DEAR, DEAR BROTHER PALMER: Yesterday was my birthday, but my heart wore crape all through its sad and mournful hours. I could think of hardly anything else than your great sorrow. And now I break in upon the solitude of your grief only because I am irresistibly impelled to tender you my deep and unfeigned sympathy. Deny me not the privilege. You are very dear to me, and I claim the right to tell you that I weep and pray with you. Alas! 'That which you feared has come upon you.' 'The desire of your eyes has been removed with a stroke,' and the center of your earthly life is gone. What will you do? Oh, woe! woe! I often cry, O Lord, spare my wife to my age—the companion of my joys and sorrows. The minister to my earthly needs! Afflict me, if thou pleasest, but oh, take not away my wife! If ever I felt another's trouble, I feel this of yours. And along with the sympathy with you comes a personal grief for one who once dispensed so kindly to me the hospitalities of her house. Suffer me to drop a tear with you over her departure. That's all I will say now. My prayers will go up for you to the God of Jacob.

"Let me thank you most heartily for your very kind letter about my late articles. I only allude to the subject now for the purpose of expressing my gratitude.

"Most affectionately yours,

"JOHN L. GIRARDEAU."

"RICHMOND, November 27, 1888.

"MY DEAR DR. PALMER: Of late years when I hear that any one of my friends has suffered a great bereavement I hesitate to send immediately the assurance of my sympathy, well knowing that such will appreciate the sympathy of silence until the sorrowing heart has had time for self-communion and for communion with the great Healer and Comforter.

"There is a sacredness in some griefs into which the tenderest affection must not too soon intrude, even when it yearns to give some expression of it.

"I trust I may now be permitted to say what my heart prompted me to say the moment I heard of your great loss.

"It *is* a loss, whatever heaven may have gained, and whatever you may have gained through the discipline of sanctified sorrow.

"Even the grace of God does not make us insensible of the deep sense of loneliness and privation when one who has been intertwined with us, life for life, and with whom every thought, feeling and plan has been associated through all the vicissitudes of long years, has been taken away.

"I suppose our Heavenly Father means that by every experience of trial we may better understand the actual character of each form of suffering which others endure, and that thus we may become qualified to comfort others by the comfort wherewith we ourselves are comforted of God.

"It is only in this way that I can interpret the purpose of the bereavement you have sustained. Hundreds of times you have spoken words of consolation to those whom death has bereft of friends, of brothers, of sisters, of parents, and now with what new tenderness will you ever speak to those to whom life can never again be what it was, because of another loss to which no other is comparable!

"My dear Dr. Palmer, I gratefully remember your gentle and loving sympathy when I was passing through a trial like your own—the greatness of which succeeding years has only made me increasingly sensible of, so that I can say:

" 'Time but the impression deeper makes,
As streams their channels deeper wear.'

"Let us look for our solace in the heavenly reunion and in our increased usefulness on earth.

"Yours affectionately,

"MOSES D. HOGE."

"PENDLETON, November 27, 1888.

"MY DEAR AFFLICTED BROTHER: I have no idea that an old *Isra-El*—an 'old soldier of God'—like you, is under any special need of consolation from your brethren under this greatest trial of your whole life, but my own heart impels me to send you a few lines of sincere sympathy. Doubtless you have ere this had hundreds of such expressions—many, very many more than you can be expected to acknowledge by even a word of reply. But you have not had too many for me also to get access to you with mine, nor is it too late for me to send it, seeing that few of your loving friends can trace back their intimate friendship with you through more than forty years, as I can.

"Your dear departed wife was but sixty-six years old. Mine, who is yet spared to me, will be seventy-six if she lives to see the approaching Christmas. And you, if I mistake not, are only seventy-one or seventy-two while on the 13th of next month, if I live, I shall have attained my seventy-eighth year. It cannot be very long before we shall all be on the other shore.

"Our Brother Thornwell has been nearly or quite a quarter of a century in the upper Sanctuary. And how many more we can each of us count that we confidently believe, once closely connected in various ways with us here, are with him there now in the presence of the King! Thither our feet are also gladly hastening forward.

"If I had to live over my past, there are immeasurable errors which I can see I would like to repair. But, dear Brother Palmer, you and I have rolled all the past upon Him who is able to carry it and will—and we look forward and not backward. What comfort and what hope is there for an old man, whether in affliction immediately or not, if he does not know the adorable Redeemer and cannot with some degree of confidence entrust all the infinite future to Him as well as all the past?

"Of course I do not look for any word of reply or acknowledgment of this letter from you. The object of it is simply to let you know that you have the very sincerely sympathetic regards of your old friend. I am Very cordially yours,

"JNO. B. ADGER."

"BERKELEY, CAL., December 3, 1888.

"MY DEAR BEN: I have just learned, through our friend, Wm. Henry Cumming, of the terrible and overwhelming affliction which has befallen you. Allow us, my dear friend, to mingle our tears with yours, as a feeble expression of our deep and heartfelt sympathy for you in your sad bereavement. Both my wife and myself have always entertained a peculiarly tender affection for you and yours; which has not abated with the lapse of time or the interposition of a continent.

"Mrs. LeConte unites with me in renewed assurances of the deepest sympathy.

"I remain as ever your affectionate classmate,

"JOHN LECONTE."

"176 SOUTH OXFORD STREET, BROOKLYN, December 21, 1888.

"MY DEAR DR. PALMER: I have just received, through the relatives of Mrs. Professor Rogers, the confirmation of the report that your beloved wife had been taken home to her rest and her reward. When I heard the report a fortnight ago I did not credit it—as I had seen no notice of it in the *Presbyterian*.

"To you—my beloved brother! who know so well where the 'Eternal Refuge' is, and how to find the 'Everlasting Arms,' I need send no fraternal counsels. But my own dear wife joins me in heart-felt sympathy and our sincerest condolence.

"I have known what it was to give up beautiful and beloved *children* —but the trial of all trials has been spared me; and to you the journey of your remaining days will be with these words on your lips—

"'Each moment is a swift degree
And every hour a *step towards Thee.*'

"May the richest and sweetest spiritual blessings fill your soul—ever 'unto all the fullness of God!' And your ministry be most abundant in the Lord!

"Please present our kind regards to your children and believe me

"Ever yours in Christ Jesus,

"THEO. L. CUYLER."

At this time, perhaps, he prepared that exquisite sketch of Mrs. Palmer's character, which appears in the "Broken Home," subsequently published; and, with the rest, these words of wonderful pathos, sublime submission, and holy aspiration:

"The earthly lights are put out, that no earthly love may come in between Him and us. It is the miracle of love—this stringing of the harp to a greater tension, that the praise may hereafter rise to its higher and sweeter notes before the throne, when we shall carry the memories of earth to heaven and pour them into songs forever. May it be the finishing lesson of the one great sorrow near the end of life —how through the few remaining days to be 'quiet as a child that is weaned of his mother;' and to know the sufficiency of the Divine fulness, before it becomes the joy and the portion of heaven!"

CHAPTER XVII

THE FINAL STADIUM OF SERVICE, NOBLE BUT BROKEN.

(1888-1902.)

DR. PALMER'S PHYSICAL CONDITION DURING THESE YEARS.—HIS ASSISTANT PASTORS DURING THE PERIOD.—SERMONS PRODUCED.—HIS PREACHING.—PASTORAL WORK.—THE PROGRESS OF HIS CHURCH.—WHY THE GROWTH WAS NOT MORE RAPID.—ATTEMPTS TO GET HIM, IN 1892, AT COLUMBIA, AND AT CLARKSVILLE.—SERVICES TO CHURCH THROUGH THE HIGHER COURTS:—OPPOSITION TO FUSION AND TO PAROCHIAL SCHOOLS.—OCCASIONAL ADDRESSES AND SERMONS. THE LOTTERY.—THE ANTI-LOTTERY FIGHT.—OTHER OCCASIONAL ADDRESSES AND SERMONS.—ORATION AT LOUISVILLE, 1900, BEFORE THE REUNITED CONFEDERATE VETERANS.—HIS CENTURY SERMON.—ETC.

THE thoughtful reader of the closing pages of the last chapter has probably suspected that Dr. Palmer was in a somewhat abnormal condition during the first months after his wife's death; that he was walking in a state of spiritual exaltation too great for his body's strength; and that notwithstanding his extraordinary self-control and a power to continue his labors, he would soon succumb for a time to illness. The precise connection between his wife's death, his grief over it and his efforts to bear his loss as he ought, and his subsequent illness we shall not attempt to trace; but about two and a half months after her death, and upon the "night of his seventy-first birthday," stricture of the urethra came upon him, like a bolt from a lowering sky. Very soon this was followed by cystitis, and that by the enlargement of the prostate gland. For two or three months he was quite ill, suffering inexpressible agonies. His pain was more tolerable when he was on his feet walking. Thus he took his necessary food, his faithful and devoted daughter, Mrs. Caldwell, walking by his side and feeding him, as together they strode back and forth across his room. He was able to enter his pulpit again in April, 1889: but his trouble continued, with periods of exascerbation and remittance, during the rest of his life. In 1893, for a period of three months, extending from June 1 to September 1, he was seriously ill. Throughout his remaining years till the fatal street car accident, though always compelled to use a catheter, which was a constant source of grief and annoyance to him, the severities of his malady were so far mitigated that he suffered no overwhelming pain. By the summer of 1896 his failing eyesight had begun to give great concern. As his session had given him leave of absence for July and August, closing the church for those months, he went to New York in search of professional skill of the highest sort. After an absence of a few weeks he wrote to his session:

"ROCKWELL HOUSE, GLENS FALLS, July 29, 1896.

"*To the Session of First Presbyterian Church, New Orleans:*

"DEAR BRETHREN: Ever since leaving home I have desired to communicate with you, and through you with as many of our beloved people as you may conveniently reach. But up to the present time there has been nothing definite to report in my case, and even now my plans are a little uncertain.

"Immediately upon reaching New York I consulted Dr. Knapp, who examined closely my eyes and confirmed the diagnosis of Dr. Pope, stating that the condition of my eyes could not be changed and nothing remained but to preserve what eyesight I still possessed. He dismissed me with the twofold direction to avoid all glare, and to give my eyes absolute rest for six months.

"As the regular profession failed to give me any hope for the future I resolved to interview a specialist in this place, who, though not recognized by the regular faculty, has had an amazing success in his treatment of the blind. He has established an eye sanitarium with three large buildings on the grounds, and with an average attendance of about one hundred patients. A large proportion of these, like myself, have been dismissed by the regular practice as incurable.

"Yet it is stated that seventy-five per cent. go away either cured or greatly relieved. I submitted to an experimental treatment of one week, and then determined to remain a month longer, which will carry me to the 22nd of August. My plan from the first upon leaving home was to return at that date, or certainly on the 29th to New Orleans.

"There remains only one contingency; if I should greatly improve with the prospect of entire recovery, with the short continuance of the treatment, I may remain through the month of September. This, however, is not at all probable. I mention it only as a possibility.

"It is needless to say that our dear church is constantly in my thoughts, and it distresses me to know that its doors are closed in consequence of my absence. Nothing but the hope of regaining sight for the better discharge of my pastoral duties affords me any comfort; still I desire in all things to be submissive to the Divine will, and it would be a sad confession if I could not in faith commend my people, as well as myself, to Him who does all things well. There is only one spectral thought which ever haunts me—the fear that my increasing age with its infirmities should prove an injury to the people who through an unwise devotion still cling to my imperfect service. But this care I also seek to cast upon the Lord, who will direct in all things—

"May grace, mercy and peace be multiplied abundantly upon you all—

"Ever truly yours in the Lord,

"B. M. PALMER."

Upon receipt of this letter the session at once took action urging him most affectionately to extend his time in the Sanitarium as fully as was needed to test the treatment. September the first found him back at his work in New Orleans, however.

The session offered him a vacation of four months beginning with June 1, for the summer of 1897. He spent June, July and August, as they desired, but the yellow fever and Dr. Palmer appeared in New Orleans, the latter getting in only a few days after the former, in early September. He was an old veteran who could not be kept in the hospital whilst a heavy scrimmage was waging.

His eye trouble was glaucomatous. His vision grew very slowly dimmer and dimmer. August 25, 1898, he wrote: "For two years I have not read so much as five pages of ordinary print. With the aid of a strong glass, good light and large print I can read a little in the Bible." Toward the last he could neither read nor write. This dimness of vision was one, and perhaps the chief, occasion of the fatal street car accident, in the spring of 1902.

Dr. Palmer continued to be a man of great physical powers for such labors as were incident to his calling notwithstanding the maladies by which he had been afflicted. But it was inevitable that, in view of those maladies and his advanced age, his people should feel it incumbent upon them to contrive some means by which to give him lighter labors. Dr. Palmer urged them in the same direction, out of regard for the welfare of his widespread and onerous pastorate. At his suggestion they elected, December 25, 1891, Dr. J. L. Caldwell, of Bowling Green, Ky., as associate pastor. Dr. Caldwell accepted the call and gave this co-ordinate service from April, 1892, to June, 1893, when, on grounds of climate and preference for a single pastorate, he resigned. As Dr. Palmer was quite sick during the summer of 1893, the session cast about for an assistant for him, writing to various seminaries for a young licentiate for the post. This effort resulted in obtaining the services of Rev. S. C. Byrd, with whom a contract was made extending through the months of December, January, February and March. By this time Dr. Palmer was in a measure recovered and able to bear his burdens without the aid of a helper. His session requested him, indeed, before the year 1894 was very far along, to correspond with the different seminaries with a view to securing an assistant; and he seems to have done some correspondence, but all without tangible results. In the spring of 1900 the minds and hearts of the venerable pastor and his people were turned toward the Rev. W. T. Palmer, of Dyersburg, Tenn., as an assistant. The invitation extended to Mr. Palmer was accepted by him; and he entered upon the work in May, 1900. In the following December he was elected as co-pastor, a relation which continued till the senior pastor was called to cross over the river. This relationship proved a happy one and lifted a vast load of care off Dr. Palmer. He had long feared that he might be suddenly taken off, and the church suffer greatly before getting a pastor suited to her needs.

From a study of sermons and briefs of this last period, it becomes clear that Dr. Palmer was no longer reading as widely as in former periods, or making as many new mental conquests. There is a larger use of old material. Nevertheless, there is no memtal stagnation. Some noble sermons are born,— sermons that marked him a man of his time and all time. His revisions of old briefs, lectures or sermons showed further study and more masterful handling of his themes; and this revision and reuse of old work was not made with the sole purpose of meeting the demands of his pulpit from Sabbath to Sabbath. One cannot refrain from the inference that it was, in part, his intention to put thus a good deal of valuable matter in shape for publication in a permanent form. Some of this matter found its way into the publisher's hands before his death, and other parts of it should yet be published.

He had always been fond of series of sermons, and series of lectures. To his people he now gave certain series, much of which had been given twenty years before. For example he gave them his lectures on the Beatitudes, his lectures on "Christian Paradoxes." The latter series increased to more than twice its original size. They were delivered between January 11, 1891, and April 5, 1891.[1] In November, 1895, he began a course of lectures on the "Beginning of Things," finding his texts in the first chapters of Genesis. They were delivered on the Sunday evenings of the winter following, and excited such interest as to give him large congregations notwithstanding the evening hour. In this course he aimed to show how "in every institution ordained of God, the principles were imbedded by which each should be regulated forever." The subjects were, "The First Man," "The First Woman," "The First Marriage," "The First Paradise," "The First Sabbath," "The First Sin," "The First Punishment," "The First Promise," "The First Sacrifice," "The First Schism," "The First Martyr," "The First Apostasy," "The Translation of Enoch," "The First Judgment," "The Institution of Civil Government and the Dispersion of Nations."

In the course of the winter of 1896 to 1897 he gave a second series of historic lectures, dealing with the early history of the race, also, and points in Hebrew history to the entrance of the tribes into the Land of Promise. In these lectures he betrays no ignorance of the teaching of modern archaeology, but a keen critical ability in the estimation of its findings. He discovers occasion, also, to rap soundly material and atheistic evolution. These lectures were heard by large audiences, and with "absolute stillness," says Rev. R. Q. Mallard, D.D., "as to sound and movement," no small tribute to the intrinsic interest of the subject, to the skill of the lecturer, or to both. Between November 20, 1898, and February 5, 1899, he delivered ten lectures on the Lord's Prayer, leaving in the final version of his briefs on that important passage the best one he had made.

If his preparation for the pulpit still continued worthy, even more can be said of his work in the pulpit. At home and abroad his hearers continued to remark his perfect grace of action. He never lost it to the last day. They noted his utter composure coupled with intense humility. They marveled at his wonderful voice by which he could express every

[1] With the exception of the last lecture in the series on "Christian Paradoxes." these appear to be ready for publication. There are only notes of the last lecture.

variety and every shade of feeling, and which carried easily to every corner of the auditorium and yet never rasped, and never broke. They wondered at his diction, copious, rich and sometimes magnificent, and at his style, which, if it sometimes reminded of Samuel Johnson, would oftener suggest the roll of Edmund Burke's or Lord Macaulay's eloquence. Many of his hearers believed that for a combination of eloquent diction and strong logical thought he was without a peer amongst the preachers of the world. This estimate was one confined to no one locality. It has before appeared that he spent a part of the summer of 1896 at Glens Falls, on Lake George. The people of the place did not learn who the modest little old gentleman, with the mouth and the swarthy complexion, was until just as he was on the point of leaving, although he had regularly attended prayer-meeting and church. He did not preach, therefore. The next summer, however, he preached and labored amongst them as pastor for four weeks (on condition that he should not be compensated), their own pastor taking a vacation at the time. He won them so completely that his departure was like the breaking of the pastoral tie.

Tradition says that Dr. Palmer's self-control was illustrated in a very remarkable way one Sunday morning about 1897: A woman, strange to all in the church, was seen making her way from time to time, from one pew to another, getting nearer each time to the pulpit. At last she took a seat in the front pew in the Amen corner. Then she arose and walked to the pulpit steps; ascending them slowly, she reached the platform in the rear of Dr. Palmer, who seeing her, turned and asked her what she wanted. She answered that she wanted to talk to him. He told her that he could not talk to her then, that she must sit down. She deliberately took a seat on his chair in the pulpit, in the sight of the entire congregation. Dr. Palmer let her remain there, continued his sermon and carried out the service as usual.

"The woman was of course crazy, a monomaniac who desired his advice in a case of unrequited love."

She told him that she was in love with a man who would not marry her. She had come to the great preacher to know what she could do to get him whom she yearned after. He frankly told her that there was no means by which to compel a man who did not love her, to marry her; and advised her to go to her home.

As a pastor the ripe old man was perhaps fitter to guide, to tend and to comfort than he had ever been before, within the sphere allowed by his increasing physical limitations. His devoted consecration to his work led him at times to disregard what to men of less resolute spirit would have been sufficient obstacles.

During these fourteen years the church hardly held its own. True, the church had 675 names on the roll of communicants in 1902, whereas it claimed a total of only 635 communicants in 1888; but at that time it had just purged its roll, and placed 135 names on a reserved roll. If the Sunday-school, or the financial statistics should be similarly compared, a like appreciable drop would appear. The church was living a vigorous life nevertheless. The brotherhood amongst the male members, after having done much through its "societies," and other devices to bring all the members together, and employed suitable persons to do Christian work amongst the members of the mission schools, finally, under the lead of the session, supported a mission church amongst the Italians, and two female Bible readers and Sabbath-school workers among the poor of the city. His church Sabbath-school for a period of ten years, beginning with 1886, maintained two missionaries in the state of Louisiana, under the auspices of the American Sunday School Union, at an annual cost of fourteen hundred dollars. During the first five years the work is said to have "resulted in getting 21,262 scholars and teachers into organized Sunday-schools." There was not only this outward activity but there were many less obtrusive signs of spirituality.

The question as to why there was no greater growth seems to have been often before the devoted pastor and his session; and they are frequently found bewailing the "apparent lack of spirituality of many" amongst them. "We are compelled," they say, "to mourn the seeming unfruitfulness of the word, as compared with that enjoyed in earlier years and far below what we might expect from the agencies and means employed. There is far too much conformity with the world in its principles and actions both of business and pleasure. Doubtless the same confession rings out from the Church all over the land. One godly minister has been heard to breathe out his fear that the Spirit of God was deserting the Church of to-day. We have few reports of precious revivals gathering large numbers into the Church of God, and we are presented with the strong spectacle of immense activity in the working machinery of the Church, with a much thinner type of religious experience in the great body whose names fill the roll of membership in the Church. This fact, coupled with the fantastic errors which around us are undermining the whole system of Grace as revealed in the Scriptures, should awake alarm in the hearts of all the godly, bringing all branches of the Christian Church into holy concert of prayer for the revival of true religion in this Christian land." [2]

Another factor explaining the rather slow acquisition of members should be adverted to, though little made of by Dr. Palmer and his session in their literary remains. The church had become a down-town church. The city had grown immensely in its area. Its people had, many of them, removed into quarters remote from the church edifice. Some of them felt it to be the dictate of duty as well as convenience to attach themselves to churches nearer their homes. Dr. Palmer seems to have thought little of saving the church by dragging it up town. He thought the down-town people needed a church, and he liked the proximity to the great hotels. He could make his church the church of strangers. There was much to be commended in his purpose to maintain his church where it had been for more than half a century; but the situation of the edifice did not favor the building up a greater membership of the sort he had hitherto been preaching to.

During these years of broken service the old pastor had gone, as far as a pastor can go, down into the Valley of the Shadow, with nearly two hundred of his people, and he and his session had dismissed to other churches about two hundred and thirty of their members. Amongst those who had died were three of his elders: Messrs. T. G. Richardson, M.D., a

---

[2] From Minutes of Session of First Presbyterian Church, New Orleans, La., under date of April 5, 1899. A paragraph in the same tone is found in nearly every narrative to Presbytery embodied in these records. Sometimes, more is made of a *refined* form of worldliness. Sometimes that worldliness is pointed to as obtaining amongst the more fashionable female members, sometimes as obtaining amongst both males and females.

man at once of scientific mind and childlike faith in God according to his revealed word, apparently cold and distant but really carrying a Johannine heart of love, an able ruler in the courts of the Lord's house, and a most generous supporter of every church enterprise; Thomas Allen Clarke, the able lawyer, who had shown himself a judicious counselor in the courts ecclesiastical; and John T. Hardie, the merchant prince of impregnable honesty and honor, the reliable and steadfast friend of his pastor and people, the liberal giver to every material and spiritual interest of the church, beloved, honored and respected by all who knew him. In 1900 the church lost another valued elder in the removal from the city of the venerable W. O. Rogers, LL.D., who during a residence of fifty-two years in New Orleans had always been closely identified with the First Presbyterian Church, and had given it service in every way open to one not a minister, a man of Christian polish, geniality, prudence and trustworthiness.

Even in this period an effort was made to carry Dr. Palmer to other fields of labor than New Orleans, as the following letters show:

"THEOLOGICAL SEMINARY, COLUMBIA, S. C., April 16, 1892.

"The Rev. B. M. Palmer, D.D., LL.D., New Orleans, La.:

"DEAR SIR AND BROTHER: We, the members of the Faculty of Instruction in Columbia Theological Seminary, now take the liberty of addressing you this letter, in order to lay before you a matter of very great importance, and at the same time to invite your most serious and earnest attention to what we shall endeavor to say in making our presentation of this matter to you.

"It is the earnest desire and final purpose of the friends of the Seminary to take further steps at an early date to enlarge the equipment of the Seminary so that its efficiency and usefulness may thereby be increased. With this object in view the Board of Directors took certain action last year, and we expect that these plans will be still further matured at the approaching meeting of the Board. The purpose is to increase the staff of teachers, to increase the endowment, and to make improvements on the buildings.

"In regard to the enlargement of the staff of teachers what we need is another regular instructor in Biblical Literature, and a professor for the Chair of Pastoral Theology, Sacred Rhetoric (Homiletics), and the English Bible. The latter is a matter of great urgency in the interests of theological education, and it opens up a field of great usefulness for the man who shall come to occupy it.

"You will readily understand that the members of the faculty are deeply interested in this matter, and in the welfare and advancement of the Seminary in every way, so that we are anxious to do all in our power to aid the Board in its efforts.

"In thinking and talking over the matter our minds have naturally gone out toward yourself, as the one man above all others who has special qualifications for the Chair of Pastoral Theology, etc., now vacant in the Seminary. Another main purpose of this letter is to express to you our hearts' desire in this regard, and to say that our earnest prayer is that you will regard with favor what we shall say in setting the matter before you as fully as we can. We are emboldened to make this approach to you partly by the fact that your congregation has called a colleague to aid you, and partly by the deep conviction that you could do great things for distinctively theological education at Columbia, and so crown your long and useful life with this lasting service to the church.

"Having these convictions we venture to approach you most respectfully and earnestly, to enquire whether you will not allow us (or, at least, not forbid us) to bring your name before the Board at its meeting a few weeks hence for this vacant chair; and we desire to assure you that we are prepared to do this with all the urgency that lies in our power, convinced at the same time that your election by the Board will be unanimous and enthusiastic.

"Permit us to mention some of the considerations which we earnestly invite you to weigh in your reflection upon this subject, and which in our judgment constitute strong reasons why you should regard with favor our proposal that you should enter the service of Columbia Seminary.

"1. In the first place, we mention the fact that South Carolina is your native State, and that Columbia is the scene of many of your early associations. We feel, therefore, that there would be an eminent fitness in having the rest of your life spent here in the service of the Church, so that the scene of your youth and early work might also be the scene of your last great service. The East gave you to the West for a long time, and you have nobly served the West; and now the East may justly claim you from the West again in the interests of theological education.

"2. In the second place Columbia Seminary is your *alma mater,* and in past years you have rendered her great service. We feel, however, that your service to her has not yet been completed, and we are surely justified in believing that we have a stronger claim upon your service than any other institution. There is at present only one of the four regular professors in the Seminary who is a graduate of the institution, and it is eminently proper that this fact should be considered by you in this connection. If you came to Columbia Seminary you would have ample opportunity to do a splendid work for our beloved Seminary and the Church.

"3. In the third place, permit us to indicate briefly the scope of the work of the chair for which your services are desired, in order thereby in some measure to show you how wide a field of usefulness it opens up before you. The whole area of pastoral theology, with its various inviting departments, lies before you. The general oversight of the congregation, and the whole work of pastoral visitation, together with ample opportunity to deal with various phases of Christian experience, would be in your hands to give instruction in. Sacred Rhetoric and Homiletics, both as a theory and an art, would belong to your chair to be treated at length; and at the present day, when the pulpit has so many agencies to compete with, and men demand the very best, this part of ministerial training is of immense importance. Your hand could do grand work in this wide field. In addition the English Bible Course, which has not yet been definitely shaped, would also form part of your field. This you could shape to suit yourself, and we are sure that you would find this a very useful department, when exposition, doctrinal statement, and homiletical suggestion would combine to make the work inviting to the professor, and useful for the student. Besides all this, your hand would lend useful aid in the general oversight of the Seminary, and in the administration of its affairs. Thus the field of usefulness which is offered you is second to none in the Church; and when we say this we speak quite within bounds, for your experience would greatly enrich every part of our work here.

"4. In the fourth place, you could by coming here render a splendid service to the Church as a whole. Seminaries are the sources whence the future ministers of our Church are largely to come, and during their course of study our young have their views and opinions formed or largely moulded. To have the influences which shall mould them aright and preserve them in sympathy and harmony with the Church is of the utmost importance in these days when there is so much to unsettle men. Now, you have watched the growth of our Church from its birth amid the throes of civil strife, up to its honored position of to-day, and in the Seminary here you would have a fine opportunity to form and fix the views of many of our future ministers in an age of unrest, and of departure, in some quarters, from 'the old paths.' This is a matter of vast moment. Our seminaries should be so well equipped that none of our students would be inclined to go North or elsewhere, and we hope in the near future to have Columbia Seminary in this desirable condition. Your coming here would do great things in this connection, and so render splendid service to our Church as a whole.

"5. In the fifth place, in your position here you would have opportunity to mature any literary work you may have in hand or in your mind to undertake. You know that Columbia is a place admirably suited for this kind of work, and we are sure that you could give attention to literary work here with much more comfort than in New Orleans, and in the midst of a people who love you so much and would constantly draw on your time and energies. In addition to all this, the Seminary vacation is fully four months, during which time you would have entire relief from any distracting duties, and would have time for any special work. This would give you an opportunity to present to the Church in permanent form the ripe fruits of your long, studious and devoted life. In this way the literature of our Church would be greatly enriched, and a legacy would be left to her at your hands of very great value.

"6. In the sixth place, you would have as frequent opportunity to preach as you desired all over the regions of Carolina and Georgia. You would moreover have this opportunity without the wear and tear of continuous pastoral work incident to the service in a settled charge. By this means you could reach a vast number of people with the Gospel, and have the opportunity to build up our Church in all these quarters. Coming here would not hamper you in regard to preaching that Gospel which you have declared so faithfully all your life in the ministry.

"7. In the seventh place, we would urge the consideration that the Seminary needs to be strengthened, in order that it may keep abreast of the times and be enabled to give the best possible returns to the Church for the resources which are invested in its property. The prospects of the Seminary are now bright and hopeful, and everything is settling down to the support of the institution. We have enrolled twenty-eight students this year, with prospects of considerable increase next year. But we need more equipment in various ways. and the Board proposes to put an agent in the field to increase our endowment, and improve the buildings. We feel assured that our churches in this region are now ready to give generous support to any appeals that are made to them. We feel that you by your presence and services here can do great things for the Seminary. All parties would gather round you as round no other man we know, and all the differences of the past would soon be forgotten almost, even as they are already no longer active. To have Columbia Seminary developed to its proper proportions is to render a service to our Church in this South Atlantic region which it is not easy fully to estimate.

"8. In the eighth place, we beg to inform you that the Charleston Presbytery at its recent session passed a resolution by a unanimous rising vote, suggesting to the Board of Directors the propriety of inviting you to the Chair of Pastoral Theology, etc., in the Seminary. This movement was not prompted by any of us who are members of the Faculty and Presbytery, but was presented by Dr. Thompson, of Charleston, who is a member of the Board.

"9. In the last place, we venture to allude to the fact that it is rumored that an effort will be made to bring you to Clarksville to take the Chair of Theology there, after the close of this session, in Dr. Wilson's place. In regard to this report we desire to say that we wish only prosperity to all institutions of our Church that are seeking to advance educational work; but we are also aware that the brethren in Kentucky are moving in the matter of setting up a Theological Seminary in the Southwest somewhere. This we fear means a conflict of opinion and policy more or less severe for years to come, with the prospect that there will not be such unity of sentiment as shall ensure success of either of the enterprises to the extent which the situation requires. Should the rumors be correct, and should you go to Clarksville we fear that the care and worry you might have would be too heavy a burden for one who has reached your time of life. But on this point we do not venture to add more, and this much is said chiefly in your own interests.

"In closing our letter we would not allude to domestic matters and ties to the living and dead further than to say that should you be persuaded to come to Columbia some of your dead lie buried here, and the ashes of the others could be moved from New Orleans here to be laid in that sacred plot near to the remains of Dr. Thornwell and family, and there, too, your ashes could be laid on the soil of your native State to await the resurrection morning. But on this tender and solemn matter we add no more, and ask pardon for alluding to it.

"Please give this matter your most favorable consideration, and reply at your convenience. In that reply we trust that you will not forbid us bringing your name before the Board at its meeting three weeks hence. This is all we now ask, and we pray that it may be granted.

"Indulging the hope of a favorable reply, and with respect and fraternal regard, we remain,

"Yours in Christ,

"J. D. TADLOCK,
"JOHN L. GIRARDEAU,
"FRANCIS R. BEATTIE,
"W. M. MCPHEETERS,
"D. J. BRIMM,
"Faculty."

"82 RICHLAND STREET, COLUMBIA, S. C., April 18, 1892.

"The Rev. B. M. Palmer, D.D., LL.D., New Orleans, La.:

"MY DEAR SIR AND BROTHER: I send this note, on behalf of the Faculty of Columbia Seminary, along with the enclosed letter, that you may know fully what our desires were in connection with the telegrams you received from us.

"We wished to have you come to Columbia Seminary, and our purpose was to send a messenger (Dr. Girardeau) bearing with him the enclosed letter, and commissioned to lay the matter fully before you. After the letter was drawn up, we received your telegram on Saturday. The message was, you may be sure, a sore disappointment to us, and it led us to change our plans in regard to sending a messenger. Still, after consultation, we have decided to send on our letter as the best explanation we can give of our action in the premises. If in the providence of God you may see your way to reconsider the matter we intended to press upon you it will give us great joy to know that the way is open for us to press our case,

"With much respect,

"Yours fraternally,

"F. R. BEATTIE."

In the higher courts of the Church and throughout its bounds, Dr. Palmer continued to exercise a vast influence, though often finding himself in a minority, as has frequently been the fortune of men of profound discernment and powerful and persistent mental and moral grasp of principle. When the Assemblies, North and South, entered, in 1889, into the so-called "Plan of Co-operation, with Reference to Foreign Mission Work, Home Mission Work, and the Evangelization of the Colored People," Dr. Palmer strongly disapproved the part taken by his Assembly. Under his lead the Presbytery of New Orleans, in the autumn of 1889, took exception to the action of the Assembly on the grounds that the Assembly had neither constitutional nor historic right to enter upon anything like joint jurisdiction with another body without previously consulting its constituent presbyteries; that the blending of jurisdiction provided for in certain cases in this plan of co-operation reintroduced the vicious principle which underlay the famous *Plan of Union;* and that in the plan of co-operation with regard to certain other cases the Assembly provided for partial dismemberment and disintegration of the Church, a proceeding to which no court of the Church from the highest to the lowest, possessed a constitutional right.[3]

In 1891, the Synod of Mississippi was somewhat agitated by the "*Kentucky Proposition.*" This was a "proposition to unite in founding at Louisville, or St. Louis, or Nashville, a first-class theological seminary for the Mississippi Valley." Dr. Palmer opposed, and the majority of his synod with him,

[3] *Southwestern Presbyterian,* October 17, 1889.

the proposition; and in no ungracious or provincial spirit. They held that they could not concur with the Kentucky brethren without sacrificing their own institution and violating covenant engagements with sister synods and with moneyed supporters of their own seminary, nor without the abandonment of the deliberately adopted policy of coördinated literary and theological courses of instruction, which had already borne good fruit.[4]

The establishing and endowment of this second seminary in the middle Southwest was not in accord with Dr. Palmer's views as to the needs of the Church. The reader will recall that he had longed for the aid of Kentucky in establishing the Southwestern University.

Throughout the period he struck at everything which looked toward organic union with the Northern Presbyterian Church. Thus he was up in arms at once upon the publication of the proposal of the Birmingham Conference in 1894, on the subject of negro evangelization, that the whole work should be put under the direction of the Northern Board at Pittsburg. The proposal was indeed so out of harmony with the genius of our Constitution that it was doomed to defeat as soon as born. He seized upon the occasion to do a little educative work, however.[5]

In the summer of 1894, he wrote to Dr. Eugene Daniel, then of Raleigh, N. C.:

"HENRY CLAY AVENUE, NEW ORLEANS, LA., July 19, 1894.

"MY DEAR DR. DANIEL: Ever since the rising of the General Assembly, it has been my purpose to write you—thanking you most cordially for the noble part you took on all the great questions which came before that body. In reading the proceedings, I could, even at this distance, feel that you were a power for good in that court, and most devoutly did I give God the homage of gratitude and praise for the same. We are in the heart of a great struggle for the truth on every side, and the battle rages along the whole extent of the line. Some of us are getting too old to mingle conspicuously in the fray: and we rejoice that others, in the vigor of their intellectual life, are taking up the defense, or carrying the Church on to further triumphs and more splendid victories. It is perhaps for the better, that the older men should retire into the background, since a measure of

[4] *Southwestern Presbyterian*, November 19, 1891, and November 26, 1891.

[5] *Southwestern Presbyterian*, January 25, 1894.

prejudice exists against them under which their influence is discounted. Hence we rejoice the more in the advent of those who come to the front with matured convictions, and are so able to maintain and defend the truth. You are now in the height of your influence and power, and I pray God's blessing upon you and your labors in all time to come.

"Your kind note has just come to hand, to which this is a reply. It is my design to write soon upon the topic which you suggest, and the importance of which you by no means overstate. I have suggested, however, reasons why it is best that others should lead off in the matter. Indeed it is hard to see how the arguments presented by yourself and others can be enforced more strongly.

"Yours in the faith,

"B. M. PALMER."

In the year 1900, he reached the pass of saying that in case the Northern Church split on the great questions dividing the Calvinists and Arminian schools, "organic union might possibly occur with the sounder wing."

Further than that he never went. He condemned the "amalgamation" of the educational institutions of the Churches, North and South, in Kentucky in the year 1901.[6] He never ceased to believe that the Head of the Church had laid on his communion the burden of testifying to the Church's non-political character, and of standing for sound and certain Calvinism.

In 1898, the Assembly met in Dr. Palmer's own church. He was a member of the body and the most highly honored member, it may be safely said, being pressed to preach the sacramental discourse notwithstanding the fact that the body were the guests of himself and his congregation. That body endorsed one scheme which he did not approve, viz.: That of instituting a system of parochial schools in connection with each church.

He held that it lay outside the sphere of the Church; that the Church should not under ordinary circumstances undertake it and that such schools would never succeed unless the Church was prepared to take up arms against the public school system.

When the Synod of Louisiana came into existence in 1901, he was its first moderator.

---

[6] Of this we have, lying before us, indubitable evidence, in a letter bearing date of July 16, 1901, and addressed to the Rev. A. C. Hopkins, D.D.

He delivered, during these years, a great many important occasional addresses and sermons; amongst them were the address before the Sophie Newcomb College of Tulane University of Louisiana, at its first commencement, June 17, 1890, in which he magnified in graceful and eloquent fashion the importance and desirability of higher education for women; a memorial address, delivered in his own church, Sunday night, April 26, 1891, in honor of General Joseph E. Johnston, an effort of great beauty and power; a memorial address delivered the night of June 14, 1891, in the Independent Presbyterian Church of Savannah, Ga., in honor of Rev. I. S. K. Axson, D.D.; and his address against the Louisiana Lottery, the night of June 25, 1891, with which this cataloguing of addresses must for a time cease.

"In 1868, the Carpet-bag Legislature of Louisiana, at the instigation of a syndicate of gamblers, formed in New York in 1863, composed of John A. Morris, Ben Wood, C. H. Murray, and others, chartered the Louisiana Lottery Company with a capital of $1,000,000, giving it a monopoly of drawing lotteries in the State for twenty-five years. This grant was notoriously obtained by bribery and corruption. At that time the public regarded it with horror, and the men connected with it were pursued with public and private condemnation and disgrace. For ten years it maintained itself, against constant legislative assault, by similar corrupt means. In 1879 the Legislature repealed this charter, a result accomplished by a majority of only two votes in the Senate. This repeal was practicaly annulled by an injunction issued by Edward C. Billings, United States District Judge for Louisiana, who held in the very teeth of the decision of the Supreme Court of the United States, rendered in the similar case of *Boyd vs. Alabama,* that an immoral bargain, such as this charter enclosed, was a sacred contract protected by the Constitution of the United States and binding upon the police power of a sovereign State. The same Legislature that repealed this charter called a Constitutional Convention. This Convention was attacked by the lottery people with money, with Judge Billings' decision, with promises to give up its monopoly, to retire from politics, and to allow a provision to be inserted in the Constitution prohibiting all lotteries after January 1, 1895.

"Several distinguished attorneys of the Lottery Company

had been elected to this body. The whole Convention was surrounded with a strong lobby of purchased respectability. Under these combined influences a provision was inserted in the projected constitution, reinstating the repealed charter without the monopoly feature, permitting the Legislature to charter other lotteries, and providing that after January 1, 1895, all lotteries should be prohibited. This provision was intended and regarded as a compromise, and rather than defeat the whole Constitution in which it was imbedded, the people adopted it with the belief that in a few years the evil would die beyond any prospect of resurrection."

But "with this new lease of life came a new lease of power and a prosperity incredible. They practically enjoyed their renounced monoply, by preventing every Legislature elected after 1880 from granting additional lottery charters. This was accomplished by the unlimited use of money, by playing upon the opposition of good men to the multiplication of such charters, and by their control, through the ownership of certain dominant politicians of both political parties, of nominations to the Legislature. The market value of their stock had risen from $35 per share in 1879 to $1200 per share in 1890; so that now it was more than double the whole banking capital of the State. They had built up the original capital, which was never subscribed, and had accumulated an enormous surplus of unknown amount, while declaring dividends from 80 to 170 per cent per annum, and that, too, out of only one-half of the net earnings, as the other half belonged to the Messrs. Howard and Morris." [7]

The scheme of their drawings had increased "from a monthly capital prize of $30,000 to a monthly capital prize of $300,000, and a semi-annual prize of $600,000." The aggregate of the schemes of the monthly and semiannual drawings had reached the fabulous sum "of $28,000,000 per annum," and the aggregate of their daily drawings over $20,000,000 more! They received "annually a million and a quarter from the writ-

---

[7] The foregoing paragraphs on the lottery, with only such changes of tenses as were necessary to accommodate it to our narrative, have been taken from an address issued by the Anti-Lottery Convention, which met in Baton Rouge, La., August 7, 1890. The remaining portion of the sketch is taken in part from the same document. For a copy of it, see *Southwestern Presbyterian,* for August 21, 1890.

ten policies sold on the numbers of the daily drawings, apart from the sale of the regular printed tickets. They received annually about $22,000,000 from their monthly and semi-annual drawings. The schemes of the last drawings were so arranged that they could sell 75 per cent of their tickets, pay 10 per cent for selling them, lose the prizes provided for in the schemes, pay $1,000,000 for expenses, and still make $3,000,-000 profit per annum!"

The company offered to distribute less than 53 per cent in prizes. The chance to win a prize of any sort was about one in thirty. What were known as the daily drawings took place every day except Sunday. The prizes paid were "out of all honest proportion to the cost of the tickets or the chances of winning." For instance, for a $1 ticket the chances of winning a prize of 85 cents was one in three; winning a prize of $1.70, one in nineteen; and of winning a prize of $4.25 was one in 1,237!

In addition to these printed tickets, written policies or bets on the number of the daily drawings were "taken at the fancy of the better, with a percentage of from 22 to 41 per cent in favor of the lottery." There were "more than a hundred policy shops in the city of New Orleans" where such tickets were written. They were placed at points where they tempted the wage-earner in his progress to and from his work. The receipts of these shops averaged $30 per day, perhaps. They daily swarmed "with slatternly women, barefooted children, bloused workmen, youthful clerks, and household servants sent to market or on some purchasing errand." "None but the poor and ignorant entered these direful doors. Some of these shops kept 'dream books' and other stimulants to aid the superstitious in selecting lucky numbers." Poor wretches became afflicted by the thousands with the "lottery craze." In order to steal as gamblers they stole as thieves—the cook, from the sum committed to him to purchase dinner for the master's family, enough to buy a lottery ticket; the shop-girl, from her employer, enough for a ticket, and the clerk, sometimes trusted and confidential, perhaps intending to repay when the lucky number had been hit upon. Nor was this depravation of morals confined to New Orleans; it was afflicting increasingly the whole country. The lottery company claimed that 93 per cent of its vast revenue came up from the people of the country outside of Louisiana.

But the lottery was not only ruining the negroes and the lowest classes of the whites; "through the purchase of stock by its stockholders and friends, it had obtained control of a large portion of the organized capital of the State. Its strong hand, on the financial springs of a commercial community, was so masterful as to silence the opposition of the cautious and to attract the support of the timid.

"By the force and glitter of its money power it had warped the judgment and conscience of many good people, making them first apologists for and then desirous of such riches, even though they were obtained without honor, and in desecration of the dignity of labor and long pedigree of toil. It had captured three-fourths of the press of Louisiana, either by control of the capital invested, or by purchase of the proprietors." Papers which, a few years before, had been outspoken in condemnation of the lottery, had become violent partisans of the baleful institution. In localities where it had not been able to purchase the local press, it had started a hireling press. "Its iniquitous business was blazoned by the advertisement of winnings, often fictitious, all over the country, and it had thus created and stimulated a thirst for gambling in tens of thousands of ignorant and credulous persons" from whom month by month, it was receiving its enormous gains.

For a long time it had used the United States Post Office Department as the principal instrument in its robbery of the people outside New Orleans. When excluded from the mails as a fraudulent lottery, it skulked under the individual name of its president, and the name of a national bank chartered by the National Government. It was estimated that, in 1890, one-third of the whole local mail matter that passed through the New Orleans post-office was lottery mail, and that $30,000 per day in postal notes and money orders were paid to its stalking horse bank. Meanwhile it had been using the express companies also.

The temptation to hold on to their power and to continue to amass wealth led the lottery people, in 1890 to violate all their promises and pledges made to the framers of the Constitution and to the people of Louisiana, and reiterated over and over; and to precipitate the conflict of that year for the renewal of their charter. The lottery people secured the passage in the Legislature, of a bill "to submit a Constitutional amendment to be voted on by the people in 1892, giving to John A. Morris, a member of the original gambling syndicate of 1868, one of the original promoters of the Louisiana Lottery Company, and then its lessee and largest stockholder, and his unnamed associates, the practically exclusive privilege of drawing lotteries in Louisiana for twenty-five years from January 1, 1894, in consideration of the payment to the State of $1,250,000 per annum. They had moved earth and hell to get this measure through the Legislature. Taking occasion of the threatened inundation from the floods in the Mississippi they had made a subtle attempt to tie the hands of her noble governor, Francis T. Nicholls, by forwarding to him a check for $100,000, to be used at his discretion to protect the people of Louisiana against the inundation apparently so imminent. This heroic man would not tie his hands. He vetoed the lottery bill; and, by his letter declining the $100,000, for use in improving the levees, by his ringing veto of the Lottery Bill and otherwise, did much to rouse the people of Louisiana to their danger.

"By the most shameful bribery and Bacchanalian orgies, such as would have disgraced Rome in her decline," the lottery people nearly succeeded in passing the bill again over the governor's veto. They secured the two-thirds vote in the House and thought they had secured it in the Senate, carrying a dying man to the chamber to cast a turning vote. Death, however, snatched him from their hands ere he could cast the necessary vote. Failing to pass the desired bill in the usual constitutional way, they suddenly professed to discover that amendments to the Constitution were not subject to the gubernatorial veto;"[8] and betook themselves to the courts, hoping to find a purchasable judiciary. Not to dwell at greater length on the history of their efforts to perpetuate their malign power, it became evident to the thoughtful that those who valued honor, patriotism and religion must bestir themselves and redeem the State and people from the all-devouring octopus.

Every Presbyterian minister of any eminence in the city had from the first been bitterly hostile to the lottery. Nor had he concealed his hostility. In the very first volume of the *Southwestern Presbyterian* the attack was begun; and the onslaught so early attempted in that organ was renewed. Every important pulpit resounded at times with denunciations of this

---

[8] See editorial in *Southwestern Presbyterian*, January 15, 1891.

College of Gambling. There seems to have been less of attack between 1880 and 1890. "This may have been due to two causes," says Dr. R. Q. Mallard: "First, the conviction that the evil, having been entrenched in the Constitution by our people through a lamentable mistake as to its character as a vested right, was incurable, and could only end in its death by statutory limitation; and, second, because some supposed that 'playing the lottery,' as it is most truthfully and significantly called, was confined to classes seldom, if ever, found in our churches, which was indeed the case at the outset." [9]

Whatever may have been true of the pulpit and the Church in the past, the fear of the charter's being renewed brought them out in bold antagonism in 1890. Denunciatory resolutions were passed in every ecclesiastical court; and their people were exhorted to take righteous measures to put the lottery evil down. The Presbyterian clergymen of New Orleans memorialized the Senate and the House of Representatives of the Congress of the United States, asking them to propose for adoption an amendment to the Constitution of the United States which should prohibit the drawing of lotteries, the chartering of lottery companies, and the sale of lottery tickets within the borders of the United States. In the course of this paper they make one of the ablest expositions of the evils of the lottery to be found in all the contemporary literature on the subject.[10] Dr. Palmer had not been behind the foremost of them in his opposition to the lottery. Of late he had seen that the time was ripe for vigorous opposition on the part of every good citizen. He had addressed the following letter to Governor Francis T. Nicholls, in the summer of 1890:

"NEW ORLEANS, July 9, 1890.

"To His Excellency Governor Francis T. Nicholls, Baton Rouge, La.:

"MY VERY DEAR SIR: Ever since the conflict opened with the lottery shame I have desired to write you a line, if only to express my individual thanks for the noble course which you have pursued in the same. Nothing has restrained me but a certain shyness lest I should seem presumptuous in approaching one in such high station with words of commendation. But the waters will sometimes rise high enough to sweep away all opposition. I read your message on its first appear-

---

[9] In *Southwestern Presbyterian,* September 24, 1891, p. 4, c. 3.

[10] A copy of the paper may be seen in the *Southwestern Presbyterian,* March 5, 1891.

ance.in the papers, and again when it was presented in pamphlet form; and I have just risen from a second perusal of your veto of the lottery bill.

"Will you permit me to speak of the dignity and vigor of thought which renders them both valuable State papers, and to acknowledge the moral courage which, in its chief executive, largely redeems the State from the humiliation into which she has been plunged! We are doomed, I suppose, to a bitter campaign, the necessity of which is, itself, a reproach to the State. But I am comforted by the confidence we should all feel in the final triumph of truth and righteousness. Ideas rule the world, and nothing is able to withstand the force of moral convictions when they gain headway and sweep like a tempest over the land.

"Yours has been the trumpet voice rousing the conscience of our people, and Louisiana may well congratulate herself that the grand leader in this struggle for integrity and honor is her own chief magistrate. Among the many chaplets which have been placed upon your brow by a grateful and loving people, I do not know one of which you should be prouder than that which you have won in the initiative of this great struggle.

"Asking pardon for the intrusion upon your notice, permit me to subscribe myself with sincere respect,

"Yours most truly,

"B. M. PALMER."

The other denominations were making similar fights; and honorable and patriotic citizens generally were waxing warm with indignation. In the summer of 1891, the Louisiana Anti-Lottery League was formed. It opened its campaign, through a public meeting held Thursday evening, June 25, in the Grand Opera House, New Orleans. A concourse worthy of the cause that summoned it crowded this grand auditorium from parquet to gallery and every vacant inch of standing room in the aisles—a representative assembly, comprising all creeds, all classes, both sexes, and all ages. On the platform sat men representing the best element in the city and State. Mr. James D. Coleman, President of the Catholic Knights of America, named Col. Wm. Preston Johnston, son of Gen. Albert Sidney Johnston, and Chancellor of Tulane University of Louisiana, as chairman. He made a brief and forcible address, after which he introduced Dr. Palmer in the following words: "It it now my privilege to introduce to you a man who by his talents, his eloquence, and his virtues, well deserves the title of the first citizen of New Orleans."[11]

Rarely has an orator had a nobler opportunity. It was his to denounce and prove worthy of destruction a monster organization that had been sucking the life blood of honor, honesty, patriotism and religion, and to plead for the redemption of a great State and the Nation. He had an audience that gave him a huge homage for the life he had lived amongst them for more than a third of a century, and that gave him a large body of sympathizers in his present contention.

There he stood, a modest little gentleman but with a mouth and eyes, a fire-tipped tongue able to pour forth a torrent of argument alike beautiful and terrible, able to lay bare iniquity in the social fabric and burn it as a surgeon an ugly sore with a hot iron. The audience approved Colonel Johnston's designation and greeted the veteran minister, noble patriot and exalted citizen with heartiest and most generous applause.

Dr. Palmer said, according to the report in the contemporary press:

"MR. CHAIRMAN AND FELLOW CITIZENS OF LOUISIANA: I lay the indictment against the Lottery Company of Louisiana that it is essentially an immoral institution whose business and avowed aim is to propagate gambling throughout the State and throughout the country. Being not simply a nuisance, but even a crime, no Legislature as the creature of the people, nor even the people themselves in convention assembled has the power to legitimate it, either by legislative enactment on the one hand, or by fundamental charter upon the other. In other words, I lay the indictment against the Louisiana Lottery Company that its continued existence is incompatible, not only with the safety, but with the being of the State.

"In saying this, sir, I desire to be understood as not simply uttering the language of denunciation. I frame the indictment and I propose to support each of its specifications by adequate proof. And I do this the more distinctly from the conviction that there are many citizens throughout our bounds who, having been accustomed to look at the lottery simply as a means of revenue, either public or private, have not sufficiently considered the inherent viciousness of the system itself. [Applause.] And it is that class which I hope this night to reach and to range upon our side in this great controversy.

"Indeed, sir, if the worst should come to the worst in this present campaign, I for one could wish that all technicalities being swept away

[11] See *New Delta,* Friday, June 26, 1891. Cf. also *Southwestern Presbyterian,* July 2, 1891.

there might be some method by which the question could be carried up to the Supreme Court of the United States, whether it is competent to any State in this Union to commit suicide. [Applause.] And if that venerable court should return an answer, which I think they would not for a moment consider as possible, I would then for my part make the appeal to the virtue and common sense of the masses of our people, that the very instinct of self-preservation may stamp out of existence an institution which is fatal to the liberties and to the life of the commonwealth.

"I have laid down a proposition sufficiently broad. Now for the proof. What would you say if a syndicate should be formed in this State or any other State of the Union for the avowed purpose of propagating leprosy [laughter] throughout the land, sending their agents with the utmost activity in order to impregnate every woman and man and child in all the country with the virus of that dreadful disease? Is there a Legislature that is competent to induct such an association into existence? Or, would the people themselves in the exercise of their high sovereignty in convention assembled undertake to render lawful the existence of such a corporation as that? Or, to vary the illustration: Suppose that a university should be endowed with many millions in this State or elsewhere, in order to persuade the people throughout the land of the great advantages of lying and of stealing [applause], sending out their agents in all the avenues of life in order to indoctrinate the people both as to the methods and the advantages of these practices. Is there a Legislature in the land, or the people themselves in convention assembled, who would not immediately recognize that in chartering such an institution they simply dissolve the State? For how can society hold together if confidence be destroyed in the veracity of man to man, or if there be no security whatever in our earthly possessions?

"Permit me to vary the illustration still further. Suppose there should be an organization effected in this city in the interests of murdering, and, by the way, we have had some little experience of that of late. When all the machinery of human justice proving inadequate to defend the safety and life of the Commonwealth, extra legal measures were necessitated under the instinct of self-preservation to stamp out the existence of the Mafia in our midst. [Applause and cheers.] Now, sir, I put the lottery upon the same moral plane with these cases which I have mentioned. [Cheering and applause.] In every view which you take of it it is an institution that antagonizes the State and the people in all their interests, and there is but one issue before this people and I announce it without hesitation upon this platform: either the lottery must go or Louisiana is lost. [Cheers and applause.] And with the point of my finger I write upon the walls of every house in this city and throughout this State, *Carthago est delenda.* Carthage and Rome could not exist side by side on the same planet, and Rome must conquer and Carthage must fall. [Cheers.]

"If I am asked to sustain by adequate proof the proposition which I have announced as to the inherent viciousness of the lottery system, permit me to say that the first physical matter which forms a basis upon which human society rests is the law of labor. There are moral laws underlying society, as for example that law which demands truth and righteousness between man and man, but as the physical basis upon which all society and government must rest, we find that basis in the law of labor. It was ordained from the beginning by the great Creator when he placed man in his primal innocence in the garden to dress and to keep it, and, when after the fall that light labor deepened into the curse, it became under the decree of heaven necessary that a man should earn his bread by the sweat of his brow. Divine grace coming after it ameliorated the curse and from that day to this under the providence of a kind heaven, labor proves a blessing, hides within its folds and under its forbidding aspect the highest blessings which can be conferred upon the human race. [Applause.]

"It is written in the best of books, that if a man will not work, neither shall he eat. So that from the creation to the time of Christ's appearance upon the earth, it has been the fundamental and universal law under which society exists that each unit in society lives by his individual and personal labor. The farmer harrows the ground, plants the seed in it and reaps the abundant harvest. He blends his industry with the fertility of the soil and with the beneficence of heaven in giving the early and latter rain, and the dews and the sunshine. The common carrier takes the cotton bloom and bears it from the barn of the planter to the distant manufacturer, and in the transportation he stamps a new value upon the original product of the field, and lives by that value which he has attached.

"The manufacturer brings his industry and his skill and his invention, spinning the staple into thread and weaving it into cloth, and stamps upon the cotton bloom a value a thousand-fold more than it originally had, and the manufacturer lives upon the value which he has contributed to the plant. And so, the wholesale merchant and the retail merchant, lifting the pile of goods from under the manufacturer's hands, transports them over the land until they are found in the remotest hamlet and are sold by the yard, and the price paid by the customer measures all the successive values which have been imparted to the original product of the field, and each class lives by the value which he has himself imparted to the same. Mr. Chairman, I am almost ashamed to repeat this earliest and simplest lesson in our political economy. But I do it for the purpose now of asking the searching question: 'What value does the gambler ever create? What new value does he ever stamp upon the value which existed antecedently?'

"What does the lottery do in all of its manipulations but simply shift the products of a preceding industry from one hand to another hand [applause] without the imparting in the process of a particle of value to that which is thus tranferred? It may be said that there are customers who not being producers are under the same charge of using up what they do not create. It only emphasizes the position already taken, for even the non-producing class, as for example professional men, live upon that which they in a sense create. The lawyer may not create a new material product, but man being as he is there could be no basis of personal property without the machinery of justice, and he is the representative and organ of that justice, and just in so far as he conserves that which others create, and protects them in the enjoyment of the same, he is worth his living though he may not be a creator of a new material product. The physician who restores health to one who is incapacitated by disease from labor, or who ameliorates the suffering which disease inflicts, becomes by virtue of his calling a necessity to society and is worth in the exercise of his profession all that it costs to maintain him.

"And the preacher, of whom I stand before you a representative, taking even the lowest economic view of his profession as a consumer and not a producer, is an important part of that necessary police force without which the order and position and prosperity of society cannot be preserved. [Applause.] All not being then producers, but consumers, yet in the exercise of their several callings add to the value of what is created and render secure the enjoyment of the same. But what value does the Lottery Company protect, not to say what value does the Lottery Company create?

"Let me illustrate this so that it shall be understood by all present to-night. That company issues, if you please, a thousand tickets of $500 value apiece, creating thus within its vaults a fund of $500,000. It has first got to take $250,000 of that and deposit it safely in its own locker as its portion of the plunder. [Laughter.] It then takes the other half, the $250,000, and divides it into twenty-five shares of $10,000 each and puts these into the wheel and the five hundred men may take their chances as to which of them shall get these twenty-five prizes. When at last the prizes are realized, what has been accomplished? Simply the transfer of $500,000 out of the pockets of one thousand individuals, one-half of it to enrich those who run the machine and the other half divided among twenty-five men, leaving four hundred and seventy-five to hold the empty bag and gain the loss. [Laughter and applause.]

"Mr. Chairman, I do not wish to appear harsh, but will you draw for me the line between this and absolute stealing? [Applause.] If twenty-five men can put their hands into the pockets of four hundred and seventy-five men and take the $250,000 by which they are enriched without giving to those four hundred and seventy-five any equivalent, where is the distinction any other than barely a metaphysical distinction without even a hairbreadth's width to mark it between that and what we call in common style a theft? [Applause.] Now, sir, I know the reply to this. There are but two methods by which we acquire property, either by gift or purchase. Now I ask whether these four hundred and seventy-five men have made a gift to the successful winners of the prizes. Each one of those four hundred and seventy-five men, so far from being willing to donate their loss so that it shall become the other's gain, each one of them has been hoping and wishing that he might put into his own pocket the coveted treasure. Was there any good will in the transfer from the loser to the gainer? Is it a purchase? What equivalent has been rendered? It is simply grotesque to speak of that being purchase money which does not amount to one-twentieth of the value of the thing purchased. But, it is urged in answer to this that the parties contract and make the bargain between themselves as to this gain and loss, and that as the losers agreed to take their chances with the rest, it is constructively although not actually a gift on their part.

"Now it appears to me, Mr. Chairman and fellow citizens, one of the plainest principles of ethics that what a man has no right to do, he has no right to bargain to do, and no contract between man and man to do a thing that is unlawful can ever be made right in the sight of man or God simply by the fact that it is a contract between them. I go beyond this and say that the deliberateness of the act when two or more men sit down together and combine to do a thing which in itself was not right to do, the deliberateness of the act makes it more criminal than if it sprung from the spontaneous and sudden act of an individual, and more than all you have in the contract to do the wrong thing not only this deliberateness, but you have the concurrence of two wills, doubling the crime on the part of both. The man who staked his property had no right to stake that property on a chance, and the man who won the property upon that stake had no original right to take it. It was neither a gift nor a purchase and consequently the agreement between the parties to stand simply by the chance was an immoral agreement and no Legislature can possibly make it legitimate. [Applause.] Here then is my first position against the lottery, when I say that it disorganizes society and is incompatible with the safety of the State. It strikes at that fundamental law of labor. It has said to these one thousand men, 'There is no need for you to work. There is a shorter way by which you can enrich yourselves and your families.' Those one thousand men are called away from their proper duties and they fail in meeting that fundamental obligation to live either by the toil of their hands or by the work of their understanding.

"But, more than this, sir. When I have said there is no equivalent given and no new value imparted when there is transfer of money from one hand to the other through the lottery and its agents, it is a lesson industriously taught the people not only to live by luck, but to live upon the misfortune of their neighbors. I beg the attention of the audience to the announcement of this principle. Sir, it is a solemn thing for any body of men to inculcate it as at all right and proper that we should live simply and alone upon the losses of those that are unlucky. If I win the $10,000 prize, those that entered into the chance with me have lost just that much and I am enriched through their poverty. Now, sir, let the lottery exist five and twenty years. If only twenty-five men out of five hundred succeed in gaining what the lottery promises, how long will it take to transfer the entire wealth of the State of Louisiana into the hands of one out of twenty of its citizens? What will be the condition of things when one-twentieth of the population own everything upon the soil? And let me ask, sir, how long is any community going to stand that sort of thing? [Applause.] When the country has been led straight up or driven up to the very verge of a precipice, do you suppose that, like a herd of buffaloes, all the people of this State are going to leap that precipice into the boiling and hissing depths below? No, sir; they must and they will recoil, and if this lottery cannot be destroyed by forms of law, it must unquestionably be destroyed by actual revolution. [Tremendous and prolonged cheering and applause.] I fear that I may be trespassing upon the time of the other speakers. [Cries of "No, no, go on, go on."]

"I sometimes hear the apology for the lottery after this sort: 'Oh, it is all wrong. It is immoral, we grant that, but then it is one of the evils which to society is incident and we cannot help ourselves. It is just like drinking. The State knows that the saloon is a deep injury to the State, and if in her power would gladly suppress it, but as men must and will drink, it is wise for the State to throw around existing saloons such restrictions as shall diminish the harm and make the evil less as it bears upon society at large.' Now, the analogy is drawn. 'Gambling is in human nature. Men will gamble, and why should not the State deal with the lottery exactly as it deals with the saloons. Give it license to do its work.' But, sir, without dwelling too long upon the statement, let me dissipate the illusion by showing where the analogy fails.

"Saloons exist, but they exist under protest. They exist under not only the protest of the government, but under restraints such as the State will be able to throw around them. It stands by itself and simply answers the wishes and demands which are made upon it by those who desire the liquor which is sold them, but if you want the parallel to be exact you must convert all the saloons in the country into one grand saloon syndicate [laughter and applause] and that syndicate must go to the Legislature and demand a charter, and in order that their rights may be beyond invasion ever afterwards it must be imbedded in the Constitution that they and they alone shall have the right to satisfy the thirst of the people. [Laughter.] What next? They open their tap-rooms upon every corner in every city where they gain access, and they hang out their prices, from the pint, earthen mug, quite up to the gallon and hogshead. [Laughter.] And according to the money the parties are willing to pay this saloon syndicate will drown the country with what they desire and what proves their ruin. Not only that, but they have their agents walking the streets thrusting invitations into your face as you walk quietly in your citizenship along the streets of this city to tell you how cheap you may get this drink that you wish, and so they become the propagandists of the saloon.

"That is the crime which I charge now against the lottery. It is not only a gambling place such as other gambling places that are in this city, meeting under the cover of night to satisfy the wishes and anticipations of those who love the gambling, but it becomes the apostle of gambling. It becomes the propagandist of gambling, it goes forth under the charter of the State to persuade man, woman and child wherever they meet them to gamble. [Applause.] It carries the solicitation into our very homes. It meets our cooks when they are going with the basket to get the master's breakfast [laughter] and induces them to gamble. How long, sir, would the country stand a syndicate of saloons, and I ask how long will Louisiana or the country stand this syndicate of gamblers? [Applause.] What I charge, therefore, upon the lottery is not simply that it is a gambling concern, but that it is a university for the instruction in gambling and a high endowment in order to stimulate the process of gambling by and through the country at large. I have only one thing more to say and I am done.

"I have said the lottery must go, because the State cannot be allowed to perish. Why, sir, before the half of twenty-five years have elapsed if this lottery should gain its charter, every man that is able to leave the State of Louisiana will abandon it. [Applause.] Whilst you are holding out our invitations to invite capital and invite population, who shall drain your morasses and stimulate industry and create the wealth of the State, you are holding up this forbidding thing to drive every desirable citizen away from Louisiana. Worse than that, sir,—when you have an institution that goes openly before the Legislature and seeks to bribe it, that in less than ten years after its recharter will carry in its pocket every governor in the State [applause], remove every honest judge from the bench, and put their men in the places to do their bidding, what then will Louisiana be worth? [Applause.] I, sir, was not born upon the soil of Louisiana, but I am her son by adoption. [Applause.] I have spent thirty-five years, almost the half of a long life, in what I believe is honest and virtuous labor for the good of this people [Applause.] It will not be in my power to abandon this State, even though I might desire to escape the odium attaching it. My dead are here and the narrow house is already built in which after a year or two of active service I expect to be laid aside to enjoy the quiet repose which heaven has afforded to them, but before that event takes place, I desire to see this land of my adoption redeemed. [Applause.] I want her redemption to be accomplished by her own act. These beautiful plains, this delicious climate, taking the year round superior to any other upon this continent, these beautiful streams which like silver threads almost convert a portion of our State into a modern Venice—are we, sir, to abandon such a land as this, created by beneficent heaven and secured by the patriotism of the fathers that went before us? Are we to deliver, her, bound hand and foot, to such an enemy as this? [Cries of "No, no."] Unless she be redeemed by her own act then the appeal must be made to the virtue and the intelligence of the entire country. Mr. Chairman, I need not say to one like you, so versed in moral truths, that the world is ruled by ideas, and it is not competent to any isolated community to live against the moral convictions of the world. [Applause.]

"Scarce recovered as a people from the blow inflicted upon us coming in that precise way, the moral sentiment of the world, right or wrong, was arrayed against the institution of slavery and it went down. The moral sentiment of mankind is against the lottery, and all the countries that have given it a temporary existence have found that it exhausted the resources of the land and have more or less divested themselves of the curse; but if, notwithstanding all these things, the curse should still be inflicted upon us, Louisiana must become a lost Pleiad in the sisterhood of States, and she will go forth an outcast pariah with the scarlet letter of shame branded forever upon her forehead."

He had spoken without notes, without a line; but of an open sore that had provoked his thought and indignation for a score of years. It does not read like one of his masterpieces; but judged by the effect produced it was a great oration. Demosthenes had uttered a Philippic. The Athenians were going to fight Philip. When he declared that the partisans of the lottery, who had corrupted legislative, judicial and public morals, might drive him and his fellow citizens to the brink of the precipice, but that they would there turn and "destroy them by actual revolution," the house cheered the bold declaration in the most enthusiastic manner. Men and women, almost the entire audience, "stood on their chairs, shouting and gesticulating," says Dr. Wm. O. Rogers, "in a frenzy of applause and concurrence that expended itself only in successive waves of excitement." It has been said that at that moment Dr. Palmer might have turned his vast audience of intelligent and characterful people into a mob and led them, with such arms as mobs seize, against the domiciles of the lottery institution throughout the city. Certainly the audience was with him that night and would have been ready to follow whithersoever he could have led.

A distinguished Jewish Rabbi has said of this address:

"I have heard the foremost American public speakers, in the pulpit, or on the rostrum. Beecher commanded a more lurid rhetoric than Palmer. For a combination of logical argument and noble and brilliant rhetoric, neither he nor any other has equalled Palmer when *he* was at his best. I heard him that night in the Grand Opera House. Always except on this occasion, when listening to an address, even a great one, I have been able to say to myself, ——, how far do you agree with the speaker? What do you reject? How far will you go with him? Where will you stop? But I give you my word, sir, that night Dr. Palmer did not permit me to think for myself, nor to feel for myself, nor to will for myself, but picked me up and carried me whithersoever he would. It did not seem to me that it was Palmer that was speaking. He spoke as one inspired. It seemed to me that God Almighty was speaking through Palmer. He had filled him with His Spirit and Message as He filled the Hebrew prophets of old."

Nor did the impression wear off. The next morning, this cultured, distinguished and able Rabbi was walking on the street. He met a man of wealth who had shown him kindness and had many lovable points of character, and who was, in the Rabbi's own words, "an all-round good fellow," but was possessed of large holdings in the lottery. After the customary salutations the Rabbi said:

"Mr. B., you had better draw out of the lottery. It is doomed."

"Why do you think so, Rabbi?" said Mr. B.

"Dr. Palmer has spoken," said the Rabbi.

"Ha! the speech of one parson cannot kill this lottery," said Mr. B.

"I repeat," said the Rabbi, "your lottery is doomed and you had better draw out."

"Pshaw! The speech of this parson cannot kill the lottery. We have the *money*."

"Once more, I say, Mr. B.," said the Rabbi, "your lottery is doomed, your holdings will soon be worthless as chaff. Not one parson has spoken! *Ten thousand parsons have spoken!* Every man, woman, and child that heard that address last night is to-day a missionary against your lottery and its doom is as certain and as inexorable as death."

This distinguished gentleman believed that without that speech the fight would have been won by the lottery people; that it was essential to the victory of the anti-lottery crusade. The compiler of this biography does not undertake to assert this. There were other heroic men engaged in the fight. Gov. Francis T. Nicholls, Hon. E. H. Farrer, of New Orleans; Hon. Don Caffrey, of St. Mary's Parish, and Hon. John H. Stone, of East Feliciana, and other leaders of equal note, and a great host of the morally best people of the State. But it was a great thing for the good cause, that he did that night. He stood forth clothed with a character, an ability, a wisdom and an experience, proven by half a century of toil consecrated to human good and Divine glory, as a representative of the highest moral and religious forces of the State, and denounced the wrong and plead for the right, even for the redemption of his city and his people—his fellow citizens of Louisiaina.

His opponents, driven to desperation, in their extremity charged him with counseling violence and threatening war. His speech itself was a sufficient answer to the charge: Revolution was counseled only as the last resort. The speech was published at once, and repeatedly, and was widely influential.

The lottery was doomed. "Conceived in the miscegenation of reconstruction, born in iniquity, sustained by a deliberate policy of bribery, an unmitigated curse to the whole country, stained with theft and the blood of many of its dupes, honest only in this, that after its large per cent of receipts was reserved for its stockholders, buyers of tickets were given the privilege of trying their luck in fortune's wheel for the balance, and the prizes won were, with blasts of trumpets, faithfully paid,"[12] this gigantic swindle was doomed. The moral sense of Louisiana had been aroused, and had issued her dictate.

To resume the cataloging of addresses made in this period: On Saturday, October 31, 1891, he delivered another notable anti-lottery address, before the Women's Anti-Lottery Mass-meeting in Tulane Hall, in which he rent the mask from the

[12] R. R. Mallard, D.D., in *Southwestern Presbyterian,* May 2, 1895, p. 4, c. 3.

huge bribe the lottery was offering for the renewal of its charter, and revealed it as a curse though represented as God's beneficence, something which would make Louisiana putrify, should she accept it, something that would exile all her worthy citizens and place the people under the very heels of the lottery swindle; the address on the "Representative Life and Character of Dr. T. G. Richardson," delivered at the Annual Commencement of the Medical Department of Tulane University, Louisiana, April 5, 1893, brilliant and able; a little later, an exquisite brief funeral address over the remains of Dr. Miles, who had lifted himself to the first rank of Christian physicians; an eloquent address, in his own church, February 16, 1897, over the remains of Mrs. A. M. Jennings, daughter of his old elder, Mr. Alfred Hennen, who had, in view of her approaching death, started back from Europe that she might be laid to rest among her own people in New Orleans, and who had died at sea; a patriotic address on the afternoon of May 11, 1898, at Camp Foster, to the First and Second Regiments of Volunteers for the Cuban War; about the same time, an address before the Counsel of Jewish Women at New Orleans, on "Liberty, Truth and Civilization; Judaism and the Jewish People Have Stood for Them in All Ages;" the address in honor of Winnie Davis, before the Memorial Meeting at Washington Artillery Hall, September 23, 1898, when "his tongue seemed shod with a grief that was almost divine;" a valuable historical address delivered, November, 1898, before his church on occasion of its seventy-fifth anniversary, in which the origin and growth of the church was succinctly brought out; an address delivered May 20, 1899, at the unveiling of the monument to the memory of Rev. Thos. R. Markham, D.D.; an address delivered upon the dedication of Waddell Hall, Clarksville, Tenn, June 10, 1899; the "Onliness of God," a baccalaureate sermon, at the Southwestern Presbyterian University, Sunday, June 11, 1899; an address before the United Confederate Veterans and the Washington Artillery, on occasion of the presentation of the historic gun, the Lady Slocum, to the Louisiana Historical Association, September 19, 1899; a memorial address in honor of William Preston Johnston, LL.D., first president of Tulane University, 1884-1899, a production valuable not only for its brilliant account of the life and work of a great educator, and of the origin and establishment of

Tulane University, but for philosophical views of the process of education itself; a speech before the Anti-Trust Meeting, held in Tulane Hall, January 29, 1900, other speakers on the occasion being Bishop Hugh Miller Thompson and Mr. Ashton Phelps; a patriotic, tender and eloquent address on Confederate Decoration Day, April 6, 1900; and the great oration before the Confederate Reunion, in Louisville, Ky., May 30, 1900.

Of this oration the introductory paragraphs and the concluding paragraph are presented to the reader that he may thus command the attitude of the grand *old* man toward certain great subjects with which American history has been deeply concerned. Having been introduced by Gen. John B. Gordon, Dr. Palmer said:

"CONFEDERATE VETERANS AND FELLOW CITIZENS: Accustomed through sixty years to address public assemblies, I am nevertheless subdued with awe in your presence to-day; for we stand together under the shadow of the past. It is the solemn reverence one might feel in the gloom of Westminster Abbey, surrounded by England's illustrious dead. Indeed, we are here the living representatives of countless comrades who sleep in lonely cemeteries throughout the land, where perchance a single monumental shaft is the ghostly sentinel keeping watch over the bivouac of the dead.

"It is five and thirty years since the Confederate War was closed, and about thirty-nine years since it was begun, and it is sometimes asked why we should stir the ashes of that ancient feud? Why should we not bury the past in its own grave, and turn to the living issues of the present and the future? To this question, comrades, we return the answer with a voice loud as seven thunders, because it is history, because it is our history and the history of our dead heroes who shall not go without their fame. As long as there are men who wear the gray, they will gather the charred embers of their old campfires and in the blaze of these reunions tell the story of the martyrs who fell in the defense of country and of truth.

"Nay, more than this; it is the story of a strife that marks an epoch in the annals of the American people. It is known to every schoolboy in the land that two parties existed at the formation of our government, who could not agree in locating the paramount sovereignty which should decide upon all issues arising between the States themselves. The Federalists, as they were termed, demanded a strong government, concentrating power in the national administration; the Republicans, on the other hand, contended for the distribution of power among the States claiming their original sovereignty among their reserved rights. Both parties were too strong to allow the question to be determined by arbitration or through forensic discussion. It was, therefore, permitted to slumber beneath certain ambiguities of expression in the Constitution itself, to be settled by the exigencies of the future, not as an abstract principle, but as an accomplished fact. I need not remind you how this issue was raised in 1832, and was postponed through the conciliatory legislation of that period. Such an issue could not, however, sleep forever. The admission of new States into the Union, with their conflicting interests, must reopen the question and compel its decision. Thus it arose in our day, leading to the establishment of the Southern Confederacy, and to the Civil War that followed.

"Fellow citizens, it is simply folly to suppose that such a spontaneous uprising as that of our people in 1860 and 1861 could be effected through the machinations of politicians alone. A movement so sudden and so vast, instantly swallowing up all minor contentions, would only spring from great faith deeply planted in the human heart and for which men are willing to die. Whatever may have been the occasion of the war, its *cardo causae,* the hinge on which it turned, was this old question of State sovereignty as against national supremacy. As there could be no compromise between the two, the only resort was an appeal to the law of force, the *ultima ratio regum.* The surrender at Appomattox, when the tattered remnant of Lee's great army stood guard for the last time over Southern liberties and rights, drew the equatorial line dividing between the past and the future of American history. When the will of the strongest, instead of 'the consent of the governed,' became the base of our national structure, a radical transformation took place. The principle of confederation gave way to that of consolidation, and the American nation emerged out of the American republic.

"It is not my design, however, to discuss these issues. On the contrary, I have traced the remote origin of the Confederate War for a purpose which is entirely conciliatory, and to explain some things which may appear contradictory. It enables both parties in this struggle to give full credit to each other for patriotic motives, though under a mistaken view of what that patriotism may have required. It shows why no attempt was ventured to bring attainder of treason against the Southern chiefs, which could not afford to be ventilated before any civil court under the terms of the American Constitution. It explains how through a noble forbearance on both sides (always excepting the infamies of the reconstruction period) the wound has been healed in the complete reconciliation of a divided people. It explains how we of the South, convinced of the rightfulness of our cause, can accept defeat without the blush of shame mantling the cheek of a single Confederate of us all; and while accepting the issue of the war as the decree of destiny, openly appeal to the verdict of posterity for the final vindication of our career. In making this appeal, veterans, in your name, I am brought to the subject of this day's discourse, which is to set before you the tribunal of history, before which all the issues of the past continue to be tried; and which in the view of many sound thinkers is rendering a proximate judgment in what is occurring before us in the immediate present."

Having thus reached his subject the orator proceeded to show, by luminous and noble historical parallels drawn from ancient, mediaeval and modern history, that peoples have often "mourned their dead and the principles for which they in vain had fought," and yet been vindicated by the true historians of the after-time.

He concluded as follows:

"What I affirm then is this: That the value of these final generalizations is scarcely impaired by the doubts as to this or that minute fact. Contemporaneous history, written in the interests of prejudice and passion, may be largely a libel, and future criticism may be sorely puzzled to distinguish between the truth and its travesty; yet in the aggregate result these, by a strange smelting process, are sifted out as not material to the issue. As we may poison a fountain, but cannot poison the ocean, so we may corrupt single facts, but cannot transmute the whole history of a people into a lie. A thousand hints of the truth will lie imbedded in the record, which antiquarian research will disentomb. The long silent voices will deliver their testimony in the court of final adjudication, and in these solemn historic retractions the good and the brave will find an honest vindication.

"Fellow citizens, the application of this discourse is left to silence and to you. That which hath been is now, and that which is to be hath already been. Invective and reproach will continue in the sacred name of history to be poured upon those who deserve only her applause. The faithful witnesses of the truth will go in cloud and sorrow to the tomb, burying their principles only in a protest. But they will do it in the certain faith of a resurrection. As for their own fame, they can afford to wait. Eternity is long, and it is their lifetime. Upon the lip of that boundless sea their prophetic gaze is fixed upon the burnished throne which human justice makes its last tribunal, and before which the nations and the centuries are burnished for trial. Defamation and slander rest as lightly on their calm spirits as the salt spray that crystallizes upon the silent rock. If, too, the warnings of the past, like the prophecies of Cassandra, are heard only to be disbelieved, still let the despots of earth know they are but sowing the dragon's teeth of an armed and fierce retribution. Constitutional freedom has not come forth from the conflict of ages to be stifled now, when her broad shield is thrown over two continents. She will reappear again and again amid the birth-throes of regenerated States, for regulated liberty is to the commonwealth what piety is to the Church—the very law of its life. Both have struggled through corruption and decay to a more complete realization. But if the day should come when despotism shall so far consolidate its power as to crush all human freedom beneath its iron heel then will be consummated the second apostasy of man after the flood in the usurpation of Nimrod. History will have completed its cycle, and nothing will remain but the call to universal judgment."

The comments of the press on the oration were highly commendatory; and for sufficient cause. The *Presbyterian Journal* said: "Apart from a few deductions with which we of course could not agree, the address is the most perfect classic we recall having seen since we laid aside our Demosthenes many years ago. Dr. Palmer, we believe, is the last of the Romans, the one solitary souvenir of that magnificent coterie of Presbyterian orators, who in their day revived the forensic age. Where are the orators of forty years ago? We have more good speakers, but fewer of those who might be called great."

Amongst the private letters which it occasioned we read in one, "I think your address unsurpassed in all time." The following will be read with pleasure:

"CHATTANOOGA, June 4, 1900.

"*Rev. B. M. Palmer, D.D.*

"MY DEAR REV. BROTHER: I cannot refrain from expressing my admiration for the noble address you delivered at Louisville, before the Veterans of the Confederacy, and the very great pleasure I enjoyed on yesterday in its perusal. It is a great comfort (not to speak of the mental joy and spiritual satisfaction I experienced) to me to read so worthy, and so true, and so able and eloquent a setting forth of the great truth you declare for us all—that God is over our defeats and disappointments, and that human actions and human conduct when inspired by a sense of duty and devotion, and glorified by sacrifice and suffering, can never be for nought! Our dead did not die in vain! Our heroic struggle was a grand struggle of duty! Our whole people did the will of God! I wish, my dear sir, I could have been present to hear you.

"You will be interested to know, that our South Carolina Legislature voted $10,000 for a monument, and stone markers on the battlefield of Chickamauga. I am here by request of the Commission, to assist them in locating the markers, especially of my own regiment, (Twenty-fourth South Carolina), and the place for the monument. The

Federal officers on the Commission are most polite and considerate, in every way,

"I am, my dear Dr. Palmer,

"Most respectfully and truly your brother in Christ and Confederate comrade, "ELLISON CAPERS."

His *Century Sermon,* delivered at the request of prominent citizens irrespective of creed, New Year's Day of 1901, deserves special notice. The audience to which he delivered it was thoroughly representative; while the body of it was made up of Presbyterians, "every denomination, race and calling was represented in the two thousand people who were packed into the great church. There were Methodists, Baptists, Episcopalians, Jews, German Protestants, Lutherans, merchants, scholars, professional men, representatives of the great business and railroad interests, shipping people, strangers in the city, young men and women, old men and women, some of them as old as the venerable pastor himself, and little children, whose lives may be prolonged far toward the coming of the next century, and who will see many of the wonderful things which will come to pass in the further march of civilization outlined in the eloquent words of the man who had for forty-four years stood in the pulpit of the First Church and uttered words of wisdom to three generations." [13]

This oration was a noble attempt to trace the hand of God in history, the part that the historical peoples have severally played, in the great drama, according to the Divine economy.

"In reading it one will recognize its noble elevation of thought, its purity of expression, its profound sympathy, its rich rhetorical allusions, its nice historical perspective, its comprehensive grasp of the forces that have fought for empires throughout the history of the earth for four thousand years, and its wise emphasis of those eternal verities which have made and kept civilization what it is to-day. All this may be recognized in the printed words. But the potent personality of the speaker is absent. The simple majesty of his presence, the strange music of his voice, the unearthly glance of his eye, the gesture dignified and impressive, the countenance luminous with intense conviction of God's eternal laws—these no artist with pen or brush can adequately describe or portray. Looking upon him one felt in all solemnity and with profound pride that a city and country that could produce such a man surely had much energy for good. 'On God and Godlike men we build our trust,' comes freshly to one's mind. For more than an

[13] *The Picayune,* January 2, 1901.

hour, in the densely crowded church, the thronging auditors sat in reverent silence, listening to the words spoken by one who was at once poet, priest, patriot, prophet and patriarch. During the solemn address the clock in the rear of the church ticked audibly throughout the congregation. No one moved. No one spoke. No one whispered. There was not even the slightest coughing so common in densely crowded halls and on days damp, cheerless and depressing. When the great Apostle of God's law had finished, a gray-haired parishioner in the gallery, who had listened attentively to every word of the discourse, turned to the man at his elbow and said . . . with strange earnestness and sincerity, measuring every word he uttered: 'Greatest man alive!' "[14]

Other addresses were the baccalaureate sermon at the University of Georgia, July 16, 1901; and an address before Tulane University, delivered during the February preceding his death, on "Love of Truth the Inspiration of the Scholar;" and many others.

The last one named was, for the most part, an old address rewrought. It is remarkable how little use he made of old speeches, notwithstanding the pressure of years and of the burdens of his office. He usually preferred to bring forth for the occasion.

This is no complete catalogue of his addresses of the period. Others of greater value than some of these might be added.

---

[14] *Times-Democrat,* January 2, 1901.

CHAPTER XVIII.

THE FINAL STADIUM OF SERVICE; NOBLE THOUGH BROKEN.—Continued.

(1888-1902.)

PUBLISHED WRITINGS OF THE PERIOD: "FORMATION OF CHARACTER."—"THE BROKEN HOME; OR, LESSONS IN SORROW."—"HINDRANCES TO UNION WITH THE CHURCH."—"THEOLOGY OF PRAYER."—"THE THREEFOLD FELLOWSHIP AND THE THREEFOLD ASSURANCE."—"REVIEW ARTICLES.—TRIBUTES TO FRIENDS AND BROTHER MINISTERS.—LETTERS OF CONSOLATION.—LETTER TO REV. W. D. SPURLIN.—LETTER TO DR. J. B. STRATTON.—LETTERS OF FRIENDSHIP AND PASTORAL CARE.

DR. PALMER published four volumes in the course of these last fourteen years. The first to pass through the press, was that on the "Formation of Character"—twelve lectures delivered on as many Sabbath evenings in his church, in 1889. The lectures had been delivered in response to a request signed by twenty-five young men of his congregation. Shortly after their delivery a stenographic report of the lectures was placed in his hands, with a request to revise them with a view to their publication. Such a request he found it hard to deny; and accordingly complied with it. The several subjects of the lectures were: *Youth, the Formative Period; Elements Which Enter Into Character; Influence of Piety in Forming Character; Obligations Arising from a Pious Ancestry; Obligation Arising from the Trust of Life; Obstacles to Piety in the Young; Choice of Amusements; Sin of Profane Swearing; Sin of Sabbath Breaking; Intemperance and Sins of the Flesh; The Sin of Gambling; The Scriptures Our Rule.* The lectures are thoroughly sane, strong, and rich expositions of correlated teachings of God's word on these subjects.

"The Broken Home; or, Lessons in Sorrow," 1890, was the next volume to appear from his pen. The production of the manuscript for this book was in this manner, viz.: After the death of his eldest daughter, which occurred in 1863, he sketched her life and character, primarily for her mother's comfort and satisfaction and to preserve the various incidents in the life and death of his dear child. Similarly, after the death of each of the other daughters who went to an early grave, he wrote down that which he and the rest of the family, left behind, would wish to recall. After the death of Mrs. Colcock, he wrote (some time in 1875, perhaps) the sketch of his firstborn, who had impressed himself indelibly on his father's memory. Mrs. Palmer treasured the sketches greatly and had them gathered into a blank book, now before us. Soon after Mrs. Palmer's death, the Doctor prepared a life sketch of her, and their one remaining daughter started to copy it into this treasured blank book. But the suggestion came to publish it and make their sorrow a means of blessing to others. The whole was carefully revised and room was made in the volume for a sketch of his mother's life and death, also. In an introductory note he says:

> "The following pages are committed to the press with no little mental conflict. The 'stricken deer,' says Cowper, withdraws,
>
> "'To seek a tranquil death in distant shades:'
>
> and so the mourner should hide his wound beneath his mantle. But the Free Masonry of those in sorrow would pour the balm into other hearts which the Spirit of Consolation may have given to each.
>
> "From the simple desire of comforting those who mourn, this story of repeated bereavements is here told. . . . Long treasured memories are now scattered upon the winds, with the prayer that they may help to bind up the broken-hearted."

It would be hard to find in all Christian literature a sweeter, or a saner, Christian spirit than runs through this whole volume. It is worthy of a place in every mourning household. If high example in the midst of affliction could have any uplifting influence, the glimpses of it given in this volume should make the book a boon to every one to whom the Gospel is a savor of life unto life. The literary style of the sketches is marvelously beautiful. They are each a poem in limpid and nervous prose. They linger on the ear like sweet, sad music. Printed on cheap paper, bound in homely guise, and insufficiently advertised, the book has had slight sale; but properly published it ought to have the widest circulation and rank as a classic in pathetic and devotional literature.

It is a queer fact that, notwithstanding its markedly *Christian* character, a Jewish Rabbi should have used it in his pastoral work in dealing with the afflicted members of his flock.

In 1891, Dr. Palmer published a pamphlet of nineteen pages, entitled "Hindrances to Union with the Church: A Letter to An Aged Friend." This letter had been actually written February 3, 1874. It was designed to reach a man believed to be a child of God but distrusting his own religious experience to such a degree as to be unwilling to unite with the Church.

The next volume to come from the press was his "Theology of Prayer as Viewed in the Religion of Nature and in the System of Grace," 1894. The work makes an octavo volume of 352 pages, consisting of two parts. In the first part he treats the subject of prayer on the plane of natural religion, "the main design being to discuss the objections raised by skeptics against it, as a universal duty." As these for the most part reject the authority of the Scriptures, the author endeavors to meet the question on their own ground; and "to show that the argument drawn from the consideration of nature itself, and especially from their own mental and moral organization, scatters these objections to the winds." In the second part, he had the more "grateful task" of interweaving prayer in the whole scheme of grace, by showing its connection with every part of the office discharged by each person of the Godhead. The work thus covers the ground of natural and revealed religion so far as the subject of prayer is concerned. It stands in a class by itself; and fills a gap which had existed hitherto in our theological literature. It is a real contribution to practical theology. Dr. Palmer's ripeness of knowledge and of grace, the products of many years of toil on the part of a brilliant mind, and of God's leading him through great and sore tribulation, went into this effort at didactic and polemic teaching concerning prayer.

His last volume was one entitled "The Threefold Fellowship and the Threefold Assurance," an essay in two parts, 1892—a modest duodecimo of one hundred and forty-four pages. His eyesight had become very dim after 1896 or 1897. This work was, therefore, dictated to his granddaughter, Miss Gussie Colcock, who produced the copy for the printer. The volume betrays no abatement of mental power. The first part begins with an admirable argument for the unity and the tri-personality of God. In successive chapters it discusses fellowship with each of the three Divine persons in turn. The second part deals with the threefold assurance of understanding, faith and hope which grows out of the fellowship in its trinal form. It is on the same general level of excellence with the "Theology of Prayer."

During this period he made an occasional contribution to reviews and newspapers. Of his review articles, one in the *Southern Presbyterian Quarterly* for April, 1898, had for its thesis the following proposition: *"The Hebrew Commonwealth enshrined the fundamental principles of political and civil liberty, which modern nations have only reproduced, and, under other forms have applied."* This very interesting thesis he argued with great ingenuity and ability.

His pen was frequently employed in the framing of tributes to the dead—deceased parishioners, deceased friends in the ministry. Many of the friends of his early mature manhood preceded him to the grave. Their other friends looked to this grand old man to say the fitting thing for the occasion. Thus in 1894, he prepared memorial sketches of the Rev. Dr. Thomas Railey Markham and the Rev. Dr. Henry Martyn Smith, able and godly men, whom he had taught, back, at Columbia, in 1854, and with whom he had sustained warm friendship, who had been his close neighbors in New Orleans, to the last. In 1898, when Dr. Robt. L. Dabney died, the most felicitously expressed tribute of all that were drawn forth by that great man's death was from Dr. Palmer's pen.

Dr. Palmer said, when Dr. Dabney died, " I am lonesome, now that Dabney's gone." This was said because they had for twoscore years fought together in behalf of the same great principles; he must often have felt lonesome, though successive days were ever bringing him new friends, for so many of his friends of forty years or more were going to the Great Beyond. That he so felt, his correspondence gives some sign. "Oh, how death is thinning our number and soon the marble slab will contain the last record of us all!" he exclaimed in a letter of September 3, 1889.

He continued, in some sense, the pastor to many far beyond his parochial bounds. In times of affliction he put forth his efforts to serve, as under-shepherd to the Great Pastor, all whom circumstances rendered it peculiarly incumbent on him to comfort. In the following letters we have instances of this kind of effort:

"NEW ORLEANS, LA., February 20, 1889.

"To Mrs. Edgeworth Bird, Baltimore, Md.:

"MY LIFELONG FRIEND AND SISTER: It distressed me greatly to hear of your severe accident, and of the illness which ensued, so graphically detailed in Saida's kind letter of information. A fall down a flight of hard stone steps, in the depths of your winter climate, would be no trifle to one even younger than yourself. It is matter of thanksgiving that no bones were broken, however severe the shock to the general system. In what wonderful ways the promise is fulfilled to us, 'He shall give His angels charge over thee, to keep thee in all thy ways; they shall bear thee up in their hands, lest thou dash thy foot against a stone.' Thus it has happened to you—'He keepeth all his bones, not one of them is broken.' Then, too, we are permitted to rejoice that the sickness which followed was not unto death; but that you are spared still longer to be the light of that home, of which you have ever been the pride and the joy. God be praised for this deliverance of yourself back into life, and of our escape from a heavy sorrow.

"My daughter Mary's reply to Saida has already told you of my own kindred distress, disabling me from replying to her letter with my own hand. On my seventy-first birthday, I was seized with one of those internal troubles with which persons advanced in years are apt to be overtaken. I am now in the fourth week of its continuance, still a prisoner in my chamber—and this but the second attempt to open correspondence with those outside. The affection involved no immediate danger, but imposed an amount of pain more than I have endured through the whole of preceding life. I realize, however, and that most fully, that it imports to me the beginning of the end. I shall never be the man I have been. With a chronic disorder deranging one of the most important of the bodily organs, I recognize the first blow of the battering-ram which is to demolish the earthly tabernacle. So be it; I shall sooner be at rest, and bow with my beloved one before the throne.

"And now, whilst both of us are in our sick chambers, let us commune together about this discipline of pain. You recall Job's pathetic words 'His flesh upon him shall have pain and his soul within him shall mourn.' Ah, Lord, why this two-edged sword? One edge for the body, another edge for the spirit—the entire man smitten, in both divisions of his complex being. And why this sword appointed to those whom Thou lovest? It is a word full of mystery, 'whom the Lord loveth he chasteneth;' and how much does it mean? Well, this among other things upon which it is impossible here to dwell—that the sufferings of believers on earth are testimonial, and bear witness to the awful holiness of that God who yet, in the infinite stretch of a Divine love, snatches us from eternal death. It is a large topic to handle in a brief letter, at a moment when bodily weakness imparts its impotency to the mind with difficulty attempting to interpret its thoughts to another. Consider how prone men are to think that God gives away a part of His holiness when He wraps a poor sinner in His bosom and kisses him with the kisses of His love. What then? God takes one of His dearest children, laying him on a bed of severe suffering—calls a witnessing world around that couch of pain, and says to them—'You have never doubted my love to this poor saint, and I bring you here to see how I deal with sin as it is found in him. He shall be my witness that, in all the love which has ransomed his soul from eternal death, there has been no relaxation of that holiness which abhors sin with an infinite and consuming hatred; redeemed though this believer is, he cannot enter into my glory until I shall have burnt away his remaining sinfulness with the caustic of these sufferings.' And what shall be the response from the sufferer himself? What but this—'I glory in tribulation also;' let the anguish of soul or body be tenfold more severe, I bear it with a supreme and holy joy if thereby I may vindicate the glorious excellence of that blessed Father who has thus chosen me in the furnace.

"Take another view of the matter. Christ Jesus, our precious Savior, comes to our suffering couch and says: 'In those agonies which I endured upon the Cross, I bore witness to the hatefulness of your sin; and now that I am glorified in heaven my humiliation on earth is continued through you and all my redeemed, who in their sufferings continue my testimony against all sin.' Thus, our sufferings are Christ's also; He is identified with us in them; whilst He lays them upon us for our good, He feels an infinite pity for us as bearing our sorrows, which are yet His sorrows as well. With this thought before you read such passages as the following: Rom. 8: 17, 18; Phil. 1: 29, and 3: 10; 1 Peter 4: 12, 13, 17 and 19. When you have pondered these awhile, you will be prepared to ask, What does the Apostle mean when he says in Col. 1: 24, 'Who now rejoice in my sufferings for you, and *fill up that which is behind of the afflictions of Christ* in my flesh for His body's sake, which is the Church?' Then that other wonderful word in Gal. 6: 17, 'From henceforth let no man trouble me, for *I bear in my body the marks of the Lord Jesus.*' I tremble while I transcribe these tremendous words. Of course they do not mean that there is any merit in our sufferings, or that they add anything to the completeness of Christ's atoning sacrifice by which we stand alone justified in God's sight. Only this is meant: that by our union with Him who is our head, we are identified with Christ in His testimony against the hatefulness of sin—He continuing his testimony through His people and through the afflictions which He is pleased to lay upon them.

"If all this be true, my dear friend, what a holy and blessed thing it is to suffer for Him who has first so suffered for us? Has not God consecrated us anew, by causing us both afresh to 'drink of Christ's cup and to be baptized with His baptism?' Can we afford to come forth from our sick chambers without looking deeper into our Lord's face than we have ever seen before? Must there not be a deeper consecration to Him who has bought us with His blood? Should we not rise to a higher plane, leaving the 'elements of the world' much lower beneath our feet? Coming back from the border of the eternal world, shall there be no reflection of its awful mysteries in our character and life? Oh, that our remaining pathway might be lighted up with a brighter testimony for the holiness and love of the blessed God!

"Pardon me for suggesting to you the questions I have been putting to my own soul. We have little longer to remain below: soon we are to be caught up into the splendor of our Lord's own presence. Let us carry up with us into that supreme glory the remembrance of a communion with our heavenly Father, such as we have never known before; leaving the light of our testimony for Christ, which shall help those who remain after us to find the way to the bright heaven which is our home forever.

"With much love to Saida and to all in the house,

"I am as ever, your lifelong friend and brother,

"B. M. PALMER."

To Mrs. Charles R. Railey on the death of her husband:

"NEW ORLEANS, LA., July 3, 1889.

"MY DEAR MRS. RAILEY: I was equally sorry with yourself to have missed your parting visit, which indeed I had no right to expect. But the pleasure of receiving your note of yesterday more than compensates for it. It is scarcely necessary for me to say that you have been much in my thoughts since your great bereavement. Passing through the same bitter loss myself, I have the keener sense of what such a loss imports: and my heart goes out in sympathy to all those who suffer under such an affliction. We think our sympathies lively enough at all times—in a general sort of way sufficient to take up the sorrows of others in their time of trouble. But it is a different sympathy wholly, when our own hearts are bleeding under the same blow, and we are able truly to put our soul in their soul's stead. Possibly, the state of widowhood means more to your sex than to mine. I cannot judge, of course, from any experience which does include a comparison between the two as actually felt. I can only know what this bereavement imports to a man: yet there is that greater feeling of dependence, that deeper and fuller leaning upon the strength of another, which belongs to woman; and this must make the sense of deprivation the greater with her. It is hard enough with either of the two, and we can well afford to bear one another's burden.

"Still, I do not doubt that you find the consolations of God most abundant in this hour of darkness. It is said (Exod. 20: 21) that

'Moses drew near unto the *thick darkness where God was.*' How much there is in that to teach and comfort us in sorrow! Our Father must needs hide himself in the cloud, for we could not endure the brightness of his glory and live: then, too, in this life of discipline 'clouds and darkness are round about Him,' even while 'mercy and truth go before His face.' So it is in 'the thick darkness' we are often able to get the nearest approach to Him; even as Moses just there spake with God face to face. We are, each of us, not far away from our Father's home, where those dear to us are already at rest: let it be our supreme desire to anticipate its joys by living as near to God as we can, and be the better fitted to behold His glory when we too shall be called higher.

"I trust that your summer trip will do you a world of good; you have greatly needed this season of rest, and the society of your kindred will make it such to you, if not of recreation.

"We are thinning out more and more down here: some thirty or more pews emptied out of the Church, to remain so until the fall. Even in our own house we are reduced: Dr. Caldwell left yesterday for North Carolina with the two boys, who stand in need of being reinforced physically after a hard season of study at college. Only Mary, with the two girls, is with me, and we draw all the closer together. They join me in kindest remembrance, and in the hope that you will return to us fully invigorated.

"Yours most truly,

"B. M. PALMER."

To Col. F. W. and Mrs. Mary J. McMaster, Columbia, upon the death of a son:

"NEW ORLEANS, LA., September 11, 1889.

"MY DEAR COLONEL AND MRS. MCMASTER: Death has at length cast its portentous shadow over your happy and united home. The Columbia *Register*, received yesterday from some kind hand, tells the story of your loss, and I come to sit beside you in your grief. Too well do I know all that it imports. Five times the same cup has been placed to my lips: and in four out of five a grown child escaped out of our hands—just now as from yours. All this happened through a term of years, until we had learned fully what submission means under this form of affliction. Since then I have passed through deeper waters still, and know now what it is to be alone. Surely I have earned the right to sit with you in the ashes, as together we cover our heads with a mantle. You have been wonderfully spared the sorrow so common to earthly households;[1] and your friends around you have looked with surprise at how such a group should gather about you,

---

[1] They had been married thirty-six years before death invaded their household.

without the invasion of disease and death. But it has come at last, and the charmed circle has been broken in the departure of your eldest son in the prime of his early manhood. Alas, we do not take in the significance of death until it enters our own dwelling. We read of its invasion of other homes, and we often follow in the melancholy procession which bears those we have honored to the tomb; but its dreadful tyranny is not disclosed until it tears our own beloved from our arms. It is in the desolation of a dismantled home that we read the full meaning of the curse, 'Thou shalt surely die.'

"But blessed be God, to us who believe the power of the curse is broken: we hear the voice of Him who hath 'abolished death,' saying, 'I will ransom them from the power of the grave; I will redeem them from death: O death, I will be thy plagues; O grave, I will be thy destruction.' And again, 'thy dead men shall live, together with thy dead body shall they arise.' 'Awake and sing, ye that dwell in dust: for thy dew is as the dew of herbs, and the earth shall cast out the dead.' Let us be quiet in our grief, as we listen to the voice of the Redeemer, who having cancelled sin, has taken away the sting of death—and can, therefore, proclaim, 'I am the resurrection, and the life.'

"My dear friends, to whom in your present sorrow my heart goes out in all the freshness of the old-time love—this hour of grief must be the triumph of faith. Our times of trial are to be the triumph, in yielding up our will in holy consecration to Him who has bought us with His blood—'made perfect through suffering, and through suffering, entered into glory.'

"My daughter, Mary, offers her sympathy in this sore bereavement; united with me in love to your dear mother and to all of your mourning household. Affectionately yours,

"B. M. PALMER."

To Rev. S. A. King, D.D., then of Waco, Texas, on the death of his son, Dr. Walter B. King, a young physician of great promise:

"NEW ORLEANS, LA., December 27, 1889.

"MY DEAR BROTHER KING: I have delayed writing the letter promised in the telegram I sent you, simply that I might learn some of the particulars of your recent great bereavement. My first impulse was to follow the message you so kindly sent me, with such fulness of sympathy as your sorrow at once planted in my bosom. But I felt that there was danger of bruising where I desired to heal, if I attempted to write in ignorance of all the circumstances of your affliction.

"And now that your more recent letter to Markham, and his cordial tribute to the memory of your son has appeared in the *Southwestern,* I know not whether to condole with you upon the greatness of your loss, or to congratulate with you at furnishing such a contingent to the happiness of heaven.

"I remember, long years ago, saying to myself (in my first domestic sorrow), 'If God gives me reason to hope that any one dear to me has gone safe to the rest above, I will never suffer myself to grieve." Of course, this was not meant to deny the right of nature to assert herself when deeply wounded; but only to acknowledge that the prospect of eternal separation would be anguish utterly insupportable. In truth, were I to press upon you the consolation you must feel in contemplating the career of a son who 'never gave you a pang'—your reply might be the same which was returned to me by a heartbroken father, whose noble son fell at the head of his company in one of the battles of our late war—'Ah, sir, that is what makes it so hard to give him up.'

"My brother, you have met with a heavy loss—none greater, unless it should be that which God has laid upon me. Still, the tears I have shed over the graves of four grown daughters, besides that of an infant son, enable me to sound the depths of your parental grief. To have reared a son of such brilliant promise, and to have seen him enter into life in the assured fulfillment of your long-cherished hopes, only to see that fine promise wither in its opening splendor, is cause for human lamentation and woe. But all this makes a sacrifice more precious, when with Christian resignation you lay this offering on the altar of your Father's pleasure. We are accustomed to teach our people, that they must serve the Master with what costs them much: and often our teaching is brought to our own bleeding hearts. Thus it is, dear King, that you and I must break our alabaster box of very precious ointment upon the Savior's head. Let us give our Lord the best we have, and which He first gave to us.

"I am not guilty of the presumption of giving counsel to a faithful servant of God, such as I know you to be; but I have so often found the advantage of bringing accepted principles again and again under review of the judgment, that I seek only to 'stir up your pure mind by way of remembrance.' It is not perhaps possible to accept a painful dispensation before it is sent. I do not know that God has ever required more than that we shall always cherish a perfect faith in His wisdom and love as manifested in all His acts. But He does not call upon us to suppress grief in the bare anticipation of it. The ends of gracious discipline require that we should feel the full force of the loss and of the grief. Let us thank Him that He allows the privilege of tears. 'Jesus wept:' and then let us adore Him that we know how from a breaking heart we are able to say 'not as I will, but as thou wilt.'

"Permit me only to add that it was in the thick darkness Moses saw God face to face; and so it is often in Christian experience, the richest disclosures of Jehovah's love are made in the heaviest earthly bereavements. I pray that special grace may be given to you, and to your more deeply afflicted wife, to glorify God in this furnace heated seven times hot. Affectionately yours,

"B. M. PALMER."

To Mrs. Macfie, Columbia, S. C., on the death of her son, Capt. J. P. Macfie:

"NEW ORLEANS, LA., April 14, 1890.

"MY DEAR MRS. MCFIE: On returning from Presbytery on Saturday, I found a copy of the *Columbia Record* marked so as to call my attention to the sad affliction which has overtaken you in the death of your only son. Alas, how sorely we are taught in advancing age that this world cannot be our home! And how willing these accumulated sorrows render us to leave it for the 'city which hath foundations and whose builder and maker is God!' Long ago the Lord left you in the sadness of widowhood, with three young children to lighten your desolate home. You were graciously spared to see them all grown and settled in life and then the new sorrow is allotted you of closing the eyes of two of them in death. Surely a world thus darkened by recurring bereavements and ending at last in the gloom of the grave for ourselves, is not meant to be a home for any of us. Blessed be God, if our treasures be laid up in heaven—a permanent inheritance to be enjoyed evermore 'without the chance and change of mortal breath.' I hope shortly to see you in the flesh, and to hear from your own lips all of sorrow or of comfort you may have to tell. Meanwhile, receive these words of affectionate sympathy from one who has so much in common with you in the memories of the past. Oh, so well do I remember, when I first came to Columbia, a youth fresh from college, and was received into your hospitable house, that little group of three —of which dear Jimmie was one. I then began weaving my own domestic ties. Two and fifty years lie between them and now: and oh, the difference to us both! A few more years press upon you than upon me: but we both sit on the edge of life, with a broken, shattered earthly being. If heaven were not beyond, what could we do with these shattered earthly joys? But heaven is beyond, and into it we throw our hopes and renew the ties of fellowship so rudely torn by the hand of death. How much more I appreciate what is written in 1 Cor. 15: 19, 'If in this life only we have hope in Christ, we are of all men most miserable.' Do you not? But with that world of life and joy just ahead we can take up the song of praise to Him who hath promised there to be our everlasting portion.

"My dear Mrs. McFie, I do not need to whisper words of Christian counsel into the ear of so ripe a believer as yourself. You have long since 'tasted that the Lord is gracious' and have learned well how to 'lean hard upon Him' in the hour of trial. It is only to 'stir up your pure mind by way of remembrance' that I recall to your thought that 'He doeth all things well:' 'Shall not the Judge of all the earth do right?' When we get home and see the interpretation of Providence in the light of the throne, I am sure that next to the gift of a Savior we shall rejoice most in the sanctified sorrows by which we were weaned from earth and made to store our affections above.

"But I will write no more; only adding that as often as I 'bow my knees to the God and Father of our Lord Jesus Christ' I will commend you and all with you to the 'Spirit of His grace.' May He be with you all in this hour of trial!

"As ever, yours,

"B. M. PALMER."

To a friend who had lost his second wife:

"NEW ORLEANS, LA., July 27, 1891.

"MY DEAR ————: The report of your sad bereavement was heralded to us, even before the paper reached us with the official announcement. It is not often that the lightning strikes the same tree twice in such quick succession; and you are young to have twice borne the supreme sorrow of human life. If I have not written you earlier, it is because it seemed impossible that any human consolation could soothe the anguish of such a stroke. Since my own great loss nearly three years ago, I am able to measure the pain of this great loss as never before: and hence a feeling of dread in touching with a sort of cold hard sympathy a sorrow such as yours. The sharpness of no affliction is known except to those who have experience of it; and each has its own particular edge, which must be felt to be known at all. There is, however, in this bereavement a sense of loneliness and desolation, which belongs to no other. The sharp blade cuts through and through and leaves but one-half to mourn the loss of what was indeed a part of our very substance. To myself, to whom the loss came at the close of a long life, the solid comfort remains that the separation is not permanent, and the reunion close at hand. But to you there stretches perhaps a long and lonesome path, before you shall again feel the touch of the hand that has vanished; and life may appear weary and sad to the very end. I would not wrest from you these mournful reflections, if I could; simply because there is for a time a luxury in our tears; and not to grieve seems as a wrong to the dead. Yet I have found that in the thickest darkness God often reveals Himself, and we see the full shining of His face. It is His way to cut us off from all created streams, that we may slake our thirst at the only fountain which is ever flowing. He puts out all lesser lights, that we may see only the glory of His presence. Nothing but this can appease the weariness of your spirit in this hour of earthly desolation. To Him then let your thoughts turn, and in the hunger of your heart, feed upon the love which is eternal and unfailing.

"We have all spoken of you in our home circle, feeling the sympathy which finds no language to utter its tenderness. And as we have found life again weaving its endearments around us, making us cheerful even in sorrow, so we hope 'the Comforter' will bring the consolation to your own bruised heart, which has bound up ours in seasons of similar bereavement.

"Yours most truly,

"B. M. PALMER."

To Mrs. Arnold Miller, Charlotte, N. C., on the death of her husband:

"HENRY CLAY AVENUE, NEW ORLEANS, LA., January 14, 1892.

"MY DEAR MRS. MILLER: It is my misfortune to have met you but once, as some years ago I passed through Charlotte and sat with you at the tea-table. But it is enough to know that the sorrow of widowhood has fallen upon you in the death of my old friend, brother and childhood's playmate—Arnold Miller. The sad news has just reached me through a letter from my dear friend, Mrs. Clarke, who pours out her burdened heart to me as one whose ancient memories prepare him to take her grief and yours into his own soul as a personal bereavement

"I shall offer no premature consolation in this hour of supreme anguish, when the breaking heart desires only to be alone with its grief. Miserable comforters are they all who seek to assuage the pain which must be felt in the first separation—and when love can pay no tribute to the dead, except to utter its own dreadful sense of loss in tears and groans. It sounds like robbing the dead of their due to be told not to mourn when mourning is the only language left to an aching and bleeding heart.

"It has been assigned to me, sorrowing sister, to drink of your cup, and I know its bitterness. It is not difficult for me to put my soul in your soul's stead, and to feel every pulse of pain which throbs within. Three years have sped since the first bitter stroke, and I am not yet like 'a sparrow on the housetop.' I know that the remaining days of your pilgrimage are to be days of mourning; but when your affliction shall be three years old, you will say with me, 'I had rather have my dead sorrow than any living joy.'

"I am emboldened in this utterance, because I knew your Arnold. We were barefooted boys together, playing in the sand. We were young men together, associated during the earlier years of our common ministry. Of late far separated in distance, I have kept the run of his career—and knew him in the strength of his rigid orthodoxy, a mighty champion for the truth of God. I have always rejoiced in his record, strengthened in my own convictions by the steadfastness and vigor of his defense of the same. But he has gone to his reward: and you must not deny him the rest upon which he has entered. The loss is greatest to you; because it is the loss felt in the sweetest affection of life, and in all the moments and in all the details of domestic relationship. It is in this sense of irreparable loss that you are called now to make the holiest sacrifice upon the altar of your heart. In the sweet submission of your will to Him who has taken what was dearest to you above all else on earth, you make the costliest offering which the human heart can render; and I would not like to think that the lessons you have learned kneeling by your husband's side have not enabled you to say, 'Not my will, but Thine, be done.' The Church, too, has suffered a heavy loss in the death of a most faithful son and servant; but the Church of God is one, and what is lost on earth is gained in heaven. He whom we all mourn is now bowing with the great company of the redeemed before the throne. Still my sympathy flows freely to you in this heavy affliction, and it pains me to think that I can do nothing except to 'sit down with you in the ashes.' Beyond this it only remains to say to you what I say also to myself, 'the time is short'—'yet a little while'—and then comes the glorious reunion with those gone before—and waiting for us in one of the 'mansions' prepared for us above. Since my own sorrow, I never bow my knee in prayer without asking a blessing upon all the children of affliction. As I do this, many forms of those dear to me rise before my thought who thus get an individual place in these poor petitions of mine. You may be assured that you will not be forgotten in these moments of prayerful memory—not only as one, like Hannah, bowed before God in sorrow, but as the bereaved one who most bitterly mourns him who was my friend and brother and playmate, and a noble champion of the cross of Christ.

"With sincere respect and Christian sympathy,

"B. M. PALMER."

"HENRY CLAY AVENUE, NEW ORLEANS, LA., September 23, 1892.

"MY DEAR MR. DYAS: Our mutual friend, Mrs. Shefton, has sent me a letter just received from your sister, giving an account of the last hours of your beloved wife. The bitterness of this bereavement I know too well to attempt any premature consolation. What we need in the first access of such sorrow is to be allowed its indulgence. There is more comfort in the full flow of our grief than in all the words of human sympathy. It is the last office of affection to feel the loss and the pain which are allotted to us, and to withhold the expression of it seems a wrong to the dead and, in some sort, a species of sacrilege. It is not then to tell you not to mourn that I pen you these lines, but rather to sit down with you in the ashes in the fellow feeling of your pain. Perhaps I would not intrude into the sanctity of your grief if she who is gone had not been at one time under my pastoral care.

It was in the early period of your married life, and I recall with great distinctness the impression which her amiable piety made upon me from the first. I remember, too, with the same distinctness my regret at your removal from our city as bringing with it the loss of her presence and friendship. Possibly, too, my kindred bereavement draws me in close fellowship with all who were called to drink of this bitter cup. I may venture therefore to make you partaker of my own comforts in their alleviation of my own sorrow.

"It is a great support to know that all these things come to us under the ordering of a wisdom infinite in its stretch, and that no mistake can occur under such an administration as that of God.

"It is an equal support to know that this world is not intended as our home, and that sooner or later all must pass across that bourne from which none return. Both the time and the way are in themselves of little importance in comparison with the imperative necessity of the departure itself.

"It is an immense comfort to be persuaded that our Heavenly Father gathers all his children thus to himself, in their eternal home.

"We can sink our sense of loss in their blessedness with him in the unselfishness of love, willing ourselves to bear the pain that theirs may be the glory and the gain.

"It abates the anguish that we feel in the remembrance of their earthly sufferings, to know that in these they were bearing witness to the holiness of God; and that it all came on them because of their living union with a suffering Christ—sharing of necessity in his humiliation here, if they are to share in his glory and triumph hereafter.

"It should be an inspiration of gratitude to you, that God gave to you, for so many years, such a happy companionship—that so near the end of life yourself, the prospect is so close to you of the reunion above, with no parting there to dread.

"I am sure that you will find an inexpressible comfort in calling up the memories of the years gone by, if only to see how fresh and green they will remain to you forever. It is an inconceivable blessing when those who go from us leave behind a memory always fragrant—a memory in which there is nothing we would have changed. Such an inheritance, I am sure, is yours; and that she will live in your thought, as one who to you, at least, can never, never die.

"But I will not waste words perhaps barren of relief under your immediate heavy pressure. It is enough to convey my sincere sympathy, and to pray that the consolations of Divine grace may not be withheld from you in this dark hour.

"Very truly yours in Christ,

"B. M. PALMER."

To the venerable mother of the late Rev. Thos. E. Peck,

D.D., LL.D., Professor of Theology in Union Seminary in Virginia:

"HENRY CLAY AVE., NEW ORLEANS, LA., October 16, 1893.

"MY DEAR, VERY DEAR MRS. PECK: I commenced a letter to you on the 7th inst., when the sharp tidings first reached me which I could not receive without a spasm of pain. It came to me not only with the feelings of a public loss, but with the sense of a personal sorrow. Unhappily, before I could finish my letter I was called out of the city, and am permitted only now to mingle my grief with yours. I am glad that our heavenly Father does not forbid us the luxury of tears; and that it is possible to mourn without repining. I am sure that you in the unselfishness of a sanctified love can bid him joy in his ascension to a world whose blessedness he has so long anticipated; and that the smitten wife, who claimed him as her own by the closest human tie, can now yield him to lie, like the sainted John, on the bosom of his Lord. Yet in the assurance that it is his translation, the sorrow and the loss are to us none the less keen. Thus it is, the human lies side by side with the Divine, the earthly along with the Heavenly.

"If I did not know how strong is your faith, and the thoroughness of the discipline through which you have already passed, I should wonder how it is possible for you, in this your old age, to sustain this great bereavement. Even to me it seems as though another light had gone out of my life, and I am more lonely than before. He was so bound up with the associations of my early ministry, more precious to memory in my declining years, that his death has broken a great link that binds me to the past. In the struggle to hold up the truth in this degenerate age, it was a comfort to know that a stalwart defender of the faith was always to be found in him. He was so strong in his convictions, so unswerving in fidelity to truth, so powerful in his humility before God to prevail in prayer, so wise and considerate in counsel, that he always seemed a strong staff on which to lean in a time of trouble and of peril to the Church. On these public grounds I always admired and loved him; while a closer personal affection for him grew out of the intercourse of the years long since gone by, and living only in the memory of so much that is precious. There are few on earth who can draw closer to you than I; as with the tenderness of a son I share with you the burden of sorrow—and then lift with you the hallelujah of praise. Dear Mrs. Peck, it was a glory to you to be the mother of such a son; and your grateful heart must often have burst into song as through the years you traced his noble career. Your grief is the more sacred, in being subdued before God; for I cannot place you before my eye as one swallowed up of sorrow, but rather as one rejoicing in praise of him who gave you this son to be the joy and crown of your own being. He has gone a little before you into the presence of the King, where it will be his glory to introduce the mother whose earlier piety had so much to do with moulding his own. You are to be envied the heritage you possess in the honors reserved for you above, when, with this beloved servant of God you shall side by side with him cast your crown before the Lamb upon his throne. Indeed, the time is near at hand with me as well as with you, when I trust we shall sit together on the mount of God, and turn our memories into praise forever. I have been three months ill myself, this summer; and through four years have found the sentence of death in my members, warning of the coming end. Spared a little while to finish up the work assigned to me, I only pray for grace to be found meet to join those who have gone before to the rest of the eternal house. I am very slightly acquainted with the bereaved widow. Will you tell her for me that I know it all, the unspeakable depths of her sorrow and her loss? My heart goes out in affectionate sympathy with her, for it is not often that death has power to give such a blow as this which has smitten her. May our heavenly Father bear you all in his holy keeping, and fill you with the comfort of his grace.

"Yours in the love of the past,

"B. M. PALMER."

On occasion of a second death in the McMaster family:

"HENRY CLAY AVE., NEW ORLEANS, LA., August 23, 1894.

"Col. F. W. and Mrs. Mary J. McMaster, Columbia, S. C.

"MY VERY DEAR FRIENDS: A copy of *The State,* a Columbia paper, has just reached me, giving the sad intelligence of your dear Shelley's death. It is the third heavy sorrow that has fallen upon you in recent years; and I can well understand how with each repeated blow the heart becomes the more exquisitely sensitive to the pain which ensues. True, with God's children submission comes with every affliction, and the lesson is easier with every repetition; but then submission does not mean insensibility. On the contrary, Divine grace by its refining power renders us more susceptible to suffering; and other things being equal, the Christian suffers more acutely because his sensibilities are strung to a higher key. Then, too, the end of discipline would not be attained if it did not hurt; and the sanctifying process calls often for the severest pain. While therefore you kiss the rod, saying with meek submission, 'Shall not the Judge of the earth do that which is right?' still there is the writhing of the flesh as it is torn by the pincers.

"I have often thanked God, in passing through my own afflictions, that he does not forbid us to grieve—that the moans which come from a breaking heart are not construed by him into expressions either of impatience or rebellion. It is a luxury to mourn for one who is gone; it is the only form in which our love can find utterance; and to which our cherished dead seem to be entitled. For this reason, it is so foolish for inconsiderate friends to rush forward with their premature consolations; robbing us of the melancholy joy of communing with our dead in the tears which are shed over their great loss. For my part, I would rather sit down with you in the ashes, and in a measure feel with you the anguish of this bereavement. Still there are great consolations given you in this dark trial. Your darling now lies safe in the Father's bosom. The everlasting arms encircle her, and she has entered into rest. Another tie binds you to the better world, and the heavenly home is enriched by every removal from the earthly. As we ourselves draw near to the border-line, we appreciate the more our gain in this increasing transfer of our ties from this to that. Each day brings to me the tidings that another of those who began life with me, has passed away. Life is growing sensibly thinner at the edges; and in the gray of the evening, the air gets more and more chill. You, too, are drawing closer to the sunset hour, and the losses and the sorrows will come thicker and faster. But if the Lord's blessed love is thrown upon them all they will become the clouds rendered gorgeous with the sun's setting glory, as you have often seen them on the western sky. The time is short and the end near; we shall soon be caught up in the clouds to meet the Lord, who says, 'Father, I will that those whom thou hast given me be with me, *that they may behold my glory.*' Is not this enough? and if a little sooner this dear child of your earthly home is now in the bosom of that glory, are you not willing yourselves to take the loss that she may have the eternal gain?

"I have received Dr. Smith's urgent request to be present at the coming anniversary of the Columbia Church; and it has cost me a pang to be obliged to forego what would be to me a great joy. But I am in 'the sere and yellow leaf'—bearing a thorn in the flesh which makes me almost a prisoner at home. I can never lose the deep affection I feel for Columbia; and though there are but two or three remaining of my old flock, I cherish their memories as a precious legacy of the past. I have room only to pray God's richest blessing upon you in this sorrow, and to hope that it will be the pavilion in which he will show you the secret of his covenant.

"Yours ever in love,

"B. M. PALMER."

To Mrs. A. A. Woods, New Orleans, La.:

"GLENS FALLS, N. Y., July 14, 1897.

"MY DEAR MRS. WOODS: At the breakfast table this morning your kind letter was placed in my hands; for which, in advance, allow me to return most cordial thanks. At the same time I desire to say, once for all, that I do not wish your good mother to feel obliged to answer my letters, tit for tat, every time. My thoughts are with her daily, as with one who is not long to be here,— and who is passing very gently through the 'via dolorosa,' by which we all pass, in our turn, into the life beyond. I sincerely hope and pray it may not be a path strewed with the thorns of much bodily suffering; but in any event it is, to most of us, a deeply shaded way—and sometimes the shadows darken into gloom and fear. I would not have it so with her; for I am sure she is one of 'the Lord's hidden ones,' upon whom his face should shine with unclouded love. Hence I am inclined to write simply from the love I feel for one of the most precious of my flock. Yet I would not tax her to do more than read, and be strengthened by whatever God may say to her through me.

"It was however a pleasure to hear directly from yourself, without regarding you as a mere amanuensis holding the pen of another. Mr. Woods and yourself stood the trial of reverse in fortune so bravely as to command the admiration and respect of all your friends. There was no foolish whimpering over 'the spilt milk;' but a dignified and quiet acceptance of your lot, and going on calmly to make things better, if might be. It is the Christian way of taking life, not as our lasting portion, but only as discipline for the life that is life forevermore. Thus we lay up our treasures in heaven, where neither moth nor rust corrupts, and where no thief breaks in to steal.

"Your mother is now, I suppose, at the Pass; where she would do well to remain quiet with your brother, during the heated months which are to follow. At any rate, it was good news that the boarding-house was to be given up, allowing her children the sweet privilege of ministering to her wants during her short pilgrimage yet remaining. It would have been wrong to deprive you of it, and of the sweet memories which will survive, after she has slept out her life in your arms. Leave the matter of the sorrow till the time comes. It will be a sacred sorrow, carrying its own solace and sweetness with it. The days of bereavement are not always days of unhappiness. The glare dies out of the sunshine sometimes, but the light is more mellow; and the great twilight of life's evening has its own charm to those who have passed through the heat of the day.

"With much love to all with you, yours truly,

"B. M. PALMER."

On occasion of Mrs. McMaster's death:

"1718 HENRY CLAY AVENUE, NEW ORLEANS, LA., October 10, 1898.
"Col. F. W. McMaster.

"MY VERY DEAR FRIEND: The telegram of Wednesday last brought the distressing tidings of your great bereavement. It sent a sharp pang through my own bosom, as I said to myself, 'Almost the last link is now broken which connects me with my old Columbia life.' Indeed, the feeling of loneliness is creeping too much upon me, deepening the shadow of the twilight, whilst thinking of those that are gone. There is Dr. Miller, of Charlotte, the playmate of my barefooted boyhood, long since departed. More recently Dr. Dabney, the great theologian of our Church, has gone to his rest. It is but yesterday that Dr. Girardeau, whom I dearly loved, has laid down his armor and sleeps. The tidings come to me of Dr. Witherspoon, whom I should have married to Nannie Thornwell—he's hopelessly ill. Sweeping thus around the circle the great magnets of our Church are disappearing one after the other, leaving only a few like Drs. Adger, Hoge and myself to feel the vacancy in our ranks. And so the heart responds when other sweet associations of the past are broken. Your sorrow ought indeed to be my sorrow when I can recall your beloved wife in her early girlhood, growing up to mature womanhood, in the hour of her marriage with yourself and finally the mother of a large family group, with the hairs whitening upon her head, the crown of the promised glory. My last recollection of her was on the Sabbath when after the first baccalaureate sermon delivered to the students of the Seminary, a group of six or eight ladies gathered around me. Among these was Jennie Thornwell, lately widowed, and her dear mother, Mrs. Thornwell, your own precious wife with her dear mother, Mrs. Macfie, Mrs. Squire, and others. They all greeted me with such affection—and now they are all gone. We see them still but only in the chamber of memory, as they speak angelic blessings upon us. It is not strange then that I should miss her who has last departed and sit down with you in full sympathy with your deep sorrow.

"This bereavement strikes at the center of our domestic life. In other sorrows we find retreat in this sacred relation which we hold only with one, and when that tie is severed, there remains no other secret place where we can find shelter on earth. It is a grief alone and by itself, and bears comparison with no other which we are called to sustain. What then remains for us, my dear friend, but to seek repose in the bosom of the Divine Father above? He has gathered into that bosom the wife of your youth; and you will find her there, when you too shall have passed through the gates of pearl. It is our privilege on earth to find comfort and strength in that Divine love which brings to us alike our sorrows and our joys. I beg you to bear me in remembrance to all of your afflicted children, who will do for you what mine have done for me—making still a home for you in the watchful sympathy with which they seek to bear a portion of your heavy load.

"I hope one of these days to visit Columbia, if only to stand once more by the graves of my first and second born; but, besides yourself and J. D. Pope, I cannot recall one survivor from the old past, who will be there to greet me.

"May God bless and comfort you in this the hour of your greatest need.

"Affectionately yours,

"B. M. PALMER."

On occasion of Colonel McMaster's death:

"NEW ORLEANS, September 15, 1899.

"To the Sons and Daughters of Col. F. W. McMaster:

"MY DEAR YOUNG FRIENDS: I address you in this group in order that I may feel that I am speaking to each one of you at once. Your father's death coming so soon after that of your mother doubles the weight of your affliction, by renewing the sorrow for her loss in that which you feel so keenly for him. But even in this first hour of anguish it must comfort you to reflect that he is permitted to be with her whom he so tenderly loved. What is all loss to you is all gain to him; and Heaven is brighter to them both in the blessed reunion of their spirits. We pluck the sting out of our deepest sorrow when we reflect upon the happiness of those with whom we are compelled so reluctantly to part. I need scarcely remind you that there are treasures of consolation to be found in Him who is styled in Scripture 'the God of all comfort.' May you be able to rest in perfect submission to him who has promised that 'all things work together for good to them that love God.'

"I am exceedingly glad now that I had the pleasure of seeing your father once more during my late visit to Columbia. It was a very happy evening with all of you gathered around me in his home. The recollection is made the sweeter now that I shall see his face no more on earth. He has left the record of a noble life as the heritage of his children. I know that you will cherish it with all that enthusiasm which filial affection can kindle in your hearts.

"We shall hold you in constant remembrance, anxious to learn whether this death will break up your home or whether you will be able to keep together in the house filled with memories and associations of the past.

"Mary, my daughter, and Gussie join me in all these expressions of sympathy and affection.

"Yours ever and truly,

"B. M. PALMER."

Dr. Palmer was always ready to aid his younger ministerial brethren with a word of friendly counsel, when desired to do so. In the summer of 1889 a young minister wrote to several brethren "of repute," requesting them to give him "the titles of a few books, that had been most helpful to them in their ministry." Dr. Palmer was the only one who replied, though he was perhaps the busiest one of them all. His reply was:

"NEW ORLEANS, LA., July 2, 1889.

"Rev. W. D. Spurlin, Monroe, La.

"MY DEAR BROTHER: In reply to yours of the 1st inst., I assume that you are in the early period of your ministry, that you have but a small and insufficient library, and possibly have need to economize in order to its enlargement. It will perhaps assist you in the selection, to recommend books to you in the classes to which they belong; and in each class, those which are the most important in the order in which they are named.

"1. *Commentaries.* Jamieson, Faussett & Brown, six volumes, Lippincott's Edition. Avoid another edition in four volumes, as not having the text for convenient reference, and omitting some valuable Dissertations, as, at the beginning of Genesis, History of Creation. *Alford's New Testament for English Readers* (not the Greek, which is costly and hard to obtain). *Godet on Luke* (2 vols.); also *on John* (2 vols.); *also on Romans* (1 vol.). *Spurgeon's Treasury of David* (7 vols.) perfectly invaluable on the Psalms. *Hodge on Romans* (1 vol.). *Haldane on Romans* (1 vol.)—admirable for the clearness and force with which he brings out the doctrine of the Epistle. *Addison Alexander on Mark* (1 vol.) and *on Acts* (2 vols.). *Meyer* has great reputation as an Exegate, but cold as an iceberg; I have not found him useful to me. *Schaff's Lange,* in 24 vols. 8vo, contains much excellent criticism as well as homiletic matter, and with a good deal of useless German trash: a valuable work to own for consultation, but requiring discrimination in its use. *Old John Owen on Hebrews* (4 vols.); a wonderful mine of theological learning and Christian experience. You ought to have a Commentary on this portion of the New Testament; and this is the best—if you cannot afford to get it, get *Sampson on Hebrews.*

"2. *Encyclopaedias. Smith's* large work in 4 vols., or *Kitto's* in three large volumes; and, if you can afford it, *Schaff's Herzog* in addition, as it supplements the others. One of the two first indispensable.

"3. *Theology. Turretin* (4 vols. 8vo.). *Hodge's Systematic Theology* (4 vols.). *Thornwell's Collected Writings* (4 vols. 8vo), especially vols. 1 and 2. *Geo. Hill's Theology* (2 vols.) a Scotch work, very excellent for the comparative view represented of the Calvinistic, Arminian and Socinian systems. *Dabney's Syllabus of Theology* (1 vol. 8vo) compact and clear. *Pearson on the Creed,* and *Beveridge on the 39 Articles;* old books, but most excellent.

"Perhaps I had better stop here, without going into special departments of theological research. Allow me to say in concluding, that if I had my life to live over again I would make tenfold more use of Hebrew and Greek. Later years I have done more of this; and I find that I get more real light from the shades of meaning in the original Scriptures, than from all the commentaries. I would advise every young brother to push his reading in the systematic and elaborate works of theology. It is a wonderfully enriching process.

"In haste, yours most truly,

"B. M. PALMER."

If Dr. Palmer was ready to sympathize with, to comfort and to guide, his brethren in the midst of affliction, or to aid them in their efforts to become more fit for their work, he was no less ready to rejoice with them when they rejoiced. The following beautiful letter to the Rev. Jos. B. Stratton, D.D., on the semi-centennial of his pastorate in Natchez, Miss., is an illustration of this, the like of which many might be given:

"NEW ORLEANS, LA., December 29, 1893.

"REV. AND DEAR BROTHER: With the longing of a great desire, I 'proposed in spirit' to be with you at this semi-centennial of your pastorate. At the last moment, I find my daily cross interposing to prevent; I can therefore only send in this letter a fraternal greeting.

"Tender and precious ties bind you to your brethren in the ministry. Perhaps the voice of one of the oldest of these, who stands close to you in a ministerial life of two and fifty years, thirty-seven of which have been spent at your very side, may be allowed to speak the affection which is felt for you by us all.

"The innate modesty which has thrown around you the charm of a touching humility has drawn to you the homage of our constant reverence. The amiable temper and genial courtesy which are ever the characteristics of a true gentleman we have recognized in you as refined and sweetened by Divine grace—with a double magnetism drawing our hearts to you. The literary taste which, like the gift of the fairy, has caused only pearls to drop from your lips has led us to sit at the feet of so delightful a teacher, to drink in the words which flow from so sweet an inspiration. But these natural graces, diffusing their delicate fragrance over and about you, do not reveal the secret of that witchery by which 'half all men's hearts are yours.' Your long and patient service in the kingdom of our Master; the steadfastness of your faith in the doctrines of grace, in this restless age, when the foundations of religious belief are with so many destroyed; the fidelity with which these have been expounded from the pulpit, the wisdom of your counsels in the Courts of the Church, above all, the saintliness of your own character and walk, which has made your entire career a living gospel to your people and to the world—these, my brother, have made yours the record of a monumental life.

"During a pastorate of fifty years, you have touched four distinct generations: the generation which was disappearing when you first came upon the stage, the generation to which you properly belong, followed soon by that of your children, and now the hand of patriarchal blessing rests upon the heads of the children's children. What a joy to be embalmed in the grateful memories of such a constituency! And, when, 'in the sweet by-and-by' you shall sit down with them all upon the mount of God, rehearsing the story of each separate life, and blending them in the universal chant of praise to Him who "stands in the midst of the throne as a Lamb that has been slain," then only will you know into how many blessed experiences your ministry has poured the moulding influence, and there only will you know how many will claim you as one of whom 'in Christ Jesus they have been begotten through the Gospel.' Even on earth, after these generations have passed with you beyond the stars, your name will go down into the history of the Church. The generations that are to come will read the story of the long and useful pastorate; and a fresh benediction will spring from the record, to purify and strengthen, to comfort and to bless, the troubled hearts which are yet unborn! Can your faith, my brother, take it all in? If so, then you will understand why I term yours a monumental life. It is a marble shaft lifting its polished face before the world, covered with inscriptions of 'peace on earth, good will to men,' and above all, of 'glory to God in the highest.'

"I wish I could be with you to speak these words with the living voice, as you sit amongst your people in the glow of your life's beautiful sunset, with the memories of the past like clustering clouds of mingled gold and purple, to form the drapery of the couch on which you sink to rest in 'the everlasting arms.' But this cold paper must speak for me the greeting which I send. We are standing, both of us, quite near the edge of the Great Beyond; on the sand of this seashore, I tender you the respect, the reverence, the love of a heart softened by sorrow and by age. Should I be found worthy to walk with you in white in the presence of the King, our united song will be adoring worship to Him who has washed us in his blood; and our joy will be none other than 'the joy of our Lord.'

"With hearty congratulations to your people, who have so much reason to make you happy in the demonstration of their affection,

"I remain yours in the faith of Christ alone,

"B. M. PALMER."

He found time for many letters, during this period, in which, he gave vent to his longing for affectionate communion with absent friends. Some of these are the following:

"NEW ORLEANS, LA., October 21, 1889.

"MY DEAR MRS. SHOEMAKER: I had almost forgotten my manners by addressing this letter 'My Dear Helen,' in memory of former years when you were a girl; until I bethought myself that a lady who is about to give a daughter away in marriage deserves to be approached with all the formality and reverence which is due to age.

"This note is written simply to advise that I send off by express a little parcel intended for Hetty, who, I learn from our mutual and dear friend, Mrs. Clark, is very soon to exchange her name for another which she likes better. It is of little value; but it will serve as a memento from myself—and especially from her who has gone from me, who would not have suffered such an occasion to pass without a token of her loving remembrance.

"May God in heaven look down upon the dear child in that sacred hour of vows, the most solemn that ever comes to a woman! and when the two are made one in the holy covenant of marriage, give Hetty a kiss for me with my blessing upon her young head,—and a devout prayer that it may prove a long union of happiness and love to them both.

"I wish I could be there to perform this office in person; but there can be no sweeter deputy than her own dear mother. Believe me, as the years lengthen and the sorrow deepens before me, the old memories and the old affections grow more and more precious. The two ends of life, the opening and the closing, are thus strangely brought together in a charmed circle—and the dotage of age is freshened into the infancy of our youth. Say to dear Hetty that all I can wish for her she will find written in 2 Sam. 7:29, last clause.

"Yours ever,

"B. M. PALMER."

"NEW ORLEANS, LA., August 26, 1890.

"Mrs. Grace Lea Hunt, Wilkes-Barre, Pa.

"MY DEAR MRS. HUNT: We were all startled some days since by the account of a cyclone, given in our papers, which passed over your beautiful city and wrought such damage. Of course, the statements were exceedingly general, with no names given of the sufferers; and we take heart in hoping that you and yours escaped all injury. This hope deepens almost into conviction, as several days have since elapsed during which the news must have traveled to us, if serious injury had happened to any of you. Still I write a brief line, if only to indicate how much your sister and yourself, with the families of both, have dwelt upon our hearts since the dread catastrophe. You may be assured that no lapse of time can dim our remembrance of you both, or weaken our affection. The memory of your dear father abides with me among the consecrated associations of the past; and with him is the living remembrance of all who perpetuate his name on earth.

"Doubtless you are not old enough to take in the singular fact that, as we draw near the close of life here, the receding years roll together as the world we look at through a telescope—very much as by Christian faith we contemplate the eternal future which is before us. How sacred it becomes, as an unchangeable inheritance which is ours by the power of memory—and of memory illuminated with the brightness of human affection! The living flit before our eyes, subject to change or forgetfulness: so many things occur to wreck the friendships we cherish, that we know not which will endure. But death comes with his sanctifying touch: and paradoxical as it may appear, those whom we call our dead are more truly the living than when they breathed and moved around us. I daily wonder at these spiritual, experimental and therefore individual proofs afforded us of the soul's immortality, of the resurrection of the dead, and of certain and eternal existence in the great hereafter. This mortal life is indeed beautiful, sweet, sometimes awful and grand—but it is all this, as it foreshadows the blessed life of immortality which is beyond—where we shall go up, and dwell forever with the gods. (See Psalm 82:6 and John 10:34, 35, for this use of the last word).

"Please give our united love to your sister Helen and Mr. Shoemaker, as well as to Hetty and her partner—whom I know only as belonging to her. Be assured of our remembrance and sympathy in all your dangers and alarms: and may the God of Peace be your protector even to the end!

"Ever truly yours,

"B. M. PALMER."

"HENRY CLAY AVENUE, NEW ORLEANS, LA., January 15, 1894.

"Mrs. S. C. Bird, Baltimore, Md.

"MY DEAR FRIEND OF A LIFETIME: In looking over a file of old letters I came across one of yours, unanswered and bearing date of February 18, 1893. How long I have been in your debt: yet you see I am determined to bring it within the year, that I may not be proclaimed and outlawed as wholly insolvent. Alas! in old age I am becoming a sluggish correspondent, and deserve to lose the confidence of all who ever put trust in me. Still, in this occasional intercourse I am not conscious of any decay of affection toward those loved in former years. Are you old enough to enter into this experience of mine—that a precious dew rests upon the hearts of the old, quite as soft and refreshing as the dew of one's youth? We outlive the hardness that encrusts us in the battles of middle life, when those we meet are our competitors who challenge us in the conflict of earthly interests. These struggles with fortune we remit to the children who bear our names; and we rest in the beautiful glow of life's sunset when the purple and the gold line the edges of the overhanging cloud which enfolds as a mantle while we fall to sleep in the arms of the eternal Father. May 'the hoary head' be to each of us 'the crown of glory' spoken of in the blessed Book!

"By yesterday's mail I sent you a copy of a work just from the press, bearing the signature of my own name. Perhaps it will serve instead of a long letter, if you can find in it the traces of the writer's individuality: for wherever this exists, it has its effluence like the fragrance of a flower. You may possibly read it with fresh interest, by knowing that the second part was written during convalescence from a painful sickness, which locked me up in my chamber through three solid months. It was a great refreshment, during those weary hours, to draw the profile of that sweet Gospel of a Savior's love, which drew down to the depths of hell to ransom a soul lost to goodness and to God. In ten days I will reach my seventy-sixth birthday—oh, how close to the better birthday, when we are born into the kingdom of glory. Standing thus upon a 'narrow ledge' of time, and looking by faith into the great Beyond, you can imagine how the comfort grew of tracing the everlasting Covenant through which a conscious sinner finds himself consciously a child of God. It is a precious, precious Gospel—if my poor effort may only help some other soul to rest upon it with the confidence of a perfect trust.

"But enough of myself—after that I have told you that my oldest grandson, John Caldwell, is now in the Theological School, in Virginia, preparing to preach during his generation 'the Gospel of the kingdom.' It is a joy to me that one of my own blood shall take up my testimony borne now through three and fifty years, and carry it perhaps himself into the middle of the next century. All are within the kingdom: the two girls, bright and happy, engaged in all manner of Christian work, and with their feet clear away from the entanglements and snares of fashionable life. Mary's younger boy, named after myself, is a pious youth, having borne a first-class repute through the College, and now following in his father's footstep in the higher walks of science.

"Now can you forgive my long silence, in the assurance that silence does not mean forgetfulness—so far at least as to write me one of your *old-time* letters, telling all about yourself and about yours? It will bring the memory of other years, with the breath of flowers upon them—the perfume of that fond friendship which has bloomed through a lifetime.

"I ask a Father's blessing upon all dear to you, as I close with simply, Yours as ever,

"B. M. PALMER."

To the venerable Mrs. Peck who had sent him her photograph from Hampden-Sidney, Va.:

"HENRY CLAY AVENUE, NEW ORLEANS, LA., June 27, 1894.

"Mrs. Sarah B. Peck.

"MY DEAR FRIEND AND MOTHER: I have no words in which to express the delight with which I gazed in the photograph sent me, on the face I once knew so well. The years which were so heavy in old age, have left their mark upon it; but I would not fail to recognize the features which even time has no power to efface. As I looked and looked upon it, the fountain of memory was unveiled; and there gathered around it all the Columbia of forty years ago. In the center of the group stood the form of her who made life happy to me, through seven and forty years: next to her stood dear Mrs. Howe and her noble husband, my dear old teacher, then dear Mrs. and Dr. Leland, then Mrs. Macfie and the Crawfords until the room was full of my old flock, who bore with me in the greenness of my youth. And most of all the face of the old mother brought before me the noble son who has just gone to his rest; leaving you a little lonesome, while waiting your own call. Then, would I think of him and of you without calling up from the tomb the noblest Roman of them all, that Prince of Theologians, that great Master of Israel with whom I walked in closest fellowship, through fourteen years—and whose portrait I was permitted to draw in the book which described him? It was but a vision of the moment, yet it was a foretaste of the heavenly reunion when in the palace of our King we will sit down together, and chant those memories in the "new song" there. For will we not tell the story of grace as we knew it here, and shall we not trace all the ministries by which we were helped along the pilgrimage to the home of eternal rest? How the throng is passing through the gates into the city, to which we of right belong. I thought your Thomas would have a leaf to lay upon my grave, but he is gone before me; then my two co-presbyters, Markham and Smith, who would surely bury me, as I thought, yet literally I have laid them side by side in my tomb! hardly leaving room for myself to sleep. And now lying by me on a chair is an Abbeville paper telling me that Morse has joined the caravan that pitches its tents over the river! Blest as I am in all my present surroundings, in a cherished home, and with the tenderest love of a people devoted to me, there does sometimes steal a shadow of lonesomeness, as I look and find my whole generation gone. Only a month since I received a letter from a college classmate beginning thus: 'Palmer, you and I are alone left of all our class.' Yes! but that was six and fifty years ago—the life of almost two generations. I rejoice in my work—possibly more than I ever did; I am grateful to Him who has preserved my physical and mental powers, as I should not expect them at seventy years. Yet I long for the companionship which I hope to enjoy in 'the sweet by-and-by.' May the gracious Father make me ready for the passage over the Jordan upon the stones of the Covenant dry-shod. I sent you a photograph of myself taken on my seventy-sixth birthday, last January. You will see changes in it, putting it perhaps beyond recognition, but my photographs all differ from each other, so that I do not know which tells the truth. My grandson tells me a great deal about you all as he spent the last session at Hampden-Sidney. I envy him the privilege of seeing you; and were it not for a chronic trouble which disables me from traveling I would make a pilgrimage to Virginia to see you once more.

"With much affection I subscribe myself,

"Yours 'in the like precious faith!'

"B. M. PALMER."

"HENRY CLAY AVENUE, NEW ORLEANS, LA., August 14, 1894.
"W. O. Rogers, LL.D., Oswego, N. Y.

"MY DEAR FRIEND AND BROTHER: Your most refreshing letter of the 9th inst. reached me yesterday; and I feel it deserves an immediate response. I am sincerely glad that you are enjoying your summer vacation amidst such pleasant surroundings, both of nature and of art. The splash of the waters playing their lullaby of rest upon the ear:—did you ever reflect how the sound echoes through all the Scriptures; from the water in the midst of the Garden of Eden parting into four heads into the river of Life springing beneath the throne in the Paradise above—while half way between, you have the 'still waters' in the 23d Psalm and the river of Ezekiel flowing from the side of the Temple by the side of the altar of sacrifice until it empties into the Dead Sea and heals it of the curse? As you look out on the bosom of the beautiful Ontario, can you help thinking of the 'sea of glass mingled with fire' on which those stand who 'have gotten the victory, having the harps of God?' I almost envy you the sight of those treasures, which only the wealth of a prince could accumulate in a single library. It is well that wealth is sometimes given to those who have the taste to enjoy it, and not (as too often the case) a jewel in a swine's snout. But ought not such treasures in the book line to find their final and appropriate home in a public institution? Let all this go, however, in order to come to more personal matters.

"Your letter was like a cup of cold water to a thirsty lip. Such expressions of kindly remembrance are a great tonic to me. I trust I am not so foolish as to expect their daily repetition, but just now they help me. Old men are so dull sometimes, as not to perceive the decay of their powers: and I have always felt that, especially in a heavy city charge, the remove of the pastor by four generations from the young who are just coming upon the stage of action, is a serious and, perhaps, a fatal disqualification.

"Of all things on earth, I dread most the decline of this noble old Church which I have been so long permitted to serve. And rather than it should shrink in my hands, dearly as I love its walls and all who worship within them I would gladly yield to some younger and superior hand at the helm. All our efforts to relieve the difficulty have so signally failed, that I have concluded to leave the whole matter in the hands of our Lord and King to be ordered as he shall please. I am greatly strengthened however by the evidence of willingness of such as your dear wife to listen to my voice.

"I have been preaching this summer to unusually good congregations. Every Sabbath, as I rise in the pulpit, the thought forces itself upon me that anyone might be glad to be allowed to remain through a hot summer to address such an audience. I feel, too, that I have been greatly drawn out the last four Sabbaths, in the themes discussed: and that my grasp of the Gospel, if not broader, is at least sweeter than ever. What language can express it, except that of the inspired Apostle, 'the glorious Gospel of the blessed God?'

"Death is removing from us many whom we can ill spare. Dr. Miles, whose departure from us you have doubtless noted, is one of these. His death, in the height of his fame and usefulness, is greatly lamented. I am happy to say that those in our own circle are still with us; and thus the sorrow does not become so painfully personal, as it might be. My own health is excellent; and my work has never rested more lightly than during this season. All in the house unite with me in grateful remembrance to Mrs. Rogers and yourself, and to Ellen when she is with you. Johnny and Palmer are off on a little excursion northward, at Northfield, Niagara, etc.—before going back to the studies of another session.

"Yours most truly,

"B. M. PALMER."

On receiving a bouquet:

"HENRY CLAY AVENUE, NEW ORLEANS, LA., January 25, 1895.

"MY DEAR MRS. BAKER: Your card, with the beautiful buds and ferns, has just been handed to me from the door. Flowers will always be to the pious soul the emblem of beauty and love. They seem to spring from the earth by that Divine grace which lightens the curse resting upon it through man's sin. The blush upon the rose is the blush of penitence still ashamed of the sin which is forgiven; and the pure white is the glory of that Divine love which extinguishes the guilt in its mercy. Accept my thanks for this thoughtful remembrance of the last mile-stone on life's highway.

"Yours most gratefully,

"B. M. PALMER."

While in New York, during the winter of 1896 to 1897, Miss Agnes McMaster, of Columbia, S. C., struck with the voice of a young shop woman, said to her, "You are not a Northerner?" "No," was the reply, "I am from New Orleans." "I do not know anyone in New Orleans but Dr. Palmer," next remarked the purchaser. "Why," exclaimed the saleswoman, "I am an Israelite and we do not let the Presbyterians claim Dr. Palmer; we all claim him." And her face beamed with delight.

When the Southern girl returned to her home in Columbia and recounted the incident, her father said, "You must write to Dr. Palmer and tell him of it." She did write and shortly afterward received the following reply:

"MY DEAR MISS AGNES: Your sweet letter has greatly refreshed me. I am full of memories running through a period of fifty years and embracing all of your lineage from your grandmother down to the youngest of your father's household. They were all sweet and lovely in their lives and the remembrance of them comes to me always as a pleasant dream. Your dear mother has left you sad in her departure, but this to her is but the entrance into the eternal home. That home, I trust, will embrace us all, and in the happy reunion heaven will be the sweeter for the earthly memories, which will there be embalmed in songs of triumphant joy.

The little story which you told of the Jewess whom you met at the North, reads like a piece of New Orleans history; for the Hebrews here seem to regard me in the light of a special friend. They do not, however, know the secret of this, which is the prophetic announcement of their being gathered at last into the Redeemer's Church at his second coming to be glorified in his saints. The Savior will have his triumph at last, even from those who have rejected him for centuries. We can all, therefore, by anticipating join in the words we so often sing:

"'Joy to the world, the Lord is come,
Let earth receive her King.'

"With love to your father and all members of the household,

"Affectionately yours,

"B. M. PALMER."

Letters to a dying saint:

"GLENS FALLS, June 26, 1897.

"MY DEAR MRS. RAILEY: With so many idle hours hanging wearily upon my hands, it is not strange that my thoughts should continually revert to my deserted home and flock. Memory easily depicts the form and the surrounding of each figure in the separate groups called up before the eye; and this poor typewriter must serve as the tongue with which to address them. You understand perfectly why I should most regret parting from yourself, and why, therefore, you should most frequently drift before me in my musing. Though your friends had long perceived your failing strength, yet the verdict of your physician fell upon most of us with a fearful shock. It is one thing to count the years and know that the sands are running low in the hourglass of life: but even this scarcely prepares us to record the last minute which is to 'measure our days.' When the revelation is made, somehow I feel that God has put upon us his final consecrating touch, making us from that instant a holy offering to himself. It seems a case similar to that of Aaron, when the Lord led him into the Mount, caused him to put off his priestly robes upon the person of Eleazer, his son, and then laid him down to his long sleep. What mean all our increasing infirmities gathered up in the final breakdown,—what is it after all but the Lord's gracious and loving undressing us, his own dear children, for the sweet sleep upon his bosom? The gray twilight is only the hour just before dark, when infants are undressed for the night—a calm, holy hour for putting off this poor world and preparing for the eternal rest.

"You perceive that I am not inclined much to condole with you; though I am far from forgetting that the end always means the breaking of precious human ties—and sometimes the pain of this is like the killing of a nerve. But then, in this lies the consecration of your Lord. This is the undressing of the priestly Aaron, giving up his robe of office to his successor. So in the dim twilight you are putting off this life and putting on the better life. Your heavenly Father is granting you this short measured interval before the end to sanctify yourself for his early and happy coming. I have no sympathy with those who wish and pray for sudden death. To my view it is a cowardly shrinking from sorrow and pain. I had rather be sanctified through both—to pass through the fire for a little, in order to come forth purified as by fire into the presence of his glory. There is to me something tender and sacred in this intelligent putting off the flesh, that we may see God. The apprehension of suffering often renders bitter the close of life; still this makes it a season of witness bearing, converting the very discipline into a crown of glory at last. This witnessing is twofold—a testimony to the deplorable nature of sin on the one hand, and to 'the exceeding riches of Divine grace' on the other hand. Doubtless we shall find in heaven that there is more than one species of martyrdom, as well as many distinct crowns with which suffering saints will be rewarded.

"But I will not weary you with reflections which possibly may strike you as over-somber: but the shading and the light belong together in every landscape. The girls unite with me in affectionate remembrance.

"Yours faithfully,

"B. M. PALMER."

"GLENS FALLS, N. Y., August 18, 1897.

"MY DEAR MRS. RAILEY: Your letter of the 13th is received with mingled feelings of surprise and regret, as well as of pleasure. The knowledge of your great weakness led me almost to hope that you would not tax it with any effort at writing; while, at the same time, the contents of your letter gave me unspeakable delight. It was a pleasure to learn thus directly from yourself that you were resting in quiet expectation of the call to 'come up higher.' It was not difficult to anticipate this from your long experience of Divine grace; but it was nevertheless a satisfaction to know it from your own lips. The discipline of patience you recognize as that which you specially needed, and therefore it was sent. The Apostle clearly puts it as the crowning grace of Christian experience: 'Let patience have her perfect work, that ye may be perfect and entire, wanting nothing.' How strong the emphasis here! You notice this in its threefold expression: 'the patience must have its perfect work;' through it 'we become perfect and entire;' and then the climax is reached in the words, 'wanting nothing.' Consider for a moment, the reason for this: It is our complete recognition of God's supremacy, in that sovereignty which he guards with the greatest jealousy; and in addition, it is the full surrender of ourselves to his Fatherly authority and love, as the children of his grace. It is the highest obedience of our creatureship to him who has both created and redeemed us. Is it not the fitting posture in which you and I should stand before God in our old age—this holy resignation and sweet submission to our loving Father's will?

"It is surely gracious in our heavenly Father to give us a brief pause before we actually encounter the realities of the future world. You, for example, have had a long and busy life—a life filled with duties, anxieties and cares. True, you have enjoyed much, and your happiness has been found in the duties which attached to the various relations you have sustained; and with these duties corresponding anxieties and care have been necessarily connected. Now all these are laid down by you at the Savior's feet—you are done with them all, and rest. You have had also your trials and sorrows, and they were in such sense your own, that you had to bear them mostly alone. Now all this is past, and you reap only the good that has come out of it all to your own soul. So your heavenly Father gives you a quiet twilight in the evening of your days, that you may put away the whole earthly past—a sort of spiritual undressing, before you are 'clothed in the fine linen, pure and white, which is the righteousness of the saints.'

"It rejoices me, too, that you are in measure free from that bodily suffering which we all so much feared for you. Our Father is tender to his child: and if the suffering does come, he means it to be brief. Your sun is setting brightly behind the clouds; the gloaming, as the Scotch call it, is lengthening out the daylight, before the night sets in, that you may praise God for all his love, and tell your children, who wait at your side 'How gently fades the departing day'—and how glorious the morning is breaking upon your ravished sight. May the dew of the evening rest sweetly upon you, blessed saint of God! We shall soon be where parting is no more.

"I add a line on this other page, only to say that we expect to leave this place on the 6th of September, reaching home before the second Sabbath. I trust you will be spared, so that we may meet again on earth. My sight is improved, but I do not expect a cure; this would require an indefinite stay, if indeed it can be accomplished at all. My daughter, Mary, came up here with a dreadfully inflamed eye with which she was afflicted a month before leaving home. It proves very obstinate, and has scarcely yielded to the treatment here, as yet.

This explains why she has not written you. She simply cannot; but bears you ever in her heart. We all chesish you with an exceeding affection. Good-bye!

"Yours in the hope of the life to come,

"B. M. PALMER."

"P. S. Give our united love to Annie. Glad she is with you."

"1718 PALMER AVENUE, NEW ORLEANS, LA., October 31, 1901.

"Mrs. Sallie C. Bird.

"MY DEAR SISTER: It was pleasant to both eye and heart to receive a letter from you after this long, long silence. Since its reception your second note has come to hand—stating, what I was glad to learn, that Edgeworth had received my letter addressed to Rev. Mr. Kirk enclosed in one to him. I sincerely hope that your wishes may be gratified in Mr. Kirk's acceptance of the call, and that he may prove a great blessing to your Church.

"I write in haste simply to acknowledge your letter and therefore cannot indulge in recollections of the past and in all these would suggest.

"We are in usual health and very happy in being permitted to live together so long. Perhaps you are already aware that another has been added to our circle, through the marriage of one of my grandsons who went so far as Richmond, Va., in search of his bride. She has entered so naturally into our home life that we feel as though we had always known and loved her. Thus God strews blessings in our path and makes old age glad as with the joys of the past.

"Love to all in your house.

"Affectionately yours,

"B. M. PALMER."

"1718 PALMER AVENUE, NEW ORLEANS, LA., November 23, 1901.

"MY DEAR SISTER: In reply to a letter from Mr. Kirk, I have just written him my assured conviction that he has done exactly right in accepting the Baltimore call. The indications of the Divine will seem to me so clear in all the circumstances of the case, that he could scarcely have done otherwise than accept the call without disregarding all the leadings of God's providence. I congratulate you and the Church upon the result and hope that the latter will enter upon a new career of prosperity and happiness. I cannot stop to write more just now, but will try to write you again as soon as I have a lull of business.

"Affectionately yours,

"B. M. PALMER."

"1718 PALMER AVENUE, NEW ORLEANS, LA., April 2, 1902.

"MY DEAR SISTER SALLIE: Your letter received some days ago came like a fresh breeze ladened with the perfume of sweet memories of the olden time. How blessed is memory, holding in its clasp all the pleasures of a long life, in which even the sorrows of the past lend the charm of a sacred sadness to soften and temper the whole. Can we imagine the higher joy which memory will bring to us in the world above—when the spirits long separated blend in the higher embrace of a purer love, and memory binds together the life that was and the life that is indissoluble forever? We are growing old, because we are mortal: but the immortal lies just beyond, where we shall live in perpetual youth. If God has given to us precious memories on earth, let us thank him that they will bloom again with still richer fragrance in the Paradise above. Forgive this little bit of sermonizing, the force of old habit, perhaps.

"I have sent you a little book of my own, just from the press—doubtless the last contribution I will be permitted to make to the literature of our time. It will teach you nothing that you do not already know; but it will serve as a remembrance from me whilst you are dwelling upon its pages.

"I read with great interest the account of your satisfaction and that of your Church with your new pastor, Mr. Kirk. I have no doubt that he is worthy of all your praise; and that he will soon repair the waste which may have been occasioned during the dreary time when you were without a guide. Tender him my congratulations and my earnest prayer that his may be a long ministry with you, and fruitful as it is long. Last summer I paid a visit to Athens, enjoying the Centennial of the University, in which I took some part. I felt like one standing upon the edge of a great chasm, when one member of my class alone with myself headed the long procession, the oldest of all the Alumni, excepting one. I enjoyed greatly the meeting with the descendants of the old stock that I knew sixty years ago—but felt all the time as though I were stepping from this into the world beyond.

"Give my love to Saida, if with a grown up son by her side she has not outgrown the sweet girlhood in which I remember her still. To Mrs. Machen say that it puzzles me to place her where her blessed mother used to stand in my thought—always trying to blend two generations together which are so distinct.

"I ought, before closing, to add that in a visit to Atlanta last summer I had the great pleasure of meeting your brother Andrew and his wife. He was the least changed in appearance of all the men in our generation—with the same face, distinct in all its features, which he had in boyhood.

"We are all in comfortable health with the exception of my daughter, Mary, who is just convalescing from an attack of pneumonia which was very severe but which has yielded to vigorous medical treatment. She is, however, still very weak and requires tender nursing.

"Affectionately yours,

"B. M. PALMER."

CHAPTER XIX.

THE FINAL STADIUM OF SERVICE, NOBLE THOUGH BROKEN.—Continued.

(1889-1902.)

DOMESTIC LIFE.—LONGING FOR HER WHO HAD BEEN TAKEN; BUT HAPPILY APPRECIATIVE OF REMAINING HOUSEHOLD BLESSINGS.—REMOVAL FROM THE MANSE INTO HIS OWN HOUSE.—CONGRATULATORY RECEPTION GIVEN HIM ON HIS EIGHTIETH BIRTHDAY.—COMMENDATION BY THE PRESS.—LETTERS OF CONGRATULATION.—SUBSEQUENT BIRTHDAYS.—TRIP TO SOUTH CAROLINA IN APRIL, 1899.—LETTERS.

THE reader of the foregoing pages has already seen that Dr. Palmer is not to be thought of as a lonely man in his home during these closing years of his life. The partner of his joys, sorrows, burdens, responsibilities and honors, between whom and himself an unwonted affection had existed, had indeed been taken away; and her loss was not and could not be replaced. But there were still left to him, his devoted daughter, Mrs. Caldwell and her honored husband and their children, one of whom bore his own name. There was also another granddaughter, left as a precious legacy and reminder of herself by Mrs. Colcock, the daughter who had been such a comfort to him; upon whom he had poured out his heart's love. He is frequently found, in the course of his pilgrimage through these later years, thanking God for allowing them all to live together in so much happiness for so long a time.

Passionate longings for her, who had forever gone, would sometimes possess him; and a wail of agony from a sense of his desolation would escape into the ear of an old and tried friend. Thus he writes to Rev. Robert H. Reid, of Spartanburg County, South Carolina, March 31, 1890: "Since the death of my wife, I have a great desire to see once more some of her relatives, whom I can never see any more on earth. . . . My visit to Columbia will be one of pain and sadness. It is the place where the ties were formed which are now broken forever . . . where children were born to us, who now sleep with their mother; and the desolation will seem most complete in the midst of those old associations. Still I have almost a pas-

TAKEN ON HIS 80TH BIRTHDAY.

sionate wish to be there . . . with a longing something like that of a pilgrim for some holy shrine."

But if he was moved with a great longing which would never be filled, he knew he had much left in his home. Accordingly, he writes, to Mrs. Caldwell, from Clarksville, Tenn., June 9, 1890:

"Yesterday was an idle day with me, and particularly lonesome as it was spent in my chamber in the hotel. I recognized most feelingly how desolate my house would be, if it were not filled with your presence and that of the dear children. Truly God has been merciful to me in this, and my heart goes out to him in daily gratitude and praise. I have no words in which to say how constant and how great a comfort you are to me. I cannot write it without a moistened eye, for I lean upon your love as I once leaned upon that of your mother. God bless you, my child and fill you with all good, for your dutifulness to your stricken father! A thousand loves to all in the house.

"Ever truly and fondly,

"B. M. PALMER."

Later, he also wrote, to his granddaughter:

"HENRY CLAY AVENUE, NEW ORLEANS, LA., October 29, 1894.

"MY DARLING GUSSIE: You must not measure my delight on receiving your favor of the 15th, by the delay of this reply. You know my dilatory habit in the matter of correspondence—especially now that my eyes are growing dim, so that I see with extreme difficulty both in reading and in writing. Perhaps, too, I was the more negligent, knowing the active interchange of letters between yourself and the other members of the family. Both Auntie and Fanny keep you posted as to the news of the home and of the town; so that I will not invade their province, but confine myself to mere sentiment. Ah, my child, you do not know how close you lie to this old heart of mine; for you are embalmed in two memories singularly dear to me. First, there is the memory of your own mother, whom it is your misfortune not to have known, and of whom therefore, you can have no recollection. She was the sweetest of women, and would have cherished you with inexpressible tenderness, had she been spared. Then there is the memory of your grandmother, into whose arms you fell as a second mother—and whose loving care you can remember. Through them both you come to me, as a most precious legacy: and in yourself have established a claim of your own, by growing up the bright, happy, loving daughter that you are. I ought to be glad of an opportunity of putting this on paper before your eye; for a certain awkward kind of reserve makes its difficult to utter in speech what might embarrass another to hear. My grandchildren, with your dear Auntie, go far to fill the gap made in my life by the death of your grandmother, who was always an unspeakable blessing to me. In this, God has been exceptionally good to me: and I do feel that I cannot be grateful enough for this last special mercy. But good-bye, darling, with ever so much love,

"From your old grandfather,

"B. M. PALMER."

Meanwhile, in 1891, Dr. Palmer had removed from the fine old manse on Prytania street, in which he and his beloved had known so much of joy and so much of sorrow, and in which she had passed away, to his own new and commodious house, on Henry Clay avenue. He had desired a home of his own for his last days, thinking that thus the church might be saved some embarrassment should he become disabled; and that his daughter would feel more comfortable were he to become the owner of the house in which she and her family were to live to take care of him. Hence he purchased a fine lot on beautiful Henry Clay avenue; and built him thereon a house, not pretentious but ample in size, admirably planned for that mild climate, suited to afford dignified comfort; excellent in materials, workmanship and appointments—a domicile worthy of the simple, unpretentious, great man who was to live in it. He is said to have enjoyed immensely overseeing its construction. The locality became increasingly charming as the years passed.

As his eightieth birthday approached the Ladies' Associations of Dr. Palmer's church planned a congratulatory reception to be given him in honor of the day, Tuesday, January 25, 1898, at his residence. They laid their plans, arranged, conducted and carried the reception to the happiest issue, the veteran pastor being a passive victim in their hands. Indeed, to achieve success in this enterprise was not difficult. The whole city held him constantly in the highest homage. To all who knew anything of his life in times when the plague covered the city with gloom and the shadow of death, he was an undoubted hero; to every lover of the Old South he was the highest embodiment of it; to the Jew he was a great protagonist for righteousness and the foe to every species of oppression and wrong from which the Israelites had suffered; to liberal Roman Catholics he was broad enough in his human sympathies to have shown himself lovely to them; to Protestants he was an exponent in whom they gloried; and to Presbyterians he was all this and more. To all men he was a man who had dignified human nature. The people seemed to be but waiting for an occasion whereon they could properly express their veneration, esteem and affection for the man.

The reception was held from four o'clock in the afternoon till ten at night, a very short respite for dinner excepted. During all these hours the grand old man stood, defying fatigue, receiving congratulations, shaking hands, listening to compliments, receiving formal addresses from societies, church officials, veterans of the Confederacy, and having, on every occasion something appropriate, amiable, eloquent in response. Every car coming up town carried passengers for Dr. Palmer's house, and the crowd "which for hours occupied the front yard in no wise deterred others, upon arriving, from waiting for their chance to gain entrance to the house." It has been estimated that fully ten thousand people called on him that day. Amongst these were many conspicuous for their position, ecclesiastical, business, social or political. Amongst them were delegations from many benevolent, historic, religious, or patriotic institutions. Representatives of the Confederate Veterans of the division of Louisiana; Veterans of the Army of Tennessee; and Veterans of the Army of Northern Virginia in large number came with kind, loving and appreciative messages to which he responded in a manner to deepen the impression his great personality had already made upon them; saying, for example to men of the Army of Northern Virginia, that the life spent in the army was not lost, that it would bear fruit in three or four generations; that they had fought for precious principles that would not only live but be recognized as the true principles of this government.

There were representatives from three Jewish synagogues, "Touro Synagogue," "Temple Sinai," "Gates of Prayer."

The representatives of Temple Sinai brought an address enscribed on parchment and beautifully bound in black morocco. The front bore a massive silver plate on which was the inscription: "To Rev. Dr. B. M. Palmer, with the best wishes of Congregation Temple Sinai, New Orleans, January 25, 1898." The back bore a heavy silver monogram, "B. M. P." The address was as follows:

"The directors of Congregation Temple Sinai, in meeting assembled, upon learning of the approaching eightieth anniversary of the birth of Rev. Dr. Benjamin M. Palmer, unanimously resolved that a committee be appointed to frame and convey on this welcome occasion the sincere sentiments of the religion we represent. Whereupon, in due course, the undersigned reported the following, which was with perfect accord adopted as the sense of the meeting:

"'For almost the lives of two generations has the Rev. Benjamin M. Palmer pursued his labor as a divine, performed his duties as a citizen and as a man in this the beloved city and our home. In the course of these several decades many trials have visited our sunny metropolis. The ravages of war, the chaos of political corruption, the raging of pestilence, threatening disaster without and acute dissensions within, have tested severely the manhood and the enlightened patriotism of the people of New Orleans.

"'From an early time our citizens of every field have learned to look for guidance and inspiration under public exigencies to one spiritual leader above others, to the man whose earnest eloquence was always held in check by a courtly dignity, whose religious fervor was balanced by sincere love for the fellow man. They instinctively admire in Dr. Palmer the noble consistency of distinctly sectarian beliefs with broadly human sympathies, the temperamental supremacy of human ardor and of lofty moral aspirations.

"'As a society banded together for the preservation of a most ancient faith, we, of Congregation Temple Sinai, entertain a deep-seated regard for the reverent tenderness with which during a lifetime of ministry Dr. Palmer has expounded our own sacred history and literature. We respond with affection to the spirit of brotherhood with which he has ever met our representatives, spoken of our institutions in the name of the religion which has experienced the greatest measure of fanatical persecution; we acknowledge with appreciation a fruitful example of the Christian teacher, who has unpretentiously left his master lessons of peace and good will. Unto our Father which is in heaven we turn in heartfelt gratitude that He has permitted this righteous man to be vigorous in his old age and rejoicing with the joy of all who hold him dear, we pray that an all-kind Providence may yet preserve him with unweakened powers very many an added year of blessed ministry.'

"MAX HELLER,
"J. WEISS, *President,*
"JOS. SIMON, *Vice President.*"

[*Seal of Temple Sinai.*]

Rabbi I. L. Leucht and the other officers of Touro Congregation brought with them a splendid solid silver loving cup inscribed with Dr. Palmer's initials, in the form of a handsome monogram; with the legend, "Presented to Rev. B. M. Palmer, D.D., by the Rabbi and Board of Officers of Touro Synagogue on the day of his reaching fourscore years, January 25, 1898;"

and with the following selection from Psalms 28 and 29: "Forever more will I keep for Him my kindness; and my covenant shall stand fast with him." After exchange of greetings, the Rabbi addressed himself to Dr. Palmer in the following words:

"Often have I had the pleasure of addressing men, and have conveyed to them my heart's sentiments, but I do not remember a single case when I had better cause to thank God than for the privilege granted me to-night to bring home to you in my name and in the name of Touro Synagogue the reverence and affection we cherish for you. Our appearance here this evening, Rabbi and teachers of another faith, is more than a simple compliment or simple courtesy. Do you remember about twelve years ago, when you were called to pay the last tribute of respect to a trusted servant of God, you said that what man views as sorrow, pain or evil, was only one string on the world's harp, and to the divine artists all sound in sweet harmony? Let me suggest to you to-night that every religious faith is but one string on God's harp, and when his divine hand touches these strings they only sing and sound together one grand and glorious hallelujah.

"Truly, this is a grand moment. When all over Europe anti-semitism raises its hoarse cry, far away from the smoke and medieval battles, down here in our Southern land, we meet to honor a beloved Christian divine, invited by our brethren to do him homage. You have not only lived and preached and worked for the narrow walls of your Church; your goodness, your eloquence, your pure life and your untrammeled manhood have deeply impressed all, and helped to form the religious sentiment of this great commonwealth, and its seed falls also blessingly in every Jewish household.

"Do you remember when, in 1882, the persecution of the Jews commenced in the dominion of the Czar and my brethren were driven from hearth and home, a cry of despair was heralded across the ocean and you, sir, were one of the first to raise your voice in solemn protest? Never shall I forget how your manly form rose before me and, with a voice trembling with emotion, you cried: 'When a Hebrew suffers, I suffer with him.' We have not forgotten all this; we cherish a feeling of gratitude; and we have come on your eightieth birthday to pray God to spare you many a day for the blessing of mankind.

"It is an old custom in Jewish households that on every Sabbath eve and on any other great festival the day is ushered in by the head of the household saying a blessing over the wine cup, emphasizing the covenant that God made once with Israel. Now, sir, this is also a great feast, and we have come with a cup filled with wine, to bring home to you, sir, the covenant existing 'between me and thee,' 'between my people and thy people.' We wish to drink to you out of the same cup —a loving cup, indeed—remembering that we all stand under the protection of one and the same Father in heaven. Please, sir, drink out of this cup, which shall henceforth be your own. And let us all join, and may God bless you. Amen."

The Rabbi having concluded his remarks, the loving cup, which had been filled with wine, was handed to Dr. Palmer. He took a sup from it and handed it back to Rabbi Leucht, and he and the several members of the delegation drank to the health of their reverend friend, and to a continuance of the affectionate and helpful regard which existed at the time between him and the Israelites of the city.

Visibly affected by the sentiments expressed by the Rabbi, it required a moment for him to recover himself sufficiently to respond. He said:

"Rabbi Leucht and Gentlemen of the Synagogue—The symbolic ceremony is wholly unexpected by me, and I assure you it touches every chord of my heart. The Old Testament and the New Testament come together under this roof to-day—the Old and the New Testaments, which are the two breasts from which the Church of God in all the ages has drunk its nourishment. There is a great deal that is in common betwixt us. Your sacred books are my sacred books, and in the pulpit when ministering to the people in God's name I take the theme of discourse as freely from one as from the other; from those grand teachings of the Old Testament as freely as from the Evangelists and the Apostles in the New Testament. There ought not to be any harsh feelings between the bodies that you and I represent. We understand, you and I, perfectly the point upon which we differ, but there is vastly much lying behind that in which we both agree. Let us, then, cherish in the future, as we have cherished in the past, the point of agreement—that we worship one God common to you and to us, according to that law which He proclaimed from Mount Sinai, which we understand to be ratified and confirmed in the teachings of the New Testament. I can hardly trust myself to utter the emotions which are struggling in my own heart. I never walk these streets and meet one of your faith without feeling a trembling in the palm of his hand, the affection which he feels toward me personally, and it is to-day a renewal of the sentiment which you have under this form reduced to a covenant. Why, sir, the great God is the God of Abraham, of Isaac and of Jacob, and the covenant that was made with Abraham planted the seed of that Church which from that day to the present moment exists upon the earth, and I feel in a spiritual sense we are of the seed of Abraham. That covenant to which you refer stands in force and will remain until the end of time, and, therefore, the Hebrew, wherever he is found upon the earth, will always be a body of interest and of affection to every true Christian heart.

"We know the part which you are called to play in the providence of God, not only in the history of the past, but as we believe in the future. I have only to invoke upon you and your people in this land and in all lands the blessing of Almighty God, your God and my God."

A letter from the inmates of the Soldiers' Home in Louisiana touched him deeply. It included the following paragraphs:

"REVEREND SIR: We still retain lively remembrances of your stirring battle addresses, which were delivered to inspire and comfort our young hearts (young then) at the outset of the great conflict when first marshaled together destined for terrible scenes of conflict. The memory of your cheering exhortations, your sentiments of patriotism for the cause of the South, and the admonition of our duty toward the land we love, and, above all, the blessing of heaven so earnestly by you invoked upon our heads, often in the dark hours of hardship and defeat, have proved a consolation, and in the 'earthquake shock of battle, the triumph and the rapture of the fray' have been to us a soul-elevating stimulus; for on those critical occasions our minds ever reverted to your words of hope and consolation.

"Reverend sir, there are now near seven score of us in this refuge, this camp, bronzed and battered veterans. Our strength and usefulness have departed. We all are more or less afflicted by disease, by the weaknesses incidental to old age. Some are maimed, have lost limbs, disabled by wounds, lameness, loss of sight partially, and in one case wholly. We have outlived everything but the memory of the great conflict, and we owe our present support and comfort to the benevolence of the State of Louisiana, for which we fought, and to the people of Louisiana, who still cheer and honor us.

"Your name, your memory, and, above all, your continued presence with us, invoke our gratitude to the everlasting Father for sparing you to us, for we recognize in you a living link with the past. In common with all the surviving soldiers of our beloved Southland, we love and esteem our battle pastor. We remember our debt to you, your fortitude and constancy in the dark hours, your striking example engendering in us those moral qualities. We are now fallen on the sere and yellow leaf, and we love you as our friend still with us."

On the day of the reception he received also the following amongst telegrams and letters:

From Cardinal Gibbons: "Cardinal Gibbons begs leave to congratulate Rev. Dr. Palmer on the attainment of his eightieth birthday, wishes him additional years of useful and vigorous life."

From Right Rev. Davis Sessums, D.D., Protestant Episcopal Bishop of Louisiana: "I deeply regret that an official appointment without the city, which cannot well be changed, hinders me from coming in person to greet you and to express my sincere wishes that your health and strength may be long continued. It has not been my privilege to know you as closely as I have wanted, but you will let me assure you of the honor in which I hold your very remarkable life and character, and of the reverence with which I recognize the power and earnestness of your witness for righteousness. In common with all your fellow ciitzens, and in common with all Christians, I feel that you have wrought good which will long endure and that your life will be cherished as a lofty and noble example of courageous and devoted service to God and man. Again wishing that the burden of years may rest lightly upon you, and that the eventide may be full of blessing and peace, I am, sincerely yours."

From Rev. Beverly Warner, D.D.: "At a called meeting of the rector, wardens and vestrymen of Trinity Church it was unanimously

"*Resolved,* That the rector, wardens and vestry of Trinity Church beg to present their congratulations to Dr. B. M. Palmer on the happy occasion of his eightieth birthday.

"That we unite with the members of his own congregation in rejoicing that so honorable a career in this community has been crowned by the length of years promised of old to those who dwell in righteousness.

"That we recognize with gratitude the power and influence of his godly life and conversation, and pray that for yet many years he may be spared to be an inspiration to good living, an example of Christian manhood and a model of a faithful pastor in this community, with whose interests for more than forty years he has been identified."

From the Chancellor of the Southwestern Presbyterian University, Clarksville, Tenn.: "The University whose foundation you helped to lay, and all whose interests have been dear to your heart, most heartily unites with your people in congratulations upon your eightieth birthday and prays that you may have more years to bless it with wise counsels and continued love." (By order of the faculty, students and committee.)

From Wm. Henry Green, Princeton, N. J.: "Mrs. Green joins me in cordial congratulations, best wishes and grateful remembrance of your exceeding kindness and courtesy during our visit to your city. Princeton Seminary faculty sends united congratulations, rejoicing in your long, useful and honored ministry and fidelity to Gospel truth, and praying for God's continued blessing upon you and yours."

Such incidents of the day as have been narrated show that all creeds and sects met on common ground in Dr. Palmer's residence, that of veneration for nobleness of aim, loftiness of character, purity of life and high morality, united with great talents and a lifelong noble use of them.

As the *Times-Democrat* of the next day well said, "Dr. Palmer's very presence in the community has been, like a greater presence of old, a pillar of cloud by day to this community and a pillar of fire by night to uphold the standard of morals, to guide the wanderers' steps in the path of rectitude, to fix their eyes on the shining heights, to cheer and comfort falterers stepping heavenward." The press of the city seems universally to have pronounced Dr. Palmer worthy in every sense of the word of the grand outpouring in his honor. One editor said: "He stands to-day before the whole world with a record that links his life to the most glorious deeds of this century. On every occasion, however arduous it may have been, and whatever sacrifices were required, Dr. Palmer was there ready to act at a moment's notice.

"Great in mind, majestic in eloquence, lofty in motives, pure and undefiled in character, brave to the core, this venerable preacher of God wielded a power for good for which his name shall endure until the end of time."

The press in many parts of the South, outside of Louisiana, also took large and approving notice of this interesting event.

The congratulations showered on him so abundantly on that 25th of January were renewed from day to day through the mails. There lie before us beautiful letters from the Rev. Drs. G. R. Brackett, Theodore L. Cuyler, A. C. Hopkins, John Hunter, Moses D. Hoge, Joseph B. Stratton, George F. Pentecost, Geo. T. Goetchins, J. C. Graham, S. A. King, R. A. Webb, etc. In one of these letters he is told that his "mode of stating the doctrine of substitution and imputed righteousness made it appear not only reasonable but adorable;" so that the writer, who before had been walking amid the baleful shadows of doubt, had ever since been able to join Paul in his doxologies. Another says, "I regard the importance of your life and influence as greatly enhanced by the recent death of our great and beloved Dr. Dabney. With special fervor, therefore, I pray that our Lord may long preserve your life and your talents unabated for the maintenance of truth and for the defense of our Church." Another well says: "I thank God for you; for the grace He has given you and the glorious work He has wrought through your voice and pen and *eloquent life.*

I thank God that He has spared you so long to *stand like adamant* for the dear old faith, and for an undiluted Gospel of redeeming love.

"Though you and I have differed on some past issue in the 'long time ago,' I have never ceased to honor your courage, your conscientious fidelity to the truth, and your unselfish devotion to the welfare of others and to the salvation of souls. In just one hearty word, Brother Palmer, *I love you.* Can I say more? My earnest prayer is that your eloquent voice may ring out for many years more until that voice shall mingle in the harmonies and hallelujahs of the heavenly world."

With these honest praises ringing in his ears, the grand old man went on his way somewhat more than four years longer. The Brotherhood in his church was wont to have his successive natal days observed now as they passed; but in a more quiet way. On such occasions he had not a little to say of the joys of old age. Hear him in his reply to Rabbi Leucht's address, on January 25, 1899; for the Jewish Rabbi has been made the Presbyterian Brotherhood's mouthpiece for the occasion. Dr. Palmer said: "There is a certain solemn and peculiar beauty and joy in old age. There is comfort and holy calm in those maturer years, when the animal passions are at rest, and when one settles down to the quiet contemplation of the past and the serene expectancy of the nearness of life to come. I have lived to know that there is beauty in old age. I saw it in the life of my father, who at the age of ninety-four laid down his work and passed away after two or three hours' notice from his King," etc.

As these birthdays recurred some of the ablest editors of the press of New Orleans seemed to think that they could not do better than to make his life the subject of an editorial. They magnified his talents and his genius, his lifelong stand for righteousness, his broad charity for men of a differing faith, and his readiness to fellowship with them in all that was right. They felt, and let him know they felt it, that he had in some of these respects morally towered aloft amongst all the great citizens of the world. They felt, and let him know they felt it, that in regard to religious toleration he had lifted his whole city high amongst the most enlightened communities of earth.

His city had, ere this eighty-first anniversary of his birth, named that part of Henry Clay avenue, which is east of St.

Charles avenue, after the veteran minister and citizen, "Palmer Avenue."

His sunset, radiant because of all the kindness shown him, was made still more so by the good he continued to do, by voice and pen and walk. To the congratulatory notes and letters went forth answers. One such answer is this:

"1718 PALMER AVENUE, NEW ORLEANS, LA., January 26, 1899.

"MY DEAR ——: Your sweet note of remembrance is just at hand; and I thank you sincerely for your good wishes—which united with the hundreds of others would procure me endless life here on earth, if it were in human power to order it so. But we are all under the care of the Father above, who knows best how to dispose of all of his children. Let us try to learn how to lie quietly in his hand, simply awaiting and also doing his blessed will.

"This, by the way, suggests to me what you say about the doubts which sometimes perplex and annoy you. If you were here, we could shift them all one by one and blow them away. But there is an easier and quicker way to dispose of the whole trouble—dealing with them in the mass and not in separate detail. Taken separately, they swarm upon us like bees and sting us to death; but a good fresh breeze from the heavenly hills will disperse them like the dust which fills the air. Settle it then once for all that the Bible is the word of God and that in it we hear nothing but truth, and then all doubts are settled by its supreme authority. We too often seek to determine divine things by the light of our natural reason alone. We cannot measure the path of the sun by our tape line—why should we undertake to measure the scope of the Infinite by the narrow stretch of that which is finite? God certainly knows the truth of all that he reveals to us; why should not his word be supreme in its authority. A calm submission to the divine testimony should settle all difficulties, leaving to us only the task of finding what the Bible actually does teach on any given point. But enough of this.

"With affectionate greetings to your mother and sister, as well as to Mr. ———, I remain,

"Gratefully yours,

"B. M. PALMER."

In April, 1899, he went up with his daughter, Mrs. Caldwell, and a granddaughter to South Carolina on a farewell visit. At Columbia an ovation was accorded him. At McPhersonville he preached again in the Stony Creek Church; into whose membership he had been received, as he told the congregation, on the profession of his faith, July 16, 1836.

The whole trip was greatly enjoyed. The following letter to Miss Helen McMaster, Columbia, S. C., refers to one pleasurable incident:

"January 30, 1900.

"MY DEAR HELEN: Your kind greeting upon the entrance of the New Year was duly received, to which a response should have been given before this. It is never, however, too late to acknowledge an obligation so pleasant to be discharged as this. The three of us who enjoyed, last April, that delightful interview with your father and his household, frequently speak of it as one of the most charming incidents of our brief visit to Carolina. The memory of it is made even more tender by reason of your father's removal to his eternal home. The twin death of both father and mother within so short a period must sanctify to his children the earthly home and fill it with most precious memories. To me, however, at this distance every death that occurs seems to rub out more and more the impressions of my early life in Columbia. Hardly one of my own contemporaries now survives, and if I should again revisit the dear old town it is only in the hearts of their descendants that I could find a resting place.

"I close in haste, with love to all the sisters and brothers.

"Yours affectionately,

"B. M. PALMER."

In the early months of 1902, his daughter, Mrs. Caldwell, was quite ill. Upon her recovery, the following letter, accompanied by a check, was received by the treasurer of the Board of Deacons of the First Presbyterian Church:

"1718 PALMER AVENUE, NEW ORLEANS, LA., March 18, 1902.

"*Mr. Duncan Galbreath.*

"MY DEAR MR. GALBREATH: As a thank offering to God for the recovery of my daughter, I enclose a check for another $100—given to Home Missions in the Synod of Louisiana.

"Please send the entire amount therefore to Rev. J. C. Barr, Treasurer of the Synod's Committee of Home Missions.

"Yours truly,

"B. M. PALMER."

The following to Mr. and Mrs. John Barkley is said to be the last note he ever wrote:

"MY DEAR MR. AND MRS. BARKLEY: You are ploughing your way through the vasty deep, with only the heavens above and the waters beneath, without a speck of land around the whole horizon.

"The captain of your vessel takes his bearings only from daily observation of the sun to learn his latitude and longitude and thus determines the exact spot of earth upon his chart where his vessel stands. What an emblem this of the voyage of human life! We are at sea within the vast horizon of God's adorable Providence: and only through daily study of the sky, with the Bible as our chart, do we know at any moment how far we have reached in the Divine life toward the home of eternal rest.

"In either voyage, whether this or that, may God bless you both and bring you with propitious winds to the desired haven.

"Affectionately yours,

"B. M. PALMER."

CHAPTER XX.

THE STREET CAR ACCIDENT, DEATH, BURIAL AND EULOGIES.

The Street Car Accident.—The Grief of His People, the City and the South-land.—Letters Illustrating This.—Resolutions of the Same Import Passed by Various Organizations.—Sinking Under the Shock.—The Last Message to His Congregation.—Effect of His Death on His People, His City, and the South.—Incidents Connected with the Burial.—Some Tributes.

ABOUT half past one by the clock, Monday, May 5, 1902, Dr. Palmer left his home to attend a meeting of a ladies' society at his church. He walked out Palmer Avenue to its intersection with St. Charles. When he reached St. Charles Avenue, no car was in sight, and he stood for a few moments watching some negro laborers who were making excavations in the street. A car approached. At the intersection of Henry Clay Avenue, just a short distance further up St. Charles Avenue, two ladies stood, waiting to take the same car, and Dr. Palmer seems to have thought that the car would stop for them to board it. He did not hurry to cross the track. But, as the car was behind time, and closely followed by another, it did not stop for the ladies. Coming speedily on, it struck him just as he reached the inner rail. Fortunately the fender threw him aside.

The cries of the motorman, who had called to him to look out, had attracted the attention of the workmen in the street. They hurried to the scene, took up the bruised form of the venerable old man and bore him tenderly back to his home. Meanwhile, sympathetic spectators of the accident had run to telephones and summoned physicians, who were soon attending him.

When his injuries were examined, it was found that his right leg had been fractured, that three toes on his left foot had been crushed, and that he had suffered contusions on the head, face and arms, one on the right and another on the left side of the forehead. He had retained full consciousness. When asked if he suffered any pain, he replied that he felt numbness in the

HIS TOMB IN METARIE CEMETERY.

right leg, and that his left foot pained him exceedingly. He bore up bravely. An hour after the terrible shock, he was resting in tolerable comfort, and his exceptionally strong constitution gave his friends some ground on which to hope for his recovery. The contusions were not serious, but the comminuted fracture of both bones of the right leg was no trifle.[1]

The event moved the city of New Orleans most profoundly. For many years he had been to the city the impersonation of Southern manhood, civic virtue, sacred eloquence and ripened piety. Nor was the motion confined to the city. The whole South was stirred, and to a less extent the entire Union. Expressions of concern poured in from every part of the land by mail and wire, to himself, to his family, to the co-pastor, Dr. W. T. Palmer, to the members of his flock, and to his brother ministers of the city. The most of these were, of course, personal and individual expressions. From half a hundred which have been preserved, the following are fair samples:

PRESBYTERIAN PARSONAGE,

"LANCASTER, N. Y., May 12, 1902.

"DEAR DR. PALMER: Your old and devoted friend, Mr. F. N. Thayer, with tears in his eyes, came to me on Saturday (10th) with a copy of the *New Orleans Picayune* for May 6, containing an account of the dreadful accident which befell you on the 5th.

"He made me promise to write you and mention his deep sorrow and tender solicitude. Mr. Thayer was more affected by this very sad occurrence than I have ever seen him affected by anything. He said he had been crying like a child.

"Accept the assurance, Dr. Palmer, that I, a perfect stranger to you, though long cognizant of your rank, influence, and Christian character, share the sorrow and solicitude of Mr. Thayer, and pray that God will be gracious to you, and that his presence may be with you in this most trying and (to us) deplorable situation.

"In years I am not far behind you. Some day we shall both, I trust, renew our youth under happier skies.

"WILLIAM WIATH."

"MADISON, N. J., May 12, 1902.

"MY DEAR MRS. CALDWELL: I was greatly shocked a few days since, when I read the telegram printed in the New York papers giving a brief notice of the injuries received by your dear father. It seemed

---

[1]This account has been reduced from that in the *Southwestern Presbyterian*, May 8, 1902, p. 8.

quite a family matter to our Madison household, because we all hold your father in affection and share a common grief and anxiety because of this distressing news. Friends have kindly sent us clippings from the New Orleans papers, by which we have been encouraged to hope that the injuries received by him will make no permanent impression upon his health, and that we may soon hope to hear of his complete recovery.

"I write simply to express my sympathy with you and the members of your family during the stress and strain of your trials, and to ask you to convey to Dr. Palmer the assurance of my deep solicitude and my earnest hope that he may soon be restored to his accustomed activities. My daughter joins me in the hope that we shall continue to hear only good news of your patient.

"Very truly yours,

"WM. O. ROGERS."

"CHARLESTOWN, W. VA., May 16, 1902.

"MY DEAR DR. PALMER:

. . . .

"I feel as if our beloved Church cannot afford to be deprived of your counsel and your influence, though I know, of course, that the Church is founded not on man but on the Rock Christ Jesus. Yet we need the wisdom of the wise and the counsel of experience. You are almost the last of the generation of men who launched our Church upon the stormy seas of her separate existence, and whose judgment has guided her safely thus far. There are rough seas still tossing our craft, and all storm clouds have not disappeared. And I for one feel the need of your piloting till these evil omens disappear. Besides, so warm is my love for you personally that your misfortune is to me a distressing affliction. Mrs. Hopkins, too, who has met you once or twice, feels similar affliction.

"Oh! that it may please God to guide your physicians and to bless the natural means employed to heal and restore you. My heart yearns over you. . . .

"Of course I do not expect you to answer this letter; but I trust that the newspapers will bear to us the glad tidings of your improvement as the days go by.

"With much sympathy to Mrs. Caldwell and a heart full of love to you, my dear doctor, I am, Yours truly,

"A. C. HOPKINS."

"BATTLE HILL, JACKSON, MISS., May 26, 1902.

"MY DEAR DR. PALMER: Ever since I heard of the accident my thoughts and poor prayers have gone out for your restoration and the prolongation of your useful and most valuable life.

"I do not see how we are to spare you from a world that, now especially, it would seem, needs all its good and strong men.

"But you, like myself, believe God is sovereign over all, life and death, this world and the other, and in His holy keeping all is well.

"I leave you there, dear friend, where your own faith holds you safe.

Sincerely yours,

"HUGH MILLER THOMPSON."

Messages expressing heartfelt sorrow at the great calamity, tender sympathy with him in his suffering, profound esteem for his character, and hope for his speedy recovery were sent by the following, among other organizations: The Executive Committee of the Eye, Ear, Nose, and Throat Hospital, in New Orleans; The Presbytery of New Orleans; The Presbytery of Lexington, in the Synod of Virginia; The Alumni Association of Columbia Seminary; The Board of Trustees of Union Theological Seminary, in Virginia; The Board of Administrators of the Tulane Educational Fund; The Presbyterian Ministers' Association, of Atlanta, Georgia; The Louisiana Division of the Association of the Army of Tennessee; The General Assembly of the Presbyterian Church in the United States, *et al.;* Similarly, The General Conference of the Methodist Church, in session at Dallas, Texas, and the Southern Baptist Convention, in session at Asheville, N. C., "each adopted a resolution of sympathy, with prayer to God on behalf of His servant, for whom they expressed the greatest love and veneration.[2]" During a conference of Jewish Rabbis, held soon after the accident, Rabbi Leucht spoke as follows:

"At the eve of our Conference, one of God's noblest men has been struck down in a minute by an electric car. He was not a Jew, but a Christian, and as such a better Jew I never knew. I saw him stand where you now stand and drop a rose on the bier of a Jewish Rabbi, and he said it was the tribute of a Christian heart to a Jewish Rabbi. In 1882, when the iron hand of the czar again drove our brethren out from Russia, he arose and said: 'When a Hebrew suffers I suffer with him.' In this great community there is not a single home where prayers are not arising for one who suffers on a bed of pain, and I ask my brethren to join with the Jewish ministers of the United States in their prayers that God may spare the life of Dr. Benjamin Palmer, which is itself the greatest Christian model in New Orleans, and I ask that all will arise in the adoption of resolutions expressing that sentiment, and I believe it will be seconded by this congregation."

---

[2]See the *Southwestern Presbyterian,* May 15, 1902.

"In adoption of the resolution every person in the crowded building arose."[8]

Receiving the best medical attention and nursing, and all the stimulus to recovery which the outpouring appreciation and love that hundreds of thousands could give, Dr. Palmer seemed to bear up wonderfully for a time. The injuries from his accident lessened to such a degree in the course of seven days that it became highly probable, other conditions continuing favorable, that he would recover; but this was not to be the case. Troubles from which he had suffered in years past recurred—notably, prostatic irritation and kidney derangement. These were assuaged for a time, but again became more severe. After Friday, May 22, his case was considered almost hopeless.

At times on Saturday he would speak, but his mind seemed to be wandering. On Sunday, occasionally he would speak. The watchers, straining to hear, could only make out the sweet words, "Jesus Savior." They seem to have been the last words he uttered. After Sunday he grew speechless. Once, Monday, he looked for a moment at his granddaughter, Miss Fannie Caldwell, with a gleam of recognition; and when she asked him if he knew her he put up his hand and drew her face down to his to be kissed, then lapsed again into unconsciousness. After that there was no further sign of recognition of those about him. At 12:15 P.M., Tuesday, May 27, his attending physician, Dr. Joseph Holt, issued a bulletin which read:

"Dr. Palmer is in complete coma and gently sinking. The end is not immediately at hand."

He continued to sink slowly through the afternoon, night and following forenoon, and expired at one o'clock Wednesday, May 25, 1902.

Once he had been so severely injured, he probably preferred to go away and be at rest. He had put in some hours, indeed, on his bed of confinement, in planning for a possible earthly future, but that future had not seemed bright. He had felt that with a broken leg he would be fearfully hampered. He had looked not without a certain willingness to the approach

[8] *Item*, May 28, 1902.

of death, therefore. With Scriptures on his lips, about God's gracious forgiveness of sins, he had passed through the first fortnight subsequent to the "accident." After his brother, Rev. E. P. Palmer, D.D., of Harrisonburg, Va., reached him, they had had one or two talks in which the dying man had given beautiful testimony as to the preciousness to him of his Lord Christ.

Sunday morning, May 18, he had dictated the following letter, his last message to his people, which was read to them that day by the co-pastor, Dr. W. T. Palmer:

"It does not seem proper that a second Sabbath should intervene without a word of communication from me to the dear people of my charge—the members of the First Church and congregation.

"I desire, first of all, to express my grateful sense of the warm sympathy and affection tendered me in this hour of trial. I can do nothing more than reciprocate most tenderly all the expressions that have been conveyed to me and to pray that they may be returned in showers of blessing upon those who have been thus lavish in their kindness to myself.

"It is even more important, however, to urge that in this period of severe discipline we should both be prepared to meet whatever may be before us. As yet we cannot anticipate the changes which insue. My only desire is to suggest on the part of us both a hearty submission to the Divine will, which will order all things for the praise and the glory of His Church upon earth. Most affectionately yours,

"B. M. PALMER."

May, 1902.

This was a thoroughly characteristic letter, full of concern for his flock, for the glory of the Church and its Divine Head, and full of gracious humility.

Throughout the city and all over the Southland the intelligence of his death was flashed, carrying that anguish which is usually experienced only when death has broken the ties of blood as well as of friendship. And because men could do no better they comforted themselves with words which had fallen from his own lips as he once stood over the cold, clammy form of a friend:

"DEAR FRIENDS: If anything is taught to us in this hour to-day, it is God's right to rule, and He means to teach us that however great may be the instrument which He shall employ in human history, however needful they may seem to be to us, He can do without them all. There is no man great enough to compete with God; there is no man so immortal and princely in his gifts but that God could lay him in his tomb and guide the affairs of His nation and of His Church without his aid. It is a lesson for us to learn, who stand beside the bier of our friend to-day, that deeply as we may be intrenched in the affections of the people whom we serve, God will eventually teach all these, and teach us before them, that we are not essential to the prosperity of the Church and the extension of the Redeemer's kingdom. Oh, let us learn this now as we cry out in the anguish of our grief, and ask what shall we do, now that our head is gone from us; let us learn that God speaks from His throne and says to us: 'Lift your eyes and your thoughts from the mortal on earth, and fix your supreme regard upon the power and the wisdom and love which are infinite in their scope.' It is a sad loss to the world when a good man dies. No man was ever taken from this world without taking from the very atmosphere of this earth the influence which this poor earth needs for its life. Yet, no man was ever taken from this world without leaving behind him his equivalent in *the influence of his counsels,* the characters which he has moulded and the memory which survives him. Men have gone up by the scores and the hundreds, one by one, so that we have not counted them, and to-day perhaps they are hanging over the battlements of the upper kingdom, looking down upon this scene of sorrow. And as friends greeted them passing through the gates of pearl, they sat down together upon the mount of God, and their memories were blended in that immortal chant of praise to Him who sitteth upon the throne, and to the Lamb forever and forever. Those who have tasted sorrow, who have put the bitter cup of sorrow to their lips and have drunk it to the dregs, will understand my speech when I say that a life of virtue and religion, crowned with a peaceful and joyous death, comes back to us who survive. And though there may be in the heart that strange hunger of love for the form that we can no longer embrace, yet the blessed memory of our dead comes to us as a sacred presence, and we hold sweet communion with what is only the memory of what is gone."

During Thursday, May 29, 1902, many were the messages of sympathy and condolence received at the family home. Telegrams came from all parts of the country. In the afternoon were many callers, and numerous gifts of fresh flowers, designed often to make visible the sentiments of the givers toward their long-time shepherd. The people of the city almost idolized him. They rejoiced in him that day as somewhat that would be theirs forever. He belonged to New Orleans. His history was an immortal part of its history, a glorious part of it. Yet their grief was beyond expression, for he would nevermore be their leader, as of yore, in fighting the battles of right against wrong, sweeping them on to victory; nevermore be their comfort and support, under God, in trouble; never feed their minds and hearts with sweet, large and ennobling discourse; never again show them Christ, to whom he had lived so close.

In the course of the day "there came a timid knock at the door, so soft that it was scarcely heard at the first; then, as if taking heart, it grew a little louder. It was from a man, and on his face was the unmistakable sign of tears. He handed a bouquet of flowers, not the magnificent tropical flowers that were coming in from every quarter, but a simple cluster that was gathered from the home garden. Attached to it was a simple card on which was written: 'With the heartfelt regrets of the motorman.'

"That was all. 'Give these to the family,' the man said, almost choking with grief, 'and tell them that I am very sorry, but that I would esteem it a favor that I will never forget to my dying day if they would give my simple offering a little place near Dr. Palmer.'

"The ladies who received the flowers were so touched that they could not find words for utterance.

"'Wait,' one of them said simply; 'we will send these upstairs to the family.'

"In another moment a message came from Mrs. Caldwell, Dr. Palmer's daughter, bidding the poor man come up to her presence; she wanted to thank him personally for his remembrance, and, in her beautiful thoughtfulness and kindness, seek to take away some of the terrible wound that was gnawing in his heart, albeit her own was the one that was suffering most grievously.

"The man went up into that hallowed chamber where Dr. Palmer had breathed his last, and where the grief-stricken family still kept sad vigil. He burst into tears, it is said, and poured out his grief at the accident in which he was one of the chief actors, and which had deprived her of such a father and the world of such a man, and the people of such a friend. He wept pitifully and assured the family again and again of his deep sorrow that would follow him to his dying day.

" 'It was a week,' he said, 'before I could even conduct my car again.'[4]

"Then seeking to comfort the heartbroken man, Mrs. Caldwell took his hand and said: 'Sir, if my father could speak one word to you now, I am sure that he would say: 'I would gladly give up my life if I could know that by doing so you would always show yourself a true and faithful follower of Christ,' and so I ask you in his name to do this for me; to take this as his last message to you. God bless you, my friend.' And the weeping man went from her presence."[5]

Then Mrs. Caldwell ordered the flowers to be placed at the foot of the casket, and there they lay; and when as the evening came on the body was carried to the church the same place was accorded the motorman's bouquet, notwithstanding all the array of beautiful floral tributes which love and admiration had designed.

It had been planned that it should be the privilege of the members of his church and his more intimate friends to call at his house ere the remains should be carried to the church. But callers could not be confined to those within these pales. Dr. Palmer had been a great friend to the poor, ever the prey of the importunate beggars of the street even, for fear lest in refusing any he might fail to give in a case of real need; and the poor came, one after another, as the hours passed, "came with tear-dimmed eyes and sorrow-laden hearts, some bringing only a simple flower, others naught but their simple love and gratitude." "Most touching was the grief of the old family servants," some of whom had been with Dr. Palmer for a great number of years and had known and loved his wife and children as they had loved him.

Meanwhile the First Presbyterian Church had been draped in mourning, turned into an "epic in black," speaking of unutterable sadness and desolation. That again had been somewhat relieved by exquisite floral tributes arranged and trained about pillar and rostrum.

At 5 o'clock P.M. Dr. Palmer's body was borne from the home to the church. A few friends had gathered at the home at the hour of leaving. Simple services were held. The small cortege was soon on its way, watched the meanwhile by peo-

---

[4] The *Daily Picayune,* May 30, 1902. [5] *Ibid.,* May 31, 1902.

ple with bared heads, to the church. A little later a stream of people was pouring by to take the last look at the form lying in front of the pulpit behind which he had so often thrilled, informed and ennobled them. The people taking this last look were thoroughly representative. "There were in the throng soldiers in war and soldiers of the cross, people of all creeds and all nationalities, from the highest to the most humble. Many women silently wept, while others sobbed audibly, and men brushed away the tears as they looked on the face of a friend who had soothed their sorrows in many a bitter crisis of life." Time-scarred veterans who had worn the gray looked on the form of their old chaplain, lying there in the majesty and greatness of a death that knew no sting; recalled his deeds of kindness when rough-visaged War his horrid front had reared high, and no less his heroic service when fearsome Pestilence had stalked the streets. It was hard for some of them to give place to those coming behind. Such expressions as the following dropped from persons in the stream as it flowed out: "I have lost my best friend," said a little girl of ten years. "He was the best friend my poverty ever knew. Sorry am I that I ever lost him, for he always sought me out in my grief and misery," said an old and poverty-struck woman. "He baptized all my children and married my sons and daughters," said another. "He officiated at the funeral of each member of my family," said another. "He wrote such kind letters to us in our affliction," remarked another. "He was the most wonderful man I ever knew, so tender and so true, and so heroic," said others. So on went the stream of comment throughout all the hours of that evening.

At ten o'clock that night the body was committed to the care of the session of his church, which sat guard over it till an early hour the next morning, when they were relieved by other important members of the church and representatives of various organizations, who kept vigil until the time of the funeral.

The funeral services were held in the church at 10 o'clock A.M. Friday, May 30, 1902. The church was opened at 9 o'clock. The seats between the galleries were reserved till 9.45 for the members of the church. A few minutes thereafter "every nook and corner of the immense edifice" was crowded. It was a "remarkable, a wonderful gathering, a massing together of culture and intellect and thought and love such as seldom, if ever, was witnessed in New Orleans before.

"They came to pay tribute to that life that had been so pre-eminently rich in its endowment, so marvelously gifted with the acquisitions of the scholar, the eloquence of the writer, the inspiration of the orator; so sanctified by religious faith and principle, so many-sided in its aptitudes and abilities, so broad and self-sacrificing in its Christianity, and so abundant in works that honored God and blessed the world. They came to testify their faith in him, their appreciation of the unswerving steadfastness with which he had pursued his convictions of what he held to be right and true in the face of difficulty or sacrifice or defeat; their sympathy with the magnificent equability of character that he had ever displayed, their admiration of his loyal heroism as a soldier of Christ, and to give public testimony of the love that followed him beyond the grave.

"From every portion of the Church that love spoke; it echoed from choir and gallery, and spoke from chancel and aisle. But especially did the old Church echo the breaking heart of the congregation that Dr. Palmer had guided for so many years. From generation to generation he had borne to their homes his tender ministry in seasons of sorrow, and his cheerful presence in their hours of joy; he had wept amid their desolation as Jesus did at Bethany, and rejoiced in their pleasures the same as did the Master at Cana; thus filling up with sympathetic service that parenthesis of varied experiences inclosed between those brackets of brightness and bitterness—the bridal and the tomb; he had offered their children in baptismal consecration, united them and their sons and daughters in wedded bonds, and received them and their offsprings into church communion; he had been their counsellor in difficulty, their helper in trouble, their friend in misfortune; he had spoken words of comfort in their hours of woe, and lifted petitions for healing beside their beds of pain; he had whispered the consolations of hope as their beloved ones entered the dark valley, and he had laid away with tears their precious dead, and afterwards he had never failed to sit with them in their darkened homes and pour the balm of comfort upon their bruised hearts. Thus was Dr. Palmer inseated into their hearts by a thousand bonds of the holiest communion, a thousand ties of tenderest associations, a thousand sweet memories."[6]

Men and women came with fresh tributes of flowers. One given the day before held the place of honor, however. Mrs. Caldwell had requested that the little bouquet of the motorman

---

[6]*Picayune,* May 31, 1902.

should be placed on the coffin just over the heart of her father. There it lay in all its simple pathos. As the donor passed down the aisle, with white, set face, and saw his flowers so honored he burst into tears again.

"By ten o'clock, the hour fixed for the final ceremonies, there was not a vacant seat in the church, the galleries were thronged, and out in the streets were many who could not even gain entrance. It was said to be the largest crowd that had ever attended any funeral in New Orleans since President Davis was laid away. It was an eminently representative gathering; there were representatives of the State and city government, the judges of the Supreme, Federal and City courts, distinguished lawyers, college presidents and professors, merchants, physicians, bankers, newspaper men, members of the Exchange, Jewish rabbis and Catholic priests, Episcopal bishops and ministers, and Methodists and Baptists and Congregational clergymen, business men of every calling, representative women of every walk of life, all gathered to do honor to the great and noble man who had passed from the busy life of this great and rushing city. And there were the old Confederate veterans, who loved Dr. Palmer with a love 'passing the love of woman;' there were the old men from the Soldiers' Home, to whom he was such a friend, all mourning the great chaplain, the consecrated man, the true friend of that cause for which many of them to-day are halt and lame, and for which he, as well as they, would have willingly shed the last drop of his heart's blood.

"Very touching, too, was the presence of a delegation of Chinamen from the Chinese Mission School, in which Dr. Palmer took such a deep and abiding interest. They came down the aisles, bringing a wreath of autumn leaves, which they deposited near the casket; then they withdrew into a further corner to pray. Dr. Palmer had made Christians of these men, and their stoical faces showed no little emotion as they passed by his lifeless corpse."[7]

The service was conducted by the Rev. Drs. R. Q. Mallard and J. H. Nall, assisted by the Rev. Drs. Alexander and C. M. Atkinson, at the church, and by Rev. J. C. Barr and Rev. Mr. Koelle at the tomb.

Dr. Palmer had twice expressed the wish that no elaborate funeral oration should be pronounced over his body. Accordingly only a very simple service was held. Drs. Mallard and Nall each made a brief address. They were simple tributes to the man, the prophet, the friend. The following excerpt is from the address of Dr. Mallard:

---

[7]*Daily Picayune,* May 31, 1902.

"But that great heart which took us all in, I am sure, were it able to use those mute lips, would not silence all expression of the love and grief struggling in our bosoms for utterance. This, then, is my personal tribute. As a student of that queen of sciences, theology, I sat a learner at his feet during the week, and on Sabbath a worshipper under his preaching; that was in the fifties. Even then he had risen to the zenith, and as a star of the first magnitude he has shone ever since, through all these years, with undiminished effulgence, until lost because absorbed in light of eternal day. Since the sixties have I sat with him in the councils of the Church, and more than any other minister has it been my privilege to hear him from this pulpit. In every perplexity, personal or public, it was my wont to seek his advice, and he was ever found the kind and sympathizing friend and wise and safe counsellor. Between us, in the awful crises which come to some lives, there passed two letters, one of which, like a sudden lightning flash, lighted up for me the inmost chambers of his soul.

"A competent witness, I only wish to say that as thus known and revealed, he was to me as good as he was great, and as great as he was good—his a greatness without eccentricity; his a goodness without flaw. His individuality was like his voice—that wonderful organ, clear, deliberate; and, even when passion moved, distinct in every syllable; filled without seeming effort, but never overfilled, the darkened parlor where lay the flower-covered form, or the public hall and this spacious audience room. Thus his personality exactly and perfectly filled every place in which God called him to be, to do, to speak.

"But I prefer to recall him now as the humble disciple of my Lord. If the Christian be the highest style of man, then was he a Saul, for spiritual stature, head and shoulders above his brethren. His was a mind which bowed with the simplicity of a child to every word of Scripture, and without questioning thought accepted the most humbling doctrines and profound mysteries. In his last conscious hours, as I learned from one close to him, he turned resolutely away from every other confidence, and cast himself on Christ, trusting to His sovereign grace alone."

The immense throng which lined the route to Washington Cemetery was further proof that the people felt that something great had gone out of the life of the city; and that, irrespective of creeds, classes, races or nationalities, they were moved by a sorrow that would not be denied expression.[8]

Tributes had already been flowing into the press and thence

---

[8]His remains were, in the year ——, transferred to the beautiful Metarie Cemetery, where his people had constructed a handsome family tomb as the resting place of all that was mortal of him and his.

over the country. Some typical instances are presented, that he may be seen as he appeared to those who knew him well:

"He was intimately connected with and powerfully influential in great movements that have made for the moral welfare and the true advancement of the city and the commonwealth. He was recognized in this country and abroad as one of the most distinguished and pre-eminent leaders in his own communion, and amidst other religious bodies he was held in profound honor and admiration for the testimony borne by his life and teaching to righteousness and the kingdom of God. He was endowed with a mighty and splendid gift of eloquence and oratory, which united the characteristics of inspiring enthusiasm and majestic self-control, and innumerable causes are indebted to this moving and victorious eloquence. He mingled the courage of the prophet with the gentleness and sympathy of the minister of consolation, and in times of pestilence he endeared to him multitudes even outside his fold and pastoral care. He was knitted in bonds of imperishable sympathy and fellowship with the soldiers of the Confederacy, and no tongue more eloquently than his could declare the pathos of the Southern cause and its rights and justification, and at the same time uphold the duty of patriotism and true citizenship under the established order. The clergy and the members of our communion unite with me in the expression of profound sympathy with the congregation of the Rev. Dr. Palmer in the death of their great leader and most dearly beloved pastor, and in the expression of the sorrow and deep consciousness of loss which we feel in common with the entire community in the departure of one so distinguished in loftiness of Christian character, so powerful as a religious teacher and so courageous in pressing upon society the moral standards of Christianity, so identified with the history of the South and representative personally of the highest strain of chivalry, so beneficent in spiritual consolation and works of charity. In his departure a great personality has passed from earth and entered into the joy and the approval of the Divine Redeemer and King, whom he served with such humble dependence, yet with such valor and might.

"His name will be perpetuated as a living and consecrated force; and in the remembrance with which he will be cherished through the coming years there will mingle gratitude and admiration for the greatness of his testimony and his services and that tenderness of reverence which attaches to those strong warriors of God who themselves have learned in suffering the knightly prowess and patience of the soul which they have taught to others.

"DAVIS SESSUMS,
"Protestant Episcopal Bishop of Louisiana."

"Some men are great as statesmen, some as philosophers, some as theologians, some as preachers; but Dr. Palmer was great in whatever relation he sustained. In the pulpit he was without a peer; as a theologian, clear, strong, logical; as a citizen and patriot, second to none. He was a man of convictions. He stood for something, and yet in such a gentle and courteous way that he made thinking men his firm friends, though they occupied positions hopelessly separated from him—witness the remarkable scene in the Jewish Synagogue the other night when Rabbi Leucht prayed for Dr. Palmer's recovery and praised him as a Christian. Yes, they were Jews and they knew he was a Christian, and they honored him as a Christian. That is a gift that few men possess—to be firm and true to one's colors and at the same time not to be disagreeable and discourteous to those who differ with you. This gift Dr. Palmer possessed as few men have ever possessed it. Hence men of all creeds loved and honored him.

"It is, however, as a preacher that Dr. Palmer must ever be remembered as pre-eminent. He is the last of the great philosophic preachers who 'justified the ways of God to men.' He never spoke without laying deep as a foundation of his discourse some great principle of eternal truth. He belonged to the Henry Clay and Webster class of orators—that class which seem to be forever passing away, and in whose passing the world is losing a glory it can ill afford to lose. There was never but one Dr. Palmer, and the mould is broken. There will be no more.

"W. McF. ALEXANDER,
"Prytania Street Presbyterian Church."

"As a child of a Presbyterian household, the name of Dr. Palmer is one of the earliest associations of my life, and I count it a precious bit of good fortune that it was reserved for me to know him, to work with him, to get strength from him and to love him. Looking over his threescore years of manhood, who shall say that human life be not capable of splendor and dignity and beauty? His passing is like the going out from this community of some elemental moral force as serene and unfailing and strengthening as the great natural forces that freshen and invigorate the earth. Two generations have looked to him for moral beauty and guidance, and he has not failed them. So pervading and insistent is the moral bigness of the man that one almost forgets his unusual endowments and graces of mind and manner—the organ tones of his voice, the passionate, artistic fire that kindled in his brain, the noble forms of his speech, the large integrity of his thought, the graciousness and sincerity of his manner.

"These powers, if given to the service of the State, would have placed him in the nation's Pantheon, along with Calhoun and Davis and Prentiss and Lamar. But he lived too intimately with the eternal verities for that sort of service. He saw God each day in his heaven, and in the wide earth. The beauty of holiness charmed his austere spirit and held him in a kind of sacred thrall. Indeed, it is hard to think of him as living in this shifty, stormy, metallic era. One wants to place him in the high statured age of prophets, priests and kings, when righteousness was the master word, and moral welfare the battle-field of the strong.

"If there be anywhere a man who looks at this human life of ours with cynicism, with weariness, or with doubt, let him reflect upon this life with such simplicity, and yet stateliness, and stirring the pulses of tens of thousands with the yearnings of a God. I hope to be able to place his portrait upon the walls of this university, which he loved and served, in order that the generations of youth who shall come hither for strength shall know the face of a man who worked uprightly before God and man, who lived loyally with the highest, who counted it a gladness and a glory to serve the humblest, and who realized in his activities the noblest conceptions of virtue, justice, tenderness, goodness and truth. "EDWIN A. ALDERMAN,

"President of the Tulane University of Louisiana."

"His mental gifts were of a very high order, and beyond doubt he is entitled to first rank among the orators of our time. In temperament and disposition he seemed always calm, and gentle also, except when denouncing what to him seemed wrong. His manners were courteous and refined.

"Above all, in my estimation, was the sincerity and earnestness of his convictions and the courage and zeal with which he championed the causes which he considered right. There was with him, in this respect, no compromising and no hesitation in either expression or action. Our country at this time needs many such men—men who do not stop from proclaiming the truth for fear they may frighten away a dollar or two.

"The Southern Confederacy had in Dr. B. M. Palmer one of its most devoted sons, and we survivors of that time of danger and trial love him for that. The Louisiana Lottery found in him one of its most pronounced and implacable foes. The old guard of that great moral campaign will ever cherish his memory for what he did in that great cause. Gambling, Sunday violations and other common wrongdoings of our city and time encountered ever his determined opposition. All lovers of morality must keep in mind his persevering championship of causes which they still hold dear.

"Despite his aggressiveness, however, I do not believe Dr. Palmer leaves behind him any but mourners. His friends and associates, of course, loved him; the mass of our people respected and admired him, and even those whom, in the discharge of duty as he saw it, he especially antagonized, acknowledging always the purity of his motives, can harbor no malice aaginst his memory.

"FRANK MCGLOIN."

Judge McGloin was a distinguished representative of the Roman Catholic Church.

"COLUMBIA, S. C., May 29, 1902.

"The news of the death of the venerable Dr. Palmer has been received in his native State with expressions of sincerest sorrow. It was not my pleasure to have acquaintance with Dr. Palmer, but I have heard him, and no man has ever impressed me more as a preacher. Dr. Palmer was one of the many bright stars of the firmament of learning produced by the Palmetto State. His name will go into our history with those of Calhoun, McDuffie, Hayne and Rutledge. In Columbia, the capital, where Dr. Palmer served for fourteen years at the opening of his brilliant career, he was most dearly loved, and to the members of the congregation he served so faithfully here the news of his death brought the deepest sorrow. Dr. Palmer undoubtedly ranked as one of the greatest preachers of the Gospel and exponents of theology that the United States has ever produced.

"M. B. MCSWEENY, *Governor of South Carolina.*"

"BATON ROUGE, LA., May 30, 1902.

"I learned of the death of Dr. Palmer only yesterday evening, on my return from Natchitoches. I can scarcely find words to express my grief at the great loss the State has sustained in the death of this good and sublime preacher of the Gospel and unstinting dispenser of that real Christianly charity that knows no differences of creed.

"His grand patriotism and faith in righteousness, sustained as it was by an intellect unsurpassed in scope in any age, was a veritable beacon light of truth for our people, which his matchless eloquence was continually spreading.

"Let us hope that the striking examples of the virtues that ennoble mankind, which he bequeaths to our people whom he loved so well and faithfully, will remain enshrined in their hearts for their uplifting and the uplifting of the coming generations. I regret exceedingly that I could not be among those who will do homage to-day to his mortal remains. "W. W. HEARD, *Governor of Louisiana.*"

"DALLAS, TEXAS, May 30, 1902.

"In Dr. Palmer New Orleans loses a figure which in its way may be unique in the world. He was a man who represented in his own denomination the stanchest orthodoxy, who made no theological concession whatever to the currents of the age, who had outspoken convictions which he never concealed.

"A man decided, who was fearless and determined in every moral crusade, knowing not friend nor foe, neither policy nor advantage in warring against what he considered wrong.

"Yet this outspoken man, whose life lay like an open book before the world, was not only honored but revered and loved by all sects, admired by those who did not share his beliefs, venerated often by those whom he was forced to attack, for his heart was rich with a love that swept away every barrier; his genial smile knew no sectarian bounds, and thus he had more than people's love and honor, more than their admiration for his transcendent ability and lofty citizenship. He was across all religious barriers, the minister of all of us, in the fine spirituality of his soul, in the reverence which refined every touch of his noble intellect, in the profound and pervasive religiousness of his personality. God bless him for all the spiritual uplifts by which he has preached to all our people and shone out afar along the difficult path of every minister of the faith who was privileged to inspire himself from this glorious example. "RABBI MAX HELLER."

One may read from the record of the Civil District Court, the judges having met *en banc,* at the request of the members of the Bar, to consider the request that the divisions of that court should stand adjourned from the evening of Friday till the following Monday in respect to the memory of Dr. Palmer:

"With members of the bar and judges Dr. Palmer was always at home. His strong analytical intellect, his love of justice, his deep sense of right, the undaunted courage of his convictions, along with his universal learning and interest in public affairs, made him by nature a lawyer. He always held that the minister of the Gospel and the lawyer were necessarily co-laborers in the cause of truth, morality and justice. His sermon at the funeral of the late Alfred Hennen, the Nestor of our Bar at the time of his death, was upon those lines, and endeared him still more to our profession for this public recognition.

"When a citizen so distinguished and so beloved by all, a man whose whole life had been so devoted to the service of his God, and for the best interests of all the people, who has never been found absent from any call of religious or civil duty, is taken from our midst, we feel that we should manifest our respect for his high character, our affection for his memory, and our appreciation of his life's work by pausing from our labors to mingle our tears and our sorrows with those of our fellow citizens.

"With this feeble expression of our sentiments on this sad occasion, it is ordered that the motion of the Bar be granted, and that all the divisions of the court stand adjourned until Monday morning."[9]

---

[9]A true extract from the minutes of the Civil District Court for the Parish of Orleans, sitting *en banc,* New Orleans, May 29, 1902. H. Messionnier, "minute clerk." See copy in *The Times-Democrat,* May 30, 1902.

During the hours for the funeral the New Orleans Cotton Exchange, the Maritime Exchange, the Board of Trade, the New Orleans Stock Exchange, etc., suspended business, some of them with similarly praiseful resolutions. Aye, this busy city stopped its very wheels of transportation and commerce for some minutes in token of its sense of loss; even as the City Council had found time to pass resolutions of regret at his death.

From *Picayune* editorials of May 29 and 30, 1902, we read:

"Although the death of this grand man and most eminent citizen has been expected for some time, its actual occurrence yesterday, when it was announced in the afternoon papers and on the bulletin boards, seemed to inflict upon the sensibilities of the community a distinct and painful shock, as if it had been the result of a blow.

"Benjamin Morgan Palmer, D.D., and LL.D., was one of the most eminent divines of the Presbyterian Church in the world, and was easily, in point of learning, wisdom, piety and devotion to the doctrines of the Church, its chiefest representative in America, and so far as the organization and polity of that Church would permit, he was the head and highest authority in Presbyterianism of the Southern Church.

"Outside of his denominational connections, Dr. Palmer was a grand citizen, shunning party politics, but so thoroughly devoted to the best interests of the people of his city, his State and of the entire Southern country that he paid strict attention to every great public question, and did not hesitate to express his views and feelings whenever such questions were up for discussion. His patriotism and public spirit were intense and abiding, and he lived up to the lofty conceptions he held concerning them with all the devotion of his profound affection and sense of duty. Dr. Palmer believed that the State is founded on the family, and therefore patriotism begins with the home and extends to the country that contains it. His conduct as a citizen was founded on this doctrine.

"Although this grand man's great heart and vast love and charity were equal to the task of embracing in their scope all his fellow-creatures, his mighty affections turned first of all to his fellow-citizens and fellow-sufferers of these Southern States. Born and bred in the South, there his great life work was wrought largely for those with whom he had passed through the fiery trials and tribulations of a terrible sectional war, and knowing how extreme had been the sufferings of his friends and neighbors and his fellow-citizens of this section, he cherished for them a pity and affection vast and abounding, and he earnestly desired always to help and lift them up, a duty in which he never failed, while not forgetting that love and charity must not be limited to any class of suffering.

"Dr. Palmer was perhaps the most eminent orator upon the continent. His fame has gone abroad over the world. His eloquence was not a mere outpouring of well-chosen words arranged in pleasing phrases. It was in the flood of ideas, always expressed in the most fitting words, moving the heart at one moment or convincing the understanding at another, that his wonderful oratory excelled, and although it was in the pulpit that his magnificent public addresses were oftenest heard, he was no less grand in the forum discussing important public interests, nor was he less gifted on some festive occasion when he arose in response to a call to speak to some sentiment that was worthy of his greatness and dignity of character.

"Those persons to whom it has been given to hear him at the reunion banquets of the Confederate Veterans' Association of this city have learned something concerning after-dinner speeches that have never been surpassed, if, indeed, they have been equalled, on any occasion in any tongue. With infinite grace and expressiveness, and with a briefness that all speakers on such occasions should emulate, Dr. Palmer would pour out a tribute to the heroic devotion of those who fell in the Southern cause, or he would minister to the survivors counsels so wise and encouragement so comforting and uplifting that the entranced listeners would gaze at the inspired speaker, almost expecting his countenance to shine with a reflection of the divine glory.

"If the oratory of Dr. Palmer has been to some extent dwelt upon in this brief review, it is because the great public speakers of his stamp are rapidly passing away, with few, if any, to take their places. The tendency in education to-day is to make men specialists. They are required, by the exigencies of the times, to devote themselves to some particular branch of study, a rule which is unfavorable to the turning out of minds of symmetrical, and, it may be said, universal development, while another favorable feature in modern study is that it discredits and disparages culture in pure literature. Doubtless the orators of coming generations will be equal to the demands that may be made upon them, but in an age which discourages and mocks at sentiment there will be no longer developed the dignity, the pathos, the might, the majesty and the dominating and abiding power that characterized the oratory of the great man who, so lately towering in our midst, now lies with the lowliest.

. . . .

"The State and city have lost a most eminent citizen, a monument of patriotic public spirit, while religion has lost one of those who, like Joshua of old, was worthy to hold up the hands of Moses, the first and greatest lawgiver. There is left not one who can take the place once so fully and completely occupied by Dr. Palmer, and it is much to be doubted if it can ever be filled, but will not remain forever vacant as a memorial of the grand and unique man who stood among the foremost of his age in service and in duty."

Mr. Ashton Phelps, in the *Times-Democrat*, New Orleans, May 30, 1902, writes:

"In speaking of Richard Cobden, Mr. Disraeli most truly declared that certain illustrious men would always be members of the House of Commons, even though they were no longer in the land of the living. It may likewise be affirmed that the name of the great teacher will be forever borne on the golden roll of our citizenship. The splendid and strenuous life of this modern prophet was indeed inseparably intertwined with the ideas and aspirations of us all. In sunlight and shadow, in peace and war, his tongue was possessed of a redemptive magic. No barriers of creed could stand against a philanthropy which was rooted in the profoundest perception of the eternal verities. To such a mind and heart, every problem presents itself in its largest aspects alone. To such an intelligence the accidents of time and place are but the light which lends to the landscape of life its unfailing perspective.

"The ordinary forms of praise are the merest impertinence in the case of him whose whole nature bore the ineffaceable impress of the Most High. He was truly 'one that feared God and eschewed evil.' With an unshakable grasp on the underlying laws of the universe, he expounded the truths of religion with awful earnestness and power. A past master of all the refinements of our English speech, the resources of his oratory were but the scabbard for a blade of celestial temper. The grandeurs and the niceties of phrase simply served to set forth the symmetry of his thought, as the toga's graceful folds revealed the giant form of the masterful Roman. Through the warp and woof of his memorable deliverances there ran the golden threads of pathos and sympathy. The immemorial streams of human achievement were mingled in that flood of intellectual and moral strength, as mighty rivers 'lose themselves in the main waters.'

"Whether Dr. Palmer spoke from the pulpit or the platform, he fused the earnestness of the Hebrew seer with the perfect beauty of which classic Greece is the matchless exemplar.

"In an age whose besetting sin is a crass materialism, the example of this heroic type is continually needed, to redeem the masses from the thralldom of passion. Controversy may rage about doubtful points of doctrine, but the essential truths of religion, as mirrored in a life so perfectly pure and consistent, are quite beyond the sphere of the casuist. We instinctively feel that such manhood will approve itself noble metal by whatever edge of experience it may chance to be tried. The declining years of these paladins of humanity are the final touches of the supreme sculptor's chisel which simply serve to draw the finest lines of beauty from the marble.

"This old city has a stormy past, and we dare not hope that the future will bring calm in its train. Standing about the bier of the foremost moulder of our public opinion, we should resolve that his teaching and example shall find an undying echo in our polity and practice. If we be tempted to substitute the suggestions of greed for the commands of conscience, let us recall the accents of a voice which was never raised to plead the merits of a creed so base. In this solemn hour all right thinking men and women must be stirred by thoughts which transcend the commonplaces of grief. The cry of sorrow will be merged in the note of triumph over the career of one who was ever 'true to the kindred points of heaven and home.' To men of this flawless fibre death is but a momentary pause in a victorious march; for them there is an eternal meaning in the glorious words of the apostle: 'I have fought a good fight, I have finished my course, I have kept the faith.'"

From his old friend, one of his hearers for forty years, we have:

"REV. B. M. PALMER, D.D., LL.D."

"A prince of Israel's prophet line lies dead.
The forum and the marts of 'change are still,
The tidings swift through all the land have sped.
A city mourns; with crowds the churches fill.
The church he loved, where long his voice was heard,
Is draped in mourning garb, with honor crowned.
A wise and mighty teacher of God's word,
On mission grand with soul inspiring sound.

"A prince who largess gave on every side,
Rich treasures gleaned of high enraptured thought,
From mountain peaks, where strong-winged spirits bide
And truth in pure ethereal realms is sought;
Its heavenly light oft on his features shone
When, soaring high on Faith's exultant wing,
He told of joys celestial and the Throne,
And the sweet hymn that ransomed spirits sing.

"He wrestled oft with some majestic theme,
As patriarch of old with angels strove,
Of Law Divine that sways all thought supreme,
And bids the circling worlds in order move.
But most, with words of sweetest grace, he showed
How Love beyond compare, in glory bright,

From Eden's dawn through all the ages glowed,
And shed on ways of God effulgent light.

"Unvexed by human praise or greed of power,
He measured all life's duties, great or small,
In sacred work that filled each passing hour,
And nearer grew to hearts and homes of all.
Calm and self-poised, when trouble stirred the land,
His strength to every righteous cause he gave,
And oft was called to lead a struggling band
'Gainst social wrong, or public issues grave.

"Oh, noble soul! On virtue's side so strong;
Beloved of God and man for pious deeds,
With thoughts so high above the idle throng,
Yet large of heart for others' faith and creed,
His loyal work and zeal for truth shall stand
On grand historic scroll with princely name,
While grateful hearts through this extended land
Shall glow with lasting love to crown his fame."

"WM. O. ROGERS."

"Madison, N. J., 1902.

Tributes were published by the score. Some of the ablest paid were those by the Rev. Drs. Nall, in the *Presbyterian Quarterly;* Mallard, in the *Union Seminary Magazine* and in the *Homiletic Review.*

The flood of affection and admiration for this great man poured itself out in like manner through the channel of private correspondence. A few specimens of the letters that came to the family, at 1718 Palmer Avenue, are presented as representative types:

From the Rev. Prof. R. A. Webb, D.D.:

"CLARKSVILLE, TENN., May 29, 1902.

"MY DEAR MRS. CALDWELL: I beg you, and all the household, to accept my sincere sympathies in the great bereavement which you have experienced in the death of your great and good and illustrious father.

"Our whole Church participates in this sorrow, and stands with bowed head by the grave of him who was the confessed prince of us all.

"All American Christendom feels the loss which has come from the silencing of that voice which so superlatively told the story of Jesus and His love.

"Many public prayers were offered in this community for his life;

that not being the will of God, the suppliants have turned to bearing his whole household to the throne of heavenly grace.

"May that Gospel which he so eloquently taught could take the gloom out of sorrow, the despair out of life, and the sting out of death, supply all your needs in this distressing hour.

"I beg to be remembered to Dr. Caldwell and all the family.

"Very truly yours, R. A. WEBB."

From Rev. S. A. King, D.D., Waco, Texas, dated June 2, 1902:

"He was the grandest man I ever knew, and by far the greatest preacher I ever heard—and I have heard the most noted preachers in America and Great Britain. I said in my telegram that there had been no greater preacher or grander man since Paul. At the same time his humility and simplicity and absence of self-assertion were as remarkable as his genius and eloquence.

"All men knew his transcendent greatness but himself."

From the Hon. Charles E. Hooker, member of the United States Congress:

WASHINGTON, D. C., June 11, 1902.

Mrs. Caldwell, No. 1718 *Palmer Avenue, New Orleans, La.*

"MY DEAR MADAME: I have heard, with profound sorrow, of the death of your honored father. I had the honor to be associated with him in many of the annual meetings of the Army of Tennessee, of which he was the battle chaplain, and of which I am an honorary member.

"A native of my old State, of South Carolina, he removed in early life to Louisiana. His long and useful life not only extends in its influence to his native and adopted States, but extends all over our own country, and covers the whole world with its Christian love and charity for his kind, whatever their text or creed or belief.

"I could not permit this sad occasion of his demise to pass without expressing to you my deep and sincere sympathy with you in the great calamity which has befallen his family and his country.

"With expressions of highest regard,

"Most sincerely yours,

"CHAS. E. HOOKER."

From the Hon. Chas. E. Fenner, of New Orleans:

"GRAND NATIONAL HOTEL, LUCERNE, June 20, 1902.

"*Prof. Caldwell.*

"MY DEAR SIR: I address this to you as the medium for communicating to the family of my dear and venerated friend, Dr. Palmer, my profound sympathy with them in the great loss which they have sustained. In my long voyage from New Orleans and the constant traveling which followed it, without view of any American papers, the sad news only reached me on my arrival here, when I received a letter from Mr. Hincks, accompanied with copies of the New Orleans papers announcing his death, with glowing tributes to his memory and touching accounts of the universal grief which fell on our entire community, without distinction of rank or race or creed.

"I was not unprepared for the news, although when I left (on May 18) all reports of his condition were favorable. Still I somehow felt that it would be little less than a miracle if at his age and with the infirmities to which he was subject he should survive so terrible a shock. While cherishing all the hope I could, I could not escape the sad foreboding that his noble life had received a fatal wound from which it could not recover. Often during my wanderings has my mind reverted to him with hope that my foreboding might prove ill founded and that the miracle of his recovery might be vouchsafed. If there were ever a life worthy of being saved by a miracle, surely it was his; but one wiser than we, who alone could have performed it, deemed it better that the grand life, having achieved the acme of its beauty and beneficence, should end and be transfigured from a living inspiration into an enduring and ennobling memory.

"I well remember hearing, many years ago, Col. Wm. Preston Johnston introduce Dr. Palmer at a great anti-lottery meeting, as 'the most illustrious citizen of Louisiana.' I echoed the sentiment at the time, and my admiration of him at that time expressed in that eulogium, has strengthened with every passing year during which I have watched the 'daily beauty in his life' and observed the expanding and far-reaching influence of his elevated character. I am quite sure that the entire people of Louisiana indorse to-day the sentiment of Col. Johnston, and feel that they have lost their 'most illustrious citizen.'

"Amongst the irreparable losses that his death inflicts on our whole community, I may be permitted to say that none will be more keenly felt than that of his presence among the administrators of Tulane University. His superb culture, broad and liberal views, long experience and practical wisdom, and, above all, his optimistic and enthusiastic determination to develop the university and to permit nothing to stand in the way of its growth, with his buoyant confidence that, however we might temporarily exceed immediate resources, new means would come to us in the future, made him an invaluable member of the Board whose loss can never be supplied.

"Personally, I have received from Dr. Palmer many evidences of his regard, which I treasure amongst my most precious souvenirs. As one who truly loved and revered him, I crave the privilege of extending to his loved ones my most sincere sympathy. In their descent from such a man they have a patent of nobility far exceeding ducal or even royal titles. "Yours faithfully,

"CHAS. E. FENNER."

Sunday evening, November 16, 1902, a memorial service was held in his honor in the First Presbyterian Church. The principal address was delivered by the Rev. Dr. Eugene Daniel, of Lewisburg, W. Va., who was in the fullest sympathy with Dr. Palmer in respect to theological and ecclesiastical views. Of this very able address use shall be made in the next and concluding chapter of this volume.

This chapter may well close with the tribute uttered on the same occasion by the distinguished Rabbi I. L. Leucht, of New Orleans:

Rabbi Leucht, in opening his address, announced his text from Job 29: 7-18, reading the passages as follows:

"'When I went out to the gate close by the city, when in the open place I established my seat; young men saw me and hid themselves, and the aged rose up and remained standing; princes stopped in the midst of (their) words and laid their hand on their mouth; the voice of nobles was arrested, and their tongue cleaved to their palate; for the ear that heard me called me happy; and the eye that saw me bore witness for me; because I delivered the poor that cried, and the fatherless, yea, that had none to help him. The blessing of him that was ready to perish came upon me; and the heart of the widow I caused to sing for joy. I took righteousness as my garment, and it clothed me; as a robe and a mitre was justice unto me. Eyes was I to the blind; and feet to the lame was I. A father was I to the needy; and the cause of him I knew not I used to investigate. And I broke the cutting-teeth of the wrong-doer, and out of his teeth I cast down his prey. And I said then, 'In the midst of my nest shall I depart hence, and like the sand shall I have many days.'

"This grand picture of a righteous, honored and pious man, unrolled by the Sacred Book," said Rabbi Leucht, "would be in itself a tribute of love and affection to the memory of the man in whose honor we have assembled here to-night. His character had been formed in the mould of the good men of the Bible, and Job's parable grew into reality in the personality of our departed friend.

"Men and women of our Commonwealth, I do not come here to-night to praise him or to add a new tribute to a sainted memory. I have come to weep a tear with you in a common grief and to point out a ray of light in our bereavement. A tear has no fatherland and knows of no theology—it is the tribute the human heart pays to its own sorrow—and it is also a symbol of joy when we have found consolation and peace, when at last a beam of hope pierces the clouds of pain and woe. This grand privilege has been accorded to me, not because I deserve to stand here in the place hallowed by him; not because my weak words can ever pay him proper homage. No; I have come because I loved him and he was my friend for so many years, and because we together were seeking light. Although seeking it upon different paths, we met and never quarreled as to its source. And here at once I touch the pivot upon which the character of Dr. Palmer revolved—broad-mindedness and large-heartedness. Only great men have the capacity of harboring strong convictions, and at the same time of allowing others to differ; only good men will take an opponent by the hand and say, 'Be my friend.' No one doubts that he clung to his faith with a pertinacity that knew no compromise. What had once crystallized into conviction—be it religion, politics or social problems—he never deviated from it for a moment. No matter how the world stormed against it, no matter what evolution would take place in the minds of his colleagues, pupils or contemporaries, he stood fast and immovable upon the rock of his judgment; and no doubt he took it unaltered and unabridged into his grave. Bigots and zealots are recruited from the ranks of such men—but Palmer rose to the level of forbearance and broad-mindedness rarely found, pardon me, among theologians.

Manhood prevails in life. With the scalpel of his intellect he exposed every proposition that came before him, and, in spite of his own findings, he had a comprehension and a deep regard for the opinions of others. And he honored probity, uprightness, loyalty to one's self and principle—with his unstinted regard, admitting, however, that after all righteousness and virtue may go furthest before the august Judge in the heavens above—and here I may quote the words spoken by him in that touching incident, when, standing in the pulpit of the late Rabbi Gutheim, paying him the tribute of affection: 'After all, it is manhood that prevails in life; it is manhood that rules, and he is the mightiest monarch of us all and sways the loftiest sceptre who reigns through the honesty of his own nature and by the majesty of his superior will.' It is the loss of such a king among men we are now called to mourn.

"He had a keen insight into human nature, and his own strength prompted his forbearance with the weakness of man and endowed him with comprehension coupled with pity for the frailty of the race. There was not a trace of self-righteousness nor pious pomposity in him; he walked in the midst of his brethren, sowing seed, correcting evil, consoling and uplifting, unassumingly and modestly, asking neither reward, neither honor, nor distinction. He did not turn away from the sinner with a feeling of horror and disgust, but as a true physician of the soul; he knew its wounds and its sores and he reached the sweet balm of consolation and faith to every bruised heart. He never gathered wisdom to hang it as an ornament around his neck, for all he knew, all he was, and all he aimed at was placed at the service of others, for guidance and for betterment. Truth falling from his lips never wounded and gave man back to himself. I believe that this whole community viewed him as being her public conscience. He was the man to whom she turned in moments of great public anxiety, in great public questions, for we all knew that after he had once spoken on which side the banner of victory would be unfurled. In such critical times he knew neither friend nor foe. His eloquence rose to a height where once the prophet of old dwelled, his voice rolled on impregnated with passion divine, and his words, inspired from the crest of his own intellect, carried conviction, sweeping us along even against our will, impelling obedience to the demands of a great, comprehensive mind. Therefore, when he went home to his Father's house, we all became poverty stricken. New Orleans had lost her foremost citizen, and many years will fall into the lap of time before another man of his power and influence arises.

"He was not simply public conscience, he was also one of the foremost architects for building character in this community. Dr. Palmer occupied a unique position in this respect. Although a Presbyterian minister, all denominations claimed him as their own. He did not preach in these four walls only; his pulpit was erected upon the height from which all could hear him, and all could admire him, and even when he dwelled with all the vigor of his intellect upon the mandates of his own faith, the very vibrations of his voice, the very trend of his thought, often impressed me as if he had risen higher than himself, gazing loftily over the wall of doctrine and dogma dividing mankind. And when he spoke of ethical truth, of the beauty and glory of the moral law governing man, holding up before him the reward of sacrifice and recompense of selfishness, he reached a degree of eloquence and force rarely equaled by any man in any pulpit throughout the land. For half a century he was a public teacher, and a teacher of the public unconsciously under his sway and guidance, accepting his conception of matters and things as a master's dictum, forming its opinion in the mould of his mind. This explains why his presence at most public functions was sought, and whenever he appeared he at once dignified the occasion above the common, and his personality dispelled any doubt as to the worthiness of the undertaking.

"And when he spoke men listened and waited and watched in silence for his counsel, and vividly I call to my mind what the rabbis of old said in their quaint way: 'When Moses dashed the tables of the covenant into fragments, the form broke, but the letters scattered to the four corners of the earth'—indicating that the breaking of the form cannot destroy the spirit. Thus it seems to me that although his body has crumbled into dust, he has imprinted the beauty of his rounded character upon hundreds and hundreds of his contemporaries, awaking daily within their hearts' shrine his blessed resurrection. We may, therefore, justly apply to him the words of the prophet: 'The law of truth was in his mouth, falsehood was not found on his lips, and many did he turn away from iniquity.'

"*Was a Friend of the Jews.*—When I was honored to come here to-night and participate in this solemn service, the pastor of this church said: 'We wish you to represent your people.' Never was I more willing, never was I more thankful, to be permitted to speak as a Jew. And in this instance it is of lasting historical interest to reproduce the words spoken by Dr. Palmer on several occasions. It was in the year 1882, I believe, when once more my downtrodden brethren were driven out of the dominions of the czar into cruel exile, in spite of the protest of the civilized world, here in our own city a mass meeting was called in order to join in public condemnation, and speakers representing all denominations had rallied, denouncing the terrible edict of the Russian ruler. Dr. Palmer was the last speaker, and when he walked toward the center of the platform there was something indescribably characteristic in his gait. I had the impression as if he was ready to set his heel upon the whole of Russia. His oration grew into a terrible arraignment, thundering against Russian crimes and barbarities, and his prediction of the coming of God's punishment and retribution reminded me of Jeremiah's imprecations against Jerusalem. Finally he turned toward the sufferers, and it was touching indeed how his voice, that had rolled in accents of manly anger, now spoke in the minor key of his soul's anguish, exclaiming: 'When a Hebrew suffers I suffer with him,' and these words since then have been the bonds that linked us to him—even unto death.

"You all yet remember the grand and glorious day when it was vouchsafed to him to behold the dawn of his eightieth anniversary. To our whole community it was like a festive day. His home was a shrine where thousands of pilgrims had wandered to pay their homage. Cardinal and priest, rabbi and rector, representing all faiths, shook him by the hand, exclaiming: 'This is the day of the Lord; let us be glad to rejoice therein.' Among those who came to wish him joy were also the representatives of Touro Synagogue, bringing him as an offering of their affection a loving cup. I see him yet before me, his eyes moist, holding aloft the goblet containing the 'wine of communion,' and his voice trembling in deep emotion as he said: 'The Old and the New Testament come together under this roof to-night, which are the two breasts from which the Church of God, in all ages, has drunk its nourishment. Your sacred books are my sacred books, and in the pulpit, when ministering to the people in God's name, I take the theme of discourse as freely from one as from the other. There ought to be no harsh feelings between the bodies that you and I represent. Let us then cherish in the future, as we have cherished in the past, the point of agreement, that we worship one God common to you and to us according to that law which He proclaimed from Mount Sinai. I can hardly trust myself to utter the emotions which are struggling in my own heart. I never walk the streets and meet one of your faith without feeling a trembling in the palm of my hand, caused by the affection which he feels toward me personally, and it is to-day a renewal of the sentiment which you have under this form reduced to a covenant.' And in referring to Abraham, he continued: 'That covenant will remain until the end of time, and therefore the Hebrew, wherever he is found upon the earth, will always be a body of interest and affection to every Christian heart.'

"*Worship One God.*—Was I wrong when I maintained that his character was formed in the mould of the prophets of old? Is this not a paraphrase of that grand old deathless dictum of humanity? Have we not all one Father? Has not one God created us? Then why shall we deal treacherously one against his brother and profane the name of the Lord? Could we honor our friend more than by writing his golden word: 'In the book of remembrance before Him, for those who fear the Lord and for those who respect His name?' At the sacred shrine of his memory let me say that I believe that it is eminently due to the life and influence of Dr. Palmer that a deep, religious peace reigns supreme in our midst. Thank God, we live in a community where in all public endeavors, in all that tends toward the good of our people, we know of no separating walls. We never ask our neighbor, 'What dost thou believe?' but 'What art thou willing to do for the best interests of our Commonwealth?' We take each other by the hand, exclaiming, 'Let there be no strife between me and thee,' and together we help to build on that great structure where in time to come will be sung a hallelujah by a united mankind. Posterity placing one day the crown of victory on his brow, his tolerance and his love for others will be its brightest gem. After having mourned with you, after I have placed a wreath of immortelles, gathered from the Eden of my own heart, upon the shrine of memory, let me rejoice with you that you had the privilege and the blessing to own him for so many years as your guide, your pastor and your friend. He has taught you, in his own life, how to accept the dispensation of Providence with dignity and resignation, and he who has read his 'Broken Home' will have learned from its pages the heroism of sacrifice and the mastery over death.

"*A Ray of Light.*—There is a ray of light in this gloom. We know that he is not dead—that he is still living, and that his memory will never pale as long as a single heart in this vast Commonwealth will love and revere virtue, honor manliness, piety and truth.

"Let me relate to you in conclusion an old Hebrew legend: When Moses, the great lawgiver, stood upon the crest of Mount Nebo to be gathered to his reward, God would not entrust the Angel of Death with the soul of His most faithful servant, and He Himself descended and kissed the life from his paling lips. When the shepherd did not return to his flock, the anxious children of Israel climbed the mountain to seek and to find him. They found him not, but, in one of the clefts they beheld the heart of Moses, which he had left behind, and the people wept and were consoled. May I not claim for our departed friend that, although we see him no more, his soul, his image and his heart are still here, pulsating among us—never to die? And it is to me as if I heard his voice: 'Weep not and mourn no more—I have fulfilled my mission upon earth. I have lived more than the years allotted to man; I have bequeathed unto you as an inheritance' 'My life and my deeds."' I hear him repeat the words of Elezar: 'Let me not tarry, the Lord has prospered my way—send me hence that I may go to my Master.' May he dwell in the realm of immortality to the end of time."

CHAPTER XXI.

SUMMARY VIEW OF THE MAN AND HIS SERVICES.

HIS PHYSICAL ORGANISM.—DISTINGUISHING TRAITS OF HIS CHARACTER.—THE ENERGY, HARMONY, EASE, POISE AND SPLENDOR OF ALL HIS MENTAL, EMOTIONAL AND PRACTICAL WORKING.—HIS ETHICAL AND RELIGIOUS CHARACTER.—THE UNION IN HIM OF UNCOMPROMISING ALLEGIANCE TO DENOMINATIONAL CREED, WITH AN INCLUSIVE LOVE FOR ALL MANKIND.—TACT.—MAGNETISM, OR CAPACITY FOR LEADERSHIP.—DR. PALMER AS A PREACHER.—AS A PASTOR.—AS A TEACHER.—AS A THEOLOGIAN.—AS CHAMPION OF THE PRINCIPLES AND LEADER OF THE HOSTS OF THE PRESBYTERIAN CHURCH, SOUTH.—AS A PHILOSOPHER.—AS A STATESMAN.—AS A PATRIOTIC CITIZEN.—AS THE HEAD OF A FAMILY.—AS A FRIEND.—AS A SOCIAL SERVANT.—AS A SERVANT OF GOD.

BENJAMIN MORGAN PALMER was under, rather than over, medium height, slight in build, though deep in the chest and somewhat stooped as age came on. He was susceptible of indefinite physical wear and tear, able to endure and equally able to wage unceasing conflict. All his bodily movements were as easy, agile and graceful as those of a leopard. His head was small; its shape would have been a *pons asinorum* to peripatetic phrenologists. His forehead, however, was relatively ample. His eyes were very fine, dark brown, sparkling and brilliant. His mouth was not handsome, but of generous proportions, the most conspicuous feature of his face, suggestive of sweetness and eloquence and strength. His whole lower face was indicative of will power; power to determine and to persist. Taking the entire face into view, one saw written thereon great kindliness, alertness, penetration and force. In his general bearing there was a still more pronounced air of power coupled with dignity, graciousness and utter freedom from self-consciousness. While his physical person did not conspicuously advertise his noble intellectual and practical endowments, it suggested to all shrewd observers, even before they had heard his name or seen his power evidenced in overt fashion, that he was an extraordinary man.

Turning from his physical organism to his faculties of mind, feeling and will, the student of his life observes in Dr. Palmer a very unusual combination of rare endowments. One is struck with the energy, harmony, ease, poise and splendor of all his mental, emotional and practical working. Glancing at his intellectual working, we see him absorbing and acquiring easily the glorious classics of the English tongue, while yet a mere lad at his mother's knee, well prepared for college at the age of fourteen; and so easily mastering the literature of theology, at the age of twenty-one to twenty-three, that his fellow students at Columbia were wont to say: "Palmer has only to put a book under his pillow and go to sleep; he will awake the next morning knowing all that is in the book." We see him taking in knowledge so naturally, easily and rapidly that all through his life only brief periods of special preparation are needed in order to his furnishing himself for noble and instructive addresses on topics outside the pale of his ordinary studies, and that, too, before exacting audiences, keyed to the highest point of expectation. We see this power of acquisition evidenced at length in the impression which he so frequently made of being approximately universal in knowledge.

His dialectical faculty worked as efficiently and splendidly as his acquisitive faculties. His vast acquisitions were stored away in his capacious memory in a logical order, and were drawn forth from that great storehouse under the same rigorous canons. His power to unfold and elaborate the logical implications in a word of truth or a dictum of error was nothing short of masterful. The possession and use of this power gave to his ministry a prophetic aspect, and an aspect of great originality. In bringing out the implications of a truth he seemed to the less logical to be bringing somewhat that was new to the mind of man. His deductions were so remorseless in their sweep of the plain involved that he was wont to make the impression upon his audiences that he was one whose teachings were as unanswerable as they were impressive.

His constructive imagination was not less active than his acquisitive and elaborative faculties. We see its operation in his permanent bent toward series of sermons, on some one particular line or other, tending to bring out the whole rotund and beautiful truth on the particular line. We see it in his love for systematic theology, which was so great that he would preach that queen of the sciences in the pulpit. We see it in his eternal effort to expound the philosophy of God's dealings with man. This faculty made it inevitable that he should plan and build structures. Had there been no systematic theology he must have taken the materials from the word of God and builded one up. The operation of the faculty is still more beautifully and generally evidenced in his trying God's truth on the whole face of nature about him, and thus vivifying it for himself and all who heard him. This faculty made him a poet, an interpreter of nature as well as of God. He understood, at least in part, the things around him; and could talk in terms of the material while expounding the spiritual.

These very remarkable mental endowments were thoroughly trained. The training was intense from the time of his conversion till he was seventy years of age. It never ceased altogether till the day of the fatal street car accident. His intellectual development placed him amongst the few very foremost men of his age in point of mind.

He was not more remarkable for the proportions of intellect than he was for those of the heart, for his susceptibilities and emotions. His was a very sensitive nature, an instrument with ten thousand delicate strings on which Providence could play with the fingers of every man, woman and child with whom he was brought into touch, and find a response in answer to every touch of any string. Answering to this sensitive endowment was another of active, emotive desire, rising in his early youth often to the pitch of passion; and not less strong but brought under almost perfect control after he reached manhood. He was a great lover. He loved his wife, loved his children, loved his parents, loved his brothers and sisters; he loved the people of his pastorate, he loved his friends everywhere, he loved the people of his city, his State, his section, his whole country. He loved all classes and conditions. He loved all men and he loved them intensely, because he loved God. He hated well and strongly, too, as is inevitable; hated evil, and the more dangerous the form of it the more he hated it. This intensity of feeling was steadily firing him to endeavor, making it inevitable that he should use his great talents.

Once these vigorous likes and dislikes, guided by his equally clear and discriminating judgments as to the true, beautiful and good and their contradictories, had issued in choices, he was no man to be easily turned from the choices. Particularly, having explored with his mind and embraced with his heart what he conceived to be the fundamental principles of proper human conduct, he became as immovable as the Alps. All the world could see in him wonderful persistence in regard to religious convictions and political theories. Many looked upon this persistence with wonder. They could not explain it. The explanation, however, is not difficult. He had adopted each set of principles for cause, and through conflict, on grounds that had appeared ample notwithstanding all objections. He had thought the matters through, had deliberately reached his conclusions, and had made his decisions. Thenceforth the matter was settled. Others might change with the passing years, but he changed not. Stonewall Jackson was no more confident that his brilliant plans for a campaign, or a battle, were correct than was Dr. Palmer that he was right as to the great principles he had chosen in the sphere of religion, morals and civil government. He never questioned whether his beginnings were essentially correct, in his mature life. It was a fixed fact in his mind and heart that they were substantially right; and that it was his duty to give himself to a life in accord with the principles. This helped to make him a hero. In every time of stress he was to be found just where these principles logically led him.

Other very remarkable features of Dr. Palmer's immaterial constitution were the harmony, ease and poise with which his great faculties worked. Some men, even men with very considerable achievement, work only with much friction, wear and tear. Along every line he seemed to do what he did with ease, as if born to do that thing and to do it easily. This was no doubt due in part to his original endowments, but also to that large mastery which he so easily acquired over himself. The quality of self-control, perfect self-mastery, was one he valued very greatly. He had struggled hard to acquire it, and he had made it his own to such a degree that when he was in the pulpit or on the platform it was hardly possible to disconcert him or to interfere in the least with the order of his mental processes. Nor is evidence wanting that in his daily life he exercised over himself from hour to hour this same mastery. His faculties wrought and wrought together, therefore, as so many well directed and well trained servants. Hence their easy, balanced working.

Another remarkable feature was the splendor with which he worked. There was a dignity and majesty about all his mental operations. This may be explained by the strength of the whole bundle of his faculties and their vigor and activity, and particularly by the great force and vitality of his faculties of the constructive imagination and the esthetic. His faculty of the constructive imagination has already been noted. His faculty of the esthetic was equally pronounced, though severely regulated. He had a great love for the beautiful and power to perceive wherein beauty lay, in nature and art, particularly in literary art. From the former of these faculties came dignity and majesty of form; from the latter came beauty. Hence his thought clothed itself in splendid garments. He could only speak in stately and beautiful phraseology. He early formed the habit of such speech. He carried it with him into the street, into the parlor, into inmost recesses of his own home. It never degenerated into stilt. It was never moved by pedantry. Simplicity was wedded to his splendor of diction and style. He spoke as one who had dwelt long on a Christian and literary Olympus, and who had while there wrought into a fixed faculty of his own the power to think in the high fashion of the place; for here, by a word, he sets the imagination a-stretch, like John Milton, or the sense of the awful or the sublime, like Dante, or Job, or Isaiah, or John the apostle in Patmos. Then, with a single stroke, he lays open an aspect of the human heart, like the Bard of Avon, or Paul the apostle, or King David, or Solomon. He shows a readiness, an excisiveness, a clearness and a sufficiency of thought which mark him as akin to those great spirits. Apparently he saw the world lit up with God's great glory, and when he talked of it to his fellow men he tipped it with the sheen of light in which he saw it.

Thus his thinking had large, noble and peculiar attraction. Men heard somewhat from his lips that was fresh and new as to form, even though as to matter it might be, in other men's mouths, a commonplace.

If his mental operations were clothed with splendor, his feelings and his will were similarly garbed. Hence men called him knightly; said that in him were embodied the highest and most knightly ideals of the old South. He was not simply heroic. His heroism was of the type of the Chevalier de Bayard. He was not simply one of the truest and staunchest friends; he was a friend who felt all the dignity of the relationship, saw and knew a beauty and a sweetness in it which it is given to but few to see, so that he gave to his friends a new apprehension of the loftiness of friendship. "A tenderer heart never beat," says one who knew him well. He was not simply a good, faithful, husband and father; he added dignity to the term "husband" and the term "father." In short, in every relationship, whether civil, ecclesiastic, social or domestic, he reflected upon the relation a moral elevation, beauty and splendor by the manner in which he bore himself therein. It is not meant, of course, that his mental, esthetic and moral machinery never creaked, much less that it was perfect in its action. Perfection is not given to mortal man. What is asserted here is that large relative excellence must be accorded to Dr. Palmer in all these respects.

Religion is the most important concern of man. A man's religion is his most important bearing Godward, or worldward. It colors the working of every faculty and of the whole soul. Dr. Palmer had a grand religion, the religion of Abraham, Isaac and Jacob, of Moses, the prophets and the psalmists, of Jesus of Nazareth and the College of the Apostles. He interpreted their teaching for himself, following, however, as they appeared to have light to give, the greatest interpreters since the apostolic age—Anthanasius and Augustine and Anselm and Calvin and Thornwell, and others of the same class. He made an honest application of the truths of this religion to his own life; and under the good hand of God led a beautiful life. One of the features of his religious life was a remarkable sense of obligation to do that which was right. A distinguished representative of the modern Jewish faith has said that, in a philosophy of Dr. Palmer's life, a large place must be given to "his sense of obligation to righteousness." "Why did he plead for oppressed Jews? Because righteousness dictated that he should so plead. Why did he condemn certain phases in the history of the Northern Presbyterians, even at the cost of being charged with narrow bitterness of hate? Because, as he saw things, that Church had gone wrong in those particulars, and he was morally obliged to condemn it for so doing." There can be no doubt that righteousness held a large place in his religion. It has always held a large place in the ecclesiastical breed of which he came. The law was the great ideal which Calvin and all his kind, since or before, back to Moses, would have realized. Yet in Dr. Palmer's religious thinking and experience righteousness was not primal. Justification by faith through the merits of the Lord Jesus Christ was primal. The sinner being thus justified and enabled by the effectual working of the Holy Spirit to strive successfully toward the keeping of the law, was a new power fully obligated—obligated by infinite love to keep God's holy law. He saw the Lord as high and lifted up, the holy, holy, holy Lord God of hosts, of whose glory the whole earth was full. He saw the law as the transcript of the great perfections of God. It was to be held aloft, honored, kept up to the limits of the possibilities. Even there man's obligation did not end. He owed it to keep the law absolutely, because it was right and because the Creator and Moral Governor of the Universe bade it. But still more imperative was the obligation to keep it because the infinite God in the second personality had incarnated himself and paid the penalty of the broken law, and because the Spirit had made him a new man in Christ Jesus.

A corollary of this magnification of righteousness was a tremendous notion of the ill-desert of sin. It has been said that no one oftener confessed his own sins and the sins of his people. It may be said with equal truth that no one made sin more heinous in his confessions. Sin was viewed as not only against a Creator and Moral Governor of the Universe of infinite excellence, but against the Redeemer God.

His conception of God's holiness and the obligation of man to righteousness and away from sin, lent a majesty to his character. His conception of Christ's sacrifice and its necessity lent a sweetness, a humility, a readiness to sacrifice himself, not in the way of expiation, but for the edification of his brethren in the flesh. He was always sweetly generous in judging his brethren. He interpreted them habitually in terms of himself, or something better still, and so saw them as fairer than they were, of larger powers and nobler, loftier character. His purse was open to every man in need as long as it contained anything. Indeed, it has been sometimes said that he was "extravagantly liberal." That he often gave unwisely can hardly be doubted. But he was careful thus not to fail to help in every case of real need. His home, too, was open. In a thousand ways he would sacrifice self and toil and suffer in the behalf of others. He followed his Lord in this habit of life without cant and without sanctimony—a pleasant, cheery, hopeful, genial gentleman.

A marked trait of the man was the union in behalf of uncompromising allegiance and fealty to a denominational creed, and the most inclusive affection for all men, even for those warring against the very creed for which he would have given his life. That he possessed this trait was recognized by all who knew him well. Those who only knew him through his polemic writings might charge him with being unforgiving and unloving. Says his neighbor, the Rev. J. H. Nall: "There could not possibly be a greater mistake; nor could graver injustice be done the noblest of men. No man was ever more free from all malice, envy, bitterness toward any human being, and disciple of the Lord, any branch of the Church. There was no man of broader sympathy, more catholic spirit." In proof of this Dr. Nall cites the assembled, bereft multitude around his open tomb, made up of Protestants of every name, Roman Catholics, priests and people, Jews and men of the world, the similar multitudes that had packed his church at the hour of the funeral service and had lined the streets with heads uncovered all the way from the church to the cemetery. They loved him, they honored the very ground he walked on, were prouder of their city because he had lived in it. They loved no cold, hard, unrelenting man. They loved him because he loved them. Yet they knew that he was a Presbyterian of the Presbyterians, a Calvinist of the Calvinists, a Christian of the Christians.

Another trait was his tact, or large common sense in dealing with his fellow men. He seemed to have an instinct for approaching problems social, political, ecclesiastical, precisely at the spot where his labors would be most easily effective. A shrewd fellow Presbyter, in illustrating this point, has said that often his brethren seemed to themselves to institute and carry on measures which they had never thought of, but for Dr. Palmer. He, the real institutor and director of the measures, seemd to be taking little part. But the thing which he desired was done. Others had come to desire it also and had, with a little public favoring help from his potent hand, done the thing. His kindliness of heart, so great that he was always on guard against giving any one a needless wound, and so great that he was ever seeking to do some service to every man with whom he came in contact, was always coupled with his power to devise wise plans, and with his vigorous and indomitable resolution in pushing his plans, so that the righteous plan, and of the least friction, was always the one he sought and wished to push.

Still another trait was magnetism, or capacity for leadership. This quality was his to a large degree. He, perhaps, never belonged to an ecclesiastical court of any rank after he was thirty-five years of age in which he would not have been counted one of the leaders. And when, on the evening of his famous address against the Louisiana Lottery, before a mass meeting of his fellow citizens of New Orleans, Col. Wm. Preston Johnston introduced him as the first citizen of Louisiana, it was only a gracious recognition of the simple truth that in the State, too, men looked to him first, in the titanic struggle with the lottery fiend, to lead them. His sanity of judgment, his recognized keenness and purity of conscience, the sufficiency of his comprehension of the gravity of every situation, and of what was demanded of himself and his fellow citizens under the circumstances, and his practical wisdom in union with his magnificent powers of impressing his views on the public, made him inevitably a leader. The same quality appeared even in a social gathering. He was a man around whom men liked to cluster. He was humble, arrogating nothing to himself. He was there to serve. In the social spheres, as elsewhere, he ever earnestly sought to give some person in need of it a friendly and uplifting word, or touch of the hand of brotherly sympathy; but in so doing he found himself surrounded by men and women who luxuriated in his conversation and society.

However crude this outline sketch of the personality of Benjamin Morgan Palmer, it will at least serve to recall the more adequate sketch given, and largely by his own master hand, through sermon and speech and familiar letter in the body of this book.

His personality being of such a sort, his endowments so noble, his acquirements so extensive and varied, his religion so august and so simple and so Christian, it was necessary that he should play many great parts in the historic drama covered by his long life. In the stirring and changeful period through which he lived, and in his particular environment, it was necessary that, under the good hand of God, he should play some very important roles, as preacher, pastor, teacher, theologian, polemic, philosopher, statesman, patriot, head of a family, as a friend, a social servant and servant of God.

AS A PREACHER.—Dr. Palmer was one of the few greatest preachers of this century, and of the first nineteen centuries of the Christian era. By the people of the Southwest this view was commonly, and perhaps almost universally, held; and in every other section whither his fame hath blown the same view has found its advocates. It is believed that a fuller knowledge of him and his sermons would result in the general prevalence of the view. He was a real preacher of the Gospel. He had studied the evidences of its being the word of God; had deliberately made up his mind that they were valid, and that the Bible is the word of God; had set that down as a fixed fact in his creed. He gave himself to preaching that word. Whatever others might preach, science, sociology, politics, literature, he would preach the Gospel, and the Gospel only, from his pulpit. It was a thing the world needed worst of all, and that need he would fill. He preached the Westminster interpretation of the Bible, preached it all; the doctrines of the Trinity and the incarnation; the doctrines of sin and grace, the doctrine of the atonement, the doctrines of regeneration and conversion, justification and sanctification. He even preached boldly and frequently on those points of Calvinism which have been so bitterly attacked in every generation, viz.: Total depravity, unconditional election, particular redemption, efficacious grace and perseverance therein unto the end. He was a theological preacher from the very order of his mind. He was bound to systematize, to theorize facts, to endeavor to discover their philosophy. He was not even afraid to use technical theological terms. He could well afford to do this, for he had the faculty of making these terms easily comprehensible to his hearers. Knowing the truth of the Bible experimentally, and preaching what by experience he knew to be true, he communicated, as by a contagion, the affection of his own mind to the truth. To the minds thus opened he poured in the great central doctrines of Christianity. He was particularly happy in preaching the great doctrine of the atonement by the cross, but the gift of popularization of all the great doctrines was his. He was a living refutation of the widely current notion that the day of doctrinal preaching is over. For thirteen years in one pulpit and forty-six years in another, he was preëminently a doctrinal preacher, and a preacher of the very marrow of the doctrines of sacred Scriptures. He delighted in preaching the great cardinal doctrines. He not only did not desire to preach the mere fringes of truth in which certain clerical hunters for the novel seem to take delight; he apparently took little pleasure in preaching the lesser doctrines of Christianity, the mint, anise and cummin of religion. Yet he preached the whole Gospel. So much for the matter of his preaching.

Capable of the finest expository preaching, he was driven by the bent of his mind to topical preaching very largely. In this method the logical and systematizing tendencies have the freest and noblest application. His plan, usually, then, upon announcing his text, was to show exactly what the text, in its historical setting connections, meant. This he did by a careful exegesis, giving often, in this preliminary step, as much matter, and in better form, as many ministers put into a whole sermon. Then having set forth in perspicuous terms the doctrinal teaching, which he had drawn from the text, he would proceed to enforce it by a series of arguments, generally powerful in themselves and so happily put as to carry general conviction to the hearts of his hearers. Following this would come an application which was often threefold, or more, in the course of which the truth, previously developed by interpretation and argument, would be pressed with all his powers of appeal and persuasion.

He was a magician in the use of the English tongue. His vocabulary was vast and, in virtue of habit in use, was choice, pure, powerful, pictorial, vivid as life. He made a large use of metaphor. Says a most competent student of his sermons: "He was not given to relating anecdotes or drawing pathetic scenes for the mere effect of exciting emotions. He did not indulge in very frequent or extended illustrations, like Henry Ward Beecher. But more than any other man I have read or heard, he would put metaphor, sometimes in a single word, and suggest the full illustration while not elaborately expressing it. And he would do this as naturally as a spring would bubble or a bird would sing. Would he oppose subordinating the Church to the State? He would say, 'Chain not the Church of Christ to the chariot wheels of Caesar.' Would he speak of humility as a prerequisite to lofty communion with God in prayer, he would say: 'The bird stoops upon the branch of the tree before it springs and soars in the air.' I took the charming book on Prayer and on one page containing eight sentences I found that six out of eight contained metaphors. This lends the charm of poetry to his preaching. The mind is delighted, often not knowing the reason."[1]

Thus Dr. Palmer gave his people rich truths in the garb of noble and poetic language, language which made his thought clear and beautiful to the ordinary capacity. And these rich truths, clothed in fitting phrase, were made more acceptable to the hearer by the bearing of the preacher in the pulpit. Divining the attitude of his audience, he took them apparently on their own ground, into the study of his subject. He carried himself as their leader with perfect grace. No monarch ever bore himself with a port more becoming his position than that of Dr. Palmer became his. His humility was manifest, his fine sense of propriety met the expectation of every audience. His physical movements were a delight and a marvel to all his auditors. He seemed so free and so easy, so evidently at home, as he strode from one side of his platform to the other, resting his hand on a chandelier, stood on tiptoe, on the very edge of the platform, swung himself back. His gestures, not very frequent were as appropriate and telling as they were graceful. Agile as a leopard, he did not have to strive for grace of movement. It was his by heredity, and it counted, amongst his minor attractions, not a little.

His perfect self-control with any theme and any audience, united with his other great gifts, enabled him to control everybody in the assembly before him. In his apparent self-mastery men saw somewhat that so won their respect, that they could not be ignoble enough not to behave aright. When now and again a fanatic attempted to interrupt the quiet course of the

---

[1]Dr. Eugene Daniel, in his *In Memoriam* address.

exercises he found to his own cost that the little gentleman in the pulpit was the master.

It will be recalled that this little gentleman had a way of seeming to grow big while he was preaching. Instances of the illusion have already been given. The Rev. Dr. R. Q. Mallard has left the following paragraph, which affords further proof of the fact of the phenomenon:

> "A lady introduced to him in my presence in a parlor in Natchez, who had never before met him out of the pulpit, exclaimed, 'Why, Dr. Palmer, I thought you were a large man!' The other was told me recently by a member of the family. A Texan, drawn by the reputation of his church, was disappointed to find, as he supposed, a stranger of unprepossessing appearance in his pulpit, and was tempted to leave, but staying, was first struck by his reading, then by his prayer, and then, as he progressed in his sermon, he grew until he seemed to be a giant. He stayed over another Sunday and told his story to the doctor himself."

His organs of speech were his greatest physical endowments for the function of preaching. His voice was "wonderful," indefinitely flexible and of great compass, adapting itself to the size of the audience room and the audience, always musical, even when thundering denunciations against sin and wrong, and often as sweet as a mother's lullaby. Apparently no description could do justice to this wonderful instrument. As he had the power by his choice of words, of calling up before the mind pictures, his own pictures of the things of which he spoke, so he had the power of expressing every emotion in his voice. His voice thrilled with joy, was swathed with woe, pulsated with hope, wailed with despair, responded to and interpreted to his congregation every phase of every emotion of his soul. So, at least, it seemed to his people. Some of them say that he never shed a tear in the pulpit, so perfect was his self-control, and that "all his tears were in his voice;" that often there were "tears in his voice," often victory, often veneration, adoration; often condemnation, reprobation; oftener solicitation, pleading; oftenest love, love for God, love for his brethren, love for all men.

Still more important was the known character of this man of great intellectual furnishing, great attractions of bearing, wonderful gifts of speech and superb voice. He was known to be a man to be found whenever wanted, and always found in the path of light and the path of duty. He was known to be living a life of self-sacrifice. He was known to be a man of heart, going out to his people, and to all men, in their joys and sorrows, having a wondrous power of sympathizing with all those in grief. "By nature, by God's grace, by his own experience, he was made with a soul to feel another's woe," says Dr. Eugene Daniel. Dr. Daniel continues: "I remember well that an elder of the first church I ever served was in this city, and heard Dr. Palmer preach on Sunday after the preacher himself had been in sorrow. The subject was 'The Holy Spirit as the Comforter.' Said this elder: 'I was never so wrought upon in my life; the tension was so great that I felt positively sick when the exhaustion of reaction from my strained elevation came on.' His power of pathos—for that is what it was, power—was plainly never sought by him or cultivated by him; it was just naturally and simply within him, and the ease with which he wielded it was nothing less than majestic."[2]

In virtue of the possession of this power, of putting his soul in the stead of his fellow's soul, and the great faith by which he endured as seeing Him who is invisible, he could flood with hope a great congregation or an individual heart bowed down with sorrow, dissipating the clouds and fog in which they walked as the sun floods hilltop and valley with his brightness. The character of a man, noble in all respects, so sympathetic and so loving, gave vast weight to every utterance.

Another feature of his preaching should be briefly noted, viz.: Its positive and assured character. He did not preach "ifs," doubts and negations of Bible teaching. Having determined for himself the fact of the inspired and infallible character of Holy Writ, he preached it as the veritable truth of God. After the careful study of a passage, and reaching the conviction that he had its meaning, he went before his people with authority approaching that of the prophet to the degree within which he felt that he approached the meaning of his text; he went before them also with the power springing from the realization of the truth of his Scripture in his own experience. He spoke with positiveness and conviction. This confidence, in the genuineness and authenticity of his massage,

---

[2] *In Memoriam*, p. 10.

was perhaps not the only reason for his ringing dogmatic method of preaching. The very order of his mind, its penetrativeness, strength and general trustworthiness in all its workings, would naturally make him a positive teacher in the pulpit. His certainty, too, that he had been called to preach the Gospel was not without its effect on the general tone of his preaching.

It was as a preacher that he did his greatest work. He was prodigiously endowed for the function. He justly ranks with the great preachers of the ages. He possessed the power of pathos of Massillon and the sustained majesty of eloquence of Bossuet. He justly ranks with Chrysostom and Spurgeon, falling below Spurgeon indeed in general popularity of style, but surpassing him in compactness of thought and power of impression produced. His ideal of worship was as beautiful and noble as the Cologne Cathedral. His ideal of the part the chief minister in the worship of the congregation should take corresponded. It was his to lead the people in the worship of God in spirit and in truth; to enable them to see God as He has revealed Himself in His works and in His word, and, as seeing Him thus truly revealed, to go out to Him with all the homage of their souls. Accordingly every part of the service was conducted with great beauty, but the sermon was the center. In it God's message was delivered to men, in it God was revealed to man. In it the preacher felt the stress of obligation to be lying heavy upon him, and so acquitted himself of the obligation, that his preaching lingered with his hearers as amongst the richest parts of all their experiences. There lie buried in the churchyard of the First Presbyterian Church of Columbia, S. C., the remains of a noted woman, who as a schoolgirl in Barhamville, S. C., had come under the influence of his ministry during his pastorate at Columbia. Forty years later, as she lay dying, she asked that her mortal part might be carried back to Columbia and deposited in the old churchyard because of the preaching of Dr. Palmer whereby she had been blessed while a schoolgirl. In this sentiment of reverence for his preaching she is but a representative of the great body of those who came under his ministerial influence, of the men, as well as of the women.

AS A PASTOR.—Dr. Palmer was a great pastor. So far as appears, he kept no record of pastoral visits; he could not have told his people at the end of the year how many calls he had made. He professed to do a good deal of purely "social visiting," went to see the people as their friend. But when his people were sick or supposed, on other accounts, to be specially open to private religious guidance, he was sure to be on hand. He is said to have visited his sick, however long their sickness, as often as their physicians. Occasionally he sat up all night with a sick member. He knew how to behave in the sick room, what to talk of with each patient and how to broach the all-important matter.

To the poor he was a most liberal pastor, giving according to the need in the case often, rather than according to his own abilities, robbing his own study of its comfortable furnishings and never forgetting that once in life he, too, had been penniless. In times of epidemic he went about day and night, ministering to body and soul without respect of persons or faiths, so that all New Orleans could not fail to see that he was a Christian hero, nor to love him for his heroism. Disease and death might "spread sable wings over a whole city, he was found at the bedside of the sick to pray for them, at the tomb to bury the dead and everywhere to strengthen the living, raising the drooping spirit and binding up the broken heart." At all times in the darkened home he was a very son of consolation. "Oh! how I miss him" has been the cry of many a heart since his death. His letters to bereaved and mourning members of his flock have rarely been equaled. Tactful, redolent of sweetest sympathy, full of pure and noble personal affection, brotherly, fatherly, commanding the flood gates of Scriptural consolation, they are to-day amongst the peculiar treasures of many of his old people or their descendants.

As a pastor his work extended far beyond the limits of his own charge, beyond the limits of his city; he was pastor to his brethren in trouble over a wide field. Says Dr. J. H. Nall: "I have known him, in response to a telegram, take the first train and go hundreds of miles to carry the message of comfort and hope to a brother minister whose wife lay dead in the home made desolate by her sudden removal and ready to be borne forth to burial. There he sat in the midst of the broken circle and, with the word of love and the prayer of faith, brought the mourners under the outstretched wing of the Divine Comforter; then, after the burial, he returned to his own home, leaving a heavenly benediction behind him."

AS A TEACHER.—His abilities as a teacher were never fairly tried save in the pulpit and lecture room of his church. He was professor of church history for two or three years in Columbia, but, except during the last year, he was also pastor of an important church. He was professor of systematic theology for a year or so in the same institution during the period of the war, but again during a good portion of this time he was acting pastor of the First Presbyterian Church in Columbia. He himself judged that he was better adapted to the pastorate than to the professoriate. This was the judgment of many of his best friends also. They said that his gifts for popularization, through great amplification, adapted him to the pulpit and rather disqualified him for carrying students through a great amount of work. But a study of his lectures, briefs, etc., shows that he was a philosophic student of history and leaves the conviction that he would have taught a vastly illuminating and broadening course of church history. The philosophy of history was the great part of history to him. It is to be remembered, too, that he was sought as a teacher by a great number of institutions—sought over and over again; and in some cases certainly not on account of his gifts as a speaker at all. This argues that they believed him quite capable of development into a great teacher. In this view the compiler of his life and letters very confidently believes, after a long study.

AS A THEOLOGIAN.—Many of his ministerial brethren of New Orleans, and elsewhere, who had long known him and his work have said that, had he run his career in a line parallel to those of James Henley Thornwell and Robert Lewis Dabney, he would have developed into a theologian ranking with them in comprehension, depth, subtlety and power. Passing by speculations as to what he might have been, it is clear that he was a masterful expounder of the theology of the Bible and the Westminster standards. He seemed ready and able to expound the profoundest teachings to the people from the pulpit. He possessed an unmeasured systematizing talent and vast power to grapple with the most abstruse teachings of the Christian religion and to handle them with edification to his people from the pulpit. His "Theology of Prayer" and his

"Threefold Fellowship" are good illustrations of his work as a theologian for the people.

As a young and susceptible minister he had come under the potent influence of that prince of theologians, Dr. Thornwell, during his pastorate in Columbia, S. C., Thornwell being during most of that period in the college of the State. These two gifted men were bosom friends. The younger man received a stimulus and an impress which he carried with him to his grave. If Thornwell had added somewhat to the teachings of the Westminster standards where they touched the matter of polity, and if he had a somewhat distinctive way of looking at certain doctrinal teachings, Palmer was usually found to have the same view. Within certain limits he was a disciple of Thornwell. But he called no man master. If he agreed with Thornwell it was because, in his view, Thornwell had gotten the truth and proven that he had gotten it. He was never a blind disciple.

Rev. Richard McIlwaine, D.D., LL.D., late president of Hampden-Sidney College, contributes the following incident illustrative of Dr. Palmer's relation to Dr. Thornwell: "One day during the meeting of the General Assembly in Staunton, in 1881, I happened to be sitting by Dr. Palmer, who, when one of the speakers endeavored to maintain his position by a repeated and earnest reference to Dr. Thornwell's views on the subject, turned to me and said with some vehemence: 'Brother McIlwaine, the time has come when men ought to stop quoting Dr. Thornwell as a final authority on every subject,' and when the member then on the floor took his seat Dr. Palmer arose, and after stating his deep reverence for the memory and opinions of his departed friend, laid down and enforced eloquently the position that the opinions of no man, however great and good, could be received safely as a final settlement of any question; and that, as for himself, he was tired of hearing the name of Thornwell bandied about in every Assembly as the arbiter of every disputed point. He wanted good and sufficient reasons given and not the authority of any man, however great, as the ground on which the decision of all questions should rest. He then proceeded to give his views briefly and powerfully."

Whether the point under dispute was strictly doctrinal or

not, it illustrates his theological attitude toward his honored friend, the great theologian of Columbia Seminary.

AS CHAMPION OF THE PRINCIPLES AND LEADER OF THE HOSTS OF THE SOUTHERN PRESBYTERIAN CHURCH.—After Thornwell's, his hand did more than any other, perhaps, to give its peculiar form to the Presbyterian Church in the United States. He came to love her because of his own work upon her and because he believed that she conformed nearly to the pattern of the Church shown in the Scriptures; and, with all his great abilities, he defended her throughout her history as long as he lived. The pages of this volume contain many instances of his defensive effort. It is to be remarked here that he was able to retain, in spite of opposition of view, the respect and the friendship of the great majority of those who fought against him, whether they were of his own communion or of the alien one which he found himself obliged to oppose.

All his apologetic and polemic efforts have been remarkable for their evident design to subserve the ends of truth and righteousness and for their freedom from personalities. There is no question that in these efforts he believed he was doing what the right obliged him to do. As Rabbi Leucht has said: "If he condemned and opposed a sister communion it was because his sense of the demands of righteousness compelled him." As Dr. Eugene Daniel says: "The principle involved must first be satisfied and honored; then, but not until then, might the outer relationship dependent upon that principle be modified or adjusted. Discussion was useless but as a means to the ends of sacred truth and righteousness."

He was at the farthest removed from those beasts of prey who delight in slinging slime and filth over the person whose opinions are attacked. He left personalities for others. He was a gentleman in the highest sense of the word. In his most strenuous discussions he preserved the proprieties and left his opponent with profound respect, and often affection, for himself. Indeed, he never replied to a mere opponent. Having fully and profoundly expressed his grounds of antagonism to the principles which he resisted, and vindicated the principles which he espoused, he let other men have their say, and then let the matter come to issue. If in any struggle he ever thought:

"Peace-lovers we—sweet peace we all desire.
Peace-lovers we—but who can trust a liar?"

he was most careful to call the other party by no uglier name than was demanded by allegiance to principle.

Hence, in part, the willingness with which his leadership was accepted by hosts of his brethren—a function which was inevitably devolved upon him in consequence of his great abilities. For as his brethren of the Reformation age took John Calvin and made him their leader, so great numbers of the brethren in the Southern Presbyterian Church looked to Dr. Palmer for leadership.

AS A PHILOSOPHER.—Dr. Palmer was looked upon by his own people as a philosopher, as well as a divine. He undoubtedly possessed the philosophic temper, and a definite philosophical system gave shape to his thinking on all subjects. This philosophic system, which furnished him with the forms under which he construed the facts of nature and revelation, was the common sense philosophy of the Scotch school. He was perfectly at home in this type of philosophy, and would have been able to expound it with the symmetry, beauty and power which he manifested in the exposition of the sacred Scriptures. In a thousand ways he betrays his easy familiarity with, and adoption of it. Being a master of this philosophy and making constant and ready use of it, it is not strange that his intelligent hearers soon came to think of him as a great philosopher as well as a great preacher. For the philosophy of common sense fits the genius of the Bible and hitherto has suited the genius of unsophisticated Anglo-Saxon common sense.

AS A STATESMAN.—Dr. Palmer was at home with representatives of the medical profession and with representatives of the legal profession, as well as with fellow ministers of Christ's Evangel. In his youth he had leaned toward the legal profession, and in that part perhaps because it prepared for statecraft. Like the sons of all Southern gentlemen in ante-bellum times he had made a study of civil government. A South Carolinian by birth and through his early manhood, it was not strange that he should have become a free disciple of the greatest of South Carolina statesmen, John C. Calhoun. At a later time he made such a mastery of the principles of the Hebrew polity, provided for in the legislation of Moses, that thenceforth he was really able to instruct most statesmen on some of the fundamental principles of constitutional government. It has been said of him that he might have ranked with Chief Justice Marshall as a constitutional lawyer had he given his attention to the law instead of the Gospel of Jesus Christ. Whether or not he be worthy of this high praise, it may be safely said that in the United States Senate, in any period of his public life, after reaching thirty-five, he would have been one of the chiefest ornaments of the body, and during no inconsiderable part, its crown and glory.

He was down to 1865 a believer in the doctrine of States' rights. Down to the day of his death he continued to believe that, up to 1865, when force determined otherwise, according to the terms of the original compact, the States had the legal and therefore the ethical right to secede on certain conditions, of which they were to be the judge. He deplored universal suffrage as a great evil. He entertained decided views touching monopolies, trusts, combines, etc. Especially did he entertain advanced and worthy views on the relation of the State toward all institutions which tend to debase the common morals and conscience. On all these and many other subjects within the civil pale he propounded well considered and sagacious teachings.

But for his remarkable power of self-control and his strong sense of the obligation to keep separate things ecclesiastical and things civil, frequently he would have turned the pulpit into a political fulcrum, so strongly did he feel on some of these subjects.

Going on to the platform during the agitation of two or three of these questions, he exercised as much, and perhaps more, influence than any professional statesman within the bounds of his Commonwealth. This was the case when, on a Thursday, he used his church to speak on the duty of preserving the original constitution made by the thirteen sovereign American States for the Federal government. It was the case again, when he led the fight, speaking in the Grand Opera House and elsewhere, against the Louisiana Lottery. From the early years of the war to the close of his life he perhaps never carried a question of civil government into the sacred desk.

AS A PATRIOTIC CITIZEN.—Dr. Palmer said, in concluding his address of November 29, 1860: "It only remains to say that whatever be the fortunes of the South, I accept them for my own. Born upon her soil, of a father thus born before me—from an ancestry that occupied it while yet it was a part of England's possessions—she is in every sense my mother. I shall die upon her bosom—she shall know no peril but it is my peril, no conflict but it is my conflict, and no abyss of ruin into which I shall not share her fall. May the Lord God cover her head in this her day of battle."

The peril that followed was his peril, the conflict was his conflict. *That* old veterans, his companions on many a march, still live to attest. They tell of his stirring battle addresses, of his ministrations to wounded and dying men on the field of carnage, regardless of danger, of his forcing weak and wounded soldiers to mount his horse and his trudging cheerily on with the "boys" when on the march. Their love for him down to the day of his death, their honor to his memory, makes it clear that they believed in his patriotism. After the war for a time he felt, indeed, in accordance with the reality that he had no citizenship on earth except in the Church of God. But he continued to love the people who had constituted the State; and when the caricature of free government began to give away to intelligent self-government and worthy citizens were once more accorded their full rights, he lent a helping hand to every endeavor that was honest, strong and true. And when, on the memorable night of his great anti-lottery speech in the Grand Opera House, Col. William Preston Johnston introduced him as the first citizen of Louisiana, he only put him on that pedestal on which the suffrages of his fellow citizens would undoubtedly have placed him.

He loved, too, not only the State of Louisiana, but the consolidated nation, which had taken the place of something that he had loved even better. That better thing being gone, he loved the country from Maine to California, and from Canada to the Gulf and the Rio Grande. He fondly hoped that she would repent of trampling on the constitution and that the principles for which the Confederacy poured out her all would again become dominant.

He was ever ready to put his great gifts at the services of the State, when his paramount duty to the Church permitted; ready to fight impurity, ready to aid every enterprise devoted to the relief of the unfortunate; ready to help every measure designed to secure justice between man and his fellow man. It would be superfluous to advert further in this place to his services in the civil realm.

AS THE HEAD OF A FAMILY.—In his conception, the family is the great institution, the spring of both Church and State, ordained of God for man in Eden. "The man as challenging the woman's love is the head of the family, and the founder of the home. The woman's submission is queenly because wholly voluntary. Parental authority is next to the authority of God. Love is the check divinely given to protect against abuse of authority. The husband is the priest of the home, responsible for offering the sacrifices of prayer and thanksgiving in daily worship, and the children are to be nurtured in the admonition of the Lord. Every home is to be the type and enfold the promise of a home in heaven." [3]

In his own domestic life it is known that he discharged well the high priesthood which was his as a husband and a father. In his little volume called the "Broken Home," in which he gives a sketch of each of his loved ones that preceded him to the grave, we are given incidentally much insight into the relations subsisting between himself and the several members of his family. These relations show that he was king and priest in the family, ruling by love and the reverence with which his character was invested. He made mistakes in this sphere as in others, without doubt. For some reason his children were not made to live a sufficiently out-of-door life, did not take sufficient physical exercise, and consequently did not develop vigorous physical vitality. He thought he overincited his eldest daughter to study and that the worry of the effort was the occasion of her early decline. He may have made other mistakes, but, for the simplicity of the family life, for beautifully disciplined children, for ready unselfishness of bearing induced in them toward one another, his family was remarkable. He had a most accomplished helper in this priesthood in his wife. He would have said that to her the beauty of their family life was due; that it was due to that peculiar union of force, gentleness and prudence for which she was so remarkable, her unyielding firmness in the maintenance of principle. She would have said that she owed much that

[3]So Dr. Eugene Daniel justly sums up his view of the family.

was in her own character to him, and that he was robbing himself to praise her. They would have both been right. He was a pattern to his people in his domestic relations, and not only as concerned his immediate family, but in regard to all under his roof. He was a model in his care for his servants, care of them physically and care of them spiritually.

AS A FRIEND.—There is a friend that sticketh closer than a brother. Dr. Palmer's friendship must have been a reflection of his Master's. It stuck. He did not say of all friendships, 'They will keep without cultivation.' He cultivated them. He kept up some of these friendships from his young manhood all through his long and busy life; and nobler examples of high, sweet, pure friendship one would have to ransack all history to discover. The intensity of his friendship for some was no barrier to a generous outpouring of his affections on many and on all mankind.

Some men are said to be so great as to be necessarily lonesome. It is possible that this was true of him at times and in regard to certain longings. Yet it was not generally true of him. He was a man amongst men, and, in his quiet, genial way, entered into all their joys and sorrows. A finished, polished, considerate gentleman, he rendered a sympathy to his fellow men as simple and unaffected as that of a child. As a Christian father, he allowed and encouraged those in need of friendship to speak to him of all their deepest feelings; and as a Christian father he responded to their appeals with fatherly sympathy, help and counsels.

AS A SOCIAL SERVANT.—For convenience we shall include under this general head not only his character as a host in his own home and in the social gatherings in his church, but the part he played as after-dinner speaker and as an orator before various literary bodies. He was a model host, not burdening his guests with attention, but exercising exquisite courtesy toward them and making them feel thoroughly at home as well as charmed with his conversation.[4] In the social gatherings of his flock he seemed ever to measure up to the high expectations of his people and to raise their anticipations with regard to all similar occasions in the future. The kindly retort, the

---

[4]It is said that some callers found him distrait and preoccupied. Such were exceptions, however.

keen wit, the ready flow of conversation and eloquence made him the personage in every such gathering. His apparent unconsciousness of this, his sincere humility, his keen appreciation of the excellences of others, but added to his charm.

But the figure of the great preacher, philosopher, statesman, patriot was often conspicuous on great social occasions as post-prandial speaker and orator. His abilities for extemporaneous speech have seldom been equaled. His adaptability to the occasion was exquisite. He knew how to say the true thing fittingly. On one occasion, says Dr. Mallard, "a dinner was given by the New Orleans Bar to a visiting Chief Justice of the Supreme Bench of the United States, and Dr. Palmer was one of the invited guests. It fell to his lot to make an after-dinner speech, and he discussed so eloquently and exhaustively the great principles of law that the delighted Chief Justice asked him afterwards where he had acquired his legal lore, and was informed that it was from studying the Hebrew Commonwealth in the Bible."

His oratorical powers often received signal illustration. Dr. Mallard says, again: "An immense audience filled one of our theatres on occasion of the service held in commemoration of Gen. Robert E. Lee, then lying a dead president in a college chapel in distant Virginia. . . . The building was crowded to its utmost capacity. The first address was by Hon. Thomas J. Semmes, a distinguished member of the New Orleans Bar. It was a masterly effort, and evidently thrilled the audience so that I, for one, trembled for Dr. Palmer (but it was unnecessary fear). He took the audience just where he found it, on the high plain, and bore it up to yet loftier heights. In the gallery where I was there sat a war-worn veteran in faded gray, and tears were streaming down his cheeks without his consciousness."

In a eulogy over Rabbi Gutheim he swayed his audience "as the trees of the wood are moved with the wind," and in describing the dead leader as "a man always to be found when wanted and always to be trusted when found," he coined the sentiment which the rabbi's friends afterwards had carved on his monument.

He was one of the greatest orators of the centuries, and his greatest orations were more than orations; they were sermons. But in the character of preacher he has already been sketched.

AS A SERVANT OF GOD.—In all these roles, in every phase of his life, he was a servant of God. His conversion had come after a bitter and protracted struggle, when he came to Jesus with the query of Saul of Tarsus, "Lord, what wilt Thou have me to do?" Henceforth he was a servant of God. He was sanctified as years passed by the gracious Spirit who applied God's truth and afflictive providences. In consequence he became more and more a servant of the Lord. We must think of him not only in his preaching, pastoral work, teaching, theologizing and philosophizing on the scheme of salvation as serving God, but as just as consciously trying to serve God as a patriot, as head of his family, friend and minister to the pleasure of social gatherings. His highest motive in all these functions was to glorify God and to enjoy Him.

Taken all in all, he was a very great man; he has often been put into a small group with which the great Head of the Church blessed the Southern Presbyterian Communion. Thornwell, Dabney, Palmer and Hoge have often been named together. Dr. Palmer was not the least of these. In some particulars, some of them surpassed him. For example, in the sheer power of thought, Thornwell and Dabney did. But when we consider his ethical and religious character, his freedom from petty vanities, his Christ-like humility, his transparent simplicity, honesty and honor, his broad and intense love for his fellow men, regardless of race or condition, his noble devotion to God; when we consider his great powers and achievements as a preacher, as a pastor, as a theologian, as a defender of the faith once delivered to the saints, as a philosopher, as a statesman, as a patriot, as an orator of Demosthenic power; when we remark the energy, the harmony, the ease, the balance and the splendor of all his mental, emotional and practical working, we unhesitatingly rank him as the peer of the great uninspired preachers and defenders of the faith of the ages, and one of the greatest of men, fit companion to other greatest leaders in the world's march into Christian civilization, whether statesmen or scientists, or philosophers, or leaders of the hosts of Jehovah.

INDEX.